Language and Life

Essays in Memory of Kenneth L. Pike

SIL International and
The University of Texas at Arlington
Publications in Linguistics

Publication 139

Publications in Linguistics are published jointly by SIL
International and the University of Texas at Arlington.
The series is a venue for works covering a broad range of
topics in linguistics, especially the analytical treatment of
minority languages from all parts of the world. While
most volumes are authored by members of SIL, suitable
works by others will also form part of the series.

Series Editors

Donald A. Burquest
University of Texas at Arlington

Mary Ruth Wise
SIL International

Volume Editors

Mary Ruth Wise
Thomas N. Headland
Ruth M. Brend

Production Staff

Bonnie Brown, Managing Editor
Margaret González, Compositor
Hazel Shorey and Kirby O'Brien, Graphic Artists

Language and Life

Essays in Memory of Kenneth L. Pike

Edited by
Mary Ruth Wise
Thomas N. Headland
Ruth M. Brend

SIL International
and
The University of Texas at Arlington

©2003 SIL International
Library of Congress Catalog No: 2003-105328
ISBN: 1-55671-140-9
ISSN: 1040-0850

Printed in the United States of America

Copies of this and other publications of SIL International may be obtained from

International Academic Bookstore
SIL International
7500 W. Camp Wisdom Rd.
Dallas, TX 75236-5699
Voice: 972-708-7404
Fax: 972-708-7363
E-mail: academic_books@sil.org
Internet: http://www.ethnologue.com

Contents

Part 1: Pike and SIL

Part II: Language and Culture

Part III: Etics and Emics

Part VII: Particle, Wave, and Field

Part VIII: Language in Relation to...

Kenneth L. Pike, circa 1988.
(Archived in the Ken Pike archives.)

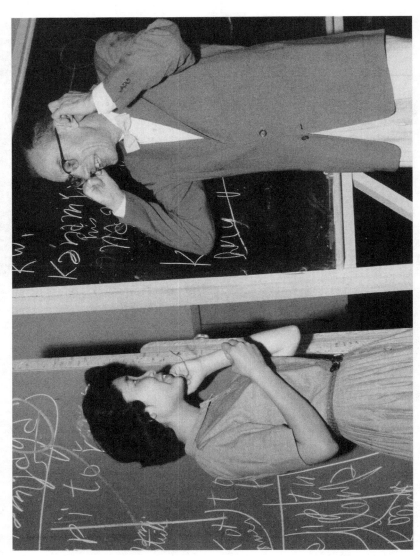

Ken Pike doing a monolingual demonstration, c 1960.
(Photograph from the Townsend Archives; used with the permission of Cal Hibbard.)

An Omnilingual Demonstration

John R. Ross

Tall, cropped dark hair, brow furrowed
intense, gray-green eyes
soft, highish voice—threw
himself always at the hardest problems.

Intonation. (any sensible linguist's nightmare)
Or learning in a scant hour
a lot of the structure of a language
he didn't even know the name of,
by asking questions of a speaker
who wouldn't even know the name
of the language he would wrap the questions in.

And doing this fieldest kind of field
linguistics anthropology philosophy music
not just before a trusted group of comrades
but before anyone, anywhere—and why?
So we would see that people speaking
one to another, in any words
could reach across the deepest gulf
could meet anyhow in learning.

Up there on the highest tower
about to plunge six stories
down through a hoop of fire

into that tiniest teacup?
[drum rolls] Fun! Off we go—

But all of that would pale beside and inside
his life's truest work—translation.
Into any language, any world.
Translating what?
The simplest most important stuff—
his Buddy's words—the guy from Nazareth.
And helping others to find the light
that soared him through a richest life.

Full of friends and challenge
free in growth and depth
rich through gentle toughness
around a widest heart,
a listening mind, the curiosity
of a kid rattling a trick box,
with something fascinating rolling
around back and forth inside it,
but there's no key, no keyhole,
maybe this corner lifts a bit,
but while you lift you gotta
do a counterclockwise twist, as
you tilt it downwards and northeast...
and then—

back to square one, where he started,
where he was always too happy to
return to, to learn new ways of seeing
understanding new always sounds, morphologies,
kinship systems, ethnobotanies,
ways of life and faith...open to all of it and us.

A permanent beginner, just like all of us
right to the end, right through it,
beyond all thought of end,
playing in the Always.

Háj
20-02-2002
Mistywood

Foreword

I have long thought of Kenneth Pike as one of the last—maybe the last—
of the New England transcendentalists and pragmatists—Emerson,
Thoreau, William James, and above all, along with Pike the most architectonic of them all, Charles S. Peirce. All were theists and thought
broadly about mind and nature, but only Peirce and Pike shaped their
worldview around the phenomenon of language itself, and built it in
threes—firstness/particle, secondness/wave, and thirdness/field.

For those of us who were his students, that image of language grew
slowly, by practice. We practiced seeing things from the different perspectives—noticing how changing perspectives changed meaning, and that no
one perspective alone was sufficient. We, his students, learned to see the
world out of his window, and it made great sense. The observer is always
part of the meaning, he would say. Person, the very root of language, is
prior to logic. Made sense. He never insisted that his students adopt his
worldview, just try it, and articulate problems we found in using it.

Pike said he wanted a worldview he could live by, a theory of practice.
For him, a major part of practice was fieldwork—learning a strange language—usually unrelated to one's own—in a strange place. The anthropologist Sherry Ortner defined fieldwork as "the attempt to understand
another life world using the self—as much of it as possible—as the instrument of knowing."

Pike would often say that for many of his students the final exam was
survival in that strange place, and that survival meant learning an unknown language very quickly. He'd say, "I'm tough on you so you'll
survive."

If there was a root metaphor for him, I would say it was fieldwork itself
—from careful phonetics to the complete parsing and translation of a

transcribed oral text. Phonetics gathers the raw materials, phonemics cooks them.

When a new insight came to the linguist from this engagement with the unknown, the architectonic theory would adjust itself, find ways to attune itself to the new insight. In my day the new insight was the matrix—a development of the traditional grammatical paradigm—first to handle morphemic complexity from New Guinea languages like Fore and North American languages like Potawatomi. It was a descriptive technique for handling fields.

There was always for us one way out of most problems—the wavy line. The wavy line marked a residue. You were safe if you were aware of a residue. The wavy line made a residue into a problem, a live issue. You'd get an A for a good problem. Pike and Pike define residue as: "That part of a preliminary linguistic analysis in which analytical indeterminacies in the data are cited (sometimes along with initial hypotheses concerning a resolution of the indeterminacies); may be marked by wavy underline in the text or formulas" (1977:482). Finding a good residue took one to the frontier—where the fun is, he would say.

There were many theories of language and linguistics then, and Pike's large work, *Language*, pays attention to most of them. There also was a sharing of issues across theories, so that, at a national meeting, the sessions were plenary and the issues were debated by many sides and from many perspectives. I recall one annual meeting of the Linguistic Society of America, in Chicago, where Pike, Paul Postal, William Labov, and several others locked horns. One got a sense of the frontier.

I think that same sense is found in the essays collected here and the live issues they engage.

A. L. Becker
Ann Arbor, Michigan

Preface

In mid-2000 some of us, former students of Kenneth L. Pike, began a project to produce a festschrift in honor of our beloved mentor and friend. Professor Pike knew nothing of our plans, because we intended to present our volume as a surprise to him on his ninetieth birthday, June 9, 2002. However, our plans changed when he suddenly passed away on December 31, 2000, at age 88. Most of the authors in the present volume were already writing their chapters when we notified them of Pike's death. Everyone encouraged us to continue with our plans for the volume. The result is this book.

As the reader will see, Pike's influence spread far and wide during the last half of the twentieth century. The authors here are just a few of thousands of scholars whose work was influenced by Pike's teaching and writing. It is our hope that this present work will help younger scholars today, and forthcoming scholars in the twenty-first century, to grasp something of the intellectual influence of Ken Pike's contribution to linguistics, anthropology, and many other disciplines. May the essays herein help them, too, to follow Pike in contributions to the academic world and to the speakers of minority languages. Long before the concept of "endangered languages" came into vogue in the 1990s, Pike was instilling in his students the importance of recording, preserving, and working to keep alive the thousands of unwritten languages spoken throughout the world, in many cases by less than a thousand people.

Pike's work with the Summer Institute of Linguistics (now SIL International) took him to many parts of the world as a consultant and lecturer. He worked with speakers of hundreds of indigenous languages as well as with the SIL field linguists studying those languages. At the same time, he interacted with scholars at international conferences and lectured at universities in many countries. Many of those he met or worked with wished to accept our invitation to contribute an essay in his honor but were unable to do so for a variety of reasons. We are pleased, nevertheless, to include the papers of authors representing at least ten countries and at least six disciplines in a volume in memory of the one who said:

> I'm interested in truth about man [human beings], about how language is related to man, about how language is related to behavior. I wouldn't ever grant that I'm interested only in languages. I'm not. (Pike 1971:162)

Ruth Brend, who worked closely with Dr. Pike for some twenty years, did much of the early editorial work on this volume. Regrettably, she had to relinquish the task before completion due to declining health. (She died on January 8, 2002.) Her contribution was invaluable; we hope she would have been pleased with the decisions we had to make without her.

We are deeply indebted to Karl Franklin and John Costello for their helpful suggestions, to Vurnell Cobbey for supplying us with the photographs on the book cover from the Pike Special Collection of the SIL International Language and Culture Archives, and to Bonnie Brown, Margaret González, Renee Isaac, Kirby O'Brien, Hazel Shorey, Frank Sinclair, and Ardella Olson for their painstaking efforts in copyediting, data entry, graphics, and typesetting. They join us in dedicating this volume to the memory of Kenneth L. Pike, our teacher, mentor, and friend.

Mary Ruth Wise
Thomas N. Headland
Dallas, Texas
April 2003

Introduction

Mary Ruth Wise and Thomas N. Headland

Our title for this volume, *Language and Life,* is borrowed from that of a collection of four lectures by Kenneth Pike published in 1958. Although he did not comment on his use of the phrase, it is clear that Pike considered *language* and *life* to be coordinate, inextricably linked nouns. He was interested not only in language but in all of life, and that as seen from multiple perspectives. Many of his key concepts are expressed in triads or dyads. They include "person and relation between persons," "etics and emics," "form-meaning composites," "contrast, variation, and distribution," "units-in-context," etc. For Pike the analysis of language and culture, of verbal and nonverbal behavior, was not "either/or" but "both/and."

This volume is not intended to explain his theoretical concepts, for that has been done elsewhere, but rather to focus on a few of the themes which appear continually in Pike's work. The essays in this interdisciplinary book are ordered according to the way they seem to us to fit into some Pikean theme, but the choice was sometimes arbitrary since some essays fit into more than one subject. Only a few of his themes are included since Pike's interests were so wide-ranging. Most of the following chapters are written within theoretical orientations other than—but compatible with—Pike's; they all echo some of his major concepts, directly or indirectly. And the authors discuss many aspects of language and life; these include, among others, language change, language in relation to history, language in relation to education, language in relation to worldview, language in relation to environmental pollution and coalitions, language in relation to religion, and language in relation to philosophy.

Part I: Pike and SIL

We begin with an eight-chapter section on Pike and SIL since the paths of the two were intertwined for over sixty-five years. The first two essays are biographical sketches of this Christian and scholar by Martha Hildebrandt and Thomas Headland, respectively. Chapter 3 is a photo essay by his daughter, Barbara Ibach. Chapter 4 is by Pike himself; it is a friendly "fireside chat" where Ken reminisces in a personal way about certain highlights of his academic career. Pike describes some of his memories of early American linguists and of major paradigm shifts in American anthropology and linguistics as he witnessed them over the last sixty years of the twentieth century. It is the last essay he ever wrote and was completed just weeks before his death in December 2000. (Earlier in 2000, however, he coauthored a paper that was published in 2002. See his bibliography in chapter 6.) Chapter 5 is a succinct, evocative review of Pike's poetry by Jana Harvey.

The last two chapters in Part I look inward to SIL and call upon its members to continue—in the manner modeled by Pike—participating in and contributing to the academic community. First, Gary Simons discusses Pike as both a Christian and a scholar and the dual SIL distinctions that come from this: Bible translation and science. Simons describes the essence of science as acting in community: it is a cooperative, social activity. He affirms that this is foundational to "the scientific approach," one of the original principles of SIL that Pike espoused. The newly-founded Open Language Archives Community (OLAC), which Simons helped to develop, is described here as a network of cooperative activity which will enable scholars around the world to work together on the puzzles of human language. He concludes by calling on SIL to renew its commitment to the academic community.

Following Simons, Joseph Grimes discusses in chapter 8 a gap that is often left unfilled by SIL linguists who focus primarily on synchronic studies rather than diachronic studies. Two twentieth-century linguists, Kenneth Pike and Morris Swadesh, helped Grimes learn the diachronic side of the discipline. Pike summarized the comparative method in an experimental syllabus, published in 1950. Through Swadesh, Grimes had live contact with comparative research. That exposure prepared him to focus on ideas that allow comparative studies a practical role in investigating aspects of language diversity that concern linguists, educators, and others.

Part II: Language and Culture

Jane Hill's essay in chapter 9 opens the discussion of the inseparability of language and culture—of verbal and nonverbal behavior. She focuses on social relations between members of two different cultures and the linguistic consequences. Hill reviews one of Ken Pike's earliest publications, "Mock Spanish of a Mixteco Indian," which details uses of Spanish by a speaker who had very little access to the Spanish language but, no doubt, had strong views about what the language stood for in a world in which he occupied a low rung on the social ladder. "Mocking" Spanish is also a practice of middle-class "Anglos" in the United States, who, like Pike's Mixtec friend, are monolingual in their home language and do not know Spanish; but they have strong views about the marginal and restricted place in their world that Spanish should occupy. Hill's paper compares "mocking from below," especially as documented by Pike, with "mocking from above," based on her own research over the last several years on Anglo mocking.

In chapter 10, George Huttar explores the interface between lexicon on the one hand and aspects of culture and cognition on the other. Developing the notion of "basic" vocabulary in terms of a continuum—or several continua specific to different semantic domains—rather than a dichotomy, he uses data from creole languages, primarily the plantation creoles of Suriname, to demonstrate that more basic lexemes tend to stabilize earlier in the formation of a creole than do less basic lexemes. In particular, more basic lexemes are more likely to derive their form from an earlier superstrate or substrate rather than from a later one. In addition, his application of these results to the ongoing discussion of the relative chronology of English and Portuguese input into the creoles of Suriname supports the case for early Portuguese input.

Chapter 11, by Stephen Wurm, is a reminder that when a culture changes, the language changes with it. Once a culture is being lost through pressures from another culture, the bearers of that old culture begin to adjust their thinking pattern to that of the bearers of the new culture, and the structure and expression of their language follows the same trend. A number of examples are given of this process from indigenous languages of the Pacific and Australia, and also from metropolitan civilizations in which cultural changes lead to changes in the nature, form, and use of language.

Chapter 12, by V. I. Subramoniam, is an example of what we may learn about ancient cultures from linguistic reconstruction. The author addresses the question: Who were the originators of the Mohenjodaro-Harappan civilization? The recent trend is to consider that it was founded by Aryans; a majority of scholars still ascribe it to the Dravidians; and a few consider it non-Aryan and non-Dravidian. Evidences that the Dravidians were iron users are presented from the earliest strata of Tamil (Dravidian) literature of the second century B.C. to second century A.D., whereas the Mohenjodaro-Harappan civilization was a non-iron using civilization. It did, however, use copper: copper is an inherited word in Indo-European languages. The culture, therefore, was probably not of Dravidian origin.

In chapter 13, Eugene Nida's essay continues the emphasis on the inextricability of language and culture by discussing the similarities, differences, interdependence, unsystematic features, and coordination of each. He affirms that cultural symbols change even more rapidly than do linguistic symbols and that, as Pike emphasized a half-century ago, words have meaning only because they relate to behavior.

In chapter 14, Carol McKinney and Norris McKinney describe Bajju proverbs as a reflection of the worldview of the speakers of Bajju, also known as Kaje, of Nigeria. Proverbs are terse traditional instructional statements, often stated in metaphors, that reflect folk wisdom. Their terseness and metaphorical nature adds to their charm, wide applicability, multivocality, and ease of memorization. They reflect general truths by referring to specific situations or phenomena. The Bajju use proverbs in daily life to teach the consequences of wrong actions, behavioral expectations, and more generally their worldview. The proverbs provide practical advice for human relationships, taking responsibility for one's actions, and avoiding foolishness. They also address the importance of having prestige and status.

Part III: Etics and Emics

Etics and Emics—the Outsider and the Insider—the concept for which Pike is best known in anthropological circles, as well as in several other disciplines, is the focus in Part III. In the first essay in this part, Dell Hymes presents an emic analysis of oral narrative. He maintains that in many languages, perhaps all, oral narratives consist of lines and sets of lines. To present them in paragraphs is like describing one language (say Takelma) in terms of another (say Latin). Boas, Sapir, and others worked to overcome that practice. We need to overcome the parallel with narrative. Just as those raised with one language may retain its grammar while using words of another, so they may retain its "narrative grammar." The narrative analyzed by Hymes, a Wishram Chinook version of the "The Deserted Boy," is an example of what an insider analysis might look like.

In chapter 16, George Mavrodes' essay on alien gods is a striking example of the application of etics and emics to the philosophy of religion. He argues that a Christian missionary such as Kenneth Pike must often speak about God to people who are themselves accustomed to speaking about God, or about the gods, for many of those people will already have a religion which makes reference to one or more gods. In this essay the author discusses the question: How are we to construe those other gods, the alien gods, the gods of other religions? He explores a variety of options ranging from universal atheism to universal theistic realism. And in the end Mavrodes argues that in many cases a modest and limited agnosticism may be the most honorable stance for us to adopt, for we as outsiders do not share the knowledge and experiences of those who worship "alien gods."

In chapter 17, David Weber attempts to discover why certain parascientific cause-effect relations are reasonable within Quechua thought by exploring some of the primary metaphors reflected in the Huallaga Quechua language of Peru. The study suggests a link between these metaphors and the dominant philosophy, fatalism.

In the last chapter in this part, chapter 18, Karl Franklin explicitly follows Tagmemic Theory, as developed by Pike, which offers a holistic approach to language and culture. In this chapter Franklin applies some of the tagmemic concepts to a view of numbers and names in Kewa. Because numbers and names represent complex cultural features—such as a body-part tally system, a four-base counting system, personal and place names, as well as various kinds of taboo naming systems—the tagmemic perspective is particularly useful. The etic and emic manifestations of the names and numbers are illustrated and discussed with their contrasts, variations, and distributions noted.

Part IV: The Observer's Perspective

For Pike, the observer's viewpoint and intrusion into observed phenomena is part of the equation in analyzing any aspect of language and culture. Although one finds the term "deixis" infrequently in Pike's writing, "I/thou," "here and now," "speaker and addressee"—the essence of deixis—occur frequently. In chapter 19, Bernard Comrie discusses deixis as it relates to person. Although suppletion for grammatical person seems to be rare cross-linguistically, a number of languages from all parts of the world show such suppletion conditioned by the person of the recipient of the verb "give." Data are presented from several languages, showing both a third person versus first/second person split and a first person versus second/third person split. A diachronic explanation for this phenomenon is provided in terms of the grammaticalization of a deictic distinction comparable to that found in "come/go." Some possibly related phenomena are discussed, and suggestions are given for further work in this area.

In chapter 20, Herbert Pilch describes a monolingual demonstration in which Pike, who almost always made a breakthrough in forty-five minutes or so, gained only an inkling of what was going on in the initial consonant mutations of Irish and the governing conditions. Pilch maintains that the mutations indicate the illocutionary force of the enunciation, that is, what the speaker is actually trying to say.

Chapter 21 is Peter Fries' analysis of the presentation of reality—as perceived by their characters—in two authors whose different styles strike the reader immediately. Henry James wrote in a very complicated style and was interested in his characters' perceptions of the complex and ambiguous world around them. Hemingway presented the world his characters inhabited as clear and obvious. Further, he had the reputation of focusing on the actions of the characters. A comparison of sections of James' *The Ambassadors* and Hemingway's *A Farewell to Arms* shows that while James used only a few more mental processes (e.g., clauses which have verbs like "think" "like," or "hear" as their main verbs) than did Hemingway, he used many more nouns and adjectives which referred to mental concepts.

Eugene Casad's contribution in chapter 22 relates Pike's Tagmemics to the more recent Cognitive Grammar. He asserts that Pike's book, *Language in Relation to…,* presents us with a comprehensive view of language, interpreted within the framework of the human mind and the collective fabric of culture and society. In this chapter, the author shows how Pike's ideas, elaborated first in the 1950s, have a more recent bedfellow in Langacker's Cognitive Grammar. Casad suggests that the latter framework corroborates and validates Pike's approach in many ways, including the characterization of linguistic units as form-meaning composites, the grounding of grammar in human mental abilities, and the centrality of viewing arrangements in accounting for language use.

Part V: Form and Meaning

Just as language and culture are inextricably intertwined so also are form and meaning. For Pike, linguistic units and societal and cultural units are form-meaning composites. In chapter 23, anthropologist Robert Canfield describes a kind of etic framework representing the relationship between human motives, human sentiments, and the forms of culture. He begins with a provisional explanation for the assiduous religious practice of the Afghanistan peoples in order to draw attention to certain assumptions common to anthropological writing. These assumptions include the implication that the sentiments of a communicating public are profiled in the repertoire of symbolic forms available to them; and that some symbols evoking complex emotional associations are the symbolic devices through which sacrificial behavior is motivated. He also argues that description of culture as a resource utilized for practical ends and of culture as a system of determining signs are not contradictory but merely different ways of seeing how the spectrum of cultural forms is engaged in social practice. Canfield's central point is to note that symbols that bear complex meanings not only represent complex sentiments but also under certain circumstances are internalized so as to induce sacrificial action.

In chapter 24, Mildred Larson discusses form and meaning in relation to translation. She asserts that the process of translation is complicated by the fact that semantic and grammatical units in a language do not match. Just as a word may have various secondary meanings, so also grammatical units and structures may have various functions. Larson's essay shows how this mismatch of grammatical units and their meanings at the level of words, phrases, sentences, and even discourses challenges the translator.

In chapter 25, Vern Poythress focuses on gender-specific pronouns in English in his discussion of form and meaning in relation to translation. He points out that elementary translation theory instructs us to translate meaning, not form, while in-depth examination of languages shows that form and meaning interlock. Such interlocking affects the translation of gender-marked generics in English. Use of "they" or "you" instead of "he" in generic statements might seem to be merely a matter of changing form. But subtle differences in nuance arise from the fact that "you" suggests the addressee as the starting point and "they" suggests a plural starting point. Likewise, the use of the masculine form "he" in English might seem to be a mere convention. But closer examination shows that with generic "he" English speakers tend to think of a single male figure as the representative example for the general principle expressed in a particular sentence.

Part VI: Beyond the Sentence

Just as language cannot be separated from its cultural context, so a given sentence cannot be understood apart from its context, the paragraph or complete discourse. This part begins, in chapter 26, with Robert Longacre's textlinguistic analysis of a psalm from the Old Testament. He describes Psalm 19 as a prayer with two embedded lyric poems—one on God's revelation of Himself in nature and the other on God's revelation of Himself in the written Word—supplying the motivation for petitions which are expressed towards the end of the psalm. A textlinguistic analysis of this psalm serves to highlight the structure of this ancient composition and reveal some of the rhetorical devices, which make it effective.

In chapter 27, Austin Hale and Kedar Shrestha present an analysis of three puzzling sentence-final particles in Newari. They begin with Pike's claim that "No item by itself has significance. A unit becomes relevant only in relation to a context...The observer interprets data relative to a context..." (1982). Hale and Shrestha examine three sentence-final constructions in Newari (a Tibeto-Burman language of Nepal)—Verb-*gu du*, Verb-*gu khə:*, and Verb-*gu*—in extended narrative contexts. They claim that such contexts provide the field analyst with a better grasp of the differences among the constructions than could be obtained working only with sentences in isolation.

In chapter 28, Linda Jones presents a study of transitive clauses with respect to their roles in texts in Yawa, a Papuan language spoken in Irian Jaya, Indonesia. In particular, the paper discusses certain transitive clauses which are marked in that they vary from the unmarked SOV pattern. The discourse functions of the marked clauses explain their occurrence.

In chapter 29, Ivan Lowe, Edwin Arthur, and Philip Saunders give an account of how they arrived at a definition of the Kouya suffix -*à* as a form-meaning composite by contrasting its occurrence with its absence in different constructions. (Kouya is a Kru language of Côte d'Ivoire.) The occurrence of -*à* marks foregrounded participants and events in the main event line of narrative.

Part VII: Particle, Wave, and Field

Multiple perspectives, according to Pike, must be invoked in order to get a complete understanding of linguistic or cultural phenomena.

> One can choose to see the world as made up largely of discreet bits, parti-
> cles....But fusion, merging, gradients [waves], change...are also part of
> experience and are difficult to capture if only a particle theory is avail-
> able....Similarly, *all* events or situations or items...can for certain pur-
> poses of the observer be viewed...as points in a set of relationships (that
> is, as making up a field). (Pike 1982:xi)

The first four essays in this part can be considered as viewing language
phenomena from a wave perspective, for they all treat some aspect of language change, a diachronic view of language structures. T. Givón's essay,
in chapter 30, deals with the typological diversity of syntactic clause
union. He first identifies the two main diachronic sources of clause union—nominalized complements and clause chaining. He then describes
how these diachronic pathways yield two distinct synchronic types of
clause union—embedding and serializing, respectively. Syntactically, the
first type displays more extensive clause integration, while the second displays incomplete integration of the two component clauses. Taken as a
whole, the data illustrates the diachronic underpinning of both typological diversity and syntactic universals.

In chapter 31, John Costello claims that independent processes of
reanalysis were carried out in the Mayan and Indo-European languages
which led to a rare and profound change in each, the emergence of a new
part of speech, the preposition. These prepositions made more specific the
adverbial relationships that a noun could have to another element in a
sentence and thus reduced ambiguity. These developments suggest that in
the evolution of language, the acceptance of a significant increment in linguistic complexity, like a new part of speech, will be associated with a
concomitant increment in the precision of human communication.

Thomas Gamkrelidze, in chapter 32, maintains that the Glottalic Theory
provides a plausible explanation for the evolution of voiced consonants in
Proto-Indo-European. He shows that an investigation into phonation types of
speech sounds indicates that voiced consonants and sounds with glottalic articulation (laryngealized consonants, including ejectives) are related and
comprise a single natural class of sounds. They are closer to each other than
are consonants with glottal articulation to voiceless consonants. This state of
active glottalic involvement in case of the articulation of voiced and
glottalized consonants conditions their articulatory (and acoustic/auditory)
relatedness evidenced in instances of their conditioned interchange and alternation, as well as their diachronic transformations observed in languages
of a vast structural spectrum. Synchronic and diachronic typology of the
ejectives points to a higher degree of plausibility and linguistic reality of

Glottalic Theory for Proto-Indo-European as compared to the classical model with plain voiced stops.

In chapter 33, Barbara Hollenbach updates our knowledge of tone in Mixtec, the language in which Pike first began fieldwork in 1935. Using data from related varieties of Mixtec to support her position, Hollenbach shows that a tone change that appears aberrant, as described by Pike, developed from the expected tone change by means of the movement of a high tone one syllable to the right. This movement left the low tone that had originally been on that syllable stranded at the end of the word. In the Magdalena Peñasco variety of Mixtec, this floating low tone affects the tone of many following words.

Chapter 34 presents a classification of French verbs—particles—as points in a field. Wolfgang Dressler and Marianne Kilani-Schoch present a model of the inflectional system of French verbs, which focuses on their class hierarchy. The three homogeneous sets (called microclasses) of verbs that are productive are described first. They represent the nucleus of the first macroclass of French verbs, whereas the second macroclass consists of various types of unproductive microclasses. All of them are incorporated into the class hierarchy of each of the two macroclasses respectively. The paper ends with typological conclusions about French verb morphology.

Part VIII: Language in Relation to...

In this final part, the title of Pike's all-encompassing volume, *Language in Relation to a Unified Theory of the Structure of Human Behavior* serves as the theme for contributions on topics ranging from rhetoric to education.

In chapter 35, Bruce Edwards describes the impact Tagmemic Theory has had on scholars and practitioners in the discipline of rhetoric and composition. In the early 1960s, Pike's publications in the flagship journals of composition, along with his interactions among rhetoricians and writing instructors in the Department of English at the University of Michigan, identified Tagmemics as a new focal point for research in rhetorical theory and pedagogical experimentation. In 1970, Pike and two University of Michigan collaborators published what was to become a very influential textbook, *Rhetoric: Discovery and Change*, a work that for the first time presented various axioms and tools of Tagmemic Theory to a broader academic audience. Between 1970 and 1990, Tagmemics was particularly harvested for its discovery and inquiry tools. Edward's description summarizes some of the main concepts of Tagmemics and their relevance for the teaching of invention in the writing process of postsecondary students. Other, fruitful applications of Tagmemic Theory for rhetoric and composition specialists await further development in the twenty-first century.

In chapter 36, Adam Makkai discusses language as "polluted environment." He describes the functional tenor of persuasion in advertising and counter-advertising and in politics. Makkai also discusses the problem of "politically correct language." He urges the reader to clean up language pollution by telling the truth.

In chapter 37, Patricia Townsend, influenced by Pike's understanding of scholarship as service, describes a dual career in academic and applied anthropology. Her paper discusses an applied research project that examined the role of religious and interfaith organizations at hazardous waste sites in three communities in the United States. Of the religious organizations studied, the Ecumenical Task Force (ETF), formed at Love Canal, was the most actively engaged with the Superfund site. The ETF regarded its role as a dual one of providing pastoral care to families facing a disaster and speaking prophetically against environmental injustice. Interfaith organizations were also engaged with the other two Superfund communities in Memphis and western Montana, though not as conspicuously so.

Chapter 38 is Stephen Walter's contribution on the crucial role of language in education. Linguists, semanticists, psychologists, and philosophers have extensively explored the relationship between language, meaning, and experience taking positions ranging from extreme interdependence to relative independence of these systems. The field of education has largely ignored such "theoretical" issues, taking it for granted that learning, the mastery of new meaning, is not highly dependent on language, specifically the language of instruction. Drawing upon recent research in multilingual education, this chapter explores the assertion that language not only mediates learning, but does so at a level of subtlety and complexity not previously suspected by most linguists, psychologists, and educators. Further, if this is the case, then the issue of the language of instruction becomes not merely an issue of general educational policy, but also one of national development policy and strategy. Pike had an intense interest in language *use* and *structure* and the relationship between language and thought. This paper on language and education is, thus, a fitting conclusion to a volume in memory of the author of *Language in Relation to a Unified Theory of the Structure of Human Behavior*.

Ken Pike, arguing a linguistic problem with Dr. Frank Robbins (left) and the late Dr. Sarah Gudschinsky, at the University of Oklahoma in the summer of 1973. Photograph by Cornell Capa. (Archived in the Ken Pike Archives; used with the permission of Cal Hibbard.)

Part I

Pike and SIL

"Sometimes I'm a horse and sometimes I'm a donkey, but I'm always a mule. I am both a missionary and a linguist." (Pike 1988)

William Cameron Townsend, founder of SIL, (left) and Ken Pike in vigorous discussion at the University of Oklahoma in the summer of 1973. Photograph by Cornell Capa. (Archived in the Townsend Archives; used with the permission of Cal Hibbard.)

1

A Portrait of Kenneth L. Pike

Martha Hildebrandt

Translated from the Spanish by Ruth M. Brend

I have the honor of presenting to this audience Dr. Kenneth Pike. His truly exceptional life and work cannot be recounted in the few minutes allotted. Nevertheless, I am going to try to give a brief résumé of Dr. Pike's academic career, as well as some necessary biographical facts.

Kenneth Lee Pike was born in Connecticut on June 9, 1912. He was the seventh of eight siblings—six boys and two girls—born into the home of a country doctor who had deep religious convictions. The youngest sibling, Eunice, became first his student, then a collaborator, and finally his biographer. I have taken the facts about his childhood and adolescence from her book, *Ken Pike: Scholar and Christian*.

Kenneth's mother, along with her husband, was a constant example and a strong influence on his character and that of his siblings. Eunice remembers her mother singing hymns while doing housework or sitting in a rocking chair with two or three of the children around her.

A longer version of this biographical sketch was originally published as *Semblanza del doctor Kenneth L. Pike*, 1988, Instituto Lingüístico de Verano, Lima, Peru. It was read by the author as her introduction to Pike, the first lecturer in the Ciclo de Conferencias: "Homenaje al Centenario de la Academia Peruana de la Lengua" (Cycle of Conferences: "Celebration of the First Century of the Peruvian Academy of Language"), Lima, September 9, 1987. Editorial emendations are enclosed in square brackets.

Kenneth's father was a classic example of the altruistic and unselfish physician, beloved by the community. He deliberately chose a rural practice where he knew he was needed. This decision resulted in his turning down the good income which he could have had in a large city. His wife, at times, wondered if the day would ever come when the eight children would finish their high school education and begin to work.

Kenneth finished high school in 1928 and went to work in a supermarket some thirty miles from home. Then his father became ill, first with appendicitis, and then with a serious infection contracted in the hospital. He was at the brink of death and was left with a greatly weakened respiratory function. The character of this man is clear: when someone in his presence blamed poor sterile technique for the postoperative complications, he rejected that idea stating, "My God is bigger than some sloppy scrub nurse. Since this has happened, it is because he permitted it."

At this time young Kenneth, agonizing over the possibility of losing his father, promised God that he would be a missionary to China if his father did not die. He did not die; and he always had a strong faith in the intellectual capacity, temperament, and will of his last-born son whose original and complex personality manifested itself from an early age.

After his recovery, Dr. Pike allowed Kenneth to fulfill his promise and to enter Gordon College in Boston. There he had to work in the kitchen to cover expenses. He graduated in 1933 and was accepted [as a candidate] by the China Inland Mission and began to prepare himself for his future mission.

Young Pike studied Mandarin and other assigned materials so hard that he was at the point of a nervous breakdown which caused the mission board to reject him. This was the official reason given for his rejection. Another reason, which fortunately he did not know then, was his inability to distinguish two types of sounds in Mandarin which could change the meanings of words. These were the voiceless aspirated stops which contrasted with the unaspirated ones—consonants which alternate in English in words like *paper*.

It is incredible and paradoxical that the future phonetic revolutionary had, in the beginning, difficulty in recognizing and reproducing the sounds of a foreign language. This failure, very difficult for the young missionary hopeful, undoubtedly molded his character and did not weaken his faith.

Somewhat later he decided to return to Gordon College to study [more Greek…]. He also attended Camp Wycliffe where future Bible translators of little-known languages were taught, and there he studied phonetics, indigenous languages, anthropology, and other subjects necessary for the life of a linguistic missionary or a missionary linguist.

And there he met William Cameron Townsend, a pioneer in the study of American indigenous languages and in translating the words of Christ into these languages.

From their first meeting, Dr. Townsend saw in that young man academic and humanitarian potential, and he became his guide and patron. Townsend's influence was that of an intellectual and spiritual father under which, during several decades, Kenneth Pike became a great linguist and a brilliant university professor. He also became an organizer and leader of the largest group of missionary linguists scattered throughout the whole world, studying hundreds of unwritten languages, giving them practical scientific alphabets [...].

In 1935, Dr. Townsend invited Pike to a three-week tour of several Mexican towns. There Pike had contact with various indigenous languages such as Otomi and Mixtec and he decided to translate the New Testament into Mixtec. That work took many years, unflagging dedication, and enormous intellectual effort. Mixtec is a tonal language—like Chinese which Pike wanted to learn first—but there had not been any previous study [accessible to Pike] of this unknown indigenous language of Mexico.

Based on earlier experience, Townsend decided that Pike should not lose time learning Spanish as an intermediate language between English and Mixtec. So Pike had to submerge himself abruptly into the Mixtec culture and begin to learn and analyze that language, trying to disentangle the complicated tone patterns. The long, hard task of studying and describing this complex language [or language family], spoken by some 200,000 forgotten people, with the objective of being able to produce an alphabet which represented not only its vowels and consonants but also its tones, was not abandoned by Pike, in spite of many interruptions, until he was able to finish it. Even today he considers the translation of the New Testament into Mixtec as one of the tasks which is closest to his heart.

The difficulties with Mixtec caused Pike to study tirelessly and to prepare himself academically in order to solve the deep linguistic problems he ran into. To teach is, without a doubt, the surest way to learn. So, in the summer of 1936, Pike taught the phonetics of indigenous languages at Camp Wycliffe in Arkansas.

Dr. Townsend approved of the progress that Pike made in his phonological studies and believed that the moment had arrived for him to put into writing his knowledge, in the form of a text for his colleagues.

But Pike did not believe that he was yet able to do this task, and furthermore, he also had great difficulty expressing himself in writing. Isn't that incredible for a man who would later have an impressive bibliography of thirty-three books and 230 articles [up to 1987]? But in spite of his reluctance, he took on the task prescribed by Townsend and turned out a few pages on indigenous phonetics.

Returning to the Mixtec town of San Miguel, a fifty-kilo bag, which he was carrying, fell on him and broke a leg. The break, at first poorly treated, left him with a permanent and noticeable blemish, and it meant that he had to spend seven weeks in the hospital.

And there, also, he was certain that God had immobilized him with a broken leg so that he could write up the phonetic material which Dr. Townsend had asked for. During his stay in the hospital, he accomplished, therefore, with his characteristic hard work and energy, the first draft of a text on phonetics. His aim was, of course, that it be an intelligible, clear, and instructive text, meant for missionaries, many of whom did not at the time have a strong linguistic background. Thus, it was that he tested the text on intelligent persons who were untrained in linguistics, and then he made the necessary changes to make it as clear as possible.

Dr. Townsend, his mentor, then felt it necessary that Pike attend the courses offered by the Linguistic Society of America at the University of Michigan in Ann Arbor, the summer of 1937. But he could not do so without a scholarship. When Pike arrived in Ann Arbor, he learned that there was no available grant. As a reaffirmation of his faith in the way God had led him, one of the grants was refused, and so it was given to Pike.

At the University of Michigan a new stage of life began for the young missionary. There he met the greatest American linguists of the day, such as Leonard Bloomfield and Edward Sapir. Pike received academic backing from Sapir after showing him his manuscript on phonetics. He also received constructive criticism from Sapir and other prestigious linguists in the academic world of Ann Arbor. And, in this world, he finally triumphed because of his intellectual capacity, the originality of his thesis, his strong tenacity and dedication to work, his gift as a teacher, and his honesty as a researcher.

The previously mentioned work on phonetics was the basis of his doctoral thesis, defended at the University of Michigan on August 11, 1941. The university published it as a book with the title: *Phonetics: A Critical Analysis of Phonetic Theory and a Technic for the Practical Description of Sounds*. This book, which appeared in 1943, was a truly Copernican contribution to work which had been done up to that time on the sounds of language [...].

Pike belongs to a generation which found linguistic science "in diapers." In the universities there were not sufficient courses to complete a linguistic degree; it was customary to study literature or philology and from there to go off into an individual study of linguistics, primarily self-taught.

With regard to phonetics, Pike had a simple and attractive premise: No language in the world could have sounds which were impossible for the human vocal system to articulate, and the human sound apparatus was basically the same for all races and peoples in the world. In addition, if one listed all the possible combinations of the diverse factors which contribute to the production of sounds in human language, there will never be a surprise—that is, a sound not anticipated—in the study of languages up to then unknown by science.

Pike then started at the beginning to produce an exhaustive table of possibilities of the sound apparatus. He distinguished proper linguistic sounds from nonlinguistic ones and from those which are marginal. He considered air [air mechanisms and directions of the air stream] to be a primary factor in the production of all of the sounds of language [...].

In this authentic treatise of general articulatory phonetics, Pike separated the study of the sounds of language apart from those in specific languages [...].

In 1943 he also published his *Tone Languages*, which resulted largely from his fruitful study of the tones of Mixtec and was designed to help all his colleagues and students who encountered similar problems (beginning with his own sister Eunice who was studying Mazatec).

Pike published [in 1945] his important work *The Intonation of American English*, designed first as a useful tool for Latin American students who, in spite of having learned to produce the vowels and consonants of English, had not succeeded in using the proper intonation of the language.

The study of sounds which function in specific languages was the subject of the book which Pike entitled *Phonemics: A Technique for Reducing Languages to Writing* [1947]. In it he established the principles which, applied with the pertinent methodology, allowed for the identification and description of the phonemes of a language, with their variants. [Once analyzed] the total phonemic or phonological system should be represented in the alphabet which should join the requirements of linguistic science with requirements of the society in which the investigated language is spoken, for example, the traditional orthography of the official language of the country.

Later Pike began the study of meaningful linguistic units which were larger than the word and their relationships within discourse. He produced, in this area, an original theory which he named "Tagmemics" and which is developed in his work which has this long title: *Language in Relation to a*

Unified Theory of the Structure of Human Behavior. Discussed by many, and considered by some to be his magnum opus, this book is doubtless an example of interdisciplinary work extending from one's main discipline, in this case, linguistics. Tagmemics, whose development took Pike many years, was the focus of discussion in an entire session of the Eleventh International Congress of Linguists in Bologna, 1972 [...].

Pike is convinced that his intellectual work would have been different, and perhaps less important, without the stimulus of the need to help solve the linguistic problems of his colleagues and students of the Summer Institute of Linguistics [now SIL International] in the translation of the New Testament into hundreds of languages throughout the world. Pike has been directly associated with that institute, founded by William Cameron Townsend in 1942. [Pike was president from 1942 until 1979 and President Emeritus since then.] Through the Summer Institute of Linguistics, Pike has become simultaneously one of the most important linguistic theoreticians of the twentieth century and the primary leader and inspirer, from an academic point of view, of the largest and most active group of linguists in the world.

Asked once about how he reconciled his position as an intellectual and as a vibrant Christian, Pike replied, "Yes, I am a hybrid of an intellectual and a Christian. On the one side, I have spent the better part of my life since 1935 making scientific analyses of many linguistic systems and writing about phonology and grammar in the context of human behavior. On the other side, I did all of this, in spite of many failures, in the context of a determination to serve God with my mind and heart as Jesus told us to do. I want to try to help others as I would want them to help me if I were in their situation, if I were a member of an isolated group of humans, without access to a written language. And this also is following the commandment of my Master and Creator."

This explains why Pike has always been considered to be the moving spirit behind the Summer Institute of Linguistics. He is also considered, throughout the world, as the supreme showman in phonetics classes and in descriptive linguistics.

The best example of this showmanship is his famous monolingual demonstration, which many of you here have had the opportunity of witnessing. For those who have not had this privilege, I will explain that it is a demonstration in which Pike, armed with a piece of chalk, and with various other objects, begins to obtain from a speaker of a totally unknown language and without using a common language, sufficient phonetic, phonological, and morphosyntactic data to make a preliminary analysis of the language, and to begin to communicate in it. This task, in public, takes Pike some forty minutes.

This admirable man of iron will and a superhuman capacity for work, nevertheless, detests routine and noncreative activity and accuses himself of laziness when his own nature rejects them.

This altruistic man, who has dedicated most of his life to helping others resolve problems of all types, accuses himself of impatience with the slowness of others.

This passionate man, who ceaselessly spurs himself on in everything, exhorts others saying, "Note that today is tomorrow because the day after tomorrow might be too late."

This nervous man, intense, and strung tight like a bow with a drawn arrow, tenses up to the point where stress gives him mouth sores and itching feet, yet he has the most enviable and absolute inner peace.

And he is a deserving candidate for the Nobel Peace Prize for his contribution, as a linguist and as a Christian, to communication between men. Personally, and through the hundreds of missionary linguists he has trained and guided for forty-five years, Pike has helped many in the Third World and many more in the so-called Fourth World in isolated ethnic groups, forgotten by the governments of their own countries. And he has helped them in his somewhat magical role as the Grand Maker of Alphabets—alphabets which allow them to read and write first in their own language and then in others in order to take their place in the global community.

Once asked about the relationship between language and peace, Pike replied, "Words explode before cannons do. It is very difficult to be at peace with someone if you can't talk to him, whether within a family or a state. The hundreds of small, isolated groups, due to their unknown languages, can't realize their legal rights, because they can't communicate with their national governments. There are still 3,000 alphabets lacking for other unwritten languages. When they have alphabets, their speakers can make themselves heard."

Thank you, Dr. Pike, for the example of a noble and useful life in which you have exceptionally joined the highest academic achievements with the highest works of love for our fellow beings.

Thank you, Dr. Pike, from a Peruvian, for what the Summer Institute of Linguistics has done for my compatriots in the jungle and in the mountains.

Thank you, from a linguist, for the direct and unforgettable teaching I had from you in that far-away summer of 1952 in Norman, Oklahoma.

And thank you, from a member of the Academia Peruana de la Lengua [Peruvian Academy of Language], for joining in the celebration of the first century of our organization.

Reference

Pike, Eunice V. 1981. *Ken Pike: Scholar and Christian.* Dallas: Summer Institute of Linguistics.

Kenneth L. Pike in 1998.

2

A Tribute to the Life of Kenneth L. Pike

A Perspective from One of His Students

Thomas N. Headland

Kenneth L. Pike, age 88, internationally recognized linguist, educator and Christian thinker, died in Dallas, Texas, on December 31, 2000, after a brief illness of only five days. Evelyn Griset Pike, his wife and closest friend since their marriage in 1938, and their oldest daughter, Judith, were at his side.

Dr. Pike was born in East Woodstock, Connecticut, on June 9, 1912, the seventh of eight children of a country doctor. He received his Bachelor's degree in 1933 from Gordon College (then in Boston). In 1935 he joined SIL and served in Mexico studying Amerindian languages. He received his Ph.D. in Linguistics at the University of Michigan in 1942 under Charles Fries—Bloomfield was also on his dissertation committee—and later served for thirty years on the University of Michigan faculty. Pike was the recipient of ten honorary doctorates/professorships from universities around the world, including the University of Chicago, Université René Descartes, the University of Lima, and Albert-Ludwigs University in Freiburg, Germany. His leadership included serving as President of the

This tribute was originally published in *American Anthropologist*, Vol. 103, No. 2, June 2001, pp. 505–509.

Linguistic Society of America, President of the Linguistic Association of Canada and the United States, and from 1942 to 1979 President of the Summer Institute of Linguistics (now SIL International). He was chair of the University of Michigan Linguistics Department from 1975 to 1977 and director of the English Language Institute at University of Michigan at the same time. For a quarter of a century he divided his time between the University of Michigan and SIL, as Director of the SIL school at the University of Oklahoma and helping to establish other SIL schools around the world. He lectured in forty-two countries and studied well over a hundred indigenous languages in the field, including languages in Australia, Bolivia, Cameroon, Côte d'Ivoire, Ecuador, Ghana, India, Indonesia, Mexico, Nepal, New Guinea, Nigeria, Peru, the Philippines, Sudan, and Togo.

Doing a monolingual demonstration in Cheyenne with
Helen Spottedhorse at the Univeristy of Oklahoma, 1963.

Ken Pike's contributions to the field of linguistics combined with his dedication to the minority peoples of the world brought him numerous honors. He was recipient of the Presidential Medal of Merit from the Philippines and the Dean's Medal at Georgetown University. He was nominated for the Nobel Peace Prize for fifteen years in a row and for the Templeton Prize three times. At the time of his death he was a member of the National Academy of Sciences, the American Anthropological Association, Professor Emeritus of the University of Michigan, and President Emeritus of the SIL. At least twenty-one encyclopedias have published entries on him. Dr. Pike published twenty books, two hundred academic articles, and over a thousand poems. For a complete list of his publications up to 1987, see Brend (1987); for a near complete list up to the year 1997, see www.sil.org/acpub/biblio/.[1] His last trip overseas was to Irian Jaya, Indonesia, in 1995, where he was the plenary speaker at the International Conference on New Guinea Languages at Cenderawasih University. He was actively lecturing and writing until 1997 when his health required him to slow down. His last book publication was his five-volume set of poems (Pike 1997a); he published three articles in 1998 (1998a, b, c) and two in 1999 (1999a, b). And he had just completed a historical essay on "Early American Anthropological Linguistics" the month before his death (Pike 2001).

   Dr. Pike's life can be seen in patterns of decades, each producing publications in its disciplines. During the 1940s, his emphasis was on the sounds of languages: phonetics and phonemics, tone and intonation. The 1950s focused on anthropology and language in relation to culture, developing his holistic view. The 1960s involved mathematics, and the 1970s were devoted to grammatical analysis. During the 1980s, Pike developed his areas of interest in philosophy, publishing his book *Talk, Thought, and Thing* (1993). His website is at www.sil.org/klp. *Current Anthropology* published "An Interview with Kenneth Pike" in 1994 (Kaye 1994), where Ken shares publicly for the first time some of his own personal experiences in academia.

Pike's Contribution to Linguistics

Pike's major *theoretical* contribution in linguistics was his development of tagmemics, an important theory in American linguistics until the paradigm shift towards Noam Chomsky's transformational grammar theory in the 1960s. Pike's (1967) magnum opus on tagmemic theory was first published in three volumes in 1954, 1955, and 1960, and then in a second edition in 1967. For those not willing to work through this mammoth 762-page volume, Pike later wrote a popularized version of just 146 pages that explains his theory at a level undergraduate students can handle. Subtitled *An Introduction to Tagmemics* (1982), and translated into Japanese, Korean, and Spanish, it became his most popular theoretical treatise. His most widely-used book, though, and a true classic, is his *Phonetics* (1943). Published almost sixty years ago, it is still in print and used as a text in courses today.

   Pike's *practical* contribution in linguistics was in his amazing ability to train so many students to learn, analyze, and publish data on unwritten

---

[1]See also chapter 6 in this volume.

minority languages. One of his major goals was to help colleagues with their linguistic challenges. To that end, he established linguistic workshops around the world, where he and his junior colleagues helped thousands of field researchers and Bible translators with difficult analytical challenges in aboriginal languages. When Pike first went to live with the Mixtec people in southern Mexico in 1935, he knew no Spanish, nor did the San Miguel Mixtecs. So he began learning their language monolingually, since there was no common language. This method eventually developed into his famous pedagogical "monolingual approach" for learning hitherto unknown tribal languages. Who would have guessed then that there were some four to five thousand such languages spoken around the world, that were unidentified even to linguists in the 1940s? This holistic approach to language learning became Pike's trademark. He eventually taught thousands of his students how to learn such languages, many of them by using the method that he demonstrated countless times in his dramatic "monolingual demonstrations" over the decades (explained by Pike 1999b, and described best by Makkai 1998). Today those students have produced thousands of linguistic documents on 1200 indigenous languages in fifty countries. (See www.sil.org/acpub/biblio/ for a bibliography of 12,000 academic publications on minority languages and cultures by SIL field workers.) Most of those languages had never been studied before, most are spoken by just a few hundred to a few thousand people, and almost all fall under the category called today "Endangered Languages"—defined as those likely to become extinct in the twenty-first century.

Collecting language data from an Aguaruna man in the Peruvian Amazon in 1956;
duplicate photo first published in Time, April 30, 1956, p. 32.

Pike's Contribution to Anthropology

Pike's major contribution in anthropology was his development of the emic/etic concept. First coined by Pike in 1954, the two terms are found in common usage in the vocabularies of most anthropologists today, and the distinction between emics and etics has proved very useful to them. (See Franklin 1997.) In fact, most anthropologists today use insights about the different perceptions of reality of various cultural groups as the principal conceptual tool of their trade. The emic/etic distinction underlies a basic contribution of modern anthropology, a tool for understanding other cultures. Anthropologists make their living at least partly because of their unique ability to make the distinction between emic and etic.

Perhaps the highlight of Pike's role in the American Anthropological Association came in 1988. At the AAA's annual meeting that year in Phoenix, a public debate was scheduled between Pike and Marvin Harris on their differing uses of the emic/etic concept. The debate, which went on for four and a half hours with 600 anthropologists in the audience, was vigorous but cordial. It resulted in a book titled *Emics and Etics: The Insider/Outsider Debate* (Headland, Pike, and Harris 1990). One unforgettable amusing incident occurred during this otherwise serious dialogue. During the discussion period a man in the audience asked Pike a question. In answering him, Pike was describing an incident that happened to him in Russia, but he couldn't remember a name. He then looked out over the audience and suddenly said, "Evelyn, are you out there? Who was that man we had dinner with in Moscow?" Evelyn was sitting in the back of the auditorium. She stood up and said, "Ken, that was Dr. So-and-So." Pike said, "That's right." And he finished answering the question. The symposium moderator then went to the microphone to call on the next person but before he did he said, "Let me stop here, colleagues, to tell you who that was in the back of the room. That was Kenneth Pike's wife, Evelyn Pike, and they are here with us this week celebrating their golden wedding anniversary." Everyone started clapping. Then Dr. Pike, without a moment's hesitation, stood up, leaned across the table and blew his wife a kiss. The audience, perhaps restless after four hours of sitting, broke forth with cheering and whistles. It was an entertaining moment in a long and otherwise humorless panel that anthropologists still remember thirteen years later.

Pike's Contribution to Religion

Throughout his career, Pike was keenly interested in the religious aspect of his work, as seen in his relationship with Wycliffe Bible Translators. He, Ángel Merecías, and Donald Stark completed the translation of the New Testament into the San Miguel Mixtec language in 1951. Pike was above all a Christian philosopher. He was a convinced theist who influenced thousands of people towards religion. He wrote numerous religious articles and books. Such books include *With Heart and Mind* (1996, first edition 1962), and *Mark My Words* (1971). In his book, *With Heart and Mind,* Ken defended scholarly and intellectual approaches to Christianity, maintaining that Christian faith and academic scholarship can be intimately integrated. As Hugh Steven wrote (Pike and Steven 1989:16),

> To understand and appreciate Pike, one must know he is both scholar and Christian; that his faith in Christ is at once full of energy, without pretense and rooted in Biblical depth.

Pike Was a Mule!

Ken Pike never had any internal conflict integrating his personal faith in God with his scholarship, nor his call to missions with his professorship at Michigan. But this was a problem for some academics who wondered if Pike left his brains at the door when he went to church. Pike wrote his *With Heart and Mind* (1996) to help those people understand that he did not. He recently wrote two shorter essays describing his dual calls to missions (1997b) and to linguistics (1998a). And his sister, Eunice Pike (1981), wrote a biography of Ken to explain his unique integration of faith and learning. Pike once told this story to help people understand his role as a Christian scholar:

> In 1980 while Evelyn and I were lecturing in China, we were honored at a dinner at Beijing Foreign Studies University. I was seated next to a Chinese gentleman who had just returned from lecturing at Berkeley. When he learned who I was he said, "Ah yes, I heard about you while I was in the USA. But I also heard you are a missionary. So which are you, a missionary or a linguist?" I thought fast and told him I was a hybrid, a mule. His expression caused me to explain myself. Mules are the result of breeding between a horse, wanted for its speed, and a donkey, wanted for its strength and ability to walk over rocks in the road. When you want to combine the

two qualities you have a mule. So sometimes I'm a horse and sometimes I'm a donkey, but I'm always a mule. I am both a missionary
and a linguist. [Recorded by Ruth Carr and Ken Pike in 1988, used
here with Carr's permission.]

An example of how this played out in Pike's life can be seen in some of
the letters he received over the decades from scholars who were influenced by his quiet faith in God. Here is an example, a letter from a Russian
scholar who Pike befriended when he was a Fulbright Scholar in Moscow
in 1988, before the fall of the Soviet Union in 1991:

Dear Professor Pike, Thank you for your paper....It is a good contribution to the development of our mentality....Many innovations are
expected here [as a result of recent political upheavals]....Thanks to
the depolitization of higher educational establishments, there has
appeared a possibility of abolishing [Communist] party meetings,
party bureau sittings, and so on....My loss of belief in [Marxism]
caused my sessation from the CP [Communist Party]. Paraphrasing
the statement made by Pascal, "There is a God shaped vacuum in
the heart of every person and it can never be filled by any creative
thing but can be filled by God we may know through Christ." I must
admit that the vacuum formed in my heart is open to Christ but it is
not very easy for a former fanatic communist and atheist to make a
decision. Your book [he refers here to Pike's biography *Ken Pike:
Scholar and Christian*] is especially dear to me now as it depicts the
ideal of the Christian gentleman in work and life....So I am trying to
study Christianity and wish I would ever dare to go to Shrebu
[pseudonym] Church to be baptised....I have to queue for hours to
buy something eatable or salt cabbage to last through the winter.
But man shall not live by bread alone. Yours sincerely. [Written to
Kenneth Pike in 1990 from Russia; the original letter was handwrit-
ten in English; the spelling here remains as in the original. Words
added for clarification are in square brackets.]

Case 75-2: Pike's Organization Accused of Ethnocide

Pike was often criticized in the academic world because of his tagmemic
theory. But he was mainly controversial because of his religion and because he was the president of SIL, an organization whose primary aim is
the translation of the Bible into preliterate indigenous languages. Pike
wrote replies to the public charges against SIL and its sister organization
Wycliffe Bible Translators. The first printed criticism of Pike came from

David Stoll (1974), now an anthropology professor at Middlebury College, in the *Michigan Daily* when Stoll was just twenty-three years old. Pike (1974) replied in the same newspaper. In 1975, some members of the American Anthropological Association filed a formal charge of ethnocide against the SIL to the AAA's Committee on Ethics (COE's "Case 75-2"). In May of that year, the AAA wrote a letter to the SIL describing the complaint and inviting SIL to formally respond. Pike replied to the AAA in a 15-page letter dated May 21. After spending a year investigating the charges, the AAA's COE submitted their report to the AAA Executive Board. The COE decided unanimously in favor of SIL against the complainants. In a letter dated September 20, 1976, to Pike, AAA Executive Director Edward Lehman stated, "At its 85th meeting in May [1976], the [AAA] Executive Board accepted that [COE] recommendation, also by a unanimous vote." The most recent attack from anthropologists, this time accusing SIL of genocide, was published in *Anthropology Newsletter* in 1997 (Edelman 1997). Pike replied also to that, and the AAA published it in a later issue of the *Newsletter* (Pike and Headland 1997). To accuse Pike's students of genocide was so extreme that even long-time SIL critic Stoll (1997) criticized Edelman's editorial.

*   *   *

Ken Pike was an extraordinary man. He loved life. He had a passion to challenge people to think. He wrote poetry. He laughed. He used his mind to solve linguistic puzzles and share the methods he discovered with others. He was a true scholar, philosopher, poet, pioneer and author. He was a man who shared his life, knowledge, and love with countless people around the globe. He was a gentleman in the highest sense of the word—an elegant man who noticed and spoke with the most unpretentious person in a crowd; a shy child would catch Ken's eye and he would engage the child in conversation.

In 1999 SIL began work on what will eventually become the "Kenneth L. Pike Special Collection." When this archival storehouse is completed, it will include thousands of documents on or by Pike, his wife Evelyn, and his sister Dr. Eunice Pike. His correspondence collected here spans almost seventy years. When it is completed, the Collection will be open to scholarly academic researchers.

Kenneth Pike is survived by his wife Evelyn; three adult children, Judith Schram, Barbara Ibach, and Stephen Pike; three grandchildren and two great-grandchildren; and one sister, Eunice V. Pike.

Dr. Pike's poem, "The End" (Pike 1997a, volume 2, p.102), expresses the feelings of his students and colleagues.

The End

Regarding Daniel 12:9–13, and "the end of the days."

In tears, then joy!
Life in contrast
Sets the pace
Of learning
Good, through bad...

Both now and "then"
Hold to trust,
In God, in time
To light our stars,
Forever there.

References

Brend, Ruth, compiler. 1987. *Kenneth Lee Pike bibliography*. Arcadia Bibliographica Virorum Eruditorum 10. Bloomington, Ind.: Eurasian Linguistic Association. [56 pages].

Edelman, Marc, ed. 1997. Nelson Rockefeller and Latin America. *Anthropology Newsletter* 38(1):36–37, January.

Franklin, Karl J. 1997. K. L. Pike on etic vs. emic: A review and interview. Online: <www.sil.org/klp/karlintr.htm>.

Headland, Thomas N., Kenneth L. Pike, and Marvin Harris, eds. 1990. *Emics and etics: The insider/outsider debate*. Newbury Park, Calif.: Sage Publications.

Kaye, Alan S. 1994. An interview with Kenneth Pike. *Current Anthropology* 35:291–298. [Reprinted online at <www.sil.org/klp/kayeint.htm>.]

Makkai, Adam. 1998 [orig. 1986]. The nature of field work in a monolingual setting. Online: <www.sil.org/klp/klp-mono.htm>.

Pike, Eunice V. 1981. *Ken Pike: Scholar and Christian*. Dallas: Summer Institute of Linguistics.

Pike, Kenneth L. 1943. *Phonetics: A critical analysis of phonetic theory and a technic for the practical description of sounds*. Ann Arbor: University of Michigan Press.

Pike, Kenneth L. 1967. *Language in relation to a unified theory of the structure of human behavior*, second edition. The Hague: Mouton and Co. [First edition published in 3 volumes in 1954, 1955, and 1960 by the Summer Institute of Linguistics, Glendale, California.]

Pike, Kenneth L. 1971. *Mark my words*. Grand Rapids, Mich.: William B. Eerdmans.

Pike, Kenneth L. 1974. Professor Pike replies. *The Michigan Daily*, March 26, p.2.

Pike, Kenneth L. 1982. *Linguistic concepts: An introduction to tagmemics*. Lincoln and London: Nebraska University Press.

Pike, Kenneth L. 1993. *Talk, thought, and thing: The emic road toward conscious knowledge*. Dallas: Summer Institute of Linguistics.

Pike, Kenneth L. 1996. *With heart and mind: A personal synthesis of scholarship and devotion*, second edition. Duncanville, Tex.: Adult Learning Systems [first edition 1962].

Pike, Kenneth L. 1997a. *Seasons of life: A complete collection of Kenneth L. Pike's poetry*. Compiled and edited by Sharon Heimbach. 5 volumes. Huntington Beach, Calif.: Summer Institute of Linguistics.

Pike, Kenneth L. 1997b. My pilgrimage in mission. *International Bulletin of Missionary Research* 21:159–161. October. [Reprinted online at www.sil.org/klp/pilgrim.htm.]

Pike, Kenneth L. 1998a. A linguistic pilgrimage. In *First person singular III: Autobiographies by North American scholars in the language sciences*. Studies in the History of the Language Sciences 88. Amsterdam/Philadelphia: John Benjamins. [Reprinted online at www.sil.org/klp/pilgrim.html.]

Pike, Kenneth L. 1998b. Mary R. Haas, January 12, 1910–May 17, 1996. *Biographical Memoirs* 76:3–13. [Reprinted online at www.nap.edu/readingroom/books/biomems/mhaas.html.]

Pike, Kenneth L. 1998c. Semantics in a holistic context—With preliminary convictions and approaches. In Udom Warotamasikkhadit and Thanyarat Panakul (eds.), *Papers from the Fourth Annual Meeting of the Southeast Asian Linguistics Society 1994*, 177–197. Tempe, Ariz.: Program for Southeast Asian Studies, Arizona State University.

Pike, Kenneth L. 1999a. Etic and emic standpoints for the description of behavior. In Russell T. McCutcheon (ed.), *The insider/outsider problem in the study of religion*, 28–36. London and New York: Cassell Academic.

Pike, Kenneth L. 1999b [orig. 1996]. On planning a monolingual demonstration. Online: www.sil.org/klp/monolingual.htm.

Pike, Kenneth L. 2001. Reminiscences by Pike on early American anthropological linguistics. SIL Electronic Working Papers 2001–001. Online: www.sil.org.silewp/2001/001/silewp2001-001.html.

Pike, Kenneth L., and Thomas N. Headland. 1997. SIL and genocide: Well-oiled connections? *Anthropology Newsletter* 38(2):4–5, February.

Pike, Kenneth L., with Hugh Steven. 1989. *Pike's perspectives: An anthology of thought, insight and moral purpose*. Langley, B.C.: Credo.

Stoll, David. 1974. Onward Wycliffe soldiers. *The Michigan Daily*, March 26, p.2.

Stoll, David. 1997. SIL and genocide? *Anthropology Newsletter* 38(3):2, March.

3

Kenneth L. Pike

A Photo Tribute by His Daughter

Barbara Pike Ibach

Kenneth Pike at the beach, in 1993 at age 81.

Christian, translator, scholar, linguist, friend, poet, husband, father, grandfather, great-grandfather.

Generations of Pike families have acknowledged the importance of the Word of God in their lives. Thus, Kenneth Pike grew up influenced by his grandfather who was a preacher and his father who had been a medical missionary. At Gordon College, Kenneth's commitment to God and his Word deepened, and his goal to be a missionary was strengthened.

Kenneth heard of Camp Wycliffe (later SIL), a new group, whose goal was to translate the Bible for people whose language had never been put into written form. In 1935, Kenneth

21

hitchhiked from his home in Connecticut to Sulphur Springs, Arkansas, to join the team. His luggage was a suitcase with "ARK" written in large print on the side. Taking classes there from W. Cameron Townsend and others, he studied language-learning techniques including phonetics.

Elvira, Townsend's wife, had a heart problem. So, Townsend asked his niece, Evelyn Griset, if she would take a year away from her studies at UCLA to live and travel with them and take care of Elvira. Evelyn did. It was during that year of 1935 that Kenneth met Evelyn and introduced her to the wonders of phonetics.

Kenneth, age 22, hitchhiking to Arkansas to attend Camp Wycliffe, spring 1935.

After a year in the field studying the Mixtec language in southern Mexico, at the urging of Townsend, Kenneth went to the University of Michigan in 1937 to study linguistics with Edward Sapir and other members of the Linguistic Society of America. God blessed Kenneth in this pursuit of excellence in scholarship. He found an academic mentor in Charles Fries.

In 1938, Evelyn joined Wycliffe and she and Kenneth were married in Mexico City. This began the dynamic Pike partnership in which Kenneth was the theoretician and Evelyn helped clarify and teach.

Kenneth continued his study of linguistics, dividing his time between studying Mixtec in southern Mexico, teaching at SIL, and studying at the University of Michigan. During that period their first child, Judith, was born. In 1942 Kenneth was awarded his Ph.D. in linguistics at the University of Michigan.

Evelyn and Kenneth on their wedding day, Mexico City, 1938.

While his focus was always on translating the Bible, he took delight in unraveling and understanding the intricacies of language. He and Evelyn wanted to help others understand the process of language learning and translation, and to be better equipped to translate God's Word.

The Pike family continued to grow with the birth of their second child, Barbara, and several years later, Stephen. The three children joined their parents in their travels. Most summers were spent at the University of Oklahoma where both Kenneth and Evelyn taught. Then followed time in fieldwork in Mexico or other countries during the fall terms. The winter-spring semesters were usually spent at the University of Michigan where

Kenneth Pike at age 30 when he was awarded his Ph.D. at the University of Michigan, 1942. (Spedding Studio, Ann Arbor, Michigan)

The Pike family in 1956 (back row from left: Judith, Evelyn, Kenneth; front row: Barbara and Stephen) Calvary Church, Santa Ana, California.

Kenneth taught linguistics. Travel time with the family was a change of focus for Kenneth. When they were in the car for days at a time, the family had his undivided attention. It was a time for telling family stories and creating new ones. It was a time of rest and, often to a child's dismay, a time to work on multiplication tables or learning to give descriptive words to passing scenery. Singing and a harmonica often fit in somewhere.

Linguistic workshops were conducted in different countries to assist Bible translators in solving problems that they encountered, and to encourage them in their work. Kenneth lectured to government and academic groups. He and Evelyn also led in starting other SIL schools in Australia, England, and Germany.

Through the years Kenneth continued, as he had begun, exploring and applying new ideas and methods. In later years he and Evelyn often took their grandchildren on trips abroad where they introduced them to different languages and cultures. As the years began to catch up with and overtake his energy, Kenneth increasingly shifted his focus and energy to encouraging young linguists and translators, and to supporting and cheering the accomplishments of seasoned ones. Just six weeks before he died, Kenneth revisited the language-learning process and beginning literacy with his great-grandson Jonathan Benison via Dr. Seuss books and videotapes, to the delight and satisfaction of them both.

Ken and Evelyn Pike, at Yarinacocha, Peru, in 1960.
(*Photograph from the Townsend Archives; used with the permission of Cal Hibbard.*)

*Kenneth Pike, second from left, with his seven siblings, circa 1916
when Kenneth was about 4 years old.*

Kenneth Pike, circa 1940 at age 28.

*Evelyn and Kenneth Pike in the field (Oaxaca, Mexico)
with first child Judith, 1941.*

Evelyn, second child Barbara, first child Judith, and Kenneth, in 1945.

Kenneth and Evelyn Pike circa 1961.

Kenneth Pike in 1988 at age 76 climbing up a cliff, Georgian Bay, Ontario.

Kenneth Pike at the lectern, taking questions from the audience after presenting a paper at the Seventh World Congress of Applied Linguistics, in Brussels, Belgium (1984).

Three generations of Pikes; Kenneth on left, son Stephen Pike on right, and Stephen's son Andrew, in 1993.

Kenneth Pike in 1992 at age 80.

*Kenneth and Evelyn Pike in 1994 at the dedication of the portrait
in the Pike Library, Dallas.
(Portrait by Angela Carson Photography, Northville, Michigan.)*

Kenneth Pike at age 82 with Tom Headland, one of his former students, in 1994.

Evelyn and Kenneth Pike in 1994, with grandson Andrew, Dallas, Texas.

4

Reminiscences by Pike on Early American Anthropological Linguistics

Kenneth L. Pike

One advantage of growing old is that as one ages one gains a better diachronic perspective of one's discipline. In my case I get to have a longer view of the history of the American Anthropological Association than most AAA members, and especially of its fourth field, linguistics. [Editors' comment: Pike was a member of the AAA and had planned to publish this in an anthropology journal. The reader should keep in mind that Pike was writing here mainly to anthropologists, not just linguists.] I enjoy that view. And I remember interacting personally with some of the forefathers of American linguistics way back before most of today's AAA members were born. I thus determined in late 1999 to write a historical essay reminiscing about highlights and historical figures in linguistics and in

Editors' note: This is the last academic paper that Ken Pike wrote shortly before his death on December 31, 2000, at age 88. In October 1999 the editor of *American Anthropologist* had asked Pike if he would write a "historical essay" on linguistic anthropology for consideration for publication in the journal. Pike began work on this essay in early 2000 and submitted a final version to the AA editor on November 8, 2000. The editor's review committee rejected that version of the manuscript saying it was too "folksy," but wrote back with editorial suggestions and an invitation to resubmit. Pike's untimely death came before he could revise the essay. While the essay published here may be too folksy for a theoretical science journal, those interested in the history of American linguistics and Pike's role in it will find that his reminiscences provide insightful glimpses into the history of linguistics. The essay was first published as SIL Electronic Working Paper 2001-001.

linguistic anthropology. This treatise is not meant to be a survey of the discipline of American linguistics. Rather it is an attempt to summarize some of my own memories of early American linguists—and a few American anthropologists and British linguists—whom I knew personally. As I write here, I try to place these recollections in the context of the discipline of the past sixty-four years.

Early Mentors

Cameron Townsend (1896–1982), Elbert McCreery (1877–1955), and Eugene Nida (1917–)

Of all my mentors, William Cameron Townsend was the one who set the underlying direction of my life for sixty-plus years. Townsend was not a professional linguist himself, although he had been studying Indian languages and doing Bible translation in Guatemala since 1917. Yet he urged me into linguistics, Bible translation, and community service. In 1935 I attended Townsend's second session of his small summer training institute (called "Camp Wycliffe" that summer, and from 1936 on, the "Summer Institute of Linguistics"). Townsend's central content was teaching us how to analyze the grammar of an unwritten language, and to translate into it. His basic model was the Cakchiquel (Mayan) language of Guatemala. He had gone to Guatemala to sell Bibles when he was twenty-one, leaving college before finishing, and decided to stay on to help the people who needed it—who needed alphabets, schools, business possibilities, and social esteem from appreciation of their language.

Townsend's grammatical theoretical presentation, which left a deep impression on me in 1935, was a metaphor in the form of a physical model. (See my "Foreword" to Townsend 1961.) It was a sheet of cardboard with a row of slots (or "windows") cut into it, one for each of the classes of affixes, and one for the verb or noun stem. A strip of paper was prepared for each slot (position); and each of these strips had written on it a specific list of morphemes that was appropriate to that slot. By lowering or raising a combination of the respective vertical strips he was able to show through the cardboard windows any one of thousands of theoretically possible complex verb forms. It was Townsend's presentation here that helped me to develop my "slot-class" tagmemic theory later on (Pike 1967, 1982).

Another enormous impact on me was a ten-day series of lectures on general phonetics in 1935 by Elbert McCreery (of Biola University), following his missionary work abroad. I do not recall what his sources were, but the impact on me was to be felt by my students for the next several decades. In the fall of 1935 I went with Townsend to Mexico, and chose to work on the Mixtec language, which I mention below in relation to tone. The following summer, 1936, Townsend brought me back to his "Summer Institute of Linguistics" school in Sulfur Springs, Arkansas, to teach phonetics—which I continued to do for some years (including my dissertation on *Phonetics*, published in 1943), until my sister Eunice Pike took over that part of my task. During that summer, Eugene Nida (mentioned below in relation to Bloomfield's book) started as a student, but because of his training in linguistics in California, he was asked to help teach morphology later in the summer. At the end of the summer Townsend urged that the three of us (Townsend, Nida, Pike) write books on linguistics! I did not like the idea. (I was then twenty-four, and my experience was not that great!) Eventually we did our assigned tasks. Nida wrote the important book *Morphology* (1946, second edition 1949)—which he used as a textbook when he taught with us for some years at SIL's linguistic courses at the University of Oklahoma. Townsend wrote his grammar (1961). In the meantime, hoping to avoid my assigned task, I chose to return to the Mixtec fieldwork area in Mexico. On the way there, in the fall of 1936, I broke my leg trying to help my Indian friends unload corn from a train to a warehouse. It took two days for my local friends to send me to a hospital in Puebla, where I eventually woke up to find my leg resting in a basket. Not sure whether it was God or Townsend who had put me in this position, I decided to get to work on my assigned phonetics book. Unable to get out of my hospital bed, with my leg now in a cast and tied to a pulley, and suffering from malaria, I wrote phonetics eight hours a day for the next several weeks.

In the spring of 1937, using a cane to start with, I walked for a month from the highlands of the Mixtec area (8,300 feet above sea level) to the coast, to survey other Mixtec-related linguistic needs on the way.

In the summer of 1937, Townsend sent me off to Michigan to study with Edward Sapir. Beginning in Guatemala, Townsend had for years been making friends with leading scholars and government officials (including corresponding with Sapir). And in 1937 in Mexico he was pushing us to write and publish linguistic articles (see two, of that date, in my bibliography edited by Brend 1987) and to attend linguistic conferences.

The Sapir-Bloomfield Era

Edward Sapir (1884–1939)

In the summer of 1937, I studied with Sapir at the Linguistics Institute of the Linguistic Society of America being held at the University of Michigan. At that time I was a young, 25-year-old naive beginner, with only one summer of previous linguistic training in 1935, and two years of field-work study of the Mixtec language in southern Mexico. In the first hour of hearing Mixtec, working through an interpreter, I knew that the language was tonal—the numbers one and nine differed by pitch only. But after two years of intense study of that language, I could still not tell how many contrastive pitches there were. Then, in one "coffee cup" session with Sapir in 1937, there in Michigan, he showed me how he had analyzed the tones of Navajo, using frames: The Navajo word *ni* with high tone meant "he said"—and nothing went higher in any sentence with it. The word for "horse," following "he said," was as high in tone pitch as "he said," but the word for "grass," following "he said," went lower. So it was clear that there were contrasting high and low tones in Navajo speech. At the end of my summer with Sapir, I went back to the Mixtec area, tried the technique, and it worked—Mixtec turned out to have three tones. And across the state, the language of the Mazatec people, where my sister Eunice worked with Florence Hansen, had four tones. I am deeply indebted to Sapir for that help so long ago, a field research technique that I have since passed on, directly or indirectly, to hundreds of students over a half-century of teaching.

Sapir taught me more than linguistics. I looked to him as a role model in handling personal relations. He was kindly to beginners. For example, one day I came into the building where he was seated. I sat down beside him, and started to show him the list of words in English, which I had just received from Bernard Bloch (who was teaching us the structure of English vowels at the LSA Institute). He took the sheet, put his finger on the first word, and said, "*Father*—now how would I say that word?" And it was through Sapir's article "Sound Patterns in Language," published in 1925 in the inaugural issue of *Language* (the flagship journal of the Linguistic Society of America, of which he was a crucial founder) that I learned to appreciate the important significance of relationships among sounds, rather than just their objective features. This became the basic philosophical foundation for my understanding of the difference between phonetics and phonemics. A phoneme, for a particular language, is considered here as psychologically a reality for the native speaker of that language. But the view of general phonetics as an approach to understanding the total list of phonetic items in the world does not have that kind of psychological "local" status.

Leonard Bloomfield (1887–1949)

However, it wasn't from Sapir that I first heard the word "phoneme." That term came to me in 1936 out of Leonard Bloomfield's classic book *Language* (1933). Eugene Nida, a student at SIL's 1936 linguistic course in Sulfur Springs put the book into my hands that summer. But my understanding of the concept grew only after I had read Sapir's "Sound Patterns" article. Bloomfield's book was more surprising to me because of the elegant way in which he described the development of historical linguistics, of which I was ignorant. His handling of morphological structure was also important to me. The whole book was a heuristic surprise to my initial thinking about how language worked.

In terms of personal relations, Bloomfield seemed to be very different from Sapir. Whereas Sapir frequently commented publicly on topics presented at the summer meeting of the Linguistic Society in Ann Arbor, Bloomfield rarely did so—and only when an important theoretical point was at issue. One linguist told me that Bloomfield was living in his home for the summer, but had instructed him not to invite visitors. Bloomfield was much more reserved, socially, than Sapir. What a surprise, therefore, when Bloomfield invited me to stay overnight in his home in Chicago, when I went on a train with him. (This was in June 1938 when I was en route to Arkansas for my fourth summer at SIL). He was following a request Charles Fries made to him to consider helping me to get credit for the summer's class in Ann Arbor, even though I had to leave early. Bloomfield asked me about Mixtec, and my work with SIL; and he requested that I write to him about my research on Mixtec as a way to complete the Ann Arbor course and satisfy Fries.

Bloomfield also encouraged me about a book I was writing on intonation. He wrote a letter in 1943 (quoted in Pike 1989:220), saying, "the book is beautiful and it is the first thing on intonation that I have read with any interest or profit." As a young aspiring linguist, one can imagine how this encouraged me in my budding career. Some time later, when I was in Bloch's office at Yale, Bloomfield came in, and suggested to Bloch that he publish my intonation volume (1945). Bloch refused. (He apparently preferred the work of Rulon Wells.) Bloomfield had known of my Christian commitment, and although his book *Language* had appeared to be behavioristic in scientific approach, he one day stated in an LSA (Linguistic Society of America) meeting: "We have no objection to someone saying that there has been a revelation from God, but we must handle our linguistic science separately." In 1945 I met Bloomfield for the last time. (He died in 1949 at age 62.) We were dining at the faculty club at Yale. But during this dinner, he leaned forward in his chair, and said: "If when I die I find that the Roman Catholic priest is right, I'm going to laugh!" He said this of himself, seriously, in a potentially humorous context, to a Christian student. I enjoyed seeing that humorous side of Bloomfield, who was a Jew. And this brings me to mention here an interesting question that arose in my mind in those days: How was it possible that so many of my great teachers (e.g., Sapir, Bloomfield, Bloch, Trager) were Jews? My own guess was that some centuries before my memory span, the Jews were not allowed to own big property, nor to play an important role in politics—but no one objected to their studying at universities—so linguistics and other academic fields were some of their outlets, to which I am indebted so deeply. There was some prejudice against Jewish professors in those days. I occasionally heard students make offhand bigoted remarks against them, and it made me uncomfortable. (Marvin Harris [1999:71] also mentions this prejudice against Jews in his new book, and that major universities did oppose admitting Jews in the 1920s.)

At the University of Michigan

Charles Fries (1887–1967)

As Townsend was my mentor for my work in SIL, Fries was my mentor for my work at the University of Michigan. He arranged for me to do my doctoral studies in the summer sessions of the LSA there, since I could not leave my SIL work in Mexico in the winter. (Students were not allowed to do their doctorates in the summers only, since many of the most experienced faculty members would be absent—but in Michigan, because of the summer sessions of the LSA, many special faculty were present.) Fries had me present my work on tone and phonetics to faculty seminars, which led to further help for me from that faculty. He arranged for the Michigan publication of several of my books, when I did not have another outlet for them. When I was on furlough from Mexico, he had me work on phonetics and later on intonation, for the English Language Institute. He arranged several grants in relation to these projects. We published an article together (Fries and Pike 1949) on "Coexistent Phonemic Systems." I am deeply indebted to him in these academic and personal ways. In gratitude, I published a poem about him in 1968 (Pike 1968, see now in Heimbach 1997(4):201), after his death:

A Great Shade Tree Has Fallen

A great shade tree
    Has fallen low.
Yet high it rose
    O'er battle shout
And lonely vigil kept.

Wail, starting sprouts—
    Grow ye must,
Fill forest gap
    With shadow young and straight,
Grow lumber tall,

While cities waiting strength
    Crave knotless planks.
Age gave seed formed
    In cones torn from limbs
By winds blown high in trees.

Leslie White (1900–1975)

In 1948 I was appointed as an associate professor in the departments of Anthropology and English at the University of Michigan. (Later, the Michigan Linguistics Department was formed, and I moved from English over to that.) Leslie White was the chairman of the Anthropology Department. Whereas I was a theist, he was a mechanist. My wife and I had him over to our house for dinner one evening in the late '40s, where he and I enjoyed talking freely about things where we differed, but were both interested. White said to me something to the effect that "We have no free choice except in the bathroom." To this I replied, "How, then, can you expect students to choose voluntarily that your teaching is to be accepted as valid or true?" His reply to me was: "What is truth?" To answer that question I responded: "Truth, for me, has to be in conclusions resulting from the careful testing of observations using what equipment and context might be available. For example," I said, "it would mean that if some population could see only in straight lines, then they would see the sun appearing on the horizon, pass above them in a straight line, disappear, only to reappear the next day doing the same thing. If all other testing confirmed that observation, then that would be truth for such individuals." White said that he liked such a statement very much, and would use it.

E. Adelaide Hahn (1893–1967)

My wife Evelyn and I first met Prof. E. Adelaide Hahn in one of the summer sessions of the Linguistic Society of America (LSA) in Ann Arbor, Michigan at the University of Michigan. This was in the early 1940s. She was a vibrant, enthusiastic, highly competent classicist, also involved in research on the Hittite language. She was on the faculty of Hunter College in New York City. She was in the organizing meeting in December 1924 of the LSA, and was elected president of the LSA in 1945.

We were intrigued and delighted with her presentation at a summer session of the LSA at the University of Texas at Austin in 1961. She was discussing the genitives in Greek. She listed illustration after illustration together with where each was to be found in the literature during that lecture. Evelyn recognized the ones that she quoted from the New Testament, so we were sure that all her sources were just as accurate. However, if she had any notes at all, they must have been on the ceiling, because that was the only place she looked when she wasn't looking directly at her audience!

Another time in Ann Arbor a phonetician was giving a paper and to emphasize his point he played a tape of some ten utterances of phonetic data, asking the audience to write down what they heard. When the dictation was finished, he gave the answers. No sooner had he finished than Prof. Hahn called out, "Gordon, you have mixed up your tapes. I'm not used to getting so many things wrong! [because his answers did not match those which she had written down]." Yes, the next day Gordon apologized to everyone; he had indeed mixed up his tapes!

J. R. Firth (1890–1960)

I knew Firth both in England, when I was lecturing there, and at the University of Michigan, where he was lecturing. Two personal items stand out in Evelyn's and my memories. In England I walked into one of his classrooms, and was talking to his students or colleagues. He walked in, and appeared a bit uneasy because I had not checked in with him first. I told him that I had been saying to his students that I felt that a hierarchical approach needed to go higher—sentence was not enough, paragraph was not enough, etc. He then said, "OK, if you want to go half way to heaven, Pike!" To which I replied: "What's wrong with that?" In Michigan, he was speaking to a local audience, discussing how phonology spread more widely than the word; and they had difficulty following him. I stood up and tried to explain Firth's position to them. Firth then said to me: "That's right, Pike, you are the only one here who understands me!" We continued to be friends.

In my 1967 book I included dozens of references—see the index—to his work, more than most other scholars (and I approved of his dealing with hierarchy beyond the word). For example (see reference in Pike 1967:619), he treats meaning as being on a "series of levels" (Firth 1951:76) where the meaning "of the whole event is dispersed and dealt with by a hierarchy of linguistic techniques descending from social contextualization to phonology." Also (in Pike 1967:616, Firth 1937:126) he affirms that words "mean what they do," being both "affecting and effective" in meaning. Hierarchy also affected phonological theory, for him. He states (in Pike 1967:415, Firth 1949:129) that "we may abstract those features which mark word or syllable initials and word or syllable finals or word junctions from the word, piece, or sentence, and regard them syntagmatically as prosodies, distinct from the phonemic constituents which are referred to as units of consonant and vowel systems."

M. A. K. Halliday (1925–)

In my view, Halliday was very much a successor to Firth. In various ways, however, many of his principles can be seen as related to some of mine. My most extensive discussion of that fact can be seen in my book *Language* (1967:506–509), in a section entitled "On Halliday's Prosodic Approach to Grammar." (I will be drawing heavily on that section, for my comments here.) In his 1961 article (p. 247), Halliday refers to fundamental categories as including "unit," "structure," "class," and "system." They are comparable to tagmemic terms, except that by "unit" he implies "syntagmatic level," rather than definition by way of tagmemic contrast, variation, and distribution.

We would differ, in that I would handle phonetic variants of a phoneme as all parts of that same unit—so that the aspirated [t] in the first syllable of my American pronunciation of "tatter" would differ from the flapped unaspirated [t] of my second syllable of that word—and he would not grant a single phoneme unit for the two. When I deal with a phoneme from the perspectives of particle, wave, and field, I leave room (in the wave perspective—compare his and Firth's prosodies) for features, which spread, from one phoneme to give partial overlap with another. Halliday also goes beyond language, for example in discussing the analysis of a meal (1961:278–279), with a "mouthful" as a "gastronomic morpheme." Compare my extensive analysis of a recorded breakfast meal in my book *Language* (1967:122–128).

The Bloch-Trager Era and Later

Bernard Bloch (1907–1965)

I have indicated above that I profited in studying about American vowel structure with Bloch in Michigan in the summer of 1937, but that he did not want to publish my intonation materials in the *Language* series. Similarly, he did not want to publish my tone volume since, as he told me, he did not like my sources about Japanese pitch. He also later rejected my essay "Grammatical Prerequisites to Phonemic Analysis," which clashed with the Bloch/Trager search for science via the autonomous analysis of different levels of language structure. (I felt that they could not be handled separately.) So I submitted the essay to the new society founded by (among others) Roman Jakobson and André Martinet. Jakobson said that they founded the new society (International Linguistics Association) because Bloch rejected his article on poetry—saying something to the effect that poetry was not appropriate for scientific study. So the new society published my essay in *Word* (1947b) (where it became one of the most widely cited of my earlier publications).

George Trager (1906–1992)

Added to his rejection of overlapping levels of phoneme and word in scientific description, Trager—like other theoretical academicians of those days—wanted scientific research, as such, strictly separated from practical language learning or analysis. This showed up in his very critical review (1950) of my book *Phonemics: A Technique for Reducing Language to Writing* (1947a). He said (p. 158) that he as reviewer "must therefore condemn the book as a theoretical work, and even more as a textbook—since as the latter it will lead astray many who might otherwise be valuable workers in linguistic science."

But our differences of theoretical viewpoint did not prevent Trager and me from having both an academic and personal interlocking friendship.

One summer, for example, about 1947 at SIL (now moved from Arkansas to the University of Oklahoma), I had Trager give two lectures, since I wanted our students to know the principle linguists of the time, in order to learn important approaches from them even when they had different presuppositions or methodology from mine.

Morris Swadesh (1909–1967)

When Townsend sent Sapir some of my materials, Sapir responded by sending me some articles by Swadesh. I found Swadesh's discussion of the pedagogy of phonemics (1934, and 1937 on long consonants) very helpful. On the other hand, when Swadesh went to Mexico, and got involved in applied linguistics there, I could not accept his view about [practical] alphabets [for indigenous languages], where—if I understood him correctly—he favored writing in a classical phonetic form rather than in an alphabet adaptable to Spanish orthography.

Zellig S. Harris (1909–1992)

Although Zellig Harris and I had some interaction many years ago, I did not know him well. I drew from his work, however, and I remain grateful to him for his contribution to linguistics. In fact, I was astonished recently when I was checking my references to Harris in my *Language in Relation to a Unified Theory of the Structure of Human Behavior* (1967). In the index there were some fifty references to him—more than to almost any other scholar! Many of these were brief mentions in relation to the work of others, but a number included relevant quotes.

Harris was a teacher of important students, including three of my colleagues from SIL (Sarah C. Gudschinsky, Robert E. Longacre, and Richard S. Pittman), Noam Chomsky, and others. Harris early (1952) published on discourse structure, even though he considered that some of the information "goes beyond descriptive linguistics" (1952:1) in that it was "beyond the limits of a single sentence at a time." This he considered to be one of two types of problems. The other "is the question of correlating 'culture' and language" (i.e., nonlinguistic and linguistic behavior). This problem led in 1948 to my developing a holistic view, to include all of human behavior, resulting in my material of 1967, discussed below.

Harris also thought of structure as a network of relations (1954:149). He considered that the grammar as a whole consists of a kernel. These made up of a "set of elementary sentences and combiners, such that all the sentences of the language are obtained from one or more kernel sentences (with combiners) by means of one or more transformations" (Harris 1957:335).

Archibald A. Hill (1902–1992)

Hill was interested in voice quality, as I have been, but he felt (1958:21) that these elements were "not parts of larger metalinguistic structures." He was also interested in various poetic elements, but felt (1955:973) "that rhyme and alliteration are structures correlated with language but not a part of it." He was also interested in other items under discussion at the time, such as the validity of movable units of language, such that it is "quite obvious that the formulae for 'deriving' a passive sentence from an active one could not be stated as a manipulation unless the active sentence contained isolable items capable of being manipulated" (Hill 1962:345).

Charles F. Voegelin (1906–1986)

Voegelin became the editor of the *International Journal of American Linguistics* in 1944 after the death of its founder Boas. In that role he continued to keep up the interest in the descriptive analysis of American Indian languages. (It was a delight to me to find in Voegelin's first issue of the journal my article on the "Analysis of a Mixteco Text" [Pike 1944].) By 1952 Voegelin and Harris (1952:325) felt that linguistic descriptive tools were "uniquely fitted to the data of language, rather than to culture in general." (This was at the very time I was drafting the first volume (1954) of the early edition of my unified theory.)

Mary R. Haas (1910–1996)

The work of Haas is of special interest to me, since she did her doctoral dissertation in 1935 on an American Indian language (Tunica; see Haas 1941), the same year I started on my study in Mexico on Mixtec; and she, also, studied with Sapir and Bloomfield. Later she worked on Thai, and its tones (e.g., Haas 1958)—which also interested me, because of my struggles with the tones of Mixtec and other American languages. Still later, she worked on historical linguistics, beyond my own studies. (For further discussion of her work, see Pike 1998.)

Floyd G. Lounsbury (1914–1998) and Ward H. Goodenough (1919–)

Lounsbury (1956) dealt with the structure of semantic fields (in relation to the universe of discourse) in defining the meaning of words. Such a field may be subdivided by one or more variables. This, which I approved of, brought semantics and discourse into attention before many scholars drew on it. That same year, Lounsbury tried to analyze kin structure by using an analogy to relate phones to kinsmen, or kin type, or kin class—relating them to phonology rather than to grammar. This approach interested me, since it carried some relation to my then-developing unified theory (Pike 1967).

Goodenough, like Lounsbury, was interested (1951:64, 1956:195, and 1957:169) in the analysis of kinship in a larger cultural setting, relating it to procedures of linguistic analysis.

Charles Hockett (1916–2000)

I met Hockett, as I did many other linguists, at the summer linguistic meetings at Ann Arbor. It was probably in 1938 that I was asked to give an informal talk about phonetics. (I had disagreed with Trager about some phonetic principles.) At the end, Hockett, who was at the meeting, asked me if he could have a copy of my talk. I told him yes. Unfortunately, for me, I had not prepared a written copy. So I left Michigan, and started to try to write up the material. But it took longer and longer—and required very much reading of the available literature, in the States, and in Mexico.

After several months, I had a draft of the material. I took it to Michigan. Prof. Fries had me talk about it to an advanced seminar (including various faculty). Fries then suggested that I write my dissertation on phonetics instead of on tone, as I had intended. I did—with the resulting 1943 book *Phonetics: A Critical Analysis of Phonetic Theory and a Technic for the Practical Description of Sounds.*

Martin Joos (1907–1978)

My impression was that Joos occupied a theoretical position comparable to that of Bloch and Trager. Specifically, for example, I mentioned above that Bloch had rejected my article (1947b) on "Grammatical Prerequisites to Phonemic Analysis." Joos (1957:96, in an added editorial note) referred to my view there as "the ghost of the slain dragon" which "continued to plague the community of linguists."

On occasion, however, he made suggestions to me that I thought were very interesting. Once, for example, he suggested that even the general height of the voice may prove to be discretely split into four "kinds" of levels which I later came to call relaxed, normal, intense, and excited.

Dell Hymes (1927–)

Hymes, an anthropologist, reviewed my 1967 book in *American Anthropologist* (1969). He was one of the first to show interest and approval of my attempt to deal with the structural analysis of culture beyond linguistics. That pleased me—although he was disappointed that in "the work Pike concludes his book by falling back on a treatment of language and society as separate parallel structures that his opening chapters had transcended" (Hymes 1969:362).

In a more recent work by Hymes and Fought (1981), we have an extensive history of American structuralism. (It goes far beyond the detail which I have given here.) It was an encouragement to me (after they pointed out that much of my material was somewhat ignored at that period) when they added that: "the more one insisted, as did Pike, that native speaker reactions, judgments, were essential tests of validity, the more one would want theory to be consistent with practice (as did Pike)."

Marvin Harris (1927–[2001]) and Pike's Etics and Emics

In the first 1954 volume of the early edition of my *Language* (1967), I took the well-known terms "phonetics" and "phonemics" and generalized on them by deleting the first syllable "phon," about sounds, and using the balance of the terms to relate to all language and human behavior, as well as to mental or social relations in a culture. I developed the terms ETIC and EMIC in order to help to capture the essential academic difference between a general approach to an etic system covering all structures of the world, and the analysis of some specific emic local structure of some particular language or culture. The emic/etic concept today has become very widely used in many disciplines, textbooks, encyclopedias, dictionaries, and anthropological descriptions (although often without reference to the origin of the terms or the concept). In some instances, also, the emic/etic terms are described differently, or are used differently, from what I had originally intended (Headland 1990).

Native reaction (both to and by language and nonverbal behavior) is important to identifying emic material relevant to a person's cultural structure. But scholars may analyze such systems differently. One general approach might be called "psycholinguistics," which does not seem to tie the parts as closely together as we wish to do in our "unified" theory of human behavior. (For a discussion of variants of this last approach, with some bibliographical references, see Pike 1967:351–354.)

Clearly, the most saliently different use of the emic and etic terms was developed in the 1960s by Marvin Harris (1964), the leading theoretician in materialist anthropology today. [Editor's note: Pike wrote this essay in the year 2000. Marvin Harris died on October 25, 2001.] Harris appears to consider the emic term to be more mental, and the etic term more physical. Harris and I constructively worked out some of our differences in meaning and use of the emic/etic concept in a public debate before six hundred anthropologists at the annual meeting of the American Anthropological Association in 1988 (published in Headland, Pike, and Harris 1990). Recently, Harris (1999:31-48) has made efforts to further clarify his use of emics and etics, and he recognized there (p. 37) that he had misread me for decades. Harris and I still do not conceptualize emics and etics in the same way, as he makes clear in his new book (1999:32, 37). For example, as I read him, he continues to equate emic and etic with ideal versus real behavior (pp. 44, 45). Still, I am glad to see that the concept has been so helpful in anthropology today. It has helped cultural materialists in their theory building for over a quarter century. I never imagined that the concept would lead others in such a direction; but I am rather satisfied that it did.

The work of etics and emics by Kenneth Pike was supplemented for phonetics by Eunice Pike and for grammar by Evelyn Pike. In 1955 my sister Eunice and I, in a small booklet titled *Live Issues in Descriptive Linguistics*, tried to survey (for graduate students) the scholars and problems discussed during the times of the two eras mentioned here (the Sapir-Bloomfield era and the Bloch-Trager era). As an introduction to each bibliographical section, we asked questions to try to highlight issues involved. A bit later, in a second edition (K. L. Pike and E. V. Pike 1960), we added more items involving publications from the Chomsky era, plus some other scholars and their publications from earlier times and from European sources.

My wife, Evelyn, and I published our classroom textbook *Grammatical Analysis*, (K. L. Pike and E. G. Pike 1977, revised 1982) and in 1983 we published our *Text and Tagmeme* to try to present to our students our understanding of the relation of grammatical to referential (content) structures (illustrated by a text), as well as the phonological hierarchical analysis of a poem from sound to text, plus a tetrahedron model for seeing the application of a matrix in practical description. Before that I published my *Linguistic Concepts: An Introduction to Tagmemics* (1982) to help students have access to a general summary (hopefully intelligible to them) of tagmemic theory.

Noam Chomsky (1928–)

In 1957 a young linguist named Noam Chomsky published a book which dramatically changed the face of descriptive linguistics in America. Chomsky emphasized formalism in terms of transformational grammar. He focused in his first book only on the sentence or below, and ignored semantics and discourse structure. I have never controlled Chomsky's approach in detail, and shall thus leave its discussion to others, including the addition of semantics or other features. I enjoyed, however, having Chomsky speak to my linguistics seminar at Michigan. I believe this was about 1964. He was pleasant to talk with, and I very much wanted my students to be acquainted with him as a person and as an innovative theoretician. I could not, however, adopt his basic starting point for mine, since I was working with unwritten languages, with no one to suggest new and unwritten sentences; and I saw no way to ignore working from a holistic viewpoint as a way to get into (and live within) the language and culture of a preliterate people. (In a related way, the philosopher Sinclair once said [1944:129] that explanation shows how "the previously unrelated fact or situation falls into a place in the pattern." I should say here that I have various SIL colleagues who have built components of some variety of transformational grammar into their own holistic approaches.)

Major Shifts in Twentieth-Century American Anthropology

I have reviewed here many interesting historical events that I have personally seen or experienced in the academy during my sixty-five years as an American linguistic anthropologist. But what do I see as being major movements since I first took up linguistics in 1935? There have been two major changes in my subfield of American anthropology during my academic career, as I see it. Both were uncomfortable for me. The first shift was the movement of linguistics away from the other three fields of anthropology. That became salient to me in the 1960s. I am glad to see the American Anthropological Association's emphasis today to try to bring linguistics back under the old four-field umbrella, where I think it belongs. [Editor's comment: Pike is here referring to the "four-fields" of

American anthropology—cultural anthropology, physical anthropology, archaeology, and linguistics—as anthropology was practiced until linguistics moved away to become a separate discipline in the middle of the twentieth century. Today linguistics is being increasingly brought back as a part of American anthropology.]

A second major change was the paradigm shift in linguistics from descriptive (or structural) linguistics to Chomskyan transformational linguistics. While this was good for anthropological linguistics—all linguistics is anthropological, by the way—it was unsettling for me personally because I came out of the Bloomfieldian descriptive linguistics school, and especially because the transformational revolution shoved my own tagmemics theory to the back burner. A humbling experience for me, but not surprising when we think of Thomas Kuhn's (1970) model.

The Condition of American Anthropology Today?

I end the above subtitle with a question mark, because while I can see far into the past where anthropology has come from, and especially its fourth field (linguistics), I struggle as I try to interpret the anthropology academy's current and future events. For me, at least, the most salient movement in American anthropology in the last decade has been Postmodernism.

While deconstructionism and postmodernist ideas were beginning to influence American anthropology before the 1990s, the growing strength of the movement didn't really impact anthropology, as I see it, until the last decade. Or at least most "modern" anthropologists didn't realize they were under attack until then. It is still going on in anthropology, though perhaps less obviously now than it was in the early '90s.

This is not the place to review Postmodernist anthropology. Suffice it to say here, it appears to me that it is not only changing the way anthropology is viewed by the public but also the way anthropologists practice their trade. I have heard numerous colleagues over the past five years say that they think American anthropology is in a major crisis today. I hope they are wrong, but I fear they may be right. I admit I am especially depressed about this as I write the final words of this essay, because of the hundreds of worldwide news stories published in recent days against anthropologists. I have never seen anthropology take such a beating in the press as it has this month (November 2000). These stinging news reports concern a book published just this month (November) by journalist Patrick Tierney (2000) accusing certain anthropologists of crimes and human rights violations against an indigenous

group in the Amazon. Two of the most critical stories against anthropologists in general were both published on October 8 (Cockburn
2000; Zalewski 2000). Exaggerated unfair stories, I suspect, but
enough to make serious anthropologists cringe. Who knows at this
point whether the stories are true? But it is clear that it is not helping
the public image of anthropology right now. Maybe journalists are
more influenced by Postmodernism than anthropologists. [Editor's
comment: Pike was right about the seriousness of this controversy. In
the weeks after he wrote this paragraph, thousands of articles appeared
in newspapers, science magazines, and on the Internet about this
"Darkness in El Dorado." Readers looking for information on this will
find "Doug's Anthropological Niche" the best place to go to begin surf-
ing on the topic http://www.anth.uconn.edu/gradstudents/dhume/
darkness_in_el_dorado/index.htm (accessed July 8, 2002).]

I objected, some time ago, to a deconstructionist approach, which
seems to me to say that words have no meaning which can be shared, with
some degree of certainty, with others. So I wrote a poem objecting to this
(see it, now in Heimbach 1997(2):12):

Inkblot Poetry—A Query

"Me, trying to say something?"
"Oh, no—you're just the author.
Someone else must say
What's said...Right?"
    (*Author's* rights
    Are semantically bankrupt,
    Faced by interpretive
    Staked-out claims
    Affirming that poems
    Are pretty inkblots
    Waiting readers'
    Dreamy impositions!...
    But *reader* "re-write" rights?...)
"And when you are
Saying I said—
Are you then 'saying'
Something to me?"
    "No, just throwing words
    At other unhearing wordless 'things'."

From Now into the Future—A Pikean Dream

In a 1999 article in *The Scientific American* on "A Unified Physics by 2050?," Steven Weinberg says (p. 68): "One of the primary goals of physics is to understand the wonderful variety of nature in its unified way. The greatest advances...have been steps towards this goal...terrestrial and celestial mechanics by Isaac Newton...space-time geometry and the theory of gravitation by Albert Einstein...and of chemistry and atomic physics through the advent of quantum mechanics..." This jolted me into remembering my experience in 1948, when I was tired of writing books on phonology and wanted to turn to write on grammar. But I did not want to lose my past experience in phonology, so I went through my *Phonemics* book to see what there was there that could carry over, in general principle. I came up with items that I now call "contrast, variation and distribution." I had no trouble seeing that [p] and [b] contrasted in "pie" and "buy"; or that "John" was distributed as subject in "John shot the dog," or as object [of a preposition] in "The dog was shot by John." But, I asked with difficulty, "What is the English language distributed into?" I replied to myself: "with different dialects, yes—but all of them together, into what?" And now the important jump: "All types of English are distributed into culture."

This set the tone of my research for years. I could no longer study just phonology, or any other topic isolated from culture when I wanted to discuss its distributional component. (I used footnotes to state that further work needed to be in done in related matters, which should now include such distribution.) Nor could I ignore hierarchy, in grammar, phonology, and lexicon, which drove me at least that far (and on up to theism—see above my discussion with Firth). So in 1948 I started working on this, published in three volumes (Vol. I, 1954; Vol. II, 1955; Vol. III, 1960) and later revised and published together (1967) under the title of *Language in Relation to a Unified Theory of the Structure of Human Behavior.* Various kinds of cultural nonlinguistic material (but with some verbal materials often involved) were mentioned (1967:27–32), e.g., a motion picture of a wedding, a banquet for departing students, bargaining (in the Mazatec language) with whistles, water polo, a basketball game, a parade, gestures; plus a football game (pp. 98–106).

These materials show that I would not be willing to stop with a separation of phonology, grammar, and social materials with their meanings, nor to stop with some feature or domain isolated from culture. In short, I wanted a unified theory. And this fact has affected my view of the past developments of linguistic theory, as discussed above. I do not want to be "neutral" or "abstract" or "domain oriented," but rather unified in an approach to human nature as I experience it.

Here, I would like to utilize the metaphor of a helix (Pike 1991) to keep graduate students from being surprised, or bothered when (1) new ideas come on the horizon which seem to challenge their favorite professors or (2) old ideas come back again into unexpected but partial focus. A helix can be thought of as a vine spiraling up a post, winding around it, so that from a certain direction it is at first seen, then lost from sight, and then seen again, and again. In linguistics, by analogy, a new idea does not necessarily destroy an old one, but may add to it or change observer focus for a moment. So, here, I wish to mention several approaches to some part of the discipline that I have enjoyed, and hope that the discipline will use such approaches in ways beyond my own experience with them. Perhaps, also, the helix would make it easier for students to deal with "both-and" rather than only "X versus Y."

Linguists need to be interested in philosophical presuppositions underlying anthropology. In the 1980s my interest focused on linguistics in relation to philosophy (see my *Talk, Thought, and Thing: The Emic Road Toward Conscious Knowledge*, 1993). There I urged students' attention to my belief that a theory of cross-cultural knowledge needs to focus upon personal interaction in a social-physical context. The observer must be included in the description of all social interaction, or of rule-oriented material. Phonological, grammatical, and referential features all affect human behavior hierarchically. Each needs to be treated in relation to features of slot (where?: context, position in behavioral structure), role (why?: function, meaningfulness or relevance), class (what?: the list of alternatives with different semantic impacts in that position), and cohesion (how controlled?: its agreement with other items in a particular context, or its control of them or by them). The outsider analyst or the insider mother-tongue analyst can choose at any one moment to focus on the function of an item as if it were a separate particle, or as if it were merely a nuclear point in a smear from one unit to another (a wave), or as if it were primarily an analyzable point in an intersecting matrix of items or events or thought [a field]. A holistic view of truth requires the search for pattern within pattern within pattern of knowledge. (But basic presuppositions, in my view, come from person, not from logic—and there is an observer at the source of every such search, varying, however, if one is a theist—as I am—or a mechanist.) In relation to such viewpoints, I choose to put person beyond logic (Pike 1992).

For a partial understanding of some of these relations between person and person, person and event, person and thing, person and feeling, person and ultimate reality, I would hope that poetry could in some way be helpful to the anthropologist. In this past decade, for example, Sharon Heimbach (1997) gathered a thousand of my poems in five volumes. Along with the study of poetry in its emotional relation to humanity, there is the need to be aware of the mode of physical pronunciation of poetry (e.g., its intonation, or the harshness of its voice quality), which carries much of the inter-social meaning of human nature, in its holistic relation to people and context.

The physical, geological, and social contexts can be seen interweaving in the following poem of mine (in Heimbach 1997(4):202). A time change, from one day to the next, occurs at a point in the Pacific called Wake Island. I have used that point as a metaphor for the need for "passing on the baton" in scholarship, from an old person (me) to the young (you!):

Placard at Wake Island

"The U.S. day begins at Wake"—
Start the clock;
Run the full race
To end—and early sleep.

String from
Pole to Pole
Marks life in two.
"Hello Wednesday!"
"Good-bye Tuesday!"
Someone must begin,
Lest all die.

Spin the world's dial:
Come the sun.
Warm hands by day,
Rest by night—
Or care for airstrip
So others may embark.

Our day is done.
Who carries on
In wind and tropic rain
Our journey round the clock?

References

Bloomfield, Leonard. 1933. *Language*. New York: Holt, Rinehart and Winston.

Brend, Ruth M, compiler. 1987. *Kenneth Lee Pike bibliography*. Arcadia Bibliographica Virorum Eruditorum 10. Bloomington, Ind.: Eurasian Linguistic Association.

Chomsky, Noam. 1957. *Syntactic structures*. The Hague: Mouton.

Cockburn, Alexander. 2000. What happens when genocide poses as science. *Los Angeles Times*, October 8, p.M5.

Elson, Benjamin, ed. 1961. *Mayan studies I*. Summer Institute of Linguistics Publications in Linguistics 5. Norman: Summer Institute of Linguistics of the University of Oklahoma.

Firth, J. R. 1937. *The tongues of men*. London: Watts and Co.

Firth, J. R. 1949. Sounds and prosodies. *Transactions of the Philological Society* 1948:137–152.

Firth, J. R. 1951. General linguistics and descriptive grammar. *Transactions of the Philological Society* 1951:69–87.

Fries, Charles C., and Kenneth L. Pike. 1949. Coexistent phonemic systems. *Language* 25:29–50.

Goodenough, Ward H. 1951. *Property, kin, and community on Truk*. Yale University Publications in Anthropology, No. 46. New Haven, Conn.: Yale University Press.

Goodenough, Ward H. 1956. Componential analysis and the study of meaning. *Language* 32:195–216.

Goodenough, Ward H. 1957. Cultural anthropology and linguistics. *Monograph Series on Language and Linguistics* 9:167–173. Washington, D.C.: Georgetown University Press.

Haas, Mary R. 1941. Tunica. In Franz Boas (ed.), *Handbook of American Indian languages*, vol. 4, 1–143. New York: J. J. Augustin.

Haas, Mary R. 1958. The tones of four Thai dialects. *The Bulletin of the Institute of History and Philology*, Academia Sinica 29:817–826.

Halliday, M. A. K. 1961. Categories of the theory of grammar. *Word* 17:241–292.

Harris, Marvin. 1964. *The nature of cultural things*. New York: Random House.

Harris, Marvin. 1999. *Theories of culture in postmodern times*. Walnut Creek, Calif.: AltaMira Press.

Harris, Zellig. 1952. Discourse analysis. *Language* 28:1–30.

Harris, Zellig. 1954. Distributional structure. *Word* 10:146–162.

Harris, Zellig. 1957. Co-occurrence and transformation in linguistic structure. *Language* 33:283–340.

Headland, Thomas N. 1990. Introduction: A dialogue between Kenneth Pike and Marvin Harris. In Headland, Pike, and Harris (eds.), 13–27.

Headland, Thomas N., Kenneth L. Pike, and Marvin Harris, eds. 1990. *Emics and etics: The insider/outsider debate*. Newbury Park: Sage Publications.

Heimbach, Sharon, compiler and editor. 1997. *Seasons of life: A complete collection of Kenneth L. Pike poetry*. Dallas: Summer Institute of Linguistics. [Five volumes.]

Hill, Archibald A. 1955. Analysis of the Windhover, an experiment in structural method. *Publications of the Modern Language Association of America* 70:968–978.

Hill, Archibald A. 1958. Linguistics since Bloomfield. In Harold B. Allen *Readings in applied linguistics*, 14–23. New York: Appleton-Century-Crofts, Inc.

Hill, Archibald A. 1962. A postulate for linguistics in the sixties. *Language* 38:345–351.

Hymes, Dell. 1969. Review of Pike 1967. *American Anthropologist* 71:361–363.

Hymes, Dell, and John Fought. 1981. *American structuralism*. The Hague: Mouton.

Joos, Martin, ed. 1957. *Readings in linguistics*. Washington, D.C.: American Council of Learned Societies.

Kuhn, Thomas. 1970. *The structure of scientific revolutions*, second edition. Chicago: University of Chicago Press.

Lounsbury, Floyd G. 1956. A semantic analysis of the Pawnee kinship usage. *Language* 32:158–194.

Nida, Eugene. [1946] 1949. *Morphology: The descriptive analysis of words*, second edition. Ann Arbor: University of Michigan Press. [First edition published in 1946.]

Pike, Kenneth L. 1943. *Phonetics: A critical analysis of phonetic theory and a technic for the practical description of sounds*. Ann Arbor: University of Michigan Press.

Pike, Kenneth L. 1944. Analysis of a Mixteco Text. *International Journal of American Linguistics* 10:113–138.

Pike, Kenneth L. 1945. *The intonation of American English*. Ann Arbor: University of Michigan.

Pike, Kenneth L. 1947a. *Phonemics: A technique for reducing languages to writing*. Ann Arbor: University of Michigan Press.

Pike, Kenneth L. 1947b. Grammatical prerequisites to phonemic analysis. *Word* 3:155–172.

Pike, Kenneth L. 1961. Foreward to Cakchiquel grammar. In Elson (ed.), 3–8.

Pike, Kenneth L. [1954, 1955, 1960] 1967. *Language in relation to a unified theory of the structure of human behavior*, second edition. The Hague: Mouton and Co. [First edition published in 3 volumes by the Summer Institute of Linguistics, Glendale, California.]

Pike, Kenneth L. 1968. A great shade tree. Originally in *Language Learning*; reprinted in Heimbach (comp.) 1997, vol. 4:201.

Pike, Kenneth L. 1982. *Linguistic concepts—An introduction to tagmemics*. Lincoln: University of Nebraska Press.

Pike, Kenneth L. 1989. Recollection of Bloomfield. In *Historiographia Linguistica* XVI:1/2.217–223. Amsterdam: John Benjamins.

Pike, Kenneth L. 1991. A revolutionary "Helix" in linguistic history—as seen over half a century by one who has lived it. In *Cairo studies in English: Essays in honor of Saad Gamal El-Din*, Special issue, 21–26. Giza: University of Cairo. [No editor's name given; ISBN number listed as 977-223-065-8.]

Pike, Kenneth L. 1992. Person beyond logic, in language, life, and philosophy. In *The Eighteenth LACUS Forum 1991*, 23–27. Lake Bluff, Ill.: Linguistic Association of Canada and the United States.

Pike, Kenneth L. 1993. *Talk, thought, and thing—The emic road toward conscious knowledge*. Dallas: Summer Institute of Linguistics.

Pike, Kenneth L. 1998. Mary Haas, A biographical memoir. In *Biographical Memoirs* Vol. 76:3–13. Washington D.C.: The National Academy Press.

Pike, Kenneth L., and Eunice V. Pike. [1955] 1960. *Live issues in descriptive linguistics*, second edition. Santa Ana, Calif.: Summer Institute of Linguistics.

Pike, Kenneth L., and Evelyn G. Pike. [1977] 1982. *Grammatical analysis*, revised edition. Dallas: Summer Institute of Linguistics and the University of Texas at Arlington.

Pike, Kenneth L., and Evelyn G. Pike. 1983. *Text and tagmeme*. Norwood, N.J.: Ablex. [Also published London: Pinter in 1983.]

Sapir, Edward. 1925. Sound patterns in language. *Language* 1:37–51.

Sinclair, Angus. 1944. *An introduction to philosophy*. London: Oxford University Press.

Swadesh, Morris. 1934. The phonemic principle. *Language* 10:117–129.

Swadesh, Morris. 1937. The phonemic interpretation of long consonants. *Language* 13:1–10.

Tierney, Patrick. 2000. *Darkness in El Dorado: How scientists and journalists devastated the Amazon*. New York: W. W. Norton.

Townsend, William Cameron. 1961. Cakchiquel grammar. In Elson (ed.), 1–79.

Trager, George. 1950. Review of Pike 1947a [*Phonemics*]. *Language* 26:152–158.

Voegelin, Charles F., and Zellig S. Harris 1952. Training in anthropological linguistics. *American Anthropologist* 54:322–327.

Weinberg, Steven. 1999. A unified physics by 2050? *The Scientific American* 281(6):68–75. December.

Zalewski, Daniel. 2000. Anthropology enters the age of cannibalism. *The New York Times*. October 8.

5

Seasons of Life Reviewed

Jana R. Harvey

In the fall of 1998, Dr. Ken Pike shared his poetry with the students of the University of Texas at Arlington's linguistics circle, Lingua. When he commented that afternoon that no one had ever reviewed his poetry, many eyes turned in my direction as I was known as being perhaps the most poetically-inclined of the group. I had also been vocal in expressing my opinions of Dr. Pike's poetry to some of the other students. The Seasons of Life* set that he donated to the group recently passed into my hands when its previous caretaker headed overseas for a career in Bible translation with SIL. What follows is my review of* Seasons of Life *by Dr. Kenneth L. Pike.*

*   *   *

Blunt. Staccato. Jarring. Plosive. Pike does not waste words; neither does he mince them. At times you wonder what he is thinking in putting those particular words together in that particular way. At times the meaning hits you instantly as the words connect with your spirit.

Not like an abstract, which hands you all the connections so you don't really have to read the article, Pike's poems are like key words, telling the

---

*Seasons of Life is a five-volume collection of Pike's poetry, edited by Sharon Heimbach and published by the Summer Institute of Linguistics in 1997.

reader searching for understanding wherein lies the relevance of life, but only if he or she knows how those key words fit together to make a whole.

Pike's poetry is insider poetry. It is deeply personal, yet the believer, the linguist, the struggling, hoping, keeping-on human are all welcomed to the inner circle. Anyone who has cried, laughed, loved, lost, won, complained, or wondered why can find a poem in these volumes that shares his or her, not just season, but moment, of life.

Stress, word play, and alliteration being prime, Pike's poetry cannot be read silently. Best, of course, is to hear him read it. With his frequent use of capitals, parentheses, and other punctuation and spacing techniques, his poetry should not be solely listened to, either. The spoken word and the printed page must be blended for optimal interaction with his poetry.

Pike's poetry makes me chuckle. Why? Because its stress-induced regularity, simple rhymes, and short phrases give it lightness. When I read his poetry, I come away feeling that simply being alive is joyous and I should not take myself and my worries too seriously. I think this is what Pike intends. He says in the introduction to "Identity-Mine" that when we trust God, relax, and work, the job gets done; but both the order and ordering of those mandates are not flexible. We are called to work, but more than that, we are called to trust God and acknowledge that he is the one who gets the task accomplished. In the poem that follows (from vol. 4, p. 112), and with which I conclude this review, Pike speaks of a lone tribesman. But he might as easily speak of any one of us.

Heaven's Orchids

ONE—of singular value—
A lone orchid
Is SINGULARLY valuable…
Person above logic.
Person above math.
You, above mountains,
Might, just,
Be Heaven's mite.

6

The Writings of Kenneth L. Pike

A Bibliography

Joan Spanne and Mary Ruth Wise, compilers

Introduction

Kenneth L. Pike's writings span sixty-five years and encompass numerous topics and genres. Whereas Ruth Brend's 1987 bibliography[1] organizes Dr. Pike's writings as linguistic, religious, or poetic, distinguishing books, articles, and other media, here the compilers felt it appropriate to present them in a simple chronological order. Many of Pike's writings defy categorization, interweaving exposition of linguistic theory, lively exhortation, and expression of deep faith—and sometimes doubt. In other words, they reflect his hallmark, the integration of faith and scholarly endeavor, the one life of heart and mind together. Among Pike's works are more than thirty books (authored or edited), over two hundred scholarly articles, another ninety articles for popular magazines, eight poetry collections, and numerous other works—Scripture translations, individual poems, instruction workbooks, video and audio recordings.

An explanation of some typographic conventions might assist the reader: where Pike alone authored the work, no explicit indication of

---

[1]Brend, Ruth M., comp. 1987. *Kenneth Lee Pike Bibliography.* Arcadia Bibliographica Virorum Eruditorum, fasc. 10. Bloomington, Ind.: EUROLINGUA, Eurasian Linguistic Association.

authorship is given in the citation; where he coauthored or coedited a work, all authors/editors are listed in parentheses ( ); where the author(s) were not attributed on the original work itself, they are listed in square brackets [ ]. Finally, notes of subsequent editions, republications, reprintings, or relations to other works are given following the citation, again in square brackets.[2]

1937

Likenesses, differences and variation of phonemes in Mexican Indian languages and how to find them. *Investigaciones Lingüísticas* 4:134–139.

Una leyenda mixteca. *Investigaciones Lingüísticas* 4:262–270.

1938

Phonemic worksheet. Glendale, Calif.: Summer Institute of Linguistics. [Reprinted (1977) in *Grammatical Analysis*, 469–474.]

Practical suggestions toward a common orthography for Indian languages of Mexico for education of the natives within their own tongues. *Investigaciones Lingüísticas* 5:86–97.

1941

A reconstruction of phonetic theory. Ph.D. dissertation. University of Michigan. Ann Arbor, 229 pp.

1942

Pronunciation. Vol. 1 of An intensive course in English for Latin-American students 1. Ann Arbor, Mich.: English Language Institute. 123 pp. [Pedagogical materials rewritten and incorporated in *An intensive course in English for Latin-American students*, by Charles C. Fries and staff (1943); research materials revised and incorporated in *The intonation of American English* (1945).]

1943

Phonetics: A critical analysis of phonetic theory and a technic for the practical description of sounds. University of Michigan Publications in Language and Literature 21. Ann Arbor: University of Michigan. ix, 182 pp. [Reprinted with corrections (1944).]

Taxemes and immediate constituents. *Language* 19:65–82. [Repub. in Ruth M. Brend (ed.), *Kenneth L. Pike: Selected writings*, 11–31. The Hague: Mouton (1972).]

Tone languages: The nature of tonal systems, with a technique for the analysis of their significant pitch contrasts. Glendale, Calif.: Summer Institute of Linguistics, 121 pp. [Rev. ed. (1945), xi, 159 pp.]

---

[2]We are indebted to David Irwin, Vurnell Cobbey, and Ardella Olson for their painstaking efforts in helping to compile this bibliography.

1944

Analysis of a Mixteco text. *International Journal of American Linguistics* 10:113–138.

1945

Mock Spanish of a Mixteco Indian. *International Journal of American Linguistics* 11:219–224.

The intonation of American English. University of Michigan Publications in Linguistics 1. Ann Arbor: University of Michigan Press. xi, 200 pp. [Repub. (1946–1949, 1953, 1956, 1958, 1960, 1992).]

(With Aileen Traver and Virginia French). Step-by-step procedure for marking limited intonation with its related features of pause, stress and rhythm. In Charles C. Fries (ed.), *Teaching and learning English as a foreign language*, 62–74. Publication of the English Language Institute, University of Michigan, 1. Ann Arbor.

Tone puns in Mixteco. *International Journal of American Linguistics* 11:129–139.

1946

Another Mixteco tone pun. *International Journal of American Linguistics* 12:22–24. [Repub. in Ruth M. Brend (ed.), *Studies in tone and intonation by members of the Summer Institute of Linguistics,* 57–61. Basel: S. Karger (1975).]

The flea: Melody types and perturbations in a Mixtec song. *Tlalocan* 2:128–133.

Phonemic pitch in Maya. *International Journal of American Linguistics* 12:82–88.

(KLP and Ángel Merecías). *Cuendú ñanga* [Reader]. México, D.F.: Instituto Lingüístico de Verano. 15 pp.

(Donald Stark, Evelyn G. Pike, KLP, and Ángel Merecías). *Cuendú ndaā* [True tales]. México, D.F.: Instituto Lingüístico de Verano. 31 pp.

1947

God's guidance and your life work. *His* 7(1):19–28. [Repub. (1955) Santa Ana, Calif.: Wycliffe Bible Translators.]

Grammatical prerequisites to phonemic analysis. *Word* 3:155–172. [Repub. in Ruth M. Brend (ed.), *Kenneth L. Pike: Selected writings*, 32–50. The Hague: Mouton (1972); Valerie Becker Makkai (ed.), *Phonological theory: Evolution and current practice*, 153–165. New York: Holt, Rinehart and Winston (1972); Erik C. Fudge (ed.), *Phonology: Selected readings*, 115–135. Harmondsworth, England: Penguin Books (1973)].

On the phonemic status of English diphthongs. *Language* 23:151–159. [Repub. in Valerie Becker Makkai (ed.), *Phonological theory: Evolution and current practice*, 145–151. New York: Holt, Rinehart and Winston (1972).]

Phonemics: A technique for reducing languages to writing. University of Michigan Publications Linguistics 3. Ann Arbor: University of Michigan (1947), xvi, 254 pp.; [Repub. (1961, 1963), xx, 254 pp.; revision and expansion of 1943 mimeographed version, revised also in 1945, 1946.]

A text involving inadequate Spanish of Mixteco Indians. *International Journal of American Linguistics* 13:251–257.

(KLP and Eunice V. Pike). Immediate constituents of Mazateco syllables. *International Journal of American Linguistics* 13:78–91. [Repub. in Ruth M. Brend (ed.), *Studies in tone and intonation by members of the Summer Institute of Linguistics*, 62–83. Basel: S. Karger (1975).]

[KLP, Donald S. Stark, and Ángel Merecías]. *Tūhun vāha nī chaa makú* (El Santo Evangelio según San Marcos). Mexico: Sociedad Bíblica Americana. 84 pp. [Rev. ed. (2000), 76 pp. Beth Merrill, rev.]

[KLP and Donald S. Stark]. *Yāhá kúu kartá jā ní chaa pálú ápoxlí nuū ñáyʌvʌ ñúū filipó* (La Epístola del Apóstol San Pablo a los Filipenses). Mexico: Sociedad Bíblica Americana. 16 pp.

1948

Living on manna. *The Sunday School Times* (May 1), 3–4.

Problems in the teaching of practical phonemics. *Language Learning* 1(2):3–8.

Tone languages: A technique for determining the number and type of pitch contrasts in a language, with studies in tonemic substitution and fusion. University of Michigan Publications in Linguistics 4. Ann Arbor: University of Michigan Press. xii, 187 pp.

(Donald Sinclair and KLP). The tonemes of Mezquital Otomi. *International Journal of American Linguistics* 14:91–98.

1948–1949

Cuento mixteco de un conejo, un coyote y la luna. *Revista Mexicana de Estudios Antropológicos* 10:133–134.

1949

A problem in morphology-syntax division. *Acta Linguistica* 5:125–138. [Repub. in Ruth M. Brend (ed.), *Kenneth L. Pike: Selected writings*, 74–84. The Hague: Mouton (1972).]

(KLP and Charles C. Fries). Coexistent phonemic systems. *Language* 25:25–50. [Repub. in Ruth M. Brend (ed.), *Kenneth L. Pike: Selected writings*, 51–73. The Hague: Mouton (1972).]

1950

Axioms and *procedures for reconstructions in comparative linguistics: An experimental syllabus.* Glendale, Calif.: Summer Institute of Linguistics. 25 pp. [Rev. ed. (1957) 32 pp.]

[KLP and Donald S. Stark]. *Yāhá cácuu carta jā ní chaa San Juan apóstol* (Las Epístolas de San Juan Apóstol). Mexico: npl. 33 pp.

1951

The problems of unwritten languages in education. In *Report in UNESCO Meeting of Experts in the Use of Vernacular Languages*, 27 pp. Paris.

We'll tell them, but in what language? *His* 12(2):8–11, 14.

[KLP, Donald S. Stark, and Ángel Merecías]. *El Nuevo Testamento de nuestro señor Jesucristo* (Testamento jaa maa jitoho-yo Jesucristo). Cuernavaca: Tipografía Indígena. 365 pp.

1952

More on grammatical prerequisites. *Word* 8:106–121. [Repub. in Valerie Becker Makkai (ed.), *Phonological theory: Evolution and current practice*, 211–223. New York: Holt, Rinehart and Winston (1952)].

Operational phonemics in reference to linguistic relativity. *Journal of the Acoustical Society of America* 24:618–625. [Repub. in Ruth M. Brend (ed.), *Kenneth L. Pike: Selected writings*, 85–99. The Hague: Mouton (1972).]

1953

Intonational analysis of a Rumanian sentence. *Cahiers Sextil Puscariu* 2:59–60.

A note on allomorph classes and tonal technique. *International Journal of American Linguistics* 19:101–105.

1954

Language in relation to a unified theory of the structure of human behavior, part 1. Glendale, Calif.: Summer Institute of Linguistics. 170 pp. [Preliminary ed.]

(KLP and Evelyn G. Pike). *Laboratory manual for Pike's Phonemics*. Glendale, Calif.: Summer Institute of Linguistics. 156 pp.

1955

Language in relation to a unified theory of the structure of human behavior, part 2. Glendale, Calif.: Summer Institute of Linguistics. [Preliminary ed.] 85 pp.

Meaning and hypostasis. In Ruth H. Weinstein (ed.), *Report of the 6th Annual Round Table Meeting on Linguistics and Language Teaching*, 134–141. Monograph Series on Languages and Linguistics 8. Washington, D.C: Georgetown University Press. [Repub. in Ruth M. Brend (ed.), *Kenneth L. Pike: Selected writings*, 100–105. The Hague: Mouton (1972).]

(KLP and Eunice V. Pike). *Live issues in descriptive linguistics*. Glendale, Calif.: Summer Institute of Linguistics. iv, 23 pp. [2nd rev. ed. (1960) iv, 41 pp.]

1956

As correntes da linguística norteamericana. *Revista Brasileira de Filologia* 2:207–216.

Towards a theory of the structure of human behavior. In *Estudios antropológicos publicados en homenaje al doctor Manuel Gamio*, 659–671. Mexico. [Repub. in Ruth M. Brend (ed.), *Kenneth L. Pike: Selected writings*, 106–116. The Hague: Mouton (1972).]

(KLP and Willard Kindberg). A problem in multiple stresses. *Word* 12:415–428. [Repub. in Ruth M. Brend (ed.), *Studies in tone and intonation by members of the Summer Institute of Linguistics, 212–226*. Basel: S. Karger (1975).]

1957

Abdominal pulse types in some Peruvian languages. *Language* 33:30–35. [Repub. in Ruth M. Brend (ed.), *Studies in tone and intonation by members of the Summer Institute of Linguistics*, 204–211. Basel: S. Karger (1975).]

Gold, frankincense and myrrh. *The King's Business* 48(12):16–17.

Grammemic theory. *General Linguistics* 2:35–41.

Grammemic theory in reference to restricted problems of morpheme classes. *International Journal of American Linguistics* 23:119–128.

Prescription for intellectuals. *Eternity* 8(8):11, 44–45.

Slots and classes in the hierarchical structure of behavior (Language and life, part 2). *Bibliotheca Sacra* 114:255–262. [W. H. Griffith Thomas Memorial Lectureship for 1956, Dallas Theological Seminary and Graduate School of Theology.]

A stereoscopic window on the world (Language and life, part 1). *Bibliotheca Sacra* 114:141–156. [W. H. Griffith Thomas Memorial Lectureship for 1956, Dallas Theological Seminary and Graduate School of Theology.]

A training device for translation theory and practice (Language and life, part 3). *Bibliotheca Sacra* 114:347–362. [W. H. Griffith Thomas Memorial Lectureship for 1956, Dallas Theological Seminary and Graduate School of Theology.]

Why I believe in God. *His* 18(2):3–7, 32–33.

(David Beasley and KLP). Notes on Huambisa phonemics. *Lingua Posnaniensis* 6:1–8.

[KLP and Donald S. Stark]. *Tuhun vaha ni chaa San Juan* (El Santo Evangelio según San Juan). Cuernavaca: Tipografía Indígena. 63 pp.

1958

Discussion of reports on "The importance of distribution versus other criteria in linguistic analysis," by Paul Diderichsen and Henning Spang-Hanssen. In *Proceedings of the Eighth International Congress of Linguists,* 204–205. Oslo: Oslo University Press.

Flaming candle. *His* 18(7):30. [Poem.]

The individual. *Eternity* 9(9):18–19

Interpenetration of phonology, morphology and syntax. In *Proceedings of the Eighth International Congress of Linguists*, vol. 2, 363–371. Oslo: Oslo University Press.

Language and Life. Glendale, Calif.: Summer Institute of Linguistics. [43 pp.]. [Reprint of essays in *Bibliotheca Sacra* (1957–1958); W. H. Griffith Thomas Memorial Lectureship for 1956, Dallas Theological Seminary and Graduate School of Theology.]

On tagmemes, née gramemes. *International Journal of American Linguistics* 24:273–278.

Serving our colleagues. *His* 18(5):5–7.

The sin of independence. *His* 18(8):5–7.

Tristructural units of human behavior (Language and life, part 4). *Bibliotheca Sacra* 115:36–43. [W. H. Griffith Thomas Memorial Lectureship for 1956, Dallas Theological Seminary and Graduate School of Theology.]

(Esther Matteson and KLP). Non-phonemic transition vocoids in Piro (Arawak). *Miscellanea Phonetica* 3:22–30.

1959

Cause and effect in the Christian life. *His* 20(1):32–34.

Finishing the sentence—a linguistic parable. *His* 19(6):39–40.

Intellectual idolatry. *His* 19(5):5–6.

Language as particle, wave and field. *Texas Quarterly* 2(2):37–54. [Repub. in Ruth M. Brend(ed.), *Kenneth L. Pike: Selected writings*, 129–143. The Hague: Mouton (1972).]

A linguistic parable. *His* 19(6):39–40.

Our own tongue wherein we were born (The work of the Wycliffe Bible Translators and Summer Institute of Linguistics). *The Bible Translator* 10(2):3–15.

Walking. *The King's Business* 50(4):10–11.

Why the angels are curious. *The King's Business* 50(9):12–13.

(KLP, Ralph P. Barrett, and Burton Bascom). Instrumental collaboration on a Tepehuan (Uto-Aztecan) pitch problem. *Phonetica* 3:1–22.

(Rachel Saint and KLP). Notas sobre fonémica huarani ('Auca'). In *Estudios acerca de las lenguas huarani (auca), shimigae y zápara*, 4–17. Publicaciones Científicas del Ministerio de Educación del Ecuador. Quito: Ministerio de Educación.

1960

Building sympathy. *Practical Anthropology* 7:250–252.

Foreword to *Cakchiquel* grammar by William Cameron Townsend. In Benjamin Elson, (ed.), *Mayan Studies I*, 3–8. Norman: Summer Institute of Linguistics of the University of Oklahoma.

Language in Relation to a Unified Theory of the Structure of Human Behavior, part 3. Glendale, Calif.: Summer Institute of Linguistics. [Preliminary ed., 146 pp.]

Linguistic research as pedagogical support. In John G. Broder (ed.), *Papers of the National Conference on the Teaching of African Languages and Area Studies*, 32–39. Washington, D.C.: Georgetown University Press.

Nucleation. *Modern Language Journal* 44:291–295. [Repub. in *ILT News* 6:1–5 (1961); *Philippine Journal for Language Teaching* 1:1–7 (1963); in Harold B. Allen (ed.), *Teaching English as a Second Language*, 67–74, New York: McGraw-Hill (1965); in Ruth M. Brend (ed.), *Kenneth L. Pike: Selected writings*, 144–150, The Hague: Mouton (1972).]

Players. *His* 20(9):41–42.

Toward a theory of change and bilingualism. *Studies in Linguistics* 15:1–7.

When failure is success. *The Alliance Witness* 95(21):5.

Why there is a moral code. *The King's Business* 51(10):10–11.

[KLP and Donald S. Stark]. *Ja ni casaha chaa apóstol* (Los Hechos de los Apóstoles). Cuernavaca: Tipografía Indígena. 99 pp.

1961

Compound affixes in Ocaina. *Language* 37:570–581.

Language and meaning: Strange dimensions of truth. *Christianity Today* 5:690–692. [Repub. in *K.L. Pike, With heart and mind*, Grand Rapids, Mich.: Eerdmans (1962), pp. 46–53; in Ruth M. Brend (ed.), *Kenneth L. Pike: Selected writings*, 301–306. The Hague: Mouton (1972).]

Stimulating and resisting change. *Practical Anthropology* 8:267–274. [Repub. in Ruth M. Brend (ed.), *Kenneth L. Pike: Selected writings*,151–159. The Hague: Mouton (1972).]

Strange dimensions of truth. *Christianity Today* 5:690–692. [Repub. in Ruth M. Brend (ed.), *Kenneth L. Pike: Selected writings*, 301–306. The Hague: Mouton (1972).]

(Arthur Glasser and KLP). Current strategy in missions: Two proposals. *His* 9(12):1–15.

(KLP and Milton Warkentin). Huave: A study in syntactic tone with low lexical functional load. In Benjamin F. Elson and Juan Comas (eds.), *A William Cameron Townsend en el vigésimoquinto aniversario del Instituto Lingüístico de Verano*, 627–642. Mexico. [Repub. in Ruth M. Brend *(ed.), Studies in tone and intonation by members of the Summer Institute of Linguistics*, 153–172. Basel: S. Karger (1975).]

1961–1962

(Arthur Glasser and KLP). Current strategy in missions. A series of articles in *His* 22(1):8–14; 22(2):2–5, 21–23; 22(3):15–16, 21; 22(4):29–31, 25–28, 21.

1962

Dimensions of grammatical constructions. *Language* 38:221–244. [Repub. in Ruth M. Brend *(ed.), Kenneth L. Pike: Selected writings*,160–185. The Hague: Mouton (1972).]

Left-handed. *His* 22(9):36–47.

Practical phonetics of rhythm waves. *Phonetica* 8:9–30. [Repub. in Ruth M. Brend (ed.), *Studies in tone and intonation by members of the Summer Institute of Linguistics*, 11–32. Basel: S. Karger (1975).]

With heart and mind: A personal synthesis of scholarship and devotion. Grand Rapids, Mich.: Eerdmans. xii, 140 pp. [Repub. 1996. Duncanville, Tex.: Adult Learning Systems.]

(Rachel Saint and KLP). Auca phonemics. In Benjamin F. Elson (ed.), *Studies in Ecuadorian Indian Languages 1*, 2–30. Linguistic Series 7. Norman: Summer Institute of Linguistics of the University of Oklahoma.

1963

Choices in course design. In Mandelbaum, Lasker and Albert (eds.), *The teaching of anthropology*, 315–332. American Anthropological Association Memoir 94. Menasha: American Anthropological Association.

The hierarchical and social matrix of suprasegmentals. *Prace Filologiczne* 18:95–104.

Modern Christianity's crucial junctures [a note in a list of comments by scholars]. *Christianity Today* 8(1):32.

A syntactic paradigm. *Language* 39:216–230. [Repub. in Ruth M. Brend (ed.), *Advances in tagmemics*, 235–249. Amsterdam: North-Holland (1974); in Andrew B. Gonzalez and others (eds.), *Readings in Philippine linguistics*, 583–600. Manila: Linguistic Society of the Philippines (1973).]

Theoretical implications of matrix permutation in Fore (New Guinea). *Anthropological Linguistics* 5(8):1–23.

(KLP and Graham K. Scott). Pitch accent and non-accented phrases in Fore (New Guinea). *Zeitschrift für Phonetik, Sprachwissenschaft und Kommunikationsforschung* 16:179–189. [Repub. in Ruth M. Brend (ed.), *Studies in tone and intonation by members of the Summer Institute of Linguistics*, 173–186. Basel: S. Karger (1975).]

1964

Beyond the sentence. *College Composition and Communication* 15:129–135. [Repub. in Ruth M. Brend (ed.), *Kenneth L. Pike: Selected writings*, 192–199. The Hague: Mouton (1972).]

Discourse analysis and tagmeme matrices. In Elmer Wolfenden (ed.), *Papers on Philippines Linguistics by members of the Summer Institute of Linguistics. Oceanic Linguistics* 3(1):5–26. [Repub. in Ruth M. Brend (ed.), *Advances in Tagmemics*, 285–305. Amsterdam: North-Holland (1974).]

A linguistic contribution to composition: A hypothesis. *College Composition and Communication* 15:82–88.

Man or robot. *Eternity* 15(2):9–11, 46.

Name fusions as high-level particles in matrix theory. *Linguistics* 6:83–91.

On systems of grammatical structure. In Horace G. Lunt (ed.), *Proceedings of the Ninth International Congress of Linguists, Cambridge, Mass., Aug. 27–31, 1962*, 145–154. Janua Linguarum, series maior 12. The Hague: Mouton. [Repub. in Ruth M. Brend (ed.), *Kenneth L. Pike: Selected writings*, 200–208. The Hague: Mouton (1972).]

Onseigaku. Tokyo: Kenkyusha Press. (Kunihiko Imai, translator; translation of *Phonetics* 1943)

Stress trains in Auca. In D. Abercrombie (ed.), *In honour of Daniel Jones: Papers contributed on the occasion of his eightieth birthday, 12 September 1961*, 425–431. London: Longmans, Green. [Repub. in Ruth M. Brend (ed.), *Kenneth L. Pike: Selected writings*, 186–191. The Hague: Mouton (1972).]

(KLP and Alton L. Becker). Progressive neutralization in dimensions of Navaho stem matrices. *International Journal of American Linguistics* 30:144–154.

(KLP and Barbara E. Hollenbach). Conflated field structures in Potawatomi and in Arabic. *International Journal of American Linguistics* 30:201–212. [Repub. in Ruth M. Brend (ed.), *Advances in Tagmemics,* 135–146. Amsterdam: North Holland (1974).]

(KLP and Mildred L. Larson). Hyperphonemes and non-systematic features of Aguaruna phonemics. In A. H. Marckwardt (ed.), *Studies in languages and linguistics in honor of Charles C. Fries,* 55–67. Ann Arbor, Mich.: English Language Institute. [Repub. in Ruth M. Brend (ed.), *Kenneth L. Pike: Selected Writings,* 209–220. The Hague: Mouton (1972).]

1965

Christianity and science. *The Church Herald* 22(4):4–6.

Language: Where science and poetry meet. *College English* 26:283–292. [Repub. in Sanford R. Rader and Susan G. Rader (eds.), *Language and literature for composition: Introductory readings,* 504–512. New York: Crowell (1973).]

Non-linear order and anti-redundancy in German morphological matrices. *Zeitschrift für Mundartforschung* 32:193–221.

On the grammar of intonation. In E. Zwirner and W. Bethge (eds.), *Proceedings of the Fifth International Congress of Phonetic Sciences, Münster 1964,* 105–119. Basel: S. Karger. [Repub. in Ruth M. Brend (ed.), *Studies in tone and intonation by members of the Summer Institute of Linguistics,* 33–44. Basel: S. Karger (1975).]

1966

Crushed. *Translation* (Spring), 12. [Poem]

The disillusioned scholar. *The Church Herald* 23:15, 30.

God in history. *The Church Herald* 23(2):4–5, 22.

A guide to publications related to tagmemic theory. In Thomas A. Sebeok (ed.), *Theoretical Foundations,* 365–394. Current Trends in Linguistics 3. The Hague: Mouton.

(Editor). *Tagmemic and matrix linguistics applied to selected African languages.* Ann Arbor: University of Michigan Center for Research on Language and Language Behavior: U.S. Dept of Health, Education, and Welfare, Office of Education, Bureau of Research, Final Report, Contract OE-5-14-065. [Repub. in Summer Institute of Linguistics Publications in Linguistics and Related Fields 23—appendix omitted. Norman: Summer Institute of Linguistics of the University of Oklahoma (1970) 122 pp.].

Tempted to quit. *The Church Herald* 23(6):14–15. [Repub. in *The Christian Athlete* Feb. 1968, 11.]

1967

Abraham, my father. *The Alliance Witness* 102(25):9, 19.

The courage to face tension. *The Church Herald* 24(21):11.

Etic and emic standpoints for the description of behavior. In Donald C. Hildum, (ed.), *Language and thought: An enduring problem in psychology*, 32–39. Princeton, N.J.: D Van Norstrand Company. [Reprint from *Language in relation to a unified theory of the structure of human behavior*, part 1, pp. 8–12.]

Grammar as wave. In Edward J. Blansitt, Jr. (ed.), *Report of the 18th Annual Round Table Meeting on Linguistics and Language Studies*, 1–14. Monograph Series on Languages and Linguistics 20. Washington, D.C.: Georgetown University Press. [Repub. in Ruth M. Brend (ed.), *Kenneth L. Pike: Selected writings*, 231–241. The Hague: Mouton (1972).]

Language in relation to a unified theory of the structure of human behavior. Janua Linguarum, series maior, 24. The Hague: Mouton. 762 pp. [second rev. ed.]

Meaning. In Donald C. Hildum (ed.), *Language and thought: An enduring problem in psychology*, 140–152. Princeton, N.J.: D. Van Norstrand Company. [Reprint from *Language in relation to a unified theory of the structure of human behavior*, part 3, pp. 89–93.]

Stir, change, create. Grand Rapids, Mich.: Wm. B. Eerdmans. 164 pp. [Cover title adds: Poems & essays in contemporary mood for concerned students; several selections repub. in *Kenneth L. Pike: Selected writings*, ed. by Ruth M. Brend. The Hague: Mouton (1972), pp. 307–320.]

Suprasegmentals in reference to phonemes of item, of process, and of relation. In *To honor Roman Jakobson: Essays on the occasion of his seventieth birthday, 11 October 1966*, 1545–1554. Janua Linguarum, series maior 31–33. The Hague: Mouton. [Repub. in Ruth M. Brend (ed.), *Studies in tone and intonation by members of the Summer Institute of Linguistics*, 45–56. Basel: S. Karger (1975).]

Tongue-root position in practical phonetics. *Phonetica* 17:129–140. [Repub. in Ruth M. Brend (ed.), *Kenneth L. Pike: Selected writings*, 221–230. The Hague: Mouton (1972).]

[KLP and Donald S. Stark]. *Tuhun vaha ni chaa San Juan jiin uni carta ni chaa San Juan* (El Santo Evangelio según San Juan y las cartas de San Juan). Mexico: Sociedad Bíblica de México. 114 pp.

1968

The day before Christmas. *Overflow* 2(1):8 [Poem].

How to make an index. *Publications of the Modern Language Association of America* 83:991–993.

Indirect vs. direct discourse in Bariba. In E. M. Zale (ed.), *Proceedings of the Conference on Language and Language Behavior*, 165–173. New York: Appleton-Century-Crofts.

Intergenerational cleavage. *Translation* 3(1):4–5.

In war—or fuss. *Overflow* 2(1):16 [Poem].

Mental tension. *The King's Business* 58(2):30–31.

Mission and social concern [a letter to the editor]. *His* 28(March):26.

Not by bread alone. *The Church Herald* (May), 11. [Poem].

Pre-literate tribe. *Translation* (Jan–Feb), 2.

Professor Charles C. Fries. *Language Learning* 18:1–2.

Review of You! Jonah! (by J. T. Carlisle). *Christianity Today* 13(2):22–23.
Termites and eternity. *His* 28(7):4–5.
(KLP and Gillian Jacobs). Matrix permutation as a heuristic device in the analysis of the Bimoba verb. *Lingua* 21:321–345. [Repub. in Ruth M. Brend (ed.), *Kenneth L. Pike: Selected writings*, 242–262. The Hague: Mouton (1972).]

1969

Fear. *His* 29(9):13 [Two poems].
Language as behavior and etic and emic standpoints for the description of behavior. In E. F. Borgatta (ed.), *Social psychology: Readings and perspective*, 114–131. Chicago: Rand, McNally. [Repub. from *Language in relation to a unified theory of the structure of human behavior.*]
(KLP and Ivan Lowe). Pronominal reference in English conversation and discourse: A group theoretical treatment. *Folia Linguistica* 3:68–106.

1970

Five poems. In Arthur J Bronstein., Claude L. Shaver, and Cj[sic] Stevens (eds.), *Essays in honor of Claude M. Wise*, 65–72. Hannibal, Mo.: Standard Printing Co.
Good out of a student strike [a letter to the editor]. *The Church Herald* 27(18):17.
Guest editorial: On finding God's role for you. *Missionary Messenger* 45(8):24, 23.
The role of nuclei of feet in the analysis of tone in Tibeto-Burman languages of Nepal. In León, Faure, and Rigault (eds.), *Prosodic feature analysis / Analyse des faits prosodique*. *Studia Phonetica* 3:153–164. [Repub. in Austin Hale and Kenneth L. Pike (eds.), *Tone systems of Tibeto-Burman languages of Nepal 1: Studies on tone and phonological segments*, 37–48. (1970).]
(Eileen Edmondson and KLP). Ranking in singular-plural prefix pairs. In Kenneth L. Pike (ed.), *Tagmemic and matrix linguistics applied to selected African languages*, 75–78. Summer Institute of Linguistics Publications in Linguistics and Related Fields 23. Norman: Summer Institute of Linguistics of the University of Oklahoma.
(Austin Hale and KLP, editors). *Tone systems of Tibeto-Burman languages of Nepal 1: Studies on tone and phonological segments*. Occasional Papers of the Wolfenden Society on Tibeto-Burman Linguistics 3:1. Urbana: University of Illinois Press. v, 380 pp.
(Austin Hale and KLP, editors). *Tone systems of Tibeto-Burman languages of Nepal 2: Lexical lists and comparative studies*. Occasional Papers of the Wolfenden Society on Tibeto-Burman Linguistics 3:2. Urbana: University of Illinois Press. 130 pp.
(Austin Hale and KLP, editors). *Tone systems of Tibeto-Burman languages of Nepal 3: Texts 1*. Occasional Papers of the Wolfenden Society on Tibeto-Burman Linguistics 3:3. Urbana: University of Illinois Press. 306 pp.

(Austin Hale and KLP, editors). *Tone systems of Tibeto-Burman languages of Nepal 4: Texts 2.* Occasional Papers of the Wolfenden Society on Tibeto-Burman Linguistics 3:4. Urbana: University of Illinois Press. 305 pp.

(Maria Hari, Doreen Taylor, and KLP). Tamang tone and higher levels. In Austin Hale and Kenneth L. Pike (eds.), *Tone systems of Tibeto-Burman languages of Nepal 1: Studies on tone and phonological segments,* 82–124. Occasional Papers of the Wolfenden Society on Tibeto-Burman Linguistics 3:1. Urbana: University of Illinois Press.

(Richard E. Young, KLP, and Alton L. Becker). *Rhetoric: Discovery and change.* New York: Harcourt, Brace & World. xxi, 383 pp.

1971

Crucial questions in the development of tagmemics: The sixties and seventies. In Richard J. O'Brien (ed.), *Report of the 22nd Annual Round Table Meeting of Linguistics and Language Studies,* 79–98. (See also Discussion: Session 2, 157–166.) Monograph Series on Languages and Linguistics 24. Washington, D.C.: Georgetown University Press. [Repub. in Ruth M. Brend (ed.), *Advances in Tagmemics,* 35–54. Amsterdam: North-Holland (1974).]

Implications of the patterning of an oral reading of a set of poems. *Poetics* 1:38–45.

The linguist and axioms concerning language of Scripture. *Interchange* 3(2):47–51. [Repub. in *Journal of the American Scientific Affiliation* 26:47–51 (1974).]

Mark my words. Grand Rapids, Mich.: Eerdmans. [Poetry commentary on King James Version text of the Gospel of Mark].

More revolution: Tagmemics. In C. Laird and R. M. Gorrell (eds.), *Readings about Language,* 234–247. New York: Harcourt Brace Jovanovich.

1972

General characteristics of intonation. In Dwight Bolinger (ed.), *Intonation: Selected readings,* 53–82. Harmondsworth, England: Penguin Books. [From chap. 4 of *Intonation of American English,* 20–41.]

Language. In Robert W. Smith (ed.), *Christ and the modern mind,* 59–67. Downers Grove, Ill.: Inter-Varsity Press.

Language and faith. In *Language and faith,* 18–30. [Ed. by Cornell Capa and Dale Kietzman] Santa Ana, Calif.: Wycliffe Bible Translators.

Morals and metaphor. *Interchange* 12:228–231.

Use what you have. Costa Mesa, Calif.: One Way Library. [Audio recordings.]

(Ruth M. Brend, editor). *Kenneth L. Pike: Selected writings to commemorate the 60th birthday of Kenneth Lee Pike.* Janua linguarum. Series maior 55. The Hague: Mouton.

(KLP and Kent Gordon). Preliminary technology to show emic relations between certain non-transitivity clause structures in Dhangar (Kudux, Nepal). *International Journal of Dravidian Linguistics* 1:56–79.

(KLP and Evelyn G. Pike). Seven substitution exercises for studying the structure of discourse. *Linguistics* 94:43–52.

(KLP and Burkhard Schöttelndreyer). Paired-sentence reversals in the discovery of underlying and surface structures in Sherpa discourse. *Indian Linguistics* 33:72–83. [Repub. in Austin Hale (ed.), *Clause, sentence, and discourse patterns in selected languages of Nepal,* part 1, 361–375. (1973).]

1973

Comments on Gleason's "Grammatical prerequisites." *Annals of the New York Academy of Science* 211:34–38.

Cultural corners: Sweep under the bed. Santa Ana, Calif.: Wycliffe Bible Translators.

Language and self image. In Charles Hatfield (ed.), *The Scientist and Ethical Decision,* 69–82. Downers Grove, Ill.: Inter-Varsity Press.

Science fiction as a test of axioms concerning human behavior. *Parma Eldalamberon* 1(3):6–7.

Seed thoughts: Jesus choosing his disciples. *His* 34(2):7.

Sociolinguistic evaluation of alternative mathematical models: English pronouns. *Language* 49:121–160.

(Kent Gordon and KLP). Paired semantic components, paired sentence reversals and the analysis of Dhangar (Kudux) discourse. *International Journal of Dravidian Linguistics* 2:14–46. [Repub. in Ronald L. Trail (ed.), *Patterns in clause, sentence, and discourse in selected languages of India and Nepal,* part 1, 313–343. Summer Institute of Linguistics Publications in Linguistics and Related Fields 41. Norman: Summer Institute of Linguistics of the University of Oklahoma (1973).]

(Burkhard Schöttelndreyer and KLP). Notation for simultaneous representation of grammatical and sememic components in connected discourse. In Austin Hale (ed.), *Clause, sentence, and discourse patterns in selected languages of Nepal,* part 1, 321–360. Summer Institute of Linguistics Publications in Linguistics and Related Fields 40(1). Norman: Summer Institute of Linguistics of the University of Oklahoma.

1974

Agreement types dispersed into a nine-cell spectrum. In Matthew Black and William Smalley (eds.), *On language, culture, and religion: In honor of Eugene A. Nida,* 275–286. The Hague: Mouton.

Don't jitter. *The Forum,* 14. [Poem].

Hacia una teoría de la estructura del comportamiento humano. Tr. by Xavier Albo. In Paul L. Garvin and Yolanda Lastra de Suárez (eds.), *Antología de estudios de etnolingüística y sociolingüística,* 103–116. Lecturas Universitarias 20. México D. F.: Universidad Nacional Autónoma de México, Instituto de Investigaciones Antropológicas.

The linguist and axioms concerning the language of Scripture. *Journal of the American Scientific Affiliation* 26(2):47–51.

New Year's resolutions. The Forum, 13. [Poem].

Recent developments in tagmemics. In Luigi Heilman (ed.), *Proceedings of the Eleventh International Congress of Linguists Bologna-Florence, Aug. 28–Sept. 2, 1972*, vol. 1, 163–172. Bologna: Mulino. [Repub. in J. C. Sharma (ed.), From sound to discourse: A tagmemic approach to Indian languages, (1992), 1–12. CIIL Conferences and Seminars series 9. Mysore: Central Institute of Indian Languages.]

Seed Thoughts: The sluggard. *His* 34(4):13.

Seed Thoughts: Chain Reaction. *His* 34(6):22.

Seed Thoughts: Attacked—Nehemiah. *His* 34(8):4.

Seed Thoughts: Flagellation. *His* 34(9):21.

Seed Thoughts: God remembers us by name. *His* 35(1).

Seed Thoughts: Power when we're weak. *His* 35(3):23.

(Howard R. Martin and KLP). Analysis of the vocal performance of a poem: A classification of intonational features. *Language and Style* 7:209–218.

(KLP and Evelyn G. Pike). Rules as components of tagmemes in the English verb phrase. In Ruth M. Brend (ed.), *Advances in tagmemics*, 175–204. North-Holland Linguistic Series 9. Amsterdam: North-Holland.

1975

Analogies to the good news (Review: *Peace child* by Don Richardson). *Christianity Today* 20(2):33.

Analogies to the good news. [Review of *Peace child* by Don Richardson.] *Christianity Today* 20:91ff.

Focus in English clause structure seen via systematic experimental syntax. *Kivung* 8:3–14.

On describing languages. In Robert Austerlitz (ed.), *The scope of American linguistics*, 9–39. Lisse, Netherlands: Peter de Ridder.

On kinesic triadic relations in turn-taking. *Semiotica* 13:389–394.

Review of *Peace child* by Don Richardson. *His* 36(5):26.

Seed Thoughts: In the interest of others—Diotrephes. *His* 35(5):21.

Seed Thoughts: Jacob valued the birthright. *His* 35(7):27.

Seed Thoughts: A spiritual democracy—Korah. *His* 35(8):5.

Seed Thoughts: Two timid men—Joseph of Arimathea and Nicodemus. *His* 35(9):12.

Seed Thoughts: An unforgiving spirit—Ahithophel. *His* 36(1):26.

Tests for prosodic features of pitch, quantity, stress. In Ruth M. Brend (ed.), *Studies in tone and intonation by members of the Summer Institute of Linguistics*, 4–5. Bibliotheca Phonetica 11. Basel: S. Karger. [Reprinted from SIL phonetic worksheet (1938).]

Three readings of a poem by Emily Dickenson. In Ruth M. Brend (ed.), *Studies in tone and intonation by members of the Summer Institute of Linguistics*, 6–10. Bibliotheca Phonetica 11. Basel: S. Karger. [Reprinted from *Language in relation to a unified theory of the structure of human behavior*, 528–532 (1967.]

(Rachel Saint and KLP). Fonémica del idioma de los huaurani (auca). In M. Catherine Peeke (ed.), *Estudios fonológicos de lenguas vernáculas del Ecuador*, 87–107. Quito: Ministerio de Educación Pública.

1976

The meaning of particles in text: A random note. In Ignatius Suharno and Kenneth L. Pike (eds.), *From Baudi to Indonesian*, 41–44. Jayapura: Cenderawasih University and the Summer Institute of Linguistics.

Pike's answers to 12 questions for Conference on Language Universals, Gummersbach, October 4–8, 1976. In *Materials for the DFG International Conference on Language Universals*. AKUP (Arbeiten des Kölner Universalien-Projekts) 25, 170–176.

A poem on disconnecting form and meaning. In Mohammed Jazayery, Edgar C. Polomé, and Werner Winter (eds.), *Linguistic and literary studies in honor of Archibald A. Hill, Vol. 1: General and theoretical linguistics* 233–234. Lisse, Netherlands: Peter de Ridder.

Review of *Naked and not ashamed*, by Lowell L. Nobel. *Christianity Today* 21(4):42.

Seed Thoughts: A mighty coral reef. *His* 36(8):7.

Seed Thoughts: How to sin righteously—Balaam. *His* 36(9):22.

Seed Thoughts: Well worth doing. *His* 37(2):8.

Toward the development of tagmemic postulates. In Ruth M. Brend and Kenneth L. Pike (eds.), *Tagmemics, vol. 2: Theoretical discussion*, 91–127. Trends in Linguistics 1. The Hague: Mouton.

(Ruth M. Brend and KLP, editors). *Tagmemics, volume 1: Aspects of the field.* Trends in Linguistics 1. The Hague: Mouton. viii, 147 pp.

(Ruth M. Brend and KLP, editors). *Tagmemics, volume 2: Theoretical discussion.* Trends in Linguistics 2. The Hague: Mouton. viii, 133 pp.

(KLP and Evelyn G. Pike). The granular nature of a construction as illustrated by 'flying planes'. In Ignatius Suharno and Kenneth L. Pike (eds.), *From Baudi to Indonesian*, 29–37. Jayapura: Cenderawasih University and the Summer Institute of Linguistics.

(Robert H. Sterner, Ignatius Suharno, and KLP). Experimental syntax applied to the relation between sentence and sentence cluster in Indonesian. In Ignatius Suharno and Kenneth L. Pike (eds.), *From Baudi to Indonesian*, 95–117. Jayapura: Cenderawasih University and Summer Institute of Linguistics.

(Ignatius Suharno and KLP, editors). *From Baudi to Indonesian.* Jayapura: Cenderawasih University and Summer Institute of Linguistics. xiv, 209 pp.

1977

Into the unknown: Learning language by gesture. Ann Arbor: University of Michigan Television Center, Produced in cooperation with the University of Michigan Dept. of Linguistics. Pike on Language series. [Motion picture.]

Introduction: On the relation between modes of argumentation in linguistic analysis versus the documentation of change of behavior in reading. In Kenneth L. Pike (ed.), *Pilot projects on the reading of English of science and technology*, 1–5. University of Michigan Papers in Linguistics 1. Ann Arbor: University of Michigan.

(Editor). *Pilot projects on the reading of English of science and technology.* University of Michigan Papers in Linguistics 1. Ann Arbor: University of Michigan. 41 pp.

Pitch and poetry: The music of the voice in speech. Ann Arbor: University of Michigan Television Center, produced in cooperation with the University of Michigan Dept. of Linguistics. Pike on Language series. [Motion picture.]

Seed Thoughts: The excuse is gone. *His* 37(6):15.

Seed Thoughts: Practical advice in marriage. *His* 37(7):9.

Seed Thoughts: Serving one another. *His* 37(4):31.

Voices at work: A fresh approach to the learning of the pronunciation of language. Ann Arbor: University of Michigan Television Center, produced in cooperation with the University of Michigan Dept. of Linguistics. Pike on Language series. [Motion picture.]

Waves of change: A consideration of how and why change occurs in language. Ann Arbor: University of Michigan Television Center, produced in cooperation with the University of Michigan Dept. of Linguistics. Pike on Language series. [Motion picture.]

The way we know: The value of theory in linguistic study. Ann Arbor: University of Michigan Television Center, produced in cooperation with the University of Michigan Dept. of Linguistics. Pike on Language series. [Motion picture.]

(Jared Bernstein and KLP). The emic structure of individuals in relation to dialogue. In Teun A. van Dijk and János S. Petöfi (eds.), *Grammars and descriptions: Studies in text theory and text analysis,* 1–10. Berlin: Walter de Gruyter.

(Ruth M. Brend and KLP, editors). *The Summer Institute of Linguistics: Its works and contributions.* The Hague: Mouton. viii, 200 pp.

(KLP and George L. Huttar). How many packages? *Hemisphere* 21(12):26–29.

(KLP and Evelyn G. Pike). *Grammatical analysis.* Summer Institute of Linguistics Publications in Linguistics 53. Dallas: Summer Institute of Linguistics and the University of Texas at Arlington. xxix, 505 pp. [Rev. ed. (1982), xxvi, 463 pp.; repub. (1991), incl. changes and additions.]

(KLP and Evelyn G. Pike). *Instructor's guide for use with Grammatical analysis.* Huntington Beach, Calif.: Summer Institute of Linguistics. 142 pp. [Rev. ed. (1988), 216 pp.]

(KLP and Evelyn G. Pike). Referential vs. grammatical hierarchies. In Robert J. Di Pietro and Edward L. Blansitt, Jr. (eds.), *The Third LACUS Forum 1976,* 343–354. Columbia, S.C.: Hornbeam.

(KLP and Stephen B. Pike). *Songs of fun and faith.* Edward Sapir Monograph Series in Language, Culture, and Cognition 1. Lake Bluff: Jupiter Press. viii, 48 pp. [Supplement to Forum Linguisticum 1:3; words by KLP, music by SBP.]

1978

Particularization versus generalization, and explanation versus prediction. In Ikuo Koike, Masuo Matsoyama, Yasuo Igaroshi, and Kozi Suzuki (eds.), *The teaching of English in Japan,* 783–785. Tokyo: Eichosah Publishing Co.

Social interaction as the break-in point for the analysis of verbal behavior. In Wolfgang U. Dressler and Wolfgang Meid (eds.), *Proceedings of the Twelfth International Congress of Linguists, Vienna, August 28–September 2, 1977,* 739–741. Innsbruck: Innsbrucker Beiträge zur Sprachwissenschaft.

Thresholdism versus reductionism. In Hansjakob Seiler (ed.), *Language universals,* 53–58. Tübingen: Gunter Narr.

(KLP and Evelyn G. Pike). *Index and glossary to Grammatical analysis.* Dallas: Summer Institute of Linguistics. 58 pp.

1979

Christianity and culture 1: Conscience and culture. *Journal of the American Scientific Affiliation* 31:8–12.

Christianity and culture 2: Incarnation in a culture. *Journal of the American Scientific Affiliation* 31:92–96.

Christianity and culture 3: Biblical absolutes and certain cultural relativisms. *Journal of the American Scientific Affiliation* 31:139–145.

Emotion in God, and its image in us. *The Banner* 114(45):4–5.

Intellectual initiative: The image of God. *The Banner* 114(46):10.

Linguistics: From there to where? In Wolfgang Wölck and Paul Garvin (eds.), *The Fifth LACUS Forum* 1978, 3–18. Columbia, S.C.: Hornbeam.

Love God with mind—and bless Babylon. *The Gordon Alumnus* 8(4):6–7.

A note on some universals of human behaviour. *Sabah Museum Annals* 1:47–55.

Notes on the academic programme of the Summer Institute of Linguistics around the world. *Sabah Museum Annals* 1:1–12.

On the extension of etic-emic anthropological methodology to referential units-in-context. *Lembaran Pengkajian Budaya* 3:1–36.

Seed Thoughts: Truth and responsibility—Pilate. *His* 39(5):13.

Social linguistics and bilingual education. *System* 7:99–109.

[Ten Poems, reprinted]. In Donna Jo Napoli and Emily N. Rando (eds.), *Linguistic Muse,* 138–144. Carbondale: Linguistic Research Inc.

Universals and phonetic hierarchy. In Eli Fischer-Jørgensen, Jørgen Rischel, and Nina Thorsen (eds.), *Proceedings of the Ninth International Congress of Phonetic Sciences, Copenhagen, August 6–11, 1979: Special lectures,* 48–52. Basel: S. Karger.

1980

Here we stand: Creative observers of language. In Maurice Reuchlin and Frédéric François (eds.), *Approches du langage: Actes du Colloque Interdisciplinaire tenu à Paris, Sorbonne, le 8 décembre 1978,* 9–45. Études, 16. Paris: Université de Paris.

An image of his debating technique: What's your opinion? *The Banner* 115(14):6–7.

A Mixtec lime oven. SIL Museum of Anthropology Publication 10. Dallas: SIL Museum of Anthropology. iv, 9 pp.

(Carl D. DuBois, John Upton, and KLP). Constraints on complexity seen via fused vectors of an n-dimensional semantic space (Sarangani Manobo, Philippines). *Semiotica* 29:209–243.

1981

An autobiographical note on phonetics. In R. E. Asher and Eugénie J. A. Henderson (eds.), *Towards a history of phonetics*, 181–185. Edinburgh: University Press.

Dreams of an integrated theory of experience. *Waiyu Jiaoxue Yu Yanjiu* [Foreign Language Teaching and Research] 45(1):24–33, 12.

Nonsense in the service of sense. *Language and Communication* 1:179–188.

Systematic planned distortion of text as a clue to translation problems—a query. In Bhatki Prasad Mallik (ed.), *Suniti Kumar Chatterji commemoration volume*, 163–166. West Bengal: University of Burdwan.

Tagmemics, discourse, and verbal art. Ann Arbor: University of Michigan. xvi, 67 pp.

Wherein lies 'talked-about' reality? In Florian Coulmas (ed.), *A festschrift for native speaker*, 85–91. Janua Linguarum, series maior 97. The Hague: Mouton.

1982

Linguistic concepts: An introduction to Tagmemics. Lincoln: University of Nebraska Press. xvi, 146 pp.

Phonological hierarchy in a four-cell tagmemic representation from discourse to phoneme class. *Forum Linguisticum* 7:65–91.

Some questions for field linguists beginning language analysis. *Notes on Linguistics* 24:3–14.

Tune and tone: Generalized syntagmatic pitch patterns constrained by particular lexical patterns. *Journal of West African Languages* 12(2):22–41.

(Jean Soutar and KLP, compilers). *Texts illustrating the analysis of direct versus indirect quotations in Bariba (Africa)*. Language Data, African Series, 19. Dallas: Summer Institute of Linguistics. 312 pp.

1983

Experimental syntax, a basis for some new language-learning exercises. *Arab Journal of Language Studies* 1:245–255.

The future for unit-in-context: The tagmeme. In Shiro Hattori and others (eds.), *Proceedings of the 13th International Congress of Linguists, August 29–September 4, 1982, Tokyo*, 881–883. Tokyo: Tokyo Press.

Grammar versus reference in the analysis of discourse. In Thomas Bearth (ed.), *Perspectives dans l'analyse du discours*, 23–41. Publications Conjointes: Institut de Linguistique Appliquée–Société Internationale de Linguistique, 6. Abidjan: University of Abidjan and Société Internationale de Linguistique.

Humor, home and holiday. In Emily Norwood Rando and Donna Jo Napoli (eds.), *Meliglossa*, 184–187. Edmonton, AB, Canada: Linguistic Research.

In rhetoric the passage from A to B is not equal to passage from B to A. *Work Papers of the Summer Institute of Linguistics, University of North Dakota* 27:135–139.

On understanding people: An integrative philosophy. In John Morreall (ed.), *The Ninth LACUS Forum*, 129–136. Columbia, S. C: Hornbeam.

Quelques suggestions pour les premiers stades d'une analyse linguistique. In Jacques Nicole (ed.), *Études linguistiques préliminaires dans quelques langues du Togo*, 8–17. Lomé: Société Internationale de Linguistique.

The translator's voice: An interview with Kenneth L. Pike (interview by Elizabeth Miller). *Translation Review* 12:1–10.

Universal terms as waves. In Frederick B. Agard and others (eds.), *Essays in honor of Charles F. Hockett*, 126–127. Leiden: Brill.

(KLP and Evelyn G. Pike). *Text and Tagmeme*. Norwood, N.J: Ablex. xiii, 129 pp. [Also published London: Pinter (1983).]

1984

Assumptions in Maxwell's article 'The generative revolution and the Summer Institute of Linguistics'. *Notes on Linguistics* 29:48–50.

Some teachers who helped me. *Historiographia Linguistica* 11:493–495.

Towards the linguistic analysis of one's own poems. In Alan Manning, Pierre Martin, and Kin McCalla (eds.), *The Tenth LACUS Forum 1983*, 117–128. Columbia, S.C.: Hornbeam.

(Mark E. Karan and KLP). Notes on phonological grouping in Kalengin (Kenya) in relation to tone, intonation patterns, and vowel harmony. *Occasional Papers in the Study of Sudanese Languages* 3:47–59. Juba: University of Juba and the Summer Institute of Linguistics.

(KLP and Evelyn G. Pike). *Changes and additions for Grammatical analysis*. Dallas: Summer Institute of Linguistics and the University of Texas at Arlington. 39 pp.

1985

Foreword to *Mei kuo ying yü ying yung yü yin hsüeh*, i–ii. [Shang-hai]: Shang-hai wai yü chiao yü ch°u pan she. [Translation of: *Applied phonology of American English* by Tsan-kun Kwei.]

Language, linguistics, and linguists: A panel discussion with Gregory et al. *Langues et linguistique* 11:1–36.

The need for the rejection of autonomy in linguistics. In Robert A. Hall, Jr. (ed.), *The Eleventh LACUS Forum, 1984*, 35–53. Columbia, S.C: Hornbeam.

Static, dynamic and relational perspectives suggested in words and phrases. In Kurt R. Jankowsky (ed.), *Scientific and humanistic dimensions of language: Festschrift for Robert Lado on the occasion of his 70th birthday on May 31, 1985*, 447–452. Amsterdam: John Benjamins.

Systematic emic pattern above abstract etic universals: A query. *Word* 36:179–181.

(KLP and Peter H. Fries). Slot in referential hierarchy in relation to Charles C. Fries' view of language. In Peter Howard Fries (ed.), *Toward an understanding of language: Charles C. Fries in perspective*, 105–127. Current Issues in Linguistic Theory 40. Amsterdam: John Benjamins.

(KLP and Barbara Keller). The integration of self in society through language. In Jos Nivette, Didier Goyvaerts, and Pete van de Craen (eds.), *AILA (Association Internationale de Linguistique Appliquée) Brussels 84: Proceedings*, vol. 5, 1877–1900. Brussels: 7th World Congress of Applied Linguistics.

1986

A further note on experimental clauses in discourse. In Benjamin F. Elson (ed.), *Language in global perspective: Papers in honor of the 50th anniversary of the Summer Institute of Linguistics, 1935–1985*, 135–138. Dallas: Summer Institute of Linguistics.

Mixtec social 'credit rating': The particular versus the universal in one emic world view. *Proceedings of the National Academy of Sciences of the United States of America* 83:3047–3049.

On the value of local languages. In Nancy Schweda-Nicholson (ed.), *Languages in the international perspective*, 13–19. Delaware Symposium 5: Proceedings of the 5th Delaware Symposium on Language Studies. Norwood, N.J.: Ablex.

Servants. *Stillpoint* 2(1):8.

(With others). Reminiscences about Edward Sapir. In *New perspectives in language, culture, and personality: Proceedings of the Edward Sapir Centenary Conference, Ottawa, 1–3 October 1984*, 371–403. Amsterdam: John Benjamins.

1987

Alas for Judas. In Edgar W. Conrad and Edward G. Newing (eds.), *Perspectives on language and text: Essays and poems in honor of Francis I. Andersen's sixtieth birthday, July 28, 1985*, 300. Winona Lake, Ind.: Eisenbrauns.

The relation of language to the world. *International Journal of Dravidian Linguistics* 16(1):77–98.

Teaching in His image: The structure of the Sermon on the Mount. *Arts & Letters* 1(2):3–11.

Today. In Ross Steele and Terry Threadgold (eds.), *Language topics: Essays in honour of Michael Halliday 1*, 229. Amsterdam: John Benjamins.

1988

Bridging language learning, language analysis, and poetry, via experimental syntax. In Deborah Tannen (ed.), *Linguistics in context: Connecting observation and understanding*, 221–245. Norwood, N.J: Ablex.

Cultural choice. *Lenguaje y Ciencias* 28(2):10.

Cultural relativism in relation to constraints on world view: An emic perspective. *Bulletin of the Institute of History and Philology* 59(2):385–399.

1989

An ILA tree. In Donna Jo Napoli and Emily Norwood Rando (eds.), *Lingua Franca: An anthology of poetry by linguists*, 130. Lake Bluff, Ill.: Jupiter Press.

Recollections of Bloomfield. *Historiographia Linguistica* 16(1/2):217–223.

Waves and spray. *Philippine Journal of Linguistics* 20(2):2.

(With Hugh Steven). *Pike's perspectives: An anthology of thought, insight and moral purpose*, xi, 196 pp. Langley, B.C., Canada: Credo.

1990

On the emics and etics of Pike and Harris. In Thomas N. Headland, Kenneth L. Pike, and Marvin Harris (eds.), *Emics and etics: The insider/outsider debate*, 28–47. Frontiers of Anthropology 7. Newbury Park, Calif.: Sage.

Pike's final response. In Thomas N. Headland, Kenneth L. Pike, and Marvin Harris (eds.), *Emics and etics: The insider/outsider debate*, 184–201. Frontiers of Anthropology 7. Newbury Park, Calif.: Sage.

Pike's reply to Harris. In Thomas N. Headland, Kenneth L. Pike, and Marvin Harris (eds.), *Emics and etics: The insider/outsider debate*, 62–74. Frontiers of Anthropology 7. Newbury Park, Calif.: Sage.

(Thomas N. Headland, KLP, and Marvin Harris, editors). *Emics and etics: The insider/outsider debate*. Frontiers of Anthropology 7. Newbury Park, Calif.: Sage. 226 pp.

1991

La relación del lenguaje con el mundo. (Enrique Carrión, tr.) Lima: Instituto Lingüístico de Verano. 25 pp.

A revolutionary 'helix' in linguistic history—as seen over half a century by one who has lived it. In *Cairo Studies in English: Essays in honor of Saad Gamal El-Din*, Special issue, 21–26. Giza: University of Cairo.

(KLP and Evelyn G. Pike). *Análisis gramatical*. (Jorge Suárez, tr.) Colección Lingüística Indígena 5. Mexico: Universidad Nacional Autónoma de México. xl, 566 pp.

1992

An autobiographical note on my experience with tone languages. In J. C. Sharma (ed.), *From sound to discourse: A tagmemic approach to Indian languages*, 21–31. Mysore: Central Institute of Indian Languages.

Etic universals and emic particulars seen through the intonation of American English. *Voprosy aiiazykoznaniaiia* 41(1):8–24.

Konsep linguistik: Pengantar teori tagmemik. Jakarta: Summer Institute of Linguistics. xvi, 123 pp. [Indonesian translation of *Linguistic concepts*.]

Person beyond logic, in language, life, and philosophy. In Ruth M. Brend (ed.), *The Eighteenth LACUS Forum, 1991*, 23–37. Lake Bluff, Ill.: Linguistic Association of Canada and the United States.

1993

A brief update on my interest in relating language to philosophy. In James E. Alatis (ed.), *Languages, Communication. and Social Meaning,* Georgetown University Round Table on Languages and Linguistics (GURT) 43, 298–304. (1992) Washington D.C.: Georgetown University Press.

Experimental linguistics and language learning. *Word* 44(2):302–308.

Matrix formatives in N-dimensional linguistics. In *Pan-Asiatic linguistics: Proceedings of the International Symposium on Language and Linguistics,* Chulalongkorn University, Bangkok, Thailand, January 8–10, 1992, 1042–1063. Bangkok: Chulalongkorn University Print House.

Talk, thought, and thing: The emic road toward conscious knowledge. Dallas: Summer Institute of Linguistics. xii, 85 pp.

(KLP and Gary F. Simons). Toward the historical reconstruction of matrix patterns in morphology. *Voprosy Jazykoznania* [Problems of Linguistics] 1:22–44.

1994

Ene kyaynyem (Shin Ja Joo Hwang and Hyon-Sook Shin, trs.). Seoul: Hankook Moonhwa Sa (Korean Culture, Inc.). xxi, 182 pp. [Korean translation of *Linguistic concepts.*]

A limited perspective on WORD seen in a transitional moment between paradigms. *Word* 45:39–43.

Paradigmatic and syntagmatic features or prosodies in sound, syllable, word, or poem. In Brigitte K. Halford and Herbert Pilch (eds.), *Intonation,* 53–68. Tübingen: Gunter Narr.

Too late for them. In Bradley R. Strahan, Donna Jo Napoli, and Emily N. Rando (eds.), *Speaking in tongues: Poems by linguists,* 59. Falls Church, Va.: Black Buzzard Press.

1995

Conceptos lingüísticos: Una introducción a la tagmémica. (Thomas Hemingway and Katherine Langan, trs.) Dallas: Summer Institute of Linguistics. xx, 166 pp.

Experimental syntax in language and in music. In V. Dehoux, S. Fürniss and others (eds.), *Ndroje balendro (Musiques, terrains et disciplines: Textes offerts à Simha Arom,* 223–226. SELAF 359. Paris: Peeters.

A holistic semantics: The semantics of phonology, grammar, and reference. In Jorge Fernández-Barrientos Martín and Celia Wallhead, (eds), *Actas: Jornadas Internacionales de Lingüística Aplicada Robert J. Di Pietro. In memoriam.* Granada, January 11–15, 1993, 63–77. Granada: Universidad de Granada.

Poems for Evelyn: From her tunnel-vision sweetheart. [For her 80th birthday along with other poems written over the years; unpublished booklet.]

Tagmemics. In Jef Verschueren, Jan-Ola Östman and Jan Blommaert (eds.), *Handbook of pragmatics,* 533–536. Amsterdam: John Benjamins.

(KLP and Evelyn G. Pike). *L'analyse grammaticale: Introduction à la tagmémique.* (Laurence Boquiaux and Pierre Dauby, trs.). Société d'Études Linguistiques et Anthropologiques de France, numéro spécial 26. Paris: Editions Peeters. 484 pp. [French translation of *Grammatical Analysis.*]

1996

Linguistic 'Venn diagrams' with their 'formative blocks' in morphology, semantics, and historical reconstruction. In Kurt R. Jankowsky (ed.), *Multiple perspectives on the historical dimensions of language,* 51–56. Münster: Nodus Publikationen.

To Dave Thomas. *Mon-Khmer Studies* 26:1.

(KLP and Donald A. Burquest). The importance of purposive behavior in text analysis. In Kurt R. Jankowsky (ed.), *The mystery of culture contacts, historical reconstruction, and text analysis: An emic approach,* 65–86. Washington, D.C.: Georgetown University Press.

(KLP and Carol V. McKinney). Understanding misunderstanding as cross-cultural emic clash. In Kurt R. Jankowsky (ed.), *The mystery of culture contacts, historical reconstruction, and text analysis: An emic approach,* 39–64. Washington, D.C.: Georgetown University Press.

(KLP and Gary F. Simons). Toward the historical reconstruction of matrix patterns in morphology. In Kurt R. Jankowsky (ed.), *The mystery of culture contacts, historical reconstruction, and text analysis: An emic approach,* 1–37. Washington, D.C.: Georgetown University Press.

1997

Eigogaku-no Kihon Gainen. Tokyo: Jiritsu Shobo. xxii, 211 pp. [Japanese translation of *Linguistic concepts.*]

My pilgrimage in mission. *International Bulletin of Missionary Research* 21:159–161.

A note on holism. In Christina Bratt Paulston and G. Richard Tucker (eds.), *The early days of sociolinguistics: Memories and reflections,* 211–212. Summer Institute of Linguistics Publications in Sociolinguistics 2. Dallas: Summer Institute of Linguistics.

Tagmemics in retrospect — a biased personal view. In Kurt R. Jankowsky (ed.), *Conceptual and institutional developments,* 91–97. Münster: Nodus Publikationen.

(Thomas N. Headland and KLP). SIL and genocide: Well-oiled connections? *Anthropology Newsletter* 38(2):4–5.

(Sharon Heimbach, compiler). *On love, laughter, and life, vol. 5: Seasons of life: A complete collection of Kenneth L. Pike poetry.* Dallas: Summer Institute of Linguistics. xvi, 204 pp.

(Sharon Heimbach, compiler). *On pain: Beyond suffering, vol. 1: Seasons of life: A complete collection of Kenneth L. Pike poetry.* Dallas: Summer Institute of Linguistics. xvi, 171 pp.

(Sharon Heimbach, compiler). *On philosophy of life: A kaleidoscope, vol. 2: Seasons of life: A collection of Kenneth L. Pike poetry*. Dallas: Summer Institute of Linguistics. xiv, 140 pp.

(Sharon Heimbach, compiler). *On scholarship and the work: Service and success, vol. 4: Seasons of life: A complete collection of Kenneth L. Pike poetry*. Dallas: Summer Institute of Linguistics. xviii, 221 pp.

(Sharon Heimbach, compiler). *On the Shepherd: Feeding the flock, vol 3: Seasons of life: A complete collection of Kenneth L. Pike poetry*. Dallas: Summer Institute of Linguistics. xvi, 206 pp.

(Sharon Heimbach, compiler). *Seasons of life: A complete collection of Kenneth L. Pike poetry*. Dallas: Summer Institute of Linguistics. 5 vols. 171, 140, 206, 221, 204 pp.

1998

A linguistic pilgrimage. In E. F. K. Koerner (ed.), *First person singular III*, 145–158. Studies in the History of the Language Sciences 88. Amsterdam/Philadelphia: John Benjamins.

Mary R. Haas, January 12, 1910–May 17, 1996. *Biographical Memoirs* 76:3–13.

Semantics in a holistic context—with preliminary convictions and approaches. In Udom Warotamasikkhadit and Thanyarat Panakul (eds.), *Papers from the Fourth Annual Meeting of the Southeast Asian Linguistics Society 1994*, 177–197. Tempe, Ariz.: Program for Southeast Asian Studies, Arizona State University.

1999

Re-LSA—and Me. *Linguistic Society of America, 1924–1999*. [75th anniversary booklet.] Washington, D.C.: Linguistic Society of America, p.12.

Tensity and pressure in structure: 'tensegrity'. In Lourdes S. Bautista and Grace O. Tan (eds.), *The Filipino bilingual: A multidisciplinary perspective; Festschrift in honor of Emy M. Pascasio (Proceedings of the Centennial Congress on Philippine Bilingualism from a Multidisciplinary Perspective, Manila, 21–23 January 1999)*, 3 pp. Manila: Linguistic Society of the Philippines.

2001

Reminiscences by Pike on Early American Anthropological Linguistics. SIL Electronic Working Papers 2001-001. Dallas: SIL International. http://www.sil.org/silewp/2001/001

2002

(KLP and Mark F. Peterson). Emics and etics for organizational studies: A lesson in contrast from linguistics. *International Journal of Cross-Cultural Management* 2(1):5–19.

7

The Call to Academic Community

Gary F. Simons

Ken Pike: Christian and Scholar

Kenneth L. Pike, the man whose memory we honor in this volume, was both a man of faith and a man of science. It was his commitment to God that led him to begin work as a Bible translator among the Mixtec Indians of Mexico in 1935. It was his commitment to pursuing a scientific approach to that work that ultimately resulted in his election to the National Academy of Sciences in 1985—half a century later—after a distinguished career as a world-renowned linguist.

This two-fold identity was one of the hallmarks of Dr. Pike and he had a colorful way of explaining it. The following, a transcription of a story he told in 1988, was one of the remembrances read at the public memorial service following his death (SIL International 2001):

> We [recently visited] China where we were honored at a dinner in Beijing. I was seated next to a Chinese gentleman who had just returned from lecturing at Berkeley. When he learned who I was, he said, "Ah, yes. I heard about you while I was in the United States, but I also heard that you were a missionary. So which are you, a missionary or a linguist?" I thought fast and told him I was a hybrid—a mule. His expression caused me to explain myself: "Mules are the result of breeding between a horse, wanted for its speed,

and a donkey, wanted for its strength and ability to walk over rocks in the road. When you want to combine the two qualities you have a mule. So sometimes I'm a horse and sometimes I'm a donkey, but I'm always a mule."

He described his identity as a hybrid in yet another way in an interview with Betty Blair (1983):

Q: You seem to put equal emphasis on being a scholar as well as being a Christian. Is this right?
A: Exactly. I am a hybrid. I'm both. On the one hand, I've spent most of my life since 1935 handling the scientific analysis of linguistic systems, writing on phonetics and grammar in the context of behavior. On the other hand, I've done this, in spite of failure, in the context of a determination to serve God with both "mind and heart," as Jesus told us to do. I want to help other people as I would wish them to help me if I were in their place as a preliterate ethnic person.

The details of that hybrid life are laid out in the biography written by his sister, Eunice Pike (1981), *Ken Pike: Scholar and Christian.* Another glimpse can be seen in his book of essays: *With Heart and Mind: A Personal Synthesis of Scholarship and Devotion* (Pike 1962).

SIL Distinctives: Bible Translation and Science

SIL, the organization that Dr. Pike led as president for the better part of four decades (1942–1979), is similarly a hybrid. When William Cameron Townsend founded SIL in the 1930s, among the distinctives he laid down for the organization were these two:
- We translate the Bible for language groups that don't have it.
- We follow a scientific approach.

When Pike first went to Mexico, his passion was for Bible translation and not for science. He initially put off Townsend's encouragement to write a book about phonetics that could help in training others. But then, when a broken leg landed him in a hospital with nothing else to do for three weeks, he began writing; and the rest is history (Blair 1983).

As president of SIL, Pike was always encouraging its members to pursue the scientific approach. He saw two keys to maintaining that aspect of the organization:

> To have a healthy academic organization, accepted as such by friends and competitors, two kinds of credentials are important: (1) degrees and (2) continuing publication. (Pike 1989:122)

Pike wrote that in 1955 he felt "academically lonely" with only one fellow Ph.D. among the ranks of SIL members (Pike 1989:168), so he made it a priority in his leadership of SIL to encourage members into advanced study programs. Twenty-six years later, in a 1981 essay, he was able to write, "We now have about 125 Ph.D.s in our group" (Pike 1989:122). After another twenty years, in 2001, the number is over 350. Why advanced degrees? For this, too, he had a colorful explanation:

> Would you want your son to be operated on for his appendix by somebody who had no degree in surgery? Wouldn't you want the surgeon to have a certificate hanging on the wall? If so, shouldn't governments and universities have a comparable right to wish for credentials if we are going to be involved in their national cultural structure—in alphabetizing, helping in community development, and lecturing in local universities to provide theory and technology for local scholars to use in their turn? (Pike 1989:98)

But having degrees was not enough. A second hallmark of Pike's leadership was an emphasis on publication: "Degrees are empty if, after people have them, [they] do not 'produce the goods.' It is expected in a top-flight graduate university that persons will continue to publish" (Pike 1989:122). Though he saw that degree holders had a special obligation in this respect, his vision for publication did not end there:

> We need to emphasize that we need to encourage publication wherever we can get it, by any of our people who are competent to handle it, whether or not they have degrees. Eventually, many people will judge us not by the degrees we carry but by our academic output. (Pike 1989:123)

He spent a lifetime urging his colleagues to:

> Publish or perish! The normal linguistic production for each language should include published (printed or microfilmed) material on some aspect of the phonology, grammar, and lexicon. We believe that as scholars we are committed to publish. The product of our work should not be limited to archived field notes. (Pike 1989:1)

Such linguistic publication was, of course, in addition to publication in the local vernaculars (such as of literacy materials and translations) that his colleagues were also doing.

Pike knew that solid publication could not issue from scholars who are isolated. Thus he encouraged his colleagues to engage in the normal activities of academic life, particularly, participating in conferences and reading the literature:

> The half-life of a Ph.D. on the theoretical frontier is brief—perhaps five years. After that they feel embarrassingly out-of-date and hesitant to publish. [SIL] branches may find a deep payoff by sending linguistic leaders (i) to congresses, preferably to present papers; (ii) to a refreshing LSA institute, or equivalent, to meet scholars. (Pike 1989:48)
> Young trained scholars should be aware of the need to check out bibliography, to see what has been done in the immediate geographical or theoretical area, to get help from the work of predecessors. Also they should be able to check bibliography of a more remote type, to try to discover general principles—worked out elsewhere—which might, with some modification, be applied locally. (Pike 1989:143–144)
> I recently met a colleague who was unaware of material published on a related language. This is inefficient, costly, and depressing to the struggling beginner....We should not have to "reinvent the wheel." (Pike 1989:79)

This belief in the fundamental importance of the academic literature led Pike, while president of SIL, to push both its training centers and its field centers to develop academic libraries. As a result there are today at least thirty-nine linguistics libraries located at SIL centers all over the world. Together these hold a total of about 210,000 volumes.

Science: Cornerstone or Stumbling Block?

For Pike, following his mentor Townsend, the scientific approach was a cornerstone of SIL's work and purpose. Unfortunately, it was more like a stumbling block to some of his colleagues. During the 1960s, a growing number of voices called for its removal. In response, the 1971 Biennial Conference (SIL's highest decision-making body) passed an official motion reaffirming the organization's historical commitment to the scientific aspects of its work (Pike 1989:58). During the following year, Pike wrote a letter to the SIL membership in which he spoke of wanting "to prevent the development of a rift between the linguistic crew and the translation crew." After reminding his colleagues of the prime command to love God with heart, soul, and mind, he observed that: "Commitment of heart and soul constrains us to help in [the task of translating the Bible for people who speak languages where it is not present]. Commitment of mind draws us into scientific research" (Pike 1989:44–45).

The place of the scientific approach as a distinctive of SIL is still questioned by some of its members. It surfaced, for instance, in 1999 when the executive leadership of SIL gave serious consideration to a generalization of the distinctive in terms of "excellence in all we do." Some felt that focusing on the broader concern with quality might be a means of mending the rift that Pike wrote of thirty years ago; others saw it as a license to reassert the rift. The executive leadership has since returned to a more specific characterization of the distinctive that reaffirms the academic and professional nature of SIL. However, the debate that was stirred up in the process of considering this proposal throughout the world of SIL points to the persistence and deep-seatedness of the issue. Why does the scientific approach continue to pose such a stumbling block for some members of SIL? I can think of four possible reasons.

The first is the centuries-old debate on "faith versus reason" that has raged ever since the Enlightenment. As Pike summed it up in one of his essays, "Mind and heart have again and again sued for divorce" (Pike 1962:22). Just 200 years ago, virtually every university was a center that integrated faith and reason, but today most major institutions of learning have disengaged from the faith component in a process that one author has dubbed "the dying of the light" (Burtchaell 1998; see also Marsden 1994). But pressure for the divorce of faith and reason has come from the faith community as well, resulting in a disengagement that another author has dubbed "the scandal of the evangelical mind" (Noll 1994). Pike commented as follows about the latter trend:

> For the past generation or two, the evangelical wing of the Christian church has viewed scholarship with suspicion. Reeling under attacks internally from higher criticism and externally from science, it has sometimes withdrawn into a defensive cyst formation in order to weather the storm. But the price it has paid for defense has been severe. While accepting joyfully one part of the greatest commandment, it has often ignored another part of the same command. Vigorously, it has attempted to obey the command to serve God with heart and soul. Belligerently, it has sometimes ignored in the same command the order to love God with *mind*. (Pike 1962:viii)

To those of the faith community who would want SIL to disengage from its founding commitment to a scientific approach, I can think of no better counterargument than to point to the efficacy of the life and work of a man like Pike who clearly integrated the two.

A second reason that the scientific approach might be a stumbling block for some today is a growing distrust of science by the public at large. SIL was founded during the height of the modern era, when there was a popular sense that science held the key to solving all our problems. But in today's postmodern era, science has lost much of its luster. After witnessing modern developments like nuclear war, eugenics, and environmental disasters, the populace has grown more wary of science. Ironically, one outcome of postmodernism is to produce a climate that is more open to the realm of spirit and thus to the possible reconciliation of faith and reason (Glynn 1997).

A third possible reason for some is more pragmatic—they fail to be convinced of the benefits or relevance of the scientific approach. They see it as distracting from what they really want to accomplish. Pike was, of course, deeply convinced of the benefits and took every opportunity to explain these to his colleagues. Now SIL has lost that voice, but the message is no less critical. Leaders throughout SIL need to pick up where Pike left off.

A fourth reason that the scientific approach continues to be questioned by some in SIL is that many are not sure what it really means. Bloomfield (1933:3), in the opening page of his classic *Language,* makes clear his assumption of a scientific approach in linguistics: "It is only within the last century or so that language has been studied in a scientific way, by careful and comprehensive observation." A few generations later, textbooks on linguistics cannot so easily take this for granted. For instance, Lyons (1981:37) remarks:

> Linguistics is usually defined as the science of language or, alternatively, as the scientific study of language. The very fact that there should be a section, in this book and in other introductions to linguistics, devoted explicitly to the scientific status of the discipline should not pass without comment. After all, disciplines whose scientific status is unquestioned—physics, chemistry, biology, etc.—feel no need to justify their claim to be called sciences. Why should linguistics be so concerned to defend the validity of its title? And why is it that, in defending his scientific credentials, the linguist so often gives the impression of protesting too much? The reader has every right to be suspicious.

Lyons goes on to identify the hallmarks of the scientific study of language (in contrast to the nonscientific approach of traditional grammarians) as being that it is empirical and objective. In other textbooks that have a section on linguistics as science, Robins (1989:7) observes that linguistics is guided in its operations by three canons of science—exhaustiveness, consistency, and economy; Crystal (1971:78) points to the three essential characteristics of explicitness, systematicness, and objectivity; Yngve (1986:7–9) emphasizes the primary place of observational evidence—that theory must answer to observed data and that assumptions not supported by data should be rooted out.

These discussions of linguistics as science focus on the nature of the results it produces. While these are basic tenets of science, I do not think they help very much to settle the question of what Townsend really meant when he laid down SIL's founding distinctive of following a scientific approach. The leadership that Pike gave as SIL's first president (as described in the second section above) indicates that participation in the scientific community was more in focus. The next section develops a restatement of the founding distinctive based on the view that cooperative, social activity lies at the heart of the scientific approach.

Acting in Community: The Essence of Science

It is generally believed that the essence of science is its method. The so-called "scientific method" involves making systematic observations, formulating hypotheses to explain what has been observed, and then validating or invalidating those hypotheses through further observation. Scientific theories result when hypotheses are confirmed by observations; such theories are held to be reliable since they were arrived at by objective means.

In *Scientific Literacy and the Myth of the Scientific Method,* Henry H. Bauer, a distinguished chemist, observes that although the method has a place in science, it does not explain how science really works (Bauer 1992:19–41). Evidence does not always have primacy over theory as the method would lead us to believe. Existing theory is often invoked to explain new evidence (though it may not exactly fit). Alternatively, evidence is often rejected when it does not align with accepted theory.

Science is not a unity defined by a unitary scientific method. Rather, the many subfields of science are characterized by different methodologies. This is because the subfields themselves differ in the extent to which they are data-driven or theory-driven, data-rich or data-poor, experimental or observational, quantitative or qualitative, and so on. Bauer argues that science is best understood not in terms of a method, but in terms of social activity—the unity of science derives from a shared commitment to certain kinds of cooperative action. Science is a process by which a scientific community generates scientific knowledge. The extent to which the community achieves consensus about a particular bit of knowledge is the extent to which it is deemed reliable.

In a chapter named "How science really works," Bauer uses two metaphors to explain the social activities that make up the enterprise of science. The first metaphor (Bauer 1992:42–44; after Polanyi 1962) is the jigsaw puzzle. Doing science is like putting together a large jigsaw puzzle with a group of people. One strategy might be to give each puzzler an equal share of the pieces and have them work independently, but this approach would be singularly ineffectual since few of the pieces given to each puzzler would actually fit together. Alternatively, one could give each puzzler a copy of all the pieces, and eventually combine their separate, partial results. This approach at least has a chance of completing the puzzle, but would lead to large-scale duplication of effort and may not be significantly faster than a single puzzler working in ideal conditions.

The only effective way to put multiple puzzlers to work at once is to have them all work together on a single copy of the puzzle in sight of each other. In this way, as one puzzler fits in one more piece, all the others will see the resulting state of the puzzle and will potentially adjust their next step in consequence of the new state. These puzzlers, like scientists, take individual initiative in determining what part of the puzzle they will seek to solve and even how they will go about doing it, but the adjustment and self-coordination that occurs as they observe the outcomes achieved by their fellows results in a joint achievement that could not be equaled by any single puzzler working in isolation.

The second metaphor is that of the filter (Bauer 1992:44–48). The process by which a scientific community generates scientific knowledge is like a process of putting ideas through a multistage filter. Each stage is manifest by social institutions that the scientific community has developed over time. The first stage is undergraduate and graduate training in which aspiring scientists learn to align their thinking and behavior with the norms of a particular scientific community. The second stage is research, or frontier science, in which a vast array of ideas get formed and tested. But the array of ideas is not unconstrained; the institution of grant funding (with its attendant mechanisms of proposal writing and peer review) serve to limit those ideas that actually get worked on. The results of research cannot contribute toward scientific knowledge until they enter the third stage, namely, the primary literature. Here the key institutions are conferences and journals and the primary mechanisms are peer review and editing. The review process serves not only to filter out poor work but also to ensure that authors frame their ideas in light of established knowledge.

The fact that an idea is published does not make it scientific knowledge; it just makes it widely available. The next stage in the filter is for published ideas to be tested and used by others. In the process some ideas will ultimately be rejected by the community; others will be refined and extended and eventually make their way into the secondary literature of review articles, monographs, and graduate-level textbooks. After the passage of even more time and testing, we reach the final stage of textbook science in which the consensus of the community gets expressed as scientific knowledge in undergraduate textbooks. But even this is not 100 percent correct and gets filtered further as the understanding of scientific knowledge is revised in future textbooks. For instance, Bauer reports that one prominent physicist has guessed that textbook science in his field is about 90 percent correct, whereas the primary literature is probably about 90 percent wrong.

Thus the essence of the filter is the force of the peer community as it shapes ideas and information into shared knowledge. Science really works by achieving consensus in the community. Results derived from applying the scientific method do not enjoy an a priori claim to reliability; they, like any ideas, must pass through the knowledge filter where they will either be rejected by the community, or they will be validated and further refined as they are used.

Note that the institutions that comprise the knowledge filter are not unique to science. They are the institutions of the wider academic community and are just as fundamental to disciplines like history and philosophy that are not scientific. The thing that distinguishes science from these other disciplines is not so much its institutions as the nature of its subject matter.

Given this understanding that science is "an inescapably cooperative, social activity" (Bauer 1992:52), it becomes easier to understand what Townsend meant when he laid down the founding distinctive for SIL that "We follow a scientific approach." The notion of scientific approach can be demystified by a reformulation like:

We are part of the academic community.

And what does this mean? Following the metaphors developed by Bauer, these are possible paraphrases:

- We work the enormous puzzle of human language in view of each other and of the rest of the academic community—both building on the work of others and permitting others to build on our work.
- We participate in the institutions of the knowledge filter—both as an organization (offering advanced training, sponsoring research, hosting conferences and workshops, publishing books and journals) and as individuals (taking training, teaching courses, doing research, joining academic societies, attending conferences, reading the literature, writing papers and monographs, participating in peer review).

This is what I believe SIL's founder meant by the "scientific approach" and these are precisely the behaviors that Dr. Pike modeled for us.

OLAC: An Emerging Community

Before concluding this essay I want to discuss a particular community—the Open Language Archives Community (OLAC)—in terms of the metaphors of the puzzle and the filter. OLAC is a newly emerging community that I have had the privilege of helping to develop in collaboration with Steven Bird of the University of Pennsylvania. It was founded as an outcome of a workshop we organized in December 2000 on the topic of "Web-based Language Documentation and Description" (Bird and Simons 2000).

The workshop brought together a group of ninety scholars and technicians who shared a vision for exploiting the World Wide Web to offer unparalleled access to information about the world's languages. The Web has already demonstrated its value as a medium for providing universal access to language documentation and description, and it does so at a much lower cost than conventional print publishing. But a number of problems have emerged; for instance, potential users cannot necessarily find the material they are interested in, different data providers use different formats and conventions, and most linguists have no idea how to prepare their material for publication via this medium. The workshop participants recognized that if all the players work independently on the problem, the result could be unparalleled frustration and confusion rather than unparalleled access.

This is essentially the problem of the puzzle. There are tens of thousands of people around the world who are working professionally on the enormous puzzle of human language; countless others are also interested in observing and sometimes contributing. The Internet offers the potential—for the first time in the history of the world—for all of the puzzlers to watch each other as they fit together the pieces. The challenge is for this community to align its practices so as to make that potential into a reality. Current practice resembles more the scenarios in which individual puzzlers work separately or in small groups.

OLAC was founded in order to develop a solution to this problem. It has the following purpose statement:

> OLAC, the Open Language Archives Community, is an international partnership of institutions and individuals who are creating a worldwide virtual library of language resources by: (1) developing consensus on best current practice for the digital archiving of language resources, and (2) developing a network of interoperating repositories and services for housing and accessing such resources.

OLAC assists the cooperative activity of piecing together the puzzle by implementing some key components of the knowledge filter. In order to meet its first objective of developing consensus on best current practice, OLAC implements a system of working groups and successive stages of testing and peer review. This provides a mechanism by which the community may process the many competing ideas on digital archiving of language resources through the knowledge filter to ultimately yield the equivalent of textbook knowledge on how it should be done.

The second objective is to develop a network of interoperating repositories and services for housing and accessing digitally archived language resources. The key to this is the notion of METADATA—structured data about data. In essence, every piece of the puzzle has a metadata record (like a library catalog card) that describes the form and content of the piece. The archives that are participating in OLAC have agreed on a standard format they will use to publish the metadata descriptions of each of their holdings. In so doing they have also agreed on a standardized way of uniquely identifying each of the world's languages so that a search for the puzzle pieces about a particular language will find every piece associated with that language and only those associated with that language (Simons 2000). The participants have further agreed on an Internet protocol based on the work of the Open Archives Initiative (Van de Sompel and Lagoze 2001) that will allow any service interested in building a catalog of archived language resources to harvest the metadata records via machine-to-machine communication. The centerpiece of the community will be a single union catalog of the holdings of all participating archives. This will provide all the puzzle builders in the world a single gateway through which they can see all the pieces of the puzzle and share the pieces they have put together. The search mechanism for that catalog, which allows individuals to locate just those pieces of the puzzle that are relevant to them, provides an essential stage in the knowledge filter for research about the world's languages.

The vision of being able to see all the pieces of the puzzle is an ambitious one. The extent to which it will be realized depends on what proportion of language resource developers actually participate. The initial results are encouraging. At the time of the public launch of OLAC thirteen months after its founding (Bird and Simons 2002), there were thirteen institutions that had implemented OLAC-conformant metadata repositories for their archives; many others have communicated their intent to participate. The union catalog that has been built by harvesting the metadata from those thirteen sites offers access to a virtual library with about 18,000 holdings. The names of the participating archives, the union catalog of their holdings, and the documents defining the OLAC standards may all be found at the OLAC Website (OLAC 2002). The interested reader is also referred to Simons and Bird (2000) for a readable statement of the OLAC vision. That document in turn points to other documents that list detailed requirements and discuss technical implementation.

For me, there is a personal and poignant association between OLAC and Kenneth Pike. In the week following the workshop at which OLAC was founded, I had the opportunity to sit with Dr. Pike at an office Christmas party. As he was the mentor who first modeled the ways of academic community to me, I was excited to relate to him the OLAC vision and its initial success. Though confessing bewilderment at some of the technical aspects of the effort, he was enthusiastic as he expressed gratitude that there were "young fellows like you" who could understand and apply these new ways of doing things. He went on to pronounce his blessing on the endeavor. That was the last time I spoke with Dr. Pike; less than a week later he entered the hospital with the illness that ended his life.

Conclusion: The Call to Academic Community

The founders of SIL were wise in observing that they could not successfully achieve the one distinctive of Bible translation without the parallel distinctive of participation in the academic community. They saw that the puzzle was too big to do by themselves; they saw that they needed the knowledge filter of the wider community to inform and validate their work. And what was true in the 1930s is just as true today—the call to academic community is as relevant as ever. I cannot think of a more fitting tribute to the memory of Ken Pike than that the organization he helped to establish in the ways of the "scientific approach" would renew its commitment, both corporately and as individuals, to participating in the academic community.

References

Bauer, Henry H. 1992. *Scientific literacy and the myth of the scientific method*. Urbana and Chicago: University of Illinois Press.

Bird, Steven, and Gary F. Simons, editors. 2000. *Proceedings of the workshop on web-based language documentation and description, University of Pennsylvania,* 12–15 December 2000. <http://www.ldc.upenn.edu/exploration/expl2000/>.

Bird, Steven, and Gary F. Simons, conveners. 2002. *The Open Language Archives Community*. A symposium at the 76th Annual Meeting of the Linguistic Society of America, San Francisco, 3–6 January 2002. <http://www.language-archives.org/docs/us-launch.html>.

Blair, Betty A. 1983. Conversations with Kenneth L. Pike. *Languages for Peace* 1:22–27.

Bloomfield, Leonard. 1933. *Language*. New York: Holt. [Reprint: 1984. Chicago: University of Chicago Press.]

Burtchaell, James T. 1998. *The dying of the light: The disengagement of colleges and universities from their Christian churches*. Grand Rapids, Mich.: Wm. B. Eerdmans.

Crystal, David. 1971. *Linguistics*. Middlesex, England: Penguin Books.

Glynn, Patrick. 1997. *God: The evidence—The reconciliation of faith and reason in a postsecular world*. Rocklin, Calif.: Prima Publishing.

Lyons, John. 1981. *Language and linguistics: An introduction*. Cambridge: Cambridge University Press.

Marsden, George M. 1994. *The soul of the American university: From Protestant establishment to established nonbelief*. Oxford: Oxford University Press.

Noll, Mark A. 1994. *The scandal of the evangelical mind*. Grand Rapids, Mich.: Wm. B. Eerdmans.

OLAC. 2002. Open Language Archives Community web site. <http://www.language-archives.org>.

Pike, Eunice V. 1981. *Ken Pike: Scholar and Christian*. Dallas: Summer Institute of Linguistics.

Pike, Kenneth L. 1962. *With heart and mind: A personal synthesis of scholarship and devotion*. Grand Rapids, Mich.: Wm. B. Eerdmans. [Second edition: 1996. Duncanville, Tex.: Adult Learning Systems.]

Pike, Kenneth L. (with Hugh Steven). 1989. *Pike's perspectives: An anthology of thought, insight, and moral purpose*. Langley, B.C.: Credo Publishing.

Polanyi, Michael. 1962. The republic of science: Its political and economic theory. *Minerva* 1:54–73.

Robins, R. H. 1989. *General linguistics: An introductory survey,* fourth edition. New York: Longman.

SIL International. 2001. *Celebration of the life of Kenneth L. Pike.* Two audio cassettes of the memorial service, 6 January 2001. The mule story is in the remarks of Ruth Carr. Available from Executive Director's Office, SIL International, Dallas, TX.

Simons, Gary F. 2000. Language identification in metadata descriptions of language archive holdings. In Bird and Simons (eds.), <http://www.ldc.upenn.edu/exploration/expl2000/papers/simons/simons.htm>.

Simons, Gary F., and Steven Bird. 2000. The seven pillars of open language archiving: A vision statement. <http://www.language-archives.org/docs/vision.html>.

Van de Sompel, Herbert, and Carl Lagoze, eds. 2001. The Open Archives Initiative protocol for metadata harvesting, Version 1.1. <http://www.openarchives.org/OAI_protocol/openarchives-protocol.html>.

Yngve, Victor H. 1986. *Linguistics as a science.* Bloomington: Indiana University Press.

8

A Gap to Fill: Language History

Joseph E. Grimes

Up to about a century ago, most linguistics aimed at reconstructing language history. The Dutch had noted systematic similarities among languages in seventeenth-century Indonesia. The British in eighteenth-century India saw the same kind of thing. In 1786 Sir William Jones, a judge in British India, presented a paper that spelled out the affinity of some languages spoken there with Greek, Latin, and other European languages, and suggested that the similarities were due to descent from a common but no longer extant ancestor. The nineteenth century saw a boom in comparative studies, with university chairs in linguistics being established all over Europe. People did go to the field and describe languages—some rather well. But the cutting edge was the development of the comparative method and the elaboration of its results. Indo-European languages were at the center of attention, and other families were also studied.

The twentieth century found scholars like Ferdinand de Saussure sorting through the insights of comparative linguistics, but viewing them innovatively. They saw that grammars of languages from any time or place followed surprisingly similar lines, so that generalizations were possible. Synchronic linguistics took shape as a counterpart to the more familiar diachronic linguistics; both perspectives were recognized as valid. Looking at the paths languages were shown to have followed as they diverged over time, scholars of that era saw the same phenomena reflected in contextually determined alternations such as assimilation and analogy.

These things could be observed in languages whose history was unknown. Linguistics took on a new form.

Linguists looked into previously unstudied languages in North America and elsewhere. What they found added fuel to the fire of synchronic studies. The new generation of linguists were trained in historical comparative studies, and they applied what they knew to their own fresh language material. That shifted their emphasis away from accounting only for how the languages they studied got to be that way. They looked more closely than ever at what those languages were like at that time—the synchronic view.

Two midcentury linguists, Kenneth Pike and Morris Swadesh, shaped my thinking about the comparative study of languages. They made me aware that it was both doable and worth doing. They also introduced me to some of the pitfalls in it.

Pike in 1950 was exploring an epistemology that relied on procedures for finding things out: his 1947 *Phonemics* was subtitled "A technique for reducing languages to writing." Mindful of the way his own mentors had been taught to think about language change as well as language structure, he wanted to get his students involved in the diachronic side of linguistics. So he put together a 25-page mimeographed guide, *Axioms and Procedures for Reconstructions in Comparative Linguistics: an Experimental Syllabus* (Pike 1950). It laid out the principles of comparative data management and analysis. From it one could get a good start on the discipline in a do-it-yourself fashion. Equally important, its bibliography pointed to some of the standard comparative works.

I did not see *Axioms and Procedures* until the next year, since in 1950 I had been totally occupied with taking Pike's introductory course, which was purely synchronic. But by the summer of 1951 I had gotten some field exposure to both Algonquian and Uto-Aztecan languages, read Trubetzkoy's *Principes de Phonologie,* sat in on a seminar by two Slavicists, and gotten acquainted with Mexican linguists who were interested in their nation's linguistic history. So when Pike brought out his comparativist's guide, I was ready for it. It turned linguistics into a three dimensional jigsaw puzzle that disclosed a history behind each synchronic pattern that I recognized. That was fun.

I do not think Pike included comparative linguistics in his courses for very many years after that. He got other people interested in doing serious comparative work, but he had too many other irons in the fire to put in the time necessary at that stage to pursue it himself.[1]

But in recent years, Pike's work has come back to my attention. I have been developing computer software in which the computer follows out the implications of all the judgments that the comparative linguist makes; the linguist formulates hypotheses in the usual way, and from that the computer stores, relates, and presents data much more reliably and rapidly than the linguist could using traditional paper, pencil, and memory means. In the design of that software, Pike's *Axioms and Procedures* proved to be a source I could use to make sure I had not overlooked anything essential, since it covered all the basics.

The other thing that happened in 1951 was that Morris Swadesh came to visit Pike and lectured on the so-called "glottochronological" approach that he had begun taking to language classification. It drew on lexicostatistical counts of a particular kind, and brought in analogies he saw with the mathematics of dating old objects by their radioactivity. At that time, measuring Carbon[14] isotope ratios in organic artifacts was a hot topic in archaeology, so everybody listened. What impressed me as we got acquainted was that he was well grounded in classical comparative linguistics and had published in that area, yet was innovative enough to explore marrying it to a physical model. He had also contributed materially to the development of the phonological theory of the time, and had done firsthand work on lots of languages.

For the next few years I concentrated on the Huichol language of Mexico, sharpening my 3-D jigsaw puzzle skills a little by plotting out the major sound correspondences between Huichol and its linguistic and geographic neighbor Cora for the appendix to a dictionary of Huichol which I helped compile (see McIntosh and Grimes 1954).

In 1960 I returned to Mexico after graduate school. While at Cornell University I had included Romance linguistics and some Indo-European in my course work and read more widely in comparative principles. I had also published an approach to quantification that was conceptually appropriate for the sets of phonological correspondences that stand behind all historical and comparative phonology; Howard McKaughan later dubbed that kind of quantification "phonostatistics" and the name seems

---

[1]Editors' note: Although Pike did not include comparative linguistics in his basic courses, he did discuss it in his seminars on Live Issues in Descriptive Linguistics, and articles published in the 1960s by Pike and colleagues on matrix analysis pointed out the potential contribution of a matrix approach for identifying morphological relations between languages. "They opened the door to the development of an approach to historical reconstruction of morphology based on comparison of matrices" (Pike and Simons 1996:34). See also Pike (1996).

to have stuck. (See, for example, Grimes and Agard 1959 and Grimes 1964.)

The National Autonomous University of Mexico at that time invited social scientists to become proficient on their new IBM 650 computer, now a dinosaur that my Pocket PC would run circles around. Two of us took them up on it: Morris Swadesh, who by then had also moved to Mexico, and I. By that time his glottochronology had attracted attention worldwide. But the more intensely scholars evaluated it, the more flaws they turned up in it. The process of critiquing it certainly enhanced everyone's understanding of how many diverse factors enter into apparent lexical similarity, and of how difficult it is to extract valid conclusions without going back to the full scale analysis of language history that classical comparative linguistics gives.

The scholarly debates put Swadesh on the defensive. Nevertheless, over the next few years, as we spent night shifts in the computer laboratory helping each other wire up plug boards to format our output, or waiting for passes on the card sorting machines to complete, I came to appreciate Swadesh's breadth of knowledge of language, even though most scholars (including me) were finding his thinking about using the lexicostatistical approach as a shortcut to language classification increasingly untenable.[2]

By the early sixties other scholars in SIL were turning out monographs and journal articles containing historical comparative studies on families of indigenous languages,[3] and I turned my attention elsewhere. Linguistics in America was undergoing a major shift in thinking under the influence of Noam Chomsky and his school. For a time comparative linguistics was focused on reformulating what linguists had been doing for almost three centuries, using the new paradigm. The idea of processes that affect phonological and morphological features came as no surprise to comparativists, who had been looking at things that way all along. Many of them appreciated the succinctness with which changes could be spelled out, and the emphasis on recognizing only changes that were rooted in general phonological theory.

The bulk of linguistic studies turned toward testing theories on data, rather than on description as an end in itself. Subdisciplines began to

---

[2]A brief summary of glottochronology and the major criticisms of it are given under "Historical Linguistics: Mathematical Concepts" in the Oxford University Press's *International Encyclopedia of Linguistics* 2:133–134 (1992). I critiqued it further as an unreliable predictor of intelligibility in Grimes (1988), since some had hoped it might become a shortcut both for language grouping and for intelligibility testing. Neither has worked out in practice.

[3]For example, Wonderly (1949), Longacre (1957), Gudschinsky (1959), Bee (1965), Davis (1966). Since the sixties a small number of SIL scholars have become conversant with the discipline, and their comparative studies continue to appear, for example, Payne (1991).

proliferate, such as developmental linguistics, sociolinguistics, computational linguistics, and psycholinguistics. These specialties drew people away from historical and comparative linguistics, which is understandable. But the other side of that specialization was that fewer linguists felt they had the time to become conversant with the diachronic side of things, which is regrettable.

As a balance to SIL's traditional emphasis on field programs as heavily descriptive, one could suggest that historical and comparative linguistics can fill several gaps:[4]

1. Margaret Milliken (1988) has done research on types of sound change that do or do not impede intelligibility. Her work suggests that there are complementary ways of approaching the question of what groups of people in an area might or might not understand each other. In other words, intelligibility tests tap into the overall effect of all factors working together. Those results are enhanced by finding patterns of sound change that pinpoint specific known factors. This gives a dual reading to back up sound decisions on where to initiate field programs.

2. Members of speech communities, educators, governments, and the general public often show great interest in studies that help them understand their own linguistic history—to situate themselves in the confusing world of language.

3. Linguists who can view the phenomena they are studying both synchronically and diachronically are better equipped to cope with language problems than those whose understanding is limited to synchronic considerations.

4. Sociolinguists, who deal with time-dependent phenomena in the short term, may fail to recognize links to longer term changes if they are not trained in the big picture.

5. Language surveyors can characterize the linguistic composition of an area with greater confidence than if they are limited to methods that oversimplify the conclusions that could be drawn from their data.

I would not suggest that everybody who does field linguistics also master historical and comparative linguistics; there is enough else to learn as

---

[4]I hasten to add that if doing comparative linguistics continues to depend on paper, pencil, and the scholar's memory, as it did in the past, the promise I envision will never be realized. To remedy that situation, I am developing the software described earlier in this paper. A user-unfriendly prototype to test the concept was done in 1992; the user-friendly version, which also supports team research, is just now getting off the ground.

is. But I would recommend that for every language family where a university, SIL, or any other agency has field projects, at least one person who is already conversant with one language of that family be encouraged to study comparative principles and become familiar with the historical and comparative studies that have already been made.[5] Then they can contribute to those studies in their turn. Others who study languages of the same family should have opportunity to learn what the comparative specialist knows. Those people can also provide data to fill out the specialist's research. This is an economical and practical approach to making sure that useful expertise on the diachronic side of language studies is available within every cluster of field teams.

References

Bee, Darlene. 1965. Comparative and historical problems in East New Guinea highland languages. *Linguistic Circle of Canberra Publications A* 6:1–37. Republished (1973) in Howard McKaughan, ed., *The languages of the Eastern family of the East New Guinea Highland stock*, 739–768. Seattle: University of Washington Press.

Davis, Irvine. 1966. Comparative Jê phonology. *Estudos Lingüísticos* 1(2):10–24.

Grimes, Joseph E. 1964. Measures of linguistic divergence. In Horace G. Lunt, ed., *Proceedings of the Ninth International Congress of Linguists, Cambridge, Mass., August 27–31, 1962*, 44–50. The Hague: Mouton.

Grimes, Joseph E. 1988. Correlations between vocabulary similarity and intelligibility. *Notes on Linguistics* 41:19–33.

Grimes, Joseph E., and Frederick B. Agard. 1959. Linguistic divergence in Romance. *Language* 35:598–604.

Gudschinsky, Sarah C. 1959. *Proto-Popotecan: A comparative study of Popolocan and Mixtecan*. Indiana University Research Center in Anthropology, Folklore and Linguistics, Memoir 15, supplement to *International Journal of American Linguistics* 25:2. Bloomington: Indiana University.

Longacre, Robert E. 1957. *Proto-Mixtecan*. Indiana University Research Center in Anthropology, Folklore and Linguistics, Memoir 5, supplement to *International Journal of American Linguistics* 23:4. Bloomington: Indiana University.

McIntosh, John B., and Joseph E. Grimes. 1954. *Niuqui 'iquisicayari: Vocabulario huichol-castellano castellano-huichol*. México, D. F.: Instituto Lingüístico de Verano.

Milliken, Margaret E. 1988. *Phonological divergence and intelligibility: A case study of English and Scots*. Ph.D. dissertation. Cornell University.

---

[5]Synchronic linguists are sometimes surprised to learn how much comparative work others have done on the languages they are interested in.

Payne, David L. 1991. A classification of Maipuran (Arawakan) languages based on shared lexical retentions. In Desmond C. Derbyshire and Geoffrey K. Pullum, (eds.), *Handbook of Amazonian languages* 3:355–499. Berlin and New York: Mouton de Gruyter.

Pike, Kenneth L. 1947. *Phonemics: A technique for reducing languages to writing.* Ann Arbor: University of Michigan Press.

Pike, Kenneth L. 1950. *Axioms and procedures for reconstructions in comparative linguistics: An experimental syllabus.* Glendale, Calif.: Summer Institute of Linguistics. 25 pages, mimeographed.

Pike, Kenneth L. 1996. Linguistic 'Venn Diagrams' with their 'formative blocks' in morphology, semantics, and historical reconstruction. In Kurt R. Jankowsky (ed.), *Multiple perspectives on the historical dimensions of language,* 51–56. Münster: Nodus Publikationen.

Pike, Kenneth L., and Gary F. Simons. 1993 [1996]. Toward the historical reconstruction of matrix patterns in morphology. *Voprosy Jazkoznania* [Problems of Linguistics] 1:22–44. (Also published in Kurt R. Jankowsky, ed. 1996. *The mystery of culture contacts, historical reconstruction and text analysis: An emic approach,* 1–37. Washington, D.C.: Georgetown University Press.)

Wonderly, William L. 1949. Some Zoquean phonemic and morphophonemic correspondences. *International Journal of American Linguistics* 15:1–11.

Part II

Language and Culture

"But what was the largest linguistic act to be distributed within? Here we were inevitably committed to the relevance of culture...as a distributional matrix for large linguistic units." (Pike 1954:156)

Ángel Merecías Sánchez and his late wife, Modesta, in 1944.

Ángel was the main co-translator with Ken Pike and the late Donald Stark of the translation of the New Testament into the Mixtec language of San Miguel el Grande, in Oaxaca, Mexico. It was published in 1951. Ángel, Ken's main research assistant on the Mixtec language in the 1940s, was born in 1914, making him two years younger than Ken. Ángel still resides in his home village of San Miguel el Grande. He is presently (in 2003) working (by regular mail) with Ken's widow, Evelyn Pike, on the production of a collection of interlinear texts to appear in Mixtec, Spanish, and English. The Pikes collected some of those texts from Mixtec speakers over a half-century ago, plus texts that Ángel has authored describing traditional customs in his community when he was a boy.

It was Ángel who first explained to Ken the meanings of the Mixtec "tone puns" that Ken analyzed and published in four articles in IJAL in 1945–1947, and which Professor Jane Hill examines in the chapter beginning on the next page.

Mixtec of San Miguel el Grande is an endangered language today, with a reported 14,000 speakers in 1990. Reports say that in the 1980s the children in San Miguel were no longer speaking the language.

9

Mocking Spanish from Above and Below

Jane H. Hill

Introduction: Pike's Spanish and Mixtec Jokes and Puns

Most linguists who work in Latin America have at least a passing acquaintance with the Spanish language. Ken Pike, as he was always willing to admit, did not—at least not at first. Pike turned his beginner's monolingual approach to learning an unwritten language into his famous monolingual method, which influenced generations of field workers who came after him. In his highly entertaining and instructive "monolingual demonstrations" (his occasional presentations at the University of Michigan in Ann Arbor, where I saw them in the late 1960s and early 1970s, were eagerly awaited and played to packed halls), Ken taught students all over the world the monolingual elicitation method he had developed in his early fieldwork among the Mixtec Indians of southern Mexico, where he simply could not use an intermediate language or local interpreters (Pike 1999; see also Makkai 1998).

While the monolingual demonstrations are the most famous result of the communicative challenges that Ken Pike faced in the Sierra Mixteca in the 1930s, sociolinguists and linguistic anthropologists can find other lessons from this early work. Immersed in a community where his English

was useless, struggling with a difficult new language, he found sympathetic friends among the Mixtec Indians, who had as well to defend themselves in a world where their native language was often not sufficient for
their communicative needs with Mexican outsiders. And they shared with
him some very funny stories about their problems, which he wrote about
in "Tone Puns in Mixteco" (Pike 1945a), "Mock Spanish of a Mixteco Indian" (Pike 1945b), "Another Mixteco Tone Pun" (Pike 1946), and "A
Text Involving Inadequate Spanish of a Mixteco Indian" (Pike 1947).
These four essays are among a series of small masterpieces of text analysis
from this period and include both rigorous linguistic analysis and insightful cultural commentary. The original texts were written down by Pike's
Mixtec consultants, Narciso Merecías, who compiled the first drafts, and
Ángel Merecías, who filled in missing letters and tone marks. They reveal
some of the strategies that were used by Mixtec speakers to "manage"
their confrontation with Spanish, the language of powerful outsiders to
their communities who had imposed upon them a violent and impoverish-
ing regime.

Pike's papers on the Mixtec "management" of Spanish resonated for me
because in recent years I have been researching the way that the people
called "Anglos"—members of the English-speaking populations of the
United States who have no Hispanic or Latino ancestry—have tried to
"manage" their own confrontation with Spanish. I have been calling one
set of strategies that they use "Mock Spanish," and I was very interested to
learn that Pike had used this same term in a publication that appeared in
1945 about Mixtec Indians. The present essay will compare ways that
these two very different communities use humor to manage the presence
of Spanish as an outsider language—the Mixtec from below, as the victims
of oppression mediated through the Spanish language, and the Anglos
from above, as the oppressors of a Spanish-speaking population in the
United States.

Mixtec "Mock Spanish"

"Mock Spanish of a Mixteco Indian" (Pike 1945b) presents *kʷeⁿdú lorensó*
"The Story of Lawrence." The feckless antihero of this tale, called *lénčú*
'Larry' in the body of the text, goes down to Puebla to work after failing as
a swineherder. When he returns to his home village, he feigns sophistication, putting on a pair of eyeglasses (like his boss in Puebla had worn) and
pretending to speak Spanish. He gets in trouble when a feast manager
who needs to buy skyrockets asks Larry to come with him to the store in

the city of Teposcolula, so that Larry can handle the negotiations with the Spanish-speaking storekeeper. Larry asks for skyrockets with the following sentences:

MOCK SPANISH: *kiérò púlgà para práàŋ práàŋ, i čitóòŋčitóòŋ čitóòŋ, ke-ásé ṣ̌ṣ̌ṣ̌ṣ̌tóòŋ pà-r̃íbà*
REAL SPANISH: *quiero pólvora* (powder) *para* (sound effects) *y* (sound effects) *que hace* (sound effects) *para arriba.*
ENGLISH: "I want flea for praang praang, and chitoong chitoong, that makes shhh shtowng, upwards."

The storekeeper, who obviously did not sell fleas that go "praang praang, chitoong chitoong," whacks Larry over the head with a measuring stick and drives him from the establishment. Larry explains to the feast manager, "He didn't understand because I speak so very eruditely. That's the reason he whacked me over the head with a stick."

"A Text Involving Inadequate Spanish of a Mixteco Indian" (Pike 1947), analyzes a story called *kʷeⁿdú čàa nì-taʔàn ʔá-náʔán*, "The Story of What Happened to a Man a Long Time Ago." In the climactic scenes of a very long and complicated narrative, two foolish Mixtec brothers find a murder victim and are caught with the corpse by soldiers. The men know only three sentences in Spanish, which they deploy in the hope that these will be appropriate replies to the interrogation. When the soldiers ask, "Who killed this person?", they reply *Nosotros señor* 'We, sir'. When the soldiers ask, "Why did you kill him?" they reply *porque simos* 'Just because (?)'. The soldiers say, "Now you must go to jail." The two men reply, *razón será* 'That would be reasonable enough.' They are thrown in jail and their more intelligent older brother has to use hard-earned money to bail them out.

"Tone puns in Mixteco" (Pike 1945a) involves a story (it lacks a title) about a priest who doesn't speak good Mixtec, but is constantly demanding chickens—expensive festival food in the Indian world—from his Mixtec parishioners. Yet he doesn't eat the whole chicken—he throws away the head and feet and offal (which would have been relished by the Indians). After watching him waste meat this way on several occasions, the Mixtec decide to save at least these parts for themselves. When they bring the priest only the meaty parts of the chicken, he actually has the crust to ask where the missing head, feet, and innards are. Pike speculates that the priest must have imposed Spanish stress and intonation patterns on the Mixtec tone contours, yielding absurd results. So the Mixtec mock him by changing the tones in their replies, yielding a whole series of hilariously surreal sentences: When the priest asks (or tries to ask) "Where is its head?," they reply, "Right here it is turning somersaults, master." When the priest asks, "Where are its feet?," the Mixtec reply, "On the branches of that tree right there it is getting married, master." And so on.

In "Another Mixteco Tone Pun" (Pike 1946), elaborated in a story called *kʷeⁿdú ʔəən sutù híín čáa ni-kà-sáa biko* "The Story of a Priest and Some Men Who Made a Feast," the priest sends the Mixtec off to collect palm branches for Palm Sunday. He tells them, "Go hunt some *žukù ñuù kwîi*." The proper Mixtec form for 'palm branches' would be *žukú ñuù kwíi*. The Indians claim that they heard *zukù ñù-kwii* 'mountain fox'. So instead of palm branches they bring a fox. He accuses them of being stupid, and they leave him standing alone with his fox.

Pike argues that these texts are subversive comments on Spanish domination. The Mixtec in the stories about the priest appear to him to be "stupid," giving ridiculous answers to his questions and bringing home a fox instead of palm branches. But in fact they have succeeded in ridiculing him without his realizing it. Furthermore, the stories implicitly criticize the Spanish power that can impose a demanding priest, who wants to eat only the most luxurious food, on an impoverished community, or impose a military presence that can throw innocent people into jail arbitrarily. But the story of Larry also critiques Mixtec attempts to recruit this power. Pike comments that

> Whenever a Mixteco speaker wishes to give the impression of dignity and power and cultural progressiveness, he will use many Spanish words mixed in with his Mixteco, even though the Mixteco words suppressed are otherwise at that moment in common use. In this way the men, in talking in public, often use Spanish words which they would not use at home and which their wives and children do not understand at all. (Pike 1945b:224)[1]

Another criticism of Spanish that is implicit in the Mixtec stories is that a world ordered through Spanish is unpredictable and violent. To use the language is as likely to produce disorder as order, and Mixtec who try to use Spanish may encounter physical violence in response.

---

[1]Ken Hill and I encountered this use of Spanish to create a "power code" in an indigenous Mexican language in our fieldwork in the 1970s and early 1980s in Nahuatl-speaking towns in the Malinche Volcano region of Tlaxcala and Puebla (cf. Hill and Hill 1986). While the Nahuatl speech of these mainly bilingual communities was always somewhat Hispanicized, the highest frequencies of Spanish loan words occurred in the speech of men at the peak of their public careers, speaking on matters of general importance.

The Mixtec texts from Narciso and Ángel Merecías illustrate the mocking of Spanish "from below." Mixtec speakers are oppressed by a dominant community that speaks Spanish, a language that comes to be associated with this dominance and with violence and rudeness, at the same time that it is associated as well with wealth, sophistication, and opportunity. Speakers must learn some of the language if they want to seem like serious, forward-looking, public-minded people. Yet they would prefer to maintain their distance from the worst kinds of behavior and values that Spanish represents. The kinds of jokes that the Mixtec tell about their linguistic dilemma attempt to "manage" this problem by exposing Spanish, and Spanish speakers, to ridicule.

Anglo "Mock Spanish"

I turn now to the use of "Mock Spanish" by English speakers in the United States, so-called Anglos. Like Mixtec Mock Spanish, American English Mock Spanish has a double meaning. Mixtec Mock Spanish, in "The Story of Lawrence," slyly criticizes the pretensions of men who try to seem worldly through the heavy incorporation of Spanish loan material in their Mixtec speech. However, "The Story of Lawrence" also implicitly associates Spanish with violence and disorder—the disorder in Larry's absurd Mock Spanish sentences and the violence of the Mestizo storekeeper's attack on him. In the theory of indexicality that has developed in recent years in linguistic anthropology (cf. Silverstein 1979, Ochs 1990), we can refer to the first function, of which the Mixtec people—and certainly Pike—were aware, as the "direct indexicality" of the Mock Spanish in "The Story of Lawrence." The second function, the critique of Spanish itself, is accomplished by "indirect indexicality"—this function can be inferred by a listener, but is not directly expressed in the text. The inference is supported not only by "The Story of Lawrence" itself, but also from a reading of all four of the texts published by Pike, where overt violence is a theme also in "The Story of What Happened to a Man a Long Time Ago," and where the disorderly speech of Spanish speakers trying to speak Mixtec, and Mixtec speakers trying to speak Spanish, is a theme in every tale. In Anglo Mock Spanish we can see the same kind of duality. The "direct indexicality" of Mock Spanish—the function acknowledged by its speakers—is to express a relaxed colloquial persona, one that simultaneously exhibits two very desirable qualities, cosmopolitanism (manifested by the use of a foreign language) and a sense of humor (since most Mock Spanish is jocular or humorous). This function is perhaps parallel to the function of Spanish in the usage of Mixtec men (and of men in many other Mexican indigenous communities; see footnote 1), that is, to meta-phorically evoke the power and wealth of Spanish speakers as an index of local political power. This overt function is satirized in "The Story of Law-rence." The "indirect indexicality" of Mock Spanish is to reproduce racist stereotypes of Spanish speakers as lazy, corrupt, disorderly, hyper-sexualized, and untrustworthy (see Hill 1993a, 1993b, 1995, 1998 for de-tailed discussion of these ideas). This is parallel to the implicit association of Spanish with violence and disorder in the Mixtec texts.

"Mock Spanish" in these functions among English speakers has quite a long history. It may date to as early as 1634 (the earliest attestation in the *Oxford English Dictionary*), when the word "peon," from Spanish *peón* 'low peasant' (ultimately from *pedón*, literally 'big-foot') was borrowed to refer to the lowest level of rural worker, thus indexing the idea that the condi-tion of peasants in lands where Spanish was spoken was particularly op-pressive. By 1792 (Cassidy 1985:508) we find in American English usages like "calaboose" for "jail," from Spanish *calabozo*, evoking the supposed vagaries of Spanish-speaking justice. Similar usages appear right through the nineteenth and twentieth centuries in American English and are richly documented in the work of writers ranging from Mark Twain to many contemporary authors. I have been interested primarily in developments during the last fifteen years, during which "Mock Spanish" has undergone a new efflorescence, appearing at a very high frequency in all forms of media and in other "sites of mass reproduction" such as greeting cards and coffee mugs. However, the oldest usages endure—I own a white cof-fee mug with the word "peon" printed on it in large blue letters, obviously intended for the desk top of some wage slave who dares to mock "the sys-tem" with a small gesture of rebellion.

There are several devices for producing Mock Spanish. One is to borrow a neutral or positive Spanish word, often a greeting, and use it in a joking or insulting way in English. Here, for instance, we find insulting or nega-tive uses of words like "el presidente," "mañana," "amigo," "nada," "adios," and "hasta la vista."

The second way of making Mock Spanish is to borrow a Spanish word that is already negative in the source language and use it in English as a sort of euphemism. A notorious example here is "cojones" (testicles), which can be safely used in English at the highest level of public dis-course—as illustrated by the use of this word by Madeleine Albright in a speech to the Security Council when she was U.S. Ambassador to the United Nations (see Hill 1998). Again, I can illustrate this usage with a coffee mug in my collection, which bears the words "Caca de toro." Even the most daring rebel would be unlikely to keep in the workplace a coffee mug inscribed "Bullshit," but "Caca de toro" (an expression that does not exist in Spanish) is acceptable.

The third way to do Mock Spanish is to add a few items of Spanish morphology to English words. This yields expressions like "el cheap-o," "numero two-o," "mucho trouble-o," and "no problem-o."

The fourth technique of Mock Spanish is what I have called "absurd hyperanglicization." This yields expressions like "hasty lumbago" (from *hasta luego*) or "fleas navidad" (this expression, from *feliz navidad*, appears every year on humorous Christmas cards that show scratching dogs).

I have collected a good deal of evidence for the overt function, or "direct indexicality," of Mock Spanish in American English, which is to convey the idea that one possesses a humorous, easy-going colloquial persona. An excellent example is found in the 1992 film *Terminator II: Judgement Day*, the source of the ubiquitous Mock Spanish slogan "Hasta la vista, baby." In the film, Arnold Schwarzenegger plays a machine who has to learn to behave like a man. In a remarkable scene, Schwarzenegger becomes a "real person" when he learns Mock Spanish tags like "no problemo" and "hasta la vista, baby," as well as some deeply vernacular English insults (see Hill 1995 for a detailed presentation of this scene). Madeleine Albright, Secretary of State in the later years of the Clinton administration, had a public image as a rather pompous dowager. But her famous sally before the U.N. Security Council, in which she proposed that the shooting down by the Castro government of two planes flown by Cuban expatriates displayed "not cojones, but cowardice," did much to change that image. The remark was greeted with delight by the U.S. media, and, when Albright was named Secretary of State, it was repeated in almost every story about the appointment in order to demonstrate Albright's toughness and "street smarts" (see Hill 1998 for a more detailed discussion of this example). In brief follow-up discussions with people I overhear using Mock Spanish, they consistently justify their usage by mentioning the two major themes noted above: cosmopolitanism and a sense of humor. The theme of "cosmopolitanism" takes the form of statements about the speaker's slight knowledge of Spanish acquired through growing up in, or working in, areas where many Spanish speakers live. (Needless to say, Anglo Mock Spanish expressions have no more resemblance to "real Spanish" than do Mixtec Mock Spanish sentences.) The idea that Mock Spanish shows that the speaker has a "sense of humor" appears also in the reactions of interview subjects to Mock Spanish printed material—Anglo respondents (and even some Spanish speakers) often remark that it is "cute" or "funny." In summary, Mock Spanish is one way through which Anglos can show that they have a desirable colloquial persona—they do not take themselves too seriously, and they have had some exposure to the world such that they can incorporate a second language into their humor.

I have argued in several papers (see especially Hill 1995 and 1998) that Mock Spanish also has a dark side, the "indirect indexicality" through which it evokes, and thereby reproduces, racist images of Spanish speakers. Examples from each of the four strategies will illustrate this. An example from the first type of strategy is Mock Spanish "el presidente." In Spanish *el presidente* is a perfectly legitimate title borne by heads of state and other leaders. But to call a leader "el presidente" in English is somehow funny and slightly insulting. For instance, I have in my collection a political cartoon from 1992 in which Ross Perot is so labeled. (The cartoon can be seen in my electronic publication, Hill 1995.) I argued that the image thus indirectly indexed was that of a tinhorn dictator. This analysis was strongly supported by material from the magazine *The Nation*. After a decision of the U.S. Supreme Court in late 2000 made George W. Bush President of the United States, *The Nation* ran a contest among its readers to decide what his title should be (because the publishers of the magazine assumed that their readers, like themselves, would find Bush to be something less than a real "president"). One of the titles suggested was "el presidente." *The Nation* commented, "a Banana Republican, of course" (March 26, 2001:5).

The second strategy, to use words that are vulgar in Spanish as euphemisms for English vulgarities, provides another example of the negative indirect indexicality of Anglo Mock Spanish. When an English speaker says "cojones" instead of "balls," or puts a bumper sticker on her car that says "Caca pasa" (instead of the more daring "Sh-t happens"), she avoids the accusation that she is foul-mouthed, and probably gets credit (as did Madeleine Albright) for being cosmopolitan and funny. However, at the same time she indirectly reinforces the presupposition that Spanish speakers are more relaxed about profanity, scatology, and obscenity, and that the Spanish language is a ready source of such usages. This implication resonates with very widely-shared racist stereotypes of Spanish speakers as sexually loose and tolerant of filth.

The third strategy provides many examples. The frame "el ...-o," which can be used with English words to create Mock Spanish expressions, is especially common with English words that are negative even in the original language. Thus, Mock Spanish forms like "el cheap-o," "el fold-o" (recorded from a Detroit newspaper after a memorable late-inning collapse by the Tigers), and "el grease-o" (a negative characterization overheard in Tucson of the food in a bad restaurant) are very common, while usages like "el best-o," "el win-o," and "el delicious-o" are, as far as I know, unattested. The "el ...-o" frame can be used with words that are not especially negative to indicate familiarity or jocularity. Thus, a favorite spot in the town of La Jolla, California, is known to local teenagers, who hang out there in spite of adult disapproval, as "El cove-o." My husband, who believes that network television news is frothy and empty but watches it anyway, always calls it "el news-o." This use of the "el ...-o" frame, to suggest that the item referred to is somehow inauthentic, is fairly common. One item in my collection, with a slightly modified version of the frame, is a piece of software from the early 90s that permits the user to design an aquarium screensaver. The name of the software is "El Fish," where the "el" signals jocularly that the user is aware that the aquarium is a fake.

The fourth strategy, the "hasty lumbago," "hasty banana," "hasta la pasta," and "fleas navidad" system of "hyperanglicizations," also exhibits indirect indexicality. While the expressions are funny in English, they also imply that Spanish is a slightly ridiculous language that sounds exactly like very silly expressions in English. An early example of hyperanglicization is "buckaroo" from Spanish *vaquero* 'cowboy'. Cassidy (1985:411) attests the attitudes toward Spanish evoked by this usage in a citation for "buckaroo" from a story by Hart, "Vigilante Girl," set in Northern California: "I can talk what they call "buckayro" Spanish. It ain't got but thirteen words in it, and twelve of them are cuss words." Such ideas link to a whole series of ideological themes that emphasize that Spanish is "easy" rather than difficult, and "common" rather than "sophisticated" (like French) or "scholarly" (like German).

An extreme example of this ideology of trivialization of Spanish is attested in the 1992 film "Encino Man," a "high school life in Southern California" film aimed at pre-teenagers. In one scene in the film the actor Pauly Shore, playing a "typical teenager," takes "Link," a resuscitated Cro-Magnon Man played by Brendan Fraser, to a Spanish class. Shore says, "Spanish is guacamole, chips, and salsa" and raises his leg and makes a farting sound. The class itself is an absurd parody, where the teacher demonstrates meaningless sentences in a ridiculous hyper-English accent. (The sentences are later put together by "Link" to create a very dirty joke that is the punch line of the movie; this example is discussed in more detail in Hill 1995.)

I have also pointed out (Hill 1993a) that "hyperanglicization," which has created a whole series of pronunciations of Spanish loans that renders their source almost unrecognizable to Spanish speakers, also creates a profound distance between English and Spanish, permitting speakers to claim cosmopolitanism at the same time that their usage demonstrates that they are neither deeply interested in Spanish nor committed to speaking it well.[2]

Summary and Conclusions

In summary, Anglo Mock Spanish "manages" the presence of Spanish in the United States, just as Mixtec Mock Spanish manages the presence of Spanish in the Sierra Mixteca. Like Mixtec Indians, Anglos are forced to live among Spanish speakers. Anglos in the U.S. Southwest owe much to this association. Historically, Spanish speakers "civilized" the southwestern deserts, christianizing hostile Indian groups, developing the forms of exploitation (for instance, the herding of free-ranging cattle) that permitted European occupation of the region, founding many of its towns and cities, and welcoming, housing, and even marrying the earliest Anglo settlers. Today, every analysis of the border region and the Southwest acknowledges that the constant influx of Spanish-speaking immigrants from Mexico and the use by U.S. firms of manufacturing plants, the so-called *maquiladoras* that employ Mexican workers at rock-bottom wages on the Mexican side of the border, are fundamental to the regional economy. Yet local Anglo ideology denies the ineluctable links, both historical and contemporary, between the two populations, seeing the persistence of the Spanish language in the region as somehow "un-American." While the Spanish-speaking population is almost entirely bilingual, Anglos hardly ever learn Spanish and discourage the use of the language even by native speakers—almost every Spanish speaker has experienced at least once what I call the "This is America" routine, where Spanish speakers conversing with one another in a public place are suddenly interrupted by an outraged Anglo who tells them, "This is America. Speak English" (see

---

[2]Readers often object that my analysis of Mock Spanish as including a racist and "racializing" function cannot possibly be correct. Many readers probably use Mock Spanish (I certainly did until I started analyzing it) and do not consider themselves racists. I intend by "racism" to label a cultural formation in which all Americans (and many people in other places) participate. This cultural formation is not restricted to what is usually known as "racism," which I prefer to call "vulgar racism" (the use of racist epithets, the use of physical violence or obvious exclusionary tactics against people of color, etc.), but includes all those cultural practices that work to divide whiteness from color and to elevate the former vis-à-vis the latter. This point is clarified in Hill (1995, 1998). I note also that in research undertaken by Dan Goldstein and myself (see Hill and Goldstein 2001), we have found that Spanish speakers often object to Mock Spanish usages and find them to be insulting.

Urciuoli 1996 for extended discussion of such incidents and their meaning).

But, just as Mixtec speakers are seldom able to mount a direct challenge to Spanish authority, direct attacks on Spanish speakers are by no means the most common way that Anglos enforce their domination. Too many direct attacks would, in fact, undo the delicate political economic balance on which Anglo well-being depends. Just like the Mixtec, Anglos are much more likely to address what for them is "the problem" of the Spanish speakers who live among them by using jokes and puns. Through these usages, they are able to continually reproduce, albeit in a covert manner, the most negative images of Spanish speakers. Not only does Mock Spanish permit them to deny this function, it even allows them to claim that, through its use, they are demonstrating qualities of personhood that are highly desirable in the Anglo community and even showing their toleration of the Spanish presence by "learning" and "using" snippets of the language. In a similar way, Mixtec Indians can express their ambivalence about Spanish and their dislike of Spanish ways without mounting a direct threat either to Spanish speakers themselves, or to those in their communities who choose to use Spanish loans to express local forms of power and influence.

The "mockery" of other languages as a way of contemplating and managing the kinds of dilemmas confronted by Mixtecs and Anglos, where an outsider language has an extremely ambivalent evaluation, was, as far as I know, first introduced in the linguistic literature by Ken Pike in the 1940s, in his essays discussed above. Additional work would no doubt identify many other examples, where the study of the fine details of linguistic usage, modeled in Pike's early work, would go far to help us understand the inner workings of ethnic and linguistic conflict and confrontation at the levels at which these are reproduced, not by violence and confrontation, but by winks and nudges, jokes and puns.

References

Cassidy, Frederick G., ed. 1985. *Dictionary of American regional English. Volume 1: Introduction and A-C.* Cambridge, Mass: Belknap Press of Harvard University Press.

Hill, Jane H. 1993a. Hasta la vista, baby: Anglo Spanish in the American Southwest. *Critique of Anthropology* 13:145–176.

Hill, Jane H. 1993b. Is it really "No problemo"? In Robin Queen and Rusty Barrett (eds.), *SALSA I: Proceedings of the First Annual Symposium about Language and Society* 33:1–12. Austin: Texas Linguistic Forum.

Hill, Jane H. 1995. Mock Spanish: A site for the indexical reproduction of racism in American English. Electronic publication: <http://www. language-culture. org/colloquia/symposia/ hill.html>.

Hill, Jane H. 1998. Language, race, and White public space. *American Anthropologist* 100:680–689.

Hill, Jane H., and Daniel Goldstein. 2001. Mock Spanish, cultural competence, and complex inference. *Textus, English Studies in Italy* 14(2):243–262.

Hill, Jane H., and Kenneth C. Hill. 1986. *Speaking Mexicano.* Tucson: University of Arizona Press.

Ochs, Elinor. 1990. Indexicality and socialization. In James W. Stigler, Richard A. Shweder, and Gilbert Herdt (eds.), *Cultural Psychology,* 287–308. Cambridge: Cambridge University Press.

Makkai, Adam. 1998 [orig. 1986]. The nature of field work in a monolingual setting. Online: <www.sil.org/klp/klp-mono.htm>.

Pike, Kenneth L. 1945a. Tone puns in Mixteco. *International Journal of American Linguistics* 11:129–139.

Pike, Kenneth L. 1945b. Mock Spanish of a Mixteco Indian. *International Journal of American Linguistics* 11:219–224.

Pike, Kenneth L. 1946. Another Mixteco tone pun. *International Journal of American Linguistics* 12:22–24.

Pike, Kenneth L. 1947. A text involving inadequate Spanish of Mixteco Indians. *International Journal of American Linguistics* 13:251–257.

Pike, Kenneth L. 1999 [orig. 1996] On planning a monolingual demonstration. Online: <www.sil.org/klp/monolingual.htm>.

Silverstein, Michael. 1979. Language structure and linguistic ideology. In Paul Clyne, William Hanks, and Charles Hofbauer (eds.), *The Elements: A parasession on linguistic units and levels,* 193–247. Chicago: Chicago Linguistic Society.

Urciuoli, Bonnie. 1996. *Exposing prejudice, Puerto Rican experiences of language, race, and class.* Boulder, Colo.: Westview Press.

10

Scales of Basicness in Semantic Domains and Their Application to Creolization

George L. Huttar

Introduction

It was axiomatic for Kenneth Pike that people are coherent wholes, that their language behavior is a coherent part of their purposeful behavior as human beings, and that the language of a community of people is an integral part of their culture and norms of behavior. Whether studying the way Mazatecs phonologically treated Spanish loans that had become part of their language (Fries and Pike 1949) or, toward the other end of his career, explicitly laying out the presuppositions uniting his linguistics and his worldview (Pike 1993), he consistently saw language, and languages, as reflecting and constituting much of what it means to be human, and what it means to be a bearer of a particular culture. While he could treat language systems as objects of mathematical manipulation (Pike 1971), at a deeper and more persistent level he saw languages as expressions of people, and of peoples—usually not languages and peoples of power, but of the powerless.

Following his mentor Sapir, Pike was also unabashedly mentalist in his view of language, long before mentalism made its way back into favor in

American linguists in the latter half of the last century. Thus, a language is in some way reflective and constitutive not only of a culture, but of patterns of thought of members of the community who speak it. In his development of purpose as a basic component of any linguistic act (see Pike and Pike 1982 and more broadly Pike 1993), this connection between language and thought came through most clearly with regard to the individual. But the connection between language, thought, and culture at the level of the community was not to be ignored; attention to such relations is found throughout his monumental *Language in relation...*(Pike 1967), for example, though the connection with thought is often indirect, mediated through behavior.

"Basic Vocabulary"

In comparative historical linguistics, another area to which Pike turned his omnivorous attention (Pike 1957), a key notion, frequently appealed to for all its lack of definition, has been that of "basic vocabulary." The term "basic" eventually came to be used in ethnosemantic studies, in more than one way but usually defined with an explicitness that Pike would have applauded. In what follows I seek to bring together some of the notions referred to by various uses of the term "basic," doing so in the context of diachronic questions about how the lexicons of creole languages are built from superstrate, substrate, and (occasionally) adstrate sources.[1] These languages, whose very label as "creole" reflects a sociopolitical categorization by those with more power (Mufwene 2001), have historically been, and largely continue to be, languages of relatively powerless peoples.

Huttar 1994 represents an earlier stage of this attempt, treating basicness first of all in terms of a continuum rather than a dichotomy. Examples of dichotomous treatment of "basic" are the common distinction made between basic and nonbasic vocabulary in discussions of borrowing and language contact; the very different, but clearly defined, use of the term in Berlin and Kay's (1969) *Basic color terms*; and its related, but partly different, use to designate a particular rank, commonly that of genus, in an ethnotaxonomy, such as a folk classification of plants (Berlin 1992). In the approach outlined here, what is defined and operationalized for some domains is not "basic" but "more basic."

---

[1] The terms "substrate," "superstrate," and "adstrate" are used here, in accord with common usage among creolists, rather than "substratum," etc.

Let's start with the familiar term "basic vocabulary," a term used on occasion by Morris Swadesh (see, for example, Swadesh 1951). It was in fact Swadesh who most thoroughly developed and refined the notion during his process of determining an ideal test list that could be used for lexicostatistical purposes. He started out conceiving of "basic vocabulary" as comprising those terms in the lexicon of a language that refer to universal, "noncultural" notions. But he continued to revise his diagnostic list in light of empirical observations that words for certain ideas were in fact replaced through borrowing. Thus, it is not clear whether he came to define "basic vocabulary" in terms of resistance to borrowing or in terms of cultural universality. Certainly his successive revisions of his list were intended to reflect his growing understanding of what terms—i.e., terms for what ideas—were least likely to be acquired by a language through borrowing.

If "basic vocabulary" is defined in terms of low susceptibility to borrowing, then the usual claim about basic vocabulary becomes virtually tautologous. For example, Thomason and Kaufman's (1988:74) statement, "we know of no exceptions—and would be astonished to find any—to the rule that nonbasic vocabulary is always borrowed first" would amount to saying that vocabulary that is most susceptible to borrowing, and hence borrowed before other terms, is always borrowed first.

But general usage has stuck with defining "basic vocabulary" in terms of notions considered universal, "noncultural," etc. By this definition, we are claiming something when we say that basic vocabulary tends to be borrowed last—or, in creole studies, that basic vocabulary tends to come from superstrate sources. But this definition has the disadvantage that nobody can be very exact about it, so that recourse to definition by example is frequent. Witness the following definition from a paragraph on "Swadesh's glottochronology" in the 1992 *International Encyclopedia of Linguistics*:

> The underlying assumption is that a list of meanings can be constructed which are found in all cultures, and which are less subject to change and borrowing than the general vocabulary of the language. This list is known as the 'basic core vocabulary' or the 'Swadesh list'; it consists of, e.g., body part terms, lower numerals, pronouns, basic actions, certain kinship terms, widespread flora and fauna, topographical vocabulary, and naturally occurring 'noncultural' phenomena. (Embleton 1992:133)[2]

---

[2]For a textbook example, see Hock (1991:215). For a very recent example, see the entry for Morris Swadesh in the *Encyclopedia of Linguistics* to be published by Fitzroy Dearborn in 2003 (http://www.fitzroydearborn.com/chicago/linguistics/sample-swadesh-morris.php3).

In other areas of linguistics, "basic" has also been an important term, but has been used in other ways than in diachronic linguistics. In particular, in lexical semantics (Andersen 1978), including ethnosemantics (Berlin and Kay 1969; Berlin, Breedlove, and Raven 1973), defining what are "basic" terms has included use of criteria such as monolexemicness (basic *yellow* versus nonbasic *yellowish*) and lack of restriction of application (basic *yellow* versus nonbasic *blonde*) (Berlin and Kay 1969:6). The notion of "basic level," defined in terms of some kind of psychological salience, has figured prominently in ethnotaxonomy (Berlin 1992), including a fairly extensive dialogue between Berlin on the one hand and Rosch and associates on the other (Rosch et al. 1976; see also the criticism of Berlin's position in Wierzbicka 1985). Criteria for establishing the basicness or salience of terms have included ready elicitability, frequency of reference, stability of use across speakers and across occasions of use, how soon a term is learned by children acquiring a particular language, and how simply a notion is labelled (one lexeme versus more than one) (Berlin and Kay 1969:6).[3]

Hypotheses Relating Degree of Basicness to the Source of Creole Lexemes

This area of investigation is one in which creole languages offer a particularly useful empirical basis for research, for we can often identify the specific etyma of many of the lexemes of a creole; and even when we cannot, we can still often tell whether a particular item derives from a substrate or from a superstrate. Especially helpful in this regard are creoles in which several different substrate languages, or groups of languages, and several different superstrate languages can all be identified. Such are the creoles of the interior of Suriname, such as Ndyuka and Saramaccan, descendants of Suriname Plantation Creole (SPC). I will use data from nouns in several different semantic domains, and more briefly from verbs, property lexemes ("adjectives"), and adpositions, to test the hypothesis and subhypotheses in (1).

---

[3]It is by no means a given that there is any equivalence between these two ideas of "basicness"—noncultural and resistant to replacement through borrowing on the one hand and psychologically and culturally salient on the other. The research described here does provide evidence for a substantial overlap between the two concepts, but detailed consideration of this question goes well beyond the scope of this paper.

(1) More basic lexemes tend to stabilize earlier in the formation of a creole than do less basic lexemes. In particular:

    a. More basic lexemes are more likely to derive their form from superstrate sources than are less basic lexemes; less basic lexemes are more likely to derive their form from substrate sources than are more basic lexemes.

    b. If more than one superstrate is involved in the formation of a creole, and one of them precedes the other in the history of the creole, then more basic lexemes are more likely to derive their form from the earlier superstrate than are less basic lexemes.

    c. If more than one substrate is involved in the formation of a creole, and one of them precedes the other in the history of the creole, then more basic lexemes are more likely to derive their form from the earlier substrate than are less basic lexemes.

As the hypotheses are tested, the results are then also used to shed light on the relative chronology of English and Portuguese input into SPC.

Kin terms

We look first at the domain of kin terms. I have argued elsewhere (Huttar 1994) that terms for consanguineal (blood) kin are more basic than terms for affinal kin (kin by marriage). Further, I take closer relations (as measured by counting nodes between Ego and Alter in a genealogical tree) to be more basic than those farther removed. The most basic consanguineal terms, then, would be those for parents and for children, with those for siblings next. Then come grandparents and grandchildren, and aunts, uncles, nieces, and nephews after that. In the case of affinal kin, I assume that spouse is Ego's closest affinal kinsperson, then count the nodes between Ego's spouse and Alter for the other affines. Thus parents- and children-in-law are the next most basic kin after one's spouse, siblings-in-law after that, followed by grandparents- and grandchildren-in-law.[4]

Given the above operationalization of "more basic" with respect to kin terms, consider the following kin terms in one of the modern descendants of Suriname Plantation Creole (SPC), Ndyuka (cf. Huttar 1994:7).

---

[4]That still leaves us with no basis for deciding how basic "co-wife" is relative to other kin terms.

(2)   Some Ndyuka kin terms

Various African languages[5]
   m(a)má 'mother'
   d(a)dá, p(a)pá, tatá 'father'

Portuguese
   tio 'uncle' > *tiyu* 'uncle'
   tia 'aunt' > *tiya* 'aunt'
   pequenino 'small child' > *pikin* 'child'
   mãe 'mother' > *mai* 'mother-in-law/daughter-in-law'
   pai 'father' > *pai* 'father-in-law/son-in-law'
   mulher 'woman' > *muyee* 'wife'

English
   brother > *baala* 'brother/male cousin'
   sister > *sisa* 'sister/female cousin'
   man > *man* 'husband; man; person'
   woman > *uman* 'wife; woman'

Dutch
   zwager '*brother*-in-law' > *swagi* 'spouse's sibling; sibling's spouse'

English/Dutch
   E *mate* / D *maat* > *meti* 'co-wife; wife's mother's mother;
      spouse's sibling's spouse; sibling's spouse's sibling'

Because it is uncontroversial, given the history of Suriname, that English input into SPC was earlier than Dutch input, we compare first the terms of English and of Dutch origin. The only term unquestionably of Dutch origin is the affinal term *swagi* 'spouse's sibling; sibling's spouse', while English is the source of the very basic consanguineal terms for 'brother' and 'sister'. (English is also the source for some of the most basic affinal terms, those for 'husband' and 'wife'; but these terms are kin terms only by extension, with 'man' and 'woman', respectively, as their central meanings.) This result is consistent with the hypothesis in (1) that more basic lexemes tend to stabilize earlier in the formation of a creole than do

---

[5]It is primarily the low-high tone pattern on these forms, in addition to the widespread occurrence of similar forms in the areas from which slaves were brought to Suriname (Huttar 1985), that argues for an African, rather than a European source; in Ndyuka lexemes from European sources, high tone placement almost always corresponds to primary stress placement in the etymon.

less basic lexemes, and specifically with subhypothesis (1b) that the more basic lexemes derive from the earlier superstrate.

Unlike the situation with English and Dutch, the temporal relation between Portuguese and English input into SPC is a matter of controversy. By the crude node-counting measure I am using here, the consanguineal kin concepts labelled by terms from Portuguese, 'aunt' and 'uncle', are no more basic than are 'brother' and 'sister', labelled by terms from English. 'Child', however, is more basic than any of these, suggesting (but no more than that) some Portuguese input into SPC before the English input. Affinal terms from Portuguese are also relatively basic (including one term for a spouse, the most basic of affinal kin concepts); but with no affinal kin terms from English, we cannot make any comparison between the two languages.

Assuming it is correct that the origin of the terms for parents is African, comparison of these terms with the others reveals a counterexample to subhypothesis (1a). No kin concepts are more basic than 'mother' and 'father', yet the Ndyuka terms are of substrate rather than of superstrate origin. If the general hypothesis—that more basic lexemes tend to stabilize earlier in the formation of a creole than do less basic lexemes—holds, even though the specific hypothesis (1a) is falsified, the implication for the history of Suriname creoles is that some of the earliest elements of the creoles are of African, rather than of European, origin. Such a conclusion would be compatible with the notion that the slaves arrived in Suriname from Africa with some sort of language in common, such as a jargon or a pidgin, with some terms for very basic concepts derived from African languages. An alternative explanation (also speculative) is that the Suriname creoles started *de novo* in Suriname, incorporating early on a few African lexical items, lexemes for very basic concepts the forms of which were recognizably similar across many of the languages spoken by the slaves.

Color

Turning to the domain of color, consider the Ndyuka color terms from English and Dutch in (3). (Ndyuka has no color terms clearly derived from Portuguese).

(3)   Some Ndyuka color terms

E *black* > *baaka* 'black, dark-colored'	D *groen* > *guun* 'green'
E *white* [D *wit?*] > *weti* 'white, light-colored'	D *blauw* > *baau* 'blue'
E *red* > *lebi* 'red' (cf. *lebii* 'liver')	D *chocolaat* > *sukaati* 'tan, purple'

For the color domain, the "more basic" terms are those occurring in the most languages of various areas and families, and the terms whose presence in a particular language is implied by the presence of other color terms (Huttar 1994:4). By the familiar hierarchy of Berlin and Kay 1969 (where the term *basic* is used very differently from how I am using it here), the three most basic color concepts are 'black', 'white', and 'red'. From (3). it is clear that the most basic terms, definitely for 'black' and 'red' and possibly for 'white',[6] are from English, while less basic terms for 'green', 'blue', and 'tan'/'purple' are from Dutch. This result fits subhypothesis (1b), just as with the Ndyuka kin terms, that the English-derived (earlier) terms tend to be more basic than the Dutch-derived (later) ones.[7]

Plant and animal terms

For biological domains, I have shown elsewhere (Huttar 1994) in some detail how Ndyuka generic terms for various plant and animal categories are almost entirely from superstrate English and Dutch, whereas the majority of more specific terms, at the genus and species levels, are from African (substrate) and Amerindian (adstrate) sources. Some examples are given in (4) and (5). In (4), the only two general terms of African origin may in fact not be generic within Ndyuka folk taxonomy (as opposed to the etic view of this English speaker), in that no hyponyms—lexemes for specific kinds of butterfly or grasshopper—are known to me for either of them.

(4)   Some Ndyuka general plant and animal terms

> *meti* 'animal, mammal, meat' < E *meat*
> *foo* 'bird' < E *fowl*
> *sineki* 'snake' < E *snake*
> *todo* 'toad, frog' < E *toad*
> *fisi* 'fish' < E *fish* (< D *vis?*)
> *mila* 'ant' < D *mier*
> *babé* 'butterfly' < A (cf. Baule *abebé* 'butterfly')
> *makonkón* 'grasshopper' < A (cf. kiKongo *ma-kónko* 'grasshoppers')
>
> *bon* 'tree' < D *boom*
> *udu* 'tree' < E *wood*
> *gaasi* 'grass' < E *grass* (<D *gras?*)
> *tetei* 'vine' = 'string' < E *tie* + reduplication

---

[6]Smith (1987:202) takes *weti* to be from English *white*.
[7]See Fleming (1966) for a similar example for color terms in Garifuna.

For the further refinement of the notion of "basic" from a cognitive linguistic or ethnosemantic perspective, however, it is worth noting that where "generic" ends and "specific" begins depends on more than level in some putatively universal, Linnean taxonomic hierarchy. Other factors, such as cultural salience, must be taken into account, since presumably Dutch-derived *mila* 'ant' is on the same level of biological specificity as African-derived *babe* 'butterfly' and *makonkon* 'grasshopper'. There is indeed both nonlinguistic and linguistic evidence for the greater salience of ants than of butterflies and grasshoppers in Ndyuka culture. For example, ants are known for their ability to inflict pain; there are many lexical items for specific kinds of ants, but few if any for specific kinds of butterflies or grasshoppers.

In (5), not only is the most inclusive term (at the rank of 'life form' in Berlin's terms) from English or Dutch, but also most of the terms in the next level down (e.g., *busi meti* 'jungle animals'), and even some at the level below that. Nevertheless, the farther we move down the taxonomic hierarchy, the less apt we are to find terms with identifiable superstrate sources. Rather, we find substrate or adstrate terms and terms with no etymon of any sort found so far, but with phonological shapes compatible with African or Amerindian origins. Ignoring these last terms, those of uncertain origin, we still see that the substrate (and adstrate) terms are confined almost entirely to the lower ranks of the hierarchy.

(5)　Some Ndyuka terms for mammals

  meti 'mammals'
    gandá meti < kiKongo *ngánda*, E *meat* 'village/domestic animals'
    busi meti < E *bush, meat* 'jungle animals'
    fo futu meti < E *four, foot, meat* 'four-footed animals'
    doti meti < E *dirt, meat* 'ground-dwelling animals'
      dia < E *deer* 'deer'
        kuyáku 'deer sp.'
        awoyo dia 'deer sp.'
      bofoo < D *buffel* 'tapir'
      pingo < Carib *pindyo* 'white-lipped peccary'
      pakila < Carib *pakira* 'collared peccary'
      tamanuwa < Tupi (Wayampi?) 'giant anteater'
      bongó < Kwa or Bantu 'armadillo sp.'
    tapu meti < E *top, meat* 'arboreal animals'
      soó < E *sloth* 'sloth sp.'
      loili < D *luiaard* 'sloth sp.'
      babun < E *baboon* 'howler monkey'

> *siná* 'howler monkey sp.'
> *ndópi* 'howler monkey sp.'
> *mongi* < E *monkey* 'monkey spp.'
>   *kesikesi* 'monkey sp.'
>   *afoítye* 'monkey sp.'
>   *yaakalú* 'monkey sp.'
>   *dyankwána* 'monkey sp.'
>   *kusíi* 'monkey sp.'
>   *mamangína* 'monkey sp.'
> *kwáta* < Tupi 'black spider monkey'

For these ethnobiological domains organized as taxonomic hierarchies, "more basic" means "more generic," as shown in Huttar 1994.[8] The above distribution of more general and more specific lexemes for plants and animals therefore confirms hypothesis (1a).

Body parts

In the domain of body parts, I assume the relationships shown in (6) with regard to basicness, based on child language acquisition studies and cross-linguistic work as summarized in Andersen (1978) and my own speculation.

(6)   Relative basicness of body parts

More basic	Less basic
parts above the waist	parts below the waist
parts in front	parts in back
head	other parts
parts of head	parts of extremities
parts of extremities	parts of trunk
hand, foot	arm, leg
external parts	internal parts
"vital" parts	other parts
"public" parts	"private" parts

Some Ndyuka body-part terms are given in (7), organized by source language:

---

[8]It is important to note that this usage differs from the use of "basic" in most ethnobiological literature not only in referring to a continuum rather than to a dichotomy, as explained above, but also in not being associated with a specific hierarchical rank, usually the "genus" rank, which is considered basic with reference to both higher and lower ranks in a hierarchy.

(7)   Sources of some Ndyuka body-part terms

English
ede 'head' < *head*
fesi 'face' < *face*
ain 'eye' < *eye*
yesi 'ear' < *ears*
nosu 'nose' < *nose*
tifi 'tooth' < *teeth*
uwii 'hair' < *weed*
tooto 'throat' < *throat*
ana 'hand/arm' < *hand*
futu 'foot/leg' < *foot*
boma futu 'thigh' < *bum, foot*
to 'toe' < *toe*
ati 'chest, heart' < *heart*
bee 'abdomen' < *belly*
baka 'back' < *back*
bobi 'breast' < *bubby*
sikin 'body' < *skin*

Dutch
nangaa 'nail' < *nagel*
kini 'knee' < *knie*
sikoo 'shoulder' < *schouder*
koipi 'calf' < *kuit*
baasi 'bladder' < *blaas*

Dutch / English
lebii 'liver' < *lever/liver*
neki 'neck' < *nek/neck*
tongo 'tongue' < *tong/tongue*
finga 'finger' < *finger*[9]

Portuguese
baiba 'chin' < *barba* 'beard'
gingimbi 'gums' < gengiva

African
fukufuku 'lung' (Yoruba)
agba 'jaw' (Igbo)
alaka 'cheek' (kiKongo)
mantama 'cheek' (kiKongo)
bansa 'side, rib' (kiKongo)
dyonku 'hip' (Awutu, Twi)
gogo 'seat'
agana 'thigh' (Bisa)
kumba 'navel' (Bantu)
kobe 'temple'
mazonzon 'brain' (kiKongo)
bwebwe 'fontanel'
popoi 'vagina'
buba 'skin' (Yoruba, kiKongo, Wolof)
dugudugu 'flesh'

(In the column headed "African," I give language [family] names in parentheses rather than preceded by ' < ', since in many cases there is more than one possible source language, or the language given has a form only somewhat phonologically similar to the Ndyuka one. I also do not list the African language forms themselves; see Huttar (1985, 1986). Where no language [family] name is listed, I am presuming the Ndyuka form to be of African origin chiefly on phonological grounds, without documentation from a specific language.)

---

[9]In terms of regular sound correspondences, *finga* could come either from Dutch *finger* or English *finger*. Because *to* 'toe' is from English, it is very likely that *finga* is as well, given that terms for upper parts of the body are more basic than terms for lower parts, and assuming that more basic terms are more likely to come from the earlier superstrate (hypothesis (1b)). But to make that assumption is to presuppose the validity of hypothesis (1b) that we are exploring here. I therefore leave *finga* in the "Dutch/English" category in (7).

Since there are only two forms from Portuguese, I will merely note that neither of these is for a particularly basic body part, though both are for parts of the head. Turning to (possibly) Dutch-derived terms, we note that two are for parts below the waist, and two are for internal organs. "Nail" is arguably less basic than "toe" or "finger," for which we have English-derived, or probably English-derived, terms. That leaves only "shoulder" (and possibly "neck" and "tongue") as a fairly basic term derived from Dutch rather than the earlier superstrate, English. Scanning very briefly the African-derived terms, we see that most refer to parts below the waist, to internal parts, or to areas (like "cheek" and "temple") not clearly delineated on the body.

Another modern descendant of SPC, Saramaccan, is more useful in sorting out the chronology of the input of English and Portuguese into SPC, because it has many more body-part terms from Portuguese than does Ndyuka, as seen in (8).

(8)   Sources of some Saramaccan body-part terms

English
hedi 'head' < *head*
fesi 'face' < *face*
yesi 'ear' < *ears*
nunsu 'nose' < *nose*
uwii 'hair' < *weed*
futu 'foot/leg' < *foot*
sinkii 'body' < *skin*
hati 'heart' < *heart*
bëë 'abdomen' < *belly*
bobi 'breast' < *bubby*

Dutch
kini 'knee' < *knie*
baasi 'bladder' < *blaas*

Dutch / English
lëbë 'liver' < *lever/liver*
töngö 'tongue' < *tong/tongue*
finga 'finger, toe' < *finger*

Portuguese
woyo 'eye' < *olho*
tanda 'tooth' < *dente*?
buka 'mouth' < *boca*
gangaa 'neck' < *garganta*?
maun 'hand/arm' < *mão*
kakisa, kasika 'skin' < *casca*
panteya 'calf' < *panturrilha*

African
asakpaa 'thigh'
dyonku 'hip'
ku 'vagina'
fukufuku 'lung'
gogo 'buttocks'
ahwa (maun) 'shoulder'
akwa 'chin, jaw'
bingo 'navel'
tutu 'throat'
tönsö 'brain'

The Portuguese contribution includes very basic terms like 'eye' and 'mouth'. Further, more basic 'hand/arm' is from P, while less basic 'foot/leg' is from E. Assuming the general principle (hypothesis 1) of earlier acquired terms being more basic, and specifically the hypothesis (1b) that more basic lexemes are more apt to derive from an earlier superstrate and less basic ones from a later superstrate, these data support the hypothesis of a Portuguese contribution to Saramaccan before an English contribution, and also to the ancestor of Saramaccan and Ndyuka, SPC. The African contribution is similar to that in Ndyuka.

Looking briefly at Hawaiian Pidgin (Joe Grimes, personal communication), we find that most body-part terms are from the superstrate, English; but the few that are not are almost all clearly "less basic" terms: words for 'buttocks', 'testicles', 'urine', 'whorl of hair on top of head', 'belly', and two words for 'penis'. In New Guinea Pidgin (Karl Franklin, p.c.), again most body part terms are from English (or German, as in *bros* 'chest'); those from substrate or unknown sources include 'afterbirth', 'brain', 'breast', one word for 'faeces', 'semen', 'groin', 'jaw', and 'navel'. Given the scheme of relative basicness of body-part terms laid out in (6), data from all these languages support the hypotheses that the more basic terms are the more likely to be derived from the superstrate (1a), or, when there are successive superstrates, from the earlier one (1b).

To this point we have looked only at nouns. Let us briefly consider verbs, adjectives, and adpositions.

Verbs

For verbs I consider only the contrast between generic and specific verbs. Just as claimed above with regard to ethnosemantic taxonomic hierarchies, "more basic" is claimed to be "more generic." The terms in (9) are a sample of generic and specific Ndyuka verbs or expressions that include verbs. All the generic ones, on the left, are from superstrate sources. All the specific ones, on the right, appear to be from African, substrate sources, although in some cases I am making that claim mostly on phonological grounds, including a pattern of trisyllabic verbs with three low tones, rather than having a specific candidate etymon available.

(9)   Some generic and specific Ndyuka verbs

Generic	**Specific**
taki 'speak' < English *talk*	*kaku* 'stutter' (cf. kiKongo *káku* 'that hinders, that makes an obstacle')[10]
siibi 'sleep' < English *sleep*	*dyonko* 'doze' (cf. Twi *tò nkó* 'doze')
waka 'walk' < English *walk*	(*waka*) *kinika* 'limp', *dyakata* 'stumble'
kaasi 'scratch' < Dutch *krassen* (< English *scratch*?)	*kapata* 'scratch, as a hen in the dirt'
taampu 'stand' < English *stand up* (and *kaí* 'fall' < Portuguese *cair*)	*bunduka* 'lean over, topple' (cf. kiKongo *bùnduka* 'fall to earth, be uprooted'.[11] Luganda *kù-bunduka* 'be on a slant, hang over')

What we see here about verbs, and what we saw above about generic and specific plant and animal names,[12] can be expressed in terms of Bickerton's (1990) core versus periphery or protolanguage versus language distinction, or degree of communicative necessity, or similar distinctions in Mufwene (1999). It appears that it is more important for a community developing a new means of communication—a new language—to be able to express certain concepts, including more general ones, than other concepts. For example, presumably it is more often necessary to be able to refer to walking than to specific kinds of walking, or more crucial for a community to come up with a lexeme for the more general concept earlier. For many generic-specific taxonomies, it appears that hyponyms, like those referring to limping and stumbling, are less basic, or more marked—and therefore likely to stabilize in a creole later—than their hypernyms, like those referring to walking.

Property lexemes

In (10) we have three pairs of Ndyuka property lexemes—for the present purpose it does not matter whether they are considered adjectives or verbs. In the first pair, the less marked, more basic, member, 'clean', is

---

[10]Laman (1936) "qui gêne, qui fait obstacle."

[11]Laman (1936) "tomber par terre; être déraciné."

[12]Other domains in Ndyuka show a similar pattern of superstrate-derived lexemes for more generic concepts, substrate-derived ones for more specific ones—e.g., *dansi* < English *dance* is the generic term for 'dance' (both noun and verb), whereas the specific kinds of dances are designated by terms of unknown or substrate origin.

from a superstrate source, English, while the more marked member, 'dirty', is from a substrate source such as kiKongo. The second pair is similar, except that in this case the superstrate is P rather than E, and the African nature of the less basic member is more conjectural. These both fit the pattern of more basic terms being more likely to derive from the superstrate, and less basic terms from the substrate (hypothesis 1a). In the third pair, we have the more basic member, 'high', from the earlier superstrate, English, while the other term is from the later superstrate, Dutch. This fits the pattern of more basic terms stabilizing sooner in a nascent creole than less basic terms—i.e., more basic terms coming from the earlier superstrate (hypothesis 1b). If these principles hold, then the last pair, *bun* versus *ogii*, with the more basic member from Portuguese and the less basic one from English, suggests a Portuguese influence early in the history of SPC, possibly before the English influence.

(10) Some Ndyuka property lexeme pairs

> *kiin* 'clean' < English *clean*   *tyobo* 'dirty' (cf. kiKongo *tsobo*, cf. *nsobo* 'saleté, vaseux, boueux, tout sale')
>
> *bun* 'good' < Portuguese *bom*   *takuu* 'bad, evil' Source? cf. Sranan *takru*
>
> *hei* 'high' < English *high*   *lagi* 'low' < Dutch *laag*
>
> *bun* 'good' < Portuguese *bom*   *ogii* 'bad' < English *ugly*

With regard to property lexemes, it is useful to recall at this point Frake's (1971) presentation of twenty adjective pairs in Zamboangueño: in each pair, the more basic, less marked member is of Spanish, or superstrate, origin, while the other member is of Philippine (chiefly Hiligaynon Bisayan) origin.

Adpositions

Finally, let us look briefly at some Ndyuka adpositions. I have assumed on a somewhat speculative, untested basis that concrete concepts expressed by adpositions—that is, locational concepts—are probably more basic than more abstract concepts such as 'besides/except' and 'without'. I also assume that temporal adpositions fall between these two groups. On that basis, I would expect that of Ndyuka adpositions, locational ones would be from English, and other ones more likely from Dutch (I'm ignoring those from African sources here). This speculation is tested in (11).

(11) Some Ndyuka adpositions/location words

English

Locational   *fesi* 'front' < *face*
                      baka 'behind' < *back*
                      tapu 'on, over' < *top*
                      ini 'inside' < *in*
                      doo 'outside' < *door*[13]
                      mindii 'between' < *middle*

Temporal   *fosi* 'before' < *first*
                      baka 'after' < *back*
                      te 'until' < *till*

Other   *anga* 'with' < *along?*
                      fu 'for' < *for*
                      eke 'like' < *like*

English/Dutch

Locational   *ondoo* 'under' < *under/onder*
                      abaa 'across' < *over/over*
                      lontu 'around' < *(a)round/rond*

Dutch

Other   *boiti* 'except, besides' < *buiten*
                      sondee 'without' < *zonder*

We see the expectations are for the most part confirmed: the only adpositions with an unequivocal Dutch source are in the "other" category; of the more concrete temporal and locational adpositions, they are all either from English or from either English or Dutch. On the other hand, there are some English-derived adpositions in the "other" category. Regarding these, a case can be made, although I do not attempt it here, that 'with' and 'for', and possibly 'like' as well, are more basic than 'except', 'besides', and 'without', two of which latter concepts have a negative component.

Conclusion

In (1) we proposed one general hypothesis and three subhypotheses; we then tested them against data on nouns in Ndyuka and other creole languages in the domains of kin terms, color, plant and animal names, and body parts, and on a small number of verbs, property lexemes, and

---

[13]Cf. *doo* 'sever' and *doo* 'arrive at' < Dutch *door* 'through'.

adpositions. As such hypotheses cannot be tested without some operationalization of the concept "more basic," the operationalization used here included the following elements:

a. more generic concepts more basic than more specific concepts;
b. consanguineal kin more basic than affinal kin;
c. close kin more basic than distant kin;
d. unmarked members of property ("adjectival") pairs more basic than marked members;
e. more widely attested color terms more basic than less widely attested ones;
f. external body parts more basic than internal parts; parts above the waist more basic than those below; those in front more basic than those in back; more public parts more basic than those more private, parts of the face more basic than other body parts; etc.;
g. "public" concepts more basic than "private" ones;
h. degree of basicness in many cases culturally defined, with culturally more salient concepts more basic than less salient ones.

No unambiguous counterexamples were found against the general hypothesis, that "more basic lexemes tend to stabilize earlier in the formation of a creole than do less basic lexemes." The fact that terms for 'mother' and 'father', among the most basic of kin concepts, are of African origin is a counterexample to subhypothesis (1a), that more basic lexemes are more likely to derive from superstrate sources, and less basic lexemes from substrate sources. This subhypothesis assumes that superstrate-derived lexemes stabilize in a nascent creole before any substrate lexemes do, an assumption challenged by this result. Hypothesis (1a) should therefore be changed to read something like this: "To the extent that superstrate features of a creole stabilize earlier than do substrate features, more basic lexemes are more likely to derive their form from superstrate sources than are less basic lexemes; less basic lexemes are more likely to derive their form from substrate sources than are more basic lexemes."

No unambiguous counterexamples were found against subhypotheses (1b) and (1c) regarding more basic lexemes being more likely to be derived from an earlier superstrate/substrate, less basic lexemes from a later superstrate/substrate.

Finally, assuming the validity of hypothesis (1b) and then comparing the English-derived and Portuguese-derived lexemes in some domains in Ndyuka and Saramaccan gives some evidence for Portuguese input into Suriname Plantation Creole earlier than the English input.

References

Andersen, E. S. 1978. Lexical universals of body-part terminology. In J. H. Greenberg (ed.), *Universals of human language*, volume 3 *Word structure*, 335–368. Stanford: Stanford University Press.

Berlin, Brent. 1992. *Ethnobiological classification: Principles of categorization of plants and animals in traditional societies.* Princeton: Princeton University Press.

Berlin, Brent, Dennis Breedlove, and Peter H. Raven. 1973. General principles of classification and nomenclature in folk biology. *American Anthropologist* 75:214–242.

Berlin, Brent, and Paul Kay. 1969. *Basic color terms: Their universality and evolution.* Berkeley: University of California Press.

Bickerton, Derek. 1990. *Language and species.* Chicago: The University of Chicago Press.

Embleton, Sheila. 1992. Historical linguistics: mathematical concepts. In Wm. Bright (ed.), *International encyclopedia of linguistics*, volume 2, 131–135. New York/Oxford: Oxford University Press.

Fleming, Ilah. 1966. Carib. In M. K. Mayers (ed.), *Languages of Guatemala*, 303–308. The Hague: Mouton.

Frake, C. O. 1971. Lexical origins and semantic structure in Philippine Creole Spanish. In D. Hymes (ed.), *Pidginization and creolization of languages*, 223–242. Cambridge: Cambridge University Press.

Fries, Charles C., and Kenneth L. Pike. 1949. Coexistent phonemic systems. *Language* 25:29–50.

Hock, Hans Henrich. 1991. *Principles of historical linguistics*, revised edition. Berlin and New York: Mouton de Gruyter.

Huttar, George L. 1985. Sources of Ndjuka African vocabulary. *Nieuwe West-Indische Gids* 59:45–71.

Huttar, George L. 1986. KiKongo, Saramaccan, and Ndjuka. In Benjamin F. Elson (ed.), *Language in global perspective: Papers in honor of the 50th anniversary of the Summer Institute of Linguistics 1935–1985*, 563–586. Dallas: Summer Institute of Linguistics.

Huttar, George L. 1994. Lexical borrowing, creolization and basic vocabulary. *UTA Working Papers in Linguistics* 1:1–11.

Laman, K. E. 1936/1964. *Dictionnaire Kikongo-Français avec une étude phonétique décrivant les dialectes les plus importants de la langue dite Kongo.* Brussels (reprinted, Ridgewood, N.J.: The Gregg Press).

Mufwene, S. S. 1999. On the language bioprogram hypothesis: Hints from Tazie. In M. DeGraff (ed.), *Language creation and language change: Creolization, diachrony, and development*, 95–127. Cambridge, Mass.: The MIT Press.

Mufwene, S. S. 2001. *The ecology of language evolution.* Cambridge: Cambridge University Press.

Pike, Kenneth L. 1957. *Axioms and procedures for reconstructions in comparative linguistics: An experimental syllabus*, rev. ed. Glendale, Calif.: Summer Institute of Linguistics.

Pike, Kenneth L. 1967. *Language in relation to a unified theory of the structure of human behavior*, second ed. The Hague: Mouton.

Pike, Kenneth L. 1971. Crucial questions in the development of tagmemics—the sixties and the seventies. *Georgetown University Monograph Series on Language and Linguistics No. 24*, 79–98.

Pike, Kenneth L. 1993. *Talk, thought, and thing: The emic road toward conscious knowledge*. Dallas: Summer Institute of Linguistics.

Pike, Kenneth L., and Evelyn G. Pike. 1982. *Grammatical analysis*, second ed. Dallas: Summer Institute of Linguistics and University of Texas at Arlington.

Rosch, Eleanor, Carolyn B. Mervis, Wayne D. Gray, David M. Johnson, and Penny Boyes-Braem. 1976. Basic objects in natural categories. *Cognitive Psychology* 8:382–439.

Smith, Norval S. H. 1987. *The genesis of the creole languages of Surinam*. Doctoral dissertation. Universiteit van Amsterdam.

Swadesh, Morris. 1951. Diffusional cumulation and archaic residue as historical explanations. *Southwestern Journal of Anthropology* 7:(1)1–21.

Thomason, Sarah G., and Terrence Kaufman. 1988. *Language contact, creolization, and genetic linguistics*. Los Angeles: University of California Press.

Wierzbicka, Anna. 1985. *Lexicography and conceptual analysis*. Ann Arbor: Karoma Publishers.

11

Culture and Language— Changing Together

Stephen A. Wurm

Introduction

Every culture is inextricably linked with the language which is the means of its expression and that mirrors in its nature, form, and system the nature and intricacies of that culture. Every culture has unique features and characteristics; likewise, every language has unique features and differs from every other language in some ways. A given language reflects and demonstrates the manner in which the bearers of the culture have resolved their problems and come to terms in dealing with and understanding the material, immaterial, and spiritual world surrounding and concerning them. The key to a full understanding of the nature of any language is a full understanding of the culture of its speakers, just as the key to a full understanding of any culture is a full understanding of the

Editors' note: Stephen Wurm met Kenneth Pike frequently at conferences and other gatherings of linguists concerned with the study of languages in the southwest Pacific and other parts of the world. He and Pike shared the view that language and culture are inextricably linked, as evidenced by his contribution to this volume. We are sad to report that Prof. Wurm passed away on October 24, 2001, before he had opportunity to review and approve the copy editors' version of this chapter. The editors take full responsibility for the changes made to the version he submitted.

language of the bearers of that culture; the two are completely interdependent and inseparable.

Neither cultures nor languages are static. They are changing everywhere in the world, some slowly, some more rapidly, for a variety of reasons, with changes in cultures leading to changes in the languages of their bearers and vice versa.

In bygone millenia and centuries long ago, such changes were, with some exceptions, slow and ponderous. However, with the at first gradual then increasingly rapid expansion of European influence, to areas of the world untouched by it until the end of the fifteenth century, the often very powerful and destructive impact on hundreds of unique cultures resulted in more and more widespread and general changes in them. These changes had far-reaching effects on the languages of their bearers. The impact was particularly pervasive towards the end of the nineteenth and the beginning of the twentieth centuries and assumed alarming proportions during the latter half of the twentieth century. At the same time, the highly sophisticated cultures of Europe, the Westernized Americas, and some countries in Asia were also subject to powerful forces leading to far-reaching, rapid changes in their cultures. These forces included ever accelerating high technology, computerization of more and more aspects of daily life, faster and faster methods of local and worldwide communication (e.g., through the introduction of mobile handheld telephones in many parts of the world), more and more sophisticated medical techniques, genetic engineering and genome, and, in general, a meteoric rise in research and the emergence of new knowledge in a vast range of fields. The changes in the cultures of the nations and communities affected by these forces and influences inevitably have had profound effects upon the languages of their respective bearers.

Examples of the Change of Culture and Language

To illustrate this view, a number of examples from different cultural situations, with background remarks and explanations, will be given.

Indigenous cultures and languages

A general observation is valid for a large number of smaller languages of the southwestern Pacific and Australia, as well as other parts of the world, for they are under pressure from languages spoken by bearers of large dominant cultures (or contact languages that came into being through the interaction of such cultures and their languages, especially pidgin languages). This results in the gradual decay of the local cultures of their speakers, and the languages tend to undergo lexical, semantic, and structural changes. These changes bring them more and more in line with features and characteristics of the languages that exert pressures upon them. Structural features affected are, for instance, noun class systems and corresponding concordances, complex verb forms, and tense systems, with the latter tending to approach the simpler tense systems of the influencing languages. Number and counting systems, also, tend to be replaced by the number and counting systems of the influencing languages.

Numbers and counting systems

Papuan languages of the New Guinea area offer many examples of changes in number and counting systems. In quite a few, traditional counting systems used the names of points on the human body or body parts as tallies. A particularly elaborate system was that used by the speakers of the Fori language at Lake Kutubu in the Southern Highlands of Papua New Guinea;[1] thirty-seven tallies starting from parts of the fingers of one hand, going up the arm naming wrist, elbow, shoulder, one breast nipple, the tip of the nose, the other nipple, the opposite shoulder, and down the other arm to the other hand were used. 'One man' meant the numeral thirty-seven (Williams 1940–1941). In other languages, counting usually started from the little finger of the left hand; the word for 'little finger of the left hand' meant 'one', 'ring finger of the left hand' meant 'two', 'middle finger of the left hand' meant 'three', and 'hand' meant 'five'. 'Two hands' meant 'ten'. Continuing with the toes of the left foot, 'two hands and the little toe of the left foot' meant 'eleven', 'two hands and the left foot' meant 'fifteen', and 'one man (equaling two hands and two feet)' meant 'twenty'. 'Middle finger of the left hand (that is, ' three' or 'times') and man' meant 'sixty', etc.

Most such counting systems have now vanished from Papuan languages and have, in Papua New Guinea, been replaced by the numerals and the simple decimal counting system of the national language, Tok Pisin. Tok Pisin is a contact language and is becoming creolized in the major towns and some rural areas. It has a fairly complex Melanesian Austronesian grammar and over 70 percent of its vocabulary is derived from English. Often, however, changed meanings and a different phonology render many of the English-derived lexical items unrecognizable to English speakers. In Tok Pisin 'twenty' is *tupela ten.*

---

[1]Editors' note: See chapter 18 in this volume in which an even more elaborate system in Kewa is described.

The Äyiwo example

Äyiwo, the language I observed over several generations, is an example of the gradual decay of a noun class system and the complex concordance system accompanying it. Äyiwo is an East Papuan language spoken by about 4,000 people on the Reef Islands in the Santa Cruz Archipelago, situated far to the east of the main Solomon Islands chain in the southwest Pacific. There are forty-seven semantically based noun classes in this language, all indicated by prefixes to nouns and verb bases to form verbal nouns. The prefixes denote the nature—and with eight of them the shape, appearance, and the specific nature of the relationship to other things—of the items referred to by the nouns or verb bases. I started work in the language in 1965. In the Äyiwo then spoken by members of the community who were born around the beginning of the twentieth century, sixteen of the noun classes were accompanied by concordance phenomena in the noun phrase. Only with five of the classes was there full concordance with qualitative adjuncts, numerals, and possessives. With four more, the numerals received one special type of class prefix only, and there was concordance in qualitative adjuncts and possessives. With another five, the numerals had no class prefix; and with two, only the numerals had the concordance class prefix of the noun (Wurm 1991).

One speaker who was well over sixty had a rudimentary recollection of the Äyiwo spoken by his grandfather who may have been born around 1850. It appears that concordance systems were formerly present with at least eight more classes and were fuller in all classes. In addition, the class system also appeared in the forms of the third person singular personal pronoun of which the speaker was able to remember those referring to ten of the classes. In his own speech, the classless third person singular pronoun was an Austronesian loan. He also mentioned that this loanword was already present in his grandfather's speech, but was regarded by him as "bad and careless" language. His grandfather's probable birthdate coincided with the beginning of major culture contact of the Äyiwo speakers with missionaries and mission-influenced Melanesians from neighboring areas. It appears that the decaying process of the Äyiwo language resulting from the gradual loss of their traditional culture had already started around 1850 and has been accelerating ever since (Wurm 1992).

In direct proportion with decreasing age, younger speakers fluctuate freely between the various types of concordance mentioned above for the speech of Äyiwos aged 65–70. Teenagers tend to use no concordances in their speech, though a language revitalization process established by educated Äyiwo has partly reversed these negative developments. Not only the concordances were decaying, but also the system of class prefixes itself has begun to be eroded. Some of the classes are rooted in the traditional culture and, with the loss of it, reasons for the class prefixes are not always understood by young speakers.

Äyiwo also has a complicated system of the classification of verbs through prefixes indicating the modes of action, e.g., whether the action is carried out using one's hand, or an instrument, or a knife, or if energy is exerted in carrying out an action, or if the action is carried out with a single violent effort. Young speakers tend to mix up these prefixes under the influence of the absence of such distinctions in the contact languages, Solomon Pijin and English. Another characteristic feature of Äyiwo is that many of the items of its lexicon are composed of small meaningful elements that do not occur in isolation and which make the lexical items descriptive in nature (Wurm 1987a). This reflects traditional Äyiwo worldview, but the composition of many such lexical elements and the precise function of their elements are no longer properly understood by the younger generation of speakers and are being replaced by loans from Solomon Pijin and English. For example: *de-lu-po-vi-li* 'cigarette' (*de-* things and nonpersons noun class prefix, *lu-* 3pl subject, *po-* prefix indicating that energy is directed at something in carrying out an action, *vi-* concept of something being bent around something else, *-li* focusing verb suffix indicating that the object is only indirectly or superficially affected by the action; literally, 'something which they wrap around something else without damaging it, exerting energy in the process, i.e., wrapping it tightly'). This lexical item is now increasingly replaced by *sigret* 'cigarette'. Another example is: *nye-ku-lu-mw-ä* 'your (sg) heart' (*nye-* location class prefix, *ku-* continuous aspect prefix, *lu-* 'to live, be alive', *-mw* 2sg subject, *-ä* 2sg possessive suffix on verbal nouns; literally, 'the place where you (sg) are continuously alive (with) yours'). This lexical item is now increasingly replaced by *hat bilong yu.*

Tok Pisin as an instrument of change

Reduction or loss of noun classification is found also in a few other Papuan languages in Papua New Guinea. The vehicle for culture clash and culture change is the national language, Tok Pisin. Like English it lacks the overtly indicated noun class systems that play an important role in many Papuan languages and has only a simple tense system, though its aspect system is rather complicated. It does reflect indigenous, but Austronesian, thinking and categorization of the surrounding world—radically different from the Papuan one.

The near-universal knowledge of Tok Pisin by Papua New Guineans is, in my view, the cause of the penetration of the thinking and worldview of an alien culture into the Papuan world. In consequence, there are changes from the traditional cultures to cultural forms approximating facets of the intrusive alien culture. This results in a reduction of the usual structural complexity of Papuan languages. Their speakers maintain or adopt grammatical and conceptual categories present in the intrusive alien culture and conceptual system and gradually discard categories belonging to their traditional culture. In many Papuan languages, categories thus affected tend to be primarily noun classes and concordance systems, complex verb morphology such as complex tense systems, and the precise indication of the number (singular, dual, trial, general plural, collective, etc.) of subject and object persons. These categories may become optionally rather than obligatorily indicated, or they may be reduced in complexity (Wurm 1986).

Examples of the disappearance of elaborate noun class systems, with the complicated concordance system accompanying it, are found in two languages belonging to the Torricelli Phylum of Papuan languages in northern Papua New Guinea. One of these, Buna, was reported by a Catholic missionary in 1926 to have a very complicated noun class system comprising twelve classes with accompanying complicated concordance systems (Kirschbaum 1926). In 1970–1971, D. C. Laycock (1975) carried out fieldwork in that area and also looked at Buna. The noun class system reported by Kirschbaum half a century earlier had completely disappeared, with not even the older speakers having any recollection of it. Their traditional culture had largely been lost by 1970–1971. Similarly, Mountain Arapesh of the same Papuan Phylum still possessed an elaborate noun class system but was found by Laycock (1975) to be undergoing a gradual breakdown. Also, in northern Papua New Guinea, the Murik language of the Nor-Pondo Group of the Sepik-Ramu Phylum, for which Schmidt (1953) had reported four noun classes, had completely lost this noun class system in the course of twenty years (Laycock 1973).

The Kiwai example

Another example of the simplification of verb forms in a Papuan language under the influence of culture change is the coastal dialect of the Kiwai language, which is spoken in southwestern Papua New Guinea on the coast of the so-called Trans-Fly area, and which I had the opportunity to study two decades ago. In this dialect of Kiwai, as is the case with standardized island Kiwai, which is regarded as the "high" form, four numbers are distinguished in the verb complex: singular, dual, trial, and plural. This distinction applies equally to the subject and object of a verb. Six tenses are distinguished: two for the past, one for the present, and three for the future. They are indicated by an elaborate combination of prefixes and suffixes, of special tense forms of the prefixes and suffixes denoting the number of the subject, and of special tense forms of the subject prefixes themselves, with tense being signaled several times in many verb forms. Repeated signaling of number in verb forms also occurs frequently. Furthermore, there are elaborate aspectual systems in the language that indicate whether an action is performed at a certain moment, or is repeated, continuing, or incompletely performed. In addition, there is indication of the spontaneity of an action, of reflexivity, or of the application of an action to a certain purpose, as well as a complex system of habitual forms, a range of different imperative forms, and many other complexities (Wurm 1987b).

It was found that in direct proportion to the decreasing age of the coastal Kiwai speakers, the verb morphology of the language is becoming more and more simplified. This simplification is proportional to an increasing educational sophistication and a better knowledge of English, which in that part of Papua New Guinea is relatively widespread. One major feature of the simplification process is that formerly obligatory markings in the verb are becoming optional. The younger the speakers, the more they reduce the number marking to singular and plural only, as in English, and only use three tenses—present, past, and future—as in Tok Pisin. Other categories mentioned above also tend to be reduced to those which correspond to or are similar to those found in Tok Pisin or English, the means of expression of the new dominant culture. Significantly, there is little reduction in the aspect forms in Island Kiwai; this reflects the multiplicity of aspects in Tok Pisin. Young speakers occasionally use more complex forms, especially for emphasis, but the very young ones tend not even to know them.

The Kamilaroi example

Moving to another language area, Australian Aboriginal languages show marked structural changes as a result of the increasing loss of the traditional culture of their speakers. The Kamilaroi (Gamilaaraay) language formerly widespread in northern central New South Wales, but now virtually extinct, provides a striking example. Over a century ago, a reasonably detailed description of its structure was produced. At that time, the language had a very complex verbal tense system which, for instance, indicated several different times of the day linked to the rising, descending, and setting sun. These reflected the points of time of the different kinds of behavior of game animals and, therefore, the advantageous and disadvantageous times for their being hunted by the Kamilaroi people. When the last fluent speakers of the Kamilaroi language were interviewed and recorded by me in the 1950s, I found that this particular feature of the tense system had disappeared and was no longer remembered by the older speakers. They had not been hunting animals for decades, but had been living on government handouts and other means of sustenance. This elaborate tense distinction relating to animal behavior was therefore no longer culturally significant for them and had disappeared from the language.

From specific to general or abstract

A general change of the manner of expression is noticeable in several Papuan languages of Papua New Guinea and in some Australian languages. The changes reflect the decay of the local cultures of the speakers and their replacement by an imitation of, or fuller adoption of, the dominant culture, along with the acquisition of a language of wider communication or a special intermediate language such as Tok Pisin. Tok Pisin reflects indigenous thinking and categories in its structure, but in a very reduced form. The change in the indigenous concept system is due to the intrusion of the concept system of an alien culture. Tok Pisin, which occupies a transitory position between the two, is the carrier of this intrusion in Papua New Guinea. The same has been true of varieties of Pidgin English in Australia (which are largely creolized at present). The manner of expression in English and Tok Pisin is usually largely abstract with a vague or generalized indication of objects, actions, demonstratives, etc., whereas in the Papuan and Australian languages it is usually very concrete with, to English thinking, an over-exact indication of such categories. For instance, the English sentence 'a bird is sitting on that tree' does not specify the kind of bird or tree, nor the manner of the action of the sitting of the bird, nor the precise direction, from the speaker's point of view. In the Papuan or Australian equivalent of this sentence, the kind of bird and tree would be precisely specified, as would whether the bird was sitting with legs outstretched or squatting down. Also, the direction, distance, and level (higher at a steep slant or not much higher at a moderate slant from the location of the observer) would be precisely indicated by the appropriate deictics. Furthermore, 'on that tree' would be expressed by 'on a branch of that tree'. Most of these indigenous languages contain abstract or generic terms such as 'bird' and 'tree', but they are rarely used, just as exact concrete terms would rarely be used in English. With the gradual loss of the indigenous cultures, the manner of expression in such languages gradually approximates the manner of expression underlying the dominant concept system, and also becomes more and more abstract and imprecise, though many structures remain the same.

Metropolitan cultures and languages

Until a few decades ago, educated Australians of English mother tongue were very sensitive to and disapproving of, the use of swear words and rude expressions by others, especially in public; such behavior was frowned upon officially. Over the last three decades, these attitudes have changed to a great extent. Behavior and language use in the Parliament, exemplified by a very high-ranking politician being broadcast by television to the entire nation, became an excuse for many. Now this change in cultural attitudes has resulted in a change in language use: the free use of swear words and rude expressions by many in public, without the authorities taking much notice.

Another interesting example of cultural change reflected in language use in the metropolitan world is seen in Japan where the increasingly strong modernization, internationalization, and social deregulation of daily life, behavior, and attitudes in the last few years has brought about quite remarkable changes. There is very much less bowing to each other; the dress of many businessmen is changing from strict jacket, white shirt, and tie to more casual for many; young women may often walk in front of their male companions, no longer behind them; and face-to-face behavior is becoming less and less determined by strict rules. This is leading to an easing up in the strict rules of language use: the complex phrases prescribed for all sorts of social behavior and social intercourse are used less and less and the use of the respect language with its many honorific expressions is becoming more and more restricted.

Recently, I made another observation of the strong interdependence of culture and language, with the change of culture being accompanied by a corresponding change of language and language use. Speaking English, I made an international telephone call to an American Japanese now living in Europe. That person was, as I had been told, totally bicultural in the American and Japanese cultures and a natural bilingual (i.e., bilingual from early childhood onwards) in English and Japanese. The person displayed a stereotypical American businessman's aggressive demeanor, speaking constantly, rapidly, and very self-assuredly, so that I was hardly able to get a word in. I finally switched to Japanese; the American

Japanese immediately switched culture, speaking more softly, more slowly and very politely, never interrupting, and fully prepared to listen, all of which led to a full mutual understanding very quickly.

Finally, I will mention an example of the change of language use accompanying a change of cultural attitudes among the Papua New Guinean elite. After the independence of Papua New Guinea from Australia in 1975, its political and administrative elite consisted largely of persons who had studied in Australia, or at least had very good knowledge of, and predilection for, English. They always used English with each other, even if they shared a local language. They also shared the views of the former Australian administrators who had overstressed the importance of English for Papua New Guinea and had introduced education almost exclusively in English. Most Papua New Guinean children did not know English before entering school; teachers recruited from Australia did not acquire a knowledge of Tok Pisin before arriving, and in many instances there was no communication between teachers and pupils. After independence, the Papua New Guinea elite continued this flawed system. After some time, the shortcomings of this educational policy became evident, and the members of the English-oriented elite became outnumbered by those who wanted to pursue Papua New Guinea-oriented policies. Many of the English-oriented members of the elite gradually also changed their minds on this. Today, every one of the 850 or so local languages has been declared an official language, elementary education utilizes about thirty different major languages, and cultural orientation is towards Papua New Guinean values. One result is that members of the government, high-ranking officials, academics, and other members of the Papua New Guinean elite—although they know English very well—use English in business situations only, if at all. Otherwise, they speak Tok Pisin (or a local language if they share the knowledge of it) with each other.

References

Kirschbaum, Franz J. 1926. Miscellanea aus Neuguinea. *Anthropos* 16–17:1052–1053.

Laycock, Donald C. 1973. *Sepik languages—checklist and preliminary classification*. Canberra: Pacific Linguistics, Series B-25.

Laycock, Donald C. 1975. The Torricelli Phylum. In Stephen A. Wurm (ed.), *New Guinea area languages and language study*, Vol. 1: *Papuan languages and the New Guinea linguistic scene*, 767–780. Canberra: Pacific Linguistics, Series C-38.

Schmidt, Joseph. 1953. *Vokabular und Grammatik der Murik-Sprache in Nordost-Neuguinea. Micro-Bibliotheca Anthropos* No. 3. Fribourg, Switzerland: Anthropos Institut.

Williams, Francis E. 1940–1941. *Natives of Lake Kutubu, Papua.* Oceania Monographs 6. Sydney.

Wurm, Stephen A. 1986. Grammatical decay in Papuan languages. Canberra: Pacific Linguistics, Series A-70:207–211.

Wurm, Stephen A. 1987a. Semantics and world view in languages of the Santa Cruz Archipelago, Solomon Islands. In Ross Steele and Terry Treadgold (eds), *Language topics: Essays in honour of Michael Halliday,* 439–451. Amsterdam/Philadelphia: John Benjamins.

Wurm, Stephen A. 1987b. Change of languages as a result of decay and change of culture. *Diogenes* 137:39–51.

Wurm, Stephen A. 1991. Language decay and revivalism: The Äyiwo language of the Reef Islands, Santa Cruz Archipelago, Solomon Islands. In Robert Blust (ed.), *Currents in Pacific linguistics: Papers on Austronesian languages and ethnolinguistics in honour of George W. Grace,* 551–560. Canberra: Pacific Linguistics, Series C-117.

Wurm, Stephen A. 1992. Change of language structure and typology in a Pacific language as a result of culture change. In Tom Dutton (ed.), *Culture change, language change—case studies from Melanesia,* 141–157. Canberra: Pacific Linguistics, Series C-120.

12

Linguistic Prehistory

Recovery of Iron and Copper in Relation to the Mohenjodaro and Harappan Excavations

V. I. Subramoniam

C. D. Buck made a pioneering effort in producing select synonyms in the principal Indo-European languages and dividing them into several subheadings. His *Dictionary of Selected Synonyms in the Principal Indo-Aryan Languages* has under each heading detailed footnotes, which are useful in recovering the "thing" or referent from the cognate "words."

Indeed, words may not always provide the clues for inferring the "things" due to sound and meaning changes, contacts leading to borrowing, nonuse leading to loss of words, etc. When no other clue is available, one has to view linguistic evidences with caution.

The ancient Mohenjodaro-Harappan civilization, which was widespread in Afghanistan, southern parts of Russia, and both north and south India, is believed to be not an iron age culture. It had copper and bronze, which is an alloy of copper and tin (Kochhar 2000:70). If the Dravidians were users of iron, then the Mohenjodaro culture, which did not have iron artifacts, could not have been created by the Dravidians. If the Aryans had

A portion of this paper was read at Deccan College, Pune as an address to the Second Convocation on October 27, 1998. It is my humble tribute to a rare example of scholarship and humanism that Professor Pike left on me after our meetings in Trivandrum, in Moscow, and in Michigan.

copper (reconstructed on the basis of synonyms found in the Indo-European languages) the Mohenjodaro-Harappan culture, which had copper artifacts, must have been the creation of Aryans. For more than three decades, the question of origin of the Mohenjodaro-Harappan civilization has been hotly disputed in India and elsewhere. Our effort is to find out whether we can contribute in solving this question by prehistoric reconstruction.

The words found in the Indo-Aryan languages for iron are *loha, ayas, yas, sastrak, rikova, pinds katays, kal,* and *asmasar.* But only *ayas* is found in R. L. Turner's dictionary under Sanskrit. The Rig-Veda has *ayas.* It is also found in Prakrit. *Loha* is found in the Mahabharata, also in Prakrit and Sindhi, along with the general meaning 'metal'. Turner's dictionary cites *tamra* 'copper' from Sanskrit and Hindi. 'Black' and 'red' as "synonyms" of iron and copper are also found in these languages.

The Dravidian etymological dictionary has *irumpu* 'iron' in Tamil, Malayalam, and Kannada. Toda has *ip* 'needle'. Kodagu has *inumu* 'iron sword', as does Telugu.

Household articles, instruments for work, and war weapons made of iron are found in all major languages and in some tribal languages of the Dravidian family. The list from the Dravidian etymological dictionary is as follows:

irampam	No. 4236 'saw' in Tamil, Telugu, and Tulu
kōḍ āli	No. 1702 '*axe*' in Tamil, Kannada, Tulu, Toda, Kolami, Naiki, and Malayalam
caṭṭukam	No. 1905 'ladle' in Tamil, Malayalam, Kannada, Kota, Kodagu, and Tulu
takaṭu	No. 2425 'metal-plate' in Tamil, Malayalam, Kannada, and Telugu
tōṭṭi	No. 2925 'elephant hook' in Tamil, Malayalam, Kannada, Telugu, and Parji
piccākatti	No. 3451 'pocket knife made of iron' in Tamil, Malayalam, Kodagu, and Tulu
vēl	No. 4556 'dart, spear' in Tamil, Malayalam, Kannada, Toda, Gondi, Kolami, Kodagu, Tulu, and Telugu

Copper *cempu* No. 2282 is found in Tamil, Malayalam, Kannada, Toda, Kolami, Kodagu, Tulu, and Telugu. T. Burrow and M. B. Emeneau, the editors of the Dravidian etymological dictionary, observe that the Prakrit word *tamra* might have influenced *cempu*. However, phonologically, it is difficult to derive *cempu* from *tamra*.

Besides the cognates in the Dravidian languages, the literature of Tamil, especially the earliest strata called the Sangam Classics (third century B.C. to second century A.D.), have extensive references to iron as a metal, how it was molded by a blacksmith, his hammer, the bellow, the sparks which fly during the beating of the iron rods, the evaporation of water sprinkled over the red hot iron, etc. In addition to direct references, metaphors are found in that classic, e.g., iron rods compared to the horns of deer and buffalo. The use of iron for manufacturing household utensils and war weapons are also noted. Such occurrences are found in all the nine works called Sangam Classics.

In India iron ore concentrates are found in thirty-five places, of which twenty-one are found in the four southern states: Andhra (nine), Karnataka (five), Tamil Nadu (five), Kerala (two).

The iron age sites are found in Brahmagiri, Masti, Piklihal, Singampalli, Halingali, Hallur, and T. Narsipur in Karnataka; Paiyampalli, Kunnattur, Tirukkampuliyur, Uraiyur, Kodumanal in Tamil Nadu.

Nagarjunakonda, Kesarapalli, Yelleswaram in Andhra Pradesh and Painkulam and Quilon in Kerala are areas from where the iron ore is unearthed. The iron age burials are also found in almost all the places noted above (*Ariviyar Kal ñciyam*1988:729).

The progressive utilization of iron in manufacturing household appliances for hunting, for agriculture and finally as war implements is attested in Tamil. Unless iron implements are widely known, their use in literature will be little understood.

Perhaps C. D. Buck's observation on iron will be more relevant at this juncture. The use of iron is comparatively late in history, long after the period of Indo-European unity. Most of the words are obscure.

The use of copper *cempu* is very rare in all phases of the life of the Dravidian people and in their literature. *Cempon, cempu, ceppu,* etc., are clear in etymology and hence, are obviously recent in origin.

The article on iron in the *Encyclopaedia Brittanica* (1981:vol. 9, p. 894) gives the date of the iron age as 1200 B.C. The pyramids of Giza, dated to belong to 2900 B.C., had two pieces of iron. The Hittites who were speakers of an Indo-European language had artifacts made of iron (1900 to 1200 B.C.), including cast iron rings. Israel had several iron smelting furnaces, especially in the Gaza strip.

Pliny the Elder in his book, *Historia Naturale*, devotes two chapters to this subject. In them he writes on iron. Thus, the high quality iron imported from Andhra to Punjab went to Persia, and then to Greece and Rome. Only Celtic and Germanic reflect prehistoric borrowing.

Copper is an inherited word in Indo-European. It is extended subsequently to bronze ore, in part, transferred to iron.

It is now generally accepted that gold, silver, as well as copper, were known to the Indo-Europeans. Only later iron was known to them. But the Dravidians knew the use of iron from a very early age. The Mohenjodaro-Harappan culture did not use iron artifacts, but copper was used. It is, therefore, probably not of Dravidian origin.

References

Ariviyar Kaḷ ñciyam. 1988. Tanjavur: Tamil University.

Buck, Carl Darling. 1949. *A dictionary of selected synonyms in the principal Indo-European languages: A contribution to the history of ideas.* Chicago: University of Chicago Press.

Encyclopaedia Brittanica. 1981. Chicago: University of Chicago.

Burrow, T., and M. B. Emeneau. 1984. *Dravidian etymological dictionary,* second edition. New York: De Good University Press.

Kochhar, Rajesh. 2000. *The Vedic people: Their history and geography.* New Delhi: Orient Longmann Ltd.

Pliny, the Elder. 1476. *Historia naturale.* Venetiis: Opus N. Iasonis.

Subramoniam, V. I., ed. 1990. *Dravidian encyclopaedia,* vol. 1. Trivandrum: International School of Dravidian Linguistics.

Turner, R. L. 1973. *Comparative dictionary of Indo-Aryan languages.* Oxford: Oxford University Press.

13

Language and Culture

Eugene A. Nida

From the beginning of my collaboration with Kenneth L. Pike in 1936 our common concern in linguistics and translation has been the reciprocal relations between language and culture, a theme developed brilliantly by Pike in his early volumes on a unified theory of human behavior. And as president of the Summer Institute of Linguistics for many years his influence on the proper concern for the role of culture in meaningful translating has been outstanding. Everyone in the field of interlingual communication is indebted to Pike for his academic and practical contributions.

Issues of language and culture also made me respond to one of the most difficult assignments in my life. I was asked by the Japanese director of a translations seminar in Japan to give a lecture that the Japanese participants would not be able to understand—the strangest request I have ever encountered. We were already a week into a conference on Bible translating sponsored by the Bible Society of Japan for Bible translators working in Japan, Korea, Taiwan, and the Philippines, and I was told that the Korean, Taiwanese, and Philippines translators were happy with my lectures, but the Japanese participants had concluded that I could not be a scholar because they could understand so readily what I had said. Accordingly, the director insisted that I would have to give a lecture that at least the Japanese participants would not be able to understand.

Kenneth L. Pike was my closest associate in SIL for more than ten years. I learned a great deal from him and I admired tremendously his linguistic expertise.

Actually, giving such a lecture would not be technically difficult but it would be so contrary to my constant concern to be understood and be helpful that I really suffered emotionally. I wanted such a lecture to be academically valid, even if some of the participants did not understand it, and so I chose to deal with possible applications of some mathematical models to translating, including graph theory, dimension theory, and isomorphs. I was quickly able to dispense with graph theory because no one can measure semantic distance between words or utterances, and dimension theory is hopelessly inadequate because the different meanings of words and the different semantic domains can represent so many different dimensions, while isomorphs are only a different way of talking about similarities. My conclusion was that the typical circles with neatly divided segments for different meanings (the usual results of Aristotelian categories) are actually misleading, since such semantic relations represent family similarities or constellations, and do not represent the neat classifications that some dictionaries inflict on languages in an attempt to subdivide meanings.

After the lecture several Japanese participants came up to thank me for the lecture, which they clearly did not understand, and the next day the director assured me that I could go on lecturing as I had before, since the Japanese delegation were now certain that I was qualified.

In some cultural settings, however, it is the absence of language that serves to communicate intentions correctly. For example, researchers in language use in the Philippines discovered that if a tradesman waits as much as four or five seconds before answering a request for help in repairing a television set or washing machine, he will never show up, even though after the pause he always insists that he will come immediately to help. In such circumstances it is the absence of speech that is crucial, but for the sake of continuing friendship a tradesman always wants to appear sympathetic. Filipinos understand the immediate absence of language and simply phone up someone else, while persons not alerted to such language behavior become increasingly angry as they wait for tradesmen who never appear.

I, however, have used a similar device to sort out recommendations of candidates seeking employment. Letters included in a Curriculum Vitae are seldom completely valid and even the names of referees are too selective. What is far more relevant is a phone call to someone who knows the applicant, but who is not listed in the application. I first explain briefly the nature of the work, and then I ask for a judgment about a candidate's qualifications. If the respondent needs a couple of minutes or more so as to determine just how to answer such a request, the candidate is almost always unqualified. Hesitation by the respondent is the key that explains so much.

In order to understand some of the important features of language and of culture, defined essentially as the totality of beliefs and practices of a society, it may be useful to talk about their similarities, differences, interdependence, unsystematic features, and coordination.

Similarities

Both language and culture may serve as signs for communicating information, for example, the word *ouch* may signal pain for the speaker or it may be simply a verbal reflex when no other persons are present. An embrace may represent at least some degree of belonging or affection. But there may be different cultural dialects within a culture. For example, Americans often greet good friends with a single kiss near the lips, while in Spain most people in similar settings kiss each other twice, but very lightly, first on the left cheek and then on the right. In Belgium, however, people in similar circumstances normally kiss three times: left, right, and left, and in France it is common for people to kiss four times: left, right, left, right.

Changes in linguistic and cultural codes seem to correlate closely with the density of communication. This means that languages and cultural behaviors change much faster in the centers of activity, rather than in the peripheries. For example, language and behavioral patterns change faster in Paris than in Tahiti and in Boston to Washington D.C. than in rural communities. In Iceland students can quite easily read eighth-century sagas, while in America, most students fail to comprehend the fourteenth-century tales of Chaucer. English has simply changed much more rapidly than Icelandic.

Differences

Language is essentially a part of culture and though exceptionally complex it cannot equal the incredible variety of behavioral symbols that people employ constantly, for example, dress to symbolize their wealth, stance to suggest their importance, office furniture to symbolize their status, diplomas on a wall to confirm their academic standing, and letter heads to define their roles.

But cultural symbols change even more rapidly than do linguistic symbols. The greater conservatism in language change is an important protection, because it is important to be able to understand one another accurately despite the fast speed of culture change and the numerous technical and personal differences.

Interdependence

Words have meanings only because they relate to behavior, but behavior may be extremely diverse and complex. For example, the statement *he ran into the house* may be understood in a literal sense if the person was physically running and ended up inside of a dwelling. But if the context indicates that the person was in a car, then obviously the meaning of the statement contains a partial idiom because the statement refers to impact and not to physical location. But a person can also say, *he ran into his friend at the book exhibit.* Such a statement presupposes that the person was not running, but that he unexpectedly encountered his friend.

Words only have meaning in terms of the culture, but how is it that one can say *he ran into trouble, he ran into opposition,* but not **he ran into a good job*? Why is *run into* used primarily with bad states? Or how is it that a verb such as *run* can occur in so many different behavioral contexts: *he ran the horse in the second race, the snake ran across the lawn, the blue fish are running, the clock is running, his nose is running, the rose ran along the fence, planes run each hour on the hour between New York and Chicago, he runs a big business, he ran the press, his sweater sleeve is running, the dye is running, he ran for election, he runs a hundred head of cattle on his ranch each summer.*

Unsystematic Features

Despite all that is said about the rules of language, most translators are impressed by the fact that whatever rules exist seem to be exceptionally lawless. Why do we say *tie up the package* as a way of insisting that the tying be done effectively? And how is it that we can also speak about *tying up traffic* to symbolize something quite different? And what about *he turned up late,* when there is no evident turning or no "upness?" And how is it that *up* can also be a verb in *he upped the price,* an adjective in *the upper level,* an old-fashioned superlative in *upmost,* or a noun *in the ups and downs of life?* Such subcategorizing is the life of language.

Coordination

A number of persons have commented on the four levels of linguistic structure: sounds, words, grammar, and discourse, and some have raised the issue of how the brain can function satisfactorily with four different structures that do not seem to be governed by any unifying or coordinating structures. The difficulty is that most people do not realize that such structures only occur in cultural contexts involving what is being talked about, to whom, in what type of setting, for what purpose, and with spoken and/or written codes.

The coordinating force comes from the communicative purposes involved. If a linguist wishes to point out that a statement made in the last number of the journal *Language* is wrong, there are several decisions that need to be made. Is the reply to be merely a letter to the author, a note for a forthcoming issue of the journal, or a full blown article to contradict the presumed error in fact or reasoning? If the choice is a personal letter, then is it to be friendly or hostile? Is it to go e-mail, in which case it may never be looked at, or faxed and quickly tossed into the waste basket, or on personal stationary? Such choices depend on a number of cultural factors.

Even after a decision is made to write a letter, the writer must determine how to organize the series of statements, including an introductory statement (emphasizing or downplaying possible differences of viewpoint), length of the statement, formality of the wording, and a brief review of certain important differences in the beginning and end of the letter. But these decisions are only the beginning. The entire letter implies a series of decisions that seriously restrict later decisions about all four levels of language structure—even spelling. In fact, a former British colleague always corrected my American English spelling before reading my letters for content.

The rules that govern the coordination of a text at all four levels of structure depend primarily on the cultural purposes, and these are dependent on the number of relevant contextual features. Texts can only be understood in terms of cultural contexts.

In order to understand the role of culture in the formation of any text, it is essential to consider the major ways in which a culture employs a language to accomplish several of its basic purposes: integration, acculturation, collaboration, aesthetic pleasure, exploring the unknown, and evaluation.

A small baby is seemingly overwhelmed by all the people who become caregivers: parents, grandparents, siblings, aunts and uncles, maids, and nurses. In this integrative phase of life not only does a baby need to recognize such people and their roles, but needs to learn how to obtain maximal benefits for minimal conformance to the demands of caregivers. But babies seem to be especially endowed with insight as to the genuineness of caregivers, and usually within a year or so babies learn how to use words instead of screams to get what they want.

Language acquisition and integration normally proceed very rapidly so that by five years of age children are ready to participate in the acculturation stage in which children learn to master the skills that the culture has determined are essential. Schools become centers for concentrated assimilation of the culture, and in most technical societies this process lasts between twelve and sixteen years, usually up to the time of sexual maturity and marriage, when in most societies young people are expected to assume responsibility for working with others to provide food, clothing, shelter, and protection from internal and external foes—the collaborative phase.

But this is not all. People also seem to have some instinct for beauty of graphic form, melodic sound, and aesthetic movement; art, music, and dance: African wood sculptures to be viewed only in dark god-houses, multirhythmic drumming (fugues of rhythm), and dance to drive away demons or to call back the spirits of the dead. And for understanding all this, language is the crucial agent.

Most people also want to know something about the unseen and the unknown, to experience the supernatural and to learn more about the world. On one occasion, I had to wait for a couple of hours in a small village in the highlands of Ecuador, but except for the saloon keeper everyone in the village was dead drunk: sprawled out on low porches, leaning against trees, or huddled beside large stones. And so I went to chat with the saloon keeper in order to find out what saint was being honored by such a fiesta. I was told that all this was to show respect for Saint Peter because this was his day. But when I insisted that the Bible never mentions Saint Peter ever getting drunk, the saloon keeper claimed that the day was actually in honor of Santa Barbara, a saint of pleasure and an increasingly popular saint among spiritists. But when I seriously questioned this explanation, the saloon keeper said to me, "Do you really want to know about our gods?" and then he pointed to the five volcanoes that could be seen surrounding the valley, "These are our gods." Life is filled with the mysteries of the unknown: conception and birth, floods and famines, sickness and death, gods and ghosts, and for many people the best way to deal with the unknown is to celebrate it with candles, images, and prayers.

In societies that have the requisite tools, people also want to investigate the reasons for plagues, the diminishing fish in the sea, and the loss of fertility in the soil. They form cooperatives to increase production and provide a market for what people make. Computers and the Internet are changing the world.

All this has increased enormously the need and desire to rethink the meaning of dyadic equity, the fundamental relation of people to one another in their expectations to receive something proportionate to what they give. People also become increasingly concerned for power and belonging, the two driving forces in community life, namely, accepting one's role in a society and finding the satisfaction of being accepted. Unfortunately, these two major social concerns are too often expressed and experienced in the neurotic forms of sadism and masochism.

Pike's academic creativity has helped thousands of students, Bible translators, and scholars to understand and appreciate better both the forms and the contents of language.

14

Worldview Reflected in Bajju Proverbs

Carol V. McKinney and Norris P. McKinney

Introduction

Kenneth L. Pike (1967) taught that language and culture are necessarily integrated and that neither can be studied or described adequately without the other. Not only did he analyze many different language genres, he also wrote in different genres, as attested by his volumes of poetry and his phenomenal contributions in the field of linguistics. Pike included proverbs, the subject of this paper, among the myriad of linguistic genres that fascinated him. Personally, we owe a tremendous debt to him for all that he taught us over the years; we had the privilege of being his students, friends, and colleagues.

We wish to thank SIL International and Wycliffe Bible Translators for funding this research. We conducted the field research from 1967–1971, 1972–1976, 1983–1984. We wish to thank the Sociology Department of Ahmadu Bello University for granting Carol a Research Associateship for the 1983–1984 period. We wish to express our thanks also to the University of Texas at Arlington, where we have adjunct status.

Earlier versions of this paper were presented at the ninety-third annual meeting of the American Anthropological Association, December 3, 1994, and at the annual meeting of the Linguistic Association of the Southwest (LASSO), October, 1993.

The Bajju[1] (pronounced [bədʒːu]) of Nigeria, West Africa, are also known as the Kaje (Gunn 1956:106; Meek 1931). Their home area is located in southern Kaduna State. Though centrally located in Nigeria, they are part of the cultural north where Hausa is the trade language. There are approximately 300,000 Bajju, making them the third largest ethnic group in the state, after the Hausa and the Fulani.

The Bajju use proverbs in daily life to teach the practical, the consequences of wrong actions, behavioral expectations, responsibility, and more generally their worldview. Winick (1977:440–441) states that proverbs are abbreviated traditional instructional statements, often stated in metaphors, that reflect folk wisdom. Okpewho similarly states, "Proverbs may be defined as a piece of folk wisdom expressed with terseness and charm" (1992:226). Their terseness and metaphorical nature add to their charm, their wide applicability, their multivocality, and the ease with which they may be memorized. Proverbs reflect general truths by referring to specific situations or phenomena.

Metaphors and symbolism are frequent features of proverbs that add to their charm, their ease in transmission, and their memorization. Metaphors are so common in Bajju proverbs that a brief consideration of the nature of a metaphor is in order. A metaphor is "a figure of speech in which a term or phrase is applied to something to which it is not literally applicable in order to suggest a resemblance" (Barnhart 1947:765). Metaphors transmit some of the most significant or deepest truths in cultures, including cultural presuppositions. They are so common in cultures worldwide as to be almost ubiquitous. Lakoff states, "Primarily on the basis of linguistic evidence we find that most of our ordinary conceptual system is metaphorical in nature" (Lakoff 1980:3). In our corpus of 165 Bajju proverbs, 117 (about seventy percent) of the proverbs employ metaphor.

Yankah (1989) portrays an African proverb as having a dynamic strategy in which form, meaning, and logic are in constant flux. Proverbs may focus on the absurd or the antithesis, irony or understatement, paradoxes or rhetorical questions. Hyperbole, an intentional exaggeration that is not intended to be taken literally, is sometimes the essence of a proverb.

Winick (1977:440–441) notes that one proverb may give advice that controverts that given in another. By giving conflicting advice proverbs point out people's need to maintain a balance between extremes. Winick also notes that proverbs often make use of rhyme, alliteration, and word play in order to reinforce their intended meanings.

---

[1]According to Greenberg's classification Jju, the language spoken by the Bajju, belongs to the Benue-Congo Plateau 2 language family (Greenberg 1966:8). In Gerhardt's classification, Jju falls into the South-Central subgroup of the Platoid Central Group (1989:364).

By using proverbs one can display knowledge of traditional wisdom as well as add wit or spice to speech. Bajju proverbs, like other forms of their oral literature, such as folktales, songs, and the Bajju Baranzan origins narrative, help to define the Bajju as a people with a common cultural heritage that makes them distinct as an ethnic group. These oral traditions provide ideals and guides to behavior that the Bajju admire and consider worthy to strive towards.

Achebe points out that proverbs help to make a main point, but they are not the main point in conversations where they are used. In fact the proverb and the topic of conversation may be only vaguely related. He further states that proverbs are like palm oil that is used with yams, the main dish (as quoted in Okpewho 1992:231).

Okpewho states that proverbs arise from three sources. Some develop from folktales, especially of the explanatory genre. Others originate as comments on historical events. But observations of the natural environment and human affairs are perhaps the most common origin of proverbs (Okpewho 1992:227–228).

The Corpus

Together with Malam Yabo Bayei, a Bajju traditional scholar from the village of Kamuru Kaje (locally known as Kamrum), we collected Bajju proverbs wherever we could find them. Although proverbs in Jju occur in a variety of contexts, only a few of those in our corpus emerged in context; we collected most of them in isolation. We excluded a few proverbs from the corpus for various reasons, for example if one appeared to be an extempore translation from another language and culture. Malam Yabo (Bayei 1983) published the corpus of 165 Bajju proverbs that we used for this study in a trilingual Jju-Hausa-English interlinear collection of *Gan Bajju* (Kaje Proverbs).

We asked various individuals[2] to give us the translation and the meaning of specific proverbs; often we could not have guessed the meaning from the literal translation. In the following sections we present forty-one proverbs in a three-line interlinear format. The first line is the proverb in Jju (pronounced [dʒ:u]). The second provides a morpheme-by-morpheme literal translation of the Jju into English. The free translation on the third line helps the reader make sense of the literal translation. Occasionally, we have added a comment or a freer translation as a fourth line for clarity. The free translations are primarily those provided by our Bajju language

---

[2]We especially wish to thank Musa Asake, a Bajju friend, who has read through this paper and added his wisdom in expounding on the meanings of the proverbs in this paper.

assistants. Sometimes a careful analysis of the Bajju lexical items provides more insight into the Bajju worldview than the free translation, e.g., in proverbs 15, 16, and 31.

Grammatical and Semantic Structures

Bajju proverbs have several typical rhetorical structures. They include cause-effect, means-end, attribution, sequence, negative results, and personification of animals.

In our corpus of 165 proverbs, five are in the imperative mood and the rest are declarative statements; none are questions, exclamations, or other sentence types. At least 123 refer only to third person referents. Of the eight referring to the first person, all except possibly one have to do with negative values.

A number of Jju proverbs begin with the impersonal third person plural subject pronoun *ba*. In many instances its use reflects the closest that Jju comes to a passive construction. While we have usually translated *ba* as an unspecified 'they', Malam Yabo Bayei translated it as 'you'. Proverbs 1 and 2 illustrate this type of construction.

(1)   Ba   na   zzek   ǝyajok   swwa bǝyokwot ba?.
      they HAB   teach one.who.eats.beans drink water   not[3]
      'They do not have to teach one who eats beans to drink water.
      You don't need to advise someone who is eating beans to drink water.'

This proverb points to the natural consequences of one's actions. Just as drinking water follows eating beans, so consequences generally follow from one's actions.

In proverb 2 the third person plural subject pronoun *ba* is used similarly to indicate an impersonal subject. The object of the verb *tssu* in the active clause becomes the subject in the passive English free translation. In both Jju and the English translation the relatives are the patient.

(2)   Ba   na   tssu   byin   ba?.
      they HAB   wash   birth (relative) not
      'Relatives cannot be washed (separated).'

---

[3]Abbreviations used in the interlinear gloss of the proverbs are: CONT continuative, FUT future, HAB habitual, NEG negative, and REL relativizer. When a gloss requires more than one English word, the parts are separated by periods.

This proverb states that although washing typically removes dirt there is no means to wash away relatives. While a person can dissolve some relationships, e.g., one can dissolve a marriage through annulment or divorce, he or she cannot dissolve the relationship with one's blood relatives.

Proverb 3 provides another example of the use of an impersonal subject.

(3) Ba   na   ya,   ə   tssu   ryei   a.
     they HAB eat   they   wash   calabash the
     'When people have eaten, they wash the calabash.'

Proverb 3 is concerned with interpersonal relations. If a person does something for another person, for example giving that person something to eat, the person who eats will do something for the food-giver, e.g., he or she will wash the calabash in which the food was served. In this proverb the food that one person gives and the calabash that the other person washes in payment for the food represent interactions between people.

The Bajju frequently use an impersonal subject such as *əyin* 'a person' (in 5 and 6), *ənyet* 'people' (in 4), and *əzzim* 'a questioner' (in 7) in a manner similar to their use of *ba* in the above proverbs.

(4) Ənyet   ə   byyi   kəwon dama   tak   ba?.
     people they   have   child bother leg   not
     'I have no child to bother me.'

(5) Əyin   nu zong   zi ya   ni,   nu əmi ə bvwo   kəret
     person the hunger it eats REL   he it.is he knows place

     kyang ya.
     thing   eat
     'The person who is painfully hungry is the one who knows where to find food.'

(6) Əyin   nu ə cat   i,   ə   ni   shya.
     person the he wants REL   he   will find
     'The one who seeks shall find.'

Proverb 6 is not a traditional Bajju one, but it illustrates the fact that proverbs continue to be developed and incorporated into Bajju life. This particular proverb comes from Luke 11:10 in the Christian New Testament (*Kpa Kaza* 1982).

(7)   Əzzim   ryen ə   bvwut ba?.
      questioner road he lost   not
      'He who asks which road to take will not get lost.'

Proverb 7 is in a different form but with the same meaning. It presents some common sense instruction that one should ask so as not to get lost. Here inquiring is valued.[4]

Reflections of Worldview in Bajju Proverbs

A worldview consists of the basic underlying assumptions that people have about reality. Kearney states that a worldview consists "of basic assumptions and images that provide a more or less coherent though not necessarily accurate way of thinking about the world" (1984:41). Worldview universal categories include concepts of the self and the other, relationships, causality, time, and space. In looking at components of worldview as applied to Bajju proverbs we examine the self and the other, cause-effect, negation, personification of animals, attribution, and classification. We have not found time and space worldview universals in these proverbs.

Self-Other

The self

In Bajju proverbs the self deals primarily with the need for an individual to take responsibility for his or her own actions. A few also relate to the importance of having prestige and by extension personal power. For example, proverb 8 asserts that everyone wants to be famous.

(8)   Ko ɲyan ə   cat   ba   ku   bvwo.
      or who   he wants they him   know
      'Everybody wants to be known.'

Several proverbs use the idiom of one's mouth, representative of one's words, which can cause problems. For example:

---

[4]This proverb can be contracted by deleting *ryen*.

(9) Kanu ə na   hwak pfwa.
     mouth it CONT cuts neck
     'It is the mouth that keeps cutting the neck.'

This description of the mouth as the cause for injury to the neck is reminiscent of the feral character of the tongue described in James 3:5–7 in the New Testament.

(10) Kanu ə na   truk   tak.
     mouth it HAB hits (once)/trips leg/foot
     'The mouth makes mistakes.'

(11) Kanu ə ndop, bvak byyik baʔ.
     mouth it ties   hand untie not
     'What the mouth has tied, the hand cannot untie.'

With words an individual can make agreements that cannot be undone; one's words can cut, and with words a person can speak mistakenly. Because there are consequences to what one speaks, by implication one should speak carefully. In the Bajju worldview a person's mouth speaks the thoughts that reside in his or her neck. Hence, words can impact a person's neck, that is, that person's thoughts, as in proverb 9.

Included under the concept of the self are general admonitions to be content with what one has.

(12) Əbibyyi   anwaan   aran   atsatsak   anyyi
     poor.thing of.yours it.is.better.than good.thing of.another

     ayin.
     person
     'Your property may not be as good as someone else's, but it does you more good than a better thing that belongs to someone else.'

(13) Ko anyan ə cat   yet.
     or who   he wants to.be
     'Everyone wants to be (important).'

Proverb 13 points to the importance of obtaining and having status, both individually and, more importantly, as a people. For example, when we worked on the Bajju language project, people would tell us that now others would know who the Bajju are. This project contributed to their status and ethnic pride.

The other

Several proverbs deal with important issues of ethnicity in Bajju relations. These proverbs illustrate Bajju relations with the Hausa.

(14) Əraɪ   kɑnu,   nu ɑmi   ə   cong ɗkpat.
     one.of.excessive mouth he   it.is he goes Hausa (onom.)
     'The one who speaks quickly (too much) is always involved in trouble.'

The word *əkpat* is onomatopoeic; its core meaning is the sound of a slap on one's face. It translates into English as "a Hausa person" or "the Hausa language." This has become the common Jju word for the Hausa people and for their language, though in its etymology it is a derogatory term. Our Bajju language assistants insisted that a free translation for this word would be "trouble" rather than the Hausa themselves. Another version of this proverb has *əkpot*, meaning 'wickedness', rather than *əkpat*. This proverb cautions a person to speak prudently, so that by the person's own words he or she does not bring trouble onto himself or herself.

Kpat[5] has also been generalized in Jju to refer to any city or town where the elite, e.g., the Hausa, live. The word in the context of this proverb refers to a city, indicating a city outside the Bajju area. In traditional Bajju society the main reason a person would be taken out of the area would be to be taken to jail. If this meaning of *Kpat* is applied to proverb 14, then the proverb states that the person who gossips, spreads rumors, or reveals Bajju secrets will end up in jail.

(15) Əyin   nu ɗvwa ɗkpat ni,   ɗkpat ə   ni   ku ya.
     person he plays Hausa REL Hausa he will him eat
     'He who invites war (lit., the Hausas), the war (lit., the Hausas) will win over him (lit., eat him).'

In this proverb, the Hausa are identified as people with negative connotations as far as the Bajju are concerned. Here the word *əkpat* is translated as 'war'. In delving into Bajju early history, we found that each dry season the Hausa slave-raided the Bajju people. Prior to and following the imposition of British colonialism the Bajju were placed by the British under

---

[5]The word *kpat* refers to the language of the Hausa, *əkpat* to the people.

two emirates or city states, some in Zaria, and the rest in Jema'a. Jema'a
Emirate paid Zaria Emirate 100 slaves per year, and Zaria Emirate in turn
paid Sokoto Emirate ten slaves annually. The area where the Bajju live,
formerly known as southern Zaria and currently as southern Kaduna
State, was part of the catchment area for acquiring slaves for these
emirates.

The English proverb "He who seeks trouble finds it" summarizes the
meaning of proverb 15. Another version of proverb 15 has *zwang* or 'war'
instead of *əkpat*, indicating that if a person causes a fight then that person
will lose.

While the proverbs above focus on the issue of ethnicity, the majority of
the proverbs in our corpus relate to practical matters of interpersonal relationships with others in everyday life. For example,

(16) Əbyyi   bʌnyet ə ya dikan   shan baʔ.
     one.who.has people he eats medicine stick not
     'One who has people does not need medicine of the stick (i.e., a
     policeman).'

Proverb 16 emphasizes the importance of the community for the Bajju.
Here it serves as a means of defense. It indicates that the person who has
many people does not need other means of defense, as for example from a
policeman or other means of law enforcement.

The compound *dikan shan* 'medicine of the stick' relates to the compound *kəwon shan* 'a policeman'. Another possible meaning of the compound *dikan shan* is 'stick medicine', a medicine that Fulani young men
take before undergoing beatings as part of their initiation rites. If a young
man takes this medicine, it is believed that he will not feel pain while undergoing his initiation beatings. Again the meaning is the same when applied to the Bajju proverb, namely that if you have people you will always
have someone there to protect you. Members of one's own ethnic group
provide security.

The "other" as a component of worldview can refer to various categories of people, such as the blind, the lame, the slave, or the thief. For
example:

(17) Wi ryi tyyi ʌntyok ɗutwan nə shei   ɗkwwo.
     not see put man   blind   he tread.on old.one
     'Failure to see is what causes a blind man to tread on his
     father-in-law.'

Because the Bajju hold elders in such high respect, they do not joke with them. They do not tread on an elderly person such as one's father-in-law. To "tread on one's father-in-law" or in any way to show disrespect for that person is a serious matter in Bajju society.

In proverbs 18 and 19 there are two other categories of the "other," namely the dumb man and the thief. These proverbs give guidance as to how an individual should relate to them.

(18) Wi   yei   əmi   tyyi   kəbvwu   əshyirwan   ka   brik.
      not   call   it is   put   dog   dumb.man   he   get.lost
      'It is lack of calling that causes a dumb man's dog to get lost.'

(19) Əkpəndang   ətang   ə   yet   ətang.
      friend   thief   he   is   thief
      'The friend of a thief is a thief.'

Sometimes proverbs indicate the fragility of human relations. For example,

(20) Ə   ndop   ədat   ətankwo.
      he   will.tie   bridge   cornstalk
      'He will make a cornstalk bridge out of you.'

While the majority of the Bajju proverbs dealing with the "other" concern relationships between humans, a few deal with beings in the supernatural realm. For example,

(21) Kətacyi   ə   yet   tak   jet   baʔ.
      witch   it   is   leg   cricket   not
      'A witch is not like a cricket's leg.'

The word that we translate as 'witch' refers to a person who operates in the supernatural realm, and the consequences of those actions result in misfortune, sickness, and even death for another person in the physical realm. This proverb points out that the actions of a witch are not small and insignificant such as a cricket's leg is.

Cause-effect

Cause-effect proverbs include those that begin with a conditional, typically *ka*, that translates into English as 'if you' or *ki'if*. Eighteen proverbs or eleven percent of the total corpus have this construction. Some examples are as follows:

(22) Kɨ ba shya əpfwu ba?, ba brek bu dican.
if they find blacksmith *not* they return with charcoal
'If they do not find a blacksmith, they return with the charcoal.'

The sense of proverb 22 is that if the blacksmith does not do the work for you, he should return the charcoal to you. The category of blacksmith is a metaphor for any person within a specific occupation who should do work requested of him or her. If that work is not completed, whatever objects or money were paid should then be returned.

(23) a. Ka byyi, a byyi bərywai.
if.you have you have friends
'If you have (wealth, possessions, etc.), you will have friends.'

b. Ka byyi ba?, a byyi ərywai ba?.
if.you have not, you have friend not
'If you have no wealth, you will have no friend.'

The pair of proverbs in 23 points to the fact that those who have possessions also have friends who are attracted by those possessions. Within an African social organization, all those within an individual's extended family expect to benefit from the wealth and prestige of the individual. An individual receives his or her identity by virtue of being part of the community, and the community in turn expects an individual to share. All must advance together.

(24) Kɨ a wan, kə a shwei, sərei ku nat kənu.
if you cook if you roast all it goes mouth
'Whether you boil something or roast it, all of it goes into the mouth.'

The meaning of proverb 24 seems similar to that of the English expression, "It's six of one and a half dozen of the other." Paraphrasing the Hausa translation found in *Gan Bajju* (Bayei 1983) yields "Whether you cook something in a pot or roast it over an open flame..."

(25) Kɨ ku rau,   ban cat   bᶏgado.
     if it too.much they look.for elders
     'If it is too much, they look for the elders.'

An idiomatic translation of proverb 25 might advise that if the matter cannot be settled otherwise, they should consult the elders.

Negation

Negation is not usually a feature in a description of worldview assumptions. However, this grammatical feature occurs in fifty-six out of the 165 Bajju proverbs; hence, almost thirty-four percent of the proverbs teach practical lessons through negative statements. Further, eighty-seven of the proverbs have to do with negative values, including undesirable behavior. Bajju use negation to teach positive values, as in proverbs 26 and 27.

(26) Ba ya ɗkrup dityin ɗkrup   ba?.
     they eat coconut base   coconut not
     'One does not eat coconut under a coconut tree.'

(27) Ba zzek ɗvwon brek   də ambyring ba?.
     they teach fool return his wife   not
     'You do not have to teach a foolish man to get his wife back.'

Proverb 27 teaches that even a foolish man knows that he needs to get his wife to come back to his home. The Bajju are a patrilineal, patrilocal people. When divorce occurs, the usual pattern is that the woman initiates the breakup by leaving her husband. A man whose wife leaves him lives with the hope that one day she will return. Traditionally, Bajju men used a number of magical means in an attempt to compel their wives to return to them. (Sentence-initial *ba* 'negative' in (28) is a loan from Hausa clause structure. It is homophonous with *ba* 'they'.)

(28) Ba zzong   kɑtuk kwwong ba?.
     NEG too.late night cook   not
     'It's never too late at night to cook.'

Bajju hospitality dictates that the host provide food for a guest at whatever time of night the guest may arrive, as asserted in proverb 28.

(29) Nsum na ya ɗang baʔ, sei awumba.
     shame it eats thief *not* only brother
     'Shame does not gnaw at a thief, just at his brother.'

While a thief may be shameless, his relatives suffer the shame of having him as a member of the family.

Personification of animals

The use of animals in metaphors is widespread in Africa in various types of oral literature, for example in trickster narratives, folktales, and proverbs. Animals as tricksters are often endearing, yet pathetic. They may seek to fool others, but they end up fooling only themselves. A personified animal or trickster is often represented by a weak animal who fools others, particularly those stronger than himself, by his cleverness. Tricksters do not act out of kindness but rather out of self-interest.

In some instances, there is something specific about the animal that is significant that the hearer needs to know in order to understand the proverb, as in proverb 39 which assumes that the hearer knows that a hyena often eats carrion rather than fresh meat. In other instances, such as proverbs 31 and 32, the animal in the metaphor can stand for any person who does something and ends up the object of ridicule because of what he or she did. Personified animals often have human characteristics and as such they serve to teach people about the consequences of their behavior.

For the Bajju this use of animals in metaphors reflects the close relationship between the human world and the animal world. The Bajju traditionally believed in reincarnation in which following death a person could be reincarnated either as another human being or as an animal or bird. This close relationship is further illustrated by the association of totemic animals with Bajju clans. For example, one clan in the village of Sokwak is named the *kəpyyi*, the 'antelope'. When a hunter from that clan encounters an antelope he is not allowed to kill it or to eat its meat even if someone else kills it. Rather he tries to capture it, talk with it as he would with a close relative, and then release it.

In our corpus fauna, from elephants to crickets, are referents in thirty-four proverbs. However, they are grammatical subjects in only ten of the proverbs and are personified in only four (proverbs 19, 20, 83, and 90 in Bayei 1983). The hearer is presumed to know the character of each animal. While some Bajju proverbs employ animals metaphorically, in other instances their use is not figurative.

Toad

(30) N   tom   pfong   ambvat.
     I   sent   messaage   toad
     'I sent a toad with a message.'

This proverb uses the toad to represent an undependable person who may or may not fulfill his duty as messenger.

Black monkey

The black monkey (kəka) emerges as a personified animal that is deceived and cheated, namely a foolish person. A black monkey can also symbolize trouble. For example,

(31) Kəka   tswwa   kəyat   nywat   əkpat.
     black.monkey   spent.the.night   inside   guinea.corn   Hausa
     'A black monkey slept in a guinea corn farm (of the Hausa).'

The sense of the black monkey's action of spending the night in the guinea cornfield of the Hausa is an action that only a foolish person would do. This proverb can perhaps be translated into English by the phrase "only a fool would do something like that" or the proverb "(s)he who seeks trouble finds it."

(32) Ba   na   kup   kəka   zzum   ba?.
     they HAB cover   monkey   hornbill   not
     'You cannot deceive a monkey by impersonating a hornbill.'

In this proverb the monkey represents a person who cannot be deceived by another person imitating another animal, namely a hornbill bird.

(33) Ba   ka   kəka   ka   shyi   tazwa   kəkon   ba?.
     they divide monkey it   is   upon   tree   not
     'You don't share out a monkey while it is still in the tree.'

While this proverb involves a black monkey, the monkey does not symbolize a foolish person. Rather it symbolizes meat for dinner. However, until the monkey is out of the tree, it cannot be served for dinner. A similar proverb in English is, "Don't count your chickens before they hatch."

Birds

Birds can also be personified. They represent persons who speak without thinking about the consequences of their words. For example,

(34) Kɑnon ka   ə yei   za   ni,   za   ni   kə tsot.
     bird   the it calls rain REL rain FUT it beat
     'The bird that calls for rain does not escape being beaten by the rain.'

(35) Ba   tssem kɑnon ǥrung ka cyang ba?.
     they catch bird   snare it watch not
     'You don't rig a snare to catch a bird in its presence.'

Proverb 35 points to the need to avoid revealing one's plans in the presence of the person you are seeking to ensnare. The same principle is to be found in the Old Testament, Proverbs 1:17.

Hares and elephants

(36) Ənsom ə kun   ba   dɨ   ɑntyok ku yrek.
     hare he cries arrival against man   him wakes.up
     'The hare cries about the man who wakes him up.'

Proverb 36 might be translated more idiomatically as, "A hare is not complaining against his killer but against the one who wakes him up." It indicates that the hare focuses on what is trivial rather than what is really important.

(37) Ənsom ə yet zzom   kɑnkrang kɑyaan.
     hare he is elephant town   other
     'A hare is an elephant in another town.'

Here we see that a small animal such as a hare, who represents an unimportant person in one context, may be a large animal or important person in another context. Again, the importance of obtaining prestige is in focus. In some instances, it helps for a person to move to another location in order to gain more status and prestige. A similar English proverb is, "One would rather be a big fish in a small pond than a small fish in a big pond."

(38) ə   tyong zzat,   ə   si   kpa zzom.
      he flee   cape.buffalo he then fall elephant
      'He runs from a cape buffalo only to fall victim to an elephant.'
      (Figuratively, "you are jumping out of the frying pan into the fire.")

The cape buffalo is the most dangerous of all the animals in Africa due to its unpredictable behavior; it will charge without being provoked. The elephant is similarly a dangerous animal. In this proverb the person flees from one dangerous animal or situation, only to fall to another dangerous animal or situation.

Hyena

The hyena is frequently a trickster in Bajju oral traditions, including proverbs. For example,

(39) Əbwi   dinam nu ba   na   pyyem kura.
      spoiled meat   it they HAB catch hyena
      'It is with rotten meat that a hyena is caught.'

Attribution

Under attribution we are looking at qualities attributed to an individual.

(40) A   n   tyyi bəyekwot kənshang.
      you me put   water   basket
      'You are like water in a basket to me.'

As water quickly drains from a basket into which it is poured, so this proverb indicates "You have disappointed me" or "I can't handle you."

Classification

While classification is one aspect of any worldview, in general we have not found classification of the Bajju world to be important in Jju proverbs. The possible exception to this concerns classification of behavior. For example, the following Bajju proverb teaches against laziness.

(41) Əbrik   kəssi ə   hywa, "N wo   n yya kəntson."
      he.who.averts   eye   he says   I will I do   tomorrow
      'A lazy person says, "I will do it tomorrow."'

The Spanish expression "*mañana!*" conveys the same meaning as the Bajju procrastinator's "*N wo n yya kəntson.*" A person might quote this proverb to motivate a procrastinator to do a task today rather than a "tomorrow" that may never come.

A Proverb as the Coda of a Narrative

Proverbs very often form the coda of a folktale, sometimes the onset, and occasionally both. As such they provide the pithy moral that the tale intends to teach. For example, in the following folktale proverbs provide the teaching point and worldview assumption in both its onset and coda.

Zaki bu Rong
'The Lion and the Fire'

Kɨ	a	ryi	əyin	nə tyong	ə	bu	nwwa	an	dong,
if	you	see	person	he flees	he	then	enters	into	fire

"If you see a person flee and enter a fire,

kyang	a	ku	nying	i	ku rʉ	rong	a.
thing	the	him	chase	REL	it	greater.than fire	the

the thing that is chasing him is greater than the fire."

Nyyai	əyin	ə	yi	nshyi	keyak	ə	hwok	zaki	ku	uwrum	bai.
long.ago	person	he	long.ago	was	farming	he	hear	lion	it	roaring	coming

Long ago a person was farming when he heard a lion roaring and coming.

Nə	kai	ənok	ə	rot	ə	tyong	ə	si	nwwa	kəyat	əshyim.
he	let.go	hoe	he	drop	he	fled	he	then	enter	inside	thorns

He let go of his hoe, dropped it, ran and entered a thorn patch.

Zaki	na	ku	ndyi	nə	nwwa	a	əshyim	a	ni,	ku	seyak.
lion	he	him	sees	he	enter	into	thorns	the	REL	he	passes

When the lion saw that he had entered the thorns, he went on by.

Kəram	ka	zaki	na	ku	n-seyak	ni
time	the	lion	the	it	REL-passed.by	REL

When the lion had passed on by,

əntyok	keyak	əyyu	ə	cat	ryen	wruk	a	kəyat	əshyim	ka	,
man	farm	that	he	look.for	way	get.out	from	inside	thorns	the	

the farmer looked for a way to get out of the thorn patch,

ə shya baʔ, ə nwwa kənak gaan .
he found not he began crying then
but he did not find one. He began to wail.

Kəram ka kəwon nu ka ka ba   kəret mpfong ka ni ,
time   the child   his the he come place of.work the REL
When his child came to the work place,

ə bu shya ətyyi nu kəyat əhyim nə shyi i kənak.
he past found father his inside thorns, he is   in crying
he found his father in the thorn patch, crying.

Ka ku zzim sisak ji nə yya nwwa əhyim a ni.
he him ask how the he do enter thorns the REL
He asked him how come he had entered the thorn patch.

Ətyyi nu ə ku kok sisak ji.
father his he him told how the
His father told him how.

Kəwon ka gaan ə drok bə nyong ə si sook som bəpyyi
child the then he left with quietness he then picked.up bundle grass
Then the child left quietly and collected a bundle of grass.

ə bu rot, ə cat ədoma ətyyi nu ə sook tswa ndong gaan,
he then drop he search bag   father his he took seed of.fire then
Laying it aside, he searched in his father's bag, took a match,

ə tyyak tyyi bəpyyi ba ə si sook ə ta ətyyi nu mi.
he scratch put.to grass the he then took he throw father his REL
struck it, and touched it to the grass, which he then picked up and threw to his father.

Kəram ka ətyyi nu nə hwok rywei ndong a ni,
when the father his he heard noise of.fire the REL
When his father heard the sound of the fire,

nə təkwang bɨ ncyi ə wruk kəyat əhyim ka.
he struggle with running he come.out inside thorns the
he struggled and ran and got out of the thorn patch.

Kəwon ka ə si hywa də nu,
child the he then said to him,
His child then said to him,

"Dikwu ami a   bu   tyong nwwa   kəyat əhyim ka.
death   it.is you PAST ran   entered inside thorns the
"It was fleeing from death that you got into the thorn patch.

Nwan bu   tyong   dikwu u   wruk."
you   then running death you come.out
You fled from death again when you came out."

(first published in N. McKinney 1972:13–14)

Discussion

From this brief examination of Bajju proverbs it is clear that their primary emphasis is practical advice for human relationships. The first proverbs concerned the importance of having prestige and status. That prestige relates to and encompasses having a large family both for acquiring more wealth and for defensive purposes. This stress on the family relates to their concept that one without children and without an extended family is a nobody. A person has importance only in the context of the community.

A related part of Bajju worldview is that respect for one's elders and especially the elderly within one's extended family is very important. This respect manifests itself in a number of ways, including the form of greeting used by a man to welcome another man who has just arrived. A man would welcome a younger man by saying *mabən;* but he would welcome an older man by saying *mahabən*, a form that shows respect. The Bajju have borrowed from their Fulani neighbors a deep respect that borders on an avoidance relationship between a mother and her oldest son.

There are proverbs that stress not being foolish, and recognizing that if a person does act in a foolish manner, there are expected consequences. Bajju proverbs also stress the need for taking responsibility for one's own actions.

There are some aspects of Bajju life that seem to be conspicuously absent from the proverbs we collected. For example, only two proverbs concern the spiritual realm. That realm is presided over by God. There is also a host of spirits, for example, the tall spirits (*əninyet*), the small spirits (*nətənyrang*), the water and mountain spirits (*gəjimali*), and the ancestral spirits (*bənyabyen*). Basically, this realm is not represented in our corpus of Jju proverbs. This is not to say that this category is unimportant, but rather that in the proverbs we collected it was not present.

Finally, in the folktale about the lion and the fire, proverbs both begin and end this tale. Folktales serve didactic purposes in an entertaining way. This paper has sought to illustrate that Bajju proverbs present important points within their worldview, and that they do so with charm and entertainment.

References

Barnhart, Clarence L., ed. 1947. *The American college dictionary*. New York: Random House.

Bayei, Yabo. 1983. *Gan Bajju, karin magana, Kaje proverbs*. Jos: Nigeria Bible Translation Trust.

Gerhardt, Ludwig. 1989. Kainji and Platoid. In John Bendor-Samuel (ed.), *The Niger-Congo languages*, 359–376. Lanham: University Press of America; Dallas: Summer Institute of Linguistics.

Greenberg, Joseph. 1966. *The languages of Africa*. Bloomington: Indiana University.

Gunn, Harold D. 1956. *Pagan peoples of the central area of Northern Nigeria*. London: International African Institute.

Kearney, Michael. 1984. *World view*. Novato, Calif.: Chandler and Sharp Publishers.

Kpa Kaza. 1982. Apapa: Bible Society of Nigeria.

Lakoff, George. 1980. *Metaphors we live by*. Chicago: University of Chicago Press.

McKinney, Norris. 1972. *Zizwa Jju*. Jos: Institute of Linguistics.

Meek, C. K. 1931. *Tribal studies in Northern Nigeria Vol. 2*. London: Kegan Paul, Trench, Trubner and Co.

Okpewho, Isidore. 1992. *African oral literature, backgrounds, character, and continuity*. Bloomington: Indiana University Press.

Pike, Kenneth Lee. 1967. *Language in relation to a unified theory of the structure of human behavior*, second revised edition. The Hague: Mouton.

Winick, Charles. 1977. *Dictionary of anthropology*. Totowa, N.J.: Littlefield, Adams and Company.

Yankah, Kwesi. 1989. *The proverb in the context of Akan rhetoric, a theory of proverb praxis*. Spritworterforschung Volume 12. New York: Peter Lang Publishing.

Part III

Etics and Emics

"Descriptions or analyses from the etic standpoint are 'alien' in view, with criteria external to the system. Emic descriptions provide an internal view, with criteria chosen from within the system. They represent to us the view of one familiar with the system and who knows how to function within it himself."

(Pike 1967a:38)

15

Emic Analysis of Oral Narrative

A Native American Example

Dell Hymes

Kenneth Pike has had a considerable effect on American anthropology. The concepts of emic and etic became a focus of discussion, not only in regard to language, but in regard to culture generally. In this tribute I want to indicate that the emic/etic distinction is essential to the study of oral narrative. Moreover, not all are aware that for Pike the emic concept is not limited to units and levels of language, but can embrace worldview and change.

When I was a graduate student in anthropology and linguistics at Indiana University (1950–1954), Ken Pike was someone from whom to learn through his *Phonetics* and *Phonemics*. His realistic sense of the interplay between rules of analysis and actual practice could be like fresh air in a closed room. And when *Language in Relation to a Unified Theory of the Structure Human Behavior* began to appear (1954), pursuing both anthropology and linguistics no longer seemed like stepping over a stream, on legs barely long enough to reach both sides. That the frontispiece of the book was a picture of Sapir confirmed that here was the regaining of an earlier, broader tradition, left in shadows by the limited Bloomfieldianism of those years.

When I taught at Harvard (1955–1960) and came to know Charles Frake and others there, Harold Conklin and others at Columbia and Yale, amid the emergence of "ethnoscience," Pike's concepts of "emic" and "etic" caught the essence of that concern to be able to study both language and behavior on common ground. For me, Ken Pike became, and has remained, a remarkable example of thinking clearly and comprehensively, of getting to the root of matters, and at the same time living a committed life. I saw him, and corresponded with him, only occasionally, but he has been very real to me for half a century.

Structure in Oral Narratives

Franz Boas made preservation and study of oral narratives a prominent concern in American anthropology more than a century ago. He was sensitive to formal features of narratives, but the kind of form he noticed consisted of repetitions, as in song texts. He was not aware of relations of form that did not require repetition (see D. Hymes 1999). Neither were others at that time. It seemed natural to present spoken narratives in paragraphs, the form in which narratives were most familiar to us in our own culture.

It now appears that spoken narratives in many languages actually are organized in terms, not of paragraphs, but of lines and groups of lines. Lines are indicated by contours of intonation. Groups of lines may be marked by recurrent conventions and are organized in terms of implicit relations. Two kinds of relations recur in the traditions of which I know: relations of two and four, and relations of three and five.

That does not entail mechanical sequences. A variety of choices are possible, as the narrative to follow illustrates. A set of five units may be a rapid run or a somewhat complex progress of interlocking triples (the middle element completing one series and initiating another). It may be amplified as a sequence of five pairs or in other ways. Altogether, there can be changes of pace and a sense of arrival. The patterns contribute to what Kenneth Burke called "arousal and satisfying of expectation" (1925).

When there is only a written record, it is still possible to discern lines and relations among them. Turns at talk are invariably distinct units, initial time words mark units, as do changes of location and of actor. Verbal exchanges between actors commonly are paired. A narrator may have characteristic ways of proceeding. On the hypothesis that there is patterning throughout, one can find it. (The narrative to follow surprised me in some respects.)

A sequence of lines is in effect a kind of poetry. To be sure, the kinds of lines most familiar to us are metrical. One keeps track of relations within lines. In many traditions of oral narrative one keeps track instead of relations among lines. They can be said to be, not metrical, but measured (cf. D. Hymes 2000a). For such traditions, paragraphs are etic; relations among lines are emic.

I don't want to claim that such relations are universal, nor that they are innate. I can say that they have been found in texts in some ninety languages. For English and a few well-studied Native American languages, there are many examples. Published English examples include stories collected in New York City by Labov (in D. Hymes 1996 and 1998 and stories from other sources in D. Hymes 1996, Part III) and V. Hymes (1995).

A Native American Example

In 1905 Edward Sapir wrote down myths and other texts at Yakima Reservation, in the state of Washington, from Louis Simpson, a speaker of Wishram (Wasco), the Chinookan language easternmost along the Columbia River. Years later I took down narratives from other speakers of the language, living at Warm Springs Reservation, Oregon. I also analyzed several narratives in Clackamas, a related language spoken on the Willamette River. One had been taken down by Franz Boas in 1892 (cf. D. Hymes 1984), the rest by his student, Melville Jacobs (e.g., see D. Hymes 2003, ch. 7). In addition, I analyzed a number of narratives in the Chinookan languages near the mouth of the Columbia, Kathlamet, and Shoalwater, all taken down by Boas over a century ago (e.g., D. Hymes 2003, ch. 6; D. Hymes 1983). In all of these the basic relations are of three and five. Indeed, recent speakers of Wasco and Wishram have been quite aware that five is a pattern number in the culture.

A myth recorded by Sapir, "The Deserted Boy," was one of the first in which I discovered such thorough-going relations among lines (see D. Hymes 1976; 1981, ch. 4). I knew as well that the ethnographer Leslie Spier had visited Wishram people (as those on the Washington side came to be called) in 1924 and 1925, publishing a monograph integrating his information with that of Sapir (Spier and Sapir 1930). The monograph contained a few stories, including a telling of "The Deserted Boy" by Mrs. Mabel Teio. Evidently, Mrs. Teio spoke in the language, since Spier refers to a Wasco man, Frank Gunyer, as interpreter (p. 124). I noted that Mrs. Teio's telling brought out the role of a woman who helps the boy, whereas Simpson had dramatized the boy's exploit as in effect a guardian spirit quest. Simpson has a lyric stanza of the relation between the boy and his now wife as a source for wealth. Once the two grandmothers who had left him means of survival are safe, he raises a storm that drowns those who had abandoned him. (Revenge is a frequent ending in other versions in the region.) Mrs. Teio has no revenge, but a continuing marriage with children. A neat example of different shading of a shared story. But I did not think to look for patterns in the published paragraphs of her telling.

Years later I realize that I should have done so. The text does contain recurring relations. There are markers of segments (e.g., phrases with "morning"); questions and answers form sets; the entire story takes shape as one gains acquaintance with it. And to my surprise, the two occurrences of line initial "So" at the end parallel each other, defining a scene in a way that implicitly marks a woman's power.

Let me display the difference between etic and emic by showing first the nine paragraphs,[1] in which Mrs. Teio's story was published (Spier and Sapir 1930:274–275).

"The Deserted Boy"

There was a very mean boy at Spedis. He fought with the other children all the time. The boy's grandmother had an underground house. An old man said; "We are going to take him into the hills across the river and leave him." Those two old women said, "No!" They cried. He said, "Yes, he is too mean." At last he took the boy across the river. The two old women never stopped crying. The men went over there to cut sticks for the hoop of the hoop and pole game. They left him there. One young man said, "We will defecate." They made a face in the faeces with a stick and told it, "If you hear a cry, you call out." They put another far inside the clump of bushes where they cut the sticks. That mean boy said, "It is a long time now. I have lots of sticks." So he shouted, "Ho!" Somebody shouted, "Ho!" He called again and then went over there. Again he called and heard the reply. He went there, but there was no one. He saw the faeces with mouths. He said, "I guess they deserted me." So he took the sticks.

When he reached home nobody was there except the magpies. Everyone else was across the river playing the hoop and pole game. He went into the house and cried. He heard something going *k'e, k'e,* like a fire. He looked around until he found it; it was something to make string of. He said, "I am going to make a trap to catch magpies." He made it and caught many of them. He dried the skins. He

---

[1]Hines (1998:169–171) has reprinted this text with a finer distinction of paragraphs, especially for turns at talk—18 paragraphs in all.

used the string to sew them together to make a blanket for sleeping. He measured it; "It is long enough for me to sleep."

Then he went fishing and caught a chub. He roasted it at the fire and ate one side. He kept the other for the morning. He said, "Oh, I am all right." So he slept under his magpie blanket. Next morning he put it on, tying it around his neck, and went fishing again. He got two fish. He cooked one and kept one for evening. "I am getting on all right." Next morning he fished again. Pretty soon he got something: it was heavy and nearly pulled him in. It was put there by a woman of the river people, the daughter of Itc!é:kian, a river man. They had tied a big basket of salmon, camas, and berries to his line. He pulled it in. "Oh, I have something." He opened it. "Oh, my." He danced. As he danced his blanket flapped straight out behind.

The people who had left him now saw him. "Something happened to that mean boy. He is dancing close to the river." He took the basket to his house. Soon he ate and slept again. He was glad.

That woman got ready at night. She was a young girl; she had long hair. She made a nice house: she put nice blankets in it. The boy had nothing but his magpie skins. She wished him to be a man now. She put him in her bed.

In the morning he looked all around. He saw the blankets. He saw himself, "My, I am big." He turned and saw the woman. He was afraid and astonished by her nice clothes. He said nothing. She knew what he thought. She said, "That food I sent you because you were poor and deserted. Now I have come to stay with you." He said, "All right."

That morning the people saw it and said, "Look, that mean boy now has a good house. Smoke is coming out of it." They thought about him.

Those two stayed there until they had a little boy and a girl. They grew quickly. He told his wife, "I guess we will go to see my grandmother. Perhaps she is still alive." She agreed. He made a bow and arrow for the little boy. She made a little basket and digging stick for the girl. The boy tried to shoot. Those people across the river saw it and talked about him. But they never came across, because they were ashamed. So the family crossed to see the man's grandmother. They travelled; the boy tried to shoot birds. "Oh, a different man is coming," the people said. He knew because his wife had given him power. His grandmother, blind and poor, was sitting in the underground house, crying continually. He went in and said, "Oh, you two are alive yet?" One said, "Eh." He told them who he was. They cried, "No, you are a man; that was a little boy." He said, "Yes, that is me," but they did not believe him. He made them believe. So they returned across the river with him.

That is all I know of this story.

Here are the words in terms of lines and relations among lines. Scenes and stanzas are indicated at the right. Every fifth line is numbered. Right-hand braces (}) indicate units that go together—in this case pairs of verses or of stanzas.

Notice that the last scene (v) has two possible interpretations. It can be taken as having five parts, or as having four parts. I give both and discuss them. There are two bases for the difference. One has to do with how one weighs certain phrases, and the other has to do with gender.

The Deserted Boy

Mabel Teio

There was a very mean boy at Spedis.   [i]   (A)
He fought with the other children all the time.
The boy's grandmother had an underground house.

An old man said,   (B)
    "We are going to take him into the hills across the river   5
        and leave him."
These two old women said,
    "No!"
They cried.
He said,   10
    "Yes, he is too mean."
At last he took the boy across the river.
The two old women never stopped crying.
The men went over there   (C)
    to cut sticks for the hoop of the hoop and pole game.   15
They left him there.

One young man said,   [ii]   (A)
    "We will defecate."
They made a face in the faeces with a stick
    and told it,   20
        "If you hear a cry,
           you call out."
They put another far inside the clump of bushes
    where they cut the sticks.

That mean boy said,   (B)   25
    "It is a long time now.
    I have lots of sticks."

So he shouted,
   "Ho!"
Somebody shouted,   30
   "Ho!"

He called again   (C)
   and then went over there.
Again he called
   and heard the reply.   35
He went there,
   but there was no one.

He saw the faeces with mouths.   (D)
He said,
   "I guess they deserted me."   40
So he took the sticks.

When he reached home   (E)
   nobody was there
      except the magpies.
Everyone else was across the river   45
   playing the hoop and pole game.
He went into the house
   and cried.

He heard something going "*k'e, k'e*", like a fire.   [iii] (A)
He looked around   50
   until he found it;
      it was something to make string of.
He said,
   "I am going to make a trap to catch magpies."

He made it   (B) 55
   and caught many of them.
He dried the skins.
He used the string to sew them together
   to make a blanket for sleeping.
He measured it   60
   "It is long enough for me to sleep."

Then he went fishing   (C)
   and caught a chub.
He roasted it at the fire
   and ate one side.   65

He kept the other for morning.
He said,
   "Oh, I am all right."
So he slept under his magpie blanket.

Next morning he put it on,   (D)   70
   tying it around his neck,
      and went fishing again.
He got two fish.
He cooked one
and kept one for evening.   75
"I am getting on all right."

Next morning he fished again,   (E)
Pretty soon he got something:
   it was heavy
      and nearly pulled him in.   }   80
It was put there by a woman of the river people,
   the daughter of Itc!é:kian,
      a river man.
They had tied a big basket of salmon, camas, and berries,
              to his line. }
He pulled it in   85
   "Oh, I have something."
He opened it.
   "Oh, my"
He danced.
   As he danced,   90
      his blanket flapped straight out behind.

The people who had left him now saw him.   (F)
"Something happened to that mean boy.
   He is dancing close to the river."
He took the basket to his house.   95
Soon he ate
   and slept again.
He was glad.

That woman got ready at night.   [iv] (A)
She was a young girl,   100
   she had long hair.
She made a nice house,
   she put nice blankets in it.
The boy had nothing but his magpie skins.
She wished him to be a man now.   105
She put him in her bed.

In the morning he looked all around.   (B)
   He saw the blankets.
He saw himself,
   "My, I am big."   }}   110
He turned
   and saw the woman.
He was afraid
   and astonished by her nice clothes.   }}
He said nothing.   115
   She knew what he thought.
She said,
   "That food I sent you
      because you were poor and deserted.
   Now I have come to stay with you."   120
He said, "All right."   }}

That morning the people saw it   (C)
and said,
   "Look, that mean boy now has a good house.
   Smoke is coming out of it."   125
They thought about him.

Those two stayed there   [v]   (A)
   until they had a little boy and a girl.
They grew quickly.   }
He told his wife.   130
   "I guess we will go to see my grandmother.
   Perhaps she is still alive."
She agreed.   }
He made a bow and arrow for the little boy.
She made a little basket and digging stick for the girl.   }   135

The boy tried to shoot.   (B)
Those people across the river saw it
   and (they) talked about him.

But they never came across,   (C)
   because they were ashamed.   140
So the family crossed to see the man's grandmother.

They travelled.   (D)
The boy tried to shoot birds.
"Oh, a different man is coming," the people said.

He knew [the situation]   (E) 145
   because his wife had given him power.

His grandmother, blind and poor,
    was sitting in the underground house,
        crying continually.   }
He went in   150
    and said, "Oh, you two are alive yet!"
One said, "Eh."   }
He told them who he was.
They cried, "No, you are a man;
    that was a little boy."   }   155
He said, "Yes, that is me,"
but they did not believe him.   }
He made them believe.
So they returned across the river with him.   }

That is all I know of this story.   160

Profile and Interpretation

An outline, or profile, makes clear relations of form. It aids interpretation as a check against oversight and inconsistency. First, some observations:

In a case such as lines 42–43, I feel sure the original Wishram/Wasco did not have 'When', and had three lines: "He reached home; nobody was there, only magpies." Chinookan narratives often enough have such three-step sequences of action in a unit aligned with other verses. One might call them "amplified verses." (On amplification, see D. Hymes 1985:412, reprinted as chapter 6 in D. Hymes 2003.)

Lines 45–46 would not have had a gerund (playing) without subject in the original language, but two predicates: "Everyone else was across the river, they were playing the hoop and pole game."

Line 49 might not have had a second predicate (= 'going'), and 'like a fire' might be explanation in translation. I can't be sure.

Line 51 would not have had 'until'.

A brace indicates pairing, as among verses in stanza E in scene [iii]. It can also indicate pairing among stanzas in a scene, as with AB CD EF in scene [iii]. In scene [iv], stanza (B), the recognition scene between the boy, become a man, and the woman, who transformed him, swells. It has three parts, and each part has not one pair, as is common enough in the tradition, but two pairs—one pair of pairs for the young man's recognition of himself (107–108, 109–110); one pair of pairs for his recognition of the woman (111–112, 113–114) and one pair of pairs for her recognition of what he thought, her explanation, and his acceptance (115–116,

117–120, 121). Such swelling within a pattern can again be called "amplification" (see D. Hymes 1985:412).

Notice also stanza (A) in scene [iv]. Here the power of the woman/young girl is salient. The focus is on her. She makes a nice house, puts nice blankets in it. The boy has nothing but magpie skins. She wishes him to be a man. That is, she uses her power to transform him. (In Louis Simpson's telling of "The Deserted Boy," the boy also becomes a man, implicitly because of the young woman, but she is not yet present. The story shows it happening in the course of his own actions.)

I take the stanza as having five parts. I think that for Mrs. Teio they express an intended contrast, foregrounding the girl as against the boy. The girl is in charge now. The boy has one line as grammatical subject, merely as having magpie skins. There are pairs of lines for the girl's characteristics three times. These doublings highlight her. They are not amplification in the structural sense just discussed (doubling of units throughout another unit), but can be considered amplification in an expressive sense (doubling within a larger unit). Perhaps "partial amplification" would serve as a name.

Form of course may depend on interpretation. Sometimes more than one interpretation seems plausible. This is the case with the final scene of Mrs. Teio's story, as we have it.

One interpretation would hold to the three and five part relationships that are overwhelmingly the norm in Chinookan narratives. That is what has been presented above for scene [v]. There is another possible interpretation which has, not five stanzas, but four. Let me present it, then discuss it.

Those two stayed there [v] (A)
    until they had a little boy and a girl.
They grew quickly. }
He told his wife. 130
    "I guess we will go to see my grandmother.
    Perhaps she is still alive."
She agreed. }
He made a bow and arrow for the little boy.
She made a little basket and digging stick for the girl. } 135

The boy tried to shoot. (B)
Those people across the river saw it
    and talked about him.
But they never came across,
    because they were ashamed. 140
So the family crossed to see the man's grandmother.

```
They travelled.                                              (C)
The boy tried to shoot birds.
"Oh, a different man is coming," the people said.


He knew [the situation]                                      (D) 145
     because his wife had given him power.
His grandmother, blind and poor,
     was sitting in the underground house,
          crying continually.                           }
He went in                                                       150
     and said, "Oh, you two are alive yet!"
One said, "Eh."                                         }
He told them who he was.
They cried, "No, you are a man;
     that was a little boy."                            }    155
He said, "Yes, that is me,"
but they did not believe him.                           }
He made them believe.
So they returned across the river with him.             }


That is all I know of this story.                               160
```

As can be seen, in both interpretations the first and last stanzas are the same. The difference has to do with lines 136 through 144. In one interpretation, they consist of three stanzas (BCD). In the other, they consist of two stanzas (BC), with the result that the last stanza is not (E), but (D).

Years ago, I would not have thought of such a possibility. Recently, the use of relations of four within narratives organized otherwise in terms of relations of three and five has been found in a number of traditions in the western United States (see D. Hymes 2000b). The use of relations of four connotes power, or at least initiation of action, on the part of a woman.

In the preceding scene the boy becomes a man because the woman wishes (transforms) him to be so, and it seems significant that the woman's power to initiate occurs three times with pairs of lines.

In the present scene, the young man knows the state of affairs to which he returns 'because his wife had given him power' (146).

The inference of four scenes, not five, within the last scene involves taking the two crossings of the river as parallel. Each is marked by 'So', ending a pair of stanzas (141, 159). The family crosses to the grandmothers, they bring the grandmothers back.

It is not that I think 'So' is quite what Mrs. Teio said in her own language. There is no word in Wishram-Wasco easily translated as 'so'. The likely word is *aqa* 'now'. Followed by *kwapt* 'then', it regularly marks the beginning of successive units in the narratives of Louis Simpson. At the end of a unit, by itself, it has a summative force. That I think is the case here. ('So' in line 69 probably also represents *aqa*).

This interpretation has support in that a summative 'So' of line 141 is followed by 'They travelled', an explicit statement of change of location. (The preceding line can be taken as part of a contrast: the others did not cross, because ashamed, so this family crossed.)

Experience with other stories clearly supports separating, as distinct parts, the doubling in stanzas (B) and (C) of this interpretation ((B) and (D) of the other) of the boy trying to shoot, the people talking about him. The question of four stanzas or five stanzas, then comes down to the status of lines 139–141. A separate stanza in the interpretation given first, part of a stanza in the interpretation given second. More exactly, the difference comes down to the status of lines 138 and 140.

In the interpretation of the scene in terms of four stanzas, these lines, 'and talked about him', 'because they were ashamed' are indented, as second parts of two verses in the same stanza (B). In the interpretation in terms of five stanzas, the lines are flush left, as separate verses, part of separate stanzas (B, C).

If one could hear Mrs. Teio tell the story, sentence-like intonation contours presumably would tell which is right. If there are such contours for each line, indicating the presence of three verses, then the interpretation in terms of separate stanzas, each with three verses, would be right. If 'talked about him' and 'because they were ashamed' do not have such contours by themselves, but are part of contours with what precedes them, then the interpretation in terms of a single stanza, having four verses would be right.

We have only a written record. I lean toward interpretation in terms of separate stanzas—partly from giving some weight to the presence of separate predicates in each of the lines, and partly because this is not the place I would expect four-part patterning, expressive of a woman's role. I would expect it rather in the final stanza, lines 145–146, where Mrs. Teio makes explicit:

> "He knew
>   because his wife had given him power.'

On the interpretation adopted here, the two occurrences of 'So' beginning the final line of a stanza still are in keeping with Chinookan patterns. They end the third and fifth stanzas, the mid-point (turning point) and the final point. That is very Chinookan.

Here is a profile of the relations of lines, verses, stanzas, and scenes in the five-stanza version.

Scenes/Stanzas		Verses	Lines	
i	A	abc	1, 2, 3	
	B	ab cd ef	4–6, 7–8; 9, 10–11; 12, 13	
	C	abc	14, 15, 16	
ii	A	a bc de	17–18; 19, 20–22; 23, 24	
	B	abc	25–27, 28–29, 30–31	
	C	ab cd ef	32, 33; 34–35; 36–37	
	D	abc	38, 39–40, 41	
	E	ab cd ef	42–44; 45–46; 47–48	
iii	A	abc	49, 50–52, 53–54	
	B	ab cd ef	55, 56; 57, 58–59; 60, 61	}
	C	ab cd e f g	62, 63; 64, 65; 66, 67–68, 69	
	D	ab cd e	70–72, 73; 74, 75; 76	}
	E	ab; cd; ef; gh; ij	77, 78–80; 81–83, 84; 85, 86; 87, 88; 89–90–91	
	F	abcde	92, 93–94, 95, 96–97, 98	}
iv	A	abc; de, f; g, h	99, 100–101; 102–103, 104; 105, 106	
	B	ab cd	107, 108; 109, 110;	
		ef gh	111, 112; 113, 114	
		ij kl	115, 116; 117–120, 121	
	C	abc	122, 123–125, 126	
v	A	ab cd ef	127–128, 129; 130–132, 133; 134, 135	
	B	a bc de f	136, 137, 138	
	C	abc	139, 140, 141	
	D	abc	142, 143, 144	
	E	ab cd ef gh ij	145–146, 147–149; 150–151, 152; 153, 154–155; 156, 157; 158, 159	
	close		160	

Change and a Personal Search for Knowledge

Pike developed the emic approach for many years, including its relation to the individual, worldview, and change (e.g., Pike 1987:88–91, 1993: ch. 5). This larger perspective is relevant to Native American narrators such as those named early on in this essay. It is important to keep in mind that Christianity reached these people before linguists and anthropologists. There is reason to think that some of them sought to make sense of a world of which Christianity was a part, along with what they had learned of their native traditions.

Not enough attention has been given to this. I remember as a student, accompanying a professor, I heard an elder discourse at length in his language, followed at intervals by translations into English by an interpreter—translations that were clearly much shorter than the original. Afterwards, I commented on that to my professor. The response was to the effect, "Oh, that was just his combination of his own tradition and Christianity."

I would like to suggest that sometimes such a combination would show itself in certain details and a single phrase. A widespread and well-known type of myth is that of the Bungling Host (better, Bungling Host, Benevolent Host [cf. D. Hymes 1987]). In Louis Simpson's telling of it to Edward Sapir, Coyote goes twice to Deer and is well fed, Deer slicing flesh from his own body and blood from his nose. Coyote invites Eagle to his place to reciprocate, and attempts to cut flesh from his wife. Deer stops him and tells him, as before, "If you should be hungry, you should come to me."

I have not come across any other telling of this widespread story with just such words, "Come to me," and the linking of flesh and blood. If one remembers that Louis Simpson was a Methodist, it is hard not to find here the influence of the eucharist.

We need to be open to the possibility that a narrative that may seem entirely traditional sometimes may reflect a personal search for knowledge, a search for which Christianity is one horizon. (For an example in Kathlamet Chinook, see D. Hymes 2000c:3–5. For a detailed analysis see Wolfart 1999.)

References

Burke, Kenneth. 1925. Psychology and form. *The Dial* 79(1):34–46. Reprinted in his *Counterstatement* (1931).

Hines, Donald M. 1998. *Where the river roared: The Wishram tales*. Issaquah, Wash.: Great Eagle Publishing, Inc.

Hymes, Dell. 1976. Louis Simpson's "The deserted boy." *Poetics* 5(2):119–155. [Reprinted in Hymes 1981, ch. 4. In both places section 5 was omitted by oversight, and also line 82, 'He stood it on the ground'. Section 5 is present in Hymes (1994:178ff.) and line 82 also restored.]

Hymes, Dell. 1981. *'In vain I tried to tell you'*. Philadelphia: University of Pennsylvania Press.

Hymes, Dell. 1983. Poetic structure of a Chinook text. In Frederick B. Agard and Gerald Kelley, and Adam Makkai, and Valerie Becker Makkai (eds.), *Essays in Honor of Charles F. Hockett*, 507–525. Leiden: E. J. Brill.

Hymes, Dell. 1984. The earliest Clackamas text. *International Journal of American Linguistics* 50:358–383.

Hymes, Dell. 1985. Language, memory, and selective performance: Cultee's "Salmon's myth" as twice-told to Boas. *Journal of American Folklore* 98:391–434.

Hymes, Dell. 1987. Coyote, the thinking (wo)man's trickster. In A. James Arnold (ed.), *Monsters, tricksters, and sacred cows: Animal tales and American identities*, 108–137. Charlottesville: University Press of Virginia.

Hymes, Dell. 1994. Ethnopoetics, oral formulaic theory, and editing texts. *Oral Tradition* 9(2):330–370.

Hymes, Dell. 1996. *Ethnography, linguistics, narrative inequality: Toward an understanding of voice*. London: Taylor and Francis.

Hymes, Dell. 1998. When is oral narrative poetry? Generative form and its pragmatic conditions. *Pragmatics* 8(4):475–500.

Hymes, Dell. 1999. Boas on the threshold of ethnopoetics. In Lisa Philips Valentine and Regna Darnell (eds.), *Theorizing the Americanist tradition*, 84–107. Toronto: University of Toronto Press.

Hymes, Dell. 2000a. Poetry. *Journal of Linguistic Anthropology* 9(1-2):191–193.

Hymes, Dell. 2000b. Variation and narrative competence. In Lauri Honko (ed.), *Thick corpus, organic variation and textuality in oral tradition*, 77–92. Studia Fennica, Folkloristica 7. Helsinki: Finnish Literature Society.

Hymes, Dell. 2000c. Survivors and renewers. *Folklore Forum* 31(1):3–16. Bloomington, Ind.: Trickster Press.

Hymes, Dell H. 2003. *Now I know only so far: Essays in Ethnopoetics*. Lincoln: University of Nebraska Press. [In press.]

Hymes, Virginia. 1995. Experimental folklore revisited. In Roger D. Abrahams (ed.), *Fields of folklore: Essays in honor of Kenneth Goldstein*, 160–168. Bloomington, Ind.: The Trickster Press.

Pike, Kenneth L. 1987. The relation of language to the world. *International Journal of Dravidian Languages* 16(1):77–98.

Pike, Kenneth L. 1993. *Talk, thought, and thing. The emic road toward conscious knowledge*. Dallas, Tex.: Summer Institute of Linguistics.

Sapir, Edward. 1909. *Wishram texts*. American Ethnological Society Publications 2. Leiden: E. J. Brill.

Spier, Leslie, and Edward Sapir. 1930. *Wishram ethnography*. University of Washington Publications in Anthropology 3(3). Seattle: University of Washington Press.

Wolfart, H. C. 1999. Authenticity and *aggiornamento* in spoken texts and their critical edition. In Lisa Philips Valentine and Regna Darnell (eds.), *Theorizing the Americanist tradition*, 121–149. Toronto and Buffalo, N.Y.: University of Toronto Press.

16

Alien Gods

George I. Mavrodes

The servants of the king of Aram said to him, "Their gods are gods of the hills, and so they were stronger than we; but let us fight against them in the plain, and surely we shall be stronger than they." (I Kings 20:23)[1]

Kenneth Pike was a Christian missionary. Of course, all of us are many things simultaneously. So Pike, even just with respect to his professional working life, was several things. He was one of the really outstanding linguists of the twentieth century. He was a university professor, a mentor to many generations of linguists. He was an administrator, and perhaps many other things. But certainly his commitment to the missionary enterprise, a commitment which he made early in life and which he maintained to the end, was a major strand in his working career. I suspect that if he were asked what is the work which he did, then some version of the "missionary" answer would be the first thing to come to his mind. And that is also how I think of him.[2]

---

[1]Here, and elsewhere, I quote from the *New Revised Standard Version* of the Bible.

[2]I met Dr. Kenneth Pike when I came to the University of Michigan as a graduate student in Philosophy in 1958. Our academic fields were rather different, and I never had occasion to study with him. But after I came back to the University of Michigan as an assistant professor in the early 1960s we met fairly often at the Faculty Christian Fellowship and I was often a guest in the Pike home—sometimes just for a family dinner and sometimes for a larger discussion group.

The Question

In this essay, I propose to explore a question that comes up in connection with missionary work (though that is not its only locus). The Christian missionary must often speak about God, the God whom he worships and serves. But his missionary work requires him to speak in this way to people who also speak about God, or at least about the gods. For, by and large, the people to whom the missionary goes will be people who already have a religion, and many of those religions make reference to one or more gods. So my question here is: How are we to construe those other gods, the alien gods, the gods of other religions?[3]

Perhaps this question is not yet clear enough. For the sense of "other" and "alien" may not be clear. And that is related to another unclarity, one that concerns the "we" of the question. But I will try to say more about those things later.

Gods

The quotation with which I began the essay comes from one of the historical books of the Hebrew scriptures. It is part of the account of an Aramean military expedition into northern Israel during the reign there of Ahab. The Arameans attacked Samaria, and the Israelis counter-attacked. In that encounter the Israelis were victorious, and the Arameans retreated with heavy losses. The story as we have it was, of course, written by a Hebrew scribe. But the quoted sentence is attributed to Aramean officers explaining to their king why they were defeated. It is an interesting explanation, and it may give some of us a view of the question about alien gods from the other side, a side that is probably not our side.

These Aramean officers refer to some alien gods—gods, that is, who were alien to them. They refer to those gods as "their gods," the gods of their Israeli enemies. But they also seem to be "realists" in their thinking about those alien gods. That is, they think of those gods as belonging to the order of reality. They do not construe them as imaginary beings, fictions, or anything like that. They take them to be real beings, at least as real as camels and onions. They think of those alien gods as acting in the ordinary world and as having real effects there. That is evident from the straightforward way in which they refer to those gods in explaining their own defeat in battle. They attribute that defeat to the fact that they fought the Israelis in the hill country, which was the home turf of the Israeli gods.

---

[3]I don't know that Pike himself ever addressed this question in a public forum. In this essay, therefore, I make no reference to his own views about it.

And they propose to adopt a better strategy next time, fighting on the plains where presumably the Aramean gods were at home. So I will say that these officers were "realists" about the gods, explicitly here about the alien gods and presumably also about their own gods. They take all these gods to belong to the order of reality.

What else do these Arameans think about gods? Most people who think about gods, and who talk about gods, will have some idea of what a god is like, some description of a god, perhaps some "concept" of god. In the high theologies that have developed through 2,000 years of Christian history such descriptions have grown into massive books, indeed into whole libraries. (And, of course, these libraries are not entirely consistent.) These massive elaborations of the concept of God, the sophisticated and detailed speculations about the exact nature of the divine attributes, etc., are largely the work of professional scholars, theologians, and philosophers.

But it is not only philosophers and theologians who may have some concept of God, or of the gods. Unsophisticated believers also have some ideas about that, an informal concept of a god. Of course, that concept may not be very well worked out, perhaps not fully explicit in the speaker's consciousness. But wherever there is speech about the gods there is very likely also to be some idea of what a god is. And so the Aramean officers, although they were not professional philosophers or theologians, may have had some ideas along that line.

In this biblical account there seem to be some fairly clear examples of such conceptual elements. For one thing, it seems clear that these men were "finitists" about the gods. Christian theologians, thinking about God, have generally favored extreme versions of the properties they attribute to Him—not merely power but omnipotence, not merely knowledge but omniscience, etc. No limits here. But clearly the ancient Aramean notion of a god comes nowhere close to that. They construe the gods as having power all right—they might turn the tide of battle—but their power fades out at the first line of hills, not twenty miles away. The gods, as the Arameans think of them, clearly are finite beings.

The Arameans were also genuine pluralists with respect to the gods. That is, they were polytheists. They refer to the Israeli gods in the plural (rightly or wrongly), and probably they were also polytheists with regard to their own gods. And they apparently thought that these gods, some of them anyway, really were distinct from one another. The plurality was genuine, and not merely apparent. For they think that these various gods might come into real conflict with one another, backing their respective human protégés.

Is the Aramean notion of a god totally absurd? Richard Swinburne, a contemporary Christian philosopher, has put forward a minimalist conception of a god that seems to fit the implicit Aramean ideas very well. He says that he will understand a god to be "a very powerful non-embodied rational agent" (1970:53).[4] If those Aramean officers could have read Swinburne's definition they might well have said, "Yes, that's pretty much what we mean when we talk about the gods."

Of course, some Christians might immediately feel that this is not nearly strong enough for their taste, that it does not capture what *they* mean by "God" (with a capital "G"). And, of course, it does not capture that meaning, at least not fully. It does not have the extreme and absolutistic flavor of the high theologies. "Very powerful" is not the same as "omnipotent," and so on. Nevertheless, it's not as though Swinburne's minimalist concept is totally inapplicable in a Christian context. For God, as He is construed in the high theologies, also satisfies the Swinburne concept. Or so, at least, it seems to me. For example, if God is indeed omnipotent then He is very powerful. And so His omnipotence would qualify Him as a god, at least with respect to one element ("very powerful") in the Swinburne concept.[5] A minimalist concept such as that of Swinburne, therefore, provides for some commonality in the Aramean and the Christian uses of god language.

There might, however, be some beings who satisfy the minimalist concept, but who are too limited, too impoverished, too local, etc., to satisfy some more exalted concept. They might qualify as gods in an ancient Aramean theology but not in the high Christian theology. (Could we say that they might be gods but not God?) In any case, however, that failure need not disqualify them from existence, from reality. In fact, many Christians believe that there are some such real beings, maybe many of them. (I believe that myself.) Angels, for example, as they are construed by many Christian thinkers, would seem to fit Swinburne's minimalist concept quite well. And since his notion makes no reference to goodness or any other evaluative element, devils would also qualify. There is a sense, therefore, in which many Christians (myself included) are polytheists.[6]

Divine aliens

I said that in this paper I would discuss alien gods. But the Swinburne minimalist concept of god does not explicitly include any element that would

---

[4]Possibly Swinburne meant merely to attribute this concept to David Hume.

[5]If God, despite being omnipotent, is not very powerful, then I don't understand at all what omnipotence is.

[6]I discuss polytheism, and its relation to monotheism, more extensively in Mavrodes (1995).

generate the idea of an alien. Neither, for that matter, do the high theologies as they are usually developed. These concepts are purely descriptive, directed entirely to the properties of the conceptualized being, the divine attributes. But the comments of the Aramean officers introduce another element, a relational element that might well anchor the idea of an alien god. They refer to some gods as "*their* gods," i.e., the gods of the Israelis. And this contrasts with the gods whom the officers would acknowledge as their own, referring to them perhaps as "*our* gods." So they think of the gods as having special, and perhaps differential, relations to people and groups of people.

This relational element seems to me to be crucial to any genuinely religious talk about the gods. No religion in which god talk is important can be satisfied with merely identifying something (or someone) as a god, determining that it satisfies the concept of a god, describing its attributes, affirming its reality, and so on.[7] If I am to be a genuine participant in a religion in which gods are important, then my relation to the gods must be important to me. They must be, in some deep sense, *my* gods. But these Arameans also realize that it is quite possible for you to identify a god without making it *your* god. They acknowledged the reality of the alien gods of the Israelis, and immediately began scheming about how to defeat those gods the next time around. So they apparently recognized differential human relations to real gods.

What constitutes the binding relation that links a god with a human person or with a people?[8] Perhaps there is no single answer to this question, and maybe the relation varies somewhat from one religion to another, or from one god to another. From the human side, at least, such attitudes and actions as worship, obedience, commitment, trust, adoration, and loyalty seem likely to be involved.

And from the side of the god? Well, some religions include the idea of a divine initiative—some divine act or choice—in generating the binding relationship. And there is, of course, some suggestion to that effect in the biblical literature.

My gods (or God), then, are the gods whom I worship, and to whom I commit my life and service. The alien gods—alien to me, that is—are the gods whom I do not worship, etc. But those alien gods may be the gods of

---

[7]Perhaps there are some religions without gods. Maybe some versions of Buddhism are of that sort. And some scholars think that Gautama Buddha himself thought that there probably were some gods. But he also thought that these gods had their own business to attend to, and they had no interest in the world nor any concern with it, and therefore we need not concern ourselves with them. There is a version of my question that relates to the "ultimates" associated with the nontheistic religions. Here, however, I will discuss only the case of theistic religions.

[8]Ruth, resolving to leave Moab and go to Israel, says to her mother-in-law, "Your people shall be my people, and your God my God" (*Ruth* 1:16). What will make that true?

other people, other religions. If so, they are not alien to them. And my question is primarily about how *we* are to think about the gods who are alien to us. It is not about how those other people—the people to whom those gods are not alien—think about them.

Three Extreme Positions

Universal atheism

Abstractly, there are many possible answers to that question. At one extreme there is the simple position which can readily be adopted by an atheistic materialist. Such a person can choose a "one size fits all" answer. He or she can say that there simply are no real beings that fit even the Swinburne minimalist concept of a god. There are no unembodied rational agents of great power (nor, for that matter, of small power). The natural, material world is all there is to reality. That's all there is, folks, you've seen the whole show. And so the whole menagerie of gods, from those of the most sophisticated religions down to the most "primitive," consists entirely of unreal beings—fictions, imaginary entities, hallucinations, priestly frauds, and so on. Such a person intends to sweep the real world clean of all the gods, high and low.

Atheistic materialists might, of course, be mistaken in this. Indeed, I believe that they are mistaken. But in this paper I will not argue that point. I simply note this as one possible position. But here I am really interested in the positions that are open to a somewhat different "we." That is a "we" that includes Kenneth Pike, and me, and, I suppose, many of those who will read this paper. It is, roughly, we Christians. We cannot consistently adopt the atheist's wholesale dismissal of the gods from the realm of reality. Whatever we may think of the Aramean gods, or of the gods of whom we hear in other cultures, we ourselves are committed to thinking that there are some real gods. Or, at the very least, that there is one real god (or God). Like the Arameans, we are theistic realists. And we think that there is at least one real god who is not alien (to us). So, what are we to think of the other gods, those who are alien to us?

Almost universal atheism

Within this context of a Christian commitment there are several possibilities. At one extreme is the view that our god (God) is real and the gods of all the other religions are unreal. All the alien gods are fictions, imaginary beings, and so on. The other religions do not connect their devotees with anything that rises even to the level of a Swinburne minimalist god. One might say that people who take this position are theistic realists with respect to their own god and atheists about all the others. I think that some Christians have adopted this view. For now, I will pose just one question about it. Do we really have some positive reason to give against the reality and existence of those other gods?

Perhaps one reason comes immediately to mind. Christians are monotheists, aren't they? And so must they not reject categorically all the other putative gods?

I think that this reply is mistaken. I said earlier that there is a sense in which many Christians are polytheists. But there is indeed another sense (and maybe more than one) in which Christians are monotheists. The deepest sense involves the relational element. We profess, and hope, to give our whole heart in worship, love, loyalty, and commitment to one god and not to many.[9] But that need not require us to reject the existence and reality of other gods. It requires instead that we not make these other gods *our* gods. And even the Arameans, though they were probably cultic polytheists, were not totally indiscriminate in their worship and commitment. They certainly do not appear to have professed any loyalty, etc., to the Israeli gods.

And what about monotheism in a more metaphysical sense, as a claim about the reality of gods? That kind of monotheism has a contrast on each side of it, atheism on one side and polytheism on the other. And these three "isms" are all claims about the true number of the gods. But such claims, to make any sense, require some notion of what it is that is being counted. There is no inconsistency in being a monotheist relative to one concept of a god and a polytheist relative to a different concept. For the two concepts may provide us with two sorts of things to be counted, and these two counts may not result in the same number.

It seems to me, therefore, that no simple appeal to monotheism can give us a satisfactory reason for a wholesale rejection of the reality of alien gods. We might, of course, have some other general argument, which would have this result. But, as of now, I don't know of any. And what if we cannot find a positive reason for that wholesale rejection? In that case some sort of modest agnosticism might be a plausible, and honorable, stance.

---

[9]Perhaps monotheists are those who, with respect to gods, take seriously Jesus' observations about the awkwardness of undertaking to serve two masters.

Universal theistic realism

Well, we have just looked at the extreme view at one end of the spectrum, the view that says that our god (or God) is real and none of the other gods are real. At the other end of the spectrum there is the view that our god is real and the gods of all the other religions are also real. All of the religions—all the theistic religions anyway—bind their participants into a relation with real beings, real unembodied agents of great power. A person who takes this position is equally a theistic realist about his or her own religion and about all the others, about his or her gods and about all the other gods.

This is no doubt an extreme view, and probably only a few people will find any initial plausibility in it. Perhaps that is because it seems to over-populate the spiritual world with an ungainly number and variety of gods. But there is a version of this extreme view that eliminates that difficulty. It reduces the total number of the gods to one, thus becoming a version of monotheism. This version consists of saying that not only are all the gods of all the religions real, but also they are in fact just one and the same god. (Maybe such a person would say that the Arameans were right in their realism but mistaken in their polytheism.) Sometimes this position goes under the slogan, "God has many names." The different religions use those different names, but they all really refer to the same being.

Abstractly, this may not be totally implausible. After all, even such a minor luminary as Mark Twain had two full names, and both of those names referred to one and the same man. Why shouldn't God have more than one name? And does not the word "God" have translations and analogues in various languages, words which might have the same referent as the English word though they do not look or sound like that English word? Are not all of those words various names of God?[10]

Nevertheless, there is a serious problem in supposing that the gods of all the religions are identical. The fact is that the different religions give such different descriptions of their gods that it is not logically possible that any one being should satisfy all those descriptions. It does not seem possible, for example, that the omnipotent God of classical Christian theology should find Himself at a disadvantage in the hill country, as the Arameans supposed their own gods to be. So there may be good reason to deny that

---

[10]The word, "God," is anomalous in that it seems to be sometimes used as a proper name (especially when capitalized) and sometimes as a common noun (especially when uncapitalized). The Hebrew scriptures contain a word—the tetragrammaton now often transliterated as "Yahweh"—which is said to be the name of God. But Jews long ago ceased to use this name in speaking about God. And Christians, for some reason, also rarely use it.

the Aramean gods, even if they really exist, are identical with the Christian God.

This is a strong argument, but there is a possible reply to it. People, after all, are not infallible. This is not really a special claim about theology. It applies everywhere. When we undertake to describe some real independent entity—your grandfather, say—we might make some mistake in the description. And to make a mistake about your grandfather we must manage to do two things simultaneously. We must refer somehow to that actual man (your grandfather) and not to someone else, and we must also say something false about him (perhaps even going so far as to deny that he is your grandfather). And so it seems unreasonable to suppose that religious people must always be infallible about their gods. Some of the things people say (and think) about their own gods may be false.[11] We could, therefore, resolve any apparent incompatibility between two putative gods simply by claiming that at least one of the descriptions is mistaken.

A person, therefore, who wants to maintain the identity of the gods might bite the bullet and say that either the Christian theologians are mistaken about the omnipotence of God or the Arameans were mistaken about the finite power of their gods. But that is a hard bullet to bite, at least if we have to bite it a lot. People can surely be mistaken about things, even (or especially?) about gods. But it may strike us as implausible, at least, to think that so many people could be so wildly mistaken about their own gods as this strategy requires. And so we might look for some alternative view.

Three Intermediate Positions

Well, we have seen three extreme views. At one end the most extreme is universal atheism—there are no real gods at all. Moving from that to views that might be consistently adopted by a Christian, one extreme is the position that our god (God) is real and none of the others are real. And at the other end is the position that all of the gods are real, along with its special version that holds that all of the gods are identical. The extremism of these positions is generated mostly by the use of the universal quantifiers, "all" and "none." But there are intermediate positions, and these are generated by using the more modest quantifier, "some," or by specifying one or more particular cases.

---

[11]Who among us would be so rash as to claim that everything we Christians say about God is true? I, at any rate, have no stomach at all for such a claim.

This intermediate set may contain an indefinitely large number of possibilities, depending on various ways of specifying the range of the quantifier "some," or on the specifying of particular cases. This is related to an important logical fact about the intermediate positions. These positions are alternatives, in that they are different from one another. But, by and large, these alternatives are not logically exclusive. Each "some" allows logical room for a different "some." And each particular case allows for other, different, cases. So a reason in favor of adopting one of these views is not automatically a reason against adopting one of the others. There are, after all, a lot of different religions in the world, and a lot of putative gods. Maybe the true story of some of these religions and their gods is different from that of others.

Limited identity

An interesting and important example of an intermediate position is the claim that the gods of *some* different religions are real, and indeed that they are identical. In fact, many Christians appear to believe this about Christianity and Judaism.[12] No doubt a large part of the plausibility of this case is generated by a historical linkage. Though they now seem to be distinct religions, Christianity and Judaism share a good bit of common history. Jesus himself was a Jew, and he remained a Jew to the end. The first Christians were all Jews, and they did not think of themselves as ceasing to be Jews when they became followers of Jesus. Even Paul, the apostle who most vigorously insisted that Gentiles need not become Jews in order to be Christians, seems to have considered himself to be a Jew (and not merely ethnically) to the end of his life. Naturally, these people continued to use the word "God" (actually, of course, the corresponding Greek and Aramaic words) without any feeling that they were changing the reference of that word. They took their Christian faith to be continuous with their Judaism, perhaps in some way a fulfillment of it, and no such change would have struck them as necessary. So the New Testament appears to be written in that way. And now, of course, the Hebrew scriptures, full of pre-Christian references to God, have been adopted as part of the sacred canon of the Christian Bible.

Two thousand years of history have widened and hardened the split between Judaism and Christianity, a split that was just beginning to show in the first century. Now, at any rate, they certainly seem to be distinct

---

[12]A recent example, not at all unusual: "It [the book, *Gentile Tales*] belongs in the library of every Christian (and, for that matter, every Jew) who is concerned about Christians and Jews, and what the former have done to the latter in the name of the God we share" (Winner 2001:25).

religions. And if they are, then together they may provide us with a good example of two religions that have one and the same god (God).

The claim that Jews and Christians *now* "share the same God," however, does seem to require us to adopt a strategy that we mentioned earlier. There is, no doubt, a lot of commonality in the respective descriptions of God—e.g., He is the creator of the world. But there also seem to be some striking differences—e.g., the doctrine of the trinity. So if we do in fact share, and refer to, the same God then some of the descriptions and claims must be mistaken. At least here we have to bite that bullet.

There is a third religion here, Islam, which also has a historical link with Judaism, and with Christianity. In this case, too, there are common elements in the classic Islamic descriptions of Allah and the Jewish and/or Christian claims about God. And there are also differences. The identification of God with Allah is probably more troublesome for many Christians than the idea of "sharing one God" with Jews. But I think that for some Christians, at least, it is a live possibility.

Are there some other cases? Could there be? Well, maybe. There is a provocative story in *Acts* that describes Paul's visit to Athens. He found the city, so it is said, to be "full of idols." But when he was invited to speak to a group of curious Athenians he went so far as to identify God—presumably our God—with the "unknown god" to whom one of the municipal altars was dedicated (Acts 17:16–34). Now, I suppose that might have been just a homiletic strategy on Paul's part, nothing more than a casual tag to give his speech a little local color. But perhaps not. What really happened (spiritually?) when that altar was dedicated and the inscription was written upon it? What if there really was someone (Someone?) out there watching and listening, someone who was interested in that dedication? And maybe that listener really did say something like, "Yes, all right. You have dedicated an altar, and I accept that dedication. I claim that altar now for my own. And someday, maybe soon, I will send someone to stand near my altar, and to speak my claim there in Athens." Could that be? To me, anyway, it seems possible.[13]

Creaturely gods

A different sort of intermediate view might hold that some alien gods (though perhaps not all of them) are real although they are not identical with our god (God). But if they are not identical with our god, then what are they? What could they be?

---

[13]Perhaps we should say that a god who is identical with our god is not really an *alien* god. There is, at most, merely the appearance of otherness because of the different religion and, perhaps, the somewhat different descriptions and names.

Well, if we go back to the minimalist concept we discussed earlier we can find a possible answer. Such a god would be an unembodied rational agent of great power, but still a creature, finite. As we noted earlier, many Christians believe that there really are beings of that sort, maybe many of them. So this would seem to be a live possibility for at least those Christians.

Angels and devils (at least as many Christians think of them) satisfy the minimalist concept. And, in fact, some Christians have thought that the gods of the "heathens" are really devils. Now, a person who says that the god of some other religion is really a devil is pretty clearly expressing a negative and disparaging judgment about that religion. But that person also seems to acknowledge that there is some significant reality associated with that religion. The whole thing is not just a fake. There is something real there—a spiritual reality, or at least a reality which does not seem to be just an element in our "ordinary" world. And so there is a sense in which the devil hypothesis pays a compliment here, the compliment of reality. But, of course, there is the negative element, too. The reality being acknowledged is an evil power, set somehow against a good and holy power. There is a warfare among the gods, god against god (or of God against the gods?).

The idea that the gods are at war is a very old idea, as is also the idea that the warfare "in high places" sometimes spills over into the earth. It is an element in many religions and in many cultures. And, of course, it is present in the Bible, too.[14] So we Christians, at any rate, should not casually dismiss it. And we might well be attracted to the possibility that Satan, the Devil, and/or subordinate and lesser devils, may in fact be the gods of some religions.[15] We would then think of the conflict between religions, or the "competition" of religions for the allegiance of men and women, to be a mirror of the greater cosmological warfare of the agents of good and evil.

But Christians who take seriously the (creaturely) reality of devils are also likely to take seriously the reality of angels. And angels—the unfallen ones, anyway—are usually construed as good. They participate, of course, in a creaturely way in the goodness of God, and they are the servants of God. Is it possible that angels are the gods of some religions? They would presumably be fulfilling some divine commission there, doing their service for God. And I

---

[14]Cf., for example, *Ephesians* 6:10–18, and the pervasive conflict imagery running through the book of *Revelation*.

[15]Ruth Brend, the first reader of this paper, reminded me that there are Satanists who say explicitly that Satan is their god. So here there is a sort of "self-identification" from within one religion in support of the devil hypothesis. For the sort of reason given earlier, we might not take this to be entirely conclusive. But it certainly looks like prima facie evidence, at least.

suppose that this service, if indeed there is such an angelic service, is probably meant to be somehow provisional and temporary. It would be intended to lead in the end to recognition of the lordship of the one high God, the God of gods and the King of kings.

Abstractly, the devil hypothesis and the angel hypothesis seem equally plausible (or implausible). I say "abstractly" because this judgment abstracts from the actual character, history, etc., of the various religions and their associated putative gods. Of course, if we had some general argument or principle that ruled out all devils, or all angels, then our situation would be easier and neater. We would move back in the direction of one or another of the more extreme positions. But I do not have such an argument or principle.

Limited atheism

Finally, there is the view that the gods of some religions are total nonentities. Maybe some putative gods really are the fakes, fictions, or frauds that universal atheists take all the gods to be. And we might have some reason to think that to be true of some particular case. For example, if we have detected some logical contradiction in a theological description, then we have good reason to think that no real being, divine or otherwise, corresponds to that description. But that may not be fully conclusive against the reality of that putative god. For here, too, there is the possibility that the adherents have simply made some theological mistake. Despite their mistake, despite some mixed-up thinking, they may still be in touch with some real god.[16] In that case, the worst that might properly be said of them is that their god does not completely match the description which they give of him.

Conclusion

Limited agnosticism

Well then, how are we to construe those other gods, the alien gods, the gods of other religions? I have no confidence in any of the extreme, universalistic positions. I do not know of good arguments that really support those universal generalizations. So that leaves me somewhere in the middle, with the intermediate views.

---

[16]After all, I think that some Christian theologies contain some contradictory elements. But I do not feel bound to think that the corresponding theologians are not worshippers of God.

There is a lot of "resiliency" in such a position, mainly because these intermediate positions are not mutually exclusive. One can adopt several of them simultaneously. "Different strokes for different folks," some gods are like this and some are like that. And that, I suppose, is the major advantage here. In the middle, we can try to tailor our judgments to fit the multiplicity and variety that we seem to find in religious cartography and religious history. We are not bound to tell exactly the same story about Jews, animists, and Satanists. In fact, some of these stories may be strikingly different from some others.

The resiliency has a price, however. The middle ground invites us to be content with a sort of vagueness, a lack of specificity. This is especially the case where we satisfy ourselves with saying "some," while declining to specify any particular example. And so it may in the end leave us with the feeling of a lot of unresolved questions, loose ends dangling. There might be different strokes for different folks, but we might also want to know just what is the right stroke for this particular folk, what is the right story about this specific god. A position which does not provide an answer for every question of that sort is bound to appear to be incomplete, and in some way unsatisfactory.

But maybe that is just the way it is, for us here and now. The judging of gods is likely to be a difficult task.[17] At the very least, it probably requires a really close and detailed knowledge of the religion involved. And maybe not merely a "theoretical" knowledge, but some knowledge of whatever spiritual reality is there (for good or evil), what are the actual experiences of the worshippers, and so on. That might be hard to achieve, especially from the outside. But if we don't have that sort of knowledge, and hence have no real information or reason on which to base a judgment, then a limited agnosticism would seem to be an honorable position. We are not bound to know the whole truth, or even to have a firm opinion, about every spiritual reality or possibility. A Christian missionary like Kenneth Pike has a divine commission to announce the Gospel, the good news. And the news is indeed good—the news from Bethlehem and Nazareth and Jerusalem, the news from the manger, the cross, and the empty grave. It is the best news in the world—or so, at least, it seems to me. But the world has also heard a lot of other news, indeed a lot of news about the gods. And it may not be our business to render a conclusive judgment about every such piece of news.

---

[17]Is it akin to the "discerning of spirits" mentioned in a list of spiritual gifts in *I Corinthians* 12:10? Perhaps it is a gift as rare as the working of miracles.

References

Mavrodes, George I. 1995. Polytheism. In Thomas D. Senor (ed.), *The rationality of belief and the plurality of faith*, 261–286. Ithaca, N.Y.: Cornell University Press.

Swinburne, Richard. 1970. *The concept of miracle*. London: Macmillan.

Winner, Lauren F. 2001. Killing Jesus all over again. *Books & Cultures* 7(3):25.

17

When the Jacaranda Flowers

Parascientific Cause-Effect Relations in Huallaga (Huánuco) Quechua

David J. Weber

In science-shaped thought ("philosophy," "worldview," "conceptual system,"...) a cause-effect relation typically involves a CAUSE directly impinging on something to produce an EFFECT, or a chain of such impingements from the CAUSE to the EFFECT. ("All science is about adjacency.")

By contrast, Quechua thought encompasses many cause-effect relations that strike us as strange or even superstitious. For example, if we pay someone begrudgingly, the money devalues (and thus will buy less than what it would have, had it been paid willingly). If we toss kernels of white corn near a pregnant cow, the calf will have white spots. If we cook *toquš,*

I first studied linguistics at the Summer Institute of Linguistics at the University of Oklahoma in the summers of 1968 and 1969, when Kenneth Pike's intellectual influence there was immense. His passion for language was contagious, inspiring generations of students. Two ideas particularly affected me. First, Pike was optimistic about mathematics illuminating aspects of language. This coincided with my interests and led me to do an undergraduate degree in mathematics, which was essential for the contributions I later made to computational morphology and automated adaptation. Second, Pike conceived of linguistics as encompassing far more than the simple mechanics of language; he saw language as pervasively interwoven with humanness. This strongly influenced my research, particularly my ventures into the Quechua lexicon and the conception of the world on which it is based. It also led me to appreciate the complementarity of formal and functional approaches to language.

a pungent pudding, near a setting hen, the eggs will rot (lit., become pudding). I will call ideas like these "parascientific cause-effect relations." The title of this paper was inspired by just such a bit of ancient wisdom shared by don Ignacio Cayco Daza: "Don't go down into the valleys when the jacaranda flowers; you will get malaria." The appendix lists many more examples of parascientific cause-effect relations.

This essay reports a preliminary exploration into some of the underpinnings of Quechua thought, in an attempt to discover what makes such parascientific cause-effect relations reasonable. The cognitive approach pursued is that of Lakoff and Johnson's *Philosophy in the flesh* (1999) and Sperber's *Explaining culture: A naturalistic approach* (1996). Unless otherwise stated the data are from Huallaga (Huánuco) Quechua, henceforth HgQ, much of which is drawn from Weber et al. (1998).[1]

First, I sketch Lakoff and Johnson's notions of spatial schema and primary metaphors and show how they apply to HgQ. Then in the second and third sections, I comment on Quechua metaphors for events and causes, and I argue that what at first blush seem to be cases of "contagion" are better understood in terms of "magnetism." I conclude with a speculation about a deep cognitive predisposition that might account for many of the observations made in this essay.

Spatial Schemas and Primary Metaphors

Lakoff and Johnson claim that two SPATIAL SCHEMAS are at the very heart of human cognition. These are as follows (1999:32, 33):

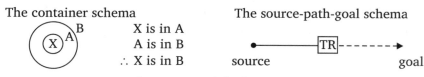

The container schema   The source-path-goal schema

X is in A
A is in B
∴ X is in B

source   goal

Figure 1. Spatial schemas.

Lakoff and Johnson (1999:30–31) state:

> Spatial-relations concepts are at the heart of our conceptual system. They are what make sense of space for us. They characterize what spatial form is and define spatial inference....

[1]Felix Cayco Zambrano, Teodoro Cayco Villar and, to a lesser extent, Pablo Villogas Javier provided most of the data on which this paper is based. Other friends, especially David Coombs, Rick Floyd, and Tom Headland, gave feedback on an earlier draft. To all I am most grateful. Of course, I—not they—am responsible for the errors.

> We use spatial-relations concepts unconsciously, and we impose
> them via our perceptual and conceptual systems. We just automati-
> cally and unconsciously "perceive" one entity as *in, on,* or *across
> from* another entity. However, such perception depends on an enor-
> mous amount of automatic unconscious mental activity on our part.

Then, according to Lakoff and Johnson, there are PRIMARY METAPHORS.
These develop because (1) our neural system involves "spreading activa-
tion," and (2) when two areas of the neural system are frequently activated
at the same time, "cross-domain co-activation" may occur. Primary metaphors are the result of the co-activation of a subjective domain and a
sensorimotor domain.

For example, the primary metaphor AFFECTION IS WARMTH involves
the co-activation of the subjectve domain "affection" and the
sensorimotor domain "temperature." Feeling warmth and affection simultaneously, whether as an infant being cuddled or as an adult being em-
braced, involves the co-activation of affection and warmth, and this
manifests itself in various ways, such as in expressions like "They greeted
me *warmly.*"

Lakoff and Johnson write (1999:56–57):

> Primary metaphors are part of the cognitive unconscious. We ac-
> quire them automatically and unconsciously via the normal process
> of neural learning and may be unaware that we have them. We
> have no choice in this process. When the embodied experiences in
> the world are universal, then the corresponding primary metaphors
> are universally acquired. This explains the widespread occurrence
> around the world of a great many primary metaphors....
>
> Contrary to long-standing opinion about metaphors, primary met-
> aphor is *not* the result of a conscious multistage process of
> interpretation. Rather it is a matter of immediate conceptual map-
> ping via neural connections.

Lakoff and Johnson (1999:50–54) list some representative primary
metaphors. For most of these my Quechua coworkers were readily able to
provide evidence for the metaphor in Huallaga Quechua (HgQ) or the
closely related Pachitea dialect (PnQ). (The following abbreviations are
used: SubjJudg: subjective judgement, SensMotDom: sensorimotor domain, EngEx: English example, PrimExp: primary experience, and QueEx:
Quechua example(s).)[2]

---

[2]The format has been changed from Lakoff and Johnson's presentation of the metaphors, but
their wording has been retained for SubjJudg, SensMotDom, EngEx, and PrimExp. The Quechua
orthography used is that used by most Quechua scholars.

Affection is warmth

SubjJudg: Affection; SensMotDom: Temperature; EngEx: "They greeted me *warmly*"; PrimExp: Feeling warm while being held affectionately; QueEx: No evidence found for Quechua.

Important is big

SubjJudg: Importance; SensMotDom: Size; EngEx: "Tomorrow is a *big* day"; PrimExp: As a child, finding that big things, e.g., parents, are important and can exert major forces on you and dominate your visual experience; QueEx: *hatun fista* 'big fiesta' (but *hatun runa* 'big man' not: 'important man'); *hatun awturida:* 'important authority'; *hatun marka* 'politically important town'.

Happy is up

SubjJudg: Happiness; SensMotDom: Bodily orientation; EngEx: "I'm feeling *up* today"; PrimExp: Feeling happy and energetic and having an upright posture (correlation between affective state and posture); QueEx: PnQ: *altuĉo kaykan* 'he has possessions and is happy' (lit., 'he is above').

Intimacy is closeness

SubjJudg: Intimacy; SensMotDom: Being physically close; EngEx: "We've been *close* for years, but we're beginning to *drift* apart"; PrimExp: Being physically close to people you are intimate with; QueEx: *huk matiaʎpita mikun* 'they are intimate' (lit., 'they eat from the same dish'); *laqwanakun* 'they are very intimate' (lit., 'they lick each other'); *rakikaška:* 'we had a parting of the ways' (lit., 'we separated').

Bad is stinky

SubjJudg: Evaluation; SensMotDom: Smell; EngEx: "This movie *stinks*"; PrimExp: Being repelled by foul-smelling objects (correlation between evaluative and olfactory experience); QueEx: *kučipa sikin* 'devil' (lit., 'pig's ass'); *asyaq* 'devil' (lit.,'one that stinks'); *kapši/či:bu* 'large male goat' (which are associated with the devil because they stink); *qanra runa* 'immoral person' (lit., 'filthy person').

Difficulties are burdens

SubjJudg: Difficulty; SensMotDom: Muscular exertion; EngEx: "She's *weighed down* by responsibilities"; PrimExp: The discomfort or disabling effect of lifting or carrying heavy objects; QueEx: Some fiesta cargos are *ankaš* 'light' requiring less money to do, while others are *hatun* 'big'; And about work one can say *pasaypa ñitiyka:man* '(my work) is overwhelming me' (lit., 'it really presses on me').

There is a related metaphor: RESPONSIBILITIES ARE PAIN, e.g., *awnišan nanan* 'what he agreed to do was difficult' (lit., 'painful').

More is up

SubjJudg: Quantity; SensMotDom: Vertical orientation; EngEx: "Prices are *high*"; PrimExp: Observing rise and fall of levels of piles and fluids as more is added or subtracted; QueEx: HgQ: *wičaša*/PnQ: *higaša* 'the price increased' (lit., 'it went up'); *hanan hanan mikuša* 'he ate more and more/again and again' (lit., 'on top of, on top of he ate'); *hanan hanan ruraykan* 'he does it again and again' (lit., 'on top of, on top of he is doing it'); *tuñiša* 'he went bankrupt' (lit., 'he fell').

Categories are containers
SubjJudg: Perception of kinds; SensMotDom: Space; EngEx: "Are tomatoes *in* the fruit or vegetable category?"; PrimExp: Observing similar objects clustered together (flowers, trees, rocks, buildings, dishes); QueEx: *tinkun* 'it is the same' (lit., 'it meets'); PnQ: *hayanakuykan* 'they are almost the same color' (lit., 'they call each other to come').

Linear scales are paths
SubjJudg: Degree; SensMotDom: Motion; EngEx: "John's intelligence *goes way beyond* Bill's"; PrimExp: Observing the amount of progress made by an object in motion (correlation between motion and scalar notion of degree); QueEx: *ʎaʎi-* 'to outdo in study, work,…' (lit., 'to beat in a race'); *yačakuyta ʎaʎiša* 'he outdid him in learning'.

Organization is physical structure
SubjJudg: Abstract unifying relationships; SensMotDom: Experience of physical objects; EngEx: "How do the *pieces* of this theory *fit together?*"; PrimExp: Interacting with complex objects and attending to their structure (correlation between observing part-whole structure and forming cognitive representations of logical relationships; QueEx: *šunqu: mana časkinču* 'it is inconsistent with my perspective (lit., my heart does not receive it)'; *šonqo:wan mana tinkunču* 'I can not accept that (proposition)' (lit., 'it does not meet with my heart').

Help is support
SubjJudg: Assistance; SensMotDom: Physical support; EngEx: *"Support* your local charities"; PrimExp: Observing that some entities and people require physical support in order to continue functioning; QueEx: PnQ: *tunkapti:pis mana ušašču* 'although I supported (upheld) him, he did not finish (e.g., school)'; PnQ: *hoqari-* 'to help (lift up) the poor'.

Time is motion
SubjJudg: The passage of time; SensMotDom: Motion; EngEx: "Time *flies*"; PrimExp: Experiencing the passage of time as one moves or observes motion; QueEx: *wañunayki o:ra čayamun* 'the hour of your death approaches'; *mikunanči o:ra pa:sašana* 'the time we were to eat has passed'.

States are locations
SubjJudg: A subjective state; SensMotDom: Being in a bounded region of space; EngEx: "I'm *close to* being *in* a depression and the next thing that goes wrong will *send me over the edge*"; PrimExp: Experiencing a certain state as correlated with a certain location (e.g., being cool under a tree, feeling secure in bed); QueEx: PnQ: *hišyaman čayaša* 'he became sick' (lit., 'he arrived to sickness'); HgQ: *mučuyčaw kayka:* 'I am lacking' (lit., 'I am in a famine'); *makinčaw kayka-* 'to be under his control/authority' (lit., 'in his hand').

Change is motion
SubjJudg: Experiencing a change of state; SensMotDom: Moving; EngEx: "My car has *gone from* bad *to* worse lately"; PrimExp: Experiencing the change of state that

goes with the change of location as you move; QueEx: *uyšapa kulurnin tikran* 'the color of the sheep changes' (lit., 'turns'); *aywaka:kun* 'he is gravely ill (he goes completely)'.

Actions are self-propelled motions
SubjJudg: Action; SensMotDom: Moving your body through space; EngEx: "I'm *moving* right along on the project"; PrimExp: The common action of moving yourself through space, especially in the early years of life; QueEx: *aʎipa aywayka:* 'my endeavors are prospering' (lit., 'I am going well').

Purposes are destinations
SubjJudg: Achieving a purpose; SensMotDom: Reaching a destination; EngEx: "He'll ultimately be successful, but he isn't *there* yet"; PrimExp: Reaching destinations throughout everyday life and thereby achieving purposes (e.g., if you want a drink, you have to go to the water cooler); QueEx: *alkaldiman yaykuša* 'he became mayor' (lit., 'he entered into being mayor'); *alkaldi kayman mana čayašaču* 'he was not able to become mayor' (lit., 'he did not arrive to being mayor').

Purposes are desired objects
SubjJudg: Achieving a Purpose; SensMotDom: Object manipulation; EngEx: "I saw an opportunity for success and *grabbed* it"; PrimExp: Grasping a desired object (correlation between satisfaction and holding a desired physical object); QueEx: *yarpaša:ta tariška:* 'I was able to do what I intended to do' (lit., 'I found what I thought').

Causes are physical forces
SubjJudg: Achieving results; SensMotDom: Exertion of force; EngEx: "They *pushed* the bill *through* Congress"; PrimExp: Achieving results by exerting forces on physical objects to move or change them; QueEx: *kaʎpaykur šamuška:* 'I came against all odds/doing whatever it took' (lit., 'exerting physical force').

Relationships are enclosures
SubjJudg: An interpersonal relationship; SensMotDom: Being in an enclosure; EngEx: "We've been *in* a *close* relationship for years, but it's beginning to seem *confining*"; PrimExp: Living in the same enclosed physical space with the people you are most closely related to; QueEx: No evidence found for Quechua.

Control is up
SubjJudg: Being in control; SensMotDom: Vertical orientation; EngEx: "Don't worry! I'm *on top of* the situation"; PrimExp: Finding that it is easier to control another person or exert force on an object from above, where you have gravity working with you; QueEx: *altučaw kaykan* 'he wins the argument' (lit., 'he is above'); *hanaqčaw ke:raša* 'he won the argument' (lit., 'he remained above').

Knowing is seeing
SubjJudg: Knowledge; SensMotDom: Vision; EngEx: "I *see* what you mean"; PrimExp: Getting information through vision; QueEx: Possibly: *reqsi-* 'to be acquainted with (someone)' This verb strongly implies seeing that person.

Understanding is grasping
SubjJudg: Comprehension; SensMotDom: Object manipulation; EngEx: "I've never been able to *grasp* transfinite numbers"; PrimExp: Getting information about an object by grasping and manipulating it; QueEx: *uma: mana čarinču* 'I do not understand' (lit., 'my head does not grasp').

Seeing is touching
SubjJudg: Visual perception; SensMotDom: Touch; EngEx: "She *picked* my face *out* of the crowd"; PrimExp: Correlation between the visual and tactile exploration of objects; QueEx: PnQ: *takanakuška:* 'We encountered each other' (lit., 'we abutted each other'). This can be said even when seeing each other at a distance.

Note that my Quechua coworkers were unable to find evidence for only two of the primary metaphors in this list: AFFECTION IS WARMTH and RELATIONSHIPS ARE ENCLOSURES. However, we did discover a primary metaphor not on this list:[3]

Favoring is facing
SubjJudg: Favor; SensMotDom: Orienting the face toward; EngEx: "At first he *looked* on me with favor but then he *turned* away"; PrimExp: Parents, sibling,…face a child when showing it appreciation; QueEx: *aʎi rikanakun* 'they are intimate' (lit., 'look at each other'); *tikrapanakuša* 'they parted ways' (lit., 'they turned their backs on each other').

Cause-Effect Relations in the Flesh —Quechua Flesh, That Is!

Beyond spatial schemas and primary metaphors, there are a host of other metaphors, some formed by combining simpler metaphors. Lakoff and Johnson (1999:49) write: "Complex metaphors are formed from primary ones through conventional conceptual blending, that is, the fitting together of small metaphorical 'pieces' into larger wholes."

I will now comment briefly on a few of the metaphors that Lakoff and Johnson mention in discussing events and causes, particularly those of their chapter 11. First, however, a couple of caveats are in order: (1) I am not a native speaker of Quechua nor have I studied these matters sufficiently to be dogmatic about anything. Sperber (1996:38) writes, "In our everyday striving to understand others, we make do with partial and speculative interpretations (the more different from us the other, the more speculative the interpretations)." For the present the reader will have to do with my "partial and speculative" interpretations. (2) I do not question

---

[3]This, of course, is not surprising given that there are probably several hundred primary metaphors.

the validity of the metaphors Lakoff and Johnson posit *for English,* only their validity *for Quechua.* Obviously different languages employ different metaphors and different expressions based on them.[4]

Lakoff and Johnson (1999:177) write:

> Here is what we have found to be the literal skeletal concept of causation: *a cause is a determining factor for a situation,* where by a "situation" we mean a state, change, process, or action. Inferentially, this is extremely weak. All it implies is that *if the cause were absent and we knew nothing more, we could not conclude that the situation existed.*

This fits Quechua nicely because the causative suffix *-či* may mean either 'to force, to make,...' or 'to allow, to permit,...'.[5] Indeed, in some cases the causative simply indicates a "determining factor for a situation," as in, e.g., *orkistapis quyan kumunkunata qačwačir* 'the band spends the day having the (people of) the community dance'. The musicians provide the determining factor, music, for the situation, the people of the community dancing.

Metaphors may come in pairs ("DUALS") differing in terms of figure and ground. Lakoff and Johnson (1999:195) give the following example:

> Harry's in trouble. (States Are Locations)
> Harry has trouble. (Attributes Are Possessions)
>
> In the first case, trouble is conceptualized as a location you are in; in the second, it is an object you can have. The difference can be seen as a figure-ground shift. In the first case Harry is a figure and trouble is the ground with respect to which the figure is located. In the second case, Harry is the ground and the figure, trouble, is located with respect to him. Grounds are, of course, taken as stationary and figures as movable relative to them.

As a further example, consider vision. Lakoff and Johnson (1999:54) posit the SEEING IS TOUCHING metaphor in which the perceiver directs

---

[4]For example, in English we speak of work multiplying (e.g., *My work is piling up, It seems each day I have more and more work*) to indicate that there is more and more *pending* work. Similar expressions in HgQ mean that one is *accomplishing* more and more work: *Aruyne: miraykan.* 'I am progressing in my work (lit., my work is multiplying)'; *Aruyta mana miračiyču. Pasaypa ñitiyka:man.* 'I am not making progress in my work (lit., I do not cause work to multiply). It is overwhelming me (lit., it is pressing on me)'.

[5]At the airport in Huánuco, Peru, it is customary for the airport staff to start the fire engine and sound its siren when an airplane is about to land. I was once waiting for a plane next to a boy about four or five years of age. When the siren began to sound I asked him (in Spanish), "Why is the siren sounding?" He replied, *"So that* (Para que) the airplane can come."

vision against the perceived. By contrast, Quechua favors the dual of this, what I will call the SEEING IS BEING TOUCHED metaphor, in which seeing is being affected by an image that travels to and impinges upon the perceiver. Grammatical evidence for this is seen in the way the directional suffix *-mu* 'toward here' is used with verbs of perceiving or emitting; see Weber (1989:section 9.2.2.4).

SEEING IS TOUCHING   SEEING IS BEING TOUCHED

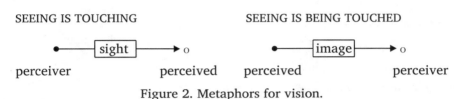

perceiver   perceived   perceived   perceiver

Figure 2. Metaphors for vision.

Lakoff and Johnson (1999:178–179) claim that there are two fundamental metaphors for events and causes, the LOCATION EVENT-STRUCTURE metaphor and the OBJECT EVENT-STRUCTURE metaphor. "Both make use of the primary metaphors Causes Are Forces and Changes Are Movements." They are duals of each other, as can be seen in the following (partial)[6] list of submetaphors:

> LOCATION EVENT-STRUCTURE metaphor:
> STATES ARE LOCATIONS
> CHANGES ARE MOVEMENTS (TO OR FROM LOCATIONS)
> CAUSATION IS FORCED MOVEMENT (TO OR FROM LOCATIONS)
> PURPOSES ARE DESIRED LOCATIONS (DESTINATIONS)
> OBJECT EVENT-STRUCTURE metaphor:
> ATTRIBUTES ARE POSSESSIONS
> CHANGES ARE MOVEMENTS OF POSSESSIONS (ACQUISITIONS OR
>   LOSSES)
> CAUSATION IS TRANSFER OF POSSESSIONS (GIVING OR TAKING)
> PURPOSES ARE DESIRED OBJECTS

Lakoff and Johnson (1999:199) say, "In the Location metaphor, the affected entity is the figure; it moves to the new location (the ground). In the Object metaphor, the effect is the figure; it moves to the affected party (the ground)."

Let us first consider the LOCATION EVENT-STRUCTURE metaphor. About this metaphor Lakoff and Johnson write (1999:194), "[The Location branch of the event-structure metaphor] is one of the most profound and most used metaphors in our conceptual system, since it lays out the

---

[6]The full list for the LOCATION EVENT-STRUCTURE metaphor is given on Lakoff and Johnson's page 179 and the full list for the OBJECT EVENT-STRUCTURE metaphor on page 198.

fundamental means of conceptualizing our most basic concepts: states, changes, causes, actions, difficulties, freedom of action, and purposes." Given this, we expect evidence to abound for the LOCATION EVENT-STRUCTURE metaphor, but for Quechua that does not seem to be the case; indeed, evidence is rather scarce. And this is also true for the metaphors that make up the LOCATION EVENT-STRUCTURE metaphor, as we will now see.

States are locations
Some evidence for this primary metaphor was given in the preceding section. However, I think that, overall, Quechua makes relatively little use of the STATES ARE LOCATIONS metaphor.[7]

Change is motion (movement)
Some evidence for this primary metaphor (Lakoff and Johnson 1999:52) was given in the preceding section. To that we may add the use of the motion verb *čaya-* 'to arrive' to mean 'to come to maturity, to become fully cooked'; e.g., *papaqa čayašanami.* 'the potatoes have fully cooked' (lit., 'the potatoes have now arrived').

Causes are forces
For the Causes Are Forces (Causation Is Forced Movement) metaphor, we might take as evidence the causative of *čaya-* 'to arrive', that is *čaya-či-*. It can mean 'to bring/take' (lit., 'cause to arrive here/there') or 'to bring to completion in cooking', 'to finish cooking'. The following illustrates the second meaning: *mirinde:raykiqa mikuyta yanukur manaraqmi čayačinraqču.* 'your midday-meal-cook is cooking your food but has not yet brought it to completion' (lit., '...caused it to arrive').

Purposes are destinations
HgQ examples were given for this primary metaphor in the preceding section; however, they are somewhat dubious because "becoming mayor" is not clearly a purpose. Perhaps better evidence can be found in the purpose-motion construction (Weber 1983: section 5.4.2). It must use a motion verb like *aywa-* 'go', as in *miku-q aywa-* (eat-agent go-) 'to go to eat'. However, the purpose does not bear a case marker indicating that it is the target of motion. The purpose is *miku-q* 'to eat', but it is not the goal of *aywa-* 'go', so this, too, is only weak evidence. Nor is evidence found with the more general purpose construction; e.g., *mikunaykipaq yanukuška:* 'I cooked it for you to eat'. This has no movement-indicating case marking. (One might expect, for example, *-man* 'goal'.)

In sum, it seems that some of the metaphors that compose (through conceptual blending) the LOCATION EVENT-STRUCTURE metaphor are only

---

[7]Also, I did not find evidence in HgQ for the ACTION-LOCATION metaphor (Lakoff and Johnson 1999:204). Apparent exceptions like *waqayman čuraka-* 'begin to cry' (lit., 'put oneself to crying') are obvious calques from Spanish *ponerse a llorar.*

weakly present in Quechua. Perhaps this is why the LOCATION EVENT-STRUCTURE metaphor itself finds only weak support.

Now let us consider some of the metaphors that make up the OBJECT EVENT-STRUCTURE metaphor.

Attributes are possessions

Lakoff and Johnson (1999:195) cite *"have* a headache" as evidence of an attribute being possessed. This is a bit strange because a headache is not a sort of property or characteristic of a person, but rather a malady that they occasionally suffer. At any rate, in HgQ one would say *uma-nanay čarimaša,* literally 'a headache grabbed me.' (Illnesses, sneezes, anger,... "grasp" or "take hold" of a person. When the affected person recovers, the malady "releases" her/him.)

There are three ways the possession, acquisition, or loss of an attribute might be expressed in Quechua.

1. It might be expressed lexically, as with the verb *čara-* 'to have' but, to my knowledge, this is never the case. When an expression like Sp. *tiene buena voluntad* 'he has good will' is transliterated into Quechua, the result is at best very amusing.

2. It might be expressed with the well-oiled genitive construction (described in Weber 1976), used to express ownership, part-whole relations, kinship relations, origin....However, its use to indicate having a property is quite limited; two cases have come to light:

    First, there are cases with expressions of dimension: *altu* 'high', *ančhu* 'wide' (both borrowed from Spanish), and *raku* 'girth, thickness'; e.g., *kay wasipa altuyninqa kimsa čunka metrumi.* 'this house is thirty meters tall' (lit., 'the height of this house is thirty meters'); *rakuynin kaša huk kiñuyaʎ* 'it's girth was one armful (as measured under the arm)'.

    And second, there are a few derived nominals: *aka-y* 'warmth' (e.g., *intipa akaynin* 'the sun's rays/warmth'), *asyay* 'odor (foul)' (e.g., *yunkapa asyayninmi kay asyayqa* 'this is certainly the smell of the rain forest'), *mušku-y* 'odor (good)' (e.g., *aʎI muškuynin.* 'its smell is good'), *muna-y* 'power, authority' (e.g., *munaynikičaw kayka:* 'I am in your power'). Note that in each of these cases the supposed attribute (warmth, odor, power) is something projected from the object, not a simple property of the object.

3. It might be expressed with the suffix *-yoq* 'having', or *-sapa* 'having much', or *-ynaq* 'not having' (described in Weber 1989: section 4.2.1). This case is well attested. In the examples that follow, note the diversity of relationships indicated (part-whole, social-kinship, origin, and so forth); it is not clear that all are based on the metaphor of a thing "possessing" an attribute.

> muruyoq 'seed bearing' ('having seeds'); kašayoq 'thorny' ('having
> thorns'); miʎwayoq 'woolbearing' ('having wool'); hučayoq 'guilty' ('having
> sin or guilt'); čaniyoq 'expensive' ('having a high price'); yačayniyoq 'wise',
> 'knowledgeable'; munayniyoq 'powerful (having power or authority)';
> runayoq 'married' ('having a man'); wasiyoq 'landlord' ('having a house');
>
> aqčasapa 'hairy' ('having much hair'); miʎwasapa 'woolly' ('having much
> wool');
>
> aqčaynaq 'hairless'; wasiynaq 'homeless'.

So there is evidence that HgQ has the Attributes Are Possessions
metaphor.

Changes are movements

There is little *direct* evidence for this metaphor. If the occurrence of -*man*
'goal' is sufficient evidence for movement, then the following (from
Weber 1989: sections 10.6.3 and 10.11.1) can be taken as evidence:
aʎčaka:čiran kašannaw sa:nu-**man** 'he cured him (so that he became) well
like he was (before)'; kumlitakan huk runa ente:ru-**man** 'he completes himself into a man (out of dissociated body parts)'.

However, given that turning is a kind of movement, *indirect* support for
the Changes Are Movements metaphor can be seen in the Changing Is
Turning metaphor (Lakoff and Johnson 1999:207), for which there is ample evidence: rumiman tikraša 'it turned into a stone'; rumiman tikračiša 'it
caused it to turn into a stone'. iškan tikraša huknayaʎman. 'the two became
one' (lit., 'the two of them turned toward only one'); and libruta tikračiša
runa-šimiman 'he translated the book into Quechua' (lit., 'He made the
book turn into people-speech').

In these examples, not only can we take -*man* 'goal' as evidence for movement but also the primary meaning of tikra- 'to turn' indicates physical motion, as in aywaykašaykičaw pitapis mana rikarqa qepaman tikranki 'while you
are going, if you do not see anyone, turn around'; and uyšapa aqiiʎnta
tikrarkur awimunki 'go rinse the sheep's intestines, turning them inside out'.[8]

Limited evidence for the third submetaphor, Causation Is Transfer Of
Possessions, can be seen in examples like hučayoqya:čiša 'he made him
guilty' (lit., 'He caused him to become one who has guilt'); pačasapaya:čiša

---

[8]Contrast this transitive use of tikra- 'turn inside out' with the derived form tikra-či- 'cause to
rotate'. Other derived forms are: tikra-pa:- ~ tikra-pU- 'to turn an evil back on the perpetrator', 'to
redirect some harm onto its source', e.g., hukta hitapar dimandučaw ga:naykaptin kikinta tikrapaša 'he
was succeeding in blaming another, but it backfired on him'; maqayta munaykapte: tikrapamaša
'when I tried to hit him, he turned it back on me' (i.e., 'he hit me'); and tikra-pu (noun) 'sickness
passed from something used in šuqpi curing to the person carrying it'. Note that these all imply the
transfer of something negative, as discussed in the following section.

'he made her pregnant' (lit., 'cause to have a big stomach'); and *munayniyoqya:čiša* 'he made him powerful'.

Evidence for the fourth metaphor, Purposes Are Desired Objects, was given in the preceding section.

In sum, there is evidence in Quechua for the four submetaphors of the OBJECT EVENT-STRUCTURE metaphor listed previously.

Given these snapshots, Quechua seems to favor the OBJECT EVENT-STRUCTURE metaphor over the LOCATION EVENT-STRUCTURE metaphor. In terms of the source-path-goal schema (figure 1) the favored metaphor presents the affected as the goal, part of the ground (stationary), the effect presented as the figure that moves to impinge on the ground. What is significant for my thesis is that the favored alternative is consonant with the affected being passive, being neither the instigator of nor the source of energy for change.

Magnetism, not Contagion

In this section I consider some parascientific cause-effect relations that, at first blush, seem to instantiate "contagion." However, I claim that they are better understood in terms of another concept, which I will call "magnetism."

Various parascientific cause-effect relations fall under what anthropologists refer to as "contagion" or "sympathetic magic":[9]

1. There are cases like those mentioned in the introduction: cooking *toqush* pudding near a setting hen, thereby causing the eggs to rot (become like pudding); tossing kernels of white corn near a pregnant cow to make her calf have white spots.

---

[9]Priest et al. 1995:13 give the following definitions:

> HOMEOPATHIC MAGIC is based on the principle of similarity or imitation—that like produces like. For example, if you can harm a doll made in someone's image, you thereby harm the person the image is of. CONTAGIOUS MAGIC stresses the principle of contact or contiguity, that physical contact transfers the character or properties of one item to another. Magic designed to heal a barren women, for example, might apply contact with a fertile hen egg, thereby attempting to transfer its fecundity to the woman. An extension of this principle is the idea that two items which come in contact with each other come to share a common essence linking them together. By acting on one such object one can affect the other. By taking a person's cast-off clothing and applying poison to it, one harms the former owner with whom the clothing is believed still to share a common essence. Magic employing these two principles is commonly referred to as SYMPATHETIC MAGIC.

2.   Floyd (1997) describes[10] many ways a fetus may be affected during gesta-
        tion by its mother's behavior or environment: her being in a place where
        she might be "grabbed by Satan," her seeing[11] or being near an animal so
        that the child is born with some characteristic (physical or behavioral) of
        that animal, and so forth.[12]
              And Floyd (1997:18) discusses how these can be cured: "Contagion is
        counteracted by recontagion with the contaminating object....The princi-
        ple of imitation, an item emanating an analogous influence on something
        around it, is at work in [the contagion and curing] contexts." Floyd
        (1997:22) concludes: "[Contagion and curing] tie the unexplainable to the
        concrete by discovering a metaphorical relationship between a physical
        condition or behavior and an element in the environment. They impute a
        transfer of this shared quality by means of contact and subsequent conta-
        gion by imitation."

3.   There is a curing practice, šoqpi-, in which something with the capacity to
        absorb (a fresh egg, a live guinea pig,...) is rubbed on the sick person's
        body, lingering particularly in the area of greatest pain.[13] The illness is
        drawn out of the body into the guinea pig, (egg,...).

These all involve the transfer of some characteristic—usually a
negative one—from one being to another, more vulnerable one. The affected always comes to resemble more closely the one that contributes the
characteristic. (There are no "dissimilations," that is, cases in which the
affected becomes somehow different from the contributor.) There are two
conditions for this transfer: PROXIMITY: the affected being must be sufficiently near the contributor and SUSCEPTIBILITY: the affected being must
be susceptible or vulnerable. Most commonly, it is either unborn (a fetus,
an egg) or recently born, that is, something that lacks characteristics and
is in the process of acquiring them.

---

[10]Floyd's research focused on a Quechua language in Huancayo, Peru, but similar beliefs and
practices are found throughout central Peru. See also Groenewald (forthcoming) which mentions
similar beliefs in Lambayeque Quechua, which belongs to the North Peruvian branch of the
Quechua language family.

[11]Being affected by perception is entirely consonant with the SEEING IS BEING TOUCHED
metaphor; see figure 2.

[12]The phenomena whereby a fetus is affected during gestation by its mother's behavior or
environment discussed by Floyd (1997) is, in Huancayo Quechua, called mipa. I posit that its
etymology is /*mi-pa/ where, /*mi-/ 'ingest, eat' is followed by an old nominalizer /*-pa/.
Evidence for /*mi-/ 'ingest' is seen in (widespread) reflexes like miku- 'eat', miči- 'to pasture', and
mirkapa 'food eaten on a trip, snacks'. Evidence for an old nominalizer -pa is seen in HgQ words
kaʎapa 'fork', kañapa 'burned place', kutipa 'relapse', mirkapa 'snack', paka:pa 'hiding place', pučupa
'leftovers', rika:pa 'lookout', riqsipa 'recognizable', qasapa 'frost', tukapa 'staff', wiʎapa 'news', etc.

[13]Mančakaypita aʎčaka:nanpaq hakawan šoqpiša. 'They cured him of fright by rubbing him with a
guinea pig'.

By the way, age is not a factor in the selection of a guinea pig to be used in the *šoqpi-* curing practice. An adult is usually used. The significant factor is the absence of color: the best guinea pig is totally black. Presumably because of the absence of color a black guinea pig—by virtue of lacking characteristics—is more "absorbant" than a colored guinea pig.

What makes the beliefs described earlier and in the appendix rational for Quechua people?[14] What fundamental aspects of the Quechua system of thought make it reasonable to believe, for example, that a child developing in a mother's womb can be affected by what the mother sees? As an initial attempt to answer this question, I posit two premises of Quechua thought: (1) beings are by nature "loosely knit" (malleable, changeable, susceptible, fluid, unstable,...), and (2) beings that come in contact tend to become more similar.

The first premise stands in contrast to the "modern" view that beings are by nature tightly knit, stable, concrete....Most Westerners, it seems, do not believe that one part of us—say our soul—can be dislodged from our body, or that we can turn into some other sort of being and then at a later time resume our human form. For us, living beings and other physical objects are extremely time-stable.

But this view is not universal. Regarding the Irish, for example, Cahill (1995:129) writes:

> ...the Irish believed that gods, druids, poets, and others in touch with the magical world could be literal shape-shifters....
>
> But however wonderful this instability may have seemed to the conscious Irish imagination, it had its dark side as well, for it suggested subconsciously that reality had no predictable pattern, but was arbitrary and insubstantial. There is within this worldview a terrifying personal implication: that I myself have no fixed identity but am, like the rest of reality, essentially fluid—essentially inessential. Of course, the Irish had no way of expressing such ideas directly. One needs a sense of identity before one can complain of

[14]Sperber (1996:38) states: "A deeper understanding of intentions involves grasping how they could be rational, or, in other words, seeing how they might follow from underlying desires and beliefs." He further writes (1996:85):

> Anthropologists and psychologists alike tend to assume that humans are rational—not perfectly rational, not rational all the time, but rational enough. What is meant by rationality may vary, or be left vague, but it always implies at least the following ideas: human beliefs are produced by cognitive processes which are on the whole epistemologically sound; that is, humans approximately perceive what there is for them to perceive and approximately infer what their perceptions warrant. Of course, there are perceptual illusions and inferential failures, and the resulting overall representation of the world is not totally consistent; but, as they are, the beliefs of humans allow them to form and pursue goals in a manner which often enough leads to the achievement of those goals.

its absence. But this wonderful and terrifying instability haunts virtually every sentence of the ancient literature.

Here are some points that corroborate for Quechua the first premise (Beings are loosely knit):

1.   It seems to underlie beliefs like, for example, when a child falls, its life-force may be dislodged from its body, causing a malady called "fright." This can be cured by rubbing the child's body with earth from the place where the child fell, which realigns the life-force and body.

2.   Quechua folklore has many cases of one thing showing up as another, as a skunk showing up as a young woman, a god showing up as a beggar, and so forth. (Adelaar [1994] discusses various cases found in the Huarochirí manuscript.)

3.   In traditional Quechua thought mountains are beings. Whereas for Westerners mountains are regarded as solid, for Quechua people they are fluid: tremors, landslides, and erosion reflect that mountains, like other beings, are loosely knit.

Regarding the second premise, consider Lakoff and Johnson's primary metaphor SIMILARITY IS CLOSENESS, which has the following properties (1999:51):

Subjective judgment: Similarity
Sensorimotor domain: Proximity in space
Primary experience: Observing similar objects clustered together
                        (flowers, trees, rocks, buildings, dishes)

This metaphor relates similarity and proximity statically. Suppose we add a temporal dimension. There are two obvious possibilities:

1.   Similarity is prior to proximity, that is, things that are similar come together. ("Birds of a feather flock together.")

2.   Proximity is prior to similarity, that is, things that are together become similar. ("One bad apple spoils the whole lot.")

The second of these possibilities is precisely the second premise stated above: beings that come in contact tend to become more similar.

Evidence for the relationship between proximity and similarity can be seen most clearly in the use of *tinku-* 'to meet', 'to encounter'. The core meaning of this verb is the meeting of two directed paths, such as the paths of two people who meet each other somewhere. Or they might be the paths of two rivers that meet; throughout Peru one finds *tinku* in the names of places where two rivers meet, e.g., *Tingo María*. It might even be the upward "growth paths" of living things, which might "meet" at the same height.

As a metaphorical extension, *tinku-* indicates identity (sameness). Two objects are identical if they "meet," that is if they end up at the same place, as in *iškanpis čay-niraqaƛ; tinkunmi* 'the two of them are alike; they are the same' (lit., 'they meet'). *manami tinkunču* 'it is not the same as the other' (lit., 'they do not meet').

The causative of *tinku* shows both the physical and metaphorical meanings. On the one hand, it can simply mean to bring two things physically together, that is, to make them meet. On the other hand, it can mean 'compare', as in *kay-man tinku-či-ša* 'he compared it to this one (lit., he caused it to meet this one').

It is particularly rational to believe that things that are together become similar when referring to a living thing in the early stages of its development, as it progresses from having few characteristics to becoming full-featured. From where do the characteristics that it acquires come? Why does a fetus in a cow develop into a cow, while a fetus in a human mother develops into a human? And why does the fetus end up resembling its mother? In the absence of an understanding of genetics, it is reasonable to believe that the fetus—being in close contact with its mother—attracts and absorbs characteristics from her, and from others near her, particularly from those who in some way impinge on her.

This belief is so reasonable that it is found in diverse cultures. David Coombs (personal communication) says:

> The view that close physical proximity between objects or people can influence their development is extremely widespread. Think of Jacob using colored sticks to influence the color of sheep and goats born to his flocks [Genesis 30:37–39], or Scandinavian beliefs that if a pregnant mother looks a lot at a person with bright red hair (or some other dramatic feature) the baby will be born with that feature.

Let us define MAGNETISM as the propensity for a being to acquire characteristics from another being to which it is sufficiently near. Magnetism, we assume, is simply a property of the world in which we live, not one we understand, but one the effects of which we can see, like gravity. And like gravity, it has a natural orientation: just as things fall DOWN, not UP, the characteristics most likely acquired are negative ones.[15]

Magnetism is at least as rational as its dual, contagion. They share the concept of transferring characteristics from one being to another, but contagion highlights (profiles) the agency of the contributor whereas magnetism highlights (profiles) the attraction and acquisition of properties by the recipient.[16]

This difference is crucial to understanding Quechua thought. In another culture a fertile hen's egg might be brought in contact with a barren woman to transfer its fecundity to the woman; see footnote 9. This would be using contagion: exploiting the egg's potential for contributing a characteristic to the woman. But in Quechua culture (and in Peruvian culture more broadly) a fresh hen's egg is often rubbed on the forehead to draw out a headache. This is a case of magnetism: exploiting the egg's potential for attracting and absorbing the headache from the person suffering from it.

I believe that—for Quechua speakers—magnetism is an intuitive belief[17] that provides the "validating context" for many parascientific cause-effect relations, for example, providing an explanation for why a newborn has some peculiarity in terms of what its mother saw.

How do Quechua children learn the concept of magnetism? Sperber (1996:92–93) writes:

> In all human societies, traditional or modern, with or without writing, with or without pedagogic institution, all normal individuals acquire a rich body of intuitive beliefs about themselves and their natural and social environment. These include beliefs about the movement of physical bodies, the behaviour of one's own body, the

---

[15]Entropy states that as time passes the degree of organization diminishes, that is, things tend to fall apart, disintegrate, deteriorate....We might say that magnetism is the opposite, that in Quechua thought the natural tendency of things is to become more uniform (an increase in the degree of organization). Interestingly, Quechua culture places a very high value on uniformity so, for example, the ideal person is one who is indistinguishable from the rest.

[16]To use the terminology of Lakoff and Johnson (1999:33), they differ by "profiling (also called *highlighting*) and a trajector-landmark relation."

[17]Sperber (1996:89) distinguishes two types of belief: *intuitive beliefs,* "typically the product of spontaneous and unconscious perceptual and inferential processes" and *reflective beliefs,* "interpretations of representations embedded in the validating context of an intuitive belief." Further, "The mental vocabulary of intuitive beliefs is probably limited to *intuitive concepts:* that is, concepts referring to perceptually identifiable phenomena and innately pre-formed, unanalyzed abstract concepts (of, say, norm, cause, substance, species, function, number, or truth). Intuitive beliefs are on the whole concrete and reliable in ordinary circumstances. Together they paint a kind of common-sense picture of the world. Their limits are those of common sense: they are fairly superficial, more descriptive than explanatory, and rather rigidly held."

effects of various body-environment interactions, the behaviour of many living kinds, the behaviour of fellow humans. These beliefs are acquired in the course of ordinary interactions with the environment and with others. They need no conscious learning effort on the part of the learner and no conscious teaching effort on the part of others....Even without teaching, these beliefs are easily acquired by everybody. The more fundamental ones are acquired quite early, suggesting a very strong innate predisposition....[18]

What role does communication play in the construction of intuitive beliefs? The answer is not simple. Intuitive beliefs are (or are treated as) the output of perceptions and unconscious inference, either the subject's own perceptions and inferences or those of others in the case of intuitive beliefs acquired through communication. Even when an intuitive belief is derived from the subject's own perceptions, the conceptual resources and the background assumptions which combine with the sensory input to yield the actual belief have, in part, been acquired through communication.

Thus, the concept of magnetism would be acquired in the course of ordinary interactions with the environment and through communication. Environmental interaction would be, for example, to see a child with some remarkable characteristic (and wonder why it was so). Communicative support would be to hear adults discuss the reason the child had that characteristic.

To take one example, Jan Benson gave birth to Kara in a clinic near Pucallpa, Peru. Before Kara was a year old, Jan moved to a Quechua community. Kara's bright red hair became part of the Quechua environment, and Jan was occasionally asked why Kara had red hair. In jest she once replied, "Because she was born in Pucallpa." *Pucallpa* derives from Quechua *puka aλpa* 'red earth', a very appropriate name for a city on the red clay banks of the Ucayali river. This explanation was readily accepted and widely disseminated. It became part of the supporting environment for the concept magnetism.

The beliefs we have been considering (eggs rotting because a pungent pudding was cooked nearby, a newborn having a characteristic because of what its mother saw while carrying the unborn child) and the fundamental concepts that underlie them, like magnetism, seem very robust. Evidence for this would be, on the one hand, the range of phenomena that magnetism seems to account for and, on the other hand, the substantial geographic area over which similar ideas are found. These suggest that

---

[18] I believe children acquire magnetism fairly early, but not so early as to suggest "a very strong innate predisposition." That is, I believe magnetism is an intuitive belief but not a "fundamental" one.

the fundamental idea, as well as the beliefs and practices derived from it, have existed for many centuries.

Sperber (1996:116) writes, "When...one encounters practices that remain stable for generations, one may suppose that they somehow maintain a sufficient level of relevance in spite of repetition, and try to see whether such is indeed the case, and why..." Sperber (1996:51–52) gives an explanation for such robustness:

> In general, there are three reasons to expect that an excessive weight may spontaneously be given to [...] cases where the failure to adhere to the practice is followed by misfortune. First, only misfortune always begs for an explanation. Second, when failure to adhere to the practice is followed by misfortune, it may appear to have caused it. Third, explaining a misfortune as caused by some people's behaviour makes it possible to assign responsibility, and to give at least a social response to a situation which, otherwise, leaves one powerless. In such conditions, following the practice does protect against at least one risk: that of being accused of having provoked misfortune. The practice does, quite objectively, have that kind of efficacy.

To take another example, about twenty years ago a Quechua friend lost a leg in an accident. A few years later he got a prosthesis, which enabled him to walk, ride a horse, and work his fields. A few years ago one of his neighbors gave birth to a child with a malformed leg. There was a ready explanation for this misfortune: the child had been affected by its proximity to P__. The child now walks, but with a limp, and people say, "She walks just like P__." Whatever precautions the mother might have taken while pregnant, no matter what the distance between her house and P__'s house, the explanation is natural and satisfying. And the case is newsworthy: it is told and retold, far and wide, propagating and reinforcing both the belief in the phenomenon and the intellectual fabric that makes it rational.

Significantly, in cases such as this, no blame is assigned to the person who "contributed" the negative attribute. P__ was completely passive. He did not "push off" the attribute onto the developing child; rather, the developing child attracted and absorbed the property from him. (If any blame were assigned, it would have been to the mother for not keeping the child away from a possible donor.)

To summarize, for Quechua the significant concept for the cause-effect relations we have been considering is magnetism, not contagion. Contagion highlights the source (cause) impinging on a target to affect it, but magnetism highlights the target, the affected, and its ability to induce change through attracting characteristics.

A Hypothesis and Parting Reflections

I wish to conclude by stating a hypothesis suggested by this study and by reflecting on the benefits of this type of investigation.

Years ago a friend considered writing a dissertation in anthropology on the psychology of oppressed peoples and considered focusing on the Quechua people. Unfortunately, she decided on another topic and I have since wondered what one might find in the Quechua psyche that reflects centuries of oppression.

The dominant philosophy among Quechua peoples is fatalism.[19] Generally, Quechua individuals see themselves as the victims of forces beyond their control. This is not too surprising since they have suffered centuries of subjugation from the Inca empire, the Spanish empire, internal colonialism from the capital,..., and now the dictates of the World Bank, the International Monetary Fund, and so forth.

Sperber (1996:115) writes:

> In general, the phrase 'cultural environment' is used very loosely, and refers to a collection of meanings, values, techniques and so forth. So understood, it has little to do with the physical environment. Its ontological status is, at best, very vague; its causal powers are mysterious. By 'cultural environment', I mean an ensemble of

---

[19]Space limitations preclude documenting this claim; I will give just one bit of anecdotal evidence. At the time the Shining Path guerilla movement was active in Huanuco, a Quechua author wrote the following story (to be included in a book for neoliterates):

> In a large town there was a huge, good, plow-pulling bull. His owner loved it dearly because it was a good plow-puller. Then it happened that a sick dog bit that bull. Because the dog bit it, that tame bull became crazy. Being crazy like that, its owner could no longer tie it. Not being able to tie it, he turned it into a corral. But that one that had been corraled escaped and went into the thicket. Then it went about in the thicket goring whatever it encountered. Although dogs would bark at it, it would chase them, goring them. In that way it would gore any people or domestic animals it met. Wherever the bull went, people were extremely afraid. People would no longer let their children go outside freely. When they slept at night, they slept watchfully, having barred their doors. Once, it (the bull) entered the town. So the people hid and watched the bull making ready his "weapons" in the plaza. So the people were sad, in no way being able to kill it. It left the plaza and went about wherever it wished. Then it became worse and went about tottering, foaming at the mouth. One or two days later that bull died. After it had really died, they buried it. After they buried the bull, people could again go about where they wished.

material items: all the public productions in the environment that are
causes and effects of mental representations. The cultural environment thus understood blends seamlessly with the physical
environment of which it is a part. The causal powers it exerts on human minds are unproblematic: public productions affect sense-organs
in the usual, material way. They trigger the construction of mental
representations the contents of which are partly determined by the
properties of the triggering stimuli, and partly by pre-existing mental
resources.

So what sort of beliefs ("representations") should we expect to find in a
cultural environment shaped over centuries by fatalism? Perhaps magnetism, and the beliefs and practices based on it, are in some measure a
product of fatalism, a way to rationalize the inevitable influence a hostile
environment will have on those not able to escape it.

I will state this hypothesis—admittedly a very speculative one—in various parts, making reference to figure 3. (By "X *is in a symbiotic relationship
with Y,*" I mean that X and Y mutually reinforce each other.)

With the source (agent):   With the goal (affected):

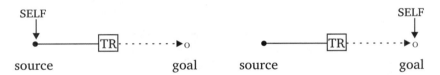

| SELF | | SELF |

source   goal   source   goal

Figure 3. Profiling and identification in the source-path-goal schema.

Conjecture 1: The source-path-goal schema is susceptible to profiling.[20] Two possibilities—profiling the source and profiling the goal—are
indicated in figure 3 by the vertical arrows.

Conjecture 2: Profiling the source would be in a symbiotic relationship
with the CAUSES ARE FORCES metaphor whereas profiling the goal would
be in a symbiotic relationship with the dual CAUSEES ARE FORCEES.

Conjecture 3: In the source-path-goal schema, an individual may have
a propensity to identify with either the source or the goal. In figure 3 this
is indicated by SELF.

Conjecture 4: The propensity for identifying SELF with the source
would be in a symbiotic relationship with the attitude "I am the captain of
my fate" whereas the propensity for identifying SELF with the goal would

[20]I have intentionally stated this vaguely, without addressing questions such as whether such
profiling applies to an individual or to a language-culture, whether its influence would be absolute
or partial, and so forth.

be in a symbiotic relationship with the attitude "I am the victim of my fate."

Conjecture 5: A language-culture can instill in its members such profiling (conjecture 1) and propensities (conjecture 3). I believe Sperber (1996) has laid the foundation for understanding how this works, as discussed above.

Conjecture 6: The propensity for Quechua is to profile the goal and to identify SELF with it.[21]

Conjecture 7: This propensity is in a symbiotic relationship with (1) the preference for the OBJECT EVENT-STRUCTURE metaphor over the LOCATION EVENT-STRUCTURE metaphor, (2) the preference for magnetism over contagion as the logic of parascientific cause-effect relationships, (3) fatalism as the dominant philosophy in Quechua culture.

Obviously, considerable work is needed to find reasons for either believing or rejecting these conjectures. And now, a final reflection. Although this exploration is brief and preliminary, I hope it demonstrates that by pursuing a cognitive approach to metaphors and beliefs one can come to understand what would otherwise probably remain a mystery.

For example, consider the HgQ sentence: *papa:ninta mikuykan* 'he is identical to his dad', which literally means 'he is eating his father'. Likewise, *tiyunwan mikunakuykan* 'he and his uncle look identical' literally means 'he and his uncle are eating each other'! When I first heard these uses of *miku-* 'eat', I was both surprised and baffled. It seemed that *miku-* 'eat' was being used to indicate identity (the end-point of similarity), but I could not imagine any relationship between eating and identity.

Now, however, I think I understand. This use depends on the notion that characteristics affect a target by moving to it and impinging on it; *miku-* 'eat, ingest' simply highlights the incorporation of the impinging characteristics.[22] It emphasizes that they are taken into the the target and "digested" by it, that is, they become part of it. Thus, if someone "eats" the characteristics of their father, they must be like him.[23]

---

[21]Let me hasten to add that I do not see this propensity as any sort of defect or handicap. It would be wrong, for example, to think that it implies passivity; David Coombs (personal communication) says, "I see Quechua people taking all sorts of actions, ritualistic and otherwise, to gain as much control as possible over the often hostile forces around them, whether these forces are natural, supernatural, or social (our categories, not theirs)."

[22]Further support for this perspective is seen in the etymology for *mipa* proposed in footnote 12.

[23]It is further believed that, in such cases of identity, one or the other must die, presumably because of competition over essential characteristics. (This was brought to my attention by Rick Floyd.) For example, a Quechua person told me that he had had a little brother that was identical to his father. As a result, his father became very ill. Then his brother suddenly died, after which his father recovered quickly. Two identicals—father-son or mother-daughter—cannot coexist.

Appendix: Sampler of Parascientific Cause-Effect Relations

The parascientific cause-effect relations described in this appendix are taken from Weber et al. (1998). In each section, the examples are presented starting with those that seem to have some scientific basis and progressing to those that seem less and less amenable to a scientific explanation. For example, we can easily imagine a causal chain that would explain why "If we look up when we are gathering snow, then later on our eyes grow dim." By contrast, it is difficult to imagine a scientific explanation for "If children play with shafts of light *(inti-pa qiaʎ-n)* they will become lazy."[24] However, I do not believe many Quechua people would regard these as different in kind[25] (except, perhaps, as he or she might be influenced by Western thought). But this merits further investigation.

Actions with negative effects

If one does not pay a reward for a lost object that has been returned, on subsequent occasions the finder will not find them. *Ñawi-čoqʎunta mana pa:qaptin yapaycawqa mana tarinnacu.*

If we make *toquš* pudding when a hen is setting, the eggs rot (lit., become pudding-like). *Waʎpa oqʎaykaptin toqušta apišaqa runtu apiyan.*

There is a sickness for one who has struck a parent. The striker goes all over the place crazy. We ask anyone going around like that what medicine will cure that sickness, should we get it. *Papa:ninta mamanta maqaqqa kaykan qešya. čaymi čay maqa:qa aywakun lo:kuyaša maypapis. čaynaw pureqta tapukunči ima hampi kašantapis qešya čarimaša čay hampiwan aʎčaka:napaq.*

It is believed that, if a person gives hot pepper to another person who receives it with the hand, those two might hate each other. *Runakuna učuta huk runa aptarkur hukaqta aptaparqa yarpan "Kapas čikinakušunmi" nir.*

If a snake startles us, fright-sickness can really take hold of us. It is said that it is very difficult to get well from this. *Kulebra mančačimašaqa mančakay fiyupaši čarimanči. čaynawpis fiyupa sasaši aʎčaka:napa:pis.*

We do not burn coca. If we do, it rains. *Kukataqa manami rupačinči:ču. Kukata rupačišaqa tamyan.*

We should not step over small children. If we do, that child remains a runt. It does not grow normally. *Takša wamrakunataqa manaši čankakunči:ču. čankakušaqa sučuʎaši ke:rakun. Manana wiñannaču.*

If anyone argues with their godfather or godmother, a fierce wind comes. *Kumpa:rinwan kuma:rinwan rimanakušanpita, lo:ku fiyu wayra yurin.*

---

[24]People believe the following: If children play with that light, they will become lazy. For that reason people do not want children to play with that light. *čay yarpay kan: wamra čay ačikyaywan pukʎaptinqa qeʎayanši. čaymi runakuna mana munanču wamrankuna čay ačikyaywan pukʎananta.*

[25]Likewise, in native Quechua thought there is at best a very weak distinction between the physical and spiritual: The Quechua world is a physical-spiritual world, not two separate spheres as in Western thought.

If we eat a huge potato alone, a rock may roll onto us and hurt us. For that reason we break up a big potato and share it. *Hatunkaray papata hapaʎanči mikušaqa kučpaši qomanči. čaymi pakipa:nakuyparaq mikunči hatun papataqa.*

It used to be that people would not allow a child to cry inside a house where there was food or in a producing field. They believed that this would make the food unhappy. The food, it was believed, would think that the child cried from hunger, so it would leave. Consequently the plants would not produce food for that person. *Unay runakunaqa wamrata manami waqačiyta munaqču wasi ruri mikuy kašančaw, mikuy wayuraykašan čakračawqa. Paykuna yarpaq "mikuy haqayanqa" nir. Mikuyši neq "Wamra yarqaypita waqan" nir. čaynaw nirši aywakoq. čawraqa čay runapa manana mikuy wayoqnaču.*

In former times, they would hit anyone who, after dark, sucked on something sweet or chewed gum, saying "You are biting your mother's nipple, failing to honor your parents." *Ñawpa kaq runakuna čakaypa miškita šoqoqta, čiklita kačoqta maqaq "Mamaykipa čučunta kañiykanki, qešya kar" nir.*

It is bad to say "I'm stuffed." If we say that, we anger the Lord God. *"Saksaška:" neyqa hučami. čaynaw nišpanči Tayta Dyustaši rabyačinči.*

ukya- 'to love an infant so much that it gets sick and possibly dies'. Because they believe this, many hide their infants. To protect them, they tie a red string about the baby's neck.

Women abort when they crave something. *Warmikunaqa šuʎun imatapis munapašpanmi.*

If someone has an intense desire for something, they say his spleen will burst. So if someone is seen to be looking longingly at something, he is invited to have some. *Imatapis fiyupa munapaptenqa runakuna riman "Ayaqnin paštanqa" nirmi. čaymi yawačin munapar rikapaptinqa.*

If someone takes a footprint that we made in mud, fries it in oil and then takes it to where ants live, the bottom of that foot will become infested with sores. *Mituman harušanči yupinči:ta kañaʎačaw mantikawan ankariykur tiksa tiyašanman qotuptin čakinči ušakan poqrur učkuyka:ʎar.*

hupay mu:la 'woman converted into a mule for having had an affair with a priest'. People believe that if a married woman has an affair with a priest, the devil will turn her into a phantom mule. Her hair turns into its halter; her breasts into stirrups. The devil rides it about at night. When that mule comes to a cross it cannot go beyond it. For that reason it weeps. *čayqa kaykan kasa:du warmi ku:rawan tiyaptin. Puñukašata dyablu tikračin mu:laman. Aqčanši tikran busalninman; čučunnaši estri:bunman. čaytaši čakaykuna dyablu muntaša puričin. Ruskunaman čayarši mana pa:sayta puydinču čay mu:la. čayši amatar waqan.*

Actions with positive effects (curative, preventative,...)

If a ball forms in the flesh, this is cured by first heating a lucuma seed and then rubbing it where the ball has formed. *Lukma ayčačaw wiñaptin lukmapa murunta akaraykačir kupašaqa aʎčakanmi.*

If a child falls somewhere and becomes frightened, to prevent the earth from "grabbing" him, we *rub* him all over with the earth from where he fell. *Wamra*

maɣčawpis tuniptinqa mančariša kaptin pača čarikurkunanta čay tunišan aɣpawan inte:runta kupanči.
If we take a cat without covering its head, he plants alder trees along the way. When we bring it to the new house, we must make it scratch the opening of the hearth. If we do that, then it will *not* leave the house. *Mišita umanta čapa:ni apašaqa rayanta lantaraykarši aywan. Nirkur wasiman čayaykačirnami tuɣpa punkuta aspičinči mana kutikunanpaq. čaynawpami wasiɣačawna qoya:kun.*
When they castrate a pig, they rub a grinding stone all over its body so that it will become fat and *round* like that stone. *Kučita kaparqa aqakuna tunaywanmi kučipa inte:runpa qaqun čay tunay ruminaw uɣušyaypa uɣušya:nanyaq wira-ya:nanpaq.*
In former times, when there would be a severe drought and the crops would dry up, the people would go *to* the wild lakes to bring water to the valley. When they would bring it from there in pots, it would rain. *Fiyupa usya kar mikuykuna čakiptinqa mas unayqa runakuna aywaq čukaru qočaman yakuta qečwaman apa-munanpaq. čaypita apamuptinqa mankawan tamyaqna.*
When there is a severe drought in the valleys and the crops are about to dry up, the people take the *images* from inside the church outside. They leave them out over night. Sometimes they parade them on a day on which they are not customarily paraded. Or, they take out images that are never taken out. The people think that God will make it rain because he thinks that even the saints are sad. And it is really that way. When they take the images, sometimes the rains come, ending the drought. *Qečwačaw fiyupa usya kar mikuykuna čakiyta munaptinnaqa runakuna santukunata horqun inlisya ruričaw kaykaqta hawaman. čayčaw wara:čin. Aybe:sir ka:ɣinpa puričin mana puričinan diyačaw. Imaypis mana horqušan santukunata horqun. čawra runakuna yarpan "'Santupis ɣakikuykan' nir Dyus tamyačimunqa" nir. čaynawmi rasunpa kan. Aybe:sirqa santukunata horqup-tin tamyamun usya kaykašanpitapis.*
People believe that one can pass all night chewing coca in competition with (the spirit of) the mountain. If one competes until dawn, the mountain will not harm him. *Runakuna yarpan hirkata wara:par binsinanpaq kašanta. čaymi wara:-paptenqa hirka mana ruranču ima mana-aɣitapis.*

Objects with negative effects

When we are gathering snow (it is said), we do not look up. If we look up when we are gathering like that, then later on our eyes grow dim (become blind). *Raštata šuntar hanaqpa manaši rika:rinči:ču. čaynaw šuntaykašanči:čaw hanaqpa rika:riša mas unaytaqa ñawinči čakan.*

Ama:pa tuɣun 'bones of pre-historic people'. Do not touch the bones of the ancient ones; it will cause your hand to break out in sores. This sore does not heal or, after healing, breaks out again. *It* is thought that this is because the ancients say "*ahay* (break out in sores)" when someone touches their remains while digging up their ruins. *Ama:pa tuɣuntaqa ama yatayču. Aha:šunkipa:mi. čay qešyaqa manami aɣčakanču, yatašan tuɣuwan mana hampišanya:qa. čaynawpis*

čaytaqa hampičinanči hampikoqkunawan. čay qeri, mana hampišaqa aƙčakar-kurpis yapay paštan.
If we do not shield ourselves when there is a sunlit drizzle, we will get that sickness (a skin ailment caused by sunlit drizzle) *Qori-čirapa čirapaykaptin mana ƙantukušaqa čarimanči čay qešya. In* rural areas it is believed that, when there is sunlit drizzle, if we drink water from springs, it will make us have a stomach ache. *čakračaw yarpan čirapaykaptin pukyu yakuta upušaqa pačanči nana:napaq kašanta.*

čiya 'earth pillar formed by erosion'. In some towns, these are highly respected. It is believed that it will cause anyone who climbs on them to get sick. *čaykunaqa wakin markakunačaw fiyupa rispita:rumi kaykan. Pukƙakuptenqa qešyačinši.*
The sac holding the brain (aracnoid membrane) is evil. If one eats it he will not achieve his goals. *Toqšupa qaran čapa. čayta mikurqa imatapis mana tarinču.*

tikra-pu 'sickness passed from something used in *šoqpi* curing to the one who carries it'. They rub the guinea pig onto the sick person. When they take the guinea pig to the mountain, the sickness may "grab" the one who carries it. When that person gets sick, they say "He is ill with that which turned back on him." This happens if the bearer becomes frightened or falls. It is at that point that the illness "grabs" the person. *Qešyaq runata šoqpin hakawan. Šoqpišan hakata hirkaman apaptin, čay apaq runata qešya čarin. čay runa qešyaptin "tikrapuwan qešyaykan" nin.*

Objects with positive effects

When heated, the leaves and seeds of the *muƙi* tree are good for treating someone sick from (lit., penetrated by) the cold. Likewise, the leaves of the *muƙi* tree are good to relieve a headache: after boiling them, the head is washed with the liquid. *Muƙipa o:han, murun aƙimi kuwariykur qasay-pa:sašata hampinanpaq. čaynawpis o:hanqa aƙimi uma nanaptin timpuraykačir paqakunapaq.*
After catching a *qoqya* frog people pass it over their face to calm a toothache. Such a frog is called a *"poƙito." Qoqyata čarirkur runakuna pa:sačin ka:ranta kiru-nanay čawa:nanpaq. čay qoqyatami kiru-nanayta hampinanpa:qa "poƙito" nin.*
The undigested matter in the stomach (of a ruminant?) is good as a remedy for curing children ill with "fright." The material is rubbed all over their body. Other people strain the juices from the material and make (the sick person) drink it. *Ašašqa aƙi hampimi kaykan mančakaywan qešyaq wamrakunata hampinanpaq. čaywanqa inte:ru kwerpunpa ašašwan kupan. Wakinqa yakuƙanta ašašta šuyšuriykur upučin.* (Compare Floyd's (1997:19–20) description of curing by placing the child inside the stomach of a recently slaughtered sheep.)
There is a tiny bone in a guinea pig's ear *(haka-pa miči-n)* that looks like a guinea pig. People used to look for this bone to swallow it, thinking that it would make their guinea pigs multiply. *Unay hakapa mičinta horquran ultananpaq "čayta ultapte: haka yača:manqa" nir yarpar.*
The linnets that make the corn ripen do not come until the corn is tasseling. They do not stay the entire year. When the corn ripens they go somewhere else.

They come from Holy Rome. The house sparrow leads off the linnet's offspring. The linnet touches the corn with hands covered with corn mush so that the corn develops quickly. *Hara poqučeqkuna hara šikšiykaptiʎanra:mi šamun. Manami watanpaču tiyakun. Hara poqurkuptenqa huk-la:pami aywakun. Santa Romapita šamun. čay a:bipa wawankunataqa pičiwsakunaši pušan. čay silgi:ruqa šatu makinwanši yatan apura: čoqʎu yurinanpaq.*

If we *place* a cross at the door of our house, the phantom mule can not enter. *Wasinči punkuman rusta čuraptinči hupay mu:laqa manaši yaykamunču.*

A child's speech development can be accelerated (or if delayed, cured) by touching *rima-rima wayta* 'speak-speak flower' to its mouth.

Indicators

The following are indicators of things to come. Although they are not parascientific cause-effect relations per se, they imply such a relation.

hitqa 'type of leafy plant'. It grows in corn fields. To eat it, it is picked before the sun rises. If it is picked after the sun rises, it is bitter. *Hara čakračaw wamun. Mikunanpaqqa paʎan manaraq inti yeqamuptinmi. Inti yeqamušata paʎaptenqa ašqan.*

When these (type of bird) swarm, it is about to rain torrentially. *Lu:ku wayanayqa purin lo:ku* tamya *tamyanaʎanpaqraqmi.* (Possible explanation: The birds swarm to get the bugs that rise because of the coming rain.)

It is believed that when soot falls it is about to rain. *Runakuna yarpan "Uʎin yaqamuptin tamyan" nir.*

waqa ñawi 'type of ant'. The black kind appears on paths when it is going to rain; the red kind, when it is going to be dry and sunny. *Yana waqa-ñawi kaminunpa purin tamyapaq; puka waqa-ñawi usyapaq.*

waqča aʎqu 'dog that indicates bad luck'. A dog that frequently defecates near a house or on the path to a house is a bad omen for those who live there.

When butchering an animal, when they remove the jaw from the head to cook it, if a bit of flesh remains on the end of the jaw, that type of animal will multiply for the person who removed the jaw. If no flesh remains, the animal will not multiply for that person. *Ima uywatapis pištar yanunanpaq umanpita kiha:danta kučupa:rir amiptin, kiha:danpa sapin kaq tuʎunčaw ičikʎapis ayča ʎoqšimuptinqa, čay uywa yačan. Mana ʎoqšimuptinqa, mana yačanču.*

If someone drops something that he was eating, it is believed that someone nearby was desiring it. *Huk runa imatapis mikuykašanta kačapakuptinqa yarpan huk runa ñawpančaw kaykaq munapašanta.*

When, in a dream, people see a man or woman doing something or in some condition they think that it has been revealed to them. When they see this, they firmly believe it. *Suyñuyninčaw runata man'ča:qa warmita rikar, imata ruraykaqta, imanaw kaykaqtapis rikar yarpan "ribilamaša" nir. čaynaw rikašantaqa fiyupa rigin.*

suwa-tamya 'a light, passing rain'. It is believed that a thief is where it rains lightly. *Runakuna yarpan čaynaw tamyaptenqa suwa čaypa kaykašanta.*

When a harbinger *(hayni)* appears, it indicates one of two things: (1) that a member of the family or someone who arrives there will get sick; (2) that a member of the family or someone who lives in the house will arrive from some other place. Hayni yuriptin iškaypaq yarpan. *(1) Hukta yarpan pipis famiʎyankuna man'ča:qa čay wasinman čayaq runa qešyananpaq kašanta. (2). Hukta yarpan, famiʎyan man'ča:qa wasičaw tiyaq huk-la:čaw kaykašanpita čayananpaq kašanta.*

When one gets a ringing in an ear, it means that someone has died; if in the left ear, for one sex; if in the right ear, for the other sex.[26] *Rinrinči:čaw čaynaw wiyakaptin musyanči pi: wañušantapis wiʎama:nanči:paq kašanta: hukaq-la: rinričaw wiyakaptinqa oʎqu wañušanta mayanapaq, hukaq-la: rinričaw wiyašana warmi wañušanta mayanapaq.*

When someone chews coca, if a stem pokes his mouth, people believe that something bad will happen to him or his family. *Kukata čaqčaykaptin šakʎun šiminčaw tukšiptinqa runakuna yarpan imapis mana-aʎi kananpaq kašanta.*

kirma- '(when divining) for the stems of two coca leaves to come out of the mouth stuck together parallel, which is a very bad sign'. When I chewed coca, two stems came out together. That indicated that my uncle was to die. *Kukata čaqčapte: kirmaša ʎoqšimuran. čayqa karan tiyo: wañunanpaqmi.*

References

Adelaar, Willem. 1994. A grammatical category for manifestations of the supernatural in early colonial Quechua. In Cole, Hermon, and Martín (eds.), 116–125.

Cahill, Thomas. 1995. *How the Irish saved civilization.* New York: Doubleday.

Cole, Peter, G. Hermon, and M. D Martín, eds. 1994. *Language in the Andes.* Newark: Latin American Studies, University of Delaware.

Floyd, Melanie. 1997. Mipa: Explaining riddles of birth in an Andean village. *Notes on Anthropology and Intercultural Community Work* 28:9–26. Dallas: Summer Institute of Linguistics.

Groenewald, Ronel. forthcoming. Prácticas y creencias sobre el embarazo entre los quechuahablantes de Inkawasi. In David Coombs (ed.) *Aprendiendo a ver con ojos andinos: Estudios etnográficos.* Comunidades y Culturas Peruanas. Lima: Instituto Lingüístico de Verano.

Lakoff, George, and Mark Johnson. 1999. *Philosophy in the flesh.* New York: Basic Books.

Priest, Robert J., Thomas Campbell, and Bradford A. Mullen. 1995. *Spiritual power and missions: Raising the issues.* Evangelical Missiological Society Series 3. Pasadena, Calif.: William Carey Library.

Sperber, Dan. 1996. *Explaining culture: A naturalistic approach.* Oxford: Blackwell Publishers.

---

[26]People argue about which ear corresponds to which sex.

Weber, David J. 1976. *Los sufijos posesivos en el quechua del Huallaga (Huánuco).* Documento de Trabajo 12. Yarinacocha, Peru: Instituto Lingüístico de Verano.

Weber, David J. 1983. *Relativization and nominalized clauses in Huallaga (Huanuco) Quechua.* University of California Publications in Linguistics 103. Berkeley: University of California Press.

Weber, David J. 1989. *A grammar of Huallaga (Huánuco) Quechua.* University of California Publications in Linguistics 112. Berkeley: University of California Press.

Weber, David J., Félix Cayco Zambrano, Teodoro Cayco Villar, and Marlene Ballena Dávila. 1998. *Rimaycuna: Quechua de Huánuco. Diccionario del quechua del Huallaga con índices castellano e inglés,* Serie Lingüística Peruana 48. Lima: Instituto Lingüístico de Verano.

18

Tagmemic Insights on Kewa Numbers and Names

Karl J. Franklin

Introduction

Numbers and names in the Kewa language represent cultural dimensions that are not obvious in a linguistic analysis, including the glossing of particular forms. Both domains require emic perspectives to fully appreciate their complexities. Although Kewa counting systems and the use of names have been discussed previously (Franklin and Franklin 1962, 1978; K. Franklin 1967, 1968), the present paper provides additional insights and analysis that benefit from Pike's tagmemic framework.

The Kewa language (with three major dialects) is spoken in the Southern Highlands of Papua New Guinea (K. Franklin 1968) by approximately 100,000 people. Ethnographic studies include LeRoy (1985), Josiphides (1985), and MacDonald (1991), as well as my own (K. Franklin 1965, 1991; Franklin and Franklin 1978).

My wife and I first met Professor Pike (he became Ken to us much later) as SIL students at the University of Oklahoma in 1956. In 1962 he went to Papua New Guinea, where we were working, and consulted with us on the Kewa language for a number of months. While there, he also trained me as a linguistics consultant. He would often eat lunch with us and encouraged me to study linguistics. Later he wrote letters on my behalf so that I could pursue graduate studies. Much later, for a number of years, we were colleagues at the International Linguistics Center in Dallas, Texas. His example and encouragement have been an inspiration throughout my SIL career.

Kenneth Pike first outlined the theory of tagmemics (once called grammemics—Pike 1957) in a series of three volumes, which were later revised and published in one volume (Pike 1967). A more condensed version of the theory appeared much later (Pike 1982), and the premises upon which his view of language and culture were built are outlined elsewhere in more detail (Pike 1976, 1983, 1988, 1992, 1993).

In tagmemics, the observer is essential, not in the usual scientific sense as an "impartial observer," but as one who enters into the definition of what things are and how they behave. In this sense, according to Pike, tagmemic theory is "a theory of theories which tells how the observer universally affects the data and becomes part of the data" (Pike 1982:3). This premise allows an analyst to inspect data from a variety of perspectives—by one analogy, in terms of particles, waves, and fields. Tagmemics also describes units as things that can be validated as having reality: represented by their contrastive components; variant manifestations; and distribution in class, sequence, and system.

As contrastive units, particles occur in some linear or special order, while waves represent clusters of nuclei and margins. Both particles and waves occur in fields, that is, dimensional patterns that represent systems of reference and meaning. Within a particular field or system of meaning, a unit is recognized by means of its contrast with other units. This can often be exemplified with patterns or matrices in paradigms and syntax. But units also have variation, so some way to recognize them in differing circumstances and environments is essential. For example, an English word must be identified as meaning the same thing, despite differences in pronunciation. And in Kewa a person is still the same entity, despite different names.

Tagmemics employs the notion of hierarchy to describe levels, with structural units manifested in the phonological, grammatical, or referential hierarchies. Words, for example, are composed of syllables, which are in turn composed of segmental and suprasegmental phonemes within the phonological hierarchy. But words make up phrases, which in turn most often build into clauses within the grammatical hierarchy. The layering in grammar is pervasive, with discourse at the top level of the hierarchy and morphemes at the lowest level. The referential hierarchy, a later addition to the tagmeme, introduces context as a crucial component for the identification of a unit. And, as we shall note, the cultural context is crucial in understanding Kewa names and numbers.

In general terms, a tagmeme is a unit of structure that displays four features: slot, class, role, and cohesion. Slot refers to the location or position of the unit, despite variations; class refers to the particular list or set of items that are substitutable in a given position; role refers to the meaning or function of the set of items; and cohesion refers to the binding structure of the field of items as a whole.

Because a tagmeme is a form-meaning composite, the various components of differing hierarchies may interlock. We will employ some of these basic tagmemic perspectives in this study.

Numbers in Kewa

The Kewa language has several numerical systems, each with significant cultural dimensions. By examining them within the tagmemic framework, we can focus upon their form-meaning dimensions from a different perspective than earlier reports. Kewa is not alone in respect to a number of the features I will outline. Lean (1986), in his volume on the Southern Highland and other Provinces (the Gulf, Western, and Enga in particular), describes similar systems in operation elsewhere.

The body part tally system

The oldest system of counting in Kewa, and one that has been documented in other parts of New Guinea (see Lean 1986), uses certain body parts to represent ordinal numbers. This system was used to recall when certain cultural events would take place, for ticking off items needed for such events, or as a generalized pointing and mnemonic device. In this system, the speaker began enumerating with the little finger of the left hand, continuing with other fingers, the thumb, the palm, wrist, further up the arm, neck, and face and finally reaching the midpoint of the count by pointing to the space between the eyes. The count then continued down the other side of the body, culminating at the right little finger. A complete count is called a *paapu*.

The body part tally system is not replicated exactly from dialect to dialect within Kewa. In East Kewa (Muli area) there were twenty-four parts enumerated on the upper left side of the body, followed by *rikaa* 'the middle' (pointing between the eyes), then the same twenty-four parts on the right side of the body, making the count a total of forty-nine (Franklin and Franklin 1962). However, in the West Kewa (Usa area), although the tally also reached forty-nine, some body parts were different from East Kewa. And in South Kewa (Erave area) only seventeen body parts were named, with the jaw enumerating the cross over point. Other variations have been noted as well. For example, Lean (1986(10):45ff.) gives information from Pumuge (representing one particular Ialibu area) showing some sixty-six body parts, with the crossover point at the nose. Extra parts are often enumerated by adding modifiers to body parts, such as *mindi* 'flesh', *pondea* 'hole', and *kuli* 'bone'. The Kewa data Lean cites from another Ialibu area is not reliable as far as the glosses are concerned, but in that dialect area some twenty-two body parts are tallied. The data for East Kewa and West Kewa are summarized in chart 1.

Chart 1. Body part counting in East and West Kewa

No.	Body part gloss	East Kewa	West Kewa	Notes
1	little finger	*kegali*	*egata*	*k* > Ø; *-li* ~ *-ta*
2	ring finger	*kegali yame*	*laapo*	*yame* < *ame*
3	middle finger	*andaa ki*	*repo*	*andaa* 'big'
4	index finger	*maala*	*maala*	'to teach'
5	thumb	*su*	*supu*	*-pu* 'collective'
6	heel of thumb	*su mindi*		*mindi* 'muscle'
	palm		*oraapu*	*-pu* 'collective'
7	palm	*waraa*		'to touch'
	wrist		*kerepo*	*-pu* sometimes added
8	wrist	*kerepo*		
	forearm		*palaa ki*	'thigh arm'
9	forearm	*palaa ki*		
	upper forearm		*noae*	
10	large arm bone	*noe*		
	inside elbow		*noae re pambu*	*re* 'base of something'
11	small arm bone	*noe luambu*		*lu-* 'hitting'
	elbow joint		*komaa*	
12	elbow joint	*komaa*		
	mid upper arm		*pini*	
13	lower upper arm	*winya ropaa*		'woman's armband'
	upper upper arm		*pini re pambu*	
14	upper upper arm	*ali ropaa*		'man's armband'
	lower shoulder		*pasaa*	
15	shoulder	*pasaa*		
	midshoulder		*pasaa re pambu*	

16	shoulder bone	*pasaa kuli*		
	top of shoulder		*kalambe*	
17	neck muscle	*pasaa mindi*		*mindi* 'muscle'
	lower neck		*ipa lo*	*ipa* 'water'
18	neck	*maa*	*maa*	
19	jaw	*yagaa*		
	cheek		*peae*	
20	ear	*kale*		
	temple		*peae re pambu*	
21	cheek	*pae*		
	ear		*aane*	
22	eye	*lee*	*ini*	
23	corner of eye	*paki*	*paki*	
24	between eyes	*rikaa*	*rikaa*	

Because there was considerable variation in enumerating the time for a cultural event (such as the building of houses, viewing of pigs and dances), it was necessary to specify when the activities would take place. This was done by pointing to a particular upper body part to represent a particular month. The series of events culminated with a large feast and "pig kill," involving multiple clans from various areas, so it was essential to make sure everyone could keep track of the activities.[1] To give some idea of how the body part counting system was used for a feast that took place in the village of Usa in 1968, note the activities that we recorded:

Month one (the little finger): preparation of the dance grounds, including the laying out of the long houses.

Month two: collection of the wooden poles and beams that would be used for the long houses.

Month three: framing the houses and collection of the sword grass for the roofs of the long houses.

Month four: continuing to build the houses and putting on the grass roofs.

Month five: additional long house built by neighboring clans.

[1] Examples of such events are the famous "pig kills" that have taken place in the Western and Southern Highlands, as well as in the Enga Province. LeRoy (1979) outlines the competitive exchanges of pork and pearl shells that took place in Kewa.

Month six: collection of additional materials for more long houses.

Month seven: preparation of more ground for additional long houses.

Month eight: building additional long houses.

Month nine: the pigs are brought in and tied to stakes in front of the long house for viewing.

Month ten: the pigs, as well as pearl shells, are again viewed and the month for the pig kill and feast is decided and specified.

Month eleven: (at the elbow joint) the first dance takes place.

Months twelve to twenty: additional house building activities take place.

Month twenty-one: (at the ear on the left side) another dance is held.

Months twenty-two to forty-eight: additional building activities, dances, viewing of the pigs.

Month forty-nine: the large pig kill and feast takes place.

Although we recorded this series of activities for a feast in Usa, it is clear from other such feasts that the monthly activities varied considerably from area to area. In most postcolonial instances, the final feast was timed to occur somewhere around "Christmas."

The four-base system

A second system of counting, equally valid in Kewa, is what Lean (1986) calls the "digit tally four cycle" system, and what we (Franklin and

Franklin 1962) have referred to as the "four-base" system. This counting system also began with the little finger of the left hand, but went only to the fourth finger. After that "extras," using the thumb as the reference point, were added to the word "four." This system counts by using what can be referred to as cardinal numbers to enumerate objects or referents. The numbers generally occur within the numerical adjective position of a noun phrase, for example: *aa laapo* (man two) 'two men'. Chart 2 illustrates this system.

Chart 2. The four-base counting system

No.	Gloss	East Kewa	West Kewa	Comments
1	one	*pamenda*	*pandane*	*pa* 'just'; *menda* 'another'
2	two	*laapo*	*laapo*	two
3	three	*repo*	*repo*	three
4	four	*ki*	*ki*	hand
5	five	*kina konde*	*kina onde*	-*na* 'possession'; *onde* 'extra'
6	six	*kina konde laapo*	*kina onde laapo*	hand-poss. extra two
7	seven	*kina konde repo*	*kina onde repo*	hand-poss. extra three
8	eight	*ki laapo*	*ki laapo*	hand two
9	nine	*ki laapona konde*	*ki laapona onde*	hand two-poss. extra
10	ten	*ki laapona konde laapo*	*ki laapona onde laapo*	hand-two-poss. extra two
11	eleven	*ki laapona kone repo*	*ki laapona onde repo*	hand two-poss. extra three
12	twelve	*ki repo*	*ki repo*	hand three
13	thirteen	*ki repona konde*	*ki repona onde*	hand three-poss. extra
14	fourteen	*ki repona konde laapo*	*ki repona onde laapo*	hand three-poss. extra two
15	fifteen	*ki repona konde repo*	*ki repona onde repo*	hand three-poss. extra three
16	sixteen	*ki malaa*	*ki malaa*	*malaa* 'index finger' (four)

The decimal system

To count the "new" way, the Kewa simply use their hands and feet, so that one doubled hand is "five," two doubled hands are "ten," two hands and one foot doubled are "fifteen," and both the hands and feet doubled are "twenty." If someone counting wishes to use this system beyond five, ten, or some larger multiple of five, then the four-base system is added. For example, sixteen is *ki laapona aa pekepu* ('fifteen', using the decimal system) and *wala pamenda* ('again one', using the four-base system). The basic decimal system is shown in chart 3.[2]

Chart 3. Decimal counting in Kewa

No.	West Kewa	Gloss
5	*ki pekepu*	hand doubled
10	*ki laapo pekepu*	two hands doubled
15	*ki laapona aa pekepu*	two hands, one foot doubled
20	*ki laapona aa laapo pekepu*	two hands, two feet doubled

Discussion and analysis

In the body part tally system in Kewa, a number is one of a set of body part names that functions as a mnemonic enumerator. There are both etic variants, as is the case between dialects, or emic variants, as is the case between a particular number in this counting system and the same one in another system. An example of an etic variant is *pandane* 'one', the first number of the four-base system in West Kewa, but *pamenda* 'one' in the counterpart system of East Kewa.

The two forms are therefore etic variants in the Kewa language. However, *egata* 'little finger' is the emic unit for the first unit enumerated in the body part system and contrasts with either *pandane* or *pamenda* 'one' in the four-base system. The units for one are therefore distributed differently in the referential hierarchy of the Kewa culture.

The nucleus for both the four-base system and the body part system is the number four, represented by the body part that refers to the hand. However,

---

[2]During the colonial era and prior to the introduction of dollar decimal currency, pounds and shillings were used. Twenty shillings made up a pound and ten pence equaled a shilling. Some of the more unusual sterling currency terms never caught on, but the Tok Pisin transliteration for shilling can still sometimes refer to any coin. And today a "pound" in Tok Pisin, if used at all, means a Papua New Guinea (PNG) *kina*. In West Kewa the terms *aana* 'stone' or *yo* 'leaf' were traditionally used for bills and *ini* or *li* 'seed' for coins.

in the Kewa language and culture, the hand may in fact represent the whole arm as well. There are also emic variants for the number four:[3] *maala,* in the body part system and *ki* 'hand', in the four-base system. The important function of the number four is seen in particular by noting its use in the four-base system, but it underlies a much older proto-system for the Engan family of languages. The Mendi language (Lean 1986 (10):30ff.), which is closely related to Kewa, is a good example of how the underlying unit of four marks each fourth body part that is enumerated. Eight is four times two, twelve is four times three, sixteen is four times four, and so on up to forty-eight, which is four times twelve. The forms in Mendi consist of the name of a particular body part in combination with *tu* (glossed 'four') at each fourth position named. In West Kewa, I have heard counts like *gupa ru repo* 'fourth three = twelve', where Kewa *ru* and Mendi *tu* are cognates. In Enga (Lean 1986(9):23), there is a sixty-cycle counting system that consists mainly of a sequence of four cycles, beginning at nine, with each cycle typically of the construction "cycle unit" + one, two, three, etc., where there are thirteen cycle units in all.

The class of items that occurs in the numeral position or slot of a Kewa noun phrase consists of a Numerical Phrase, manifested by Number Adjectives or Number Phrases. Some examples are:

(1) digital: *mone ki lapo pegepu*
money hand both doubled-up = 'ten units of money'

(2) four-base: *akua laapo*
moon two = 'two months'

(3) body part: *sekere egata*
pearl.shell little.finger = 'one pearl shell'

If the particular object is specified, a numerical class marker *ipa* may be used:

(4) *irikai ipa laapo kaba.wa*
dog class two buy.I did = 'I bought two certain dogs.'

(5) *ona ipa laapo wae pe.pe.de*
woman class two bad do.they.complete = 'There were two certain women who were bad.'

---

[3] I consider different terms for the "same" number, used in the different emic systems, to be emic variants.

In other cases, the marker *ma* specifies the object enumerated as constituting a single instance of a class or category of objects:

(6)   *yapa pandane ma piri.sa*
      possum one only sit.it did = 'There was only one possum.'

(7)   *nipu pandane ma.re*
      he one only.concerning... = 'Now, regarding only him...'

Finally, the four-base system of numbers may be reduplicated or conjoined in a Numeral Phrase:

(8)   *aa pandane pandane laata.pu.mi...*
      man one one line.continuing.agent = 'men who were lined up one by one...'

(9)   *akua ulu laapo repo pope.sa*
      moon full two three went.it did = 'Two or three full moons went by.'

As already indicated, multiples of four may also be indicated by the use of *ru*:

(10) *aa ru laapo ru repo gupa...*
      man fourth two fourth three like.that = 'Like eight or twelve men...'

Sometimes the combination of the basic numbers of two and three when conjoined simply means 'a few':

(11) *aa laapo repo.me ni.simi*
      man two three.agent eat.they did = 'A few men ate it.'

Names in Kewa

Names of people, flora and fauna, clans, and places are represented by cognitive units that are highly creative, with many possibilities. There are also taboo names.

Personal names

Kewa personal male names may end optionally in *aa* or *ali* (both meaning 'man' in West and East Kewa, respectively) or, in the case of females, in *-me* and *-nu*. Sometimes individuals are named according to the clan residence, but this is more often a secondary name or alias. Any person may also be referred to by the personal name, modified by the clan or residence name (generally the name of the dance grounds). For example, *Muli Kalo*, would refer to 'Karl, from *Muli*', whereas *Ekerepaa Kalo* would mean 'Karl, of the *Ekerepaa* clan'. Chart 4 gives some examples of names, their variations, and the social settings in which they are used.

Chart 4. Personal name variations and social settings

Gloss	Contrastive forms	Variations	Social settings
man's name	*Kirapeasi*	*Kira*	son of Yapua
clan name	*Nemola*	*Nemola Kirapeasi*	member of clan
sub-clan name	*Asa-Kindipa*	*Asa repaa; Kidipa repaa*	member of sub-clan
taboo name	*Nabawan*		in-law relationships

Personal names also include those used for mythical beings, special domestic animals, as well as ancestors and spirits. The names are significant and powerful because they represent a relationship between the person and the referent. Babies are not named for several months, usually until their survival is assured, and then they are generally named according to the characteristic(s) of the child or in accord with a particular event that took place about the time of the birth. For example *Maaku* 'vomit' may indicate that the baby threw up a lot, whereas *Yandawe* 'fight' may refer to a particular battle that the parents wish to remember. Marriages change relationships and therefore new names come into existence. The list of personal names in chart 5 is illustrative, indicating the variety and context of various words that are used as names.

Chart 5. Illustrative personal names

Given name	Taboo name	Baptized Lutheran name	Catholic name
Kamaa 'outside'	*Nali* 'outside'	*Adano* 'I should see it'	*Pita*
Ame 'brother'	*Negaa* 'last born'	*Epe-kone* 'good thoughts'	*Dominik*
Yapa 'marsupial'	*Sikame* 'type of possum'	*Giape* 'give it to me'	*Meri*
Nalisa 'he did not hit it'	*Kadupilisa* 'he closed his eyes'	*Epeta* 'it is good'	*Teresa*
Remaa 'story'	*Agale* 'talk'	*Pago-mea* 'hearing-taking'	*Tobias*
Rabuaa 'tread on'	*Loma* 'splinter'	*Ripinape* 'hold fast'	*Katarina*

Clan names are also cognitive units that are based upon how a group of people classify themselves (or some other group). The clan, known as a *ruru* (or in some cases sub-clan), has a particular name that often has -*repaa* attached to it. In the case of compound names, the parts may represent the names of brothers or the name of a particular place followed by the putative founder of the clan or sub-clan. Chart 6 presents some examples.

Chart 6. Illustrative clan names

Isolated clan/ Village name	Clan marked with -*repaa*	Compound clan name
Moi	*Adalurepaa*	*Kagua-Rakili*
Mui	*Ekerepaa*	*Pale-Ali*
Nemola	*Eparepaa*	*Palame-Ekerepaa*
Perepe	*Ibirepaa*	*Parepaa-Rakili*
Rakili	*Kipurepaa*	*Raili-Wagai*
Subulu	*Kanaarepaa*	*Pudia-Rakili*
Mirupa	*Lawagerepaa*	*Rigilimi-Alinu*
Kagopoiya	*Marepaa*	*Walua-Perepaa*
Menakiri	*Mumugurepaa*	*Yarena-Ekerepaa*
Koiali	*Mogarepaa*	*Rawami-Ali*

Name taboo and aliases

The Kewa people commonly have taboo names, not just for the more common and expected kinship in-law relations and relationships, but also for objects that are associated with cults and spirit worship. For this reason the principal personality of a particular cult, as well as objects associated with cult activities, often have taboo names. I have commented upon this elsewhere (K. Franklin 1972, 1975, 1977), but the system is so important to names, that I will briefly review it here.

First of all, aliases are a type of name taboo. One does not mention the name of certain in-laws because saying a name implies a relationship with that person. Calling out a name at a pig festival invokes the power of the clan or sub-clan founders and is not simply calling attention to an individual who will receive something, such as pork. It is also a practical way to associate a person with the name of his clan, e.g., *Rimurepaa Yandawae,* means '*Yandawae* of the *Rimurepaa* clan'. This is necessary because clans other than *Rimurepaa* may also have someone named *Yandawae.* The same logic follows in the use of aliases used between in-laws or when in-laws call each other by the particular kinship term. New names imply new relationships and subsequent obligations.

Aliases are also given at government censuses, i.e., in addition to a person's given name there is often a census name that is recorded in the "government's book." In the case of baptisms, aliases are used to represent the new way of life, again a new relationship, so that *Yandawae's* new name may become *Epe-kone* 'good behavior'.

In the case of cult activities, it was not the names of people, but the names of cult objects that were renamed, e.g., parts of pigs (used in ritual activities), dogs (associated with magical properties in selected areas where wild pandanus grows), or the cult deities themselves (because cures and the deities were traded and borrowed from area to area). New words are coined or substituted for the names of people who die, for certain affines, for objects associated with the argot of the former men's clubs, for important spirits, and, in a more general and pidginized manner, in the ritual pandanus language.

Mainly aliases are lexical substitutions for common words that are derived on the basis of semantic relationships, such as association (calling a baby "runny nose" because of his/her problem), metonymy (calling a little girl "water mother," where one term is thought of as the cause of the other), synonymy (calling a brother-in-law whose first name is "possum" a particular kind of possum), antonymy (calling a light skinned person "black one"), and so on.

Finally, names are recognized because they contrast with each other, they vary according to certain rules, and they are spoken in a particular social context. Pike considered contrast, variation and distribution as essential features to describe a unit. This distinction can be seen in chart 7.

Chart 7. Pike's emic unit applied to selected Kewa words

Gloss	Contrastive forms	Variations	Social settings
dog	*irikai*	*yana* *abuliri*	pre-Kewa pandanus language
pig	*mena*	*mena-sipisipi*	coined loan word for 'sheep'
man's name	*Kirapeasi*	*Kira*	son of Yapua
brothers' names	*Asa-Kidipa*	*Asa-repaa; Kidipa-repaa*	sub-clan
man's name	*Mano*	*Kama* (taboo name)	Muli village
sweet potato	*saapi* *modo-mapua*	*etaa* (taboo name)	garden/house spirit house

Place names

Village names most often refer to the location of the dance grounds for the clan or sub-clan. In fact, in Kewa areas the rivers, mountains, and dance grounds all have names that are considered one word.

Each stream, river, swamp, hill, and mountain has a name. Such a name is also an identity factor for the individual showing his or her relationship to the environment, so early on each child learns the names of the particular objects that describe where he or she belongs. This entails knowing the names of the trees in the area, the owner's of the gardens and trees, as well as the general topography of the area.

Summary

Numbers and names have functions in Kewa society that are determined by cultural context. Both categories have emic and etic contrasts and variations within the cultural systems. By understanding the particular distribution of the form-meaning class, we can also best note the referential meanings of numbers and names. Tagmemics provides a framework or perspective that integrates the grammatical and cultural aspects of such units of behavior.

References

Franklin, Karl J. 1965. Kewa social organization. *Ethnology* 4(4):408–420.

Franklin, Karl J. 1967. Names and aliases in Kewa. *Journal of the Polynesian Society* 76(1):76–81.

Franklin, Karl J. 1968. *The dialects of Kewa.* Pacific Linguistics, Series B 10.

Franklin, Karl J. 1972. A ritual pandanus language of New Guinea. *Oceania* 43(1):66–76.

Franklin, Karl J. 1975. A Kewa religious argot. *Anthropos* 70:713–725.

Franklin, Karl J. 1977. The Kewa language in culture and society. In S. A. Wurm (ed.), *New Guinea area languages and language study,* Vol.3: *Language, culture, society, and the modern world, fascicle 1.* Pacific Linguistics C 40:5–18.

Franklin, Karl J. 1991. Kewa. In Terence E. Hays (ed.), *Encyclopedia of World Cultures. Volume II: Oceania,* 114–117. Boston: G. K. Hall and Co.

Franklin, Karl J., and Joice Franklin. 1962. The Kewa counting systems. *Journal of the Polynesian Society* 71(2):188–191.

Franklin, Karl J., and Joice Franklin [assisted by Yapua Kirapeasi]. 1978. *A Kewa dictionary: with supplementary grammatical and anthropological material.* Pacific Linguistics C 53.

Josiphides, Lisette. 1985. *The production of inequality: Gender and exchange among the Kewa.* London: Tavistock.

Lean, G. A. 1986. *Counting systems of Papua New Guinea, Volume 9: Enga, Western Highlands, Simbu Provinces; Volume 10 Southern Highlands Province; Volume 11: Gulf Province.* Lae: Dept. of Mathematics, University of Technology.

LeRoy, John D. 1979. The ceremonial pig kill of the South Kewa. *Oceania* 49 (3):179–209.

LeRoy, John D. 1985. *Fabricated world: An interpretation of Kewa tales.* Vancouver: University of British Columbia Press.

MacDonald, Mary. 1991. *Mararoko: A study in Melanesian religion.* New York: Peter Lang.

Pike, Kenneth L. 1957. Grammemic theory. *General Linguistics* 2:35–41.

Pike, Kenneth L. 1967. *Language in relation to a unified theory of the structure of human behavior.* Janua Linguarum, series maior 24. The Hague: Mouton. [2nd ed., rev.]

Pike, Kenneth L. 1976. Toward the development of tagmemic postulates. In Ruth M. Brend and Kenneth L. Pike (eds.), *Tagmemics, Volume 2: Theoretical discussion,* 91–127. *Trends in Linguistics 1.* The Hague: Mouton.

Pike, Kenneth L. 1982. *Linguistic concepts: An introduction to tagmemics.* Lincoln: University of Nebraska Press.

Pike, Kenneth L. 1983. The future for unit-in-context: The tagmeme. In Shiro Hattori et al. (eds.), *Proceedings of the 13th International Congress of Linguists, August 29–September 4, 1982, Tokyo,* 881–883. Tokyo: Tokyo Press.

Pike, Kenneth L. 1988. Cultural relativism in relation to constraints on world view: An emic perspective. *Bulletin of the Institute of History and Philology* 59(2):385–399.

Pike, Kenneth L. 1992. Person beyond logic, in language, life, and philosophy. In Ruth M. Brend (ed.), *The Eighteenth LACUS Forum, 1991,* 23–37. Lake Bluff, Ill.: Linguistic Association of Canada and the United States.

Pike, Kenneth L. 1993. *Talk, thought, and thing: The emic road toward conscious knowledge.* Dallas: Summer Institute of Linguistics.

Part IV

The Observer's Perspective

*"The observer adds part of himself to the data
that he looks at or listens to."*
(Pike 1964:129)

*"When man studies 'things,' he injects part
of himself into their definition."*
(Pike 1982:3)

19

Recipient Person Suppletion in the Verb 'Give'

Bernard Comrie

I am honored to dedicate this essay to the memory of Kenneth L. Pike. His work has accompanied me since my first steps in linguistics, when I tried pronouncing the more exotic sounds described in his Phonetics as I strolled around Cambridge, England, much to the consternation of passers-by. This chapter is not much to give, but perhaps an essay on 'give' is nonetheless appropriate for one who gave so much.

Introduction

According to Bybee (1985:23, 93), suppletion for person is the rarest kind of suppletion to be found in verb conjugation. Examples of such suppletion are, of course, found across the languages of the world, including even in European languages, but it usually involves either very

In addition to people cited in the text or in notes as the source of data and analyses, I am grateful to the following for drawing my attention to data or for discussing the general phenomenon with me: Gontzal Aldai, Martin Haspelmath, Stephen Levinson, Paulette Levy, Anna Margetts (who also inspired me to work intensively on this topic), Igor Mel'cuk, John Newman, David Peterson, Malcolm Ross, and all those who replied to my query posted on the Linguist List (http://linguistlist.org/issues/11/11-1012.html#1). Earlier versions of this paper were presented common verbs that also have a high degree of suppletion elsewhere in their conjugation (e.g., the copula in English, with first person singular *am*, third person singular *is*), or the suppletion parallels an irregularity in pattern that is found in other verbs. An example of the latter is found in the conjugation of the French verb 'go', which has the forms singular first person *vais*, second person *vas*, third person *va*, plural third person *vont*, but plural first person *allons*, second person *allez*. The different stems correlate with the distinction between stem- versus desinence-stress and parallel exactly the vowel alternation found in such verbs as *vouloir* 'want', *pouvoir* 'be able', *mourir* 'die', as in the corresponding forms of the first verb *veux, veux, veut, veulent; voulons, voulez*.

Somewhat surprisingly, then, a number of languages of the world use distinct forms, at least providing a prima facie case of suppletion, for the verb 'give', depending on the person of the recipient. In the following section, data illustrating this phenomena from a range of languages are provided along with a possible explanation for the occurrence of this phenomenon. Then some apparently related but probably, at least historically, distinct phenomena are discussed.

Examples of Recipient Person Suppletion in the Verb 'Give'

My first encounter with the phenomenon in question was when teaching a field methods class using Malayalam in the early 1980s. I had elicited a sentence something like 'I gave him the book', and then proceeded to change the pronoun forms (Malayalam has no other verb agreement) to get something like 'he gave me the book'. My attempt at creating the corresponding Malayalam sentence ended in failure, and when I asked the consultant to give the correct form I was surprised to see that an apparently completely different verb was used! Since then, and especially during the past two years, I have been collecting parallel examples from across the languages of the world. This section will present some of the relevant data.

to the VI Encuentro Internacional de Lingüística en el Noroeste at the University of Sonora (Hermosillo, Mexico) in November–December 2000, to the conference "Verb Categories and Sentence Structure" held at the St. Petersburg Institute of Linguistic Studies (Russian Academy of Sciences) in May 2001, to an informal seminar at the Max Planck Institute for Evolutionary Anthropology (Leipzig) in June 2001, and to the Fourth Meeting of the Association for Linguistic Typology held at the University of California Santa Barbara in July 2001.

I should emphasize that the sample of languages represented here, though covering many different language families and language areas, is very much a "chance" sample. Grammars of languages that I know to have the phenomenon often do not discuss it, perhaps on the grounds that this belongs more properly to the lexicon, and the number of languages for which there are extensive dictionaries from that language to English or some other widely used reference language is not too large. Thus, it is often by chance that I myself have stumbled across an example or had my attention drawn to an example by someone else. The aim of this section is, therefore, to show that the phenomenon in question is widespread across the languages of the world, but no conclusions concerning its frequency or geographical distribution beyond this should be drawn. I am, incidentally, currently investigating further instances of this and related phenomena in other languages.

The data in this section are divided into two parts. First, I discuss examples where the suppletion is between one form for third person recipients, another form for first and second person recipients (i.e., nonspeech act participants versus speech act participants). Then, I discuss examples of suppletion between one form for first person recipients, another form for second and third person recipients (i.e., ego versus non-ego). I have encountered no examples of second person versus first and third person.

Third person versus first and second person recipients

In Malayalam, a Dravidian language spoken in Kerala (India), completely different verb roots are used for 'give' with a third person recipient (*koTukkuka*) (upper-case represents a retroflex consonant here) and with a first or second person recipient (*taruka/tarika*) (Asher and Kumari 1997:348)—the forms are here cited in the infinitive.[1] Completely different roots are also found in the Yukaghir languages of northeastern Siberia, as in Kolyma Yukaghir *tadi:-* 'give (to 3)', *kej-* 'give (to 1/2)' (Maslova 2002). In Lepcha, a Tibeto-Burman language spoken in Sikkim (India) and neighboring areas, the distinction is between *byî* 'give (to 3)' and *bo* 'give (to 1/2)' (Mainwaring 1876:127–128).[2]

Several Papuan (non-Austronesian) languages of New Guinea show the same phenomenon, e.g., Enga (West-Central group within East New Guinea Highlands) has a distinction between *maíngi* 'give (to 3)' and *díngi* 'give (to 1/2)' (Lang 1973:17, 62), here cited with the habitual suffix *-ngi*;

---

[1]Burrow and Emeneau (1984:185–186, 269; items 2053, 3098) note that some, but by no means all, South Dravidian languages and dialects have the same distinction.

[2]Further data provided by Heleen Plaisier suggest that the actual distribution may be somewhat more complex than this, but the person of the recipient is clearly a relevant factor.

the same phenomenon is found in another very closely related language, Ipili, with *mai* 'give (to 3), *gi* 'give (to 1/2)' (Frances Ingemann, personal communication), and also in Kewa, another language of the West-Central group, with *kala* 'give (to 3)' and *gi* 'give (to 1/2)' (Franklin and Franklin 1978:135, 145). In Hamtai, also known as Kapau, an Angan language spoken in Morobe province, we find *-i-* 'give (to 3)' (always occurring with a third person indirect object prefix, i.e., as *w-i-*) versus *täp-* 'give (to 1/2)' (Oates and Oates 1968:23).

A slightly more complex example is provided by Saliba, an Oceanic language spoken in Milne Bay province, Papua New Guinea, with forms *mose-i* 'give (to 3)' versus *le* 'give (to 1/2)' (Margetts 1999, which is also the source for the following discussion). In *mose-i*, *-i* is the applicative suffix, but this verb never occurs without this suffix. Unlike in all the other languages cited for which I have relevant data, in Saliba the two verbs do not have the same argument structure. In Saliba, a verb can cross-reference at most one object noun phrase (the primary object). With *mose-i*, two patterns are possible: in the first, the cross-referenced noun phrase is the recipient, while the patient appears as a secondary object (i.e., without a postposition but also without cross-referencing in the verb); in the second, the patient is cross-referenced in the verb, while the recipient appears as a postpositional phrase. With *le*, only the patient is cross-referenced in the verb, with the recipient (if expressed) encoded in a postpositional phrase; however, this verb obligatorily requires one of two directional suffixes, *-ma* 'towards speaker' or *-wa* 'towards addressee'; I return in the third section to such interrelations between the person of the recipient and marking of deixis.

Several (though not all) Zapotecan languages, belonging to the Oto-Manguean family and spoken in Oaxaca (Mexico), provide the interesting phenomenon of a group of languages sharing a distinction between roots for 'give' with third person and non-third person recipients, but where the actual forms may vary from language to language (Smith Stark 2001).[3] In Zaniza Zapotec, the forms are *zed* 'give (to 3)' and *bij* 'give (to 1/2)' (Natalie Operstein, personal communication). In Otomí, another group of languages within Oto-Manguean and spoken in a broad band running from just southwest of Mexico City, to the north of the city and towards the Gulf of Mexico, we find similar suppletion, e.g., in San Ildefonso Otomí *uN-* 'give (to 3)' (where *N* represents a nasal archiphoneme) versus *'ra-* 'give (to 1/2)' (Enrique L. Palancar, personal

---

[3]Smith Stark (2001) cites examples from elsewhere in the Oto-Manguean language family, and also some examples of a similar phenomenon in some of these languages with the verb 'say'. I had not myself come across person suppletion with 'say' before, so this is clearly something that needs to be investigated more widely cross-linguistically.

communication). In Miskitu, a Misumalpan language of Nicaragua, one finds (citing infinitive forms) a distinction between third person *yâb-aia* and the forms with other recipients first person exclusive *ai-k-aia*, second person *mai-k-aia*, first person inclusive *wan-k-aia*—in the non-third person forms, the first morpheme cross-references the recipient, in the third person form there is no such cross-referencing affix (Ken Hale, personal communication).

In the examples presented so far, the forms of the root used in connection with the person distinction in the recipient have been completely different, and indeed one might argue that one is dealing with two verbs rather than with suppletive forms of a single verb, a point to which I return in the section on residual issues. In some languages, however, the two forms are clearly related, at least etymologically. For instance, in Tsez, a Northeast Caucasian language spoken in Daghestan (Russia), we find the forms *teλ-* 'give (to 3)' versus *neλ-* 'give (to 1/2)'. These forms contain two etymologically identifiable deictic prefixes, *t-* and *n-*, although it is not clear that these prefixes are segmentable synchronically, at least not in all dialects.[4]

In some languages, there is at least a suspicion that the two roots might be related etymologically, although the evidence is not clear and is based on superficial similarity. This is the case in Manambu, a Ndu language spoken in East Sepik province (Papua New Guinea), with *kwiy* 'give (to 3)' versus *kwatay/kwatiy* 'give (to 1/2)' (Alexandra Y. Aikhenvald, personal communication). In Nandi, a Kalenjin language of the Nilotic family spoken in western Kenya, the forms are *ki:-ka:-ci* 'give (to 3)', *ke:-ko:n* 'give (to 1/2)' (Chet A. Creider, personal communication, also forming the basis of the following discussion). In the first form, *-ci* is a dative/applicative suffix indicating the presence of a recipient; this verb does not occur without this suffix. Since third person objects are always indicated by zero in the verb, there is no possibility of overt person-number marking of the recipient in the third person recipient verb; as with all finite verb forms, prefixes encode person-number of the subject. Turning to the first/second person recipient verb, its finite forms, like other transitive verbs, have a prefix encoding person-number of the subject and a portmanteau suffix encoding person-number of the subject and (non-third person) object; in the case of *ke:-ko:n*, the relevant object is the recipient.

---

[4]Tsez simple transitive verbs take a suffix *-o* in the imperative, while derived transitive verbs take no suffix. Some speakers of Tsez have the imperative forms *teλ-o*, *neλ-o*, suggesting that for them these verb stems are monomorphemic. Other speakers have *teλ*, *neλ*, suggesting that for them the verbs are derived, i.e., contain an internal morpheme boundary. Some of the related Tsezic languages have generalized one variant, e.g., Bezhta uses *niλ-* irrespective of the person of the recipient. Tsez and Bezhta data are from my own field work, with added thanks to Arsen Abdulaev for Tsez and Madjid Khalilov for Bezhta.

Finally, I will note an example that belongs equally in this section and in the following. In the Mongsen dialect of Ao, a Kuki-Chin-Naga language within the Tibeto-Burman family spoken in Nagaland (India), in the imperative and only in the imperative we find a distinction between *khi-ang^{33}* 'give (to 3)' and *kh-ang^{33}* 'give (to 1)' (the superscripts here indicate tone); since the imperative is implausible, if not actually excluded, with a second person recipient, this language is neutral between the speech act participant versus non-speech act participant type and the ego versus non-ego type (data from Alexander Robertson Coupe, personal communication).

First person versus second and third person recipients

Although I have fewer illustrative languages in this section than in the preceding section, they nonetheless come from three continents. Completely different roots are found in Kenuzi-Dongola, also known as Dongolese Nubian, a Nubian language within the Eastern Sudanic family spoken in Sudan and Egypt, where we have the forms *tír* 'give (to 2/3)' versus *dến* 'give (to 1)' (Armbruster 1960:315).

In Maori, a Polynesian language spoken in New Zealand, the distinction is expressed by means of different deictic suffixes: *-atu* 'direction other than towards speaker' versus *-mai* 'direction towards speaker', to give *ho-atu* 'give (away from speaker)' versus *ho(o)-mai* 'give (towards speaker)' (Bauer 1993:471). Given the high productivity of these deictic suffixes, one might question whether Maori is properly included here, but there is one irregularity in the combination of the root *ho-* with the second deictic suffix, namely the optional lengthening of the root vowel. But Maori is certainly close to the dividing line between suppletion and a minor irregularity, a point to which I return in the discussion of residual issues.

Another language that comes close to an ego versus non-ego distinction in its verb 'give' is Japanese, which has completely different forms. Indeed for each recipient defined deictically there are two forms distinguished by the relative social status of giver and recipient: *yaru/ageru* 'give (in social direction away from speaker, to outgroup)' versus *kureru/kudasaru* 'give (in social direction towards speaker, to ingroup)'. In Japanese, moreover, the distinction is clearly not precisely a distinction in the person of the recipient. The forms *kureru/kudasaru* are used for any giving which comes towards the speaker and would be used, for instance, if the teacher gave something to my brother, since although the recipient is third person ('my brother'), the gift is nonetheless coming towards me, from an outgroup into my ingroup. The Japanese system has been discussed extensively in the literature, and one is left wondering whether some of the departures from a strict person system that are known to occur in Japanese might also be found in some of the other languages cited had they been examined in more detail. This must remain a question for future investigation.

Recipient Suppletion and Deixis

Given that suppletion for person agreement is so rare across the languages of the world, one is naturally led to seek some other explanation, whether synchronic or diachronic, for the widespread occurrence of such suppletion with respect to the recipient of the verb 'give'. This becomes even more natural when one notes further that in several (not all) of the languages cited in the preceding section there is no other agreement with indirect objects (e.g., in Tsez), or even with any noun phrase (e.g., in Malayalam), and that the suppletion is restricted to person, not extending, for instance, to number, despite the widespread cross-linguistic treatment of person-number as a single parameter in verb morphology. In this section, I will suggest that the diachronic origin of person suppletion for the recipient of 'give' is to be sought in the phenomenon of deixis, although in at least most of the cases discussed this deixis seems to have been grammaticalized according to the grammatical person of the recipient.

Deictic distinctions in the lexicon

Deictic distinctions corresponding at least roughly to person oppositions are found frequently in the lexicons of the languages of the world, indeed for some semantic areas, like 'come/go', it is probably more frequent to find a lexical deictic opposition than not to find one. In English, the distinction between *come* and *go* corresponds roughly to a person distinction, with the former denoting motion towards the speaker or the addressee, the latter motion towards a third person, as in (1). This thus corresponds to the opposition between speech act participant and non-speech act participant, as with 'give'.

(1)   a. *I will go to him.*
      b. *He will come to me.*
      c. *I will come to you.*

In Spanish, by contrast, the "translation equivalents" *venir* 'come' versus *ir* 'go' distinguish rather motion towards speaker versus motion towards addressee or third person, so that the Spanish for 'I'm coming!' (to the addressee, e.g., in response to a summons) is *¡Voy!*, which is the irregular first person singular of *ir* 'go'. Spanish thus parallels the ego versus non-ego distinction.

Even closely related languages can differ as to whether or not they have a deictic distinction with verbs in the general semantic area of 'come/go', and if so as to the precise nature of the distinction, another phenomenon that was touched on in the preceding section (e.g., in the case of Dravidian languages). Thus, English has a deictic distinction in the case of *take/bring*, as in (2).

(2)   a. *I will take it to him.*
      b. *He will bring it to me.*
      c. *I will bring it to you.*

The German translation equivalents *bringen/nehmen*—the former is even an exact etymological cognate—are not deictic, so that the German translation of (2a) likewise uses *bringen*, as in (3).

(3)   *Ich bringe es ihm.*

Finally, there are languages like Russian that lack deictic oppositions even in the semantic domain 'come/go', where a single verb *idti* covers both, as in (4).[5]

(4)   a. *Idi v magazin!*
          'Go to the store!'

      b. *Idi sjuda!*
          'Come here!'

---

[5] Russian has ways of expressing the distinction, e.g., by prefixation: thus, *prijti* (for *pri + idti*) is more specifically 'come, arrive', whereas *pojti* (for *po + idti*) is more specifically 'go, set out'. But crucially the distinction is not obligatory, in contrast to English, and the semantic distinction is also not quite the same.

Although there is a high correlation between, on the one hand, the choice between the members of such deictic pairs as 'come' and 'go' and, on the other hand, the grammatical person to whom the motion is directed, this is not an absolute correlation, since it is always possible to adopt a deictic center other than the actual here-and-now, in which case one can even have examples like (5), where it is explicitly the referent of the first-person pronoun that is moving towards the deictic center Xanadu.

(5)   *And finally, we came to Xanadu.*

In other words, such deictic distinctions in the lexicon are not in general grammaticalized as indicators of grammatical person. It is this further stage of grammaticalization that seems to characterize person suppletion for the recipient of the verb 'give'.

Deixis and the verb 'give'

Interaction between deixis and the recipient of the verb 'give' is clearly attested in a number of languages, including both some of those cited in the second section ("Examples of recipient person suppletion") going beyond the phenomenon of suppletion conditioned by the grammatical person of the recipient, and also in a number of languages that do not show this phenomenon. First, I will recapitulate some of the relevant phenomena from the languages referred to in the second section. In Saliba, it is obligatory to include in the morphology of the verb 'give', if the recipient is first or second person, a deictic suffix indicating, respectively, 'towards the speaker' and 'towards the addressee'. In Maori, the distinction according to the person of the recipient is indicated primarily by the opposition between the deictic suffix indicating 'direction towards speaker' and that indicating 'direction other than towards the speaker'. In Tsez, the initial consonant that distinguishes the two verbs 'give' is etymologically, at least, a deictic prefix. According to Armbruster, in Kenuzi-Dongola the initial *t-* of *tír* is a "demonstrative or deictic of other than speaker" (1960:315).

I will cite two languages to show interaction between deixis and recipient person independent of suppletion. In English, the verb *give*, except in certain highly restricted usages, requires overt expression of both direct and indirect objects, so that (6a) is possible while (6b) is not.

(6)   a. *Give it to Mary!*
      b. **Give it!*

However, with an understood first person recipient, it is possible, at least
in colloquial usage, to use, instead of a first person pronoun, the deictic
place adverb *here*, as in (7a).

(7)   a. *Give it here!*
      b. **Give it there!*

As the ungrammaticality of (7b) shows, this is not part of a general license
to use deictic adverbs to indicate recipients of *give* in English, but a quite
specific possibility restricted to first person recipients.

   A more complex example is provided by Ik, a Kuliak language spoken in
northeastern Uganda. The data in (8) are taken from Serzisko (1988) and
use the following abbreviations: AND — andative, GOA — goal, PRF —
perfect, SG — singular, VEN — venitive; an upper-case letter indicates an
ejective consonant.

(8)   a. *ma-ida-ka.*
          give-2SG-PRF
          'You have given it (to him).'

      b. *me-et-ida-ka.*
          give-VEN-2SG-PRF
          'You have given it (to me).'

      c. *maa-ka.*
          give-PRF
          'He has given it (to someone).'

      d. *maa-Kota-ka.*
          give-AND-PRF
          'He has given it (to someone).'

      e. *me-eta-ka.*
          give-VEN-PRF
          'He has given it to me.'

   f. *me-et-ia*   *lotoba*   *bi-ke.*
      give-VEN-1SG tobacco 2SG-GOA
      'I gave you tobacco.'

   g. *maa-Kot-ia*   *rag*   *na*   *bien-e.*
      give-AND-1SG bull DET 2SG-GOA
      'I gave this bull to you.'

While the data presented by Serzisko do not permit a complete analysis of all issues relevant to present concerns—they were of course originally used by Serzisko in a somewhat different context—we may note the important distinction between the venitive suffix *-et(a)* and the andative suffix *-Kot(a)*, corresponding, as the Italianate terms suggest, to the distinction between 'come' and 'go'. With a first person recipient, occurrence of the venitive suffix seems to be obligatory, as in (b) and (e). With a third person recipient, the andative suffix seems to be optional when the subject is also third person (and non-coreferential with the recipient), as in (c) and (d), and excluded when the subject is second (or presumably first) person, as in (a). With a second person recipient, one seems to have the choice between venitive and andative, as in (f) and (g), at least if the subject is first person. At least one can recognize the distinction between deictic choices with first and third person recipients, and the borderline status of the second person.

    The Japanese data, presented briefly in the second section now take on added importance. As indicated in that section, the distinction in Japanese is primarily a distinction of deixis (towards or away from the speaker, in social terms, i.e., from outgroup to ingroup or from ingroup to outgroup) and does not correlate absolutely with person differences, so that a sentence with a second or third person recipient could take a verb from either of the two sets. Indeed, as pointed out to me by Shigeko Nariyama, it is even possible to use the verbs appropriate for an outgroup recipient with a first person recipient, provided a particular, unusual deictic perspective is adopted. Thus Japanese, at least, belongs properly not in the set of languages that make use of suppletion according to the grammatical person of the recipient, rather the relevant pairs of Japanese verbs are distinguished more directly in terms of deixis. To the best of my knowledge, this is not true of the other languages described, where the distinction is strictly one of grammatical person. In fairness, however, I must point out that in few of these languages has the phenomenon been investigated in as much detail as in Japanese, so it is always possible that future studies will show that for some of these languages we are not dealing, strictly speaking, with suppletion conditioned by the grammatical person of the recipient. But as a provisional conclusion, I will state that these languages seem to have grammaticalized an earlier deictic distinction, in some cases historically reconstructable (e.g., Tsez), in other cases hypothesized, into a distinction based only on the grammatical person of the recipient.

Some residual issues

In this section, I wish to deal with some further issues that arise in the consideration of the kinds of data discussed so far.

In the preceding section, I presented a diachronic explanation for the existence of suppletive relations in the verb 'give' depending on the grammatical person of the recipient. But a further question arises even given this diachronic explanation, namely why it is precisely the recipient which conditions this kind of distinction, even if not strictly grammaticalized as a grammatical person system. At least in part, this question can be answered by reference to deictic distinctions expressed by means of lexical distinctions or deictic particles, where a basic distinction seems to be, precisely, that between actions directed towards the deictic center versus actions directed away from the deictic center. This applies as much to 'give' as it does to 'come/go' or to any of the other pairs that are found in individual languages.

This does not, of course, exclude the possibility that a language might have suppletion for, for instance, the patient of the verb 'give', in particular if the language has a more general pattern of suppletion according to features of the patient. In the Uto-Aztecan language Huichol, for instance, spoken in Nayarit and Jalisco states (Mexico), the verb 'give' shows suppletion for features of the patient, as in the examples in (9) taken from the dialect of San Andrés Cohamiata (Gómez 1999).

(9)   *kʷei-tïa-rika* 'give (something long)'
       'ii-tïa-rika 'give (something flat)'
       huri-tïa-rika 'give (something without permanent shape)'
       hani-tïa-rika 'give (something folded)'
       tui-tïa-rika 'give (something bulky)'

But note that these are just the kinds of features that are relevant in general in Huichol for verbs that show suppletion for their patient. Indeed, all of the verbs cited in (9) are morphologically causatives (with the productive causative suffix *-tïa*) of monotransitive verbs meaning 'take', and these monotransitive verbs are likewise suppletive for precisely the same features of their patient, i.e., 'take (something long)', etc.

An important issue to consider in connection with the phenomena considered in the second section ("Examples of recipient person suppletion") is whether they are really to be subsumed under the phenomenon suppletion. An alternative would be to say, that for each pair of items, we are in fact dealing with two distinct lexical items, just as in English *come* and *go* are considered two distinct lexical items rather than as variants of a single lexical item. This question is particularly important for the general theory of suppletion (Mel'cuk 1994), but is, I think, less crucial for the concerns that are at issue in this article. Even if one considers that one is dealing with distinct lexical items rather than with suppletively related items within a single lexeme, it is still the case that to have two distinct lexical items that are differentiated only by the grammatical person of one of their arguments is an extremely rare phenomenon cross-linguistically, if indeed it is attested at all, so the basic question would require only minor reformulation: Why is it precisely with the concept 'give' that one finds distinct lexemes (instead of: suppletively related distinct forms of the same lexeme) used according to the person of the recipient? But returning to whether or not we are dealing with suppletion, one can try and apply tests—with all their attendant difficulties—to see if one is dealing with a single lexical item or not. For instance, suppose that in one of the languages cited in the second section one asks the question, *Who did John give the book to?* with the verb appropriate to a third person recipient. Is 'to me' a possible response, without any sense of the response contradicting presuppositions of the question? In at least some of the languages referred to, this is the case (and the others still need to be tested). Contrast this with the case of English *massacre*, which is not an optional suppletive form of *kill* used with a plural patient, because as a possible response preserving presuppositions to *How many people did they massacre?* one cannot say *One*.

From the opposite end of the problem space, one might question whether all the examples given really involve suppletion, with some of them perhaps being less radical instances of morphological relationships within a paradigm. In the second section, I noted explicitly that in some cases completely different roots are used, the strongest form of suppletion, whereas in other cases there are at least similarities between the roots, with Maori and (at least possibly for some speakers) Tsez using the same root but with different affixes. However, a weaker characterization of suppletion would characterize as suppletive all instances where the relation between the variants is idiosyncratic in the language in question.

In Tsez, the verb 'give' is the only one that shows a synchronic reflex of the deictic prefixes *t-* and *n-*; in Maori, which admittedly comes closest to a pair where one can simply talk about a single root occurring regularly with distinct productive deictic suffixes, there is nonetheless the optional idiosyncratic lengthening of the root before the deictic suffix *-mai*. Thus, in a broad sense of suppletion, all the examples considered in the second section satisfy this part of the definition.

Other Phenomena

There are several other phenomena that might, at least at first sight, seem to be related to the kinds of person suppletion for the recipient discussed above, but which are probably either synchronically or diachronically distinct phenomena. I will discuss two such cases here.

Richer person-number suppletion

In some languages, one finds at least apparently much richer systems of suppletion for the person-number of the indirect object than in the languages cited above. For instance, in Amele, a Madang language spoken in Madang province (Papua New Guinea), one finds the forms for the verb 'give', in the infinitive, as in (10), depending on the person-number of the recipient (data and analysis from Roberts 1987:279, 386–387, 390).

(10)   *ut-ec* 'give (to 3sg)'
        ih-ec 'give (to 2sg)'
        it-ec 'give (to 1sg)'
        al-ec 'give (to 2/3du)'
        il-ec 'give (to 1du)'
        ad-ec 'give (to 2/3pl)'
        ig-ec 'give (to 1pl)'

In these forms, *-ec* is the infinitive suffix for this verb class. However, on closer examination, it turns out that the first morpheme in each of these forms is identical to the indirect object cross-referencing morpheme for that person-number combination, as in (11).

(11)   *-ut* '3sg indirect object suffix on verb'
        -ih '2sg indirect object suffix on verb'
        -it '1sg indirect object suffix on verb'
        -al '2/3du indirect object suffix on verb'
        -il '1du indirect object suffix on verb'
        -ad '2/3pl indirect object suffix on verb'
        -ig '1pl indirect object suffix on verb'

This suggests that the forms of the verb 'give' are not really suppletive, but contain an invariable zero root which is followed by the appropriate indirect object suffix. Such zero roots are not unusual in some Papuan languages, and in Amele there is also a monotransitive zero root with the meaning 'get', distinguishable from 'give' in that it belongs to a different conjugation class (with infinitive in *-oc*).

However, one could easily imagine such a system being reinterpreted as a richer suppletion system, and this seems to have happened in another Madang language, Waskia, with distinctions according to person-number of the recipient as in (12) (Ross and Paol 1978:43).

(12)   *tuiy-* ~ *tuw-* 'give (to 3sg)'
        kisi- 'give (to 2sg)'
        asi- 'give (to 1sg)'
        idi- 'give (to pl)'

According to Ross (personal communication), the forms seem to include indirect object markers etymologically, but not with sufficient transparency to permit precise reconstruction. Especially since Waskia does not synchronically have any object agreement, the data in (12) appear to illustrate a system with suppletion for the person-number of the recipient of 'give', but with a completely different origin from the examples discussed in preceding sections.[6]

Person suppletion and politeness

Another possible source of person suppletion would be politeness phenomena. For instance, in Russian, in addition to the ordinary verb 'eat',

---

[6]The lists of translation equivalents of 'give' in Z'graggen (1980a; 1980b) suggest that phenomena of the Amele and/or Waskia type are widespread in the Madang languages, though detailed analysis of the individual languages is needed to identify the precise system in each case. Koasati, a Muskogean language spoken in Louisiana and Texas, also has a verb 'give' with a zero root and obligatory object prefixes cross-referencing the recipient (Kimball 1991:102–104); as in Amele, the system seems synchronically transparent.

namely *est´*, there is also a polite verb *kušat´*, expressing politeness towards the subject of the verb. In the standard language, this verb may not be used in the first person singular. One could imagine such a system leading eventually to person suppletion, although I have no clear examples to date. Japanese, incidentally, provides an example of such politeness with respect to the recipient of 'give', with (roughly speaking) *ageru* and *kureru* being used when the recipient is socially higher than the giver, and *yaru* and *kudasaru* when the giver is socially higher than the recipient, but this distinction is orthogonal to the deictic distinction.

Conclusion

At the very least I hope to have shown that the phenomenon of person suppletion for the recipient of the verb 'give', despite the fact that it has hitherto been virtually neglected in the typological and other linguistic literature, is a topic worthy of greater attention. If this essay serves to lead others to uncover new instances of the phenomenon, and especially if it leads them to provide better overall accounts of its synchronic functioning and diachronic origin, I will consider my task to have been accomplished.

References

Armbruster, Charles Hubert. 1960. *Dongolese Nubian: A grammar.* Cambridge: Cambridge University Press.

Asher, R. E., and T. C. Kumari. 1997. *Malayalam.* London: Routledge.

Bauer, Winifred. 1993. *Maori.* London: Routledge.

Burrow, T., and M. B. Emeneau. 1984. *A Dravidian etymological dictionary.* Second edition. Oxford: Clarendon Press/New York: Oxford University Press.

Bybee, Joan. 1985. *Morphology: A study of the relation between meaning and form.* Amsterdam: John Benjamins.

Franklin, Karl J., and Joice Franklin. 1978. *A Kewa dictionary with supplementary grammatical and anthropological materials.* Canberra: Department of Linguistics, Research School of Pacific Studies, Australian National University.

Gómez, Paula. 1999. *Huichol de San Andrés Cohamiata, Jalisco.* México: El Colegio de México.

Kimball, Geoffrey D. 1991. *Koasati grammar.* Lincoln: University of Nebraska Press.

Lang, Adrienne. 1973. *Enga dictionary with English index.* Canberra: Department of Linguistics, Research School of Pacific Studies, Australian National University.

Mainwaring, G. B. 1876. *A grammar of the Róng (Lepcha) language, as it exists in the Dorjeling and Sikim hills.* Calcutta: Baptist Mission Press.

Margetts, Anna. 1999. *Valence and transitivity in Saliba, an Oceanic language of Papua New Guinea.* Nijmegen: Max Planck Institute for Psycholinguistics.

Maslova, Elena. 2002. *A grammar of Kolyma Yukaghir.* Berlin: Mouton de Gruyter.

Mel'cuk, Igor. 1994. Suppletion: Toward a logical analysis of the concept. *Studies in Language* 18:339–410.

Oates, W., and L. Oates. 1968. *Kapau pedagogical grammar.* Canberra: Department of Linguistics, Research School of Pacific Studies, Australian National University.

Roberts, John R. 1987. *Amele.* Beckenham: Croom Helm.

Ross, Malcolm, with John Natu Paol. 1978. *A Waskia grammar sketch and vocabulary.* Canberra: Department of Linguistics, Research School of Pacific Studies, Australian National University.

Serzisko, Fritz. 1988. On bounding in Ik. In Brygida Rudzka-Ostyn (ed.), *Topics in cognitive linguistics,* 429–445. Amsterdam: John Benjamins.

Smith Stark, Thomas C. 2001. Supletivismo según la persona del receptor en el verbo 'dar' de algunas lenguas otomangues. *Caravelle* 76–77:95–103.

Z'graggen, J. A. 1980a. *A comparative word list of the Northern Adalbert Range languages, Madang Province, Papua New Guinea.* Canberra: Department of Linguistics, Research School of Pacific Studies, Australian National University.

Z'graggen, J. A. 1980b. *A comparative word list of the Mabuso languages, Madang Province, Papua New Guinea.* Canberra: Department of Linguistics, Research School of Pacific Studies, Australian National University.

20

The Celtic Mutations

How Unique Are They?

Herbert Pilch

Kenneth Pike's Study of Celtic

Kenneth Pike gave many of his famous monolingual demonstrations at Albert-Ludwigs-Universität of Freiburg i.Br., his first in 1964, his last in 1994. Usually, we assigned him speakers of languages that appear "exotic" to the student of what Benjamin L. Whorf tellingly called "Standard Average European." Pike handled them easily. During his last visit, he performed three times: first on Daco-Roumanian (a dialect of Roumanian spoken on Greek soil), then on Irish, finally on a West African tone language. It took him an unusually long time to unravel the Irish. Was this because the Celtic languages, even though a branch of Indo-European, are "the odd man out" among the "Standard European" lot (Pilch 1999:275)? Are they so, perhaps, even among the languages of the world?

I do not know the right answer, as I know very little about all those non-European languages that Pike used to work on so brilliantly and that the SIL people still work on. So I am going to single out the phenomenon known as the INITIAL MUTATIONS, i.e., phonemic alternations of word-initial consonants. The phenomenon is ubiquitous in the Celtic languages, but appears to be rare among the languages of the world. It gives much trouble both to the learner and to the native speaker who wish to use a dictionary. The problem is compounded with Welsh and Breton by the spelling. The word-initial consonants are spelled phonemically without any indication (which Irish does provide) of the RADICAL consonant, i.e., the one under which the word is entered in the dictionary.

Kenneth Pike, working on Irish, had an inkling of what was going on with the initial consonants, but he did not see through the problem in the short span of time allotted for the demonstration. My present hope is that some readers with wide-ranging linguistic experience can enlighten me on a typological analogue somewhere else in the world (if one exists).

The different Celtic languages show a remarkably high degree of isomorphism in their syntax (which sharply deviates from Standard Average European) including the syntactic conditions which govern their initial mutations, so we present the latter just once for the Celtic languages as a whole. Still, we will have to quote our examples from the individual languages. So for the benefit of the nonspecialist reader, we will briefly mention the Celtic languages that are alive today. They are usually divided into two sub-families: Goidelic and Brythonic.

Goidelic

Goidelic, i.e., Irish, is spoken in Ireland and in Scotland. The Irish of Scotland is also known as Gaelic (Gael.). There is a fair amount of mutual intelligibility between spoken Gaelic and the spoken Irish (Ir.) of Ireland, less so today between the written languages.

Irish consonants come in two phonemically different consonantal timbres called "broad" and "slender." When necessary, we mark the slender timbre by a comma /,/ placed after the consonant. The Irish timbre correlation is isomorphic to, but does not sound the same as, the palatalization of Russian and Roumanian.

Brythonic

Brythonic, i.e., Welsh (W.), is spoken in Wales and Breton (Br.) is spoken in Brittany (Western France). Vannetais (Vann.) (as it is known in French) is spoken in the Southeastern *département du Morbihan* between Vannes and Quimperlé. It is usually categorized as "a dialect of Breton," even though it has its own writing system and there is practically no intelligibility with the other dialects of Breton.

Nothing would be gained for the present purpose by also listing the Celtic languages that have died out.

Typological Analogues

Let us now look at some examples of alternating consonants or mutations.

(1)   /t/ in W. *tad* 'father', /d/ in *ei dad* 'his father', /þ/ in *ei thad* 'her father', /nʰ/ in *fy nhad* 'my father'.

(2)   The same in W. *talaf* 'I pay', *(faint) dalwch chi?* '(how much) are you going to pay?', *thalaf fi fawr iawn* 'I am going to pay very little', *fy nhalu* 'pay me'.

(3)   Gael. *faoda-idh* /fi·ti/ 'may', *chan fhaod* /χæ ´ni·t/ 'must not', *am bhfhaod thù* /ə´ß i·tu/ 'are you allowed to?'

These alternations are governed by pragmatic and/or syntactic conditions. They occur initially in lexical words regardless of the suprasegmentals. For government by pragmatic conditions witness W. *tal-* /tɑl/ above for affirmation, *thal-* /þal/ for negation, *dal* for the question. For government by syntactic conditions, witness the object of a finite verb in Welsh. It undergoes mutation, e.g., *caeth Jones gi* 'Jones got a dog' (radical /ki·/), but not so the object of a nonfinite verb form, e.g., *mae Jones wedi cael ci* /ki·/ 'Jones has gotten a dog'.

True, orthographic Welsh places the proclitics *ni* before the verb for negation, as in *ni thalaf* 'I don't pay'; similarly *a* for the question *a dalwch?* 'are you going to pay?' So the grammar rules claim that the mutation is governed by the preceding proclitic. In spoken Welsh, however, there is no such proclitic, but the mutation is still there. Those grammar rules have, at best, diachronic value, but they no longer operate on the spoken language.

Two typological analogues have been alleged among the languages of Europe, namely Greek and Canary Islands Spanish, and a few more could be considered. We believe, however, they are spurious, as they are governed by phonemic or, at best, morphophonemic conditions, not by pragmatic and syntactic ones.

Old Greek

The Old Greek alternation between initial voiceless stops and spirants is governed by the presence or absence of a voiceless spirant first in the following consonantal slot, as in (4).

(4)   /þ/ in *thriks*   'hair'   gen.sg.   *trichós* /t/
      /þ/ in *thréps-ô* 'I will nourish' pres.   *tréf-ô* /t/
      /f/ in *feýg-ô*   'I flee'   reduplicating perfect   *péfy-ka*

More precisely, the initial voiceless spirants /f þ χ/ change into the corresponding stops /p t k/, if the next consonantal slot has a voiceless spirant as its first member. This is phonemic conditioning.[1]

Canary Islands Spanish

Magne Oftedal's analysis of Canary Islands Spanish carries long lists of examples in which /p t č k/ are voiced between vowels and/or liquids: "A lenition-favouring position is the position between two vowels or between a vowel and a liquid" (1985:66). This should come as no surprise, as the voiced stops of Spanish have spirant allophones in this very position according to the received analysis (which Oftedal notes). So, diachronically speaking, the voiced allophones of the stops /p t k/ fill the empty spaces left in the system by the spirantisation of /b d g/.

This is, at the same time, the sort of standard phonetic conditioning into which morphophonemic alternations are reconstructed, and such reconstruction is a routine matter for the Celtic mutations (Martinet 1952:192–217). Even though we synchronically consider the intervocalic [b d g] of Canary Islands Spanish as allophones of postconsonantal [b d g], the implicit alternation /p t k/ ~ /b d g/ hardly qualifies as a typological analogue of the Celtic mutations synchronically, as it is governed phonemically.

Breton

There is a situation in Breton similar to Canary Islands Spanish (and also in Russian). Breton neutralizes the voice correlation finally in lexical words. The amount of voicing depends on the initial phoneme of the next word, more voice before vowels and voiced consonants, as in *ar c'hazh du* [χaˑz dyˑ]

---

[1]The alternation is known to Indo-Europeanists as "Grassmann's Law of Aspirate Dissimilation." In Old Greek, the alternation was between aspirated stops which are spirants today, and unaspirated stops.

'the black cat', less voice before voiceless consonants and before pause, as in *ar c'hazh foll* [χaˑs fol] 'the mad cat' (Pilch 1990:34). This is allophonic variation at best, not even morphophonemic alternation—again the sort of situation into which we routinely reconstruct morphophonemic alternations.

Swiss German

In Swiss German, there is morphophonemic alternation between two rows of voiceless initial stops and sibilants, one "fortis" /p t k s/, one "superfortis" /P T K S/. The superfortis /K/ is realized as affricated [kχ] (Pilch 1977:187f.), as in the examples in (5).

(5)   *Tasse* /tasə/   'cup'   ≠ *die Tasse* /Tasə/ 'the cup'
      kaufen /kaufə/ 'buy'   ≠ *gekauft* /Kauft/ 'bought'
      Susi /suzi/   (girl's name) ≠ *das Suzi* /suzi/ (hypochoristic)

    The alternation is motivated by the fusion of adjacent morphemes, as in */tə-tasə/ → /Tasə/ (where /tə/ is the definite article feminine), /ssuzi/ → /Suzi/ (where the first /s/ is the definite article neuter). Again, the situation is not comparable to the Celtic mutations, as no such fusion is involved in them (even though some of them are reconstructed into such fusions).

Fula

Oftedal (1985:32f.) also mentions Fula, a West African language, as a typological analogue, but again the initial consonant alternations of this language "seem to be conditioned by the following stem," i.e., morphologically. It would be very hazardous for me to venture a generalization on the basis of Oftedal's sketchy account. Therefore, my appeal for enlightenment to those readers who have studied Fula.

The Three Phoneme Paradigms

After arguing what the Celtic mutations are not, let us describe what they are, strictly limiting ourselves to the phenomena which are relevant to their typological status. They are paradigms of phonemic alternation (not allophonic variation) governed by syntactic and/or pragmatic conditions (not by phonemic ones, nor by morphological ones).

True, in the Celtic languages there are also some initial alternations governed by phonemic and/or morphological conditions—similar to Grassmann's Law in Greek and to the morphophonemic fusions of Swiss German (see also the discussion of "Sandhi paradigms")—and dictionaries and grammars lump them all together in one basket. Even a recognized Celtic scholar like Magne Oftedal quotes them as evidence of the nonuniqueness of the Celtic mutations to the point of asserting their isomorphism with the *liaisons* of French (Oftedal 1985:36). But is it really a good idea (as is implicit in Oftedal's assertion) to analyze the /z/ of (say) Fr. *les hommes* /lezom/ as the initial consonant of *hommes* rather than as the final one of *les* in the prevocalic position?

Our inquiry is, however, about their uniqueness. What is possibly unique about them is, we claim, the extent to which they are conditioned syntactically and/or pragmatically.

There are, in the Celtic languages past and present, several different paradigms of initial mutation, each of them defined *not* by the phonemic features of the alternants, but by the specific conditions which govern them (see "The Governing Conditions"). They are notably lenis, nasal, and spirant.

Lenis

The LENIS mutation is one under which a tense consonant (technically called the RADICAL) alternates with a laxer one of the same place of articulation (technically called the LENITED alternant). The arrows in our notation in (6) point away from the radical to the alternant. The lenis mutation involves the voiced stops and /m/ in all Celtic languages.

(6)   /b m/   →   /v/
       /d/   →   /ð/
       /g/   →   /ɣ/

Under more recent sound changes Ir. /ð ɣ/ have coalesced under /ɣ/; W. /ɣ/ has changed into Ø (zero); Br. /ð/ has changed either into /z/ or /χ h/ (depending on the dialect).

Within the same paradigm, the voiceless stops alternate with the voiceless spirants in Goidelic, but with the voiced stops in Brythonic.[2]

---

[2]This difference between Goidelic and Brythonic is irrelevant typologically.

(7)   Goidelic   Brythonic
       /p/   →   /f/   /p/   →   /b/
       /t/   →   /þ/   /t/   →   /d/
       /k/   →   /χ/   /k/   →   /g/

In modern Irish (including Gaelic), /þ/ has changed into /h/.

Certain additional alternations under this paradigm are limited to Goidelic, Welsh, and Breton, respectively.

(8)   Goidelic   Welsh   Breton
       /s/   →   /h/   /λ/[3]   →   /l/   /s/   →   /z/
       /f/   →   Ø   /rʰ/   →   /r/   /š/   →   /ž/

There are some minor deviations in the government of the Welsh liquids, but they concern the specialist only.

Nasal

The NASAL mutation is one under which a voiced stop alternates with a nasal at the given place of articulation and a voiceless one and /f/ alternate with the corresponding voiced consonant.

(9)   /b/   →   /m/   /p/   →   /b/
       /d/   →   /n/   /t/   →   /d/
       /g/   →   /ŋ/   /f/   →   /ß/

This paradigm is productive only in the Irish of Ireland today, but there are some relics in Welsh and Gaelic (notably with the numerals from 'seven' to 'ten' as in W. *saith mlynedd* 'seven years', radical *blynedd*) which indicate that it was productive, at one time, in all Celtic languages.

The nasal mutation is governed, for instance, by prepositional phrases containing a DETERMINATE noun, i.e., one that is a proper noun, or one determined either by the article, by a proclitic pronoun, or by a genitive as shown in (10).

---

[3]What we write with the Greek letter *lambda* /λ/ is a voiceless, unilateral spirant spelled *ll* in Welsh. The visitor to Wales will note it in the numerous place-names with *llan-* 'church premises'. They have been carried over into North America in names like Llangollen, Kentucky.

(10) Ir. *caoi* /ki·/ 'manner' → *ar an gcaoi*-se /ərən´gi·s,ə/ 'in this
        manner'
      Ir. *Baile ´Atha Cliath* /bəla·kliə/ 'Dublin' → *sa Mbaile ´Atha
        Cliath* /sə mə´la·kliə/ 'in Dublin' (literally, 'in the city of the
        wattle-ford', with *átha*, gen.sg. of *´ath* 'ford', determined
      by *cliath* nom.sg. 'wattle')

Spirant

The SPIRANT mutation is one under which *zero* alternates with /h/ in all
Celtic languages, as shown in (11).

(11) Ir. *athair*   'father' →   *a hathair*   'her father'
      W. *ewyrth*   'uncle'   →   *ei hewyrth*   'her uncle'

In Brythonic this paradigm extends to the voiceless stops, in Welsh even
to the nasals, in Vannetais even further to the liquid /l/.

(12)   Brythonic   Welsh and Vannetais   Vannetais
         /p/ →   /f/   /m/ →   /m^h/
         /t/ →   /þ/   /n/ →   /n^h/   /l/ →   /l^h/
         /k/ →   /χ/

In Breton, /þ/ has changed into /s/ or /z/ (depending on the dialect).
   In all Celtic languages, this paradigm operates on noun phrases governed by the proclitic pronoun of the third-person singular feminine, as in
W. *ei thad* 'her father' in (1). In spoken Welsh, the pronoun is *zero* when
another word in /i/ precedes it, as in *mae hi wedi ei chladdu* /maidi´χlaði/
'she is dead' (literally, 'she is after her burial'); so the government is syntactic and signals a reflexive construction.

Sandhi Paradigms

There are several more *alternation* paradigms of initial consonants, but
they are limited to Welsh, Breton, and Gaelic, respectively. Moreover,
they are similar to sandhi phenomena. What happens is that a word-initial
consonant fuses with a proclitic consonant that immediately precedes it.

Welsh

The Welsh stops /pʰ tʰ kʰ b d g/ fuse with the preceding nasal of the two homophonous proclitics /ən/, which represents either the first-person singular pronoun or the localizing preposition 'in'. The fusion yields the nasals /mʰ nʰ ŋʰ m n ŋ/, as shown in (13).

(13) */ən´ tʰa·d   →   /ənʰa·d/   'father'
      */əŋ´ kəmri/ →   /ə´ŋʰəmri/   'in Wales'

The fusion occurs with those two proclitics only, not with the homophonous proclitic governing the verbal noun, as in *yn cofio* 'remember'.

Orthographic Welsh misleadingly spells the pronoun *fy*, while the normal spoken form is /ən/ (cf. Vann. *men*) in all phonemic environments, e.g., *fy afal* /ə´naval/ 'my apple'.

Gaelic

The situation is similar in modern Gaelic. However, as Gaelic /p t k/ are unaspirated (they are aspirated sometimes for emphasis), they fuse with /n/ into the corresponding nasal or voiced stop. The two results of the fusion seem to be in free variation.

(14) /mp/ → /b/   ∼   /mm/
      /nt/ → /d/   ∼   /nɳ/
      /ŋk/ → /ŋg/ ∼   /nŋ/

(15) *an cù* /ən´ ku/   →   /ə´gu·/   'the dog'
              /əm pun´tæ·te/ →   /mmə´dʰæ·tə/   'the potatoes'
              /ən´ tæ·i·χ/   →   /ən´ɳæ·i·χ/   'tomorrow night'

As these examples show, the proclitics governing the fusion are not the same in Gaelic as in Welsh. Moreover, there is much free variation in Gaelic (which we have indicated by the tilde ∼). Sometimes, the fusion does not happen at all, so we hear from the same speaker /ən´ ku/ ∼ /ən´ gu·/ ∼ /eŋ gu·/, and also the aspirated versions with [kʰ gʰ] for emphasis. Gaelic spelling disregards the nasal fusion.

Breton

Another sandhi involving initial consonants can be observed in Breton. The initial voiced stops fuse with the proclitic spirant /χ/ into voiceless stops. The fusion is morphologically conditioned to the extent that it occurs only with the proclitics *oc'h* (second-person plural pronoun), with its homophone governing the verbal noun, and with *ec'h* 'that' (governing a subsidiary clause).

(16) */oχ ´dond/ → /o´tond/ 'come'
      */oχ ´brœ·r/ → /o´prœ·r/ 'your brother'
      */eχ ´dœ·/ → /e´tœ·/ 'that he comes'

Breton spelling writes the proclitic /χ/ (as *c'h*) only before vowels, so the written forms such as *breur* → *o preur* look as though they involve a mutation paradigm on the same footing as the lenition paradigm. Indeed, it looks like a reversal of the latter with /b/ → /p/ instead of /p/ → /b/.

The Governing Conditions

Celtic grammars usually describe the government of the mutations in terms of lexical sequence rules such as: "Welsh words are lenited after the numeral *dau* 'two'." The syntactic relationship between the two words is taken for granted. However, it is crucial. The mutation implies that *dau* and the following noun form a noun phrase syntactically, as in *dau ddyn* /dai ði·n/ (radical /di·n/) 'two men', but there is no mutation in *oedd yna ddau, dyn a dynes* 'there were two there, a man and a woman' (where *dyn* also comes after *dau*).

Moreover, the governing particle and the lenited consonant are not necessarily adjacent to each other. The object of a finite verb is lenited in Welsh (as we saw earlier), even when the subject is placed between them. Similarly, the determinate noun in Irish prepositional phrases undergoes the nasal mutation, even though the article is placed between them (see the third section, "The Three Phoneme Paradigms").

In some instances, there is no governing syntax at all, but the mutation indicates what pragmatists call the ILLOCUTIONARY FORCE of the enunciation, i.e., what the speaker is actually trying to say (Hervey 1982:113).

For instance, W. *mawr*[4] *iawn* 'very big' appears lenited /m/ → /v/ as *fawr iawn* /ˈvaur ˈjawn/ 'not very big', i.e., 'very little', as in *thalaf fi fawr iawn* in (2). There is no express negation in this phrase, but the negative illocution is conventional. It is indicated by the spirant mutation of the verb *thalaf* and the lenis mutation of its object *fawr iawn.*

Those governing conditions are essential to each mutation paradigm; the particular phonemic pairs involved are incidental. The governing conditions are, by and large, the same in all Celtic languages. (Certain differences of detail do exist, but they are irrelevant to our inquiry.)

For instance, in feminine singular noun phrases, all constituents are lenited except the first,[5] e.g., W. *dynes* /dənes/ *dlawd* 'a poor woman' (radical *tlawd*), but *y ddynes* /ðənes/ *dlawd* 'the poor woman'.

There is, however, one reservation: the article *y* commutes both with the proclitic personal pronouns and with other noun phrases carrying the article.

(17) | y
      | ei | (d)dynes
      | y pysgod |

The word order demands that the commuting noun phrase *y pysgod* 'the fish' be placed after *dynes* in this construction, so the whole phrase is *dynes y pysgod* 'the fish woman', i.e., 'one who sells fish'. The nonmutation of *pysgod* is conditioned by the fact that *y pysgod* is not feminine singular.

The commuting personal pronoun, on the other hand, remains in the same position as the article, but it governs its own particular mutation of the nucleus, as in *ei ddynes* 'his woman', but not of the remainder of the noun phrase, as in *ein dynes dlawd* 'our poor woman'.

Generalizing on these two examples, we say that the government (of mutations) within the smaller syntagm takes precedence over the government within the larger one, assuming that the smaller one is a constituent of the larger one.

In accordance with its incidental status, a given alternation as defined in phonemic terms does not necessarily imply membership of a particular paradigm of initial mutation. For instance, the alternation /k/ → /χ/ belongs to the lenition paradigm in Irish, to the spirant paradigm in Welsh, and it is an isolated one in Breton, i.e., it is not a member of a

---

[4]The word will be familiar to American readers in the place-name *Bryn Mawr* 'big hill' of Pennsylvania.

[5]The lenition is (almost) the only mark of gender in the Celtic languages. We could argue that it is not worth invoking gender as a category under such circumstances, but that we should simply set up two classes of nouns, one governing lenition of noun phrases, the other not.

paradigm of several alternating pairs. The Breton alternation /k/ → /χ/ is, in fact, governed by the masculine singular article both definite and indefinite, as in *kazh* 'cat', *ar c´hazh* 'the cat', *ur c´hazh* 'a cat', plural *ar c´hizhier* /ə´χišeχ/ (radical *kizhier*). At the same time, the phonemically same alternation of Irish is governed (as we saw above in this section) by the feminine singular article, inter alia.

The alternation /t/ → /s/ is one in the spirant mutation paradigm in Breton, as we saw earlier. Irish (including Gaelic) carries the reverse alternation /s/ → /t/ as an isolated one. Again, the governing conditions are totally different. For instance Ir. /s/ → /t/ in masculine singular genitival phrases with the article, as in *sagart* 'priest', but *teach an tsagairt* /tagərt,/ 'the priest's house'.

Speakers' Attitudes

All this sounds fairly complicated—no wonder Kenneth Pike did not sort it out within forty-five minutes. In fact, the complexity of the mutation paradigms, notably of their governing conditions, is such that children do not master it till the age of seven or eight. After that, they experience no serious difficulty.

I knew a non-Welsh speaker who was received at the age of twelve as a visitor to a Welsh family. Three months later, he was fluent in Welsh, including impeccable mastery of the initial mutations. He did not analyze them, of course. He just used them.

When I was first struggling to learn Welsh, a senior member of the community asked me how I managed to cope with the mutations. I replied (truthfully) that I had not yet been paying more than cursory attention to them, as I felt that intelligible communication should take priority (Welsh remains more or less intelligible even when the learner messes up the mutations). The gentleman was surprised at first. Then he pronounced a few random examples to himself, concluding: "In fact, if one does not pay attention, the mutations come out just naturally"—a typical native-speaker misjudgment, and one that goes to show how natural the mutations do appear to the competent native speaker. Indeed there is, among the learned class, a sense of pride of "their" mutations. The unsophisticated speakers are not aware of them, of course. They fail to understand even multiple-choice questions of the type: "Would you say *gwelais i gi* or *gwelais i ci?* 'I saw a dog'." If pushed they claim not to hear the difference.

Contrary to widespread claims, I see no reason to believe that the mutations are recessive or dying out. Such claims are invariably based on the observation that actual usage does not always agree with grammar rules as prescribed in textbooks, and that there is also quite a bit of fluctuation in actual usage.

For instance, in spoken Breton and in Irish, lenition regularly fails to materialize in the cluster /nd/ even in feminine singular noun phrases, as in Br. *poan dent* 'a tooth ache' /´poan´den/ (radical *dent*), but *poan galoun* 'a heart ache' (radical *kaloun*).

Irish grammarians accept this. I have not seen it mentioned in treatises on Breton, so it is presumably not "grammatically correct."

For Welsh, grammar rules prescribe the spirant mutation after *a* 'and' and after *tri* 'three', but the people use it only after the proclitic pronoun *ei* /i/ of the third-person singular feminine. Inversely, textbooks emphatically prohibit the spirant mutation of /m/ and /n/, as in *ei mham* 'her mother', *ei nhain* 'her grandmother'. The people do not care. They still say it.

As they are not consciously aware of the initial mutations, the phonemic spelling does not promote such awareness even on the part of those who are literate in their Celtic mother tongue; the latter are difficult to elicit in mass interviews conducted by psycholinguists. It would, in my opinion, be rash to infer that "the younger generation is abandoning the mutations."

Some nonnative speaker educationists have argued that the mutations should be abolished, because they are too hard to learn. Do they speak for themselves or for the native children? The mutations have been in existence for at least fifteen hundred years (the experts disagree on how much longer exactly), and all those generations of speakers learned them, and are still learning them.

References

Hervey, Sándor. 1982. *Semiotic perspectives*. London: Allen and Unwin.

Martinet, André. 1952. Celtic lenition and Western Romance consonants. *Language* 28:192–217.

Oftedal, Magne. 1985. *Lenition in Celtic and in Insular Spanish*. Oslo: Universitetsforlaget.

Pilch, Herbert. 1977. Baseldeutsche Phonologie auf Grundlage der Intonation. *Phonetica* 34:165–190.

Pilch, Herbert. 1990. Breton phonetics, a new analysis. *Studia Celtica Japonica* 3:9–50.

Pilch, Herbert. 1999. The Celtic languages—Eurolinguistics' odd man out? In Norbert Reiter (ed.), *Eurolinguistik—Wege in die Zukunft,* 275–288. Wiesbaden: Harrassowitz.

21

The Presentation of Reality in James and Hemingway

Peter H. Fries

Introduction

It is an honor and a pleasure to be invited to contribute to a volume of papers collected to celebrate the life and work of Kenneth L. Pike. On a professional level his attitude toward language, his insistence that language always be considered in relation to the larger behavioral context in which it occurs, and his insistence that we do not have a complete grammatical description until we can describe how clauses and sentences are used in a larger context (see Pike 1967) are principles which influenced my thinking (and still do) from the very beginning of my career. On a more personal level his encouragement and his giving an audience for my thinking provided me a means to discover what I had to say. Indeed, many of my early articles began their life as personal letters to him. Since his interests were so wide-ranging there is little I could discuss—phonology, grammar, or discourse analysis; application, description, or theory—which would not reflect one of Pike's interests and, more importantly, some of his influence on me. Since others in this volume are likely to address more typical theoretical and descriptive topics, I have finally decided to approach an applied topic, the discussion of literature.

Pike's work on literature (as well as that of his wife Evelyn—it is difficult to talk about Kenneth without talking about Evelyn's work as well) was a natural extension of his work on discourse. Kenneth and Evelyn typically examined the grammatical and referential hierarchies of narrative texts. Nevertheless, the narratives they usually addressed were oral renditions of folktales or personal accounts; literary analysis was not their major focus. However, they did analyze several literary works (e.g., Pike 1981) or other narratives (Pike and Pike 1983, chapter 1), and Kenneth was also interested in writing his own poetry. I therefore take this cue to build on his work by applying linguistic analysis to two literary works. In general, Kenneth's and Evelyn's analyses of particular texts can be described as detailed explorations of the particular way in which individual texts developed. For example, in the second chapter of Pike 1981, he traced the levels of observer relationship demonstrating the relevance of differences in point of view of the participants. Let me refer to detailed analyses of this type as taking an ethnographic approach. In such an approach, one addresses the sequential nature of the text and provides an account of the situated nature of the various language features used in the text and their interpretations.

I would like to suggest a complement to the ethnographic approach— a statistical analysis of the features of language used in a text. Such an analysis would not simply count a group of language features selected more or less at random, but would look at a particular set of features which have some common semantic or rhetorical thread, chosen because that semantic contribution is important to the interpretation of the text as a whole. I call the approach I am suggesting an "interpreted statistical analysis of a text." It is true that one fundamental assumption underlying this approach is that the language of a text is related to the interpretation of that text in predictable ways. This assumption is by no means universally agreed on. I am reminded of a discussion I once had with a friend who had just given an interesting paper on the grammatical characteristics of several narratives (Mills 1992). I approached him saying that I had found his paper very interesting, but had missed any attempt to tie his counts of grammatical features to the meanings expressed in the texts. His reaction was that it was impossible to find such a link. In his opinion the tie between grammar and meaning was so variable that interpretation of statistical results was impossible. He felt that while the different texts he had examined differed both in their grammar, and in their interpretation, one could not relate the different statistical tendencies in the texts to differences in their interpretations. For example, every author has to describe and all descriptions require similar language.

In my opinion, such an attitude does not take language seriously. I would like to claim that if two texts differ in interpretation, then we should be able to find features of the language of these two texts which relate to that difference of interpretation. Further, I would claim that in general such differences should show up in statistical tendencies in the particular lexico-grammatical choices made in the texts. In this paper I illustrate one attempt to tie features of language to the interpretation of texts through statistical counts. We can take one of two possible approaches to this task. In the first, we would make as complete an analysis as possible of the language of the texts to be considered. In such an approach we would provide a complete analysis of all the clause structures, the nominal and verbal group structures, and so forth. Once we had analyzed everything that we had time for, we would then attempt to summarize and interpret what we had found. Such an approach has the advantage of being relatively objective in that one has not chosen exactly which features to analyze based on the text. But in part that objectivity is not real in that **all** analyses are partial. We typically begin with the portions of the analyses which (a) we expect to be relevant, and (b) we have the tools for. Thus, if we have a beautiful tool to analyze clauses with, we typically analyze clauses.

The second approach to the analysis of texts makes a virtue of necessity, and says, "Since all analyses are partial, why not simply focus on those aspects of the language that I, as a proficient reader, suspect are going to be relevant?" That is, based on my reading of the text (or other peoples' readings of the text), certain meanings are found to be important. Given that interpretation (or set of interpretations), the problem for the linguist is to discover how those meanings are conveyed. Wherever a text can be said to have a clear meaning, it makes sense for the linguist to ask "just exactly how is this meaning signaled?" **How** does this text mean what it does? Can the linguist link choices in the language used to the language system in such a way that we can account for the meaning of the text? Such an approach would end up with a set of statistical counts of language features. However, these counts would be focussed around counting various forms which contribute in some potentially obvious way to the perceived interpretation of the texts. It should be obvious that since the basis for the choice of features is the semantic or rhetorical effect, the lexico-grammatical features which are examined are likely to come from **several different portions** of the grammatical system. In this approach, we may be examining not only the clause structure but the structure of nominal groups, of modals and of the relations between clauses, etc. I say that this approach involves "interpreted statistics" on the grounds that the relation between language features and meaning is the basis for choosing what to count. I do not claim to be original in using this approach to discuss texts. Many previous studies of texts have examined various language features to see how these features contribute to the interpretation of the text. Some studies—such as Benson and Greaves (1982), Burton (1982), Eggins and Slade (1997), Halliday (1970 and 1971), Hasan (1985/1989), Kies (1992), and Samudji (1999)—focus on the special effects achieved in individual spoken or written texts and the grammatical means used to achieve these effects. Other works, such as Biber and Finegan (1988, 1989) and Conrad and Biber (2000), focus on the expression of a particular semantic effect, e.g., stance toward what is said, in a range of texts.

To illustrate "interpreted statistical analysis" I have chosen to examine two works which present radically different views of reality: *The Ambassadors* by Henry James and *A Farewell to Arms* by Ernest Hemingway. Both are highly crafted works and each went through many revisions. James has been described as an impressionist writer (Stowell 1980) and preoccupied with the mental states and social relations that his characters enter into (Chatman 1972). Further, these mental states and social relations are presented as unclear and difficult to make out. Some of this complexity is illustrated in the following quotation when the narrator says of the main character, "He was burdened, poor Strether—it had better be confessed at the outset—with the oddity of a double consciousness. There was detachment in his zeal and curiosity in his indifference" (J-12–13).[1] This passage illustrates

a. James' overt interest in consciousness and in perceptions and

b. the complexity and doubtfulness of these perceptions.

By contrast, Hemingway seems to take the other extreme approach. Cowley (1929) described his style as "subtractive," a term which he amplified by saying that from the novel of previous generations Hemingway "has subtracted all the descriptions, the meditations, the statements of theory and he has reserved only the characters and their behavior" (quoted in Donaldson 1990:9).

Similarly, Savage (1970:92) describes Hemingway as a stylist who has, "within very narrow limits,...brought to something like perfection a curt, unemotional, factual style which is an attempt at the objective presentation of experience. A bare, dispassionate reporting of external actions is all that Hemingway as a rule attempts in presenting his characters and incidents."

---

[1]The code J-12–13 indicates that the example is taken from James and that the sentences in this particular example are the twelfth and thirteenth in the data.

In contrast to the worlds that James' characters inhabit, the worlds created in Hemingway stories are clear. There is no doubt as to what Hemingway's characters experience and what happens in the novel. While Hemingway **is** interested in the development of his characters, this interest is not the focus of the **language** of the novel. It is not expressed overtly, but rather is communicated through juxtapositions of various voices within the novel. (See Phelan (1990) for an interesting discussion of how Hemingway achieves this effect.)

Analytical Framework

The question then arises "What linguistic means can be used to convey these different interpretations?" Implicit in any interpreted statistical approach is the relevance of paradigmatic relations within language. That is, the interpretation of the choices that are made in the production of a text is closely related to the options that were not chosen. Since paradigmatic relations are emphasized within systemic grammar, e.g., Halliday (1994:15) and Matthiessen (1996:12–17), I will use that model in my analysis. The basic linguistic structural concepts I will use are presented in Halliday (1994). Matthiessen (1996) discusses these structural concepts in relation to the paradigmatic relations they encode.

Interest in mental phenomena

Since the two novels differ primarily in the different realities they project, the most obvious place to begin the analysis is to look at that aspect of language which has the basic function of presenting reality: the ideational metafunction. In Systemic Functional grammar, the ideational metafunction addresses the events and states that are described and the entities that are constructed to take part in these events and states. More technically, systemicists talk about the process types (the events or states with their associated participant roles) and the things (the participants themselves). Processes are typically expressed by clauses, while the participants are typically realized by nominal groups.

Process types

Halliday 1994 uses grammatical criteria to distinguish six process types for English. It should be noted that the classification of processes is a classification of **clauses** not of verbs. Hence the participant roles which are found within a clause contribute very much to the identification of the process type. As a result, the examples provided in (1) are not simply verbs. (See Martin (1996) for a discussion of the theoretical underpinnings of the analysis of processes.) Of course, while the justification for the classes which are constructed is a grammatical justification, the classes so created have semantic implications. These process types are presented in (1).

(1)   English process types
       a. **Material processes**: These are the prototypical actions such as *John ran, I will walk,* and *It hit me.*
       b. **Mental processes:** These are processes of reaction, perception, and cognition such as *I like it, Mary saw it,* and **He thinks** *that they will come.*
       c. **Verbal processes:** These are processes of saying and reporting and include examples such as **They say** *he will do it. Tell me a story,* and *I asked him a question.*
       d. **Relational processes:** There are two subtypes of relational processes: Those relational processes which are attributive, as in *John is happy, John is a doctor.* Those relational processes which are identifying, *John is the leader.*
       e. **Existential processes:** Existential processes posit the existence of some entity and are typically used in discourse as a means of entering that entity into the text. For example *There's a man at the door who wants to talk to you.*
       f. **Behavioral processes:** Behavioral processes are actions but can only be engaged in by entities which are considered sentient. For example, *Bill laughed, they cried,* and *Henry breathed quietly.*

Mental nouns and adjectives

Interestingly, English has a great many ways to move these process types into nominal groups. As a result, the analysis must also examine the uses of nominal groups as well as the clauses. Because of the nature of the particular works being examined, I will focus on entities which are related to mental processes. Obviously, like mental processes, mental nouns and adjectives concern mental phenomena. However, mental nouns and adjectives may be recognized by the following grammatical properties: something in the immediate context of the noun or adjective, e.g., a modifier, expresses a Senser and/or a Phenomenon, or an expression of Senser or Phenomenon may reasonably be added to the example. Similarly, most mental nouns or adjectives may project an embedded clause. Example (2) provides an example of a mental noun and a mental adjective taken from the James text.

(2) J-8 ...had been indifferently *aware* of the number of persons...

J-4 ...there was little *fear* that in the sequel they shouldn't see enough of each other.

J-8 expresses the Phenomenon as a modifier. J-4 is an example of a noun which projects an embedded clause. While these categories of process types and of nouns and adjectives have semantic consequences, they are recognizable based on their **grammatical** characteristics. Again, as in the classification of process types, the categories used here are not simply categories of vocabulary items—of words. Rather, each occurrence of a word must be examined in context with the expectation that the same word may constitute a mental noun in one context but not in another. Thus, the word *acquaintance* sometimes is considered to be a mental noun and at other times it is not. In example (3), this word refers to a person. It cannot express the Phenomenon nor can it project in this use, therefore this occurrence was *not* counted as a mental noun.[2]

(3) J-26 ...Strether's new *acquaintance*...

By contrast, example 4 was included as a mental noun since both the Senser and Phenomenon are expressed in this use.

(4) J-41 Her *acquaintance* with the place...

Given the descriptions of the two styles described in the introduction, we would predict that Hemingway used many material processes and relatively few mental processes, mental nouns or adjectives. By contrast we would predict that James used relatively few material processes and many mental processes, mental nouns and adjectives.

Interest in the difficulty of perception

The point was made in the introduction that not only was James interested in the perceptions of his characters, the worlds they inhabited were

---

[2]Of course this analysis is very conservative. This example certainly expresses the Senser, and one could say that the Phenomenon is included within the reference of the noun itself. I have chosen the approach I use here to make sure that the counts I arrive at are not inflated. In a similar study, Chatman (1972) considered many more items to concern mental activity.

complicated and difficult to interpret. One set of language features by which this difficulty might be constructed would be those which show the speakers temporizing on the validity of what they are saying. Here we include the occurrence of modal verbs and adverbs, and the expression of conation, modulation or reality phase; the frequency and distribution of hedges; the frequency of the author temporizing over the truth of his claims; and the frequency of similes. Though these features come from quite different parts of the grammar, all have the effect of drawing back from a simple assertion of information as fact. Examples of each of these features are provided in (5).

(5) Features of language which relate to difficulty of perception
    a. Frequency and distribution of expressions of modality: modal verbs and adverbs, and expressions of conation, modulation, or reality phase
        J-1 ...Waymarsh was *apparently* not to arrive till evening...
        J-34 ...there *seemed* nothing else to serve.
    b. Frequency and distribution of hedges
        J-1 ...he was not *wholly* disconcerted.
        J-2 ...the understanding...remained *to that extent* sound.
        J-5 ...his business would be a *trifle* bungled...
        J-43 ...the high finish of which had a *certain* effect of mitigation.
        J-45 ...a *superficial* readiness...
    c. Frequency and distribution of similes
        J-33 ...they were left together *as* over the mere laid table of conversation.
        J-40 It was almost *as if* she had been in possession...
    d. Frequency of the speaker temporizing concerning the truth of his claims
        J-8 There were people on the ship with whom he had easily consorted—*so far as ease could up to now be imputed to him*...
        J-11 ...these things, *it is to be conceived*, were early signs...

Data

The data for this paper constitute two roughly 2,000-word samples of each of the two texts. The sample of Henry James *The Ambassadors* is the first 1,996 words of chapter 1. In the case of Hemingway *A Farewell to*

Arms, the complete first chapter was sampled (603 words). Then, since this chapter was felt to be untypical of the book as a whole, a portion chosen randomly from the middle of the book—the first 1,392 words of chapter 20—was examined to create a sample of comparable size to the James text. Preliminary analyses of the two sections of the Hemingway novel indicate that they differ significantly. Chapter 1 is **not** a narrative in the normal sense of the word, but sets the scene for the story. It is a description. The portion of chapter 20 that was analyzed does constitute a narrative in the more usual sense. Since the two Hemingway chapters differ as much as they do, I will present results for each Hemingway chapter separately and then for the two Hemingway chapters combined. Table 1 presents a preliminary summary of the data obtained.

Table 1. Data

Hemingway: *A Farewell to Arms*			
Chapter 1			
603 words	66 nonembedded cl.	11 embedded cl.	77 total clauses
A portion of chapter 20			
1,392 words	221 nonembedded cl.	19 embedded cl.	240 total clauses
Henry James: *The Ambassadors*			
A portion of chapter 1			
1,996 words	136 nonembedded cl.	102 embedded cl.	238 total clauses

Results

One result is obvious from the preliminary description of the data provided in table 1; James uses far more embedding than does Hemingway.

Hemingway ~ 10% of clauses are embedded (30 of 317)
James ~ 43% of clauses are embedded (102 of 238)

Further, in Hemingway, **all** the embedded clauses are simple, while many of the embeddings in James are embedded clause **complexes,** and these embedded clause complexes may themselves contain embeddings. Clearly, James and Hemingway differ grammatically. However, we cannot simply tie these preliminary results to our interpretations of these texts since there is no simple way to link the amount of embedding in a text to the degree to which perception—or even complexity of perception—is foregrounded. In other words, not every statistically significant difference is significant (= important) for our purposes. In this case, these results may indicate that we are on the right track, but they are not sufficient in themselves to account for the different impressions conveyed by the two works.

Let me turn now to analyses which are more directly relevant.

Mental phenomena—process types

Hypothesis: Hemingway uses more material processes and fewer mental processes, while James uses fewer material processes and more mental processes.

Table 2 presents the results of the analysis of the process types. Shaded areas indicate results that seem particularly of interest. In general the hypothesis was confirmed.

45% (=143) of Hemingway clauses are Material processes
33.3% (= 80) of James clauses are Material processes[3]
13% (=41) of Hemingway clauses are Mental processes
19% (=45) of James clauses are Mental processes

In addition other differences appear which were not part of the original hypothesis. In particular, James uses relatively many relational and existential processes.

The two patterns of occurrences differ significantly (at the level of $X^2 = .001$), however the difference in numbers hardly seems sufficient to account for the dramatic difference in the effects of the two samples. That is, when one reads these two works, one has the impression that they are creating entirely different worlds. The results obtained here are different, but only marginally so, and thus are not sufficient to account for the entirely different experience that readers of these two texts obtain.

---

[3]Christian Matthiessen (personal communication) notes that this figure of 33% material processes resembles the percentage of material processes used in scientific language in his studies of the registers associated with different genres. Thus giving some support to half of the aphorism quoted in Chatman (1972) that William James (the psychologist) wrote like a novelist, while Henry James (the novelist) wrote like a scientist.

Table 2. Frequencies of process types in Hemingway and James

Length (words)	Hemingway Chapter 1 603 Non-embed clauses	Embed clauses	Chapter 20 1,392 Non-embed clauses	Embed clauses	Totals 1,995 Non-embed clauses	Embed clauses	Total all clauses	James Chapter 1 1,996 Non-embed clauses	Embed clauses	Total all clauses
Material	26	8	98	11	124	19	**143** 45.1%	48	31	**80** 33.3%
Behavioral	1	0	11	0	12	0	**12** 3.8%	4	4	**8** 3.4%
Mental										
Affective	0	0	17	0	17	0	**17** 5.6%	2	3	**5** 2.1%
Perception	5	1	8	0	13	1	**14** 4.4%	5	15	**20** 8.4%
Cognitive	0	0	8	2	8	2	**10** 3.2%	12	8	**20** 8.4%
Relational										
Attributive	20	1	38	2	58	3	**61** 19.2%	43	39	**73** 30.8%
Identificational	4	1	2	1	6	2	**8** 2.5%	4	1	**5** 2.1%
Verbal	0	0	34	3	34	3	**37** 22.7%	14	9	**23** 9.7%
Existential	10	0	5	0	15	0	**15** 4.7%	3	1	**4** 1.7%
Ellipses/Partial			12					0		
Total Clauses	66	11	221	19	287	30	**317** 100%	136	102	**238** 100%

26% (= 84) of Hemingway clauses are Relational or Existential processes (34 of these are found in chapter 1)
34% (= 82) of James clauses are Relational or Existential processes

Mental phenomena—mental nouns and adjectives

It turns out that the differences in relational and existential processes contribute to the difference in prominence of mental phenomena by providing a means to move mental phenomena into a position as attribute or existent. Thus, examples such as (6) (repeated from (2)) show that these clauses are not simply relational clauses with normal attributes or existents. Rather the use of *aware* and *fear* causes these clauses to focus on mental phenomena.

(6) J-8   ...had been indifferently *aware* of the number of persons...
     J-4   ...there was little *fear* that in the sequel they shouldn't see
           enough of each other.

As a result it is useful to make a careful search of the data for all instances of these terms to see how often they appear in the two texts and how they are used when they appear. The list found in James is given in table 3. The list of words found in Hemingway is given in table 4. There is clearly a big difference. James contained forty-six mental nouns and adjectives, while Hemingway used only three.

Table 3. Mental nouns and adjectives in Henry James—46

*acquaintance (with x)	*difficult	*recognition
appearance (of x)	*disappointment	*relieved (to x)
*apprehension (proj)	*disconcerted	*reserves (about x)
attentive	*eager	response
*attitude	enjoyment (of it)	sense
*aware (of x)	*fear(proj)	sense (of x)
aware (of x)	hope	sense (of x)
*aware (of x)	*impression (of x)	sense (proj)
*consciousness (of x)	*impulse (proj)	*shock (of x)
consciousness	*indifference	*taste (of x)
consciousness (of x)	*instinctive	*thought (proj)
*consciousness (of x)	intention	*thought (proj)
*curiosity	*no doubt	*understanding (proj)
delightful	observer	vision
detachment	recognition	vision
		*zeal

(proj) indicates that the noun or adjective projects in its use in the text.
*Indicates that the occurrence is in a nonembedded clause.

Table 4. Mental nouns and adjectives in Ernest Hemingway—3

Chapter 1	Chapter 20
feeling	obligated (proj)
	sure (proj)

Of course, it is worthwhile to see how these nouns and adjectives are used in these works. It is quite conceivable that though James uses many such words, they are typically deeply embedded within the grammar of each clause and hence are not so prominent as they could be. Table 5 provides more detailed information focusing on the distribution of mental nouns and adjectives in James. The two rows indicate grammatical prominence, with the figures in the top row of data indicating how many of these nouns and adjectives are found in nonembedded clauses (grammatically more prominent), and the bottom row of data indicating how many of these nouns and adjectives are found in embedded clauses (grammatically less prominent).

Table 5 also provides information about the internal structures of groups headed by mental nouns and adjectives. Column 1 reports figures for mental nouns and adjectives which project a clause (in bold in J-4 *There was little* ***fear that in the sequel they shouldn't see enough of each other***). Column 2 shows how many examples express a nonclausal Phenomenon (in bold in J-37 *He was **aware**...of his strange inconsequence...*). Column 3 shows the number of examples which neither project nor express a phenomenon (e.g., J-13 *There was **detachment** in his **zeal***). I take these three codings as three stages of explicitness. Mental nouns and adjectives which project "hit you over the head" with their mental character. Mental nouns and adjectives which express a nonclausal phenomenon are obviously mental, but not quite so obvious as those which project a clause. Mental nouns and adjectives which neither project nor express a phenomenon are less obviously mental. The figures in table 5 show that eight of the forty-six ($=\sim17\%$) mental nouns and adjectives are very dramatically mental, and another fifteen ($= \sim33\%$) are prominently mental.

Table 5. Distributions of mental nouns and adjectives in Henry James

	Projecting	Phenomenon expressed	Simple
Nonembedded clauses	7	9	12
Embedded clauses	1	6	12

A further point to be made is that the mental nouns and adjectives are often grammatically prominent in James. Three statements can be made concerning the distribution of mental nouns and adjectives in James.

Eight attributive clauses have mental nouns/adjectives as Attributes.

One attributive clause has a mental noun functioning as postposed Subject. (Therefore it is informationally prominent.)

Twenty-seven mental nouns and adjectives play some direct role, e.g., Subject or Complement, in a nonembedded clause.

A fourth statement, looking at the same phenomenon as the third, but from the point of view of the nonembedded clauses, can be made:

In twenty-four ($= 24/136 = 17.6\%$) nonembedded clauses, a mental noun or adjective fills a major grammatical role of the clause.

Note that this last statement does not consider the distribution of mental processes discussed previously. Remember that the portion of James which I examined contained nineteen mental processes in nonembedded clauses. Of these nineteen processes, only one also directly contained a mental noun or adjective. Thus, forty-two nonembedded clauses ($= 18 + 24$) involved some mental concept. There were only 136 nonembedded clauses in the entire selection, thus 30.9 percent (almost one-third) of the nonembedded clauses in Henry James involved some mental concept in a prominent way. Clearly, mental issues are being foregrounded in this text. (By contrast with the results for James, table 2 indicates that Hemingway used only three mental nouns or adjectives. Of these, all were found in nonembedded clauses, and two projected a clause.)

One consequence of coding a process as a noun or adjective is that the participants may or may not be expressed. Tracing the expression of participants in processes which have been coded metaphorically is an interesting exercise in James. Eleven of the mental nouns contain an explicit expression of Senser in the Deictic, as in example (7),

(7)   J-17 and he would as little have been able to say what had been the sign of her face for him on the first occasion as to name the ground of *his present recognition*.

or in the Qualifier, as in example (8).

(8) J-6 Mixed with everything was *the apprehension*, already, *on Strether's part*, that he would, at best, throughout, prove the note of Europe in quite a sufficient degree.

In these two examples there is no doubt of who is the Senser. The reader does not need to work to figure out that information. In other cases, though the nominal group does not actually *express* the Senser, it is still clear from the general context of the sentence who is involved in the process. Thus *consciousness* and *taste* in example (9).

(9) J-7 That note had been meanwhile—since the previous afternoon, thanks to this happier device—*such a consciousness of personal freedom* as he hadn't known for years; *such a deep taste of change and of having above all for the moment nobody and nothing to consider*, as promised already, if *headlong hope* were not too foolish, to colour his adventure with cool success.

On the other hand, there are several examples which are not so obvious at first glance, as in *hope* in the previous example. Since *hope* is coded as a noun, the grammar allows James to give it an independence from the one doing the hoping and the phenomenon sensed. It becomes a thing in itself. *Hope* can be foolish. The reader must **work** to figure out who is hoping.

James regularly plays with this aspect of language, not restricting himself to mental nouns. Thus *moments* can place people as in example (10).

(10) J-14 After the young woman in the glass cage had held up to him across her counter the pale-pink leaflet bearing his friend's name, which she neatly pronounced, he turned away to find himself, in the hall, facing a lady who met his eyes as with an intention suddenly determined, and whose features—not freshly young, but on happy terms with each other—came back to him as from a recent vision.

J-15 For a moment they stood confronted; then *the moment placed her*:

J-16 He had noticed her the day before, noticed her at his previous inn, where—again in the hall—she had been briefly engaged with some people of his own ship's company.

Related to this phenomenon is James' tendency to use words in unusual senses. For example, J-14 ends with the words *a recent vision*. It is clear from J-16 that this phrase simply refers to a previous "sighting." But when we look at the dictionary meaning of the word *vision*, we see that the word is typically associated with something dramatic—"seeing" something which has some importance. Indeed the typical vision does **not** involve perception through the eyes. One has visions of the future, visions of Christ—things of that nature.[4] By contrast, in J-14, *vision* has an everyday sense. Strether simply saw this woman recently in the past, and sort of remembers her. Notice again that James's use of this word in this way gives the perception an independence—a status as independent "Thing."

The difficulty of perception

Table 6 presents the results of the investigation of features of language which contribute to the impression of difficulty of interpretation and perception.

The differences in the counts for these features in Hemingway and James clearly indicate that James presented the world his characters inhabited as much more problematic than Hemingway did. When James writes in example (11), he hedges with *almost* and uses a simile in *as if*.

(11)   J-40 It was *almost as if* she had been in possession and received him
           as a guest.

In such a sentence, James both gives and refrains from giving information at the same time. Was she or was she not in possession? Exactly what was her status?

---

[4]Collins COBUILD English Collocations (Sinclair 1995) (based on the Bank of English) cites *future* (as in *visions of the future*) as the most frequent collocate of the word *vision*.

Table 6. Frequency and distribution of expressions of modality, hedges, similes,temporizing and descriptions from the characters' point of view

| | Hemingway *Farewell* | | | James *Ambassadors* |
	Chapter 1	Chapter 20	Totals	Chapter 1
Modalities	1	5	6	47
Hedges	1	5	6	22
Similes	2	0	2	8
Temporizing	0	0	0	11
Description from character's point of view	0	0	0	2

Finally, let me end by mentioning a feature that is impossible to treat statistically. I have said that James attempts to represent the difficulty his characters have in interpreting the world they inhabit, and I have tried to provide some grammatical evidence showing that this issue is the focus of his language. I cannot end without saying that James is difficult to read, because it is often difficult to figure out exactly what he means. Chatman refers to James' tendency to use pronouns where several of the characters are possible referents, and the reader must figure out just who is intended. Similarly, much of the novel has more than one interpretation. Chatman illustrates this last point by taking a sentence from an introduction to one of James' novels and demonstrates that this sentence has 960 similar but different readings. *The Ambassadors* requires a close reading, and that very difficulty of reading is a way James has of creating a complex world for his characters to inhabit. In a way, an iconic relation is set up between James' difficult language and the message he is conveying of the difficulty of perceiving.

Summary

Let me summarize what has been done in this chapter. I first examined the two texts to be analyzed and discovered differences in the interpretation of those texts. The differences in interpretation on which I focussed centered around two issues: (a) the overt interest of James (but not Hemingway) in how his characters perceived the world and (b) the fact that the world the characters inhabited in the James novel was very complex. I then examined samples of the two texts focussing on certain lexico-grammatical features chosen specifically because their meanings related to these two interpretations. This examination showed that James used far more language which concerned mental phenomena. Indeed, it was found that roughly one-third of the nonembedded, i.e., grammatically prominent, clauses in his text referred to some mental phenomenon very prominently in the grammar. It showed further that James used many more expressions which drew back from simply asserting the facts. In other words, the examination of the lexico-grammatical features of the two novels showed that the nature of the reality presented by James differed from that presented by Hemingway.

The technique of analysis used here is an example of what I call "interpreted statistics." I am suggesting that interpreted statistics be used as one of several approaches to account for or explain differences in the impressions conveyed by texts. By *interpreted statistics* I mean two things.

Statistics: the examination of the frequencies of use of certain lexico-grammatical features (in particular grammatical functions).

Interpreted: the choice of which features to examine is made on the basis of **semantic** issues, not on the basis of grammatical ones. I chose to examine **all** structures which could be interpreted as communicating "perception," "doubt," or "complex world" regardless of where in the language system these features were found.

It is critical that the features examined construct patterns of **repeated meanings.** For example, though we looked for words, we did not interpret each **individual** word by itself. There was no attempt to say, "Oh, James used *acquaintance* twice. Surely he is concerned with mental concepts." Indeed, notice that for grammatical reasons, the word *acquaintance* was only counted once. Further, it was only because there was a long list of such words, and that long list was accompanied by **other** features, and these features were regularly placed in grammatically prominent positions—all of this needed to occur before we could use these figures to account for the interpretation that James was interested in perception. Ruqaiya Hasan (1985/1989) used the phrase *patterns of patterns* as she discussed the interpretation of literature. These patterns of patterns of language are exactly what we are looking for as we address the interpretation of texts. The patterns may be found in any aspect of the language of the text—the phonology or any aspect of the lexico-grammar. This paper has attempted to illustrate one way that the search for these patterns of patterns might be performed.

References

Benson, James D, and William S. Greaves. 1982. Textual meaning in Trollop's Barchester Towers: The foregrounding of adversative conjunctions. In Waldemar Gutwinski and Grace Joly (eds.), *The Eighth LACUS Forum: 1981*, 428–436. Columbia S.C.: Hornbeam.

Biber, Douglas, and Edward Finegan. 1988. Adverbial stance types in English. *Discourse Processes* 11:1–34.

Biber, Douglas, and Edward Finegan. 1989. Styles of stance in English: Lexical and grammatical marking of evidentiality and affect. *Text* 9:93–124.

Burton, Dierdre. 1982. Through glass darkly. In Ronald Carter (ed.), *Language and literature: An introductory reader in stylistics*, 194–214. London: George Allen and Unwin.

Chatman, Seymour. 1972. *The later style of Henry James*. New York: Barnes and Noble.

Conrad, Susan, and Douglas Biber. 2000. Adverbial marking of stance in speech and writing. In Susan Hunston and Geoff Thompson (eds.), *Evaluation in text: Authorial stance and the construction of discourse*, 56–73. Oxford: Oxford University Press.

Cowley, M. 1929. (October 6, 1929). Not yet demobilized. *New York Herald Tribune Books*, 1, 6.

Donaldson, Scott ed. 1990. *New essays on* A Farewell to Arms. Cambridge: Cambridge University Press.

Eggins, Suzanne, and Diana Slade. 1997. *Analyzing casual conversation*. London: Cassel.

Halliday, M. A. K. 1970. Descriptive linguistics in literary studies. In Donald Freeman (ed.), *Linguistics and literary style*, 57–72. New York: Holt Rinehart and Winston.

Halliday, M. A. K. 1971. Linguistic function and literary style: An inquiry into the language of William Golding's *The Inheritors*. In Seymour Chatman (ed.), *Literary style: A symposium*, 362–400. New York: Oxford University Press. (Reprinted in Halliday. 1973. *Explorations in the functions of language*. London: Edward Arnold.)

Halliday, M. A. K. 1994. *Introduction to functional grammar*. London: Arnold.

Hasan, Ruqaiya. 1985/1989. *Linguistics, language and verbal art*. Victoria: Deakin University Press. (Also Oxford University Press.)

Hemingway, Ernest M. 1929/1977. *A farewell to arms*. London: Grafton Books.

James, Henry. 1903/1973. *The ambassadors*. Harmondsworth, England: Penguin.

Kies. Daniel. 1992. The uses of passivity: Suppressing agency in *Nineteen Eighty-Four*. In Martin Davies and Louise Ravelli (eds.), *Advances in systemic linguistics*, 229–250. London: Pinter Publishers.

Martin, James. 1996. Metalinguistic diversity: The case from case. In Ruqaiya Hasan, Carmel Cloran, and David Butt (eds.), *Functional descriptions: Theory in practice*, 323–374. Amsterdam: John Benjamins.

Matthiessen, Christian. 1996. *Lexicogrammatical cartography: English systems.* To-
    kyo: International Language Sciences Publishers.
Mills, Carl. 1992. Discourse, style and measurement: Narrative. In Ruth Brend
    (ed.), *The Eighteenth LACUS Forum: 1991*, 404–414. Lake Bluff, Ill.: LACUS.
Phelan, James. 1990. Distance, voice, and temporal perspective in Frederic
    Henry's narration: Successes, problems and paradox. In Donaldson, 53–73.
Pike, Kenneth L. 1967. *Language in relation to a unified theory of the structure of
    human behavior.* Mouton: The Hague.
Pike, Kenneth L. 1981. *Tagmemics, discourse and verbal art.* Ann Arbor: Michigan
    Studies in the Humanities.
Pike, Kenneth L., and Evelyn G. Pike. 1983. *Text and Tagmeme.* Norwood, N.J.:
    Ablex.
Samudji. 1999. *Mentalization in Henry James's "The Ambassadors."* Ph.D. disserta-
    tion. Macquarie University. Sydney, Australia.
Savage, D. S. 1970. Ciphers at the front. In J. Gellens (ed.), *Twentieth century in-
    terpretations of* A Farewell to Arms: *A collection of critical essays,* 91–102.
    Englewod Cliffs, N.J.: Prentice Hall.
Sinclair, John. 1995. *Collins COBUILD English Collocations.* London:
    HarperCollins.
Stowell, H. Peter. 1980. *Literary impressionism, James and Chekhov.* Athens: The
    University of Georgia Press.

22

Language in Relation to... and Cognitive Grammar

Eugene H. Casad

Introduction

Pike's *Language in Relation to a Unified Theory of the Structure of Human Behavior* presents us with a comprehensive view of language, interpreted within the framework of the human mind and the collective fabric of culture and society. It is a carefully crafted piece of work that merits careful reading and study. Although I am not a practitioner of Tagmemics, I continue to be amazed at the breadth of Pike's theorizing and am stimulated by many of his stated assumptions, formulations, and ideas, which, in fact, fit very nicely into the framework in which I carry out my own research.

In this chapter, I will show how Pike's framework, elaborated first in the 1950s, and insightfully applied to a wide variety of languages and

---

Ken Pike was my mentor in a variety of ways, both in linguistics and in life, especially over the last fifteen years. His encouragement to be active in the academic arena was augmented by his and Evelyn's generosity to me in the financial realm: they partially funded almost every trip that I made for attending linguistic conferences between 1987 and 2000. Ken's sharing with me of some of his own personal struggles and disappointments in the academic arena was a terrific help to me spiritually.

linguistic problems, has a more recent counterpart in Ronald W. Langacker's Cognitive Grammar. I will suggest that the latter framework corroborates and validates Pike's approach in many ways, including the grounding of grammar in human mental abilities, the characterization of linguistic units as form-meaning composites, and the centrality of viewing arrangements in accounting for the patterns of language use. Although there are significant differences, to be sure, nonetheless Cognitive Grammar owes a debt to Pike and confirms many of the points that he makes. For example, Cognitive Grammer sees the grammar of a language as consisting of both schematic patterns (= rules or constructional schemas) and lists of items that instantiate those rules (Langacker 1990b:264–265). This formulation is at least highly reminiscent of Pike and Robert Longacre and that is non-coincidental (Ronald W. Langacker, personal communication).[1] As another example, Nathan's work in Cognitive Phonology, with its conceptualization of a phoneme as a class of related phonological entities (Pike 1955:21–22), as well as its entertaining a mentalistic aspect to the nature of phonemes (cf. Pike 1955:12–13), is also based squarely on Pike's work.[2]

Language and Human Behavior

In Pike's view, language is a form of behavior, a human activity that is intimately connected to the structure of nonverbal behavior (Pike 1954:2). This implies that there is no unique language facility totally distinct from other conceptual abilities, as has been claimed by Chomsky and associates (Langacker 1988a:4; 1999:1). Pike's statement here accords well with both Langacker and Lakoff in what Cognitive Linguistics terms the "Cognitive Commitment" (Lakoff 1990; Langacker 1987; Gibbs 1996), i.e., the

[1] I would like to thank Ron Langacker for detailed comments that he made on this essay and on the one from which the Cora data presented here is taken. This chapter is very much the better for his help.

[2] When I remarked about this to Geoffrey Nathan after his lecture at the Santa Barbara Cognitive Linguistics Association Conference in July 2000, he affirmed it and told me that he personally had mentioned this to Pike (Geoffrey Nathan, personal communication). A similar story of the influence of Pike's thinking on Fillmore's work in Case Grammar and Construction Grammar could easily be told (Ken McElhanon, personal communication). See also Fillmore's own comment on the parallels between Case Grammar and Tagmemics:

> There is an easy conversion from underlying representations of case grammar to 'tagmemic' formulas, too, as long as the case categories unarily dominate NP's. Or, for that matter, a case grammar diagram could simply be read off as a tagmemic formula as long as certain symbols were designated as function indicators....The crucial difference between the modifications of transformational grammar that I have been suggesting and the typical tagmemic study is in the insistance here on discovering the 'deepest' level of 'deep structure'. (1968:88)

statements that we make about how language works must accord with what we know more generally about cognitive processing. In Langacker's terms, language use is a special case of the human problem-solving ability that involves the speaker's exploiting the symbolic resources of language to make categorizing judgments (Langacker 1988a:13).

Langacker summarizes the basic cognitive abilities that are crucial to an adequate account of lexical semantics and grammatical structure as follows: (a) we possess an inborn capacity for sensual experience, that is, we perceive colors, sounds, tastes, smells, and textures; (b) we are aware of spatial extension and perceive all kinds of spatially distributed configurations; (c) we experience different kinds of emotions; and (d) we perceive the passage of time. Beyond this, we can compare entities, both in terms of similarities and differences. This, of course, calls to mind Pike's notion of the Identificational-Contrastive features of the Feature Mode (cf. Pike 1954, Vol I:82). We categorize one entity in terms of another and we can talk about entities and events with a wide range of specificity. We direct our attention to entities and situations and focus that attention on certain things as opposed to others. We conceive of many kinds of relationships in terms of reference points. We group experiences and entities in various ways and manipulate them as unitary entities. We track entities through time and space and base many of our characterizations on Image Schemas and metaphor. All of these different conceptual abilities figure highly in language usage (Langacker 1999:2–3).

Pike states that the linguist's goal is to "discover the structure of language behavior" (1954:2) and he quite correctly notes that to do this, the linguist must often look to the broader behavioral field in order to find the proper context that would allow him to explain the data. As he states the case:

> Since this behavior is a part of total human behavior, and obtains its structuring in reference to that larger behavior field, and relative to the structural units of that larger field, the linguist must on occasion refer to that larger field in order to get access to that frame of reference within which the linguistic units obtain part of their definition. (1954:27)

Not only is language behavior situated within a broader context of nonverbal behavior, as Pike notes, but it finds its meaning in specific contexts within that broad field. This is crucial to Langacker's view of semantics. For Langacker, the speaker draws on his full range of knowledge and his varied cognitive capacities for constructing and understanding utterances (Langacker 1988a:13). The "frame of reference" for defining meanings is a set of conceptual domains, basic and abstract, and all meaningful linguistic units are contextually defined (Langacker 1988a:14; 1999:4). Pike's choice of words "obtain part of their definition" implies another important aspect of the meaning of a linguistic unit: it is only partially compositional and there are almost always emergent properties attendant to the unit's conventionalized usage (Langacker 1990:10, 18, 25; 1999:16, 94, 109).

The Form and Meaning Correspondence

Foundational to Pike's formulation is the idea of a linguistic unit as a form-meaning composite. He states this in the following terms:

> In the present theory, I am attempting to develop a point of view within which form and meaning must not be separated in theory; there are rather form-meaning composites concerning which we, for convenience, may on occasion discuss the form and meaning aspects as if they were separate, while taking pains to indicate that such an expedient is a distortion which must be corrected at proper intervals and in the relevant places in the discussion. (1954:24)

The pairing of form and meaning is equally foundational to Langacker's framework. To begin, in this framework grammar is characterized as a "structured inventory of conventional units" (Langacker 1988a:11; 1990:15). To be sure, the structuring in Langacker's account is distinct from the trimodal structuring of Pike's framework. Nonetheless, there are significant overlaps and I will mention three of these here.

First, in Langacker's terms, the inventory is structured in the sense that lower order units function in slots of higher order units. This reflects Langacker's view that grammar consists in forming more complex structures from less complex ones (1988a:24–25; 1990:10, 296). Pike, of course, discussed this combinatory aspect of language structures in detail (1954:66). Second, the form-meaning correspondence derives precisely from the inherently symbolic nature of grammar (Langacker 1988a:18). Linguistic units have both a semantic pole and a phonological pole; these are related to one another via symbolization (Langacker 1990:105). For Langacker, lexicon, morphology, and syntax are all constituted of symbolic units, and the kinds of symbolic structures that reflect each unit grade into one another in kind. Thus there is no rigid distinction between lexicon, morphology, or syntax (1988a:12).

Langacker's view of the symbolic nature of linguistic units seems to be reminiscent of the Saussurean conception, but it is actually very much in accord with Pike's conceptualization of the form-meaning composite relation: one can look at the semantic pole and talk about the characteristics of semantic units, but those semantic units do not exist abstractly or in a vacuum. Likewise, one can look at the phonological pole and talk about the units at that level. For an example, David Tuggy, in a recent paper, discusses in detail the units at both the semantic pole and the phonological pole for reduplication in Náhuatl (Tuggy 2003). Langacker's Content requirement assures that no abstract signs without any connection to linguistic substance are allowed: language is comprised of semantic structures, phonological structures, and the set of symbolic links between these two kinds of units (Langacker 1999:1, 28, 98).

There are, indeed, significant differences between Pike's approach and Langacker's. One of the most obvious is Pike's rejection of the semiotics of de Saussure and Hjelmslev in contrast to Langacker's explicit recognition within his theoretical framework of the basic semiological function of language. Langacker characterizes grammar as an inventory of symbolic resources and notes that this function is what allows speakers to symbolize their conceptualizations by means of phonological vocalizations (1988a; 1999:1).

It seems to me that Pike's term "form-meaning complex" actually implies just this semiological function: Each linguistic unit has a meaning that is paired with a form. This suggests to me that Pike missed the implication that the pairing is a semiological one. The question becomes: Why did he miss it? I think it goes back to his methodology illustrated in the following quotation.

> One of the most difficult of the theoretical problems, which must be faced by such a theory as this one, is the balance to be struck between giving priority to the relationships themselves on the one hand or to be given to the items which are at the poles of the relationships, on the other. (Pike 1954:93)

Pike's position here reflects the common human tendency to force distinctions that should not be forced. Here he is forcing himself to choose between "units" and "relations," a valid and useful distinction in itself, but one such that there is no real need to give priority of one over the other. Pike actually did, however, make such a choice, as evidenced by the following.

> As the theory worked out, however, it appeared more satisfactory in the long run to set up the units as basic and treat the contrastive relationships between units in part as subsidiary to them...and in part as the interlocking of these units within still larger units in their respective hierarchies of units and systems of units. (1954:93)

Pike's characterization of the relationships as consisting in part of "the interlocking of these units within still larger units in their respective hierarchies of units" seems to me to corrrespond to the integrational relationships that hold between lower level units that jointly form a construction at a higher level. What he seems to exclude here is the linking of specific units of meaning with specific vocalizations, i.e., the ubiquitous symbolic relation. In summary, it seems to me that he rejected too much unnecessarily. On the other hand, Langacker adopted the semiotic function as fundamental in his framework while distancing himself from a narrow interpretation of *la arbitreire du signe* (1987:10–11). By broadly interpreting the term "conventional," Langacker (1988a:11) gives no special status to structures that are arbitrary, unmotivated, or unpredictable.

Etics and Emics

Prominent in Pike's formulation of his framework is the distinction between what he calls the ETIC and EMIC viewpoints. He notes that these terms represent two different viewpoints that an observer (= analyst) can take to the data that he has under study. Both viewpoints have their purposes and place. He characterizes the etic view as one in which the analyst concerns himself with making generalized statements on the basis of his prior collection and categorization of data. This entails specifying criteria for classification as well as the organizing of the data into types or classes. The overall activity of classification includes updating the system by integrating newly found data and precedes the analyst's focusing on a particular culture (Pike 1954:8).

The emic viewpoint is specific to a given culture and language. Pike assumes relative homogeneity within and significant integration to the culture and the behavior displayed by the people who constitute the population of that culture. He describes the activity of arriving at an emic analysis in the following terms.

> It is an attempt to *discover* and to describe the pattern of that particular language or culture in reference to the way in which the various elements of that culture are related to each other in the functioning of that particular pattern. (Pike 1954:8)

One parallel between Pike's systemic view here and Langacker's is the latter's characterization of Cognitive Grammar as incorporating a network model for both lexical items and grammatical constructions (Langacker

1988b:51; 1999:19–20). Even more, Langacker states that our entire field of knowledge can be modeled as a vast set of interlocking networks (Langacker 1987:163). Pike's insistence on the need to study all emic units in reference to nonverbal cultural behavior (Pike 1954:10–11), clearly implies its counterpart in what Langacker calls an encyclopedic view of meaning, which is opposed to the so-called narrow "dictionary" meaning of lexical items (cf. Haiman 1980; Langacker 1988b:58). This simply means that in understanding what something means or in using a grammatical pattern properly, the speaker draws on his/her general knowledge of the world around and on his/her various cognitive capacities (Langacker 1988b:53, 57).

Another of Pike's comments about the etic-emic distinction is noteworthy at this point: "It must further be emphasized that etic and emic data do not constitute a rigid dichotomy of bits of data, but often present the same data from two points of view" (1954:12).

Pike's observation here parallels Langacker's observation about a variety of dichotomies made in linguistic theory that are actually not rigidly distinct. These include syntax versus semantics, pragmatics versus semantics, morphology versus syntax, lexicon versus syntax, transitive versus intransitive, active versus passive, and stem versus affix (cf. Tuggy 1992; Langacker 1988c:128; 1990:105). Pike's discussion of indeterminacies of categories throughout his work reflects a similar sensitivity to the plasticity of human categorization and his sensitivity to retaining accuracy in descriptive detail.

Pike's notion of etic versus emic seems to have its most direct Cognitive Linguistic analogue in the distinction that Langacker makes between two kinds of "instance" planes of cognitive representation, the STRUCTURAL PLANE and the ACTUAL PLANE (Langacker 1999:270). For Langacker, the structural plane represents the generalizations that one makes about "the structure of the world," whereas the actual plane relates to the phenomenal world, the domain where events take place and situations arise (Langacker 1999:274–5). Interestingly, Pike's characterization of etic versus emic as reflecting two different points of view of the data is mirrored by Langacker's view that the structural plane and the actual plane should be thought of as two distinct facets of the "instance" plane (Langacker 1999:274). The "instance" plane itself is paired with the "type" plane of representation; grammatical correlates of these include lexical nouns versus verbs and full nominals versus finite clauses (Langacker 1999:270). Langacker further points out that the "type" plane and the "instance" plane are not totally distinct levels nor do they have different cognitive representations, but the analyst needs to refer to both planes in order to achieve descriptive adequacy (Langacker 1999:271).

In another way, Langacker's notion of construal seems reminiscent of Pike's etic-emic distinction. In both cases, these notions are very broadly defined and widely applied within the respective frameworks. I think that what relates the two is the human capacity for imposing structure on the object of perception or conception. Pike states:

> Items as experienced take some of their perceived characteristics from that experience. The individual is unable to experience his background coldly and interpret it completely neutrally. All phenomena, all "facts," all "things," somehow reach him only through perceptual and psychological filters which affect his perception of the structuring of and relevance of the physical data that he observes. (1960:115)

Pike's view as expressed here underscores the point that Langacker repeatedly makes that semantics does not reflect objective reality but rather speakers construe situations and events in the world around them in a myriad of alternate ways (Langacker 1999:5).

Construals and Perspective

At this point, I begin detailing the framework for what Langacker calls the VIEWING arrangement. Reminiscent of Pike, Langacker notes that the primary conceptualizers in the speech situation are the speaker and the addressee, that our concern with the linguistic expressions that they use is with the conceptualizations that those expressions evoke and that the speaker and addressee can never conceive of or portray a situation in wholly neutral terms (Langacker 1999:203, 206). Instead they always construe that situation in one form or another. For Langacker, the construal relationship is characterized as follows:

> Though largely ignored in traditional semantics, construal is crucial for both semantic and grammatical structure. It is a multifaceted phenomenon whose various dimensions reflect some of the basic cognitive abilities noted previously. They can be grouped under five general headings: *specificity, background, perspective, scope* and *prominence.* (Langacker 1999:5)

The term SPECIFICITY refers to the variable degree of detail that is included in the meaning of a given term. Take, for example, the terms *Drakeoceras drakei, Drakeoceras, Lower Cretaceous ammonite, ammonite, cephalopod, invertebrate fossil,* and *fossil.* These terms, in left to right order go from the highly specific, i.e., the name of a particular species of fossil from a particular time period, on through more inclusive categories of fossils and are summed up with the category label *fossil* that includes hundreds of thousands of kinds of traces of life forms from past geological ages. Verbs also show the same kind of variation in specificity: note the following: *hang Sheetrock, build a house, do construction work, do manual labor, work.* Whereas *hanging Sheetrock* is a particular kind of activity carried out at a specific stage in the building of a house, *doing manual labor* subsumes myriads of jobs, many of which have nothing whatsoever to do with building houses, and *doing one's work* may involve no manual work at all.

Pike noted that the FIGURE-BACKGROUND relationship as set out by the Gestalt psychologists might well clarify a range of questions related to the entire question of focus (Pike 1960:56). Cognitive Grammar complements Pike's work at this point by explicitly invoking the concepts of *figure* and *ground* in the account that it gives of linguistic meaning and grammar. One way in which figure and ground relate is in linguistic categorization: speakers again and again construe one entity against the background of another. Sentences such as *He is in front of the house* versus *He is behind the house* are typical. The background entity may be a conceptual network of relations, as when we designate someone as "my uncle" or "my brother." Other backgrounds include things like the previous discourse, which is the framework for focus, anaphora, and the distinction between given and new information. Finally, the source domain for metaphor is the background for the target structure of the metaphor (Langacker 1999:5).

Langacker includes a variety of factors under the rubric of PERSPECTIVE. These include spatially based notions such as the speaker's VANTAGE POINT that he/she assumes for viewing an ongoing situation. In Cora, for example, you would refer to a waterfall one way if you were on the side of the canyon over which the water pours, whereas you would express things in a different way if you were on the opposite side of the canyon looking across at the waterfall (Casad 1993:620). A second factor is that of MENTAL SCANNING, a cognitive process that accounts for the difference between sentences such as *The hill falls gently to the stream* versus *the hill rises gently from the stream.* A third factor is whether the speaker construes an entity OBJECTIVELY or SUBJECTIVELY. What Langacker means by this is, whether the Speaker conceives of his/her own role as being simply the Subject of Perception as opposed to the entity he/she is describing, which is his Object of Perception, or whether the Speaker also puts him/herself on the stage of focus as the Object of Perception. In the latter case, Langacker would say that the Speaker functions both as Subject of Perception and as Object of Perception.

A fourth factor is the SCOPE of an expression. This term refers to the full array of conceptual content that an expression typically invokes. One way to talk about this is in terms of the set of domains that the usage of that expression calls on and exploits for a given purpose. This notion is most easily grasped by considering partonymies: e.g., in a sequence of terms such as *arm* > *hand* > *finger* > *knuckle,* we observe a series of nested spatial configurations which, starting at the left, provide the immediate scope for defining the next rightward term. Thus, "the conception of an *arm* provides the spatial scope for *hand*" (Langacker 1999:6).

The final factor in perspective is PROMINENCE. As Langacker uses the term, this includes the relative ranking of particular domains in the overall meaning of lexical items. For example, the kinship domain is central to the meaning of *aunt,* but quite peripheral to the meaning of *woman* (Langacker 1999:6–7). Prominence also has to do with the subjective or objective construal of an entity. Those entities construed objectively are the locus of attention and are therefore more salient than entities which are construed subjectively and thus fall outside the focus of attention. Finally, the status of an entity as the conceptual referent is another way in which some entities in a situation are more salient than others.[3] The conceptual referent is selected as the focus of attention and, thus, in Langacker's formulation, is placed in the "onstage" portion of the viewing arrangement (Langacker 1999:7).

In summary, all of the factors described in the preceding paragraphs interact in various ways within the speaker's viewing arrangement that he/she assumes in his/her use of given expressions and in discourse. All of this both explains and underscores the importance of the following observation by Pike.

> "Things" and "man" are not divorced from each other but are involved in a larger complex such that man's own structure is involved directly in his perception and discussion of either. (1960:115)

---

[3]Cook's recent analysis of Hawaiian *'o* is a good example of a grammatical marker of nominals that are more salient to the meaning of a sentence than other nominals in that sentence (Cook 2003).

The Viewing Arrangement

Echoing Pike's statement given above, Langacker notes that the link between an observer and what he observes is intrinsic to the statements that
the observer makes about the situation in focus. With respect to language,
Langacker equates the observer with the speaker. The speaker's observational role is that of apprehending the meanings of linguistic expressions
(1999:204).

Langacker's characterization of the prototypical viewing arrangement for
language use includes two isomorphic sets of constructs. For the prototypical
visual perception situation, he posits the VIEWER, who is the SUBJECT of perception. That viewer has a prototypical viewing stance in which he/she is
facing in a particular direction and has a MAXIMALLY EXTENDED FIELD of vision with an indeterminate periphery and a central region of high visual acuity. Langacker invokes a theater model at this point and states that the
central region of visual acuity is the "onstage" region of the overall field of
vision. This "onstage" region is the portion of the situation in focus and represents the *object* of perception (Langacker 1999:204–205). These elements
are represented diagrammatically in figure 1.[4]

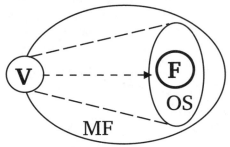

Figure 1. The Perceptual Arrangement
(From Langacker 1999:205, figure 7.1.a).

The notational conventions employed in figure 1 include the following:
(V) = Viewer, (MF) = Maximal Field of Vision, (OS) = Onstage Region
and (F) = Focus. In addition, the broken arrow running between the
Viewer and the Focus in this context represents the perceptual relationship between the Perceiver and the Perceived Entity. This is the prototype
for a variety of possible configurations, each of which can be termed a
VIEWING ARRANGEMENT (Langacker 1999:205).

---

[4]I would like to thank Anke Beck of Mouton de Gruyter for permission to reprint figures 7.1.a
and 7.1.b from Langacker (1999) in this paper.

The conceptual counterpart to the prototypical viewing arrangement of figure 1 is more general and more widely applicable in semantic analysis. The constructs in this case include the CONCEPTUALIZER (C), who is also the SUBJECT of conceptualization. The MAXIMAL SCOPE of the conceptualization (MS) includes the full range of conceptualized content, both central and peripheral. The analogue of the "onstage" region of the visually based viewing arrangement is the set of central notions that we have in focus. In this case, Langacker uses the term IMMEDIATE SCOPE (IS) to designate the general locus of attention. This IS comprises the full set of elements which *potentially* can be put in focus as the OBJECT of perception, the entity that Langacker terms the PROFILE of the conceptualized situation (P) (Langacker 1999:5). The profile, then, is the SPECIFIC focus of attention within this general general region. The conceptual counterpart to the perception relationship of figure 1 is the construal relationship, indicated by the arrow that relates the Conceptualizer to the entity he holds in focus. This represents the full range of ways that the speaker has at his/her disposal for structuring what he/she has to say and how he/she is going to say it. In short, the overt inclusion of the construal relationship in this arrangement effectively opens the door for accounting for all of the components of value, meaning, purpose and belief that Pike specified in his work (1960:113, 115, 118). The elements of the conceptual viewing arrangement are depicted diagrammatically in figure 2.

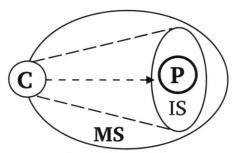

Figure 2. The Conceptual Arrangement
(From Langacker 1999:205, figure 7.1.b).

At this point, I will turn to an analysis of some data from the Cora language of northwestern Mexico in order to illustrate variants of the viewing arrangements discussed by Langacker and show how the speaker structures his/her content in a few particular contexts.

Some Cora Examples

Cora, a Southern Uto-Aztecan language, is characterized by an intricate and highly integrated system of spatial language. This includes a set of sentence-initial locative particles, an even more elaborate set of locative adverbs that are oriented to the lay of the land and an extensive inventory of locative and directional verbal prefixes that sketch out in highly schematic terms the physical and geographical settings within which conditions are observed and events are realized (Casad 1977, 1982, 1989, 1993, 1996, 1999; Casad and Langacker 1985; Langacker 1990b).

Beyond the clear morphological characteristics that separate the sets of Cora spatials, the subjective-objective distinction, discussed by Langacker (1990a, 1990b, 1999) relates to the usages of these spatials in various ways, some obvious, others not so obvious. In this section I examine this distinction and show that, in general, the locative particles construe the Speaker in a highly subjective manner in their usages in the grammar and discourse, whereas the locative verbal prefixes are highly objective in their viewing arrangement of the scene on stage. Nonetheless, there are degrees of subjectivity and objectivity observable in the usages of all three sets of spatials.

I find a variety of Langacker's notions crucial to my analysis. These include "viewing arrangement," "profile," "ground," "search domain," "immediate scope," "maximal scope," "point of reference," and "reference point."[5] In particular, all of these notions are necessary for exploring in adequate detail the notions "Subject of Perception" and "Object of Perception" and for showing how these two are reflected in specific usages of Cora spatial terms. I begin my discussion with examples that illustrate the contrast between the maximally subjective construal of the Subject of Perception and the maximally objective construal of the Object of Perception. As this description will also show, a degree of subjectivity accompanies all of these usages (cf. Langacker 1999:298; also, Verhagen 1995; Harder 1996).

Maximally subjective construal of Subject of Perception

In presenting a maximally subjective construal of his/her role, the speaker excludes himself/herself completely from "the on stage" portion

---

[5]I distinguish between the general term "point of reference" and the specific term "reference point" as detailed in Langacker (1993). A POINT OF REFERENCE is a point with respect to which some other entity is situated or calculated. It may often be offstage and implicit and in many cases may be the conceptualizer him/herself. A REFERENCE POINT, in the narrow sense, is onstage and salient. It is part of a reference-point model and is the focused element that the speaker accesses in order to reach another focused element (Ronald W. Langacker, personal communication).

of the viewing scene. The profile is the focus of conceptualization and, by definition "is construed with a high degree of objectivity" (Langacker 1999:297). The profile may be a person, a thing, an event, a relation, or an area. The Cora locative particles and topographic adverbs saliently profile an area. They constitute a striking example of what Langacker calls "Reference Point Constructions." The reference point in the relationships that these morphemes signal is, of course, a locative reference point. One of the interesting things about the semantics of these elements is the elaborate nature of these constructions: most of them are morphemically complex; each morpheme in the construction signals a distinct locative relationship; and in all cases, the Subject of Perception is construed subjectively, albeit with a variety of construals of the grounding entities. I begin with the simple examples of (1a) and (1b).

(1) a. á   pʷa'ake
         there.out   outside
         'off there outside (the house)'

     b. ú   či'i-ta
         there.in   house-in
         'off there inside the house'

These two examples illustrate two slightly different locative phrase constructions; (1a) is a locative particle + locative adverb construction, whereas (1b) is a locative particle + postpositional phrase construction. The locative particles *á* and *ú* indicate that some entity is distally located with respect to someone's position, whether speaker or other person, and that the distally located entity is to be found either within an indefinitely expanded exterior region, as in the case of *á*, or within a clearly enclosed area, as in the case of *ú*. In what follows, I intend to characterize only *á* and *ú*; the roles of *pʷa'aké* and *či'itá* are not characterized in detail, rather their citation here is simply to illustrate typical situations which are construed as either "outside" or "inside" ones.

In each case, the scenario includes an area that we can characterize as the "search domain" of the locative particle (Hawkins 1985). This "domain" summarizes the totality of locations where the Target of conceptualization might be situated (Langacker 1999:173–174). It is indicated overtly in figures 3 and 4 and elsewhere when essential to the discussion.

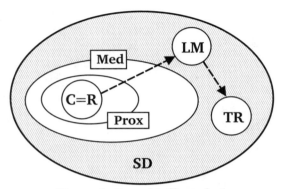

Figure 3. Cora á 'off yonder'.

In figure 3, two entities, the locative landmark (LM), and the Target of Conception (TR), are shown in a stative relationship set at a distal distance from the ground, i.e., the conceptualizer. As suggested by figure 3, the distance relationship in Cora is conventionally organized into three successively more inclusive spatial areas which I label "proximal," "medial," and "distal," respectively. The proximal area is construed as the speaker's location, whereas the medial area is viewed as taking in the speaker's point of visual reference and the distal area is conventionally understood as being out of range of the speaker's neighborhood (Casad 1982:81).

In figure 4, the trajector is shown as located within the search domain of a bounded landmark area set outside of the second largest circle in the diagram, labelled "Med." As suggested by the labels on the circles, this broad area subtends the Proximal Neigborhood of the conceptualizer, who is the default point of reference (R) for the relationship. This neigborhood is thus labelled "Prox." This divides the area of immediate scope into "near" and "far" regions vis à vis the Reference entity. Following Langacker's notation, the conceptualizer's role as a nonfocal point of reference, indicated by the circle marked "C=R" is completely "off stage" and the broken arrow linking C=R with LM indicates the path the conceptualizer follows for making mental contact with both the Locative Landmark and the Trajector of the conceptualized locative relation (Langacker 1999:174, 177, 179, 182, 197, 236, 395).

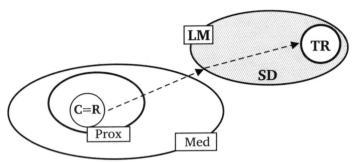

Figure 4. Cora *ú* 'off yonder in there'.

Figure 4 presents a diagram of *ú* 'off yonder in there'. The conceptualizer, as the nonfocal point of reference and part of the ground of the expression, is shown as mentally viewing a stative relationship, one that is anchored by a locative landmark that is distally removed from the proximity of the ground. Again, no element of the ground is on stage in this usage. The distal interior relationship is confined to a physically bounded region that consists of the landmark and the trajector of the locative relationship situated at some point within its search domain (SD). This conceptual content is being construed objectively and is tantamount to the speaker's locus of viewing attention, i.e., the immediate scope of the expression (Langacker 1999:6–7, 49–51, 60–61).

The topographic particles

The adverbials *á* and *ú* are the morphologically and semantically simplest of the Cora locative adverbs. The next simplest set of locative particles are the topographically oriented ones, illustrated in table 1.

Table 1. The topographic locative particles

Slope vs. Distance	Foot of slope		In slope		Head of slope
	Inside	Outside	Inside	Outside	Outside
Here	yuu	yaa	yuh	yah	yan
There	muu	maa	muh	mah	man
Off there	uu	aa	uh	ah	an

The topographic particles consist of three paradigmatic sets that involve variants of a slope predication which fit into complex semantic structures along with variants of the distance and boundary predications.

The presence of two predications in the meanings of *á* and *ú* implies the accessing of multiple landmarks which the speaker uses simultaneously for calculating specific spatial relationships. We will observe this invoking of multiple landmarks again and again in the following discussion. The slope predication is reflected in the morphological shape of the locative particles in one of three ways: 'foot of the slope' is marked by a long *a* or *u* vowel, 'in the slope' is marked by a syllable-final *-h*, and 'head of the slope' is marked by syllable-final *-n*. The three sets of resultant forms correspond to each of the locations in the slope gradient.

The locative particles are arranged vertically along the points of the distance predication. They are also set in parallel columns to display the contrastive 'inside-outside' categorization of the boundary predication. The following analysis of a single contrastive pair of topographic particles, *áh* 'off up there at the side of the slope' and *úh* 'off there straight up in the slope' shows how the Subject of Perception is construed and illustrates the reference point nature of each.

Before describing the composite semantic structures of this pair of slope-oriented locative particles, it will be necessary to consider the nature of the slope predication itself and its relation to the boundary predication. The abstract domain of the slope predication includes three interrelated regions that I call "foot," "face," and "head," which, taken together, constitute the slope domain base. Each of these regions may serve as the locative reference point area. Figure 5 presents a generalized form of the slope domain and the relationship between it and the line of sight boundary area.

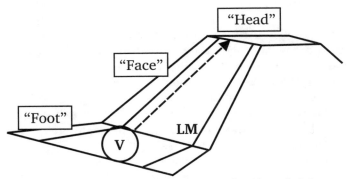

Figure 5. Slope as abstract domain for line of sight.

The slope domain in figure 5 turns out to be the base relative to which the boundary area is defined. Within this complex base, the locative point of reference bounded area is equivalent to a speaker's canonical line of sight, i.e., what he/she would see were he/she at the foot of the slope looking up the gradient. Specifically, the line of sight begins at the horizontal foot of the slope, follows the vertical axis of the slope and continues to the skyline at the head of the slope. As a natural restriction, it does not curve around to cover the head of the slope.

It is important to note that the line of sight bounded area is not equivalent to the slope domain, but is rather a second landmark with its own specialized search domain. As figure 5 shows, one reason that the two are not equivalent is that the line of sight bounded area takes in the "foot" and "slope" elements of the slope domain, but excludes the area internal to the "head" element. In short, the two domains are not equivalent by virtue of not being isomorphic. In addition, the speaker's canonical position is not necessarily his/her actual one and the line of sight landmark region is a relatively narrow strip along the face of the slope.

The morphemes *ú* 'inside' and *á* 'outside' take on specialized meanings when the boundary domain is linked to the slope domain. Specifically, *ú* 'inside' is broadly construed as being within the search domain of the canonical speaker's line of sight, whereas *á* 'outside' is broadly construed as being outside that line of sight (or, directionally), at an oblique angle to it.

A consideration of the semantics of *úh* 'off there straight up in the slope' shows the need to characterize the medial and distal ranges in highly schematic terms and invoke a set of related variants that instantiate them in the appropriate contexts. Specifically, for the Trajector as Object of Conceptualization to be in the line of sight of the speaker, but also to be outside the medial range of the speaker, which I originally defined as the limits on his visual field (Casad 1982:58, 88) is contradictory. However, if I construe the medial range as a highlighted focal reference point, then the various components fit. It is quite consistent for the Trajector as Object of Conceptualization to be outside of the search domain of the speaker's proximity at the same time that he/she is still within the speaker's line of sight along the slope. Figure 6 gives a diagrammatic representation of central aspects of the semantic representation of *úh* 'off there straight up in the slope'. In this diagram, the viewer's status as the nonfocal point of reference is indicated by "V = R."

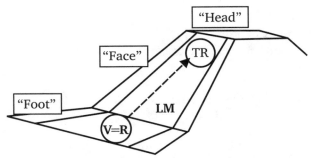

Figure 6. *úh* 'off there straight up in the slope'.

The next locative particle I discuss is *áh* 'off up there at the side of the slope'. This particle occurs not only with spatial meanings (2a), but also with temporal ones (2b). In addition, it occurs as a bound prefixal configuration in various kinds of constructions with topographic suffixes (2c), verb and adjective stems (2d–e), and incorporated nominal forms (2f).[6]

(2) a. á-h   tú   wa-rá'a-kɨ
     outside-slope we EXT-corner-leave
     'We came back from off out at the side of the hill.'

   b. á-h   pú   nu'u í   i-rá
     outside-slope SUBJ QUOT SEQ NARR-face

     'a-h-cuná
     outside-slope-spring up
     'Then, so they say, she jumped right up to meet him.'

   c. á-h-tʸi   tɨ́   a'-u-h-méh
     outside-slope-uphill SUBR ABL-away-slope-go.from
     'The guy who is going uphill along the trail.'

   d. šá-'a-h-wii-ši'ɨ   mʷán
     you.PL-outside-slope-stand-DISTR.IMP you.PL
     'Get up out of bed, you guys.'

---

[6]I use the following abbreviations for simple glosses of the individual morphemes in the examples used in this paper: ABL: ablative, ART: definite article, EXT: extensive, MED: medial, NARR: narrative, NEG: negative, PERF: perfective, PL: plural, QUOT: quotative, SEQ: sequential, SUBJ: subject, SUBR: subordinator.

e. á-h-tʸee   tʸámʷa'a mí   či'i
   outside-slope-long   really   ART   house
   'That building is really tall.'

f. ka-pú   á-h-kʷasi   mí   pina'a
   NEG-SUBJ   outside-slope-tail   ART   bird
   'That bird has no tail feathers.'

A schematic representation for *áh* in its topographical uses is given in figure 7. As usual, this schema subsumes various specific configurations. The one I have in mind here locates the speaker at the canonical viewing position from the foot of the slope. This is a point of reference for defining the landmark region, and the viewer is again indicated by the circle labelled "V = R." As in all of our previous examples, the speaker is offstage and the Trajector may be located in any number of locations within the search domain of the landmark area. In this usage, the Trajector is located well outside of the line-of-sight landmark region. Also, the speaker's vantage point relative to the target's position is flexible in the distinct and felicitous usages of *áh*; the meaning of *áh* includes no specific mention of this information, and, since the speaker is not specifically mentioned, he/she is being construed highly subjectively.

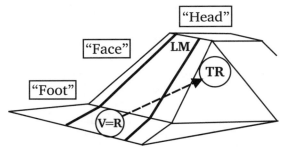

Figure 7. *áh-* 'off up there at the side of the slope'.

Conclusion

Pike's conceptual framework "Tagmemics," treated in his work *Language in Relation to a Unified Theory of the Structure of Human Behavior* is a comprehensive theory of language structure and its grounding in human experience (Pike 1954, 1955, 1960). This approach to linguistic analysis was applied to the description of data from a wide variety of languages and addressed an awesome array of theoretical problems (Pike 1964).

Langacker's Cognitive Grammar is another conceptual framework that seeks to give a comprehensive account of linguistic structures and language use. This account invokes a variety of basic cognitive processes for its theoretical constructs and explanations. It characterizes meaning as being encyclopedic in nature and reducing to the way that we conceptualize the world around us (Langacker 1990:2, 149). In Langacker's view, the speaker is the conceptualizer and the meaning of any given expression that he/she uses reduces to the idea that he/she has in mind, i.e., his conceptualization.

Langacker's approach overlaps in significant ways with a number of the main points that Pike makes in his work, in some cases complementing and validating a number of key ideas given in Pike (1954, 1955, 1960). In other cases, not only does Langacker's approach agree with Pike, but also goes beyond Pike's original formulations and gives us a more detailed account of things. The primary case in point is that of the viewing arrangement and the speaker's role in shaping the content of his/her expressions, i.e., the way that the speaker construes the situation that he/she is describing. I have illustrated this with an analysis of some Cora spatial expressions.

Although I have also pointed out some of the ways that Cognitive Grammar differs from Pike, and I have indicated one instance in which I think that Pike missed an important implication of his own formulation, this discussion in no way amounts to a critique of Pike's work. What I really hope to have shown is that many of Pike's ideas are solidly based, eminently useful, and are still alive and well.

References

Casad, Eugene H. 1977. Location and direction in Cora discourse: I. *Anthropological Linguistics* 19:216–241.

Casad, Eugene H. 1982. *Cora locationals and structured imagery.* Ph.D. dissertation. University of California, San Diego.

Casad, Eugene H. 1984. Cora. In Ronald W. Langacker (ed.), *Studies in Uto-Aztecan grammar, Volume 4: Southern Uto-Aztecan grammatical sketches,* 159–453. Dallas: The Summer Institute of Linguistics and the University of Texas at Arlington.

Casad, Eugene H. 1988. Conventionalization of Cora locationals. In Brygida Rudzka-Ostyn (ed.), 345–378.

Casad, Eugene H. 1993. Locations, paths and the Cora verb. In Richard A. Geiger and Brygida Rudzka-Ostyn (eds.), *Conceptualizations and mental processing in natural language,* 593–645. Berlin/New York/Amsterdam: Mouton de Gruyter.

Casad, Eugene H. 1996. What good are locationals, anyway? In Martin Putz and René Dirven (eds.), *The construal of space in language and thought,* 239–267. Cognitive Linguistics Research 8. Berlin/New York: Mouton de Gruyter.

Casad, Eugene H. 1998. Lots of ways to 'give' in Cora. In John Newman (ed.), *The linguistics of 'giving'* 135–174. Amsterdam/Philadelphia: John Benjamins.

Casad, Eugene H., and Ronald W. Langacker. 1985. 'Inside' and 'outside' in Cora grammar. *International Journal of American Linguistics* 51:247–281.

Cook, Kenneth W. 2003. Hawaiian 'o as an indicator of nominal salience. In Eugene H. Casad and Gary B. Palmer (eds.), *Cognitive linguistics and non-Indo-European languages,* 157–171. Berlin and New York: Mouton de Gruyter.

Fillmore, Charles J. 1968. The case for case. In Emmon Bach and Robert T. Harms (eds.), *Universals in linguistic theory,* 1–88. New York: Holt, Rinehart, and Winston.

Gibbs, Raymond W. 1996. What's cognitive about cognitive linguistics? In Eugene H. Casad (ed.), *Cognitive linguistics in the redwoods,* 27–53. Berlin and New York: Mouton de Gruyter.

Haiman, John. 1980. Dictionaries and encyclopedias. *Lingua* 50:329–357.

Harder, Peter. 1996. *Functional semantics: A theory of meaning, structure and tense in English.* Trends in Linguistics Studies and Monographs 87. Berlin and New York: Mouton de Gruyter.

Hawkins, Bruce. 1984. *The semantics of English spatial prepositions.* Ph.D. dissertation. University of California, San Diego.

Lakoff, George. 1987. *Women, fire and dangerous things.* Chicago and London: The University of Chicago Press.

Lakoff, George. 1990. The Invariance Hypothesis: Is abstract reason based on image-schemas? *Cognitive Linguistics* 1:39–74.

Langacker, Ronald W. 1987. *Foundations of Cognitive Grammar I: Theoretical prerequisites.* Stanford, Calif.: Stanford University Press.

Langacker, Ronald W. 1988a. An overview of Cognitive Grammar. In Brygida Rudzka-Ostyn (ed.), 3–48.

Langacker, Ronald W. 1988b. A View of Linguistic Semantics. In Brygida Rudzka-Ostyn (ed.), 49–90.

Langacker, Ronald W. 1988c. A usage-based model. In Brygida Rudzka-Ostyn (ed.), 127–161.

Langacker, Ronald W. 1990a. Subjectification. *Cognitive Linguistics* 1:5–38.

Langacker, Ronald W. 1990b. *Concept, image, and symbol: The cognitive basis of grammar.* Cognitive Linguistics Research 1. Berlin and New York: Mouton de Gruyter.

Langacker, Ronald W. 1993. Reference Point Constructions. *Cognitive Linguistics* 4:1–38.

Langacker, Ronald W.1999. *Grammar and conceptualization.* Cognitive Linguistics Research 14. Berlin and New York: Mouton de Gruyter.

Nathan, Geoffrey S. 1986. Phonemes as mental categories. *Proceedings of the Annual Meeting of the Berkeley Linguistics Society* 12:212–223.

Nathan, Geoffrey S. 2001. Cognitive Phonology: The embodiment of sounds. Paper presented to the 7th International Cognitive Linguistics Conference, held at the University of California, Santa Barbara, July 22–27, 2001.

Pike, Kenneth L. 1954. *Language in relation to a unified theory of the structure of human behavior, Part I*. Preliminary edition. Glendale, Calif.: Summer Institute of Linguistics.

Pike, Kenneth L. 1955. *Language in relation to a unified theory of the structure of human behavior, Part II*. Preliminary edition. Glendale, Calif.: Summer Institute of Linguistics.

Pike, Kenneth L. 1960. *Language in relation to a unified theory of the structure of human behavior, Part III*. Preliminary edition. Glendale, Calif.: Summer Institute of Linguistics.

Pike, Kenneth L. 1966. A guide to publications related to Tagmemic Theory. In Thomas A. Sebeok (ed.), *Current trends in linguistics, Vol, III: Theoretical foundations*, 365–394. The Hague: Mouton.

Rudzka-Ostyn, Brygida, ed. 1988. *Topics in Cognitive Grammar*. Amsterdam and Philadelphia: John Benjamins.

Tuggy, David. 1992. The affix-stem distinction; A Cognitive Grammar analysis of data from Orizaba Nahuatl. *Cognitive Linguistics* 3(3):237–300.

Tuggy, David. 2003. Reduplication in Nahuatl: Iconicities and paradoxes. In Eugene H. Casad and Gary B. Palmer (eds.), *Cognitive Linguistics and non-Indo-European Languages*, 91–133. Berlin and New York: Mouton de Gruyter.

Verhagen, Arie. 1995. Subjectification, syntax and communication. In Dieter Stein and Susan Wright (eds.), *Subjectivity and subjectivisation: Linguistic perspectives*, 103–128. Cambridge: Cambridge University Press.

Evelyn and Ken, with two of their three children (Stephen Pike and Barbara Pike Ibach), in front of their thatch-roofed home at Yarinacocha, Peru 1960. (Photograph from the Townsend Archives; used with the permission of Cal Hibbard.)

Part V

Form and Meaning

"A language [or behavioral] unit is identifiable and describable only when both form and meaning are somehow involved either explicitly or implicitly: 'A language unit is a form-meaning composite'." (Pike and Pike 1982:4)

23

Symbol and Sentiment in Motivated Action

Robert L. Canfield

A Problem: The Relation of Culture to Human Motivation

Human action is by definition motivated—but how are the forms of culture engaged in human motivated action? Whatever our view of human motivation we cannot talk about it without referring to the symbolic forms that enable human experience and action, for humans exist by dependence on symbols. As Richard Wilks says, "issues of motive [lurk] beneath every modern social science theory of practice and decision making" (Wilks 1993:191). Consider the debate between Obeyesekere (1992) and Sahlins (1995 and earlier works) over how to interpret the Hawaiians' response to Captain Cook. Obeyesekere takes the Hawaiians to be pragmatic, calculating, and rational; Sahlins takes them to be informed by a "total cultural system of human action." The debate is essentially over how to describe the relation of motivated action to culture. Obeyesekere accuses Sahlins of reifying culture and so making the

Acknowledgements: I thank the following persons for comments on these ideas presented orally in various contexts as well as on written drafts of this paper: Jon Anderson, Ruth Brend, Thomas Headland, Nancy Lindisfarne, Mustafa Mirseler, Audrey Shalinsky.

Hawaiians into mere irrational primitives, "overdetermined by signs." Sahlins accuses Obeyesekere of imputing to the Hawaiians the utilitarian rationality of modern bourgeois society. So they make contrary assumptions about how the forms of culture work in actual practice: from one point of view culture serves as a "tool" of reflective, calculating actors (Obeyesekere); from another it is an authoritative source of understanding, an orientation to an axiomatic "reality" (Sahlins). It is a familiar clash exemplified in many debates in the past (Andrew Lang versus Max Müller, Malinowski versus Radcliffe-Brown, Harris versus Sahlins, and so on).[1]

This is an essay about the relation of human motivations to culture. It aims essentially to articulate certain assumptions already implicit in anthropological practice but not generally recognized, specifically to formulate the nature of motivated behavior, especially sacrificial behavior. I begin with a brief reference to the problem of the assiduous religious practice of the peoples of Afghanistan and then offer an explanation for their practice and propose a way to understand religious motivations generally, especially acts of self-immolation. The presentation is programmatic in the interest of brevity, offered as a kind of etic exercise in the sense intended by the late Kenneth L. Pike, who introduced the term "etics" to indicate the attempt of a discipline to formulate frames of reference, concepts, and priorities, ways of "seeing," by which to examine its object (Headland, Pike, and Harris 1990).[2] In this case, I propose an analytical scaffolding composed of concepts about human motives and sentiments as they relate to the forms of culture.

---

[1]For an anthropologist to discuss human motives is to blunder as a novice into realms beyond his competence. For one thing there is the nether world of human motives claimed by psychoanalysts, a subject so fraught with pitfalls that Victor Turner once, having ventured into it, withdrew with a shudder. I persist however because, like it or not, human motivations are inescapably implicit in the work of anthropologists. Here I merely seek to identify the motivations already implied in anthropological writing, with the hope that I will avoid affronting the sophisticated tastes of the psychotherapists who consider motivation to be their particular preserve. The other realm beyond his competence that a cultural anthropologist enters when discussing human motives is that of evolutionary psychology (sociobiology), where the explicit quest is to dissolve all "altruistic" motives into the assumption that there must be a selective advantage for every human trait. Here I merely take as given the motivational patterns that we find in humans as constituted; how they ever came to be that way is the problem yet to be resolved.

[2]I want to express here the deep influence that Kenneth Pike's teaching and writing had in the development of my own career in anthropology. My first exposure to Pike was when I was a teenager. He was demonstrating his monolingual approach to language learning and linguistic analysis. Later, in the summer of 1952, I took Pike's course in phonetics and phonemics at the University of Oklahoma. But it was in 1955 as a Master's degree student in linguistics at the University of Michigan that I encountered Pike's now celebrated expansion of the concepts of etics and emics in the comparative study of languages and cultures. We read an early 1954 edition of his *Language in Relation to a Unified Theory of the Structure of Human Behavior* (1967). He called his approach "grammemics" then, although it would later be known as tagmemics.

The Problem of Assiduous Religious Practice in Afghanistan

I was led into the question of how to describe motives for human action by the evident religiosity of the Afghanistan peoples among whom I lived off and on in the 1950s and 1960s. I was struck, as were other visitors to the country including Muslims from elsewhere, by the assiduous religious practice of the Afghan people. Limitations of space prohibit specific elaboration of their religious behavior here—and anyway the anti-Soviet *Mujahedin* fighters displayed a religious zeal that is now considered typical of Afghanistan in the West. So I ask you to accept without further evidence my claim that the Afghan people in the pre-war period (before 1978) were relatively more faithful in their ritual observances than Muslims elsewhere. But I must add three codicils. First, Afghanistan, unlike almost any other place in Asia, was never subjugated by Western powers, so that its inhabitants practiced their faith as a common sense way of life, with a naturalness quite different from the aggressive tone of the now notorious extremists who deploy Islamic idioms to legitimize their causes. Second, the Soviet-*Mujahedin* conflict heightened among many Afghans the importance of Islamic practice as a public statement of national solidarity. Third, the religion of the Taliban who dominated most of the country between 1996 and the end of 2001 bore little resemblance to that of most Afghans before the war (Rashid 2000).

My solution: three answers that taken together seem to provide a necessary and sufficient explanation

How can we explain the predominant assiduity of religious practice among the Muslims in Afghanistan in the 1950s and 1960s? Three answers, taken together, seem to provide a necessary and sufficient explanation.

Answer 1. Social and political conditions fostered a sense of religious identity.

The first answer refers to the social and political conditions within the country. For generations Islam has been the dominant religion and has provided the idioms of moral obligation. Islam was characteristically invoked to legitimate authority and public causes. The "founder" of the country, Ahmad Shah Abdali, took a religious title after he was "crowned" Amir by a notable religious authority, and every other ruler after him similarly claimed a special Islamic title (at least until 1973). Furthermore, among the ordinary populations religious practice was considered a form of communal solidarity. Also, sectarian loyalties were important idioms of social definition; the sectarian groups sometimes clashed so that dogmatic differences became important indicators of social and political identity. In addition to these internal sociopolitical relations international conflicts with non-Muslim imperial powers in the past—notably the British and Russians in the nineteenth century—helped to strengthen the conviction among the local inhabitants that they stood as Muslims against a threatening non-Muslim world. So a commitment to the religion of the community was taken to be a sign of solidarity.

Thus, briefly, the political and social conditions inside the country and in the wider international scene generally fostered a sense of religious identity; religious practice was a kind of public statement. Since the overwhelming demands of the social and political situation supported Islam as the public idiom of virtue, the residents of the country had good social and political inducements for observing Islamic rituals to express their communal loyalty.

Answer 2. Islamic rituals of many sorts are a resource for coping with life.

Among the Afghan people I knew, who generally had little access to biomedical resources, definitions of disease, and misfortune, were informed by a tradition associated with Islam. For most people, especially the rural populations but also many educated urbanites who otherwise had secular inclinations, the conceptions of what caused disease and misfortune were informed by a "folk" understanding of Islam, so that certain rituals were considered means of efficacy. Attendance to shrines, wearing of amulets, the recitation of prayers, and incantations were presumed helpful in curing, divining, and maintaining well-being.

Thus, another reason for the assiduous religious practice of many Afghan Muslims was their belief that it was profitable or beneficial for their personal and social welfare.

Answer 3. Islamic practice expresses and shows deference to virtual truths.

Now, while many of the people I knew would accept that these two considerations were reasons for religious practice, none of them would have offered them as reasons for their own religious observance. If I asked them why they prayed or kept the fast during Ramadan or sacrificed a sheep on the Id-i Qurban festival, or why they chose to pay a costly visit to a shrine to fulfill a vow (as some of our American-educated friends did), they would tell me that their acts of worship were only what was right to do before God. Their behavior was an acknowledgement of a moral universe to which good people should submit. Indeed, an honorable person was, in common speech, a *musulmân âdam*. Such a person seeks to relate to spiritual things for what they are; and God's requirements, whatever they are, enjoin compliance.

Certainly, the pietistic tradition of Afghanistan Islam takes this view. Its literature is replete with stories about the heroes of religion whose devotion reveals a commitment to God's will. In *Qasas-ul-Anbiya*, 'Stories of the Prophets',[3] there is a story about Job (according to Islam he was tormented by worms) who, when a worm fell from his body, picked it up and returned it to its place, lest in any way he should seem not to accept God's will. He would never, so the story goes, act for his personal comfort. In the abstract and ideal sense action for selfish or practical interest is unseemly, unworthy of authentic obedience to God. Of course, the Afghan people I knew believed it was permissible to use means to get relief from distress, and those means could include religious activities. Practical motives for religious behavior was acceptable when necessary, but they also took it for granted that obedience to God was after all axiomatic.

So another reason for the assiduous religious practice of at least some Afghans at least some of the time was their deference to the higher moral values entailed in the Islamic revelation.

Summary and review of the scope of these answers

These explanations for the assiduous religious practice of the Afghans point to the distinctive sociocultural contexts of such practice. Answer 1 (the political and social context of religious practice) directs attention to the specific social and political conditions of life among those people. Because the whole moral ambiance of social life was framed in Islamic terms, moral discourse and the rituals of collective loyalty were explicitly Islamic. Islamic practice was a mark of public loyalty. This answer explains, I think, why people *in Afghanistan* appeared to be so assiduous in their religious practice, at least in public circumstances. Answer 2 (the presumed advantages for health and well-being of religious observance) directs attention to the benefits of religious practice for the individual.

---

[3]It should not be assumed that this medieval text has no relevance to current religious thought among the Afghanistan peoples. A similar work on the Islamic saints has recently been translated into Pushtu by Professor Khushal Habibi (2000).

Like all human beings, the Afghanistan peoples were under stress, and their religion offered them efficacious means for dealing with their distresses, either to cure them, avoid them, or relieve them. This explanation suggests reasons why *Muslims generally* believe it is good to practice their faith. The rituals are beneficial, profitable. Answer 3 directs our attention to reasons for religious practice that transcend practical or beneficial interests. People deferred to the enduring, pervasive qualities of the cosmos that gave meaning to their existence and constrained them to behave morally, to do things that on other grounds might seem unduly costly and unprofitable. This explanation directs our attention to why *devoted people generally* practice their faith: that is, because they recognize and defer to entities taken to be transcendent, morally compelling.

Assumptions about Human Experience, Motives and Culture in this Explanation

This argument assumes a relation of human experience to human motivations that bears on the concept of culture, specifically on the broadly accepted notion that the dispositions of human beings are realized in and sublimated in cultural (that is, symbolic) forms. As culture is the human mode of apprehending reality, it constitutes the distinctive human niche. Everything "real"—bales of hay, yokes of oxen, the calendar, justice, God, jinns, fear, love—is by definition identified and understood by means of symbolic forms. From this broadly accepted concept of culture I draw three implications not widely appreciated: (1) that the shared experience of a communicating public is reflected in the repertoire of symbolic forms that characterize their social life; (2) that the more nuanced, complex symbols of the repertoire are the symbolic devices through which sacrificial or altruistic behavior is motivated; and (3) that explanations of human action in terms of "utilitarian rationality" or "determining signs" are not necessarily contradictory, as they focus on different ways the spectrum of symbols in the cultural repertoire are entailed in human action. The latter distinction enables us to identify some critical ways cultural forms are enlisted in social and political action, especially to note a difference between the way they are used for social or political purposes and the way they function in actions that seem altruistic or self-sacrificial.

The complexities of human sentiment are traced in the elements of culture

I assume that human beings live in "a world of essential ambiguity and multivalence" (Wikan 1993:13), that their "'imaginative' and 'emotional' life is always and everywhere rich and complex" (Turner 1969:3), and in concert with this circumstance, the multiplicity of human sentiments is mirrored in the symbolic forms that make thought, word, and action possible. Symbols accomplish this seeming correspondence by acquiring meanings as they are deployed in practice, as people attempt to make their lives more comfortable, secure, predictable, and understandable. As human beings interact with their social and existential "reality" the symbolic forms through which they apprehend it take on an apparent likeness to it and an image of their experience of it, conforming to that "reality" according to symbolic schemes that are never the only ones possible.[4]

Symbols have a semantically simple or denotative sense, in which case they refer to the surface levels of human experience, those aspects of human experience and understanding that are concerned with the conscious attempt to deal with issues of life and social affairs. Symbols in this sense refer to or correspond with "surface level" feelings and stand for entities presumed to exist substantively and to operate mechanistically. But in the repertoire of a communicating public some symbols are semantically more complex than others and bear a range of other nuances associated variously with more subtle levels of human experience, some of which are emotionally "deep." The more diverse in meaning symbols are, the more emotional complexity they may represent. The "milk tree" among the Ndembu people of Africa, for example, stands for many things: women's breasts, breast milk, the tie of nurturing between mother and child, domestic social ties, the matrilineal bonds of the Ndembu community, the principles and values of Ndembu social organization, tribal custom, the unity and continuity of the community, even "powerful unconscious wishes" (Turner 1967: 20 ff.). Such meanings are enacted—and therefore taught, internalized, and reproduced—through the rituals associated with the milk tree, notably those celebrating the arrival of puberty.

Multivocalic symbols like the milk tree among the Ndembu can represent emotional struggles and may become the terms for deep psychic turbulence. They may stand for moral entities in the sense that they objectify feelings of anchorage into a world whose principles and values are of

---

[4]The number of works that address how meanings are constructed in social contexts is too numerous to mention. See for example, besides the ones cited here, the writings of such authors as Fredrik Barth, Clifford Geertz, Bruce Kapferer, Lisa Malkki, Marshall Sahlins, and Katherine Verdery.

enduring and general significance. While symbolic forms taken in their matter of fact sense index only specific things and mechanistic processes, those symbols that also carry additional nuances may represent entities that are moral, transcendent, and emotionally engaging. In this sense, multivocalic symbols can represent much that is important to the self—not only the overarching cosmology of higher values but also the more visceral of human sensibilities, deeply felt worries, and anxieties. Turner says such symbols anchor not only "up" in the rarified strato-sphere of ultimate values but also "down" in the inexpressible depths of bodily pain (Turner 1967:27 ff.). So they are more than a storehouse of ideas that sort the world into usable categories; they are also a "power-house," representing ideals deeply longed for and profoundly sensed (Turner 1968:2). Such symbols can be metaphors for the ideals, hopes, and fears of individual subjectivities.

This relationship of symbolic repertoires to the subtleties of experience can be graphically indicated as in figure 1, on which the cultural elements (such as the lexicon) of a communicating public are arranged according to their relative semantic weight or vocality, those bearing the heaviest se-mantic load clustered at one end of the scale and those bearing a rela-tively light semantic load at the other.[5]

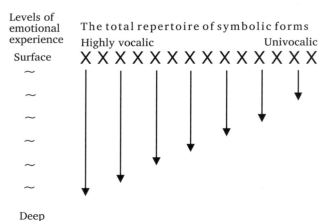

Figure 1. The semantic complexity of the symbolic repertoire.

The scale represents the collective life of a people, their emotional ontol-ogy, as it were, as it is manifest in the repertoire of symbols available to

---

[5]This diagram is roughly similar to Edmund Leach's chart of the various forms of symbolic representation (1976).

them.[6] That is, all the forms in a cultural repertoire, since they objectify thought and feeling, are alike in having a denotative sense, but the symbolic forms that bear a variety of meanings have more emotional value in that they are forms through which individuals conceptually and emotionally engage with entities believed to have significance beyond their quotidian affairs (Lewis 1961). Such imagined "realities" are in this sense taken by individuals as ready-made, as representations of things and processes of general significance. In Lewis's terms they are "received." Through the semantically complex forms of culture people acknowledge some entities as transcendent and axiomatic—receiving the kingdom of God like a child, granting certain axioms the power to enchant, accepting some principles as solutions to the great questions. Also, through such heavily-nuanced symbols people come to visualize themselves, identify with certain entities of enduring importance, place themselves in meaningful "worlds," on stages of cosmological significance.

The more nuanced, multivocalic symbols in a cultural repertoire are the symbolic devices through which sacrificial behavior may be induced

The whole semantic repertoire is of course available for use, that is, for practical ends, but the effect of multivocalic symbols representing transcendent values is to objectify moral constraints on behavior. The most extreme behavioral manifestations of internalized notions of transcendent values is self-immolation. When people sacrifice themselves—Irish separatists hunger-striking in Belfast, Tamilese assassins blowing themselves up along with targeted Sri Lankan officials, al Qaeda assailants bombing an American warship—they appear to be acting out of a commitment to causes whose importance they believe supersedes their own interests, even their own lives. Motivation of this sort seems to challenge our

---

[6]To keep the presentation simple I assume a view of culture that was once more generally accepted among anthropologists than it is now, namely that the members of a communicating public share a common culture, so that their "culture" is in some unspecific sense "shared" by individual members of the society. I realize that it is more common today to regard a society's culture as a repertoire of symbolic forms available for use by competing interests in the society; cultural forms are in this sense deployed to define situations according to people's respective interests; from this point of view the members of a communicating public may hold competing cultural orientations, are differentially positioned, and for these and other reasons may clash over how situations are defined. From either concept of culture—whether as the name for a shared worldview among members of a society or as the name for a body of symbolic resources that may be used variously by competing elements within a society—anthropologists' conceptions of how culture functions in social life recognize the different ways that the cultural repertoire functions, in some cases as a tool, in others' as a means of apprehending a world, as a source of information and orientation.

usual assumptions about human motivations. If a Palestinian youngster courts death in a clash with Israeli troops (*New York Times*, Oct 8, 2000), is it not necessary to identify the special sense in which his semantic "world" not only informs but also induces action? Behavior of this sort reveals that some conceptions of the world are not only received as axiomatic but as compelling.

It seems crucial that a human science worthy of its name recognize the particular way that this sort of self-sacrificial action is symbolically driven as well as symbolically informed. Let us call this kind of inducement to action "deference motives" to distinguish such intentions from the "instrumental motives" that are generally assumed in social science discourse. By *instrumental motives* we mean, of course, practical or gainful inducements to human action. Instrumentally driven behavior pursues interests, establishes cultural practices, conventionalizes and legitimizes behavior as people seek sustenance, security, and comfort (Harris 1979: 55 ff.). The "reality" driven by instrumental concerns is a reality apprehended for use; if it is not easily apprehended there is the presumption that eventually it could be specified, identified, and so its mechanisms could be predicted and modified or otherwise tooled for use. From the instrumentalist point of view humans are driven by practical quests so that even relations that appear altruistic, without interest, are taken to be at base driven by a search for gain: kinship, neighborhood, and cooperative enterprises, says Bourdieu, are "inevitably interested"; and "giving is a way of possessing" (Bourdieu 1977:171; 1991:24). So the conventions of social life turn out to be devices for seeking gain. They are (a la Malinowski, Marvin Harris, and other "materialists," of course) tools.

By *deference motives* for action, I mean inducements that arise out of the human propensity to internalize and visualize transcendence, to grasp "the order and natural structure of the universe" (Bateson 1972 [1949]:119). Deference motives for human action are linked to symbols that "refer to values that are regarded as ends in themselves, that is, to axiomatic values" (Turner 1967:20). Turner believes such symbols enshrine "...the crucial values of the believing community,...whose ultimate unity resides in its orientation towards transcendental and invisible powers" (Turner 1968:2). Symbols of this sort "instigate social actions....They may even be described as 'forces,' in that they are determinable influences inclining persons and groups to action" (Turner 1967:36; Kapferer 1988; Hollan 2000). In so far as they do so, they engage deeply sensitive levels of experience, feelings that are visceral, sometimes expressed subconsciously as in dreams. There are instrumental uses for all symbols, but multivocalic symbols can represent deep sentiments and commitments that can be engaged in action.[7]

The "reality" that a person driven by deferential motives deals with (to describe them in stark terms) is informed by symbols bearing many nuances—words like sincerity, justice, and purity, and objects like the Vietnam Memorial, the cross, the swastika, images of the Virgin of Guadalupe—which evoke notions of universality, immutability. They imply entities worthy of respect, perhaps enchanted, even wild, untamable—great truths to be accepted, taken for granted, too sublime for manipulation or exploitation. But having multiple meanings they are essentially ambiguous. They are the kinds of symbols invoked in politics and religion, representing values of a normative sort, to which a diverse public can attach various meanings (Wilner 1984). Because their nuances are diffuse they may be applied to a variety of contexts to represent significant notions, but always with a greater chance for confusion or disagreement as to the proper context of their use.

The term "deference motives" is intended to objectify the notion that human beings act (sometimes) as if their lives (to some degree) are framed by axiomatic principles. In such instances notions of transcendent significance connected to notions of a moral reality seem to have been internalized and so constituted as the moral context of life and behavior.

Recognizing that no behavior is driven by a single motive, we can put the matter in simple terms: behavior driven by "reason" or conscious intention entails the use of cultural forms for instrumental purposes; behavior driven by deep convictions of moral import entails the internalization of ideals enshrined in multivocalic symbols. We regard these two kinds of motivation as merely the two ends of a continuum, in between which there is a mixture of inducements to action, partly practical and partly deferential, in which both kinds of motives are to some degree involved (Wilks 1993). Just as human experience is a mélange of feelings, human action is normally impelled by several motives, some practical, some

---

[7]Renato Rosaldo in his essay (1989) on his sense of grief at the loss of his wife, Michelle Rosaldo, draws attention to the intensity and complexity of human emotion but he stresses that they are manifest in diverse expressive forms, not only in ritual. He points out that rituals don't always represent much that is deeply personal or significant; they can merely be conventions whose meaning is merely formal, not emotionally ("deeply") engaging. He appeals for more sensitive treatments of deep human experience, which is always expressed in local conventions of practice. And he calls for a recognition of the "cultural force" of human emotion, because deep feelings motivate action. Among the Ilongot, he says, it impels such extreme acts as the decapitation of human beings, which they say enables bereaved men to "cast away their life burdens, including the rage in their grief" (1989:16). The force of deep feelings, Rosaldo says, is not represented in the amount of words expressed, for in fact some of the most profound feelings may be unexpressed in words, but rather in other manifestations of feeling (1989:20).

deferential. There can be several motives for a particular action, all of them symbolically constituted.

This is what figure 2 represents: In the abstract there are two kinds of motives for human action and they relate to the cultural repertoire in a different way. The whole repertoire can be deployed for instrumental purposes. At the same time some symbolic forms in the repertoire are the means of orientation to a moral, transcendent reality and so inform and shape behavior of the sort we call deferential.

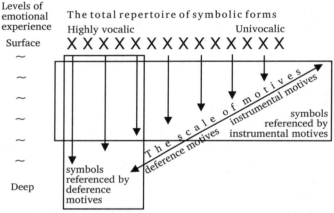

Figure 2. Relation of motives to the symbolic complexity of the symbolic repertoire.

Descriptions of culture as a resource utilized for practical ends and of culture as a system of determining signs

Studies of cultural practice as impelled by instrumental concerns or as driven by deferential concerns produce different kinds of ethnographic reports, but they are not contradictory. They can be complementary. Each approach to human action provides a certain insight into the human condition. Compare for example two works on South Asian Culture. Steve Derné (1995:vii–viii) takes the action of North Indian Hindu men to be instrumentally driven. They are "motivated by social pressures" and their cultural context "constrains individuals and affects their emotions, social life, and social institutions." The central question is how people "manipulate cultural components to attribute meaning to action." Derné assumes that social life is carried on at a self-aware level of experience: People are vitally engaged with their circumstances, events are consciously perceived, the causes of sensations are presumed to be known, and thoughts are (or can be) rationally articulated. In that sense the cultural forms index "surface" experiences, as if human sentimental worlds were semantically simple.

Regula Qureshi (2000), on the other hand, describes how a musical instrument, the *sarangi*, has become iconic for some modern South Asians. Its timbre and melody have acquired a profusion of associations—images of sensual feminine dancers amid the sumptuary elegance of bygone princely courts, pious jogis singing devotional ballads "to the unseen God" in which they express "profound sadness and detachment from the world," and (in the modern period) the convoluted tales of romantic Hindu films. Encoded in its sound and form are "pasts remembered,...stories both detailed and dim...," "layers of locally specific, historically situated, materially perceived musical practices...that both cue nostalgia and sustain identification that is socially as well as religiously, culturally, and politically referenced" (Qureshi 2000:813, 829). The sounds of the *sarangi* have at times served as a medium for sharing deep emotions: it has been played on All India Radio upon the deaths of notable persons (Nehru, Indira Gandhi), enabling the individual feelings of a dispersed audience to become "public, shared, and exterior." In such moments "bonds of shared responses [become] as deep and intimate as they are broad and universal" (2000:810). It is from such public wellsprings of collective sentiment that cooperative action is inspired.

Each of these studies presents the human condition in India in a certain light. People in India are no doubt motivated by practical concerns as Derné so eloquently describes. At the same time people in India presumably live with anxieties about fundamental issues that are symbolically linked to various kinds of cultural forms, and Qureshi explicates how *sarangi* music in certain contexts objectifies shared feelings of nostalgia, sadness, and worldly detachment among the peoples of India. The two reports on social conventions in India are complementary, not contradictory.

Rhetoric, Commitment, and Sacrificial Behavior

Our focus on variations in connotative complexity in the forms of a symbolic repertoire, it should be noted, contrasts with the variations in meaning recognized by de Saussure. For him the signs in symbolic systems map semantic relations by mutually determining each other's meanings, in which case the variance among them is denotative. We note here a different sense in which symbols vary, that is, in their connotative richness.

Those symbols most pregnant with meaning and nuance have a particular importance for anthropologists because, as they enshrine deeply felt sentiments—anxiety, dread, joy—they may be enlisted for social and political purposes.

By noting a distinction between instrumental and deference motives for action we identify different ways that the cultural repertoire is engaged in political action. The forms of a culture function differently when they are deployed to define situations from when they are "received" as authentic characterizations of situations. The difference may be expressed with respect to the role of leadership versus that of followership. Those who would frame the nature of public situations ("leaders") so as to enlist the support of others ("followers") do so by appealing to "axiomatic values" of the sort enshrined in multivocalic symbols—as when Franklin Roosevelt quoted the Bible in his fireside chats during the depression, when Ayatullah Khomaini appealed to the sacred authority of Hosain in his sermons to the Iranian people, or when Franjo Tudjman drew upon Catholic icons to legitimate his appeal for a separate Croatia (Wilner 1984:154–156; Mersipassi-Ashtiani 1994; Denich 1994). In so far as such appeals win broad support, they do so because, in their respective contexts, they infuse issues of immediate and broadly shared concern with locally accepted notions of ultimate truth. This kind of conjuncture of meanings is possible when the symbolic forms deployed to define situations successfully fuse two "realities": that of immediate and practical concern and that of compelling moral significance. Behind every ideological claim stand axiomatic truths that resonate with deeply felt notions of value.

When action is taken in response to such claims it is informed by two kinds of circumstance: a material one, in which practical interests are at stake; and a moral one, in which ultimate values seem to be entailed. It is in this latter sense that multivocalic symbols may be said to "instigate social actions," to be "forces" that incline persons and groups to action. In so far as an action seems sacrificial, "altruistic," or self-immolative, it is driven by notions of a sublime and principled reality.[8]

---

[8]This view of experience and culture is, I suppose, consistent with Maslow's concept of the "self-actualized" individual, who may have "peak experiences," which are difficult to describe but may involve a momentary loss of self and feelings of transcendence. Maslow believed that everyone is capable of having peak experiences, but he believed that self-actualized persons have these experiences more often. (*Britannica Online*: "motivation: self-actualization.")

References

Bateson, Gregory. 1972 [1949]. Bali: The value system of a steady state. In Gregory Bateson, *Steps to an ecology of mind*. New York: Ballantine.

Bourdieu, Pierre. 1977. *Outline of a theory of practice*. Cambridge: Cambridge University.

Bourdieu, Pierre. 1991. *Language and symbolic power*. (Edited and Introduced by John B. Thompson). Cambridge, Mass.: Harvard University.

Denich, Bette. 1994. Dismembering Yugoslavia: Nationalist ideologies and the symbolic revival of genocide. *American Ethnologist* 21(2):367–390.

Derné, Steve. 1995. *Culture in action: Family life, emotion, and male dominance in Banaras, India*. Albany: State University of New York.

Habibi, Khushal, translator. 2000. *Tazkerat-al awliya* [Remembrances of the saints] by Sulaiman Maku [in Pashtu and English]. Peshawar: Habibi's Research Center.

Harris, Marvin. 1979. *Cultural materialism: The struggle for a science of culture*. New York: Random House.

Headland, Thomas N., Kenneth L. Pike, and Marvin Harris, eds. 1990. *Emics and etics: The insider/outsider debate*. Newbury Park: Sage.

Hollan, Douglas. 2000. Constructivist models of mind, contemporary psychoanalysis, and the development of culture theory. *American Anthropologist* 102(3):538–550.

Leach, Edmund. 1976. *Culture and communication: The logic by which symbols are connected; An introduction to the use of structuralist analysis in social anthropology*. Cambridge: Cambridge University.

Lewis, C. S. 1961. *An experiment in criticism*. Cambridge: Cambridge University.

Kapferer, Bruce. 1988. *Legends of people myths of state: Violence, intolerance, and political culture in Sri Lanka and Australia*. Washington, D.C.: Smithsonian.

Mersipassi-Ashtiani, Ali. 1994. The crisis of secular politics and the rise of political Islam in Iran. *Social Text* 12(1):51–84.

New York Times, Oct 8, 2000. "When a 12-year-old Palestinian boy courts martyrdom, the hopes of his family are divided."

Obeyesekere, Gananath. 1992. *The apotheosis of Captain Cook: European mythmaking in the Pacific*. Princeton, N.J.: Princeton University.

Pike, Kenneth L. 1967. *Language in relation to a unified theory of the structure of human behavior*, second edition. The Hague: Mouton. [First published in three volumes in 1954, 1955, and 1960.]

Qureshi, Regula. 2000. How does music mean? Embodied memories and the politics of affect in the Indian *sarangi*. *American Ethnologist* 27(4):805–838.

Rashid, Ahmad. 2000. *Taliban: Militant Islam, oil and fundamentalism in Central Asia*. New Haven, Conn.: Yale University.

Rosaldo, Renato. 1989. *Culture and truth: The remaking of social analysis*. Boston: Beacon.

Sahlins, Marshall. 1995. *How "natives" think: About Captain Cook, for example*. Chicago: University of Chicago.

Turner, Victor. 1967. *The forest of symbols*. Ithaca, N.Y.: Cornell University.

Turner, Victor. 1968. *The drums of affliction: A study of religious processes among the Ndembu of Zambia*. Ithaca, N.Y.: Cornell University.

Turner, Victor. 1969. *The ritual process: Structure and anti-structure*. Ithaca, N.Y.: Cornell University.

Wikan, Unni. 1993. *Managing troubled hearts: A Balinese formula for living*. Chicago: University of Chicago.

Wilks, Richard. 1993. Altruism and self-interest: Towards an anthropological theory of decision making. *Research in Economic Anthropology* 14:191–212.

Wilner, Ann Ruth. 1984. *The spellbinders: Charismatic political leadership*. New Haven, Conn.: Yale University.

24

Translating Secondary Functions of Grammatical Structure

Mildred L. Larson

Surely we are all agreed that the goal of a translator is to transfer the meaning of the source text into the natural forms of the receptor language. Why then are so many translations produced which as a matter of fact are not natural sounding at all? They sound foreign, like someone trying to learn the language and carrying over the patterns of his/her first language. This happens even when the translator is truly bilingual and handles both languages perfectly when not translating.

Much of the complication in the translation process is the result of the fact that the grammatical structures and the semantic structures of languages do not match. Furthermore, the mismatches found in one language are not isomorphic with the mismatches in another language.

This paper was originally published in *Translation and Meaning, Part 2: Proceedings of the Łódź, Session of the 1990 Maastricht-Łódź Duo Colloquium on "Translation and Meaning,"* 251–258, Barbara Lewandowska-Tomaszczyk and Marcel Thelen, eds., 1992. Maastricht: Rijkshogeschool Maastricht. It is published here, with minor revisions, by permission of the editors of that volume.

Much of the early analysis of Aguaruna (see, for example, Larson 1963), which is used for the examples in this paper, was originally done in Pike's Tagmemics framework (see Pike 1954). Relations between form and meaning (or function) first came to my attention while studying under Pike during an M.A. study program at the University of Michigan (1957–1958). Additional study of Aguaruna form-meaning relationships was done in a Ph.D. program under the guidance of Longacre (for example, his 1976 work) with heavy influence from Stratificational Theory, especially as expounded by Gleason (1973) and by Lamb (1973).

A single form in a language may be used for a number of meanings or functions. One meaning may also be encoded by various forms. This is true both of lexical forms and of grammatical structures. We are all familiar with this in dealing with individual words. We know from many years of using the dictionary that lexical items have many secondary meanings. The primary meaning of a word can usually be translated by the corresponding word in another language without any problem, but secondary meanings can almost never be translated directly by the corresponding word. Consider example (1).

(1)   English to Spanish
               key — llave   'key of a lock'
               key — clave   'key of a code'
               key — tecla   'key of a typewriter'

       Spanish to English
           llave — key
           llave — faucet
           llave — wrench

Notice that the English word *key* is translated by three different Spanish words, depending on the context. It may be translated with *llave* for its primary sense, but with *clave* or *tecla* when used in a secondary sense. In the same way the Spanish word *llave* is translated by at least three different English words, depending on the context. Only its primary sense, 'key', can be translated directly. The secondary senses will require different words—*faucet* and *wrench*.

Just as a single word may have various senses, as in the examples in (1), the opposite is also true: one meaning may be represented by several different forms, as in (2).

(2)   the white kitten
       the kitten that is white
       the kitten, the white one

In the natural use of the language, the form chosen will depend on the context and the other grammatical structures in the sentence or paragraph.

However, in this essay our focus is on the use of a single form in secondary or extended meanings. Just as a word may have several meanings depending on the context, so grammatical structure may have secondary or extended usages. These secondary functions present a challenge to the translator. They cannot usually be translated with a matching form in the receptor language except in closely related languages.

There is a basic principle, which if put into practice by the translator, will go a long way in preventing unnatural-sounding translation. It is not the total answer, of course, but it is helpful. This principle is that, while primary meanings may often be translated literally, secondary meanings (or functions) may almost never be translated literally. I will illustrate this with examples at word level, phrase level, clause level, sentence level, and even at discourse level.

We have already looked at an example at word level. Example (3) is also at word level but shows the correspondence between three languages—English, Spanish, and Aguaruna, an Amerindian language of northern Peru.

(3)	English	Spanish	Aguaruna
	The boy *runs*.	El nino *corre.* 'The boy runs.'	Uchi *tupikawai.* 'boy runs'
	The motor *runs*.	El motor *funciona.* 'The motor functions.'	Motor *shinawai.* 'motor makes noise'
	The clock *runs*.	El reloj *anda.* 'The clock walks.'	Etsa *weawai.* 'sun goes'
	His nose *runs*.	Su nariz *chorrea.* 'His nose drips.'	Nuji *kitawai.* 'nose drips'

In English *the boy runs, the motor runs, the clock runs,* and *his nose runs* illustrate four meanings of the word *run*. Only the first of these is a primary meaning. The other three are secondary and cannot be translated literally into either Spanish or Aguaruna. In Spanish the motor *functions,* the clock *walks,* and his nose *drips.* In Aguaruna the motor *makes noise,* the sun *goes,* and his nose *drips.* All three languages have a word the primary sense of which is 'moving rapidly by means of moving the legs', and the translation is direct or literal. The English word *run* has many secondary senses, however. These cannot be translated by the equivalent form, *corre,* in Spanish, or by *tupikawai* in Aguaruna. A completely different word will be used for each secondary sense.

I will not go into further detail about secondary senses of words, a matter familiar to all of us. I simply want to use this characteristic of the

lexicon as a basis for understanding the mismatch between the meaning
and the grammatical structures of the larger units of a text or of a text as a
whole. Just as a word has secondary senses, so a grammatical construction has secondary functions. Just as *run* cannot be translated by the literal form when a secondary meaning is present, so a grammatical
construction cannot be translated directly if the function is other than its
primary function. A question, for example, will not always be translated
with a question. A procedural text may need to be translated by a narrative structure. Grammatical forms in the source-language text, if they are
being used in a secondary function, can seldom be translated by a corresponding grammatical form in the target language.

Let us look first at examples of prepositional phrases beginning with *on*.
The primary meaning of *on* is 'location'. But not all prepositional phrases
beginning with *on* mean 'location'. Note the examples in (4).

(4)   English   Spanish

      John found a book *on the floor*   ...*en el piso*
                                            'on the floor'

      John found a book *on mathematics*   ...*sobre/de matematica*
                                            'about mathematics'

      John found a book *on Tuesday*   ...*el martes*
                                            'the Tuesday'

      John found a book *on sale*.   ...*en oferta*
                                            'at reduced price'

The form of the grammatical construction is the same in all four examples, but only the first, *on the floor*, has the primary meaning of 'location'.
It is translated directly by the Spanish equivalent *en* 'in, on'. The other
three examples have a secondary meaning of the prepositional phrase;
therefore, each is translated with a different form in Spanish. (In the last
example *en* is a figurative use of 'location'.)

A simple English possessive phrase may have a variety of meanings
other than possession, as shown in (5) (adapted from Larson 1998:8).

(5)   my car   'possession, ownership'
        my uncle   'kinship'
        my hand   'part-whole (part of my body)'
        my speaking   'actor-activity (I speak)'
        my book   'the book I own (possession);
                                    the book I wrote'
        my town   'the town where I live'
        my bus   'the bus I ride on; the bus I drive'
        my route   'the route I use for travel; the route I
                                      use in deciding a matter'

The possessive form's primary meaning, of 'possession', is not usually a problem in translation, but its other meanings will probably be translated with very different forms.

Just as words and phrases may have secondary meanings, so also sentences are often used with secondary functions, also called extended usages. For example, a question form may be used for a noninterrogative meaning, even though the primary function of a question is to ask for information. The question *Alice, why don't you sweep the floor?* in some contexts may be asking for information, but in other contexts may be used with the meaning of 'command' or even 'rebuke'. In this case, it is a rhetorical question. In yet other contexts, *Alice, why don't you sweep the floor?* is a friendly suggestion and the answer would be, *All right, I'd like to*. If it were a real *why* question, asking for information, the answer would give a reason. Something like, *Because I'm just too busy*.

The secondary usage of a *why* question would need to be translated by an imperative sentence in many languages. If it is not, the meaning would be distorted. The translation might simply be *Alice, sweep the floor*. If translated directly as a *why* question in many Amerindian languages it would indicate a 'rebuke'. A simple imperative would need to be used. To convey the correct meaning of 'a friendly suggestion' in Yaweyuha of Papua New Guinea, a question form would never be used, rather a negative statement: *Alice, you didn't sweep the floor*. On the other hand, if this negative statement were translated directly into English it would not carry the meaning of 'a friendly suggestion' but rather would be a 'rebuke'.

In English a question form may be used to show 'rebuke' but it would most likely be a *when* question. A mother who is angry with her daughter for not doing her part of the family chores may say *When are you going to sweep the floor?* She has told her before. The daughter knows it is her duty. The mother wants to convey all of this meaning—the command and the emotion she feels about it. To do so, she will not use a command form, but rather, a question—not a *why* question, but a *when* question: *When are you going to sweep the floor?* If she had not told her daughter before, and if she were not angry or exasperated, she would have used a command form such as *Please sweep the floor* or another question form, *Would you sweep the floor, please?*

Many languages do not use question forms with a secondary function of 'command' in the same way as English. If a source text is translated literally, the question in the target language would be understood to be asking for information, even though that was not the intent of the writer of the source text. The important thing for the translator to know is whether or not the question form of the source text has a true interrogative meaning or is a secondary usage. The target-language form should communicate the same information and the same emotion as indicated by the source-text question, but need not have the same form, that of a question. (For more on English questions see Larson 1976.)

For those who are translating into or from Amerindian languages of South America or the languages of Papua New Guinea, the secondary usages of quotations and dialogue present special challenges. When quotations are used to recount speech acts, that is, to report that a certain person expressed a certain idea in spoken words, then the quotation form is used in its primary function. Something was actually said. There is no problem of equivalence as one translates. A direct quotation form may be used to translate the quotation.

But in many languages the quotation form has several secondary functions not found in Indo-European languages. (There are many examples in Larson 1978.) For example, in Aguaruna, cause-effect or purpose and reason relations are encoded by quotations, as in (6). (A literal English back-translation is given for Aguaruna in the rest of this article.)

(6)   English: He hangs it up to dry.
                    He hangs it up in order for it to dry.
       Aguaruna: He hangs it up, "Let it get dry," saying.

In English, we say *He hangs it up to dry* or *He hangs it up in order for it to dry*. But this form, the infinitive *to dry*, would not communicate 'reason' in Aguaruna. A quotation would be used. The Aguaruna form, literally, is *He hangs it up, "Let it get dry," saying*. In this case, the use of the quotation is a secondary usage. An English translation from Aguaruna would not need a quotation but would simply use an infinitive.

(7)   Aguaruna: He carves it a little bit more, "Its prow that-risen
                  let-it-be," saying.
      English: He carves it a little more so that the prow will be
                  a bit higher.

Example (7) gives the literal back-translation of an Aguaruna sentence:
He carves it a little bit more, "Its prow that-risen let-it-be," saying. A less literal, more natural English translation would be *He carves it a little more so
that the prow will be a bit higher.* The quotation form is not retained in the
translation into English because it is a secondary usage of the quotation
form in Aguaruna and is not the natural way to express the same meaning
in English. On the other hand, every 'reason' clause of English must be
translated into Aguaruna with a direct quotation. It is not always easy to
know what words to put into the mouth of the speaker, that is, how to express the content of the quotation, since nothing was actually said. Speech
is not being reported, rather, the form of reported speech is being used in
a secondary function.

Quotation forms are also used to encode thought and cognition in some
languages. In (8) we have two examples of this use of quotations in
Aguaruna. Notice that they are translated into English without the quotation form.

(8)   a.   Aguaruna: "Bird will it maybe appear?" saying, again I went.
           English: Thinking that another bird would surely appear, I
                       went.

      b.   Aguaruna: Since the things made by Incas are well preserved,
                       "They are those who surely worked like that,"
                       saying, we know.
           English: We know how the Incas did (made) things because
                       the things which they made are well preserved.

There are also other secondary uses of quotations in Aguaruna. Concepts such as 'to believe', 'to agree', and 'to thank' are expressed with a
quotation, but the quotation would not be kept in translation into another
language. Conversely, many English sentences which have no quotations
would have to be translated using a quotation in Aguaruna.

We have looked at examples of secondary functions of words, phrases,
and sentences with a view to showing that primary functions can usually
be translated literally into another language, but secondary functions
must always be considered suspect—a different form is often needed in

the translation. This does not mean that the target-language translation will be free of forms used with a secondary meaning. It simply means that the forms will not match the forms of the source language. Appropriate secondary usages will be incorporated in the translated text, but they will be used because they are the most natural, not because they were used in the source text.

The principle of nonliteral translation of secondary meanings and functions has implications for whole texts also. Do literary genres also have primary and secondary functions? If so, how does this affect the form used in the target-language translation? Might it be possible that a text that has the form of a narrative in the source language should be translated into another language as dialogue, and that what is dialogue in the source language should be translated as straight narrative in some target language? Yes. This is indeed true.

"In English short stories, as we all know, the narrative may be carried by dialogue. In fairy tales, however, it is the description which is carried by the dialogue. For example, in *Little Red Riding Hood*, the description of Grandmother is all in the dialogue" (Larson 1998:420). "Grandmother, what big eyes you have!" On the other hand, Grimm's tales in German include description outside the dialogue. For English speakers some translations into English sound strange, not like fairy tales at all. The description outside the dialogue makes them sound foreign. Perhaps if they were written in English with the description in dialogue they would seem more like fairy tales.

Aguaruna folklore often has the narration told in the dialogue, and stories of present-day events use dialogue for description and highlighting. For example, in the story of a visit to a lake where there was a boa, the description of the boa in the setting of the story, translated more or less literally in (9), is encoded as a remark.

(9)   When it began to quake like that, since there were three of them, they said to one another, "There is a boa here and he is angry and wants to eat us. That's why it is quaking like that. Also, the buzzards which are here are spying for the boa, and so seeing us, they called telling the boa that we are here." (Larson 1998:421)

In a language in which dialogue is not used to encode the setting of the story, the translation of the same example might need to be more like the following:

> Then the earth began to quake where the three stood. There in the lake lived a boa. If he became angry he would grab them. There were some buzzards nearby who had made a promise to the boa to let him know if someone came. When the buzzards saw the men, they began to make noise to let the boa know they were there. (Larson 1998:421)

Each language has a primary form appropriate for each genre and for the many subtypes. A narrative told in narrative style is easily translated into the narrative style of another language, since there is no mismatch. It is the primary function of the genre. But a narrative story told by the dialogue forms of English may not necessarily be best translated by dialogue into the target language. The dialogue may need to be changed to narrative (declarative sentences) and dialogue used only at the peak to highlight or only for certain major events or to add description. In other words, the form of the text may need to be drastically changed.

Secondary functions of genres also occur in languages. For example, the total discourse may be written in the form of a narrative discourse, with third person, past tense, etc., when as a matter of fact the semantic function is that of a procedural discourse. In some languages the narrative genre would be inappropriate for a procedural discourse and so procedural forms of second person, present tense, etc., would need to be used. It has been reported that there are Australian Aboriginal languages (Longacre 1972:155) in which dramatic discourse is used to communicate procedural texts. Semantically, the text is procedural but the form is that of drama. A translation to English would not use drama structure but rather change to a normal English procedural text with second person imperative sentences.

Example (10) is an excerpt from a Mexican tourist brochure. It uses procedural discourse (second person) to encode a descriptive text.

(10)   Leaving charming, tourist-ridden Cuernavaca, you continue your journey southwestward through a beautiful region of picturesque villages, rugged mountains, small streams, and dense vegetation.... Turning your eyes upward, you get a wonderful view of the great long stalactites...

These are the grammatical forms of an English procedural discourse, but the meaning, the semantic structure, is descriptive. This kind of mismatch of genre types, with a skewing of the grammatical forms and the meaning, is not uncommon. Just as there are secondary functions of words, phrases, and sentences, so also there are secondary functions of discourse types. A description written with grammatical forms characteristic of description does not create a problem for the translator, but a description written with procedural forms can probably not be translated as a procedural text in another language. The natural forms of the receptor language will need to be used.

A mismatch between the semantic genre type and the grammatical form used is, of course, part of what makes literary art. Literature would indeed be dull if mismatching of this kind were not used to liven the text. If only primary forms were used, there would be little art. The secondary usages are also part of the language. But the principle I wish to emphasize is that a text written in a nonprimary form may need to be translated by quite different forms in another language, depending on the secondary usages of genres peculiar to that language.

At all levels of language structure, there are primary and secondary functions of grammatical forms. All secondary functions pose potential adjustments of form in translating into a target language. Even the genre may need to be changed in the translation process if it is being used in a secondary function.

In summary, just as words have secondary and figurative meanings that cannot be translated literally, so grammatical forms and genre types have secondary and rhetorical functions that cannot be translated literally into the target language. The translator must always be alert for these secondary usages and change the form to one that will most effectively communicate the meaning—both the informational content and emotion—intended by the source text author.

References

Gleason, Henry A. 1973. A contrastive analysis in discourse structure. In Adam Makkai and David G. Lockwood (eds.), *Readings in stratificational linguistics*, 258–276. Tuscaloosa: University of Alabama Press.

Lamb, S. M. 1973. The semantic approach to structural semantics. In A. Makkai and D. G. Lockwood (eds.), *Readings in stratificational linguistics*, 205–228. Tuscaloosa: University of Alabama Press.

Larson, Mildred L. 1963. Emic classes which manifest the obligatory tagmemes in major independent clause types of Aguaruna (Jivaro). In B. Elson (ed.), *Studies in Peruvian Indian languages* 1, 1–36. Publications in Linguistics and Related Fields 9. Norman: Summer Institute of Linguistics and the University of Oklahoma.

Larson, Mildred L. 1976. The communication situation and rhetorical questions. *Notes on Linguistics* 8:14–18.

Larson, Mildred L. 1978. *The functions of reported speech in discourse.* Summer Institute of Linguistics and the University of Texas at Arlington Publications in Linguistics 59. Dallas.

Larson, Mildred L. 1984. The structure of Aguaruna (Jivaro) texts. In Robert E. Longacre (ed.), *Theory and application in processing texts in non-Indoeuropean languages,* 155–209. Hamburg: Buske.

Larson, Mildred L. 1998. *Meaning-based translation: A guide to cross-language equivalence,* second edition. Lanham, Md.: University Press of America.

Longacre, Robert E. 1972. *Hierarchy and universality of discourse constituents in New Guinea languages: Discussion.* Washington, D.C.: Georgetown University Press.

Longacre, Robert E. 1976. *An anatomy of speech notions.* Lisse, Netherlands: Peter de Ridder Press.

Pike, Kenneth L. 1954. *Language in relation to a unified theory of the structure of human behavior,* part 1. Glendale, Calif.: Summer Institute of Linguistics.

25

Gender and Generic Pronouns in English Bible Translation

Vern Sheridan Poythress

Elementary translation theory instructs us to translate meaning, not form. Gender in the linguistic sense (in contrast to the biological categories of male and female) is a grammatical category, that is, a "form," differing from language to language.[1] Some languages possess no gender-marked forms. Others possess two, three, or more genders. They differ also in the ways in which they draw the boundary between different genders (Carson 1998:77–98). So it is not only misguided but impossible to translate gender in a one-to-one fashion. One might therefore conclude from the elementary theory that gender is irrelevant. But more advanced examination of languages shows that form and meaning interlock, so that the simple recipe of ignoring form overlooks subtle meaning nuances. Kenneth L. Pike years ago noted the complexities in the relation between form and meaning and developed a distinctive emphasis on the "form-meaning

---

This chapter was originally presented as a paper at the annual meeting of the Evangelical Theological Society, November 15, 2000, in Nashville, Tennessee. It has some overlap with material from Poythress and Grudem (2000). The Poythress-Grudem book includes an expanded discussion of many of the points here. In fact, many of the examples given here were originally intended to be included in an appendix, but were in the end left out in order to shorten the book. I appreciate the contributions of Wayne Grudem both with respect to the larger issues and with the particular examples.

[1]In subsequent discussion of "gender" I always mean linguistic gender, not the biological categories of male and female.

composite" to express the complexities involved in such phenomena (Pike 1967:62–63, 516–517; Pike 1982:115–117).

We may illustrate the interlock of form and meaning by considering the complex challenge of translating sentences with gender-marked generic pronouns. In English the issue comes to a head only with the third-person singular personal pronoun, because all the other pronouns are unmarked for gender. The third-person singular has three genders, "he," "she," and "it." Until recently the masculine forms, "he/him/his/himself," served as default forms in generic statements. But now some people frown on this use, and so-called gender inclusive translations have sought substitutes.[2]

Changing from "he" to "you"

One possibility they have tried is the use of the second person "you" instead of the third-person singular.[3] Consider Proverbs 12:14. The *New International Version* (NIV) reads: "From the fruit of his lips a man is filled with good things as surely as the work of his hands rewards him." *The Good News Bible* (GNB, 2nd ed.) reads: "Your reward depends on what you say and what you do; you will get what you deserve." The NIV and the Hebrew, by using the third person, invite readers to start with a sample case "out there," and then to apply the truth to anyone whatsoever. Certainly, each reader may apply the truth to himself. But he may also apply the truth to others whom he is counseling, just as the father counsels his son in the early chapters of Proverbs. By contrast, the second-person pronouns in the GNB invite each reader to apply the truth first of all personally. Applying the truth to others by offering them counsel is an afterthought. The directness of focus on application to the individual reader is different in the two cases. The same differences crop up again and again in changes from third person to second person in Proverbs.

---

[2]For an extended critique of gender inclusive translations, see Poythress and Grudem (2000). Defenses of gender-neutral translations appear in Carson (1998) and Strauss (1998). Roughly speaking, Carson and Strauss represent a point of view opposite to Poythress and Grudem. But the opposition is qualified in two ways: (a) in a few individual cases Carson and Strauss admit that some gender-neutral translations have made mistakes; and (b) Carson and Strauss misunderstand our position at a number of points, so that what they claim to oppose is not our actual position. These matters come up for discussion in Poythress and Grudem (2000).

[3]In some translations one will also find uses of the first-person plural, "we": "We can gather our thoughts, but the LORD gives the right answer" (Prov 16:1 *New Living Translation* [NLT]; similarly, in the *Contemporary English Version* [CEV]). The NLT and CEV also introduce "we" in other places in Proverbs even where there is no problem with generic "he" (Prov 16:33; 16:2, CEV).

Complexities in meaning

But what difference does it make, since either wording implies the same propositional generalization? Meaning and communication involves more than abstract propositions. They involve relations between author and reader, a reader and his actions, a reader and other actors, and so on. We must resist the temptation to reduce meaning to a mere basic core.

We must also resist arguments based on simplistic appeals to the distinction between form and meaning. One argument might go as follows. Pronominal systems, like gender systems, differ from language to language. Pronouns are forms, and what we are after is the meaning expressed by whole sentences. Hence, changing from "he" to "you" in a generalized statement changes form but preserves meaning.

But in fact the situation is more complex. The forms that distinguish first-person, second-person, and third-person pronouns vary from language to language.[4] But some of the meaning functions remain similar across languages, because all over the world people distinguish speakers from addressees and addressees from third parties. And all over the world statements of general truths are not purely abstract, but anchor themselves in the situational and personal realities of one person making a statement to another, within a certain personal, social, and temporal context. (Thus, Kenneth Pike considered the situation and culture as a necessary context for linguistic analysis [Pike 1967:25–149].) The differences between first, second, and third person have subtle but pervasive effects on the orientation of people to the truths about which they speak.

The changes also affect the genre of the middle section of Proverbs, 10:1–22:16. Second-person exhortations abound in Proverbs 1–9 and in some parts of the later chapters of Proverbs. But the middle section contains almost nothing but third-person sayings. The strategies of the different sections make a difference. The tone of the third-person middle section invites readers to be wise observers of life. Yes, they will discover in the end many concrete, practical applications to their own lives. But the atmosphere begins more with contemplation than with action. Proverbs encourages us to learn something about the ways of others, and to learn from observing the blessing of the Lord on some and his punishments on others. Converting third-person sayings into second-person sayings tends to break down the distinctiveness of this middle section of Proverbs and makes English readers less aware of its overall reflective mood.

---

[4]In addition, some languages have a "fourth person" form, for more distant references.

Different meanings of "dynamic equivalence"

The GNB, the *New Living Translation* (NLT), and the *Contemporary English Version* (CEV) often change to second-person in the book of Proverbs. They sometimes do so even when the change is not necessary in order to eliminate a generic "he" (for example, Proverbs 12:17 GNB; 12:24 NLT; 11:3 CEV). Some of the changes seem almost random. One wonders what reason there could be for such alterations. Were the translators insensitive to nuances, so that they did not realize that they were changing meanings? Were they not aware of the distinct tone of the middle section of Proverbs? Did they freely make changes because all they cared about was some basic core of meaning?

One wonders. The GNB, NLT, and CEV share conspicuously a pronounced commitment to dynamic equivalent translation. The tradition of dynamic equivalent translation advises us to translate meaning, not form. But everything depends on how much one includes under the term "meaning." At times it seems that dynamic equivalent translation has become a broad umbrella. It can cover at one end the meticulous attempt to reproduce as far as possible every nuance of meaning. But it can also be used as a fig leaf to cover questionable practices that appear to ignore anything beyond a minimal core meaning. Consider the following example.

Proverbs 18:16

> NIV: A gift opens the way for the giver and ushers him into the presence of the great.

> NLT: .Giving a gift works wonders; it may bring you before important people.

The two translations express a similar meaning; each indicates that a gift may be effective in obtaining an audience before a prominent person. Once again the temptation arises to say that the meaning of the two is the same, but the form differs. But subtle differences in meaning accompany the changes in form. Some of these differences arise from the general paraphrastic policies of the NLT. For example, the word "wonders" in the NLT introduces the connotation of the marvelous, which is not expressed in Hebrew or in the NIV.

But what about the change to "you"? It also results in a noticeable change in meaning. Just as we observed in the earlier example, by using a third-person statement the NIV invites the reader to start with a sample situation involving a giver out there in the world. This sample situation functions as the starting point for generalizing about life. The NLT, by using "you," invites the reader to think of himself as the actor and then to generalize from there. The resulting generalization may be similar, in the two cases, but the starting point is different.

Some further effects crop up in this example. The NIV's third-person statement leaves open the question of ethical evaluation. It merely observes that giving gifts to obtain favor is an actual practice among human beings. Maybe the practice is okay. But maybe not. Maybe people should not be so readily influenced by gifts. Granted that people are so influenced, maybe an individual should give in and follow the trend for purely pragmatic reasons. But maybe also he should resist the trend and see the use of gifts in this way as a form a manipulation. Neither the Hebrew nor the NIV explicitly commit themselves to answer these "maybe" questions about ethically evaluating the process.

On the other hand, when the NLT shifts to "you," the proverb sounds more like shrewd advice. Because it develops its sample case by means of the pronoun "you," it invites the reader to think of himself as giving a gift. And by inviting the reader to picture himself in this way, it seems indirectly to invite the reader to *perform* the action suggested in the picture, because, after all, the results may be advantageous. As long as the sample case is "out there" in the world, as the Hebrew and the NIV have it, one can from a distance raise questions about the rectitude of various aspects of gift giving. Once the text pushes the reader into more direct involvement using "you," the more contemplative attitude recedes.[5]

Changing to plural "they"

The *New Revised Standard Version* (NRSV) and the *New International Version Inclusive Language Edition* (NIVI), as less adventuresome translations, have sometimes shifted to the second person. But more often, they have preferred to change a third-person singular statement with "he" to a third-person plural statement with "they." Consider some examples.

1 Corinthians 14:28[6]

> NIV: If there is no interpreter, the *speaker* should keep quiet in the church and speak to *himself* and God.

---

[5]The GNB produces the same problem: "Do you want to meet an important person? Take a gift and it will be easy." The CEV is similar: "A gift will get you in to see anyone."

[6]Wayne Grudem originally drew my attention to this example. With some of the other examples below, I cannot remember whether Grudem or I first noticed the example.

NIVI: If there is no interpreter, the *speakers* should keep quiet in the church and speak to *themselves* and God.

The NIVI has changed the singular "speaker" to plural "speakers," in order to avoid the subsequent occurrence of generic "he" in the form of "himself." But in doing so, it has introduced an ambiguity. In the NIVI, the verse may mean that all the tongue-speakers are to go off *together* and speak "to themselves," that is, to one another in their own private meeting, separate from the rest. Or does the NIVI mean that each speaker is to go and speak to himself rather than to anyone else? The latter, not the former, is basically the meaning of both the NIV and the original Greek. By converting to plurals, the NIVI introduces an ambiguity in English.

John 6:56

NIV: *Whoever* eats my flesh and drinks my blood remains in me, and I in *him*.

NIVI: *Those who* eat my flesh and drink my blood remain in me, and I in *them*.

The language of "eating my flesh and drinking my blood" will suggest to many the picture of celebrating the Lord's Supper. And the Lord's Supper surely symbolizes the spiritual communion about which Jesus speaks. The NIVI, because of its plurals, suggests the picture of the church *together* eating the flesh and drinking the blood (similarly, NRSV, NLT). The idea of "remaining," both the church in Christ and Christ in the church, then becomes corporate. But then the individual focus of John 6:56 is lost from sight.

John 15:5

RSV: ...*He* who abides in me, and I in *him*, he it is that bears much fruit, for apart from me you can do nothing.

NRSV: *Those* who abide in me and I in *them* bear much fruit, because apart from me you can do nothing.

As with John 6:56, the NRSV's change to plural "they" shifts the focus to disciples in their *plurality*. When the text says "I in *them*" instead of "I in *him,*" it is no longer clear that Christ is dwelling in each disciple rather than simply corporately in the church, "them" as a group.

John 6:44

> NIV: *No one* can come to me unless the Father who sent me draws *him,* and I will raise *him* up at the last day.

> NLT: For *people* can't come to me unless the Father who sent me draws *them* to me and at the last day I will raise *them* from the dead.

The focus shifts from the individual in the NIV to the group in the NLT. In the NLT, we may think of crowds coming to Jesus because the Father draws them. The Father brings whole groups, but perhaps each individual makes up his own mind within the group. It is not clear whether the Father acts on any individual in a way distinct from another individual. Perhaps he just draws the group as a whole. The doctrine of individual calling is lost from sight. The group as a whole is raised at the last day, but perhaps some people within the group have fallen away by that time. The doctrine of individual assurance of salvation is lost from sight.

We find in John 6:65 the same problems as in John 6:44.

John 6:65

> NIV: ...no one can come to me unless the Father has enabled *him.*

> NLT: ...people can't come to me unless the Father brings *them* to me.

The subtle shifts in the meaning, and the ambiguities between a corporate and an individual meaning, do not seem to be merely random. Though at first blush it might seem that a singular form and a plural form express the same meaning, a closer examination shows subtle differences in meaning. The singular "he" is not only singular in form, but has an effect on meaning. The language suggests as a starting point a single individual who becomes a sample case for the general truth. The plural "they" is not only plural in form, but results in a plural meaning: the starting point contains a plurality of individuals, about all of whom *together* we make the assertion in question. In the one case, we derive a general principle from a single starting case; in the other, we derive application to each individual from a direct assertion with respect to a plurality.

By itself, this difference in starting point is a difference in meaning. And it results in a further difference, namely that what is explicitly in the foreground in one case is derived in the other. But in addition, the difference in starting point introduces in some contexts a potential ambiguity between corporate and individual interpretations. The singular "he" implies unambiguously that the truth holds for each individual within the scope of the general statement. The plural "they" leaves open, in some contexts, the possibility that the truth might apply primarily or exclusively to the people *as a group*, in their relations to one another or in their corporate wholeness.

Thus, changes in person and number in generic statements involve not only changes in form, but subtle changes in meaning as well. Therefore, these changes are not in general acceptable in English Bible translation. (But see Poythress and Grudem [2000:343–344] for one kind of exception, in cases of unusual switches between pronouns within a short piece of text.) We should continue to use generic "he" whenever it is needed, in order to preserve these nuances.

Does generic "he" carry male connotations?

All this only serves to bring into focus the question of whether we can indeed use generic "he." If generic "he" were genuinely unavailable in English, we would have to do the best we could without it, and there might be no choice except to settle for some approximation that unavoidably loses nuances of meaning. What do we say here?

The topic is too extensive for me to address here. I must refer readers to the discussion in Poythress and Grudem (2000:111–232). We shall have to content ourselves with three observations.

First, generic "he" still occurs in major secular publications like *The Chicago Tribune, Newsweek, U.S. News and World Report,* and *Reader's Digest* (see Poythress and Grudem 2000:203–210). It is acknowledged as a reasonable usage in *The Associated Press Stylebook and Libel Manual* (1994:94) and the latest edition of Strunk and White, *The Elements of Style* (2000:60–61) (see Poythress and Grudem 2000:210–211). Since it is still in use, let us use it when we need it.

Second, using generic "he" invites us to start not only with a single sample case of the truth in question, but to think to a certain extent of a male rather than a female example for this sample case. Consider the difficulty of the following sentence: "When a typical American comes home from work, he wants to be comfortable. He removes his coat, takes off his panty-hose,[7] and puts on slippers. A specifically male detail such as "takes off his tie" would be less jarring than the specifically female detail "takes off his panty-hose."

The *American Heritage Dictionary* perceptively observes, "Thus *he* is not really a gender-neutral pronoun, rather, it refers to a male who is to be taken as the representative member of the group referred to by its antecedent. The traditional usage, then, is not simply a grammatical convention; it also suggests a particular pattern of thought" (1996:831). The "pattern of thought" in question involves starting with a male example when stating a general truth. The masculine form of "he" turns out not to be mere form, but to have meaning-connotations even when used generically (Poythress and Grudem 2000:135–161).

Analogously, third-person masculine singular generic masculine nouns and pronouns are customary in biblical Hebrew and Greek. This custom, too, may seem at first glance to be mere "form." But careful examination suggests that an analogous phenomenon of starting with a male example occurs in Hebrew and Greek. Leviticus 14, for example, discusses the procedure for a person who is to be pronounced clean from leprosy. Leviticus 13:29 and 38 have already clearly indicated that the regulations for leprosy include both men and women. When Leviticus 14 discusses the ceremony for cleansing, it designates the leper with masculine singular forms, and then in 14:9 says that "he must shave his head, his *beard*, his eye-brows and the rest of his hair" (NIV). At this point the fact that a male example is in view comes to the surface (Poythress and Grudem 2000:142–146, 335–347). Thus, in all three languages a meaning component attaches to the use of the masculine form.

Third, and finally, some writers adopt a style in which they oscillate between using generic "she" and generic "he." This oscillating use is not objectionable to feminists. The oscillating use shows not only that people still understand generic "he," but also that the real objection is not to a single occurrence of generic "he." Rather, the objection is to any pattern in which male examples predominate over female ones. The objection is to a pattern of thought. Authors writing in English may of course adapt to the contemporary scene as they see fit. But a translator, in distinction from an author, is not free to change the pattern of thought in Scripture, even if it should prove offensive to some.

---

[7]The idea for this example comes from Meller and Swift (1980:46), who in turn cite C. Badendyck in the *New York Times Magazine*.

Interlocking of form and meaning

In sum, the use of pronouns shows interlocking between form and meaning. From these phenomena we may generalize. Specific forms within a specific context often carry meaning nuances that cannot be completely reproduced by substitute forms. Translation must indeed translate meaning, not merely form. But meaning includes nuances, not just a basic core.

References

The American heritage dictionary of the English language. 1996. Third ed. Boston/New York: Houghton Mifflin.

The Associated Press stylebook and libel manual. 1994. Reading, Mass.: Addison-Wesley.

Carson, D. A. 1998. *The inclusive language debate: A plea for realism.* Grand Rapids, Mich.: Baker.

Casey, William, and Kate Swift. 1980. *The handbook of nonsexist writing.* New York: Lippincott & Crowell.

Pike, Kenneth L. 1967. *Language in relation to a unified theory of the structure of human behavior.* Second revised edition. The Hague/Paris: Mouton.

Pike, Kenneth L. 1982. *Linguistic concepts: An introduction to tagmemics.* Lincoln: University of Nebraska Press.

Poythress, Vern S., and Wayne A. Grudem. 2000. *The gender-neutral Bible controversy: Muting the masculinity of God's words.* Nashville, Tenn.: Broadman and Holman.

Strauss, Mark L. 1998. *Distorting Scripture? The challenge of Bible translation & gender accuracy.* Downers Grove, Ill.: InterVarsity.

Strunk, William, Jr., and E. B. White. 2000. *The elements of style.* Fourth edition. Boston: Allyn and Bacon.

Part VI

Beyond the Sentence

"Beyond the sentence lie grammatical structures available to linguistic analysis." (Pike 1964a:129)

26

A Textlinguistic Analysis of Psalm 19

General and Special Revelation

Robert E. Longacre

Introduction

Continuing in the tradition of Kenneth L. Pike that we serve God with both heart and mind, I present here a discourse analysis of Psalm 19, which, as we shall see, has praise of the written Word. This is, therefore, a part of the scriptures in which motivation and vindication are found for the commitment to Bible translation which characterized Pike's life and the lives of many of us who have been influenced by him.

Psalm 19 is a prayer. The petitions proper are in vv. 12–13. They are preceded by expressions of motivation in vv. 1–11 and followed by closure in v. 14. The motivation is expressed in two embedded lyrics. The first lyric, vv. 1–6, treats of God's general revelation of himself in nature; the second lyric, vv. 7–11, treats of God's special revelation of himself in his written Word. In the four sections of this paper I treat in order the first embedded lyric, the second embedded lyric, the petitions proper, and the closure of the whole psalm.[1]

---

[1]The analysis is implicitly tagmemic. Everywhere slot-class relations are assumed as in K. L. Pike's earlier version of that theory before subsequent elaboration into the four-celled tagmeme. Cf. Longacre 1965.

God's General Revelation of Himself in Nature

The glory and wonder of God's revelation of himself in nature are celebrated in the first embedded lyric, vv. 1–6. The first part of the lyric develops the thesis and amplifies it, followed by a comment concerning the
limitations of even so glorious a revelation. The lyric comes to a climax in
presenting the sun as a supreme example of God's creative activity. Two
similes are employed and there is a final statement regarding the all per-
vasiveness of the sun in his diurnal path. Specifically, v. 1 states the initial
thesis:

> "The heavens are declaring the glory of God;
> the skies [firmament] show his handiwork."[2]

This thesis is expanded and amplified in v. 2:

> "Day unto day pours out speech;
> Night unto night displays knowledge."

Nevertheless, in spite of the glowing affirmations of these two verses, v. 3
goes on to assert the *muteness* of God's creation:

> "There is no speech,
> There is no word;
> Their voice is not heard."

Various exegetical expedients have been adopted to mitigate the oxymoron occasioned by these verses and the assertion of speechless speech and
wordless words. A few versions insert the word "where" to read "There is no
speech nor word where their voice is not heard," with Luther and Calvin
lending their support to such a rendition. Not greatly different is the suggestion of Delitzsch (1971, vol. 1:282) which in effect supplies "whose": "There
is no speech nor language whose voice is unheard"—even though this rendition (cf. the Septuagint) borders on nonsense. Better to follow the majority of
the translations in English, French, and Spanish as represented in the sort of
rendition which I give above.

Immediately, however, the following verse takes up again an affirmation similar to that found in the first two verses of the Psalm:

---

[2]Here and elsewhere the translation of portions of the psalm is essentially mine; however, it may
concur with or echo various contemporary translations.

"To all the world has gone out their line,
And unto the ends of the earth their words."

Bratcher and Rayburn (1991), recognize the difficulties inherent in this verse and counsel, in effect, that translators say something that makes sense while at the same time avoiding any term which implies specifically verbal activity.

What then? We are translating poetry not somber prose nor the language of a theology book. What these verses apparently affirm is that while nature communicates a great deal about God's glory and power as displayed in creation, in the end nature is mute. The witness is *iconic* rather than verbal. In the words of St. Paul in Romans 1:20, "what may be known about God is plain to us because God has made it plain," but the revelation of nature concerns God's eternal power and divine nature—and little more. It is enough, however, to provide us with no excuse in our human rebellion against God. The verses in this psalm constitute, as we have already suggested, an oxymoron, i.e., a semantic clash between revealed and not revealed, speech and nonspeech, eloquence and muteness. For one who knows God, nature provides an iconic representation of himself, but icons are not words whatever words they may suggest to the already initiated.

Our passage continues, however, to its climax in the references to the sun, and the similes which are associated with this reference:

"In them [the heavens?] he has pitched a tent for the sun,
Which is like a bridegroom coming out of his marriage chamber
And rejoices as a strong man/hero to run a race."

Here the sun is singled out as the noblest and most glorious of God's works. He comes out of his quarters at sunrise like a bridegroom coming joyfully from his marriage chamber where his heart's desires have been satisfied. He's ready to run his race like a strong athlete. Somewhat more prosaically the passage continues:

"His going forth is from the end of the heavens
And his circuit unto the ends of it—
And there is nothing hid from his heat."

Although this lyric posits an exegetical problem at its core, it builds to a resounding climax with the passage on the sun—that wonderful object on whose light and warmth we are all dependent, but which is meant to reveal its Creator, not to be worshipped as a deity in itself.

God's Special Revelation of Himself in His Word

Without the least hint of transition, without any conjunction whether coordinating or adversative, the psalm now shifts into a lyric which celebrates the written Word wherein God is more adequately revealed. Deity, referred to simply as God, *'el* in verse 1 of the psalm is now referred to as *Yahweh*; that is, the generic name for God gives way to his personal name as the covenant-keeping God who enters into relations with people. This name is used six times in vv. 7–9, and a further time in the closure of the psalm in v. 14.

Before going into this section in detail, we may well raise the question as to how the two embedded lyrics are to be understood as related to each other in the overall structure within the motivation section of this psalm. Are they implicitly in contrast? Are they simply coordinated? This question is probably unanswerable. The psalm is sparing in its use of overt conjunctions. We could consider that the revelation of God in nature and of God in written scripture are simply juxtaposed—for us to revel in them both. On the other hand, the stronger language used regarding the revelatory role of the written scriptures may lead us to believe that a contrast is intended and that the contrast is weighted in favor of the second. I proceed to examine the second lyric, its affirmations, and the way that it also builds to a climax. Verse 7 affirms:

> "The law of Yahweh [is] perfect, converting the soul,
> The statutes of Yahweh [are] trustworthy,
> making wise the simple."

In each half of the verse a Hebrew verbless clause states a thesis and a participial clause gives the result. The first of several words that are used here and in subsequent verses to describe God's written revelation is *torah*. While the primary lexical meaning of the term *torah* is instruction or direction, it has come to be applied specifically to the first five books of the Hebrew Bible, the Law of Moses, for which rabbinical Judaism has the greatest reverence and affection. For this law of God, perfection is claimed; in the words of Delitzsch "spotless and harmless, as being absolutely well-meaning, and altogether directed towards the well-being of man" (1971:286). This claim is followed by a participial clause "converting the soul." Again, I quote Delitzsch (1971:286), who interprets the participle and its object as signifying "restoring, bringing back, i.e., imparting newness of life, quickening the soul." The second half of the verse is exactly parallel in structure and not dissimilar in meaning. Here, the Hebrew word <*idut* 'testimony' is used, which Cohen succinctly paraphrases as "a regulation which attests the will of God" (1992:54). Of this testimony it is affirmed that it is trustworthy or sure, i.e., it can be relied upon to direct one's life. The participial clause which follows affirms that its function is "making wise the simple (uninstructed)."

The claims made in the two verbless clauses and in the following participial clauses are striking and provocative. The written scriptures, whether called law or testimonies to the will of God, are affirmed to be altogether complete and reliable and capable of quickening our moral nature and ethical perception. The following verse, v. 8, continues much in the same vein and with exactly the same structure of verbless clause and following participial clause:

> "The precepts of Yahweh [are] right, rejoicing the heart,
> The commandments of Yahweh [are] radiant, enlightening
> the eyes."

Here the use of the terms "precepts" and "commandments" reminds us that God's revealing himself includes the resort to particular rules often expressed in imperatives. But these regulations are not only right; they also have a certain radiance. In exercising their function on us we, in the end, come to rejoice in them and are brought out of sorrow and bewilderment into a gratifying light.

Verse 9 continues with the same structure of Hebrew verbless clause followed by participial clause but substitutes for a reference to the Word of God "the fear [reverence] of Yahweh"—which as a response to the Law of God, is affirmed to be clean and standing forever. Then, in the second colon, a further synonym for the written Word is again used, the "judgments," perhaps especially referring to the regulation of one's life with his neighbor. Of these judgments it is asserted that they are true and righteous altogether. Delitzsch comments that all these are "encomiums of the Law, of which every two are related as antecedent and consequent, rising and falling according to the caesural scheme, after the manner of waves" (1968:265). Just as the first embedded lyric has its climax in a two-fold metaphorical reference to the sun so this lyric climaxes in a two-fold metaphorical reference to the Law as better than gold and sweeter than honey (v 10):

"More desirable are they than gold, than even the purest gold
And sweeter than honey and the droppings from the
honeycomb."

Regarding the latter, Cohen comments (following Kimchi, a medieval Jewish commentator), "One may become sated with the sweetness of honey but not with the joyful effects of faithfulness to God's will" (1992:55).

Verse 11 states a further function of God's revealed will and provides a transition to the remainder of the composition:

"Moreover [Heb. *gam*] by them is your servant warned
And in keeping of them there is great reward."

The conjunction *gam* is essentially additive and indicates the addition of a further related thought.

The Psalmist's Petitions

Thus motivated—by God's revealing himself in the cosmos and in his Word—the psalmist proceeds to pray. He begins his prayer with a rhetorical question which implies "no one" as its answer; it is simply a stylistic device for stating that no one can know his own faults and moral shortcomings in their entirety. Therefore, prayer must be made for cleansing from secret failings:

"One's errors, who knows?
Cleanse me from secret sins."

In the next verse, v. 13, the psalmist further prays that he may be kept back from more insolent and willful types of transgressions which, if yielded to, can come to dominate him:

"Keep back your servant also [Heb. *gam*] from presumptuous sins,
Don't let them dominate me."

Again, in a psalm that is sparing in the use of connectives the occurrence of *gam* 'also' is significant. It links the two prayers of the psalmist, one for cleansing from secret sins, the other from willful sins.

Still another conjunction, *'az* 'then', indicates here logical consequence in v. 13b:

> "Then I shall be innocent/just,
> And I shall be free of great transgression."

This verse is further weighted by the use of a wqtl form [or :waw-consecutive with the perfect] in "I shall be free" which in this case marks its climactic nature. In that wqtl forms are extremely rare in the Psalms, the use of this form here is necessarily significant, presumably as a marker of climax.

The Closure

The closure of the psalm, after the climax of petition found in the preceding verse, subsides to a more thoughtful and reflective sort of request given in modal imperfects/jussives rather than in imperatives:

> "Let the words of my mouth and the meditation of my heart
> Be acceptable in your sight, Yahweh, my strength and my redeemer."

One final word: the psalm ends with the word *go'aliy* 'my redeemer'. In the whole Hebrew Bible the word "redeemer" with the first person singular possessive suffix is found only here and in Job 19:25 where it marks Job's confidence in the darkest hour of his life. The word "redeemer" with other person-number affixes, is not infrequently found in Isaiah. Occurring at this place in the psalm with its highly personal reference, it reinforces the salvific claims made for the truth of God as revealed in his Word, and the psalmist's hope of being righteous before God.

Conclusion

In conclusion, I simply note that although one may consider the two embedded lyrics—one in praise of God's general revelation and the other in praise of his special revelation—to be either coordinated or contrasted, the latter lyric seems to outweigh the former and to be the more immediate occasion for the petitions found at the end of the composition.

As an appendix to this paper I include a stepped diagram to present the constituent structure of the psalm, to demonstrate its interweaving of lyric and hortatory elements, and to show the various Hebrew verb forms used as the psalmist plies his craft—inviting our comparing the composition to a painting or a tapestry in which the various verb forms function like paints or colored threads.

Appendix: Tree of Psalm 19

In this diagram, I do not give the Hebrew text itself but give the verb parsing in brackets and distinguish by differing fonts the translation of each form.

On a hortatory template with motivation, petition, and closure as discourse-level constituents, paragraph-level relations are as in Longacre 1996:101–151. Strophes 1 and 2 are lyric/expository; strophe 3 is hortatory. In the diagram, para is an abbreviation for 'paragraph'; for other abbreviations see note 2 of this appendix.

MOTIVATION vv. 1–11 Coordinate/Contrastive para [Strophes 1 and 2]

Thesis 1: E Exemplification para. vv. 1-6 [Strophe 1]
Thesis: E Comment para
Thesis: E Amplification para
Thesis: E Paraphrase para
[1]   Thesis: The heavens **are declaring** [par] the glory of God.
Paraphrase: And his handiwork **shows** [par] the firmament.
Amplification: E Coord para
[2]   Thesis 1: Day to day it *pours forth* [yqtl.o] speech
Thesis 2: Night to night it *displays* [yqtl.o] knowledge
Comment: E Contrast para
Thesis: Paraphrase para
[3]   Thesis: E Paraphrase para
Thesis: No speech
Paraphrase: No words.
Paraphrase: Their voice *is not heard* [qtl.pr]
Antithesis: E Paraphrase para
[4]   Thesis: To all the world *has gone out* [qtl.pr] their
line
Paraphrase: And unto the ends of the earth, their word
Example: E Comment para
Thesis: E Simile para
Thesis: For the sun *has he set* [qtl.pr] a tent in them [the heavens].
Simile: E Coord. para

[5]   Thesis 1: And he (Heb. hu') # like a bridegroom
                            coming out [par] of his marriage-chamber.
                            Thesis 2: And he *rejoices* [yqtl.o] as a hero
                            to run his race.
                Comment: E Coord. para
                    Thesis 1: E Paraphrase para
[6]   Thesis: **His going forth** [par] # from the end of
                            heaven
                Paraphrase: And his circuit # unto the end of it.
                    Thesis 2: And there is nothing **hid** [par] from his heat.
        Thesis 2: E Coord para vv. 7–11 [Strophe 2]
            Thesis 1: E Result para
[7]   Thesis: The law of Y. # perfect
                Res: **Converting** [par] the soul
            Thesis 2: E Result para
                Thesis The statutes of Y. # trustworthy
                Res: **Making wise** [par] the simple
            Thesis 3: E Result para
[8]   Thesis: The precepts of Y. # right
                Res: **Rejoicing** [par] the heart
            Thesis 4: E Result para
                Thesis: The commandments of Y. # radiant
                Res: **Enlightening** [par] the eyes
            Thesis 5: E Result para
[9]   Thesis: The fear of Y. # clean
                Res: **Standing** [par] forever.
        Thesis 6: E Result para
        Thesis: The judgments of Y # true
        Result: They altogether **are righteous** [qtl]
        Thesis n: E Coord. para
            Thesis 1: E Coord. para
[10]   Thesis 1: They # more desirable than gold,
                            than much pure gold.
                Thesis 2: They # sweeter than honey,
                            than droppings from the honey comb.
            Thesis 2 E Coord. para
[11]   Thesis 1 [gam] By them your servant *is **warned*** [qtl.pr]
                Thesis 2: And in keeping them there # great reward.

PETITION vv. 12-13 [Strophe 3] v. 13 Result para

    Thesis: H Coord. para
            Thesis 1: H Reason para
[12]   Reason [as Rh. Q]: [his] errors, who *knows* [yqtl.o]?
            Thesis: <u>Cleanse</u>-me [impv] from secret sins
        Thesis 2: H Coord para

[13]   Thesis 1: [gam] Also <u>keep back</u> [impv] your servant
            from presumptuous sins
            Thesis 2: Don't let them *dominate* [yqtl.j] me.
       Result: P Coord. para
            Thesis 1: Then ['az] I *shall be innocent/justified* [yqtl.f/m]
            Thesis 2: And I shall BE CLEARED [wqtl] from great transgression.
            [this is weighted by use of wqtl]

CLOSURE v. 14 [Strophe 4] Let them <u>be</u> [yqtl.j] acceptable, the words of my
    mouth, and the meditation of my heart in your sight, Y. my Rock and MY
    REDEEMER

NOTE 1. In v 12, weighting is not diagrammatically represented. Thus, while thesis 2
of result (v. 13) is weighted by use of wqtl, I do not see any way to diagrammatically
recognize it. The conjunction *'az*, initial in the preceding clause may possibly also
mark the two clauses as weighted. Aside from two occurrences of *gam* 'also', the only
other conjunction besides *waw* is the *'az* which is found in this verse. These two features are a kind of peak marking which underscores v. 13 as constituting the
petitionary target of the whole psalm.

The yqtl of v. 14 is of lower rank than the preceding imperatives, in that it is a
jussive/modal yqtl; I therefore make this verse closure to the whole discourse,
rather than a second petition which is correlate with the petition found in the result paragraph. I consider that imperatives outrank jussive/modal yqtl's in salience. I therefore relegate v. 14 to the periphery of the whole psalm.

NOTE 2. List of abbreviations and font encodings

qtl = perfect; qtl.pr are like the English or Greek perfect tense. Translations of qtl
    are italic bold.
yqtl = imperfect; yqtl.o are open-ended as to present/future while
    yqtl.f/m = yqtl,future/modal. Translations of yqtl are italic.
yqtl.j = jussives which often are not distinguished from the imperfects.
    Translations of jussives, as third person command forms, are underlined
    italic.
wqtl = w-consecutive with the perfect. The translation of the one occurrence of
    this form is small capitals [the last word of the psalm is also small caps,
    bold, to highlight its semantic importance].
par = participles as main verbs of clauses. Translations of par. are bold.
# = absence of verb in a verbless clause.
impv = imperatives. Translations of imperatives are underlined.
....
E = expository/lyric discourse, where verbless and participial clauses dominate.
H = hortatory discourse, where command forms, imperatives and jussives
    dominate.
P = predictive discourse, where yqtl and wqtl dominate.
....
coord = coordinate (i.e., the parts of this paragraph are coordinate with each
    other).

Res = result (i.e., this part of the paragraph encodes semantically the result of the Thesis of the paragraph).

References

Bratcher, Robert G., and William D. Rayburn. 1991. *A translator's handbook on the book of Psalms.* New York: United Bible Societies.

Cohen, Abraham. 1992. *The Psalms.* Second revised edition by Rabbi Oratz assisted by Rav. Shalom Shahar. London/Jerusalem/New York: The Soncino Press.

Delitzsch, Franz. 1971 [translated from the 1968 second German edition by Francis Bolton]. *Biblical commentary on the Psalms, Vol.1.* Grand Rapids, Mich.: Wm. B. Eerdman.

Kimchi, David. 1933. *Hebrew grammar (Milchol) systematically presented and critically annotated by William Chomsky.* Philadelphia: Dropsie College for Hebrew and Cognate Learning.

Longacre, Robert E. 1965. Some fundamental insights of Tagmemics. *Language* 41:65–76.

Longacre, Robert E. 1996. *The grammar of discourse,* second edition. New York: Plenum Press.

27

Three Newar Sentence Finals
Seen in Context

E. Austin Hale and Kedar P. Shrestha

Throughout his long and productive career, Kenneth Pike was motivated by the desire to provide field linguists with a perspective that would facilitate an understanding of the relationship between linguistic forms and their meanings. Tagmemics is a theory of *unit in context* (Pike 1982:xiv). "The meaning of a word comes from an experience of its behavioral and lexical contexts" (Pike 1982:16). "No item by itself has significance. A unit becomes relevant only in relation to a context....The observer interprets data relative to context" (Pike 1982:30). The relevance of context was a foundational principle which made it unthinkable to attempt to understand and analyze the form and meaning of sentences in isolation without reference to the larger contexts in which they occur.

This essay presents one personal experience of the value of this principle in field analysis.

Hale was initially attracted to the field of linguistics through a series of lectures that Pike gave at Norman, Oklahoma during the summer of 1956. From 1969 to 1973, Pike led a series of workshops in Kathmandu, Nepal. It was at these workshops that Hale received his apprenticeship as linguistic consultant and editor. He is deeply grateful for the stimulation and enrichment of these formative experiences and for the inspiration that Dr. Pike and his wife, Evelyn, have been to him over the last thirty years.

Three Nominal Sentence Constructions

For years Hale had unresolved questions as to the difference between Newar[1] sentences ending in -*gu du* and those ending in -*gu khə:*.[2]

(1) herama: sənnukhɛ: he   təithəka**gu**   **du**
    diamond.garland chest.LOC EMP put.CM.leave.PC.PRD **exist.ST**
    'The diamond necklace I have put into the chest.' (Knew 12.13)

(2) chitə: la   ə̃:   nəyemag:**gu**   **du**
    you.R.DAT EMP mango eat.INF.need.ST.PRD **exist.ST**

    ə̃:manapə   chu mətləb məkhu   la
    mango.tree.with   what concern NEG.be.ST EMP
    'You needed to eat a mango. Your concern was not with the mango tree.' (Name 5.5)

(3) rajkumarə̃: dhalə megu   la   chũ: məyana   tho
    prince.ABL say.PD other.ATR EMP anything NEG.do.PC this

    kətā:məhri dɛ:ku:gu   sĩtwa: jĩ: həi**gu**
    doll   make.ST.ATR wood.long.thin I.ABL bring.PC.PRD

    khə:
    be.ST
    'The prince said, "I did nothing but bring the piece of wood from which the doll was made."' (Doll 12.2)

---

[1]Newar (also known as Newari or Nepal Bhasa) is a Tibeto-Burman language spoken by some half million speakers living in Kathmandu and in market centers throughout Nepal.

[2]The following abbreviations are used as glosses in the interlinear examples: ABL = ablative (also includes instrumental and ergative); ASC = associative; ATR = attributive; CLF = animate classifier; CM = concatenation marker; DAT = dative; EMP = emphatic; FC = future conjunct; FD = future disjunct; GEN = genitive; INF = infinitive; LOC = locative; MISC = miscellaneous classifier; MNS = means; NEG = negative; NF = nonfinal (="conjunctive participle"); PC = past conjunct; PD = past disjunct; PRD = predication; PUR = purposive; SIM = simultaneous; ST = state; you.R = you, respect (honorific degree). The reference in parentheses after each free translation indicates the location in the text from which each example is taken.

(4)   gubəlẽ: gubəlẽ: thəthe   nə̃:   juiphu
      sometimes sometimes this.like also happen.INF.be.possible.ST

      dhəigu   chəgu: udahərən jəkə nheboya**gu**   **khə:**
      say.PC.ATR one.MISC example only present.PC.PRD **be.ST**
      'I'm just presenting an example of something that might happen
      like this sometime.' (Wrtr 3.5)

Native speakers presented with such sentences in isolation find it very difficult to describe the difference in meaning between sentence-final *khə:* and
du.[3] The free translations given above are ones that are natural within the
contexts from which these sentences were drawn. Both are thought to be in
some way equivalent to the English perfect, an intuition that is to some extent supported by further investigation, since both forms highlight the current relevance of the proposition in which they occur, even though the
English perfect is not always the most natural free translation. As will be
shown below, an important difference between *du* and *khə:* is in the way such
forms relate to context. Both are currently relevant to their contexts, but for
different reasons.

    To make things still more interesting, there are also sentences ending in
-*gu* which, though they have the form of nominalized sentences, they are
consistently translated by native speakers as fully finite independent sentences in English.

(5)   woya   kəlatə̃:   əʂtəmi: punhi: ekadçi: wo
      that.ATR   wife.ABL 8th.day.LOC full.moon.LOC   11th.day.LOC and

      sə̃:lhu: pəttĩ: əpəsə̃ cona: dyoyake məca chəmhə
      1st.day   on.every   fast be.NF/SIM god.ASC child one.CLF

      phoni:gu
      beg.FD.PRD
      'Fasting on every Asthami, Full Moon, Ekadasi, first day of the
      month, his wife would beg for a child from the deity.' (Knew 1.4)

    Again, the precise difference in meaning between the -*gu* sentences and
those in -*gu du* and -*gu khə:* was elusive. How do the functions of these
three forms differ?

---

[3]One could construct "minimal" pairs by replacing **du** with **khə:** and **khə:** with **du** in these
examples without changing the English translations. Where possible, however, we prefer not to use
constructed examples.

Over the years it has been possible to collect and analyze a small corpus of Newar texts.[4] Though not large enough yet to provide anything like full exemplification of Newar sentence finals, it does provide enough of the right kinds of material to give us a good start on understanding the meaning differences among these three sentence-final constructions.

Evidence from Simple Sentences

The forms *du* and *khɔ:* are sentence-final verbs in their own right. When they occur as main verbs, the meaning differences between them are transparent.

The verb *du* is existential. It occurs in existentials of location and existentials of possession. It is a stative finite verb and as such it has no conjunct forms.[5] Since it cannot be an intentional act it also has no imperative. It does have an honorific counterpart, *di* which replaces *du* when the argument for which existence is predicated is an honored person. This replacement pattern can be taken as support of the claim that the argument for which existence is predicated is the "subject"of this verb.[6]

(6)   chəgu: thasɛ: chəpwa: pwalɛ: chəmhə cəkhũ:ca **du**
      one.CLF place.LOC one.hole hole.LOC one.CLF sparrow **exist.ST**
      'In a certain hole in a certain place there was a certain sparrow.'
      (Fece 1.1)

(7)   woya   yeko   səmpəti **du**
      that-GEN much   property **exist.ST**
      'He had a great deal of wealth.' (Fece 1.2)

The verb *khɔ:* is equative and is used to assert the truth of an equation, as shown in (8).

---

[4]Our Newar text corpus currently contains approximately 200,000 words.

[5]Conjunct forms of the verb occur only with (logophoric) intentional actors. See Hale (1980) for further discussion.

[6]With intentional verbs it is the honorific status of the actor that controls honorific suppletion or the occurrence of an honorific auxiliary following the verb.

(8) sītwa: həya: kətã:məhri dɛ:ketə
     wood.long.thin bring.NF/MNS   doll   make.INF.PUR

     ma:gu   jolə̃:   ta:lakamhə   nə̃: la ji he
     need.ST.ATR ingredients prepare.PC.ATR   also EMP I EMP

     khə:
     be.ST
'By bringing the piece of wood, I was also the one who prepared the
materials needed for making the doll.' (Doll 7.26)

Sentences ending in *-gu* reflect presupposed activities. Bendix
(1974:51) claims that they are similar to relative clauses and nominals of
the same form in that they do not become assertions of the action itself
but remain presuppositions. His example:

(9) A1. wõ: yatə   'He did it.'
     B1. gu balɛ: ya:**gu**   'When did he do it?'
     A2. mhigə: ya:**gu**   'He did it yesterday.'

In (B1) the speaker presupposes (A1). In (A2) the content of (A1) need
not be reasserted.

In traditional narratives, *-gu*-final sentences often occur in recaps of
past action and in elaborations of situations which provide motivational
background for episodes or whole narratives.

(10) cihrimã:mhesya punəkhũ: məĩ:ca mikha bagələ̃: he soye məyə:
     'The stepmother couldn't stand the sight of Punəkhũ: Məĩ:ca.

     əkĩ: wõ: nhesumhyæ:yatə nəkẽ: syai**gu**
     'So she would feed her stepdaughter very little.' (Goat 1.5-6)

Evidence from Question-Answer Exchanges

Sentences in *-gu*, *-gu du*, and *-gu khə:* typically answer different questions.
Consider the following exchanges:

A -*gu* response: (request for elaboration)

(11) gənə wone tena**gu**?   'Where were you about to go?'

     yẽ: wone tena**gu**.   'I was about to go to Kathmandu.'

The question presupposes "You were about to go somewhere." It asks in essence, "Please elaborate as to where you were about to go." The response is an elaboration on the "where" of the question.

A -*gu du* response: (check on the activation of situational setting)

(12) chə khopɛ: wona**gu du** la? 'Have you ever been to Bhaktapur?'

     wona**gu du**.   'I have been.'

A natural context for such an exchange would be one in which the one who asks the question is about to tell his addressee something about Bhaktapur, and he is checking to see just how much background he needs to supply in order to bring the addressee into the picture. The question explores the addressee's familiarity with a new setting proposed by the speaker. The response assures the questioner that the situational setting referred to is familiar to him and is activated in his consciousness.

A -*gu khə* response: (request for an identificational assertion)

(13) chə khopɛ: wonagu la?   'Was it Bhaktapur that you went to?'

     ji **khopɛ**: wonagu **khə**:.   'Yes, it was Bhaktapur that I went to.'

The question presupposes "I know you went somewhere." It asks, "I think perhaps it was Bhaktapur. Am I right?" The answer makes the assertion, "Yes, you are right, I went to Bhaktapur."

Evidence from Narrative Folktales

When seeking explanations for puzzles we encounter at the lower levels of analysis it is important to consider the wider context. It was Pike who impressed Hale with the importance of this expectation. Illustrating its fruitfulness is a major concern of this essay. We present here some examples of how various manifestations of the Newar sentence-final constructions come to life when seen in their broader discourse context.

We have been working through Prem Bahadur Kansakar's little volume, *nyaṁkaṁ bākhaṃ* [Tales Told] and have found it to be a rich source of relevant examples. In the fifteen stories in this little volume we have identified some 206 examples of the *-gu*-final sentence. In the first two stories we have found thirty-two examples of *-gu khɔː*, eight examples of *-gu du*, and forty-one examples of *-gu*.

Though the stories are of comparable length, the use of the *-gu* sentence is quite variable, ranging from one story with only one example to one story with twenty-four examples. It is up to the narrator to determine how much of his material is presented as background elaboration and how much is presented as events on the main line, assertions, or settings.

Sentences ending in *-gu khɔː* assert situations as true or false

The assertive nature of a sentence becomes clear when it functions to counter a contextually evoked expectation. The following examples are from the Goat text, *Dhōːcolecā*.

(14) 1.1 In a certain country there was a girl named *Punəkhū́ː Mə̄̃ːca*.
    1.2 Her mother had already died when she was a small child.
    1.3 So her father married someone else.
    1.4 There was also a daughter by that one.
    1.5 The stepmother couldn't stand the sight of *Punəkhū́ː Mə̄̃ːca*.
    1.6 So she would feed the stepdaughter very little.
    1.7 As for her own daughter, she would feed her rice with milk, meat, and ghee. She would feed her as much good tasty food as she would ask for.
    1.8 But she would feed *Punəkhū́ː Mə̄̃ːca* only bread made with rice chaff.
    1.9 As for work, she would order her to do as much as the eye could see.
    1.10 Her father was aware of this.

By this point one might have the expectation that the father would do something to correct the situation. But what we get next is an assertion that counters that expectation.

(15) 1.11a tərə wõː chūː dhaye cha**ːgu mə**khu,...
        'But he did not dare to say anything.'

The context for example (17) runs from Goat 1.2 through 4.17. To save space we summarize in (16).

(16) *Dhõːcolecā,* **the family pet goat saw how** *Punəkhǖː Məïːca* was being underfed and overworked and took pity on her. When *Punəkhǖː Məïːca* took him to pasture he would vomit black dal and broken rice to feed her. *Punəkhǖː Məïːca* thrived on this and soon became more beautiful than her younger sister. This aroused the suspicions of the stepmother, and she decided to send the younger sister along to spy when *Punəkhǖː Məïːca* took the goat to pasture. *Punəkhǖː Məïːca* feared she wouldn't be able to eat the day she took her younger sister along, but when the younger sister had an urgent need to pass a stool, *Punəkhǖː Məïːca* and the goat took their chance. The younger sister, however, saw it and came running. *Punəkhǖː Məïːca* quickly hid the evidence but it was too late.

(17) YS: "What have you eaten, Older Sister? Give me some too, I'm hungry."

   PM: "I haven't eaten anything. If I had eaten I certainly would have given you something. How could I eat without giving anything to you?

   YS: chə̃ː nəː**gu he khəː**,...
      'You certainly have eaten!' (Goat 4.18a)

Sentences ending in -*gu du* introduce currently relevant settings

The existential *du* is often used at the beginning of a story to move the audience from the 'here-now-I-thou' of the speech situation to the 'then-there-they' of the narrative world. The goat story begins:

(18) chəguː deçɛː punəkhǖː məïːca dhəyamhə chəmhə **du**
   'In a certain country there was a girl called *Punəkhǖː Məïːca*.' (Goat 1.1)

Punəkhǖː Məïːca is the subject of the existential verb. This construction is a normal way to introduce the central figure of a folktale. Later in the story a SITUATION is introduced in (19) in a way that is parallel to the PARTICIPANT introduction in (18).

(19) punəkhū: məĩːcapini dhõːcoleca chəmhə ləhinatəː**gu du**
'*Punəkhū: Məĩːca*'s family had been keeping a goat as a pet.' (Goat 2.1)

In (19) the entire *-gu* construction could be viewed as the subject of the existential. Syntactically, then the *-gu du* construction can be seen quite naturally as the introducer of a new situation, and its function as a device for introducing new settings in the course of a folktale. As it turns out, the fact that the family keeps a goat is of pivotal significance for all that follows. A crucial new piece of setting information indeed!

Similar introductions of new situations can be found in the story, "The woman who knew the language of the birds and animals" (Knew text).

(20) After much prayer and fasting a merchant and his wife got a son. They spoiled him rotten. When he attained marriageable age they looked for a wise young woman who would be able to make something of this friendless, ill-mannered young fool. They found a young woman and the two were married. The woman knew the language of the birds and animals. One evening when the family had gone to bed and the young woman was cleaning up in the kitchen, a jackal comes and cries out:

(21) hū:kənə khusi sithɛː mənuː chəmhə sinacõː**gu du**
'Over there on the bank of the river a person **has died**.'
(Knew 5.6)

This is the first clue the reader gets of this situation, and the entire episode which follows is concerned with its various ramifications.

A parallel change of setting is triggered later in the story. The relevant context continues in (22).

(22) (The dead person had a diamond necklace on, which prevented the jackal from eating the corpse. The jackal asked the woman to remove the necklace so that he could eat.

Her husband out of curiosity got out of bed and followed her to the river where he saw her tussle the necklace with her teeth in an attempt to get it off. It looked to him like she was eating the corpse, and he decided she was a monster. With this he persuaded his parents to send her back to her parental home.

The merchant, however decided to accompany the woman home, and on the way we are confronted with the following new situation:

11.6 Early the next day a crow landed on the roof and croaked in an unbearable manner.

11.7 While the woman woke from sleep she heard what the crow said: "Over yonder in the forest there is a waterpot filled with jewels.

(23) 11.8 woya dyone dhəubəji chə bhegə: təyatə:**gu du**.
'On top of it has been placed a large clay pot filled with yogurt and beaten rice.'

(24) 11.9 wo dhəubəji kwɛ: təyabiusa rənəya ghə: chəntə dəi, ji dhəubəji nəyedəi.
'If you put the yogurt and beaten rice down [for me] the waterpot filled with jewels will be yours and I will get to eat the yogurt and beaten rice.'

This newly introduced situation ushers in the climactic turning point in the story. The merchant is set straight on the incident with the jackal and the diamond necklace, the crow gets the yogurt and beaten rice, and the merchant returns home with the woman, where he convinces his son and his wife that this remarkable woman is no monster.

Clearly in this story *-gu du* serves to introduce two pivotal situational settings in (21) and (23).

Sentences ending in *-gu* present elaborations and recaps

The suffix *-gu* is used within the noun phrase to link demonstratives, attributive clauses, and complement clauses to head nouns. Within the verb phrase it links complement clauses to complement-taking verbs. Example (25) (from the Goat text) contains a *-gu* complement clause embedded to the complement-taking noun head, *tagət* 'power'.

(25) **kəla:ya nhyone nocu he lhonegu** tagət woyake məru.
'He did **not have** the power **to lift a word in opposition to his wife**.' (Goat 1.11b)

The following (also from Goat) is a relative clause modifying the noun head *du:khəya* 'trouble'.

(26) **punəkhũ: məĩ:cayatə juyacõ:gu** phukkə du:khəya khə̃ wõ: bã:lakə thu:.
'He understood quite well all **the trouble that was happening to Punəkhũ: Məĩ:ca.**' (*Goat* 2.04)

The suffix *-gu* also nominalizes clauses and sentences, enabling them to function as subjects, objects, and adverbials within the clause or sentence. The following (also from Goat) is an example of a *-gu* clause functioning as subject of the predicate *berthə thẽ: julə* 'became meaningless'.

(27) **mwanaconegu** he nə̃: berthə thẽ: julə.
'Even just **staying alive** became meaningless.' (Goat 1.13)

Examples (25)–(27) are presented here to illustrate the linking function that *-gu* often has.

The question then comes, to what does *-gu* link a *-gu* nominal sentence? Here we have sentences which translate into English as fully finite independent sentences, yet they have the form of a noun or a dependent clause. The literature on this kind of thing is large and growing,[7] and this is still very much work in progress, so we limit ourselves here to a few examples that typify what we have found in folk narratives.

Sentences ending in -gu *may elaborate a theme*

Eventive (perfective) verb forms present a situation as a highly transient state of affairs. Nouns present a relatively stable, long-term state of affairs. The most frequent use of *-gu* nominal sentences that we have found thus far in folk narrative text has been that of elaboration. The narrator introduces a "theme" and then elaborates it with *-gu* nominal sentences. These are backgrounded sentences. They contribute to the long-term context against which long stretches of the narrative are played out. One example from Goat:

---

[7]Notably with contributions from Bendix (1974), Bickel (1999), DeLancey (1989), Malla (1985), Matisoff (1972), Noonan (1997), Hargreaves (1986), Watters (2003), Genetti (1992, 1994), Varenkamp (1999), Kölver (1977), and others.

(28) 1.2 Her mother had already died when she was a small child.
      1.3 So her father married someone else.
      1.4 There was also a daughter by that one.
      1.5 The stepmother couldn't stand the sight of **Punəkhũː Məĩːca**.

This suffices to establish a "stepmother" theme which then can be elaborated with -*gu* nominal sentences, as seen in (29).

(29) 1.6 əkĩː wõː nhesumhyæːyatə nəkẽː syai**gu**.
            'So she would feed her stepdaughter very little.'
      1.7a thəː mhyæːyatə dhaːsa ghyəː, duru la təyaː ja nəkiː**gu**
            'As for her own daughter, she would feed her milk, meat,
            and ghee with her rice.'
      1.7b saːsa bhĩːbhĩː dhako nəkiː**gu**
            'She would feed her as much good tasty food as she would
            ask for.'
      1.8   tərə punəkhũː məĩːcayatə himo jəkə walaː məhri chunaː
            nəkatəː**gu**.
            'But she would feed **Punəkhũː Məĩːca** only bread made with
            rice chaff.'
      1.9   jya dhaːsa mikhãː khə̃ːko boi**gu**.
            'As for work, she would order her to do as much as the eye
            could see.'

Sentences ending in -gu *may recapitulate prior events*

Retellings are also a prime use for -*gu* nominal sentences. The first time
something is told it is often asserted. When it is retold it is typically
treated as background. One of many good examples of this is found in the
story *kehẽː papiː gwaragwara* 'Younger Sister is a Sinner, GwaraGwara'
(Sist text).

(30) In a certain country there were two very beautiful sisters who loved
      each other very much. They were inseparable. One day the King
      proposed to marry them and so as not to separate them he married
      them both. The King loved them equally.

The younger sister thought of a way to become the King's favorite. Once when the two of them were dressing up she said, "How beautiful we look in the mirror. Let's go and see how our reflections look in the well." While they were admiring their reflections the younger sister pushed the older sister into the well, where she drowned. While the King mourned the loss, the older sister was reincarnated several times. First it was as a lotus, which only the King was able to pick. Jealous that the King was more attracted to the lotus than to her, the younger sister crumpled the lotus up and threw it away.

Next it was as a pigeon, which only the King was able to catch. Again the younger sister killed the pigeon, cooked it, and tried to feed it to the King, but since the boiling pigeon stew seemed to be saying something he would not eat it.

Finally it was as an orange which only the King was able to pick. When the King peeled the orange he found the older sister inside.

(31) 7.6   səntrasiya dune chə gɛ: latə? dhəka: jujũ nẽsẽ:li
      'After the King asked "How did you get inside the orange?"'

      juko khə̃ chəsikəthə̃: kənahələ —
      '[she] told him everything in proper sequence'

      tũ:thii kosoyaconabəlɛ: kehẽ:mhesyã: ghwana: kurkecho:**gu**.
      "I was pushed by the younger sister when I was looking into the well."

   7.7   pəleswã: juya: jənmə kəya**gu**.
      "I was reborn as a lotus."

   7.8   kehẽ:mhesyã: pəleswã: kacakucu yana: wã:choyabiu**gu**.
      "The younger sister crushed the lotus and threw it away."

   7.9   ənə̃:li bəkhũ: juya: jənmə kəya**gu**.
      "I was reborn as a pigeon."

7.10 bəkhũ:yatə syana: la dayeka: jujuyatə nəke dhəka:
      kehẽ:mhesyã: tatũ:**gu**.
      "The younger sister had hoped to kill the pigeon, boil it, and
      feed it to the King."

7.11 kehẽ: papi: gwaragwara dhəka: hala**gu**
      "I cried out 'Younger sister is a sinner *gwara gwara*'."
      jujũ: thuike məphu**gu**.
      'The king was not able to understand.'

7.12 əlɛ: jujũ: sə̃:kha yana: la phukkə sa:galɛ: wã:choku:gu.
      'Then the King became suspicious and had the meat thrown
      out on the compost heap.'

7.13 ənə̃:li səntrasima juya: jənmə kəya**gu**.
      'After that I was reborn as an orange tree.'

7.14 thəthe chə**gu**: chə**gu**: dəttəle khə̃ jujuyatə kənedhũ:ka: wõ:
      dhalə—
      'When she had told the King everything one by one like this
      she said,'
      nhyagu jənmə ka:sã: kehẽ:nə̃: jitə: məhi:.
      "in spite of each rebirth the younger sister disliked me."

7.15 jitə: syə̃ketə he jəkə soi**gu**.
      "She tried to kill me."

7.16 əki: a: hanə̃: mənu: jənmə woya**gu** **khə:**.
      "So now I have come, reborn again as a person."

It is interesting to note that this long string of *-gu* nominal sentences
which recap events that the King had observed not knowing that the older
sister was involved is terminated in (Sist 7.16) with a *-gu khə:* with which
the older sister asserts her own identity.

Conclusion

In our experience a careful look at the larger context is essential for an understanding of forms such as the Newar sentence-final *-gu du, -gu khə:,* and *-gu.* From the examples given in this essay, we see that *-gu du* is used to introduce situations in narrative which constitute pivotal settings for what follows, *-gu khə:* is used for making assertions as to the truth of a proposition, and *-gu* nominal sentences serve to elaborate themes or recap prior events. The picture is not yet complete. Preliminary studies of Newar news reports, for example, highlight other facets of meaning that these sentence finals have. As we pursue the study of Newar sentence finals in other genres, our respect for Pike's emphasis on the importance of context continues to grow.

References

Bendix, Edward H. 1974. Indo-Aryan and Tibeto-Burman contact as seen through Nepali and Newari verb tenses. *International Journal of Dravidian Linguistics* 3(1):42–59.

Bickel, Balthasar. 1999. Nominalization and focus constructions in some Kiranti languages. In Yogendra P. Yadava and Warren W. Glover (eds.), *Topics in Nepalese Linguistics,* 271–296. Kathmandu: Royal Nepal Academy.

DeLancey, Scott. 1989. Relativization and nominalization in Tibeto-Burman. Unpublished manuscript, University of Oregon.

Genetti, Carol. 1992. Semantic and grammatical categories of relative clause morphology in the languages of Nepal. *Studies in Language* 16:405–428.

Genetti, Carol. 1994. *A descriptive and historical account of the Dolakha Newari dialect.* [Monumenta Serindica No. 24] Tokyo: Institute for the Study of Languages and Cultures of Asia and Africa.

Hale, Austin. 1980. Person markers: Finite conjunct and disjunct verb forms in Newari. In R. L. Trail et al. (eds.), *Papers in South-East Asian Linguistics,* No. 7 [= Pacific Linguistics A-53] 95–106.

Hargreaves, David J. 1986. Non-embedded nominalizations in Newari: The interaction of form and function. Paper presented at the Conference on the Interaction of Form and Function, University of California, Davis.

Kansakar, Prem Bahadur. 1966 [B.S. 2023] न्यँकँ बाखँ [nyaṁkhaṁ bākhaṁ (Tales Told)]. Kathmandu: Himancal Pustak Bhawan. (Goat text, 1–11; Knew text, 12–21; Doll text, 22–34; Fece text, 40–44; Sist text, 55–60).

Kölver, Ulrike. 1977. Nominalization and lexicalization in Modern Newari. *Arbeiten des Kölner Universalien-Projekts, 30.*

Malla, Kamal P. 1985. *The Newari Language: A working outline.* [Monumenta Serindica No. 14] Tokyo: Institute for the Study of Languages and Cultures of Asia and Africa.

Matisoff, James A. 1972. Lahu nominalization, relativization, and genitivization. In John P. Kimball (ed.), *Syntax and semantics* 1:237–257. New York: Seminar Press.

Noonan, Michael, 1997. Versatile nominalizations. In Joan Bybee, John Haiman, and Sandra Thompson (eds.), *Essays on language function and language type dedicated to T. Givón,* 373–394. Amsterdam: John Benjamins.

Pike, Kenneth L. 1982. *Linguistic concepts: An introduction to tagmemics.* Lincoln: University of Nebraska Press.

Shrestha, Bhūsan Prāsād. 1981. [N.S. 1101]. कुकुल्यां कू [kukulyāṃ kū (Cock-a-doodle-doo)]. Kathmandu: Lyāmha pucaḥ / jyāḥbahāḥ. (Name text, 9–12; Wrtr text, 19–22).

Varenkamp, Bryan K. 1999. A look at *-ba* in Central Eastern Tamang. Paper presented at the 5th Himalayan Language Symposium, 15 September, 1999.

Watters, David E. 2003. *A grammar of Kham.* Cambridge: Cambridge University Press.

28

Marked Transivity in Yawa Discourse

Linda K. Jones

Introduction

This essay presents a study of transitive clauses with respect to their roles in texts in Yawa, a Papuan language spoken in Irian Jaya (Papua), Indonesia.[1] In particular, certain transitive clauses which are marked in that they vary from the unmarked SOV pattern will be examined in light of their functioning in discourse.

Forerunners to this type of analysis include Hopper (1979), Hopper and Thompson (1980), Givón (1982), and others in Hopper and Thompson, eds. (1982). But for me personally, the true forerunner of this study is Kenneth L. Pike's hefty *Language in Relation to a Unified Theory of the Structure of Human Behavior* (1967) and *Grammatical Analysis* by Pike and his wife Evelyn (1977). I cut my linguistic teeth on these Pike books (along with the 1947

I take delight in honoring Kenneth Pike, one of the great linguists of the twentieth century, by means of this linguistic essay. I suppose it is not inappropriate in a memorial volume to briefly state my connection with him. I studied and taught under him while I was a graduate student at the University of Michigan and hold the distinction of being the last Ph.D. student he supervised at UM; I defended my dissertation exactly one day before he retired from the university in May of 1977.

[1]Yawa was classified as a language isolate in the minor Geelvink Bay Phylum by Wurm (1975). However, Reesink (2000) suggests that Yawa, and probably the other Geelvink Bay Phylum languages, should be grouped together with Wurm's West Papuan Phylum languages in a single grouping, which is genetically related, albeit remotely, to the Trans-New Guinea Phylum.

edition of his *Phonemics*). *Language in Relation to a Unified Theory of the Structure of Human Behavior* advocated and modeled discourse analysis, long before it became an acceptable, much less a popular, topic of serious linguistic inquiry. For me, it was the beginning of a lifelong interest in discourse studies. *Grammatical Analysis*, a methodological approach, presented detailed analyses of clause types based on features of transitivity.

With this Pikean heritage, imagine my delight when I found, upon undertaking field studies in the Yawa language, that the language exhibited well-defined contrastive features between transitive and intransitive clauses. For example, all transitive verbs begin with *ra-* (in their citation form) and there is a special set of transitive subject pronouns—features lacking from intransitives. This paper will focus only on transitives, since I have dealt elsewhere (Jones 1986) with the intransitive verb system. Yawa has a split-intransitive system, with the subjects of one set of intransitive verbs marked "nominatively" or "subject-agreeing" and the other marked "absolutively" or "object-agreeing" (see table 1). The matter of ergativity in Yawa, which is essentially morphological only, is dealt with in Jones (1986).

After a brief overview of the unmarked transitive construction in Yawa, the present paper will examine four marked constructions as they occur in discourse. This inquiry is in the spirit of Pike's "form-meaning composite" where form and meaning are viewed as inextricably linked together, and also based on his fundamental principle of "context," where language is nested in context—both the message (text) and real-world context (extralinguistic). The four marked constructions, in order of presentation, are:

1. verb-only transitive clauses (V);
2. subject omission in independent transitive clauses (OV);
3. object fronting (left-dislocation) (OSV);
4. "reduced" transitive verbs.

Unmarked Transitives

We begin by stating the linguistic facts pertaining to unmarked transitive clauses in Yawa. The unmarked transitive clause in Yawa has strong SOV order. An example is given in (1).[2]

---

[2]Abbreviations used in the glosses and elsewhere are as follows: 1, 2, 3 '1st, 2nd, 3rd person', f 'feminine', m 'masculine', sg/Sing. 'singular', du 'dual', pl 'plural', ex/excl 'exclusive', in/incl 'inclusive', CLFT 'clefting marker', CONT 'continuative', DEP 'dependency marker', LOC 'locative', NOM 'nominalizer', NP 'marker for end of noun phrase', O 'object' OBL 'oblique', PERF 'perfective', S 'subject', SPEC 'specifier', STV 'stative/adjective', TOP 'topic marker'. For simplicity I have generally not indicated the morpheme break for the final *-e* that marks the end of a noun phrase, along with

(1)   Ingkoa   mo ansune   r-apapi.
      my.mother 3f.s clothing 3f.o-wash
      'Mother is washing clothes.'

Here the subject noun phrase is tagged by the postpositional pronoun *mo*, which is inflected for person/number/gender. Use of such a pronoun is (nearly) obligatory, even in the absence of an overt subject noun phrase, and uniquely marks the transitive subject. There is object marking in the transitive clause as well, indicated by a pronominal agreement prefix on the verb, again inflected for person/number/gender.

Table 1. Person markers in Yawa

	Subject-agreeing*			Object-agreeing			Adjective/stative		
	Sing.	Dual	Plural	Sing.	Dual	Plural	Sing.	Dual	Plural
1	syo	(ri)rimo	(in) wamo	in-	(ri)rins-	(in) wans-	(r)i-	ririN-	(in) waN-
			(ex) reamo			(ex) reans-			(ex) reaN-
2	nyo	(wu)ripo	w(e)apo	n-	is-	was-	(wi)N-	wuri-	wa-
3m	po	yo	wo	Ø-	y-	mans- ∼ m-	Ø	(-)y-	u-
3f	mo	yo	wo	r-	y-	mans- ∼ m-	N-	(-)y-	u-

*These are forms for transitive subject pronouns; final -o is dropped for subject-agreeing intransitives.

The transitive subject pronoun set differs from the object set. (See table 1.) The subject set is similar in form to one of the intransitive person-marking sets while the object set is identical to the other intransitive person-marking set, i.e., Yawa has a split-intransitive system. The person-marking for adjectives/statives is more reduced, with perhaps the most striking similarity being to the object set.[3] For ease of comparison, (2) presents a transitive clause along with the two different intransitive types ("subject-agreeing" and "object-agreeing") and the stative/adjective clause type.

---

any preceding epenthetic consonant (*g, j, y*); I have only indicated these with the abbreviation NP in cases of atypical nominals. Similarly, I have avoided abbreviations when English words would do, e.g., 'his' instead of '3mPOSS'.

[3]Choosing labels to use for the person markers has been rather vexatious, and I agree with Dixon's (1994:78) lament on the difficulty of selecting appropriate labels in a split-intransitive system. I am using "subject-agreeing" and "object-agreeing" for the two types of intransitives, but then "adjective/stative" (abbreviated STV) doesn't seem a very parallel label and, worse, it seems downright inappropriate for the "reduced" transitives which will be discussed in the section on "Reduced" Transitives. Dixon's discussion of split-intransitivity is very helpful but does not solve the labeling problem. See also Merlan (1985) and Van Valin (1990) regarding split-intransitivity.

(2) a. Arikainye wo barije r-ambaon.   (transitive)
         children 3pl.s ball   3f.o-play
         'The children are/were playing ball.'

     b. Arikainye nao w-ugoen.   (subject-agreeing intransitive)
         children   pl   3pl.s-laugh
         'The children are/were laughing.'

     c. Wanya so   r-anayanambe//mans-anayanambe. (object-
         woman this 3f.stv-happy//3pl.stv-happy   agreeing
                                                         intransitive)
         'The woman is/was happy.//The women are/were happy.'

     d. Wanya so   n-sauman akato//u-sauman. (stative/adjective)
         woman this 3f.stv-well again//3pl.stv-well
         'The woman is well again.//The women are well.'

The intransitive type of (2b) ("subject-agreeing") includes nearly all the motion verbs ('go, run, walk, move', etc.) and the directional verbs ('ascend, descend, go out, go in', etc.). This intransitive type, along with the transitive clause type, is especially prevalent in narrative and procedural texts in Yawa. They are the dominant types for telling foregrounded events (also called the "backbone" or "primary storyline"—terms from Longacre and Levinsohn (1978) and Longacre (1996). This is illustrated by the following piece of text, taken from the account of a young man who was attacked by several *anakakai* ('demon being'). The transitive verbs and the subject-agreeing intransitives just described are boldfaced in the text; it is evident that they constitute the foregrounded events.

(3) Wetiva Ø-tutar   **p-anonae-yo** namanewi, java
     so   3m.stv-shiver 3m.s-groan-DEP   all.night   until

     anakakaije **u-dija-de,**   wo   **Ø-anaun** tiva
     demon   3pl.stv-follow-come 3pl.s 3m.o-hear   so

     u-de-sea   no   tentene akari-jo naije. **U-sae**
     3pl.s-come-up LOC ladder head-DEP there 3pl.stv-stand

     yara   wo   **Ø-aera-sisa**   wo   **Ø-aen.** Wo **Ø-aen**
     and.then 3pl.s 3m.o-look-enter 3pl.s 3m.o-see 3pl.s 3m.o-see

tiva wo **Ø-aubaisy** akato, wo apa isyisye so **r-aotar**
so 3pl.s 3m.o-kill again 3pl.s his throat this 3f.o-cut

dave ti m-patimu.
very so 3f.sTv-split

'So he shivered and groaned all night until the demon beings came following; they heard him so they came up to the top of the ladder there. They stood and looked inside (and) saw him. They saw him so they gave him another fatal blow, they really cut his throat so it split open.'

Inspections of a large number of natural texts in Yawa[4] show that nearly all transitive clauses have *both* the distinctive transitive features described above: a transitive subject pronoun and object marking on the verb. This is true even in highly anaphoric contexts that might be expected to produce zero-anaphora. Many of the clauses in (3) lack overt NPs; the subjects and objects are indicated solely by use of transitive subject pronouns and person markers on the verbs. In addition, the SOV order is highly rigid, with a very high percentage of transitive clauses following this word order. Study of many texts, however, reveals that there are occasional transitive clauses which do not conform to these patterns and which speakers confirm not to be errors. It is these marked occurrences that are of special interest in this chapter.

Verb-Only Transitive Clauses

One of the most common departures from the canonical SOV pattern is stripped-down verb-only clauses (V-only). Actually V-only clauses are not altogether devoid of objects, since the usual object prefixes are still required. But these clauses *are* devoid of subjects; even the nearly-omnipresent transitive subject pronouns are lacking.

While not morphologically marked in any way as dependent clauses, V-only transitives are in fact syntactically or contextually dependent. They have been found to have a special discourse function: they link one sentence to the next via what is known as "tail-head linkage," in which the verb which ends one sentence is picked up and repeated (or sometimes paraphrased) at the very beginning of the next sentence, before the

---

[4]The discourse database consists of twenty-five conversations, more than fifty texts (procedures, sermons, descriptions, personal experiences, legends, tales, etc.), and numerous native-authored letters.

sentence moves on to state its main proposition or event. The English free translations in the examples below have been rendered to convey the effect of this type of linkage, which Foley (1986:201) says is "extremely common in Papuan languages, especially in narrative texts. Such texts are littered with dozens of examples of this usage."

Tail-head linkage in Yawa might be compared to a string of beads, where the events which form the foregrounded storyline of a narrative text are the beads, and the string on which they are strung are the linking devices. Tail-head linkage is one of these devices. (Certain time and logical connective words are another.) The links are not themselves significant other than that their presence alerts the listener (or reader) to the prominence of both of the events being linked. The tail-head linkage subtly says, "Here are two important happenings in the text, each of equal importance."

In Yawa it seems that tail-head linkage is a stylistic device, rather heavily used by some speakers and less so by others. Intransitive verbs of motion are the most common linkages, but single transitive verbs occur as well, exemplified in (4) where the linking V-only transitive clauses are boldfaced.

(4) a. Ø-seo   po   nyoe umaso r-arijati.   **R-arijati,**
        3m.stv-get.up   3m.s tree   this   3f.o-go.after 3f.o-go.after

        p-are   indamu...
        3m.s-say   in.order.to
        'He (the dog) got up (and) was going after the tree. Going after it, he was intending to...'

   b. Anakakai wo   vatane mans-aubaisy. **Mans-aubaisy,** wo...
       demon   3pl.s people 3pl.o-kill   3pl.o-kill   3pl.s
       'Demon beings fatally attack people. Attacking them, (then) they...'

Subjectless Transitives

There are a few syntactic conditions that trigger deletion of a transitive subject. They include expressions involving instrumentals and certain complement clauses, where the second subject is obligatorily deleted under conditions of identity with the first subject or with the object. This is especially common in "zoom-focusing," in which there is a (temporary) shift in focus from a discourse participant as a whole to one of his/her/its body parts. Here are some examples of "zoom-focusing." (In the following examples, the position where a transitive subject pronoun might be expected to occur if the clause were SOV is marked with parentheses. Note that 'rat' and 'dog' here are masculine, but their body parts are feminine.)

(5) a. Umba kaimire Ø-sen-a   ( ) Ø-akarije
       then rat 3m.STV-go.up.out.of-CONT   his-head

       r-arean-seo no ateme maran.
       3f.o-stick-up LOC hole outside
       'Then the rat went up and stuck his head up out of the hole.'

    b. Naije make ( ) Ø-awa r-ayak.
       then dog his-mouth 3f.o-open
       'Then the dog opened his mouth.'

Aside from syntactically-triggered deletions of subject, there are also discourse conditions that permit suppression of the subject. There is no true passive in Yawa, as is the case with most Papuan languages, but the language may achieve a passive-like function by simply omitting the subject. This includes omission of the normally obligatory transitive subject pronoun, resulting in an OV (rather than SOV) clause. In procedural-type passages (where a procedure is spelled out step by step), it is not unusual to suppress the subject, because the focus is on what is happening to the object (or undergoer/patient). An agent/actor is presumed, but his/her identity may not be important to telling the procedure.[5]

(6) Karevane ama kokome r-aritar, ama kea r-atata
    banana.tree her bark 3f.o-peel her fiber 3f.o-separate

    moen, umba r-anyinyae.
    finished then 3f.o-dry.in.sun
    'The banana tree bark is peeled and after its fibers have been separated, then it is dried in the sun.'

More interesting examples involve cases where there is suppression of subject for particular reasons. The sentences in (7) are from three different texts.

---

[5]Because there is no passive in Yawa, the transitive subject is always a prototypical agent/actor and the object is associated with the undergoer/patient. Hence, I use the terms a bit interchangeably in the discussion, depending on what makes for the clearest statement in the context.

Example (7a) is the first sentence in a text in which one of two major participants is introduced in object position. The subject is probably omitted because either it can be inferred (parents) and/or because whoever it is really
does not figure in the rest of the story. In (7b) the subject is omitted because
again it's not the agent who matters here, but the undergoer and the fact that
he got a raw deal. In (7c) the speaker suppresses the identity of the subject in
order to surprise his addressee as to who really prepared the food (the
speaker did).

(7) a. Wusyinoe-amo   arikain   tuvan m-augav-amo   u-ta   no
        long.ago-TOP   children   small 3pl.o-carry-TOP 3pl.s-go LOC

        unat-o   akokoe warae.
        mountain-DEP   huge   above
        'Long ago, small children were carried up to the huge mountain.'

     b. Uge ama atevane bo   r-augaje po   r-aisy.
        pig her tail   only 3f.o-give 3m.s 3f.o-eat
        'Only a pig's tail was given him to eat.'

     c. Anaisye mi   rati r-atayao   ti n-tuna   no   naije.
        food   SPEC CLFT 3f.o-prepare so 3f.STV-sit LOC there
        'There is food prepared, sitting there.'

Even though the clauses considered in this section lack subjects, they
are clearly transitive in their morphosyntax. They are subjectless transitive OV clauses. Their discourse behavior suggests that they are *not* so
much (S)OV types with a deleted subject as they are O(S)V types. In other
words, their discourse behavior is more suggestive of object-promotion
linked with subject-demotion, quite like passives in some languages.

Marked OSV Order

The logical *sequitur* is to consider true OSV clauses, where both subject
and object are present in the clause and in which the object has been promoted past the subject to the front of the clause. OSV order for transitive
clauses is a highly marked order in Yawa, occurring only rarely in texts.
Fronted objects may occur without any special marking, but are more
generally marked with the topicalizing particle *amo* (inflected for
person/number/gender) or the specifier phrase *i rati* (also inflected for

person/number/gender).[6] For our purposes in this paper, the three types of fronting may be lumped together and regarded as marked OSV order.[7]

As might be expected, one discourse function of OSV order is to highlight an object. Two major uses of OSV order are to introduce the topic for a section of text (example 8) or to keep track of a major participant/object in contrast with a competing one (examples 9 and 10).

One Yawa-authored letter uses the OSV construction twice, in both cases tagged with the topicalizing particle *amo*. The letter introduces itself with an OSV sentence and one of the major topics in this letter—the medicine house—is introduced as well by OSV order, seen in (8b). (In examples 8–10 the fronted object is in bold face.)

(8)　a.　**Nyovara waoe so**　m-amo syo　r-atoe　　indamu
　　　　　letter　　paper this 3f-TOP　1sg.s 3f.o-write　so.that

　　　　injaye　　nyo　r-aen...
　　　　my.father　2sg.s 3f.o-know...
　　　　'This letter, I write it so that you know...'

　　b.　**Yavaro obatije**　m-amo reamo　r-anari-ja　　moen-to.
　　　　house　medicine 3f-TOP　1excl.s　3f.o-build-CONT　finish-PERF
　　　　'The medicine house, we have finished building it.'

We have seen another sentence in (7a), which opens a text in a way not too different from the opener in (8a). In (7a) the object was not promoted in front of the subject; rather the same effect was achieved by omitting the subject altogether. The discourse purpose seems to be similar as well: in (7a) it was to introduce a major participant in the story, while in (8a) object promotion introduces the letter itself. It is worth noting that in each the topicalizing tag *amo* cooccurs as well. These discourse similarities argue for the subjectless OV clauses being regarded as variants of OSV clauses.

Besides introducing a new topic, OSV order may be used when two or more objects are contrasted. Contrastive use of OSV order is seen in one text which contrasts two kinds of traditional clay dishes which the ancestors used with the decorative Chinese porcelain dishes introduced when

---

[6]Both the topicalizing particle and the specifier phrase may be used to highlight subject as well, and even indirect object, instrument, and time phrases. In fact, their use with subject is far more frequent than with object, but these are not documented here, since the focus is on departures from unmarked word order.

[7]Probably only the unmarked fronted construction should be called "fronting." When either of the special markings is employed, the construction might be more accurately termed "left-dislocation" rather than "fronting," since the object in these cases stands outside the matrix clause—at least this is true for constructions with the specifier phrase, which are a type of cleft.

the Sultanate of Tidore extended its influence over the Yawa area. In the very first line of the text (see 9), the porcelain chinaware *(more-more)* is introduced using OSV order. In the next sentence, the clay dishes are introduced in an equational structure, and then immediately represented anaphorically by *wem* in a fronted position in the next clause. The following clause again fronts the object, the clay dishes. These sentences about the clay dishes are immediately followed by further sentences about the chinaware. We can see that the OSV order helps track the two sets of objects as they are contrasted in a back-and-forth manner in the text.

(9)   **More-more so**   arono   wusyinoe   anena   p-antukambe
       chinaware   this   when   long.ago   ancestor   3m.s-not.know

       r-ai.   Yara   arono   wusyinoe   anena   p-isyi-dai-je
       3f.o-OBL   but   when   long.ago   ancestor   3m.s-eat-OBL-NP

       m-amo   kavinoname   muno   vabiuge.   **Wem**-i
       3f-TOP   kind.of.clay.dish   and   kind.of.clay.dish   3f-SPEC

       rati   anena   po   r-ave...   **Ananugo   kavinonam**
       CLFT   ancestor   3m.s   3f.o-use   things   kind.of.clay.dish

       muno vabiuge   so   wem-amo   anena   po   veano
       and   kind.of.clay.dish   this   3f-TOP   ancestor   3m.s   use

       apa   ana   daisy-e.
       his   NOM   eat-NP
'The chinaware dishes, long ago our ancestor didn't know about them. Rather long ago, our ancestor's dishes were different kinds of clay dishes. Those were what the ancestor used....The various clay dishes, our ancestor used (them) for his eating.'

OSV order may also be used to keep references straight in passages with several characters. For example, in a fanciful account involving the misadventures of a boy and his dog (major characters) in their encounters with a host of other creatures (minor characters), the boy and dog at times are doing different things, and since both are referred to in Yawa with masculine pronouns, they are kept track of frequently by use of either the topicalizer *amo* or the identifier *i rati*, usually in SOV order but every now and then by OSV order, as in the following.

(10) **Makeye** p-i   rati   anyivan   mo   Ø-awatan.
     dog   3m-SPEC   CLFT   bee   3f.s   3m.o-chase
     'It was the dog that the bees chased.'

In (10), a major character, the dog, is acted upon by a minor one, the bees. OSV order here accomplishes what a passive might do in another language—it promotes the object while demoting the subject.

"Reduced" Transitives

Yawa has a special type of construction that seems morphologically intermediate between a transitive and an intransitive, but it is neither a traditional "middle" construction nor a "medial" verb.[8] I will call these "reduced" transitives, for lack of better terminology. The stems are always obviously derived from transitive stems, but the object agreement prefixes seem to be missing and there are no free transitive subject pronouns in these clauses; instead, subject marking occurs as a bound prefix to the verb, using exactly the same set of person prefixes as stative/adjectives (see table 1). Compare the subject marking and verb stems of the following.

(11) a. Reamo r-aisy.   (regular transitive)
       1excl.s   3f.o-eat
       'We eat/ate it.'

    b. Ream-isyisy.   (regular subject-agreeing intransitive)
       1excl.s-eat
       'We are/were eating.'

    c. Rean-daisy.   (reduced transitive)
       1excl.STV-eat
       'We eat/ate it.'

---

[8]Nor do "antipassive" and "detransitivization" seem to be appropriate terminology. The person marking of these verbs is at first suggestive of antipassives. However, according to Dixon (1994:146) true antipassives demote the object to a peripheral non-core function (e.g., instrument) or omit it altogether. While it is the case that objects may optionally be omitted from this type of clause in Yawa, when the object *is* present, it is not necessarily marked as a peripheral. The term "detransitivization" also seems inappropriate since both subject and object are still present in some form.

d. Rean-gwanen.   (stative/adjective)
   1excl.stv-sick
   'We are/were sick.'

There is an important constraint on reduced transitives: the object must be one that normally takes third person feminine verb marking (and is usually, but not always, inanimate). This significantly restricts the use of reduced transitives and helps explain their relative infrequency in texts. The semantic constraint limiting the objects to mainly inanimates also sheds light on the phonological shape of their stems. The obvious phonological connection between *r-* initially in regular transitive stems, and *d-* initially in reduced transitive stems is easily explained, since *r-* is the object agreement marker for third person feminine, which includes most inanimates.[9]

In this brief survey, we will only consider reduced transitives which occur as independent verbs, although some of the generalizations drawn here apply to other occurrences as well.[10] We will examine three that seem to have specific discourse patterns: association with fronted objects (left-dislocation); cataphoric usage (right-dislocation); and verb serialization. What is in common is that in each case the reduced transitive signals that the object is not in its customary place between the subject and verb and is to be found dislocated either to the right or to the left (within or outside the same clause).

Object fronting, the topic of discussion in the previous section, is commonly associated with reduced transitives. When we say an object is fronted or left-dislocated, we mean that it has been moved in front of the subject in the clause, inverting the normal SOV order to OSV. When OSV order occurs, a reduced transitive may optionally be employed to signal that the object has been dislocated from its normal place between the subject and verb. In the first line of (8), object displacement is not signalled in the verb, but it could be by substituting *idatoe* 'I write (it)' for *syo ratoe.*

Examples of reduced transitives are given in (12). In (12a) the fronted object is marked as topic by *mamo,* while in (12b) the fronted object is unmarked. In both, that there has been object displacement is signalled by use of reduced transitive verbs (boldface in examples 12–19).

---

[9]This raises the possibility for the reduced transitives that there is both subject and object marking, which is not permitted for any other kind of verb. The reduced transitive verb schemata would be: subject marker – object marker (*d-*) – verb stem.

[10]Significant omissions include these constructions as part of nominal structures such as relative clauses and nominalizations, as well as occurrences in dependent verb constructions such as following a causative.

(12) a. Tomateye kamije so   m-amo **n-daugav-o**   are
       tomato   seed   this 3f-TOP 2sg.STV-get-DEP who

     Ø-arijat-a?
     3m.O-with-CONT
     'These tomato seeds, who did you get them from?'

   b. Reama sambaya so   **wan-dausen**   no   Amisye win.
       our   prayer this 1incl.STV-raise.up LOC God   you
       'This our prayer, we raise it up to you, O God.'

A frequent use of reduced transitives is in 'what' questions, in which the question word (*animaisye* 'what') is queried of an object. Since fronting is required in this type of interrogative, the object is necessarily dislocated, a fact which is commonly registered in the verb by use of a reduced transitive rather than a regular transitive, as in (13).

(13) Animaisye m-i   rati **wan-daisy**?
     what   3f-SPEC CLFT 1incl.STV-eat
     'What are we going to eat?'

The preceding discussion focused on left-dislocation of objects. Right-dislocation may occur as well, but is much rarer. Since the natural position for object is to the right of subject already, right-dislocation does not affect object prominence vis à vis subject prominence like left-dislocation does. Right-dislocation in Yawa seems less a matter of shaping discourse focus than it is a matter of lexical verb choice coupled with syntax: complement clauses of certain types are right-dislocated, possibly because they are too "heavy" to appear in normal object position. The ones which are right-dislocated are the object complements of certain speech and perception verbs, especially *daniv* 'hear/perceive', *daura* 'say', *daen* 'know'. For example, in (8a), *nyo raen* 'you know' is a regular transitive which the speaker could have replaced by a reduced transitive *ndaen* to signal that the object of 'know', which is the complement clause, is right-dislocated. The text examples in (14) are instances where the speaker *did* use a reduced transitive to cataphorically point ahead to the displaced object.

(14) a. Anena **Ø-dani**   no rani-jo varet katitir-o   akokoe.
     ancestor 3m.stv-hear loc side-dep west thunder-dep huge
     'Our ancestor heard to the west a great clap of thunder.'

   b. **N-daura**   m-ai   u-jani   nora.
      2sg.stv-speak 3pl.o-obl 3pl.stv-afraid not
      'Tell them not to be afraid.'

Right-dislocation that is not associated with one of the speech or perception verbs is truly rare in Yawa, probably because Yawa permits rather
"heavy" NPs in both subject and object position. Right-dislocation is employed by some languages to move heavy NPs to the end of the sentence, but
I have found it in Yawa only rarely. One of these rare examples is given in
(15), consisting of a long list of foods, which has been right-dislocated with a
reduced transitive verb used to signal the dislocation.

(15) Ream-amo **rean-dai**   no Urosibori   anane, kareye,
      1excl-top 1exclstv-eat loc place.name sago   banana

      kambore,   ansyawae, timburu, rainsyone,   injeye,
      kind.of.taro papaya   cassava   sweet.potato kind.of.taro

      apisyi.
      squash
      'As for us, we eat in Rosbori sago, banana, taro, papaya, cassava,
      sweet potato, another kind of taro, and squash.'

The final usage of reduced transitive that we will examine is in series
with one or more other clauses. Several verbs in a series is a common feature of Papuan languages, where they are often associated with switch
reference. Yawa does not have switch reference, nor does it display the in-
dependent/dependent clause combinations often associated with switch
reference. But in narrative passages, it is common to quicken the pace by
reducing the number of NPs, using person marking on the verb along with
the transitive subject pronouns to carry the participant reference. An extract from one text nicely shows this:

(16) Arikainye umawe Ø-seo   p-ansanan Ø-de   po
      child   that   3m.stv-get.up 3m.s-run   3m.stv-come 3m.s

      Ø-aneme r-aijar   umba Ø-gwain   p-are...
      his-hand 3f.o-take   then   3m.stv-call 3m.s-say
      'That child got up and ran, he came and took his (another person's)
      hand, then he called out, saying...'

In (16) there are six verbs (*seo, pansanan, de, raijar, gwain,* and *pare*) but
only two NPs *(arikainye umawe* and *aneme).* In this example, the flow of
events is mainly carried by intransitive verbs; only one of the six *(raijar)* is
transitive. Example (3) has a similarly high ratio of verbs to NPs, but with
more of the verbs being transitive.

Reduced transitives are ideally suited to achieving quick text flow, because not only can NPs be omitted but even the nearly-omnipresent transitive subject pronouns can be eliminated. Example (17) has an instance
of both a reduced transitive and a subjectless clause, both of which
quicken the pace in this exciting account of headhunting by the ancestors.

(17) Po   vatan inta Ø-aubaisy, Ø-akarije r-aotar **n-daugav-o**
      3m.s person one   3m.o-kill   his-head   3f-cut   3f.stv-take-DEP

      arove.
      captive
      'He killed a man, chopped off his head (and) took it captive.'

Reduced transitives are not limited, however, to simply quickening the
pace of a text. Another frequent use is anaphoric—to signal that the referent for the missing object is found elsewhere (generally within the preceding few clauses). Example (18) consists of three clauses, the first a full
transitive clause, the second consisting of just a reduced transitive verb
indaug 'we two carried it', and the third also consisting of a single
verb—the intransitive verb *inajiv* 'we two went home'. There is no overt
object in the second clause; it is only implied by the reduced transitive
verb, which is understood as pointing anaphorically back to the preceding
clause for the referent to the object.

(18) Irimo ateye   r-apintai   ingkuja ambayane r-ai,
      1du.s remainder 3f.o-fill.bag bag   sago.bag   3f.o-OBL

    in-daug,   in-ajiv.
    1du.STV-carry 1du.STV-go.home
    'We two put the remainder in a sago bag, we carried it (and) went
    home.'

Sometimes the referent for the object implied by a reduced transitive
verb is not found in the immediately preceding clauses, but is understood from a topic of the discourse. The sentences in (19) are taken
from a text about how sago, the staple food of coastal Yawas, is processed and used. Since sago is the topic of the entire text, it is the most
accessible referent and it is the referent for the two clauses below
which lack overt object NPs. The first is a regular transitive clause with
the usual cross-referencing to the object in a regular transitive verb,
while the last clause employs a reduced transitive verb. The fact that
these occur one after the other in the same text, both lacking an overt
object NP, yet both referring to the same object, indicates some degree
of style optionality.

(19) Umba syo   r-augave   uisy-o   no   repon. Umba sya   wanya
      then   1sgs 3fo-carry lead-DEP LOC front   then   my   woman

    sya arikainye m-awain-de,   ream-anunugambe,
    my   children   3plo-call-come 1excl.s-gather.together

    rean-daisy.
    1excl.STV-eat
    'Then I carry it out to the front (of the house). Then my wife and
    children are called to come, we gather, we eat it.'

Conclusions

Most discourse features seem to be optional choices, not obligatory. For
example, tail-head linkage in Yawa is an optional stylistic device, one of
various devices that a speaker uses to tie a text into a coherent whole.
Similarly, in studying reduced transitives, one is struck by their
optionality: a regular transitive is nearly always possible where a reduced
transitive was chosen. But the optionality does not mean the choice is

unexplainable. Why does Yawa have a reduced transitive verb structure in addition to the regular transitive and intransitive verbs? The answer is found in its usefulness in signalling object dislocation.

It is easier to predict that a particular feature *could* occur (that it is possible because of the discourse environment) than that it *must* occur. We look for the explanation of its occurrence not in rules that are tightly predictive but in pragmatic and discourse functions. The occasional occurrence of OSV transitives in a nearly rigid SOV language begs an explanation. We found one explanation of OSV order in Yawa in its discourse function of highlighting an object, while another function is to contrast one discourse participant or object with one that rivals it in prominence. We also examined transitive clauses where the subject is totally missing (OV clauses). OV clauses are associated with "zoom-focusing" in which there is a temporary focus not on a participant in the text but on one of his/her/its body parts. OV clauses may also be used when there are discourse reasons to suppress the subject (e.g., for anonymity or mystery or to spell out object-focused procedures). Hence, for the four marked departures from the unmarked transitive type in Yawa that we examined in this paper, we were able to establish discourse functions.

References

Dixon, R. M. W. 1994. *Ergativity*. Cambridge Studies in Linguistics, 69. Cambridge: Cambridge University Press.

Foley, William A. 1986. *The Papuan languages of New Guinea*. Cambridge Language Surveys. Cambridge: Cambridge University Press.

Givón, Talmy. 1982. Transitivity, topicality, and the Ute impersonal passive. In Paul J. Hopper and Sandra A. Thompson (eds.), *Studies in transitivity*, 143—160. Syntax and Semantics, 15. New York: Academic Press.

Hopper, Paul J. 1979. Aspect and foregrounding in discourse. In Talmy Givón (ed.), *Discourse and syntax*, 213–241. Syntax and Semantics, 12. New York: Academic Press.

Hopper, Paul J., and Sandra A. Thompson. 1980. Transitivity in grammar and discourse. *Language* 56:251–299.

Hopper, Paul J., and Sandra A. Thompson, eds. 1982. *Studies in transitivity*. Syntax and Semantics 15. New York: Academic Press.

Jones, Linda K. 1986. The question of ergativity in Yawa, a Papuan language. *Australian Journal of Linguistics* 6:37–55.

Longacre, Robert E. 1996. *The grammar of discourse,* second edition. Topics in Language and Linguistics. New York: Plenum Press.

Longacre, Robert E., and Stephen H. Levinsohn. 1978. Field analysis of discourse. In Wolfgang U. Dressler (ed.), *Current trends in textlinguistics*, 103–122. Berlin: Walter de Gruyter.

Merlan, Francesca. 1985. Split intransitivity: Functional oppositions in intransitive inflection. In Johanna Nichols and Anthony C. Woodbury (eds.), *Grammar inside and outside the clause,* 324–362. New York and Cambridge: Cambridge University Press.

Pike, Kenneth L. 1947. *Phonemics: A technique for reducing languages to writing.* University of Michigan Publications in Linguistics 3. Ann Arbor: University of Michigan Press.

Pike, Kenneth L. [1954, 1955, 1960] 1967. *Language in relation to a unified theory of the structure of human behavior,* second edition. The Hague: Mouton.

Pike, Kenneth L., and Evelyn G. Pike. 1977 [revised edition 1982]. *Grammatical analysis.* Dallas: Summer Institute of Linguistics and the University of Texas, Arlington.

Reesink, Ger. 2000. West Papuan: roots and development. Paper presented at the Conference on Papuan Pasts, Canberra.

Van Valin, Robert D., Jr. 1990. Semantic parameters of split intransitivity. *Language* 66:221–260.

Wurm, Stephen A., ed. 1975. *New Guinea area languages and language study,* vol. 1. Pacific Linguistics C38. Canberra: Australian National University.

29

Eventivity in Kouya

Ivan Lowe, Edwin Arthur, and Philip Saunders

Introduction

This paper is an account of how we arrived at a gloss for the low-tone suffix -à in Kouya, a Kru language of the Central Ivory Coast with SOV word order. All data are taken from text.[1]

The low-tone suffix -à occurs on main verbs, on the verb 'be', on verbal auxiliaries, on modals, on the negator, and on certain adverbs. In none of these occurrences is it obligatory. Our goal was to provide one uniform, consistent gloss for this morpheme which would describe its function in

[1]The data include some forty texts of various genres, mostly narrative. We are indebted to the Kouya people for their patient teaching, and for their insights into the language. Many of the examples are identified by text and sentence and clause number, e.g., the first line of (9) is marked S06 022 to identify the text and location in the text.

The consonant phonemes of Kouya are:

	labial	alveolar	palatal	velar	labio-velar
stops: voiceless	p	t	c	k	kp
voiced	b	d	j	g	gb
implosive	ɓ				
fricatives: voiceless	f	s			
voiced	v	z		ɣ	
nasals	m	n	ɲ	ŋ	
laterals		l			
semi-vowels	w		y		

all of the contexts in which it occurs and thereby provide an important generalization. In Pikean terms we wanted to define -*à* as a form-meaning composite.

We begin by citing previous hypotheses for the gloss of the suffix -*à*. Then we present data that represent all the usages of the suffix -*à*, except the verb 'be'. Following this we present data illustrating the usages of the -*à* suffix on the verb 'be'. Finally, we present an integrated hypothesis which covers all the data.

Previous Suggestions for the Gloss of -à

Earlier glosses for the suffix -*à* are 'imperfective aspect', 'declarative', and 'realis'. In some other Kru languages (Marchese 1986), perfective aspect is not overtly marked, and imperfective is marked with something like -*à* on the verb. However, in Kouya both perfective and imperfective verbs take the suffix -*à*, as shown in examples (1) to (5). Because of this, and other problems, we have from the outset glossed the suffix -*à* as '-EVN' (for 'eventivity').[2] This gloss anticipates the eventual analysis.

The vowel phonemes of Kouya are:

+ATR		−ATR	
i	u	ɩ	ʋ
e	o	ɛ	ɔ
	a		

There are four contrastive tones in Kouya: high is represented with acute accent, thus *á*; mid high is unmarked, thus *a*; mid low is marked with dieresis, thus *ä*; and low is marked with grave accent, thus *à*.

The practical orthography for Kouya uses the same symbols as above except for the voiced bilabial implosive *ɓ*, the voiced velar fricative *ɣ*, and *ɲ*. which are written as *bh*, *gh*, and *ny*, respectively. Tones in the practical orthography are written as indicated in the preceding paragraph except that high tone on the first syllable of a word is represented by apostrophe before the word and low tone on the first syllable of a word is represented by minus sign before the word.

[2]Abbreviations used in this paper are:

ATR	advanced tongue root	PC	pro complement
AUX	auxiliary	PL	plural
COND	conditional	PNH	plural nonhuman
DEM	demonstrative	POSS	possessive
EMPH	emphatic	Q	interrogative marker
EQV	equative	REL	relativizer
EVN	eventivity	SG	singular
IMP	imperfective	SGH	singular human
LOC	locative	SGNH	singular nonhuman
NEG	negative	SUB	subordinator
NOM	nominalizer	TOP	topic

(1) bòbò   yäbhlò   à   yĩà
    bòbö   yäbhlò   à   yĩ-à
    pig   one   1PL   see-EVN
    'We saw a pig.' (perfective aspect)

(2) nɩmɛ   ɩ̀n   bhúà   zlïmë   wʊ́
    nɩmɛ   ɩ̀n   bhú-à   zlïmë   wʊ́
    meat   2SG   take-EVN   before   PC
    'You took the meat before.' (perfective aspect)

(3) ĩn   nà   yìà   nanʊ̀
    ĩn   ɩ̀n.IMP   yĩ.IMP-à   nanʊ̀
    and   2SG.IMP   see.IMP-EVN   yours
    'You will see your (meat).' (imperfective aspect)

(4) däadɛ́   na   wölüà   ɔ
    däadɛ́   ɩ̀n.imp   wölü-à   ɔ
    right.here   1SG.IMP   wait.for-EVN   3SG
    'Right here I will wait for him.' (imperfective aspect)

(5) mnï   nà   yɔ̀   we   mnïà   yì?
    mnï   nà   yɔ̀   we   mnï-à   yì
    go   2SG.IMP   with   it   go-EVN   Q
    'Are you going away with it?' (imperfective aspect)

The imperfective aspect forms (examples 3, 4, 5) have the following surface properties:
- One of the mid tones on the final syllable of the verb stem (many verbs are monosyllabic).
- Special imperfective pronoun forms *na* '1SG.IMP', *nà* '2SG.IMP'. Other persons have no special imperfective pronoun forms.

Another early suggestion was that *-à* means 'declarative'. It is indeed true that *-à* never occurs on imperative verbs (6), nor on main verbs in negations (7) and (8). However, there are many declarative sentences that do not have *-à* on the verb, as in the first two lines of example (9). The two verbs *gbli* 'bow' and *gbä* 'speak' in clauses 022 and 023 of (9) are not marked with *-à*, even though the illocutionary force is declarative. Note also that (5) has interrogative illocutionary force, yet its main verb still carries the suffix *-à*.

(6) tide   na   bhʊ   yí
     tídè   ɪn.poss   bhʊ   yí
     leave   1SG.POSS   leg   alone
     'Let go my leg.' (no suffix on verb)

(7) àmìa   gwézi   ní   we   ŋwɛɛ́   nynï
     àmìa   gwézi   ní   we   ŋwɛɛ́   nynï
     our   money   NEG   3SGNH.POSS   value   arrive
     'Our money did not amount to that sum.' (no suffix on verb)

(8) ɔ   ní   weè   kwláä   bhú
     ɔ   ní   weè   kwláä   bhú
     3SGH   NEG   that   tortoise   find
     'He never found that tortoise.' (no suffix on verb)

(9) *S06 022*
     zùgbà   na   gbli   Làgɔ̃   ylà   wlú   la,
     zùgbà   ɪn.IMP   gbli   Làgɔ̃   ylà   wlú   la
     at.that.time   1SG.IMP   bow   God   to   head   PC
     'And during that time I (at various times) bowed my head to God,

     S06 023
     na   gbä   ɔ   ylà   na   nökplàgbʊ̈,
     ɪn.IMP   gbä   ɔ   ylà   ɪn.POSS   nökplä-gbʊ
     1SG.IMP   speak   3SG   to   1SG.POSS   stomach-affair
     and told Him (at various times) what was in my heart.'

     S06 024
     We   zʊ̀   nyä   ɪn   yíà   na   jizaméë.
     we.POSS   zʊ̀   nya   ɪn   yí-à   ɪn.POSS   jizaméë
     3PNH.POSS   year   in   1SG   PASS-EVN   1SG.POSS   exam
     'That year, I passed my exam.'

Yet another early hypothesis was that -à means 'realis'. Now, it is true that irrealis situations like negatives and imperatives do not take -à on the verb. But repeated actions, as exemplified in (9), are realis and they do not take -à.

The Eventivity Hypothesis

Our hypothesis is that the suffix -à marks a situation as eventive if that situation is close enough to the prototype event. Otherwise the situation is not marked. For working purposes we define a PROTOTYPE EVENT as a situation which:

1. is a one-time, realized, punctilear event,
2. has deictic anchorage to time and place in the actual world (or in a world defined by a conditional clause), and
3. has an agentive (human) subject (who therefore has intentionality and control over the realization of the event).

The following contrasts are implicit in the above definition:

MORE EVENTIVE	LESS EVENTIVE
one-time	multiple action, or habitual
punctilear	durative, or stative
deictically anchored	no deictic anchorage
agentive (with intentionality and control)	non-agentive (no intentionality or no control)
realized	not realized, e.g., negative, subjunctive, imperative

The criteria of one-time, realized, punctilear, agentive event correspond closely to the Hopper-Thompson (1980) characterization of a highly transitive event. The criterion of deictic anchorage corresponds to Halliday's (1997:75) idea of finiteness.[3] Thus our definition of eventivity is a conflation of the concepts of high transitivity and finiteness.

Contrasts of constructions with and without -à

In this section we contrast constructions with and without -à, except those with the verb 'be'.

---

[3] Halliday (1997:75) states:

> The Finite element, as its name implies, has the function of making the proposition finite. That is to say, it circumscribes it; it brings the proposition down to earth, so that it is something that can be argued about. A good way to make something arguable is to give it a point of reference in the here and now; and this is what Finite does. It relates the proposition to its context in the speech event. This can be done in one of two ways. One is by reference to the time of speaking; the other is by reference to the judgement of the speaker.

Main event line verbs in narrative

The verbs in clauses 022 and 023 in (9) are not marked with -_à_ and they report actions on the main event line that were repeated several times. But the verb in 024 is marked with -_à_ and it reports a one-time event, passing an exam.

Imperfective verbs without -à and with -à

Repeated or habitual actions of an individual or of a small group are not marked with -_à_. In (10) the speaker is talking about a place where his mother and some other women from the village used to draw water. Only a small number of people are involved and it is a habitual noncurrent action. The verb _pli_ 'draw water' is _not_ marked with -_à_.

(10)	ín	bhà	wa	pli		bhaà	nyú
	ín	bhà	wa	plí		bhaà	nyú
	and	there	3PL	draw.water		before	water

'And there they used to draw water formerly.'

Again, example (11) describes a habitual action by a restricted group of people. The verb _mnì_ 'go' is unmarked.

(11)	sá	à	mnï	bhaà	kpaá	gùà
	sá	à	mnï	bha	kpaá	gʋ̀-ä
	thus	1PL	go	before	field	sleep-NOM

'Like that, we formerly used to go to the fields to sleep.'

Contrast these with customary, contemporary actions practiced by the whole community (from a procedural text on how to make _foutou_, a valued food item).

(12)	_S07 003_			
	gwï	nà	dïà	bhà
	gwï	ìn.IMP	dï-à	bhà
	palm.seed	2SG.IMP	put-EVN	there

'You put palm seed there (everyone does).'

S07 004

ìn	kà	bhà	gwi	ylí	dï	nï,
ìn	kà	bhà	gwi	ylí	dï	nï
2SG	when	there	palm.seed	fire	put	SUB

'When you put palm seed there on the fire,'

S07 005

ìn	kà	wʊ́	sɔ̀
ìn	kà	wʊ́	sɔ̀
2SG	when	PC	get.up

'when you get up,'

S07 006

nyʊ́gbàá	nà	mnïà;
nyʊ́gbàá	ìn.imp	mnï-à
water.source	2SG.IMP	go-EVN

'you go to the water source (everyone does).'

Clauses 004 and 005 in (12) are subordinate adverbial clauses and their verbs are not suffixed. But the verbs in the main clauses (003 and 006) are both marked with -*à*. Note also that the pronouns in these clauses are *nà,* the imperfective form of the pronoun; thus, these main clauses have imperfective verbs with -*à* marking. (Compare examples 3, 4, 5.)

What this passage describes is a procedure, a *customary action by the whole community,* and something which is *done today,* rather than something that used to be done. This makes it much more of a real event than a former habitual action that used to be done by a restricted group of individuals. Every time these days that a woman makes *foutou* anywhere in the Kouya community this is what she does.

The auxiliary yi 'come'

The auxiliary *yi* 'come' can occur either with or without the suffix -*à*, and the differences are very marked. The auxiliary *yi* with -*à* (*yi-à*) can occur with an unsuffixed main verb (MV), or with a main verb suffixed with mid tone -*ä*. In the former it marks a foregrounded, realized, punctilear event, as in examples (13) and (14); in the latter it indicates a certain prediction, as in (15).

The construction *yi-à* + MV is the true perfective in Kouya. It describes a foregrounded, realized, punctilear event. These are the verbs that make up the main event line in a narrative text, and they always mark punctilear, one-time events. A verb so marked is never found in any procedural text.

(13) ín   ɔ   yïà   bhà   mí   ylï,
     ín   ɔ   yï-à   bhà   mí   ylï
     and   3SG   come-EVN   there   1SG.DO   find
     'and she (my mother) found me there.'

(14) ìn   yïà   na   kɔ   nyú   lʊ   vitèlì,
     ìn   yï-à   na   kɔ   nyú   lʊ   vitèlì
     1SG   come-EVN   1SG.POSS   hook   water   into   throw
     'I threw my hook into the water,'

The construction *yi-à* + (MV + *-ä*) describes a highly certain prediction. The mid-tone suffix *-ä* which is found on the main verb in example
(15) is glossed LOC (for location). This is because the basic meaning of this
suffix is indeed 'a physical location'. However, in this example, the meaning of the suffix has been grammaticalized to mean something like 'purpose'. This example is from the viper and falcon folktale. The falcon has
done a dirty trick on the viper, and the viper is lying in wait for the falcon
at the river bank, knowing that for sure the falcon will sooner or later
come to the river for a drink.

(15) dënïdɛ́   ɔ   yïà   yïä
     dënïdɛ́   ɔ   yï-à   yï-ä
     right.here   3SG   come-EVN   come-LOC
     'Right here he is going to come (sure prediction).'

The *yi* + MV construction without a suffix on the main verb or the auxiliary is used to describe a situation that is perhaps in another world, with
no deictic anchorage. It is very vague with regard to the likelihood of its
realization. There are not many examples of this in text, but they do occur, as in (16). This is taken from a text about traditional methods of healing. If a man gets sick, people will ask a diviner what to sacrifice, and
whatever he says they will sacrifice. One possible option would be a
chicken, but no one is sure that it will be.

(16) we   yï   nynu   zɛ̀
     we   yï   nynu   zɛ̀
     3SGNH   come   chicken   become
     'It may become a chicken (it may be a chicken that the diviner
     says).'

Negations

Although negated clauses never take the suffix -*à* on their main verbs, there are some negated clauses where the negator *ní* itself carries -*à*. In examples (7) and (8) the negator *ní* is without -*à*. They are the usual straightforward negations where there is no strong expectation that the positive counterpart would be realized. Contrast these with examples (17) and (18), where a strong expectation of the positive is indeed present (and so the negation is a contraexpectation in some sense).

(17) ɔ   nía   vàfú   mnï

      ɔ   ní-à   vàfú   mnï

      3SG NEG-EVN Vavoua go

      'He did not go to Vavoua (or he will not go to Vavoua) (though it was expected that he would).'

(18) *S03 067*   *S03 068*

      We ka glɔ̀   nìmä   weeè túlü   wa   nɛɛ

      we ka glɔ̀   nìmä   weeè túlü   wa   nɛɛ

      3SG AUX domestic animals all   tell   3PL say

      'He (the cat) told all the domestic animals,   they say...'

      S03 069

      wa nía   we   ŋwnu.

      wa ní-à   we   ŋwnu

      3PL NEG-EVN it   accept

      'They (would) not accept it (although they should have).'

In the preceding context of (18), an important rich man has fallen very sick and the cat has asked all the domestic animals to go and find medicine for the sick man. This was a reasonable request and, in fact, the narrator is at pains to point out that this was normal procedure if someone important ever got sick. But on this occasion none of the domestic animals would help. Their refusal was socially a contraexpectation—it was an antisocial, reprehensible attitude, which is marked by -*à* on the negator *ní*. In other words, their acceptance was socially expected, but, in fact, they did not accept.

The ká *modal*

The *ká* modal can be used either with or without the suffix *-à*. Without the suffix the modal expresses prediction, lack of control, purpose, subjunctive (including an imperative).

Kouya predictions express what could be translated as 'future' in English, as in (19). But, in fact, it should be noted that Kouya has no affixes which could be consistently glossed as 'tense markers'.

(19) ín   à   ká   we   zɔä   yï
     ín   à   ká   we   zɔ-ä   yï
     and 1PL AUX 3SGNH buy-LOC come
     'And we will come and buy it.'

(20) zùgbà ɔ   mì ylígbedá ɔ   yú ká bhá plíῒì gbú
     zùgbà ɔ   mì ylígbe-dá ɔ   yú ká bhá plíῒì gbú
     then 3SG be stand-LOC 3SG.POSS child AUX there pass reason
     'She (the mother) was standing there because her son was about to pass by.'

Note that there is no *-à* on the *ká* auxiliary in (20). This is because the topical participant (here referred to by ɔ '3SG') has no control over the action of passing by of her grown-up son. In examples (21) and (22) *ká* expresses the idea of purpose or 'in order to'. Again, there is no *-à*. Example (22) is from a text about traditional healing; the medicine man would cut a chicken's throat as part of the healing ceremony.

(21) we   mï yïdá   we   ká   nyú   má
     we   mï yï-dá   we   ká   nyú   má
     3SGNH   be come-LOC 3SGNH AUX water drink
     'It was coming in order to drink water.'

(22) wa   dɪà   we   bῒí   ɔ   ŋní   nya
     wa   dɪ-à   we.POSS bῒí   ɔ   ŋní   nya
     3PL   cut-EVN 3SGNH.POSS throat 3SG.POSS name in
     'They cut its throat in his (the patient's) name

     nὺ   wa   ká   ɔ   züzü   wú   zizè
     nὺ   wa   ká   ɔ   züzü   wú   zizè
     that 3PL   AUX 3SGH.POSS   spirit PC   hide
     so that they might hide his spirit.'

Examples (23) and (24) are subjunctive (including a weak imperative)—again, without -*à*.

(23) Jejìtàpè ká lubhò kádʊ nʊ
    Jejìtàpè ká lubhò kádʊ nʊ
    Lord AUX work great do
    'Lord do a great work.' (part of a prayer, but beyond the speaker's
    control)

(24) à yɔ̀ we ká zɔ́ɔ́ mnï
    à yɔ̀ we ká zɔ́ɔ́ mnï
    1PL with it AUX village go
    'Let us go to the village with it.'

The *ká* modal with -*à*, i.e., the *ká-à* combination, marks:
- an event as being under the control of the participant under
  attention,
- or strong intentionality of the participant under attention,
- or high probability of realization of the marked event.

Example (25) comes from a text in which a farmer describes his daily
work routine. His work plan is completely under his control, and there is
one hundred percent probability that his intentions will be realized.
Hence the suffix -*à* on the *ká* modal.

(25) wè ìn káà le nʊ tià
    wè ìn ká-à le nʊ tià
    REL 1SG AUX-EVN PC do first
    'What I will do first is...'

In example (26), a warrior sets out to go to war. He controls his own actions and his intentionality is high. Hence the -*à* suffix on the *ká* modal.
Contrast (26) with example (20), where the mother is watching him going. The mother has no control over the son's actions—especially as seen
in the son's world!—and hence the *ká* modal in (20) is unmarked.

(26) sá ylí yabhlò nya ɔ káà tʊ gʊä mnï
    sá yĺ yabhlò nya ɔ ká-à tʊ gʊ-ä mnï
    thus day one with 3SG AUX-EVN war fight-LOC go
    'In this way one day he set out to go to war.' (and he did, in fact, go)

The suffix -à on certain adverbs

The suffix -à is also found on a restricted subclass of adverbs. Those found to date are: sá 'thus, in this way', bha 'before', and yá 'again'. When marked, these adverbs always occur in a clause that conveys the idea of a *specific realization in the real world of an established pattern.* The more common manner adverbs like 'quickly' are never found carrying the suffix -à. We illustrate the use of -à with the adverbs sá and yá.

Example (27) is from a text given by a young boy telling about his adventures one day down by the side of the Kogbayizale River. The data sample here splits up logically into two chunks. The first chunk, consisting of clauses 006 to 008, establishes a pattern. Clauses 006 and 007 tell us that formerly people would customarily sleep in the field in order to do their work (in the field). The next clause 008 then tells us that we (that is to say the boy who is the narrator and his group) adopted the same custom. Thus, these three clauses all speak of patterns of customary events. For this reason, the suffix -à is *not* found on any verb in any of these three clauses.

But then in 009, -à occurs on the verb *mnɪ* 'go'. This shows us that the event reported in clause 009 is a specific event on a specific occasion; not just a pattern of events. Finally in clause 010 we get the same event as 009 reported again but this time the report has -à on the adverb sá 'thus' rather than on the verb itself. This tells us that clause 010 is *not* reporting a new event, but rather that the event already reported in 009 is *a specific event after the pattern of customary events* reported in the previous clauses (006 to 008).

(27)   *S04 006*

ɔ	kà	bhaä	mì	ɔ	mï	ɔ	kpaá	yɔ̀,
ɔ	kà	bha	mï	ɔ	mï	ɔ	kpaá	yɔ̀
3SG	COND	before	be	3SG	be	3SG.POSS	field	beside

'If there was someone formerly, he would be beside his field

   S04 007

ɔ	kɔ́ɔ	lübhö	nö.
ɔ	ká-ɔ	lübhö	nö
3SG	AUX-3SG.POSS	work	do

in order to do his work.'

S04 008

Sá	à	mnï	bhaà	kpaá	gʋ̀à,
sá	à	mnï	bha	kpaá	gʋ̀-ä
thus	1PL	go	formerly	field	sleep-NOM

'In this way, we formerly used to go to the fields to sleep.'

S04 009

bhὲdë	Kɔ̀gbàyízälë	gʋ̀	bhà	à	mnïà	kpaá	gʋ̀à.
bhὲdë	Kɔ̀gbàyízälë	gʋ̀	bhà	à	mnï-à	kpaá	gʋ̀-ä
near	river.name	on	there	1PL	go-EVN	field	sleep-NOM

'There beside the Kogbayizale River we went (on a specific occasion) to sleep.'

S04 010

à	mnï	sáà	bhà	kpaá	gʋ̀à,
à	mnï	sá-à	bhà	kpaá	gʋ̀-ä
1PL	go	thus-EVN	there	field	sleep-NOM

'We went to sleep there in the field on that occasion after the former pattern.'

The adverb *yá* 'as well' can also take the suffix *-à*, and when it does so, the clause in which it occurs will describe a specific event which is "once again an instance of a general established pattern." So the suffix *-à* once more brings us back to a specific concrete event.

(28) *A08 029*

Sä	àmìà	nʋ̈à	dä	àmìa	nʋ
sä	àmïä	nʋ̈-à	dä	àmìa	nʋ̀
thus	we	do-EVN	place	us	for

'This is the way we do in our situation

A08 030

wɛɦ	weeè	túù	gbʋnyúü	à	nʋ̈à	lɛ	sä	à	gbäà	we
wɛɦ	weeè	túù	gbʋnyúü	à	nʋ̈-à	lɛ	sä	à	gbä-à	we
word	all	all	sins	1PL	do-EVN	PC	thus	1PL	say-EVN	them

all our words, the wrong things that we do, like this we confess them

A08 031

sá	wamìà	gbä	yáà
sá	wamìà	gbä	yá-à
thus	3PL.EMPH	say	as.well-EVN

they confess like that once as well.'

The data in (28) is from a text about how the Kouya cure sick people. In the third clause (031) the form *yá-à* 'as.well-EVN' occurs. Clauses 029 and 030 make up the immediately preceding context. In these two clauses, every verb has mid tone and every verb has the suffix *-à*. Thus these verbs are imperfectives and describe a habitual situation, i.e., what people habitually do when confronted with sickness. Note also that all the subjects in these two clauses are 1PL, i.e., everyone does it this way.

Then 031 tells what they do with the sick man. Note that the subject of 031 has changed to 3PL. Note also that in 031 the *-à* is not on the verb but on the adverb *yá* 'as well'. This means that what is described in 031 is yet another specific realization of the general habitual pattern of behaviour already established in the preceding clauses.

Summary

The following table contrasts the absence versus the presence of *-à* in the different constructions described thus far.

Construction	Without -à	With -à
main event line verb	realized repetitive actions, imperatives	realized punctilear actions
imperfective verbs	former habitual actions of an individual or small group	contemporary habitual actions of all or most individuals in a community
negator	no contraexpectation	with contraexpectation, the positive was expected
ká modal	prediction (including 'future'), purpose, subjunctive, unmarked for control	with control, strong intentionality near certainty of realization
certain adverbs	established pattern	specific event in pattern of customary events

The Verb *mɪ* 'be' and the Suffix -à

We now consider the possible suffixation of -à on the verb *mɪ* 'be'. Here we are no longer in the realm of events, but rather in the realm of participants and props. For these the concept of eventivity does not fit. What replaces it?

The verb *mɪ* in Kouya can carry either mid or low tone on its stem. The low tone stem can never be suffixed with -à. However, a mid tone stem sometimes occurs suffixed with the -à, and sometimes it does not.

Mid tone *mɪ* marked with -à: foregrounding in the actual world

When the verb *mɪ* 'be' with a mid tone stem is marked with the -à, the construction always relates to a *foregrounded* entity in the actual world of the story.

One of the most frequent functions of the mid tone marked verb *mï-à* is to PRESENT an important entity, by which we mean that the narrator has singled out an entity for special attention because that entity is important at this point in the story. The term "entity" here is used as a cover term for a participant, prop, location, situation, or abstract entity. The entities that are presented by use of the *mï-à* can be either foregrounded new information or foregrounded given information. (Foregrounded often means "current.") Often the entity that is presented becomes topical in the immediately ensuing discourse and persists as a topic for quite a long stretch of discourse after it has been presented. At other times an entity can be important even though it does not prove to be topically persistent.

In (29) Sibhia Zayi is presented in the first clause with a suffixed verb be *mï-à*. This participant is very current, important, and foregrounded. In fact he is topical in the last two clauses of (29), and he persists for the next twenty-two clauses of the story.

(29) *Bassam 046*
   ɔɔ̀ Síbhia Zàyi mï-à, mɔ wà tʊgʊnyɔ kádʊ, mɔ wa sɔ-à.
   DEM Sibhia Zayi be-EVN TOP EQV warrior great TOP 3PL fear-EVN
   'There was Sibhia Zayi. He_{TOP} was the great warrior, him_{TOP} they feared.'

In the first clause of (30b), the leader is introduced using the marked verb 'be' *mï-à*. This leader becomes topical in the second clause, 'he fell', which reports an extremely important event in the history of the Kouya people; his fall led directly to the war's being stopped.

The verb *mï-à* can be used to present important situations as well as important participants, props, and places. The marked verb 'be' in the first clause of (30d), presents the situation of the two leaders both dropping dead at the same time (see 30c). This situation is very important because it determined the future of the two villages concerned and, hence, the eventivity marked verb *mï-à* 'be-EVN'.

(30) a. *Bassam 073*

tɔʊn	wà	wa	yɔ̀	wa	mï-à	tʊ	gʊ̀-da
then	REL	3PL	with	3PL	be-EVN	war	wage-LOC

'then those with whom they were fighting'

b. *Bassam 074*

màa	tʊ	yúgaɭ̀nyɔ	mï-à	mɔ	bhli-à
3PL.POSS	war	leader	be-EVN	TOP	fall-EVN

'there was their leader, he_{TOP} fell'

c. *Bassam 075*

'ɪn	wadɛ	'sɔ	yi-à	tɭ̀	da	yabhlo.
and	3PL.same	two	AUX-EVN	die	LOC	one

'and the two of them died there in the same place'

d. *Bassam 076*

wè	mï-à	da	nì,	mʊ	ylígbeli-à	wee	tʊ.
REL	be-EVN	LOC	SUB	TOP	stop-EVN	that	war

'What happened then, that_{TOP} stopped that war, i.e., it was this that stopped the war.'

Example (31a) presents the important location of Gbeklee. In fact this part of the story is about the various different locations, that is, the locations are topical and important.

(31) a. *Bassam 082*

Gbɛklɛɛ	mï-à,	we	ní	da	yabhlo	tʊ̀.
Gbeklee	be-EVN	3SG	NEG	LOC	one	stay

'There is Gbeklee. It hasn't stayed in one place.'

b. *Bassam 083*

wè	ka	gbʊ-à	'gbe	sɔ́,	gbé	ta,	mʊ	zɛ̀-à
REL	have	reason-EVN	village	two	village	three	TOP	become-EVN

Gbɛklɛɛ.
Gbeklee
'The reason for this is that, two villages, three villages, they be-
came Gbeklee.'

An important entity (usually a participant) in an important state or important ongoing process is marked by *mì-à* plus a main verb with the suffix *-dá*. Example (32) describes an important entity taking part in an
important ongoing process. The nature of the ongoing process is expressed by the main verb. The rich man is an important participant in the
story and his sickness is an important process. In fact, the rich man's sickness is one of the main themes of the story.

(32) *S03 001*

ŋnìmnìnyɔ	mïà	gü	nüdá.
ŋnìmnìnyɔ	mï-à	gu	nü-dá
rich.man	be-EVN	sickness	do-LOC

'A rich man is sick.'

Mid-tone *mɩ* not marked with *-à*

When the mid-tone verb *mì* 'be' is *not* suffixed with the eventivity suffix *-à*,
the absence of the suffix marks a backgrounded situation in the story. In
example (33a) there is a current but backgrounded entity (here, the cat)
in a locational setting. Note that (33a) has a mid tone *mï* verb with no
eventivity marker since the information that "the cat is in the house" is
backgrounded. The next clause (33b), on the other hand, has a perfective
verb form with the 'come' auxiliary and is thus foregrounded. In fact,
clause (33b) is the first action clause in a sequence which leads rapidly to
the climax of the story.

(33) a. *A01 021*

we	mï mɔ̀	weè	bùdü	zɔ
we	mï mɔ̀	weè	bùdü	zɔ
3SGNH	be there	3NH.DEM	house	in

'He [the cat] was in the house,'

b. *A01 022*

ín	gwì	mʊ̈ʊ̈	yïà	yï
ín	gwì	mʊ̈ʊ̈	yï-à	yï
and	dog	TOP	AUX-EVN	come

'and the dog, he_{TOP} came.'

In describing a process or state of affairs that is simultaneous with the current situation but not foregrounded, the verb *mï* 'be' (with mid tone) is an auxiliary, and the main verb takes the progressive (glossed 'LOC') suffix *-dá*. The whole string describes a backgrounded ongoing process, simultaneous with the current foregrounded process. The adverb *zùgbà* 'meanwhile' is nearly always found in these examples, as in (34c), and it marks both simultaneity and backgroundedness.

(34) a. *A12 024*

sabɔ	ká	bɛä	mnï
sabɔ	ká	bɛ-ä	mnï
night	AUX	approach-LOC	go

'Night was going to approach.'

b. *A12 025*

lʊɛ	ka	sïä
lʊɛ	ka	sïä
elephant	AUX	tire

'Elephant became tired.'

c. *A12 026*

zùgbà	nynu	mï	lïdá
zùgbà	nynu	mï	lï-dá
meanwhile	chicken	be	eat-LOC

'Meanwhile, chicken was eating.'

For nonexistent situations or those outside the actual world of the story, the verb *mì* has a low stem tone, and is never marked with the suffix *-à*. Example (35) shows negation; a nonexistent situation, and there is no *-à* EVN. (Note that at times there are marked situations where the negation marker itself is foregrounded.)

(35) *S01 020*

    ŋwnɔ́   nì   mì.
    ŋwnɔ́   nì   mï
    wife   NEG   be
    'there was no wife (to be seen)'

No lexical verb of any sort within the scope of a *kà* conditional ever takes the eventivity suffix *-à*, so, as we would expect, the verb 'be' in that environment does not do so either. The verb 'be' in (36) carries a low stem tone and there is no *-à* suffix since the clause does not report a realized, punctilear event, but rather a conjecture on the part of the participant under attention.

(36) *S01 024*

    Aà,   we   kà sá   mì nï,
    á   we   kà sá   mì nï
    ah   3SGNH if thus be SUB
    'Well, if that's how it is,'

Summary

The spatio-temporal verb 'be' in Kouya can appear in three different surface forms, *mï+-à, mï, mì*. These three forms correspond to the three discourse-oriented function types: foregrounding *(mï+-à)*, backgrounding *(mï)*, and the world outside the actual story *(mì)*. In all the usages of *mï+-à*, the marked verb presents an important entity (often a participant) that is immediately involved in the current events on the main event line of the story. Bearing this in mind, and recalling the discussion of main event line verbs with and without *-à*, we can explore the functional links between the usages of *-à* on action verbs, and the usages of the same suffix *-à* on *mï-* 'be'.

With event verbs: *-à* marks prototype events on the main event line.
With 'be' verb: *-à* marks a verb that presents important entities which
    will immediately be involved in events on the main event line.

Prototype events are one-time realized events, and it is the events that are either prototypes or near prototypes that take the eventivity suffix on the action verbs or on the 'come' auxiliary. Now by its very semantic nature, the verb *mï-* 'be' cannot itself directly describe a current event. However, the marked *(mï+ -à)* 'be + EVN' verb presents an important entity that is an indispensable component in the next current event.

By contrast, when the verb *mï-* 'be' is not suffixed with *-à,* its functions are backgrounding, and not related to current events. And similarly, when an action verb is not suffixed with *-à,* the verb never describes a realized, punctilear action, but rather is an imperative, or describes repetitive actions, backgrounded habitual actions, etc.

Hence, we are justified in glossing *-à* as 'eventivity', whether it is suffixed onto the verb 'be' or onto an action verb, the perfective auxiliary *yi* 'come', certain adverbs, or the negator. In the process of defining *-à* as a single form-meaning composite, we were obliged to have recourse to discourse considerations such as the nature of prototype events and finiteness.

Although we have not explicitly referred to any of his tagmemic postulates, the influence of Kenneth L. Pike can be seen at every step of the analysis presented in this paper. First, there is the concept of a unit as having three modes: contrast, variation, and distribution. With special reference to contrast, Pike insisted that you do not know what a unit is until you know what it is not. Following this, the analysis of the low tone suffix has not only thoroughly examined the environments where the suffix is used, but also the environments where it is not used. Then, respecting Pike's insistence on the importance of the social dimension of language, we have examined the use of the low tone suffix in clauses describing a wide variety of linguistic and social environments. Finally, the idea of the eventivity suffix as marking a prototypical event follows Pike's wave perspective on language. A wave-like unit has a peak and fuzzy boundaries. Had we tried to gloss the low tone morpheme in terms of necessary and sufficient conditions, we would have regarded it as a simple particle with sharp, clear-cut boundaries. Such an analysis did not lead to consistent results. We have tried to show that its unity as a form-meaning composite becomes clear when it is considered in contexts "beyond the sentence."

References

Halliday, M. A. K. 1997. *Introduction to Functional Grammar,* second edition. London: Arnold.

Hopper, Paul R., and Sandra A. Thompson. 1980. Transitivity in grammar and discourse. *Language* 56:251–299.

Kotey, P.F.A., and H. Der-Houssikian, eds. 1977. *Language and linguistic problems in Africa.* Columbia, S.C.: Hornbeam.

Marchese, Lynnell. 1986. *Tense/aspect and the development of auxiliaries in Kru languages.* Summer Institute of Linguistics Publications in Linguistics 78. Dallas: Summer Institute of Linguistics and the University of Texas at Arlington.

Part VII

Particle, Wave, and Field

"A static (particle) view leads to performer focus on units, objects, things, events as wholes; a dynamic (wave) view leads to performer focus on change, progress, decay...and a relational (field) view leads to performer focus on relations between elements..."
(Pike 1976:93)

30

Verb Serialization and Clause Union

T. Givón

Introduction

This chapter deals with an intersection of issues, chief among which is the claim that typological diversity is often less than trivial. If one is to be realistic about universals of grammar, one must first confront cross-language variation—head on.

By the same token, while diversity cannot be responsibly argued away as trivial or superficial, neither can it be allowed to deflect us from our search for language universals. The challenge we face as empirical investigators is thus to discover the balance between universality and its limits. Our challenge as theorists is then to explain this balance.

The existence of serial-verb constructions and their peculiar areal and genetic distribution strike at the very heart of the universality of grammatical structure and the interaction between grammar and cognition. My own initiation into this topic occurred rather haphazardly, when as a young and incredibly innocent editor of a new journal, *Studies in African Linguistics*, I solicited as lead article for issue 1.1 a paper by Herb Stahlke (1970), then a graduate student at UCLA. Only long afterwards did I stumble upon two earlier works of whose existence I should have known, since taken together they suggested a much wider geographic distribution of the phenomenon: Jim Matisoff's (1969) paper on serial verbs in Lahu, and

Ken Pike's (1966) prescient, if informal, foray into verb serialization in Africa.

From the prevailing Aristotelian perspective of the early 1970s, verb serialization seemed a quaint piece of syntactic exotica, summarized in the naive definition:

(1) "Verb serialization is the use of two or more verbs in a *single clause* that codes a *simple single event.*"

That definition (1) is problematic is fairly obvious, since in the absence of a language-independent cognitive definition of "simple single event," verb serialization boils down to a mundane observation about cross-language translation equivalents:

(2) "Verb serialization is revealed in the cross-language variation whereby what some languages code as a simple *clause* with a *single verb*, other languages code as a *complex clause* with multiple verbs."

But clearly, the definition of "simple clause" in (2) depends crucially on the implicitly Aristotelian assumption of "one predicate, one proposition." That is:

(3) "A *single* clause has a *single verb* at its syntactic core."

It is indeed the Aristotelian assumption (3) that animated the early debate on the formal status of verb serialization, launched by Stahlke's paper (1970). Implicitly or explicitly, all the participants in that debate subscribed to assumption (3) (see Hyman 1971; Awobuluyi 1972, 1973; Bamgbose 1972; Schachter 1974, *inter alia*). We all accepted then the status of serial-verb constructions as *multi-clausal* structures. Given the Chomskyan *zeitgeist*, we only argued about whether they were conjoined or subordinate.

Only somewhat later, within a more diachronically-inclined corner of the field, was the multi-clause interpretation of verb serialization challenged, and then only implicitly, with the realization that many serial verbs became—at least semantically but on occasion also syntactically—*grammaticalized* over time (Li and Thompson 1973a, 1973b; Givón 1975).

The perspective from which this paper is written owes much, in an obvious way, to the insights of diachrony. As I have suggested in an earlier study (Givón 1991b), serial clauses, falling under a single intonation contour, are indeed single syntactic clauses coding single cognitive events. However, they are the product of the diachronic process of *clause union*, via which two or more erstwhile simpler clauses coding simple events have been condensed into a single clause coding a complex single event. What I try to show here is that the condensation of simple into complex-event clauses can follow two major diachronic-typological routes, thus giving rise to two types of clause union.

Multi-Verb Single-Event Clauses

Preamble

Multi-verb clauses are found in a number of distinct syntactic configurations, chief among them are *embedding* and *serial*. While the two may code similar semantic-cognitive patterns, the syntactic means via which they code them are often starkly different, representing two distinct diachronic routes to clause-union, respectively *complementation* and *clause-chaining*.

Embedding languages: Complementation and grammaticalized auxiliaries

One of the areas that best illustrates the differences between embedding and serializing languages is the diachronic evolution of tense-aspect-modality (TAM) morphemes, usually via an intermediate stage of auxiliary verbs. The very same lexical verbs can give rise to the very same TAM markers through either an embedding or a serializing grammaticalization strategy. But the syntactic end results are often rather different. In embedding languages, the most common syntactic configuration through which grammaticalized auxiliaries arise is that of modality-verb-plus-complement, as in:

(4)

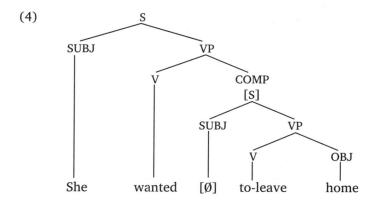

She   wanted   [Ø]   to-leave   home

In this process, the finite main verb becomes re-analyzed semantically as a tense-aspect-modal marker, while the less finite complement verb surfaces as the semantic main verb. English auxiliaries, such as 'have', 'be', and the various modals have all arisen through this route, which is widely attested elsewhere. (See Givón 1971, 1973; 1984 ch. 8; Steele 1978; Heine 1993; *inter alia.*)

Auxiliaries arising through the embedded complement configuration tend to have strong morphosyntactic dependency ("control") relations with their complements, a fact that is well documented in the distribution of finite morphology across the complex clause. Finite morphology in embedding languages invariably gravitates to the main verb, while the complement tends to be less finite or nonfinite. This pattern merely transfers itself to the auxiliary-cum-main-verb configuration that emerges as the first step toward grammaticalization. As an illustration of the point-of-origin of this process, consider the following examples from Swahili. The attraction of most finite morphology to the main verb is obvious if still incomplete, in that the object of the complement verb in (5b) does not "climb" to the modality verb.

(5)   a.   *'Want' as a simple verb*:
           Juma a-li-ki-taka
           Juma 3s-PAST-it-want
           'Juma wanted it'

      b.   *'Want' as a modality verb*:
           Juma a-li-taka   ku-**ki**-soma
           Juma 3s-PAST-want   INF-**it**-read
           'Juma wanted to read it'

However, the full "upward migration" of an object pronoun is possible in other languages, such as Spanish:

(6) a. *'Want' as a simple verb*:
         Juan lo-quería
         John it-wanted/3s
         'John wanted it'

     b. *'Want' as a modality verb*:
         Juan **lo**-quería   leer
         John **it**-wanted/3s   INF/read
         'John wanted to read it'

The verb 'want' can also pattern as a manipulation verb, with the equi-NP condition then being between the object/manipulee of the main verb and the subject of the complement. Such a construction then follows the syntactic pattern of a manipulation verb such as 'tell' or 'force'.

(7)

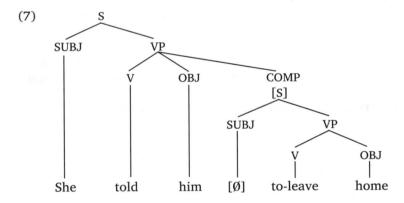

Further, in some Bantu languages, the verb 'want' can take either a more finite *subjunctive* complement or a less-finite *infinitive* complement, the latter with a "raised" object/manipulee. Thus consider the following from Bemba:

(8) a. *Subjunctive complement*:
         Joni a-à-fwaaya   ukuti Malia   a-ly-e
         John 3s-PAST-want   SUB   Mary   3s-come-SUBJUN
         'John wished that Mary would come'

    b. *Infinitive complement with raising*:
        Joni a-à-**mu**-fwaaya   uku-lya
        John 3s-PAST-**3s**/OBJ-want   INF-come
        'John wanted her to come'

This variation in Bemba parallels a similar variation in bona fide manipulation verbs, as in:

(9) a. *Subjunctive complement*:
        Joni   a-à-koonkomeshya   ukuti   Malia   a-is-e
        John   3s-PAST-order   SUB   Mary   3s-come-SUBJUN
        'John ordered Mary to come'

    b. *Infinitive complement with raising*:
        Joni   a-à-**mu**-koonkomeshya   uku-isa
        John   3s-PAST-**3s**/OBJ-force   INF-come
        'John forced her to come'

In (8b) and (9b), a full array of finite morphology—subject pronoun, object pronoun, tense-aspect—is clustered on the main verb, leaving the complement bare, i.e., nonfinite.

    Modality verbs that take verbal complements are the most common source for tense-aspect-modal morphology in language. The grammaticalization of modality verbs into TAM markers seldom stops at the auxiliary verb stage, but eventually proceeds toward full cliticization. To illustrate this in a VO language, consider the Swahili pattern:

(10) Grammaticalized verbs as TAM markers in Swahili:
    a. *'Want' as modality verb*:
        ni-na-taka   ku-ki-soma
        I-PRES-want   INF-it read
        'I want to read it'

    b. *'Want' as future*:
        ni-**ta**-ki-soma   (-ta < -taka 'want')
        I-FUT-it-read
        'I will read it'

    c. *'Finish' as modality verb*:
      ni-li-maliza   ku-ki-soma
      I-PAST-finish   INF-it-read
      'I finished reading it'

    d. *'Finish' as PERF*:
      ni-**me**-ki-soma (-me- < *mele = 'finish/PERF')
      I-PERF-it-read
      'I have read it'/'I finished reading it'

    e. *'Have' as PRESENT*:[1]
      ni-**na**-ki-soma (-na- < -na 'have/be with')
      I-PROG-it-read
      'I'm reading it'

    f. *'Be' as PAST*:[2]
      ni-**li**-ki-soma   (-li = 'be')
      I-PAST-it-read
      'I read it'

In embedding OV languages, a mirror image of the same configuration is seen, both in complementation and in the grammaticalization of erstwhile main verbs as TAM markers. As an illustration, consider the pattern of complementation and TAM cliticization in Ute:[3]

(11) a. *Loose modality verb complementation*:
      'uwas-'ura sari-ci   tṵka-**vaa-ci̱** 'asti-**kya**
      he-TOP   dog-OBJ eat-IRR-NOM want-ANT
      'He wanted to eat (the) dog'

    b. *Bound modality verb complementation*:
      'uwas'ura sari-ci   tṵka-maku-**kwa**
      he-TOP   dog-OBJ eat-finish-ANT
      'He finished eating the dog'

---

[1]The development of *-na* 'have/be with' as a present tense probably followed an indirect route, most likely first through *perfect* or *immediate past*.

[2]The development of *-li* as past tense probably followed an indirect route, most likely with several intermediate steps, with the first one most likely being the *progressive past*.

[3]See Givón (1980). The language currently has pragmatically controlled ("free") word order, but most grammaticalization still conforms to the earlier SOV pattern. Subject and object pronominal agreement is optional in Ute. When used, anaphoric pronouns appear as second position clitics.

c. *Anterior aspect*:

'uwas-'ura sari-ci   tuka-**qa**   (-ka/-ga = 'have'/'be')
he-TOP   dog-OBJ   eat-ANT
'He ate (the) dog'

d. *Habitual aspect*:

'uwas-'ura sari-tuka-**miy**   (-miya = 'go')
he-TOP   dog-eat-HAB
'He eats dogs'

e. *Future tense*:

'uwas-'ura sari-ci   tuka-**vaa-ni** (-va/pa = *'go', 'pass')
he-TOP   dog-OBJ   eat-IRR-FUT
'He will eat (the) dog'

The less finite form of the complement of the nonimplicative 'want' (11a) still involves an irrealis morpheme, in addition to a nominalizer. The implicative 'finish' (11b) is colexicalized with its complement, essentially at the same suffixal position as a TAM suffix. The intermediate diachronic stage of finite auxiliary verbs is not currently attested in Ute.

The fact that in an embedding language auxiliaries tend to retain all finite morphology, and the fact that they eventually cliticize as TAM markers on the main verb, are both predictable from the hierarchic embedding structure of the VPs involved in this grammaticalization route. Within such a structure, the complement clause is reduced and often nominalized, and it is tightly embedded into the main-clause VP structure. Such embedding does not necessarily confer on the complement clause the status of grammatical object. But in some sense complement clauses in embedding languages are analogous to objects. The tightly packed, hierarchic embedded structure of the contributory VP, with its "controlled" complement verb, is a syntactic template that virtually guarantees eventual clause union and full cliticization of the erstwhile main verb. The migration of finite affixes—particularly pronouns referring to the logical object of the complement verb—to the auxiliary verb is but an intermediate step on the way to full clause union, whereby all arguments now bear grammatical relations to a single verb.[4]

---

[4]The subject most commonly remains unexpressed on the embedded verb due to coreference with the main-clause subject or object.

Complementation and grammaticalized auxiliaries in serializing languages

Compare first the progressive and perfect auxiliary constructions in the highly-embedding English with their equivalents in the serializing Tok Pisin, an equally rigid SVO language (see Givón 1991b).

(12) a. *Serial 'be' as* PROG:

    em   brukim   **i-stap**

    he   break   PRED-**be**

    '...he keeps breaking (it)...'

    b. *Serial 'finish' as* COMPL:

    em   wokim   paya   **pinis**

    she   make   fire   **finish**

    '...she gets the fire started...'

When erstwhile serial verbs are reduced to TAM markers in such serial-verb clauses, nothing of the hierarchic, asymmetrical distribution of finite morphology seems to occur. In part, this may be due to the fact that in transitive clauses, object NPs intersperse between serial and main verbs and prevent "upward migration" of the bound morphology to a single verbal locus in the clause. As illustrative of such "dispersed" TAM morphology, consider the following examples from Supyire (Senufu, Voltaic). Senufu languages are historically SOV languages, but with postverbal indirect objects and verbal complements. Both postverbal constituents are derived historically from chained clauses (Carlson 1991). The rigid word order of Senufu languages is thus:

(13) a. S (DO) V IO

    b. S (DO) V COMP

The oldest TAM-marking auxiliaries are most commonly postsubject ("second position") clitics. So that the simple-clause order tends to be:

(14)   S-AUX (DO) V IO/COMP

Further, all TAM markers and/or auxiliaries are probably derived historically from erstwhile serial verbs. Consider first the serial complementation pattern in Supyire (Carlson 1990):[5]

---

[5]The very same word order situation (S-AUX-DO-V-IO) is found in Guaymí, a Chibchan language from Panama. The evidence for serial-verb origin of the auxiliaries there is just as

(15) a. *Simple-clause order:*

  nǫgǫ-lyengi **si**   ngkuu   kan   u-a
  man-old.DEF AUX chicken give   him-to
  'My father gave him a chicken'

  b. *Serial complement of modality verb:*

  mu   **aha' bu**   lyi   à   kwǫ...
  you COND MOD   eat   PERF finish
  '...when you finally finish eating...'
  (Lit.: '...when you finally eat and finish...')

  c. *Serial complement of manipulation verb:*

  mii à   u   karima à   pa
  I   PERF him   force   PERF come
  'I forced him to come'
  (Lit.: 'I forced him and he came')

  d. *Serial complement of manipulation verb:*

  u   à   pi   yyera   à   pa
  she PERF them call   PERF come
  'She called them to come'
  (Lit.: 'She called them so that they come')

In addition to the old subject-clitic TAM markers, many of the more recently grammaticalized TAMs in Supyire are still, rather transparently, serial verbs, often with the overt *consecutive* prefix *N-*. Some of the more
common serial auxiliaries are:

(16) a. *Inchoative aspect with 'come':*

  kà   u   pyệnge   **si**   **m-pa**   m-pee
  CONJ his   family   AUX CONJ-**come** CONJ-big
  '...and his family became big...'
  (Lit.: 'and his family *came* and was big')

  b. *Irrealis modal (* 'go'?):*

  mii **sí**   u   lwǫ   **n**-kan   yii-a
  I   FUT him   take   CONJ-give you-to
  'I'll take him to you'
  (Lit.: 'I *go* take him and give (him) to you')

---

compelling (Young and Givón 1990). Serial TAM constructions are also found in SVO languages,
such as Tok Pisin, Krio, and Kwa languages.

c. *The pluperfect aspect with 'be':*
fyinga **à** **pyi** **à** mpii jo
python PERF **be** PERF those swallow
'...the python had swallowed those...'
(Lit.: '...the python *was* and swallowed those...')

d. *The repetitive aspect with 'release':*
ka **asi** **laha** **à** wu
CONJ HAB **let.go** PERF pour
'...and it would again pour out...'
(Lit.: '...and it would *release* and pour...')

e. *The repetitive aspect with 'return':*
maa ' **nura** **à** u kuntunu-sẹẹge wwu
conj ASP **return** PERF her monkey-skin take
'...and she again took her monkey-skin...'
(Lit.: '...and she *returned* and took her monkey-skin...')

f. *The quickly aspect with 'hurry':*
mu **ú** **fyala** **à** pa
you MOD **hurry** PERF come
'You must come quickly'
(Lit.: 'You must hurry and come')

g. *Progressive copular auxiliaries:*
caawa **saha na** **wa** u mẹẹni-**na** **na** n-cee
warthog **stay PROG** **be** his song-LOC PROG CONJ-sing
'...Warthog was still singing his song...'
(Lit.: 'Warthog *was still* at his song and singing')

Just as serial are the deictic-directional 'come' and 'go':

(17) a. ka u **ú¹** wyẹrẹngi lwọ **à** **pa** naha
CONJ she AUX money.DEF take PERF **come** here
'...then she brought the money here...'

b. ka mii **í** cingikii lwọ **à** **kare** pyenga
CONJ I AUX poles.DEF take PERF **go** house
'...then I took the poles (away) home...'

The same dispersed configuration for serial directionals can be seen in the SVO-ordered Tok Pisin. (See Givón 1991b.)

(18) a. em tromwey   sospan   **i-go**...
         she threw.away saucepan PRED-**go**
         '...she threw the saucepan away...'

   b. em karim   sospan   **i-kam**
         she carry   saucepan PRED-**come**
         '...she brought the saucepan over...'

One must emphasize that there are serial-verb languages where finite inflections gravitate to a single "main" verb. This is clearly the norm in Kalam, an SOV Papuan language (see Givón 1991b).

(19)   mon   konay-nep   timb rik   tip   pang yok-**sap**...
         wood   much-very   chop cut   chop break throw-PRES/**3s**
         '...he's chopping and cutting and throwing much more wood...'

Only the last of five serial verbs in clause (19) carries finite inflection, the other four are bare stems.

   Other serial-verb languages spread finite morphology to all the verbs in the clause. An example of this may be seen in Akan (Osam 1993a):

(20) a. wo-yi-**i**   no   fi-**i**   Mankesim
         3p-take-PAST OBJ/3s leave-PAST Mankesim
         'They transferred him from Mankesim'

   b. Kofi **á**-nantsew **á**-kǫ   Mankesim
         Kofi PERF-walk   PERF-go Mankesim
         'Kofi walked to Mankesim'

   c. wo-**e-nn**-yi   Kofi **a-mm**-ba   fie
         3p-PAST-NEG-take Kofi PAST-NEG-come home
         'They did not transfer/bring Kofi home'

   d. ǫ-**a-nn**-yę   edwuma **a-mm**-ma   Ebo
         3s-PAST-NEG-do work   PAST-NEG-give Ebo
         'She didn't work for Ebo'

But even in Akan, two tenses—progressive and future—do not spread across the clause. Rather, they mark only the initial verb in the clause. All other verbs carry a neutral 'narrative' prefix:

(21) a. wo-**be**-yi   no   **e**-fi   Mankesim
    3p-FUT-take OBJ/3s NAR-leave Mankesim
    'They will transfer him from Mankesim'

   b. wo-**ri**-yi   no   **e**-fi   Mankesim
    3p-PROG-take OBJ/3s NAR-leave Mankesim
    'They are transferring him from Mankesim'

The vagaries of finite marking in serial-verb languages have given considerable headaches to formal linguists. Thus, for example, Byrne (1992) notes the following three options for placing the finite inflection of tense in Saramaccan:

(22) a. *Only on the first verb*:
    Kofi **bi** bai di buku da di muyee
    Kofi TNS buy the book give the woman
    (i) 'Kofi bought the book and gave it to the woman' (nonserial)
    (ii) 'Kofi bought the book for the woman'

   b. *Spread on all verbs*:
    Kofi **bi** bai di buku **bi** da di muyee
    Kofi TNS buy the book TNS give the woman
    'Kofi bought the book for the woman'

   c. *Only on the last verb*:
    Kofi bai di buku **bi** da di muyee
    Kofi buy the book TNS give the woman
    'Kofi bought the book for the woman'

Byrne makes a valiant attempt to give a configurational account of the fact that only in (22a), where the second verb does not carry its own tense marking, can one obtain a non-serial, conjoined-clauses interpretation. But there is no glossing over the fact that morphological finiteness is one of the most reliable correlates of independent main verb status. So that if anything, on normal iconicity grounds (see discussion in Givón 1990, chapters 13, 19), one would expect (22b) to be the more likely variant that allows a conjoined interpretation.

In Akan, one finds the spreading of some TAM markers to all verbs in the conjoined clause-chains (Osam 1993a).

(23) *Spreading tense-aspects*:
  a. *Past*:
     Araba to-ǫ   nam,   kyew-**ee,** tǫn-**ee**   nya-**a**   sika
     Araba buy-PAST fish   fry- PAST sell-PAST get-PAST money
     'Araba bought fish, fried it, sold it, and got money'

  b. *Perfect*:
     Araba **á-**tǫ   nam, **á-**kyew, **á-**tǫn   **é-**nya   sika
     Araba PERF-buy fish   PERF-fry PERF-sell PERF-get money
     'Araba has bought fish, fried it, sold it, and got money'

Other TAM markers do not spread at all, but rather mark only the clause-initial verb, with all subsequent verbs carrying the less finite and semantically neutral 'narrative' marker:

(24) *Non*-spreading *tense-aspects*:
  a. *Progressive:*
     Araba **ro-**tǫ   nam, a-kyew, a-tǫn   e-nya   sika
     Araba PROG-buy fish   NAR-fry NAR-sell NAR-get money
     'Araba is buying fish, frying it, selling it, and getting money'

  b. *Future*:
     Araba **bǫ-**tǫ   nam, a-kyew, a-tǫn   e-nya   sika
     Araba FUT-buy fish   NAR-fry NAR-sell NAR-get money
     'Araba will buy fish, fry it, sell it, and get money'

As we shall see further below, the very same distribution holds for serial clauses in Akan.

The Verb Phrase in Serializing Languages

Configurational accounts of serial clauses

The phenomenon of verb serialization has bedeviled generative grammarians for over thirty years now. In the early days, when the only recognized level of conjunction was the clause (S), a universal VP node could be preserved only if multi-verb serial clauses were interpreted as *complex clauses*, either embedded or conjoined. And so, many of the formal arguments in the early 1970s centered on selecting the *right* configurational interpretation—conjoined or subordinate—as the underlying deep structure of serial clauses. The fact that the semantics of serial event clauses fitted neither deep-structure configuration, and that both configurations thus played havoc with Chomsky's (1965) concept of semantically-supportive deep structure, did not seem a major worry at the time.

GB grammarians have only recently joined the fray, albeit with relish (see Sebba 1987; Byrne 1987, 1992; Lefebvre, ed., 1991; *inter alia*). Within the resurrected debate, both Sebba (1987) and Larson (1991) review the range of configurational alternatives and then argue for specific ones. One upshot of the latter-day configurational debate is that it is now permissible to conjoin or subordinate a lower node such as VP. A major conceptual hurdle has thus been dismantled, in that formal descriptions are now realigned with the cognitive and rhythmic facts (see again Givón 1991b). Multiple-verb serial clauses are *single* event clauses. Within this new context, Sebba (1987) argues for an analog of the subordination versus coordination contrast of the 1970s. The theory-laden nature of his approach is acknowledged:

> Theoretical paradigms are themselves responsible for the problems researchers have to tackle within them. For Christaller, writing about Twi in 1875, it did not seem to be problematic that some Twi sentences had more than one verb....Subsequently linguists working within the Chomskyan framework found that this *was* a problem, and tried to argue that serial sentences contained sentences embedded within or conjoined with other sentences....My own analysis is based on the notion of multiple right-branching VPs. (Sebba 1987:211)

Sebba posits *both* subordinate and coordinate configurations to account for different types of verb serialization within the same language.[6] Both configurations involve multiple VP nodes. That is, for a VO language (Sebba 1987:149–170):

---

[6]In one of the languages he discusses, a dialect of Akan, it turns out that the crucial data of TAM-spreading had been misrepresented by a nineteenth century linguist (Christaller; see Osam 1993a).

(25) Coordinate configuration:

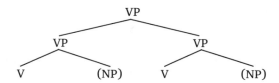

(26) Subordinate (right-branching) configuration:

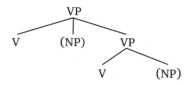

Verb serialization and the distribution of finite verbal morphology

Larson (1991) takes a somewhat different formal approach, noting "the general connection between serialization and secondary predication."

> The distinction between serializing and non-serializing languages would reflect neither a "deep" difference in X-bar theory (as for Baker), nor a difference in the availability of particular lexicalization rules (as for Lefebvre and Li),[7] but instead a rather "shallow" difference in how the inflectional requirements on secondary predicates are met. Such a parameter could presumably be set on the basis of simple sentences involving agreement and inflection... (1991:207)

Serial constructions thus contain "secondary" (=serial) predications in addition to the primary (=main) ones. But to Larson this is a "shallow" typological deviation from the "standard" hierarchic-embedding type. Larson recommends that we look at the rules governing the assignment of finite inflections in single-verb non-serial clauses, then draw from them predictions about what to expect from inflections in multiple-verb serial clauses.

---

[7]The possibility of *lexical* verb serialization had been suggested by Les Bruce (1985), in the context of a functionalist account of serial verbs in Alamblak. In that Papuan language, some serial verbs are clearly colexicalized. A similar suggestion was made for Kalam in Givón (1991b). Lefebvre's (1991) formal treatment purports to "lower" the scope of serial branching to the level of lexical nodes, at least at some stage of the derivation.

Unfortunately, the rules of finite inflection assignment in single-verb clauses do not extend quite as easily. To begin with, the most general prediction that can be derived from single-verb clauses, regardless of typological variation, is:

(27) "Attach all finite verbal inflections to the main verb."

In an embedding language, this rule extends rather neatly to multi-verb clauses, with semantic main verbs hogging up most finite verbal inflections. But even in such well-behaved languages, the notion of "semantic main verb" dissolves when that verb is grammaticalized into a TAM marker, directional marker, or causative affix. In embedding languages, grammaticalized auxiliaries retain the syntactic properties of main verbs long after they have lost all vestiges of semantic verbhood. But is the notion "main verb" more secure in a serializing language? If semantic criteria are put aside, can one identify the "main verb" of a serial clause by purely structural criteria? In a noncircular fashion without reference to finite verbal morphology? As we shall see, the answer is often "no."

Next, finite inflection assignment rules in serial clauses in many languages are neither fully coherent nor fully predictable. And finite inflections certainly do not always cluster around the *semantic* main verb. One could probably predict that *diachronically* the inflections would (eventually) gravitate toward one verb in the clause, as in Kalam and many other serial-verb languages. But in the diachronic interim, the facts of Akan, Saramaccan, Tok Pisin, etc., suggest that serializing languages can tolerate synchronic states where a less than coherent patchwork of rules govern finite inflection assignment. And Larson's study (1991) notwithstanding, those rules are not mere extensions of finite inflection assignment in single-verb clauses.

The role of diachrony in predicting the synchronic behavior of verbal inflections is considerable. Thus in Tok Pisin, the verbal inflection *i-*, the so-called 'predicate marker' (PM), is the diachronic offspring of the anaphoric pronoun 'he'. Its synchronic distribution is somewhat reminiscent of that diachronic origin, in that it is almost obligatorily on main verbs in contexts calling for an anaphoric subject; it cannot appear if the subject is the independent pronoun *em*, but may appear when the subject is a full NP (see Givón 1991b).

(28) a. *Zero-anaphoric subject*:
　　　 i-wok-im　　　paya
　　　 PM-work-TR　　fire
　　　 '...she makes a fire...'

b. *Independent pronoun subject:*
   em   wok-**im**   paya
   she   work-TR   fire
   '...she made a fire...'

The parameter "INFL" in Larson's framework will have to presumably be set separately for each discourse-pragmatic context. And when the subject is overtly expressed, the PM appears only on the serial verb but not on the main verb (see Givón 1991b).

(29) a. *Zero-anaphoric subject:*
   i-wakabaut   **i**-go
   PM-walk.about   PM-go
   '...she walks away...'

b. *Independent pronoun subject:*
   em   wakabaut   **i**-go
   she   walk   PM-go
   '...she walks away...'

Further, the Tok Pisin PM appears on some serial verbs but not on others (see Givón 1991b).

(30) a. **i**-wakabaut   **i**-go
   PM-walk.about   PM-go
   'she walks away...'

b. **i**-wakabaut   **i**-kam
   PM-walk.about   PM-come
   'she walks toward (there)...'

c. **i**-wakabaut   **i**-stap
   PM-walk.about   PM-be
   'she is walking around...'

d. em   wok-im   paya **pinis**
   she   work-TR   fire   **finish**
   'she has made a fire...'

In Akan, Kalam, and the Misumalpan languages, the inflection rules in serial clauses reflect rather faithfully the rules that govern conjoined

same-subject(SS)-chain-medial clauses. This is so because serial-verb constructions arise diachronically from the condensation of clause-chains
(see Givón 1990, chapter 19; 1991b). Thus in Akan, the same tense-aspect
"spreading" rules that govern conjoined clause-chains also govern serial-
verb clauses (see 20, 21, and 23, 24).

In Kalam, the final "main" verb of the SS-chain-medial clause has the
least finite morphology of all clause types, and the morpheme involved is
often dispensed with altogether, to the point where only intonation can
distinguish an SS-chain-medial verb from a clause-internal serial verb (see
Givón 1991b).

In Miskitu (Misumalpan), SS-chain-medial verbs, equi-subject complement verbs, and serial verbs all carry the same nonfinite (participial) inflection, reflecting the common serial origin of all three constructions.
The participial suffix *-i* can be readily interpreted as a cataphoric SS-
medial marker. Thus (Hale 1991):[8]

(31) a. *SS-chain-medial verb*:
  Baha ulu-ka   pruk-**i**   ik-**amna**
  that wasp-UNS hit-PAR/SS kill-FUT/**1**
  'I will hit that wasp and kill it'

  b. *Complement of a modality verb*:
  Naha w-a-tla   mak-**i**   ta   alk-**ri**
  This house-CNS build-PAR/SS end reach-PAST/**3**
  'He finished building this house'
  (Lit.: 'He built the house and reached the end')

  c. *SS-serial-verb* clause:
  Baha usus-ka   pali-**i**   wa-**n**
  that buzzard-CNS fly-PAR/SS go-PAST/**3**
  'That buzzard flew away'
  (Lit.: 'The buzzard flew and went away')

In rigid SOV languages like Miskitu, the most common rule assigns the
most finite verbal inflection(s) to the clause-final verb, but the most finite
verb need not be the semantic main verb (cf. 25c).

The very same carry-over of chain-medial morphology into complementation and serial clauses is found in switch-subject (DS) concatenations. Here, it is the *cataphoric DS-medial* verbal inflection that is
transferred from the DS-chain-medial configuration into the other two

---

[8]This diachronic observation was made in Hyman (1971).

syntactic structures. This inflection, here as in other clause chaining OV languages, is more finite than the cataphoric-SS inflection. Thus, again from Miskitu (Hale 1991):[9]

(32) a. *DS-chain-medial verb*:
  Man   naha yul-a   pruk-**rika** plap-**bia**
  you   this dog-CNS hit- DS/2   run-FUT/**3**
  'You will hit this dog and it will run'

  b. *Complement of nonequi verb*:
  Yang witin-nani aisi-**n**   wal-**ri**
  I   they-PL   speak-DS/**3** hear-PAST/**1**
  'I heard them speak'
  (Lit.: 'They spoke and I heard (them/it)'

  c. *DS-serial-verb clause:*
  Yang truk-kum atk-**ri**   wa-**n**
  I   truck-a   sell-DS/**1** go-PAST/**3**
  'I sold the truck off'
  (Lit.: 'I sold the truck and it went off')

Other serializing languages such as Kalam and Tairora also display this *resultative* serial structure. And it is in fact the very same structure found in the rigid SVO Tok Pisin (Givón 1991b) and Mandarin Chinese (Thompson 1973)—but without any switch-reference morphology. Again, the clause-final finite verb in (32c) is not semantically the main verb, unless one interprets the construction literally as, still, a coordinate structure.

Predicting the assignment of finite verbal inflection in serial-verb clauses is just as problematic in Ijo (Niger-Congo). In this rigid SOV language, the main verbal inflection, the 'past' suffix -*mi*, attaches to the clause-final verb in non-serial clauses (Williamson 1965):[10]

(33) a. *Simple intransitive*:
  eri bo-**mi**
  he come-PAST
  'He returned'

---

[9]In these contexts, Hale (1991) labels the participial SS-medial suffix -*i* of Miskitu 'proximate', and the DS-medial marker -*ka* 'obviative', thus suggesting that a direct versus inverse contrast is involved. It is not clear that this is a necessary conclusion, although the two contrasts—proximate/obviate and SS/DS—have a certain functional overlap.

[10]The Ijo data cited in (33) dispense with tone and vowel height markings, with apology to Kay Williamson.

b. *Simple transitive*:
arau ingo deri-**mi**
she trap weave-PAST
'She wove a trap'

The most general rule for finite inflection placement is thus the same in Ijo as in Miskitu:

(34) *Finite inflection assignment in an OV language*:
"Attach the finite verbal inflection to the clause-final verb."

This rule is retained in serial clauses, but other—nonfinal—verbs sometimes take the "spread" inflection *-ni* and sometimes do not:[11]

(35) a. omini nama tuo fi-**mi**
they meat cook eat-PAST
'They cooked and ate the meat'

b. ta-maa bele seri-**ni** aki-**mi**
wife-DEF pot remove-INF take-PAST
'She took the pot off the fire'

(36) a. eri ogidi aki-**ni** indi pei-**mi**
he machete take-INF fish cut-PAST
'He cut the fish with the machete'

b. arau zu-ye aki buru teri-**mi**
she basket take yam cover-PAST
'She covered the yam with a basket'

(37) a. eri weni-**ni** ama suo-**mi**
he walk-INF town go-PAST
'He walked to town'

b. eri weni bo-**ni** ama la-**mi**
he walk come-INF town reach-PAST
'He walked reaching town'
(Lit.: 'He came walking and reached town')

---

[11]Williamson (1991) calls the inflectional suffix *-ni* that appears on some nonfinal verbs "euphonic."

   c. eri oki   mu toru benin-**mi**
      he swim go river cross-PAST
      'He swam away across the river'
      (Lit.: 'He went swimming across the river')

Again, the *semantic* main verb need not be the clause-final one (cf. 37a, b, c).

   The problem is just as vexing with Ijo serial causative constructions, where the semantically main verb 'make' is clause-medial, sometimes with and sometimes without the inflection (Williamson 1965):

(38) a. woni u-mie-**ni**   indi die-**mi**
        we   him-make-INF fish share-PAST
        'We made him share the fish'

    b. ari u-mie   mu-**mi**
        I   him-make go-PAST
        'I made him go'
        (Lit.: 'She chased him away')

    c. arau tobou mie   bunumo-**mi**
        she child make sleep-PAST
        'She made the child sleep'
        (Lit.: 'She soothed the child')

    d. eri bide mie   fumumo-**mi**
        he cloth make dirty-PAST
        'He made the cloth dirty'
        (Lit.: 'He dirtied the cloth')

   One could, of course, argue that a subrule for marking the main verb 'make' is clearly discernible in (38). That is:

(39) "The causative main verb 'make' takes the inflection if its complement verb is transitive (cf. 38a), but not if it is intransitive (cf. 38b, c, d)."

While rule (39) may do the job, it is theoretically both opaque and inelegant; nor is it formulated in terms of the simple clause. Rather, the rule makes inflection assignment on the semantic main verb depend on the transitivity of the semantic *complement* verb. So that when the main verb 'make' is used alone in a simple transitive clause such as (40), the rule is different (obligatory inflection):

(40) eri ogidi   mie-**mi**
      he   machete make-PAST
      'He made a machete'

And the transitivity hypothesis is further dampened by the alternation found in serial comparison clauses:

(41) a. ari dangai-**ni** u-dengi-**mi**
         I   tall-INF   him-pass-PAST
         'I am taller than he (is)'

   b. eri duma tun-**ni**   i-dengi-**mi**
       he   song sing-INF   me-pass-PAST
       'He sang more songs than I did'

   c. eri kure bangi saramo tobou dengi-**mi**
       he   can   run   fast   child pass-PAST
       'He could run faster than a child'

In (41a) the intransitive main verb 'be tall' carries the inflection, while in (41c) the intransitive 'run' does not. And the most likely verb to carry an inflection is still the clause-final, semantically-serial verb.

Finally, modality verbs in Ijo, as in Miskitu and Supyire, also appear in a serial construction;[12] but sometimes they come with and sometimes without the inflection:

(42) a. eri kurei-**ni** eke fi-a[13]
         he   can-INF   rat eat-NEG
         'He could not eat the rat'

   b. eri seri   you-**mi**
       he   start cry-PAST
       'He started to cry'

   c. eri koro-**ni** oki-**mi**
       he   start-INF   swim-PAST
       'He started to swim'

---

[12]If they were embedded complement constructions, the main verb in a strict SOV language should precede its complement (cf. Young and Givón 1990).

[13]In (41c) the very same modality verb 'can' comes *without* the inflection.

    d. ari la   bo-**mi**
       I   succeed come-PAST
       'I succeeded in coming'

    e. eri inbali-**ni**   oki-**mi**
       he struggle-INF swim-PAST
       'He tried to swim'

    f. eri bari-**ni**   inbali   koro-**ni** oki-**mi**
       he repeat-INF struggle start-INF swim-PAST
       'He tried to begin to swim again'

Similar problems crop up in the rigid SVO Akan, for tenses that do not "spread" beyond the clause-initial verb. The rigid rule for those tenses is the converse of the OV rule (34) and is equally insensitive to the semantic status of the verb:

(43) *Finite inflection assignment in a VO language*:
    "Attach the finite verbal inflection to the clause-initial verb."

But some clause-initial, semantically empty serial verbs cannot take TAM inflections at all, having reached a more advanced stage of grammaticalization (see Osam 1993a for the gradual grammaticalization of Akan serial verbs). The second verb in the clause then carries the inflection, as in (44b).

(44) a. Araba **re**-yẹ   asọr   **a**-ma   Kofi
        Araba PROG-make prayer NAR-give Kofi
        'Araba is praying for Kofi'

    b. Araba de   sekan no **re**-twa   ahoma no
        Araba take   knife the PROG-cut rope   the
        'Araba is cutting the rope with the knife'

Clearly, one cannot follow Larson's (1991) advice and apply the inflection attachment rule of simple one-verb clauses to serial clauses. The assignment of finite inflection in many serializing languages is governed by more complex rules, rules that are more subtle, inconsistent, and on occasion also semantically and pragmatically sensitive. These rules often reflect the specific grammaticalization pathways through which the serial clause arose and often also the diachronic stage of its evolution.

What serializing languages do not always reflect is the idealized iconicity principle of finite morphology assignment. This principle, implicit in Larson (1991), is well-attested in hierarchic embedding languages. It predicts that:

(45) *Finite inflection assignment in embedding languages*:
"Finite verbal morphology will cluster most prominently around the semantic main verb of the clause."

In verb-serializing languages, finite verbal morphology is more scattered across the clause in ways that cannot be derived neatly from principle (45).

The Typological Divide

As a final illustration of the profound, nontrivial syntactic difference between embedding and serializing languages, compare the benefactive construction in two VO languages that have utilized the very same—near universal—source for benefactive marking, the verb 'give'. The verb-serializing language is Akan; the embedding language is Highlands Ecuadorian Spanish.

(46) *Serial benefactive construction in Akan* (Osam 1993a):
  a. Araba **re**-yę   asǫr   **a**-ma   Kofi
     Araba PROG-make prayer NAR-give Kofi
     'Araba is **praying** for Kofi'

  b. Esi **ro**-tur-**no**   **a**-ma   Kofi
     Esi PROG-carry-**her** NAR-give Kofi
     'Esi carries her (the child) for Kofi'

  c. Esi **ro**-tur   abofra no **a**-ma-**no**
     Esi PROG-carry child the NAR-give-**him**
     'Esi carries the child for him (Kofi)'

(47) *Embedding benefactive construction in Highlands Ecuadorian Spanish (Haboud 1993):*
   a. él **le**-dio   preparando el   pan   a   ella
      he **her**-give/PRET/**3s** prepare/PAR the bread OBJ her
      '*He* prepared the bread for *her*' (> instead of *her* doing it for herself)

   b. **se-lo**-dio   preparando
      her-it-give/PRET/**3s** prepare/PAR
      'He prepared it for her' (> instead of *her* doing it for herself)

In the hierarchic embedding syntax of Highlands Spanish, the semantically empty, grammaticalized 'give'—unattested in other Ecuadorian dialects—follows the normal pattern of Spanish auxiliaries: It persists as the syntactic finite main verb and attracts all finite inflection, including the direct-object pronoun that belongs, semantically, to the nonfinite main verb. In the verb-serializing Akan, on the other hand, the semantically empty grammaticalized 'give' is the second ("serial") verb. It either carries the "spread" finite inflection or the less finite "narrative" prefix. And object pronouns remain dispersed, following their logical verbs.

   When a semantically empty grammaticalized auxiliary—the syntactic main verb—finally cliticizes in an embedding language, clause union most often ensues, and the finite inflections that were carried on the auxiliary now attach themselves, together with the auxiliary, to the growing morphology of the complex verbal word. This can be seen with the causative 'make' in Spanish (VO):

(48) *Clause union in the Spanish causative:*
      se-lo-hizo   comer el   pan   a   su   esposa
      her-it-make/PRET/**3s** eat   the bread OBJ his wife
      'He made his wife eat the bread'

When the embedding language is OV-ordered, the mirror image construction is obtained. This pattern may be seen with the benefactive suffix *-ku* in Ute. Ute has, strictly speaking, no verb 'give'; the verb 'feed' with an obligatory dative pronoun is used to render this sense. The benefactive suffix *-ku* is most likely the grammaticalized verb *-kuu* 'take', 'pick up', perhaps through the sense 'take to', thus 'give to'. The benefactive use may be seen in (49). (See Givón 1980.)

(49) *Clause union in the Ute benefactive*:

mama-ci ꞌuwa-y tṳka-pi ꞌuni-**kṳ-xay-ꞌu**
woman-obj DEM/AN-OBJ food-OBJ make-BEN-ANT-**her**
'(He) made food for the woman'

In the serial-verb languages like Akan or Ijo, the "shallow" dispersal of verbs among their logical (or historic) objects makes it much less likely for a grammaticalized serial verb to stand adjacent to—and thus colexicalize with—the "main" verb. True clause union, in the sense of assembling one finite verb to which all grammatical relations pertain in an erstwhile multiverb clause, is diachronically much harder to effect in serializing languages. While semantically the very same verbs grammaticalize in both configurations, the syntactic consequences of the grammaticalization are rather different, which is another way of saying that the typological difference between embedded and serial VPs is profound.

Discussion

The theoretical paradigm as problem generator

> Theoretical paradigms are themselves responsible for the problems researchers have to tackle within them (Sebba 1987:211).

The paradigm that engendered the universal VP node, and with it the need to define grammatical relations (and other grammatical phenomena) configurationally, marches to a distinct theoretical drummer. It answers to a coherent set of core assumptions that pertain, all of them directly or indirectly, to the nature of language universals and the balance of universality versus diversity:

(50) *Core assumptions of the generative paradigm*:
   a. The abstractness of universals:
      The UG *components* of language are highly abstract and formal.

   b. *The uniform application of universals*:
      The UG components are present in all languages to exactly the same degree.

   c. *The superficiality of cross-language diversity*:
      Surface typological diversity is only superficial.

d. *The discreteness of grammatical categories*:
   Grammatical categories are discrete either/or entities.

e. *The inviolability of grammatical rules*:
   Grammatical rules are exceptionless and impervious to
   semantic and pragmatic context.

The conflation of assumptions in (50) impels theoreticians within the generative paradigm to posit one (highest) universal VP node that is unambiguously present in all languages. Cross-linguistic typological diversity that challenges the validity of such a higher node poses a genuine distress within the paradigm. The various formal accounts of verb serialization since the 1970s have been motivated by an implicit need to preserve the paradigm at all costs.

Of all the paradigm's salient features, it is assumption (50c)—that cross-language diversity is only superficial—that fairly guarantees the successful preservation of the paradigm. The configurational accounts of verb serialization as lower level branching under the highest VP node (Sebba 1987; Larson 1991) or even all the way down to lexical nodes (Lefebvre 1991) seem to both take their cue from assumption (50c) and guarantee its preservation. The universal "highest" VP node and a universal configurational rendition of grammatical relations are both central to this preservation effort.

One formal account that, to my knowledge, has never been entertained, is the depiction of serial clauses as lacking a "highest" VP node. Rather, they may have two or more VPS that branch directly under the clause node(s):

(51)

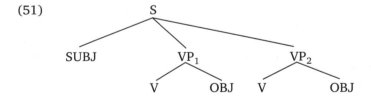

The most substantive argument against (51) would be essentially semantic: It does not provide the same formal configurational account of subject-predicate relations in verb-serializing languages as has been provided for embedding languages. But as noted above, the very same argument can be made against the various higher-in VP configurational accounts of verb serialization, whether coordinate or subordinate. To illustrate this contrast again the Miskitu SS- and DS-serial clauses in (31c) and (32c). In the SS-serial clause (31c) a single subject-predicate configurational account can be given, with the single subject pertaining to a single (higher) VP node and thus to its conjoined daughter VPs. In the DS-serial clause (32c), this account will work only for the first (serial) verb, but not for the second (finite) verb, whose subject is different and is in fact the object of the first (serial) verb.

The reality of typological diversity

The problems inherent in (51), and in all other configurational accounts of verb serialization, do not arise from the specifics of the account—deep versus shallow level of embedding. Rather, the problems are inherent in all universalist configurational accounts of grammatical relations. This approach dates back to Chomsky's (1965) injunction that deep structures must support semantic interpretation. Chomsky's sensible position has the ring of an empirical claim, perhaps translatable into the equally sensible observation that simple clauses are semantically more transparent, while complex clauses are semantically more opaque. This observation is indeed empirically well supported, reflecting a general principle of markedness (or meta-iconicity); (see Givón (1990).

(52) *Isomorphism between syntactic and semantic markedness:*
    "Clauses that are more complex semantically will also
    tend to be more complex syntactically."

The semantic opacity that arises via synchronic embedding or synchronic coordination can always be "handled"—transformationally or otherwise—by mapping complex surface structures back to their semantically transparent deep structures. But as always, diachronic processes of grammaticalization gum up the simple formal works. Thus, diverse diachronic pathways to clause union yield diverse synchronic types of semantically simple clauses. In the case of embedding languages, grammaticalized auxiliaries, directionals, and causatives retain main-verb syntactic status long after becoming desemanticized. In the case of serializing languages, grammaticalized case markers, grammaticalized TAM markers, directionals, and causatives retain their conjoined-verb status long after becoming equally desemanticized.

Configuration (51) does account rather well for the distribution of grammatical objecthood, whose scope is restricted to the more concrete ("lowest") VP nodes. (For a discussion of this in Akan, see Osam 1993b.) This is equally true of most other configurational accounts. But to the

generative paradigm, configuration (51) may have a more profound theoretical drawback: it elevates typological diversity to much-too-high a
level within the hierarchic structure of the clause. And it thus suggests
that typological syntactic diversity may be far less trivial and that the balance between universality and diversity may have to be settled on more
empirical ground, dispensing with many pre-empirical predilections
about what the outcome should be.[14]

The reality of diachronic change

A less extreme approach to language universals would also entail that
synchronic complexity of clausal syntax does not necessarily mean
synchronic complexity of clausal semantics. Put another way, a naive belief in the iconicity of grammar, *a la* principle (52), has considerable limits. In the course of diachronic change, syntax can and often does become
less natural or less iconic. And syntactic "unnaturalness" can persist for a
long time. Put another way, the diachronic source of a construction may
leave its indelible syntactic imprints on it long after it has been semantically re-analyzed (see discussion in Givón 1979, chapter 6). This is especially true when the change involves the condensation—via clause
union—of an erstwhile multiclause sequence into a single clause. Clause
union may thus be viewed as a profoundly—perhaps primarily—
diachronic process, parallelling the semantic process of event integration
(see Givón 1990, chapter 13). But while the semantic process may go to
completion, its syntactic counterpart leaves indelible marks on the syntactic structure of the erstwhile multiclause. And those marks are different depending on the diachronic venue of clause union.

In embedding languages, erstwhile multiple predicates most commonly
wind up as adjacent to each other in clause union, with all finite morphology attached to a single verb. Predicates that have been semantically
grammaticalized can easily become bound morphology. In serializing languages, on the other hand, erstwhile multiple predicates often remain dispersed in clause union, due to their conjoined clause-chain origin. What is
more, their finite morphology often remains dispersed as well. As a result,
clause union in serializing languages may preserve multi-verb or even
multi-VP structures long after such configurations have ceased to reflect
semantic reality.

Different diachronic pathways to clause union thus yield different
synchronic clause types. So that however universal the semantic-pragmatic

---

[14]No empirical work is wholly free of such presuppositions, but clear bounds must be imposed
on the *extent* they are allowed to proliferate, compete with, and on occasion altogether submerge
empirical considerations.

base underlying language may be, typological diversity remains less than trivial.

References

Awobuluyi, A. 1973. The modifying serial construction: A critique. *Studies in African Linguistics* 3.1.

Bamgbose, A. 1973. The modifying serial construction: A reply. *Studies in African Linguistics* 4.2.

Bamgbose, A. 1974. On serial verbs and verbal status. *Journal of West African Languages* 9.

Bruce, Leslie. 1985. Serialization: The interface of syntax and lexicon. Ukarumpa, Papua New Guinea: SIL. ms.

Bybee, J. 1985. *Morphology*. Typological Studies in Language 9. Amsterdam: John Benjamins.

Byrne, F. 1987. *Grammatical relations in a radical Creole*. Creole Language Library 3. Amsterdam: John Benjamins.

Byrne, F. 1992. Tense, scope and spreading in Saramaccan. *Journal of Pidgin and Creole Languages* 7.2.

Carlson, Robert. 1990. *A grammar of Supyire: Kampwo dialect*. Ph.D. dissertation. University of Oregon, Eugene.

Carlson, Robert. 1991. Grammaticalization of post-position and word-order in Senufu languages. In B. Heine and E. Traugott (eds.), *Approaches to grammaticalization*, vol. 2, Typological Studies in Language 19. Amsterdam: John Benjamins.

Chomsky, Noam. 1965. *Aspects of the theory of syntax*. Cambridge, Mass.: MIT Press.

Givón, T. 1971. Historical syntax and synchronic morphology: An archaeologist's field trip. Chicago Linguistic Society 7. University of Chicago.

Givón, T. 1973. The time-axis phenomenon. *Language*

Givón, T. 1979. *On understanding grammar*. New York: Academic Press.

Givón, T. 1980. *Ute reference grammar*. Ignacio, Colo.: Ute Press.

Givón, T. 1984. *Syntax: A functional-typological introduction*, vol. 1. Amsterdam: John Benjamins.

Givón, T. 1990. *Syntax: A functional-typological introduction*, vol 2. Amsterdam: John Benjamins.

Givón, T. 1991a. Isomorphism in the grammatical code: Cognitive and biological considerations. *Studies in Language* 15.1.

Givón, T. 1991b. Some substantive issues concerning verb serialization: Grammatical vs. cognitive packaging. In C. Lefebvre (ed.).

Gruber, J. 1965. *Studies in lexical relations*. Ph.D. dissertation. MIT: Cambridge, Mass.

Haboud, M. 1993. Grammatical change and language contact in Ecuadorian highlands. University of Oregon, Eugene. ms.

Haiman, J. 1985. *Natural syntax*. Cambridge: Cambridge University Press.

Haiman, J., ed. 1985. *Iconicity in syntax*. Typological Studies in Language 6. Amsterdam: J. Benjamins.

Hale, K. 1991. Misumalpan verb sequencing constructions. In C. Lefebvre (ed.).

Heine, B. 1993. *Auxiliaries*. Oxford: Oxford University Press.

Heine, B., U. Claudi, and F. Hünnemeyer. 1991. *Grammaticalization: A conceptual framework*. Chicago: University of Chicago Press.

Hyman, L. 1971. Consecutivization in Fe'fe'. *Journal of* African *Languages* 10.2.

Larson, R. K. 1991. Some issues in verb serialization. In C. Lefebvre (ed.).

Lefebvre, C. (ed.). 1991. *Serial verbs: Grammatical, comparative, and cognitive approaches*. SSLS 8. Amsterdam: John Benjamins.

Li, C. N., and S. A. Thompson. 1973. Serial verb constructions in Mandarin Chinese: Subordination or coordination. *CLS Comparative* Syntax *Parasession*. University of Chicago, Chicago Linguistics Society.

Li, C. N., and S. A. Thompson. 1974. Co-verbs in Mandarin Chinese: Verbs or prepositions? *Journal of Chinese Linguistics* 2.3

Matisoff, J. 1969. Verb concatenations in Lahu. *Acta Linguìstica Hafniencia* 12.1.

Osam, K. E. 1993a. From serial verbs to prepositions in Akan. University of Oregon, Eugene. (ms)

Osam, K. E. 1993b. Grammatical relations in Akan. University of Oregon, Eugene (ms).

Pike, Kenneth L. 1966. Multi-verb clauses in West African languages. ms.

Schachter, P. 1974a. A non-transformational account of serial verbs. *Studies in African Linguistics,* supplement 5.

Schachter, P. 1974b. Serial verbs as verbs: A reply to a reply. *Studies in African Linguistics*, supplement 5.

Sebba, M. 1987. *The syntax of serial verbs*. Creole Language Library 2. Amsterdam: John Benjamins.

Stahlke, H. 1970. Serial verbs. *Studies in* African *Linguistics* 1.1

Steele, S. 1978. The category AUX as a language universal. In J. Greenberg, C. Ferguson, and E. Moravcsik (eds.), *Universals of Human Language*, vol. 3. Stanford: Stanford University Press.

Thompson, S. 1973. Resultative verb compounds in Mandarin Chinese: A case for lexical rules. *Language* 49.2.

Traugott, E., and B. Heine, eds. 1991. *Approaches to grammaticalization*. Typological Studies in Language 19(1/2). Amsterdam: John Benjamins.

Williamson, K. 1965. *A grammar of the Kolokuma dialect of Ijo*. West African Language Monograph 2. Cambridge: Cambridge University Press.

Williamson, K. 1991. The tense system of Izon. *Afrikanistische Arbeitspapiere* 27. Cologne: Institut für Afrikanistik.

Young, P., and T. Givón. 1990. The puzzle of Ngabere auxiliaries: Grammatical reconstruction in Chibchan and Misumalpan. In W. Croft, K. Denning, and S. Kemmer (eds.) *Studies in typological diachrony*, Typological Studies in Language 20. Amsterdam: John Benjamins.

31

The Evolution of Prepositions in Mayan and Indo-European

A Case of Reducing Ambiguity

John R. Costello

Introduction

In this essay I propose that the development of a set of prepositions[1] (also la-belled relational nouns and relational markers) in the Mayan languages

Almost none of my research would have been possible without the work of Ken Pike, and I am happy beyond words to have the opportunity to contribute to this volume in his honor.

I would like to express my deepest appreciation to those investigators of Mayan languages whose works were consulted here. Without their publications, the present study would have been impossible. I would also like to thank Jill Brody for valuable comments on an earlier draft of this essay, and Nora England for very helpful comments on Mayan in general, and Mam in particular. Needless to say, the responsibility for the contents of this essay is mine alone.

[1]Mayan languages are rich in constructions that correspond to prepositional phrases in Indo-European languages. In this chapter, I restrict myself to those described in this section. Other types, such as [tan 'in' + Noun], [Verb + Noun], [hun + Noun + Noun], etc., found in Colonial Yucatec (cf. Smailus 1989:149–156), and [/s/ + Erg + Noun], found in Ixil (cf. Ayres 1991:94ff.), merit separate treatment, and go beyond the scope of this study. Italicized Noun in-dicates the noun which will appear as the "object" of what will become, or correspond to, a preposition.

closely parallels the development of prepositions[2] in Indo-European (IE) languages. In particular, I will attempt to demonstrate:

1.   The Mayan construction [ti + *Noun*][3] corresponds to the IE construction [*Noun* + Affix], each representing the earliest stage in the development of noun syntax in the two language families.

2.   The Mayan construction [ti + [Erg + Noun] + *Noun*] corresponds to the IE construction {Adverb, [*Noun* + Affix]},[4] each of which underwent a reanalysis whereby Mayan [Erg + Noun] and IE Adverb were reinterpreted as a new part of speech, the preposition. In each language family, this represents the second stage in the development of noun syntax.

3.   The Mayan construction [Preposition + *Noun*] corresponds to the IE construction {Adposition, *Noun*}, both representing the third stage in the development of noun syntax.

I will first review the evolution of prepositions in the IE family of languages. Next, I will present an overview of a method for syntactic reconstruction which combines tagmemic theory, as developed by Kenneth L. Pike, and comparative reconstruction, as codified by Henry M. Hoenigswald. I shall then present data from four languages, each representing one of the four branches of the Mayan family (along with corresponding data from IE languages) which permit the reconstruction of Proto-Mayan (PM) syntactic structures, and suggest a relative chronological development for these structures. I shall then comment about the loss of the adverbial marker *ti* in some Mayan languages, paralleling the loss of a corresponding element, namely the affix indicating case, in some IE languages. Finally, I shall draw several

---

[2]As will be discussed below, there is evidence that the placement of adverbs, and the adpositions which evolved from their reanalysis, was relatively free in Proto-Indo-European; these elements could appear before or after the noun with which they became associated. Although the postposing of adpositions with respect to the associated nouns still survives in IE languages, preposing is by far the most common placement in the languages cited in this article, and because of this development, I shall in general refer to these elements as prepositions.

[3]I tentatively identify the reconstruction of the adverbial marker under discussion in this paper as *ti* for Proto-Mayan, since the reflexes found in the languages representing each of the four branches of the Mayan family all evidence *t-*, and three out of four evidence *ti*: in the Huastecan branch, cf. Huastec *ti*; in the Yucatecan branch, cf. Colonial Yucatec *ti*; in the Western branch, cf. Ch'ol *ti*; in the Eastern branch, cf. Ixil *t- ~ tu*. As with all reconstructions, *ti* is subject to revision in light of additional evidence.

[4]I will use curly brackets to indicate a construction whose constitutents, separated by a comma, may occur in any order; thus [Adverb + [*Noun* + Affix]] and [[*Noun* + Affix] + Adverb] are both possible.

conclusions concerning the incrementation of complexity in language, and the concomitant incrementation of precision in human communication.

The Evolution of Prepositions in the IE Family of Languages

One of the earliest accounts of the evolution of prepositions in the IE languages was presented by Delbrück (1893:660–665). He noted that in Proto-Indo-European (PIE), adverbs could modify nouns as well as verbs. Also, nouns in all cases except the nominative and vocative could function as substantival adverbs. In a clause which contained both a substantival adverb and an adverb modifying a verb, the typical word order of the constituents was [[Noun + Affix] + Adverb + Verb]. Under such conditions, the role of the adverb could eventually be reinterpreted as modifying the substantival adverb, i.e., the noun along with its affix, rather than the verb. At this point, such an adverb could be reanalyzed as a new part of speech, an adposition, and the noun that it modified was reanalyzed as the "object" of the adposition. Also, as part of the reanalysis, the adposition was seen to call for, or "govern," the case of the noun. At a later point, the adposition could appear before as well as after the noun.

A generation later, Hirt (1927:15) elaborated further on the emergence of adpositions in IE. In a statement referring only to IE languages, but which amazingly has great relevance with respect to the development of Mayan prepositions, as well, Hirt identified two formal sources of adpositions, which he referred to simply as prepositions; also, he commented further on the "governing" of cases in IE.

> Prepositions are adverbs which enter into a syntactic relationship in part with a verb (as a pre-verb), and in part with a noun...One distinguishes between direct and indirect prepositions. Indirect prepositions are oblique forms of nouns, and consequently a noun in the genitive will enter into a syntactic relationship with them. Direct prepositions, on the other hand, are primeval particles that do not enter into syntactic relationships with nouns in any of the three cases, nominative, genitive, or dative, but rather only with nouns in the accusative, locative, ablative, and instrumental. They [i.e., the particles] do not, however, govern the cases; rather, they come to be syntactically associated with them in a supplementary

relationship. If that were not the case, then a preposition could not govern several cases [translation mine — JC].[5]

These accounts of the evolution of adpositions in the IE languages are echoed in later discussions of IE syntax, as well, although in recent years, interest has focussed more on the placement of the adposition in PIE than on the more important question of the process whereby the adposition evolved from an adverb. In these discussions, it is sometimes difficult to determine precisely what a scholar is claiming, and whether or not he has contradicted himself in a series of publications. Thus, Lehmann 1974:234 states, "As a further development, preverbs [i.e., adverbs—JC] were used as postpositions....Indo-Europeanists have long noted this development and also the further development of such postpositions to prepositions (Delbrück 1893:643-744)." Friedrich (1975:34) responds, "The units that function variously as preverbs, adverbs, prepositions, and postpositions pose a key problem that calls for a new interpretation....The reanalysis of these units entails a long-overdue challenge to the dogma that 'PIE uses postpositions' in the sense that it 'had no prepositions' (Lehmann 1972a:985)." After presenting numerous data from the earliest descendant languages of PIE, Friedrich (1975:38) concludes, "With respect to adnominal position, then, the dogma that Proto-Indo-European only had postpositions turns out to be strongly supported by the evidence from only one language: Hittite." It will become clear from data presented in this essay that one need look no further than Sanskrit and Greek to find evidence that PIE, as well as its descendant languages, had neither exclusively postpositions nor exclusively prepositions; both prepositions and postpositions existed in the parent language.

Comparative Syntactic Reconstruction

Before proceeding with the presentation of data from the modern Mayan languages that point to the reconstruction of certain syntactic structures and their development in PM, it would be well to discuss briefly a method for syntactic reconstruction that combines tagmemic theory (cf. Pike

---

[5]"Die Präpositionen sind Adverbien, die teils zu einem Verbum (Präverbien), teils zu einem Nomen hinzu treten...Man hat echte und unechte Präpositionen unterschieden. Unechte sind Kasusformen von Substantiven, und mit diesen verbindet sich daher ein Substantivum im Genitiv. Die echten Präpositionen dagegen sind uralte Partikeln, die sich nicht mit den drei Kasus, Nominativ, Genitiv, Dativ, verbinden, sondern nur mit dem Akk., Lok., Abl., Instr. Sie regieren aber nicht den Kasus, sondern treten zu ihm ergänzend hinzu. Wäre das nicht der Fall, so könnte eine Präposition nicht mehrere Kasus regieren" (Hirt 1927:15).

1954, Pike 1958, and Pike and Pike 1977, among numerous other publications) with comparative reconstruction (cf. Hoenigswald 1960).

Tagmemics

The TAGMEME is a constituent of a syntactic construction which is called a SYNTAGMEME. The tagmeme, like the morpheme, is a linguistic unit that unites content or meaning and form. Whereas the content of a morpheme expresses a root, derivational, or inflectional word-level concept, the content of a tagmeme (also known as the slot) expresses a grammatical function, such as subject or object. While the form of a morpheme may be a root (or variants of a root) or an affix (or variants of an affix), the form of a tagmeme may typically be a noun phrase or a pronoun or a clause, etc. In tagmemic notation, the name of the grammatical function or relationship appears to the left of a colon, and the name of the form or filler appears to the right, e.g.,

> Subject: Noun Phrase / Pronoun / Clause,

or in an abbreviated notation,

> S: NP / Pro / Cl.

Also, just as morphemes are distributed in contrastive and characteristic environment sets, so are tagmemes.

Syntax is characterized by a hierarchical structure: constituents (tagmemes) make up a construction (syntagmeme), which in turn, together with other constructions at the same level, join together and function as constituents of a construction at the next higher level, and so on. To illustrate the hierarchical structure of syntax from a tagmemic point of view, let us consider the following tagmemes (where not all of the possible forms or fillers have been indicated); the full notation will be followed by an abbreviated notation in parentheses.

(1)   Determiner: definite article / indefinite article (Det: def. art. / indef. art.)
(2)   Noun Modifier: adjective (NM: adj)
(3)   Head of a Noun Phrase: noun (HNP: n)
(4)   Auxiliary Verb: auxiliary verb (Aux: aux)
(5)   Head of a Verb Phrase: verb (HVP: v)
(6)   Base: transitive clause (Base: trans. cl.)

The tagmemes in (1), (2), and (3) may function as the constituents of a construction called a noun phrase:

NP [±Det: def. art. / indef. art. ±NM: adj +HNP: n],

where "±" indicates that the following tagmeme is optional, and "+" indicates that the following tagmeme is obligatory. The tagmemes in (4) and (5) may function as the constituents of a construction called a verb phrase:

VP [±Aux: aux +HVP: v].

The tagmeme in (6) may function as the constituent, or one of the constituents, of a construction called a sentence:

Sent [+ Base: trans. cl.].

Noun phrases may manifest the syntactic function subject (S) as well as direct object (O) (and other syntactic functions as well), and verb phrases may manifest the syntactic function predicate (Pred); these tagmemes in turn join together as constituents of the construction at the next higher level, the (transitive) clause. Such a construction, either alone, or together with other such constructions, may function as a constituent or constituents of a construction at the next higher level, the simple, compound, or complex sentence. Thus the hierarchical structure of the sentence

(7)   The Mayan artisan was carving an inscription

is evident in the following representation in (8).

(8)   Sent [+Base: trans. cl. [+S: NP [+Det: def. art. +NM: adj
       +HNP: n] +Pred: VP [+Aux: aux +HVP: v] +O: NP [+Det:
       indef. art. +HNP: n]]]

The comparative method

The comparative method enables one to recover some aspects of the proto-language of a language family, provided that one apply certain principles of comparative reconstruction to corresponding linguistic units in at least two descendant languages which represent different branches within a family. In phonological and morphological reconstruction, the phoneme and the morpheme are the linguistic units that are employed, respectively. In syntactic reconstruction, the linguistic units are (1) the tagmeme and (2) the syntagmeme.

The first axiom of comparative reconstruction has been followed by historical linguists since the early decades of the nineteenth century;[6] however, to my knowledge, it was not stated explicitly until 1957 by Greenberg (1957:49f.):

(9) ...occurrence in at least two separate branches of a family is the common reason for assigning a feature to the ancestral language of a family as a whole...[7]

Hoenigswald (1960:119) utilized this axiom in his efforts to establish a set of formal procedures to reconstruct phonological and morphological units. If we generalize his procedures to include other linguistic units, in particular, the tagmeme and the syntagmeme, then we may paraphrase his introductory remarks on phonological reconstruction as follows:

(10) If an emic unit A of the ancestor language appears as an emic unit M in one descendant language and as an emic unit T in another descendant language, corresponding strings in the two descendant languages will be matched in such a way that M in one corresponds to T in the other. Such a pair of emic units, one in the first descendant language, and one in the other, is a set of correspondences, which may be represented as

M 1, 2 :: T 1, 2

where "1" stands for the contrastive set of environments, and "2" stands for the characteristic set of environments, and "::" stands for "corresponds to." This leads us to posit A in the ancestor language.

This may be expressed graphically via the reconstruction diagram in figure 1, where the Arabic numeral 1 at the right of the symbols A, M, and T

---

[6]Pedersen (1962:274) reports that Fick expressed a vague indication of the awareness of this axiom as early as the last half of the nineteenth century, in the rhyming motto that adorned the title page of his *Vergleichendes Wörterbuch der indogermanischen Sprachen* [Comparative dictionary of the Indo-European languages] (1870–1871): "Durch zweier Zeugen Mund wird alle Wahrheit kund" [All truth becomes known through the testimony of two witnesses].

[7]A feature such as a phoneme, a morpheme, a tagmeme, or a syntagmeme may occur in two or more languages for two reasons, in additon to inheritance from a common ancestor: (a) borrowing or (b) chance. Thus, one must first eliminate the possibility of borrowing or chance before one applies the axiom of (9) to the data.

represents the contrastive set of environments of that linguistic unit, and the Arabic numeral 2 represents the characteristic set of environments.

	1 2	M 1 2
		Descendant Language 1
Parent Language	A 1 2	Descendant Language 2
	1 2	T 1 2

Figure 1.

With specific reference to tagmemes and syntagmemes, then, one may conclude that

(11) Sets of correspondences of tagmemes and syntagmemes between two descendant languages may be considered to be continuations of respective proto-tagmemes and proto-syntagmemes in the parent language, just as sets of correspondences of phonemes and morphemes between two descendant languages may be considered to be continuations of respective proto-phonemes and proto-morphemes in the parent language.

For further details concerning syntactic reconstruction, cf. Costello 1983, 2001.

Mayan and Indo-European data

Let us now turn to data from four Mayan languages, Huastec, Colonial Yucatec (CY), Ch'ol, and Ixil, each representing one of the four branches of the Mayan family, Huastecan, Yucatecan, Western, and Eastern, respectively. The Mayan data are followed by data from Sanskrit and Lithuanian, representing two branches of Indo-European. Some data from Greek are also presented in the discussion of the emergence of prepositions.

Substantival adverbs

Mayan [ti + Noun]

As evidence from the various Mayan languages shows,[8] *ti* in the phrase [ti + *Noun*] functions as an adverbial marker in the sense that it indicates that the following noun has an adverbial syntactic relationship to the verb of the clause. The precise role, e.g., time, location, source, direction, etc., of the substantival adverb in such a phrase is not specified in any way; rather it is interpreted by context.

Time

(12) Huastec (Ochoa Peralta 1984:107)
ti ʔakal koʔ ol tin beleʔ k'ayu:m
at night need at-I travel slowly 'I must travel slowly at night.'

(13) CY (Smailus 1989:151)
ti ca kal kin
at forty day 'for forty days'

(14) Ch'ol (Whittaker and Warkentin 1965:35)
che' mi' majlel ti chobal ti i chol, che' ti säk'ajel, mach abi anik mi' ñijkan...
when Aux-he go at clearing at his cornfield, thus at morning, not as-they-say is-not Aux-he move...
'When he went in the morning to clear his cornfield, he did not move...'

(15) Ixil (Ayres 1991:102)
¿Ma tu oxva'l q'ii kat tx'a'n kat naj Luukas?
interrogative at three day recent eat recent the Lucas
'Has Lucas eaten in three days?'

---

[8]As is well known, numerous systems have been devised for the written representation of Mayan languages. Since individual investigators of Mayan languages have chosen the different systems that they employ for good reasons, and since this does not (seem to) seriously impede comparative work, I have decided to cite data exactly as they appear in the sources that I have consulted. The one exception to this is that in representing Ch'ol, I have used ä, employed by Keller and Luciano (1997) for Chontal, rather than the carat which is usually used for Ch'ol *shwa*. The gloss lines are not morpheme-by-morpheme and therefore are not aligned word-by-word.

Figurative Location

(16) Huastec (Ochoa Peralta 1984:102)
      nana:? ?ešom ?u ?ehtowal k'ayu:m tin te:nek
      I Aux-continuation I understanding slowly at-my Huastec
      'I am slowly learning Huastec.'

(17) CY (Smailus 1989:150)
      nonoh ti Mayathan
      skillful at Maya-language 'skillful in Mayan'

(18) Ch'ol (Whittaker and Warkentin 1965:57)
      mi yälob che' ti mero k t'an lojon
      Aux they-say thus at very our language our-exclusive
      'Thus they say in our very own language.'

Concrete Location

(19) Ch'ol (Whittaker and Warkentin 1965:17)
      Che' bä ya' añob ti cholel...
      when there they-are at cornfield...
      'When they were there in the cornfield...'

(20) Ixil (Ayres 1991:102)
      Echen in tu Xlau'
      be I at Quetzaltenango 'I was in Quetzaltenango.'

Figurative Source

(21) Ch'ol (Warkentin and Scott 1980:98)
      melel ti tye'
      made at wood 'made of wood'

Concrete Source

(22) CY (Smailus 1989:150)
      ¡hokez Juan ti matzcab!
      take out John at jail 'take John from the jail!'

Figurative Direction

(23) Huastec (Ochoa Peralta 1984:107)
hwa:n wenk'on ti ɵiman
John turns at sorcerer 'John turns into a sorcerer.'

(24) Ch'ol (Whittaker and Warkentin 1980:18)
cha'an abi mi kaj i yochel ti k'in
because it-is-said Aux start he become at sun
'because, it is said, he would turn into the sun'

Concrete Direction

(25) Huastec (Ochoa Peralta 1984:107)
wanač ti bi¢ow
let-us-go at village 'Let us go to the village.'

(26) CY (Smailus 1989:150)
lubi ti ch'en
I fall at well 'I fall into the well.'

(27) Ch'ol (Whittaker and Warkentin 1965:13)
mu' abi i majlel ti cholel jini i yäskun
Aux it-is-said he go at cornfield the his older-brother
'It is said, his older brother would go to the cornfield.'

(28) Ixil (Ayres 1991:102)
ma't in t muunte
go I at cemetery 'I am going to the cemetery.'

Instrument

(29) CY (Smailus 1989:150)
u hidzahen ti che
he beat-me at stick 'He beat me with a stick.'

(30) Ch'ol (Whittaker and Warkentin 1965:18)
mu' abi i bik'ti t'oj ti machit jini ch'iton
Aux it-is-said he small cut at machete the boy
'It is said that he would cut the boy into small pieces with his machete.'

Agent

(31) Ch'ol (Warkentin and Scott 1980:64)
      José ti ilänti ti Juan
      Joseph Aux was-being-seen at John 'Joseph was seen by John.'

(32) Ixil (Ayres 1991:102)
      Qat q'osox axh t ixoq
      recent beat you at her 'You were beaten by her.'

Purpose

(33) CY (Smailus 1989:151)
      talen ti chan missa
      I-come at celebration mass 'I come for the celebration of mass.'

(34) Ch'ol (Whittaker and Warkentin 1965:36)
      che' mi' säk'an mi' cha' majlel ti chobal ti' chol
      when Aux-it dawn Aux-he again go at clearing at-his cornfield
      'When dawn would come he would again go to clear his cornfield.'

(35) Ixil (Ayres 1991:102)
      seb' t tilto'k
      early at see-it '[he is entering] early to see it'

Respect

(36) CY (Smailus 1989:150)
      in tupah vol ti hanal, tu ukul, ti baxal, ti coil
      I satisfy mood at food, at drink, at play, at cheating
      'I satisfied myself with respect to food, drink, play, and cheating.'

(37) Ch'ol (Whittaker and Warkentin 1965:50)
      Ojlil jach abi mi' yajñel tsuk ti te'
      half-way only it-is-said Aux-he arrive rat at pole
      'It is said the rat would only reach half way regarding the pole.'

Indo-European [Noun + *Affix*]

The use of substantival adverbs in IE languages corresponds to that of Mayan languages; however, whereas in Mayan, only one preposed adverbial marker, *ti*, functions to signal the adverbial syntactic relationship that the noun has to the verb, in IE languages, several oblique cases function to signal this relationship. Moreover, just as the interpretation of the specific adverbial role in Mayan is dependent upon context, so it is in IE, as well. In other words, each of the specific adverbial roles, such as time, location, source, etc. may be expressed by several oblique cases, and each oblique case may express several adverbial roles.[9]

Because of limitations of space, I will restrict the presentation of IE data below as follows:

1.   For each adverbial role, I will cite data from only two branches of the family, Indic (Sanskrit) and Baltic (Lithuanian); this will suffice, in light of (9), (10), and (11), in order for us to be able to reconstruct the adverbial roles in question for PIE.

2.   For each adverbial role, I will cite data exhibiting only one of the oblique cases employed to express that role in Sanskrit (Skt.) and Lithuanian (Lith.); I will, however, identify any other cases that are used to express that role in both languages, should they be present. Copious data may be found in Whitney 1889:90–103 and Senn 1966:385–436.

Time

In addition to nouns in the locative case, nouns in the genitive, dative, accusative, and instrumental may also function as substantival adverbs expressing time.

(38)   Skt. locative (Whitney 1889:101)
dvādaçe varṣe
twelfth year 'in the twelfth year'

(39)   Lith. locative (Senn 1966:436)
spalyje
October 'in October'

---

[9]It is possible that reconstructed PIE, characterized by multiple correspondences of case and adverbial role, was preceded by a stage in which each case was associated with only one adverbial role, and vice versa; however, this is simply conjecture, since the data available to us in the oldest IE languages only allow us to reconstruct a proto-language characterized by the multiple correspondences described above.

Location

In addition to nouns in the locative case, nouns in the accusative and genitive may also function as substantival adverbs expressing location.

(40) Skt. locative (Whitney 1889: 101)
      daçame pade
      tenth step 'at the tenth step'

(41) Lith. locative (Senn 1966:435)
      Prūsuose
      Prussia 'in Prussia'

Source

(42) Skt. genitive (Whitney 1889:100)
      yo rajñaḥ pratigṛhṇāti lubdhasya
      who of-king gifts-accept greedy
      'whoever accepts a gift from a greedy king'

(43) Lith. genitive (Senn 1966:405)
      senovės radiniai
      of-antiquity discoveries 'discoveries from antiquity'

Direction

(44) Skt. locative (Whitney 1889:103)
      papāta medinyām
      fell at-earth 'He fell to the earth.'

(45) Lith. locative (Senn 1966:436)
      išjojo broleliai svetimoj šalėlej
      our brothers rode foreign country
      'Our brothers rode into a foreign country.'

Instrument

(46) Skt. instrumental (Whitney 1889:94)
      çastreṇa nidhanam
      by-sword death 'death by sword'

(47) Lith. instrumental (Senn 1966:426)
      rankomis dirbti
      hands work 'to work with one's hands'

Agent

(48) Skt. genitive (Whitney 1889:99)
      hantavyo 'smi na te
      slain I-am not you 'I am not to be slain by you.'

(49) Lith. genitive (Senn 1966:397)
      motina kudikio mylima
      mother by child loved 'The mother is loved by the child.'

Purpose

(50) Skt. dative (Whitney 1889:96)
      iṣum kṛṇvānā asanāya
      arrow making hurling 'making an arrow for hurling'

(51) Lith. dative (Senn 1966:414)
      pietums mėsą pirkti
      meat meal buy 'to buy meat for lunch'

Respect

(52) Skt. accusative (Whitney 1889:93)
      amuṣṇītam paṇim gāḥ
      you-robbed Pani cows 'You two robbed the Pani of the cows.'

(53) Lith. accusative (Senn 1966:423)
      rankas kojas pailsau
      hands legs I-am-tired 'I am tired in my arms and legs.'

Reconstruction of substantival adverbs

As noted previously, there is only one adverbial marker in Mayan, whereas there are five distinct case suffixes represented in the IE data, and this would, at first blush, seem to indicate that the case suffixes are significantly different from *ti* in that they carry more information than simply 'adverbial marker'. In other words, the IE cases would seem to indicate not only the information 'adverbial marker', but additionally, (a) the locative indicates 'time', 'location', or 'direction'; (b) the genitive indicates 'source' or 'agent'; (c) the instrumental indicates 'instrument'; (d) the dative indicates 'purpose'; and (e) the accusative indicates 'respect'. However, if we go beyond the eight roles illustrated in the above data, we note that for Sanskrit and Lithuanian alone, not to mention other IE languages:

1. The locative may indicate all together six roles: 'time', 'location', 'direction', 'manner', 'circumstance', and 'condition' (cf. Whitney 1889:101–103; Senn 1966:434–436).

2. The genitive may indicate all together six roles: 'source', 'agent', 'possession', 'partitive', 'respect', and 'time' (cf. Whitney 1889:98–101; Senn 1966:385–411).

3. The instrumental may indicate all together five roles: 'instrument', 'manner', 'respect', 'medium', and 'time' (cf. Whitney 1889:93–95; Senn 1966:425–434).

4. The dative may indicate all together four roles: 'benefit', 'respect', 'purpose', and 'direction' (cf. Whitney 1889:95–96; Senn 1966:411–417).

5. The accusative may indicate all together five roles: 'respect', 'time', 'extent of time', 'extent of distance', and 'cognate accusative' (cf. Whitney 1889:90–93; Senn 1966:417–425).

Viewed in this way, then, each of the IE cases cited above corresponds closely to Mayan *ti* in that the cases and *ti* indicate explicitly the adverbial function of the associated noun, and only ambiguously one of several roles; the ambiguity is then reduced, if not eliminated, by context.

In tagmemic notation, a simple independent declarative clause containing an adverbial modifier of a noun or a verb or an adjective could be represented at clause level as follows:

(54) Sent [+ Base: trans. cl. [+ S: NP + Pred: VP ± O: NP
± Adv: RR / NP / adv]]

where Adv: RR / NP / adv represents a tagmeme with the function 'adverbial modifier', and the fillers are either a Relator-Related Phrase (for details, see the following paragraphs) or a Noun Phrase or an adverb. In particular, what is meant by ADVERBIAL MODIFIER is the function of any phrase or part of speech which modifies a noun, a verb, an adjective, or an adverb, in an adverbial manner, as a constituent in a syntactic construction. This function is manifested by the filler Relator-Related Phrase in Mayan, and by the filler Noun Phrase or adverb in IE.[10]

If the Relator-Related Phrase of Mayan is further specified, its structure may be represented as in (55).

(55) Adv: RR [+Relator: *ti* + Related: NP]

If the Noun Phrase of IE is further specified down to the morpheme level of analysis, its structure may be represented as in

(56) Adv: NP [+HNP: n [+nnuc: nst + Affix: case]]

where the Noun Phrase consists of a Head of a Noun Phrase, which is filled by a noun nucleus manifested by a noun stem and an affix manifested by a case morpheme. Thus, while the formal fillers of the Mayan and IE tagmemes Adv: RR and Adv: NP, respectively, are structurally different from one another, they share the same function, and thus they represent corresponding tagmemes.

If we refer to the Mayan data presented in (12)–(15), for example, it is clear that each citation exhibits the tagmeme whose representation is found in (55); in other words, each of the four languages, Huastec, CY, Ch'ol, and Ixil, representing each of the four branches of the Mayan family, contains the tagmeme in (55). Thus, any conceivable pair of the four languages produces a correspondence set

Adv: RR :: Adv: RR.

The same is true of all the data presented in examples (12)–(37), with the exception that some subsections contain only three or two correspondence sets, from three or two of the branches, rather than four. If, with reference to figure 1, we select the data on *time*, and represent the adverbial tagmeme in Huastec, for example, as M, and the corresponding tagmeme in either CY, Ch'ol, or Ixil, as T, they yield a correspondence set. Viewing this correspondence set in conjunction with the axiom stated in

---

[10]Although the tagmemes in (54) have been presented in only one particular sequence, other sequences, not listed here, may also be possible. Also, not all of the possible fillers are indicated for any of the tagmemes represented in (54).

(9), and the principle stated in (11), we may then reconstruct the adverbial tagmeme Adv: RR, with its constituent syntagmeme

[+ Relator: *ti* + Related: NP],

as formalized in (55), for PM.

If we return to the IE data presented in (38)–(39), it is clear that each contains the tagmeme whose representation is found in (56); in other words, each of the two languages, Sanskrit and Lithuanian, representing the Indic and Baltic branches of IE, respectively, contains the tagmeme in (56). Thus they produce a correspondence set

Adv: NP :: Adv: NP.

The same is true of the data presented in (40)–(53). If we now treat this correspondence set as we did the correspondence set Adv: RR :: Adv: RR, we may then reconstruct the adverbial tagmeme Adv: NP, with its constituent syntagmeme

[+ HNP: n [+ nnuc: nst + Affix: case]],

as formalized in (56), for PIE. We note that in so doing, we have provided a formal reconstruction of the earliest stage of Indo-European noun syntax referred to by Delbrück (1893).

Thus, what our two reconstructions show is that for each language family, Mayan and IE, we have reconstructed a tagmeme whose function is adverbial modifier. In Mayan, that tagmeme is manifested by an adverbial marker *ti* and a *Noun*; in PIE, that tagmeme is manifested by a *Noun* and an *Affix* for case. Clearly, the formal element accompanying the Mayan noun differs from that accompanying the IE noun with respect to morpheme status (root versus affix) and position (preposed versus postposed); nevertheless, these differences are superficial, since both the preposed root *ti* and the postposed affix essentially serve to signal the same syntactic function of the associated noun, as adverbial modifier. That this is an inefficient and imprecise way to communicate information is clear from the accompanying data; it is characterized by ambiguity which can be delimited in Mayan only, and in IE largely, by context. In the following section I will deal with a development in Mayan and in IE in which a new part of speech emerged via reanalysis, and which resulted in an increase in efficiency and precision with respect to adverbial modifiers.

The emergence of prepositions

Mayan [ti + [Erg[11] + Noun] + Noun]

The following evidence from the Huastecan, Yucatecan, and Western branches of Mayan illustrates a development beyond the original state of Mayan noun syntax, namely the addition of a possessed noun to the original phrase consisting of [ti + *Noun*], to yield [ti + [Erg + Noun] + *Noun*]. As the data show, the function of the possessed noun is to specify the role of the following substantival adverb, hence reducing the ambiguity in role characterizing substantival adverbs presented in examples (12)–(37), and at the same time reducing the dependence on context to perform this task. The glosses of the data will show that these Mayan possessed nouns are translated with IE prepositions, and indeed, it will be argued that in Mayan, a reanalysis has taken place which has resulted in an interpretation of these noun phrases as a new part of speech, roughly corresponding to IE adpositions.

Location

(57) Huastec (Larsen 1997:82)
c'uajat tin tamet an inic
it-is at-his front the man 'It is before [in front of] the man.'

(58) Ch'ol (Aulie and Aulie 1998:88)
Ya' t'uchul jini winic ti' pam otot
there climbed the man at-its forehead house
'The man climbed there on the house.'

(59) Ch'ol (Aulie and Aulie 1998:124)
T'uchul jini ch'iton ti' ni' te'
climbed the boy at-its nose tree 'The boy climbed up the tree.'

(60) Ch'ol (Aulie and Aulie 1998:89)
Wa'al juntiquil winic ti' pat otot
standing one man at-its back house
'A man is standing behind the house.'

---

[11]Erg is an abbreviation for Ergative, a Mayan case which has two functions: (a) it marks what corresponds to the subject of IE transitive verbs; and (b) it marks what corresponds to an IE possessive adjective. It is this latter function which will be the object of attention in the data to follow.

(61) Ch'ol (Aulie and Aulie 1998:123)
Ya' jach chumul ti' t'ejl cotot
there only living at-its side my house
'He lives beside [next to] my house.'

(62) Ch'ol (Aulie and Aulie 1998:158)
Päcäl xña'mut ti' yebal ch'ac
brooded hen at-its bottom bed
'The hen brooded beneath/underneath the coop.'

Direction

(63) Huastec (Ochoa Peralta 1984:102)
ka kʷ'ahba? ti nake:l ?an be:l
may-you put-it at side the road 'Put it to the side of the road.'

(64) CY (Smailus 1989:156)
manan tu calapil tziminob la
pass (by) at-his gap horse all 'pass between the horses'

Agent

(65) CY (Smailus 1989:155)
cinpahan a pixan tumen cizin[12]
is-hurt your soul at-his-cause devil
'Your soul is hurt by the devil.'

Cause

(66) CY (Smailus 1989:155)
cimil in cah tu cal vijh
die I do at-its neck hunger 'I am dying of hunger.'

---

[12]This sentence could arguably be classified as an example of 'cause' as well as 'agent'; hence it illustrates that a certain degree of role ambiguity remains even with the addition of a possessed noun to the associated substantival adverb. Also, it is especially interesting in that it reveals the conceptual connection between 'causative' and 'passive' in noun syntax; the phenomenon has been observed in IE languages, but in verb syntax; cf. Lehmann 1974:108f. *et passim* for a proposal to derive the IE passive voice from causative verbs.

Indo-European {*Adverb*, [Noun + *Affix*]}

With respect to function, the addition of adverbs in IE to the original structure of the substantival adverb, [*Noun* + Affix], yielding {Adverb, [*Noun* + Affix]}, corresponds to the addition of the possessed noun to the original structure of substantival adverbs in Mayan, [ti + *Noun*]. As the following data will show, the function of the adverb is to specify the role of the substantival adverb, hence reducing the ambiguity in role characterizing substantival adverbs, and at the same time reducing the dependence on context to perform this task. The glosses of the data from Sanskrit and Greek (rather than Sanskrit and Lithuanian) will show that the adverbs are translated with Modern English prepositions. It will be argued that in IE a reanalysis has taken place which has resulted in an interpretation of these adverbs as a new part of speech, the adposition (which in many of the descendant languages changed its preferred position with respect to the substantival adverb with which it was associated, from following it to preceding it).

Postposed adverb

(67) Skt. (Delbrück 1893:653)
      parā me yanti dhītayo gāvo na gavyūtīr anu
      away my go prayers cows as meadows toward
      'My prayers go forth as cows to the meadows.'

(68) Greek (Goodwin and Gulick 1930:29)
      toutōn peri
      these [matters] about 'about these matters'

Preposed adverb

(69) Skt. (Delbrück 1893:653)
      mā mādhi putre vim iva grabhīṣṭa
      not me-over children bird like seize
      'Do not grab me like a bird [sitting] on its brood.'

(70) Greek (Goodwin and Gulick 1930:252)
      eks okheōn sun teukhesin ālto
      from chariot with arms leapt
      'He leapt from the chariot with [his] armor.'

Reconstruction and reanalysis

We observed that the addition of the Mayan possessed noun to the original substantival adverbial phrase consisting of [ti + *Noun*] corresponds functionally to the addition of the Indo-European adverb to the original substantival adverbial phrase [*Noun* + Affix] in that the new constituents serve to specify the adverbial role, e.g., location, direction, agent, that was ambiguous in the original phrases.

If we refer to the Mayan data presented in (57)–(66), it is clear that each citation exhibits an adverbial modifier tagmeme which may be represented as

(71) Adv: RR [+ Relator: *ti* + Related: NP [+ Modf: poss. adj. + HNP: n + Pos: NP]]

(cf. the representation of the original construction in (55)).

Thus, while the lexical content of each citation differs from that of any other citation, including specifically the lexical content of the Related: NP tagmeme, it is true nevertheless that the constituents of the NP of the tagmeme are identical in each of the citations in each of the three branches of Mayan that are represented, namely the Huastecan, Yucatecan, and Western branches. Thus any conceivable pair of the three languages, Huastec, CY, or Ch'ol, will produce a correspondence set, each member of which is the adverbial modifier in (71). If, for example, with reference to figure 1, we select the data in examples (57)–(62), and represent the modified adverbial tagmeme as realized in the Huastecan example in (57), as M, and the corresponding modified adverbial tagmeme as realized in the Ch'ol example in (58), as T, they yield a correspondence set. Viewing this correspondence set in conjunction with the axiom stated in (9), and the principle stated in (11), we may then reconstruct the adverbial tagmeme formalized in (71) for PM.

If we refer to the IE data presented in (67)–(70), each citation exhibits an adverbial modifier which may be represented as

(72) Adv: NP [+ Adv: adv + HNP: n [+ nnuc: nst + Affix: case]]

(It should be borne in mind that various sequences of constituents, i.e., tagmemes, of a construction are possible; in particular, in (72), the tagmeme Adv: adv may appear before or after HNP: n.) Once again, although the lexical content[13] of each citation differs from that of any other citation, including the lexical content of the Adv: adv tagmeme, it is nevertheless the case that the constituents of the NP of the tagmeme are identical in each of the citations in each of the two languages, Sanskrit and Greek. Thus they will produce a correspondence set, each member of which is the adverbial modifier in (72).

Thus, once again carrying out a comparative syntactic reconstruction according to the second section of this essay, if we select the adverbial modifiers in (67) or (69) to represent M, and the adverbial modifiers in (68) or (70) to represent T, respectively, they yield a correspondence set, and we may then reconstruct the adverbial modifier tagmeme represented in (72) for Proto-Indo-European.

As was mentioned previously, the Mayan structures presented in (57)–(66) and the Indo-European structures presented in (67)–(70) underwent a reanalysis which resulted in a reinterpretation of the Mayan possessed noun and the Indo-European adverb as a new part of speech, the Mayan preposition, and the Indo-European adposition, the latter of which originally could appear both before or after its object, but which in many of the Indo-European languages of today appears primarily or exclusively before its object.

For Mayan, the adverbial phrase whose structure is represented in (71) was reanalyzed such that the possessor noun was reinterpreted as the object of a new preposition, and the possessed noun was reinterpreted as a preposition (also known as a relational noun or a relational marker). This noun is often the name of a part of the human body, such as Ch'ol *pam* 'forehead', *ni* 'nose', or *pat* 'back'; the use of these nouns with "possessors" like *otot* 'house', and *te* 'tree', and the fact that the possessed nouns no longer have their original meanings, but rather exhibit metaphorical meanings in their new function as prepositions, demonstrates their reanalysis (and as many would say, their grammaticalization). Also, the ergative pronoun which precedes the possessed nouns no longer functions as a true possessive adjective, but rather serves as a function word linking the new preposition with its new object; cf. Smailus (1989:153, 155) for his analysis of CY.

For Indo-European (following Delbrück's and Hirt's accounts), further data indicate that the adverbial represented in (72) is actually a reanalysis of an older structure which is well attested in Sanskrit and Ancient Greek, where the adverb had a syntactic relationship to the verb of

---

[13]Note also that three out of the four sentences exhibit different cases: (67) accusative, (68) genitive, (69) locative, and (70) genitive. However, as was demonstrated in the previous section, above, what is significant here is only that case *qua* case is the original marker of the syntactic relationship of the substantival adverb as adverbial modifier.

the clause, rather than to the substantival adverb; cf. the Sanskrit and Greek sentences (73) and (74), respectively, where the adverb precedes the verb that it modifies, and the Sanskrit and Greek sentences (75) and (76), where it appears elsewhere, respectively.

(73)　ut pātayate pakṣiṇaḥ (Delbrück 1893:648)
　　　up makes-fly birds '[she] makes the birds fly up'

(74)　patri apodounai (Goodwin and Gulick 1930:252)
　　　father back-give 'to give back to the father'

(75)　gavām apa vrajaṃ vṛdhi (Delbrück 1893:648)
　　　cows forth stall open 'open the stall of the cows'

(76)　apo patri philō domenai kourēn (Goodwin and Gulick 1930:252)
　　　back father dear to-give maiden
　　　'to give back the maiden to [her] dear father'

Because the position of the adverb modifying the verb was thus free, allowing the adverb to appear immediately after a noun, as in (67) and (68), or immediately before a noun, as in (69) and (70), a reanalysis took place by which the function of the adverb was interpreted as modifying the substantival noun, rather than the verb of the clause. Thereupon another reanalysis took place, whereby the adverb was seen no longer as an adverb modifying the noun, but rather as a new part of speech, an adposition. Accompanying this reanalysis of the adverb was a reanalysis of government of the case of the substantival noun; the case was no longer seen as an affix functioning to mark the adverbial relationship of the noun to the verb, but rather as an affix governed by the new part of speech, the adposition. Interestingly enough, the stages of this process may be observed even in contemporary German, with respect to the adverbs *entgegen* 'towards', *entlang* 'along', and *gegenüber* 'opposite'. For example, in (77), *entlang* modifies the verb *gehen* 'go', and precedes it; in (78), *entlang* again modifies *gehen*, but does not precede it; in (79) and (80), *entlang* is perceived no longer as an adverb modifying *gehen*, but rather as an adposition—a postposition in (79) and a preposition in (80), with an object, *Tal* 'valley', and "governing" the accusative case; cf. Curme 1922:362 and Grebe 1959:305, 596.

(77)　Wir wollten das Tal in Ruhe entlanggehen
　　　we wanted the valley in peace along-go
　　　'We wanted to go quietly along the valley.'

(78) Wir gingen das Tal in Ruhe entlang
we went the valley in peace along
'We went quietly along the valley.'

(79) Wir gingen das Tal entlang
we went the valley along 'We went along the valley.'

(80) Wir gingen entlang das Tal
we went along the valley 'We went along the valley.'

Perhaps the most interesting thing of all about the process of reanalysis in Mayan is that it may be seen to reflect Hirt's observation concerning the sources of prepositions, and accordingly, their behavior, in IE. We recall that Hirt stated that indirect prepositions are oblique forms of nouns, and consequently a noun in the genitive will enter into a syntactic relationship with them. One may see how this operates by again observing data from German, a language rich in newly created prepositions. An oblique form of the noun *Weg* 'way' is *wegen*, which functions as a preposition (sometimes as a postposition) with a metaphorical (grammaticalized) meaning 'by way of, because of'; used in a prepositional phrase, its "object" appears in the genitive case: *wegen des Geldes* 'because of the money'. While Mayan languages do not formally correspond to IE in general, and German in particular, with respect to case, there is nevertheless a notional correspondence in the antecedents of their reanalyzed prepositional phrases which may be seen if one aligns the analysis of a Mayan prepositional phrase, e.g., Ch'ol *ti' t'ejl otot* 'beside the house', with that of the German one, and bears in mind that (a) a Mayan noun accompanied by *ti* corresponds to an IE noun in an oblique case; and (b) a Mayan possessor noun corresponds to an IE noun in the genitive case; cf. figure 2.

Oblique noun	Possessor
wegen 'way'	des Geldes 'the money's'
ti' t'ejl 'at its side'	otot 'the house's'

Figure 2.

The Loss of the Relational Marker *ti* in Mayan and the Case Affix in Proto-Indo-European

A final development in the evolution of prepositions in some Mayan languages has an interesting parallel in the evolution of prepositions in some IE languages, namely the loss of the Mayan adverbial marker *ti*, and the loss of the IE case affix, leaving the newly created part of speech, the preposition, as the sole marker of the adverbial relationship that its object has to the verb of the sentence.

Mayan data

Because the phenomenon is attested in languages belonging to two branches of Mayan, e.g., CY in the Yucatecan branch (where the loss is partial) and Mam (where the loss is complete, according to Nora England, personal communication) in the Eastern, as may be seen in (81)–(85), it may be appropriate to attribute the phenomenon to PM.

Colonial Yucatecan (Smailus 1989:154)

(81)   u lah akab
        its all night 'during the night'

(82)   u lah haab
        its all year 'during the year'

(83)   u lah kin
        its all day 'during the day'

Mam (England 1983:72)

(84)   jawleet jun xaq kyee7yax t-jaq' yooxh tx'otx' tkub'
        go-up one rock precious its-cushion red earth go-down
        'A precious stone appeared below the red earth.'

(85)   maaxtzan ktzaajal asta maax t-wi7 witz
        up-to-well come up-to to-there its-head hill
        'Well, it has come from there above the hill.'

Indo-European data

As far as I have been able to determine, the loss of case affixes[14] in prepositional phrases with noun objects is not attested in any of the oldest recorded languages of any branch of IE; rather, it appears to be a fairly recent phenomenon. Because of this, it would not be appropriate to attribute it to PIE. The following examples in Spanish (Italic branch), along with their English (Germanic branch) translations, illustrate the phenomenon.

(86) Lo puso en la canasta
      it put in the basket 'She/he put it in the basket.'

(87) Fue a la milpa
      went to the cornfield 'She/he went to the cornfield.'

Conclusion

What is noteworthy about the developments in Mayan and in IE discussed above is that two unrelated language groups, each starting with a different formal device to express adverbial relationships, and each augmenting these with different parts of speech, carried out a process of reanalysis that yielded the same new part of speech, the preposition. Without a doubt, the use of prepositions makes more specific the adverbial relationships that a noun can have to another element or elements in a sentence, and thus reduces ambiguity.[15] The appearance of a new part of speech is a rare and profound change in a language, and developments like the independent but parallel emergence of prepositions in Mayan and in IE strongly suggest that in the evolution of language, the acceptance of such an increment in linguistic complexity will be associated with a significant increment in the precision of human communication.

---

[14]Note that in the languages cited here, pronouns—which may or may not be analyzed as having case affixes—do not always resemble noun prepositional objects in failing to reflect case.

[15]As Huffman (2001:30–31), summarizing the views of Diver and the Columbia School, observed, language is, by its very nature, characterized by ambiguity: "Linguistic forms encode much less than the messages they are used to communicate...they are very sparse tools, and...a large part of communication is accomplished not by the linguistic code, but by humans themselves through inference and their ability to jump to conclusions."

References

Aulie, H. Wilbur, and Evelyn W. Aulie, compilers. 1998. *Diccionario ch'ol de Tumbala, con variaciones dialectales de Tila y Sabanilla*. México, D. F.: Instituto Lingüístico de Verano.

Ayres, Glenn. 1991. *La gramática ixil*. La Antigua Guatemala: Centro de Investigaciones Regionales de Mesoamérica.

Costello, John R. 1983. *Syntactic change and syntactic reconstruction: A tagmemic approach*. Summer Institute of Linguistics and University of Texas at Arlington Publications in Linguistics 68. Dallas.

Costello, John R. 2001. Tagmemics and the analysis of non-verbal behavior: Pike and his school. In E. F. K. Koerner, Silvain Auroux, Hans-Josef Niederehe, and Kus Versteigh (eds.), *History of the Language Sciences*, Vol. II, 1966–1985. Berlin and New York: Walter de Gruyter.

Curme, George O. 1922. *A grammar of the German language*, second edition. New York: Frederick Ungar.

Delbrück, Berthold. 1893. *Vergleichende Syntax der indogermanischen Sprachen*. Part 1. Strassburg: Trübner.

England, Nora. 1983. *A grammar of Mam, a Mayan language*. Austin: University of Texas Press.

Friedrich, Paul. 1975. *Proto-Indo-European syntax: The order of meaningful elements*. *Journal of Indo-European studies*, Monograph 1. Butte, Mont.: College of Mineral Science and Technology.

Goodwin, William W., and Charles B. Gulick. 1930. *Greek grammar*. Boston: Ginn.

Grebe, Paul, ed. 1959. *Duden Grammatik der deutschen Gegenwartssprache*. Mannheim: Dudenverlag des Bibliographischen Instituts.

Greenberg, Joseph H. 1957. *Essays on linguistics*. Chicago, Ill.: University of Chicago Press.

Hirt, Hermann. 1927. *Indogermanische Grammatik*. Part 3. *Das Nomen*. Heidelberg: Winter.

Hoenigswald, Henry M. 1960. *Language change and linguistic reconstruction*. Chicago, Ill.: University of Chicago Press.

Huffman, Alan. 2001. "The linguistics of William Diver and the Columbia School." *Word* 52(1):29–68.

Keller, Kathryn C., and Plácido Luciano G., compilers. 1997. *Diccionario Chontal de Tabasco*. Serie de Vocabularios y Diccionarios Indígenas "Mariano Silva y Aceves," 36. Tuscon, Ariz.: Instituto Lingüístico de Verano.

Larsen, Ramón. 1997. *Vocabulario huasteco del estado San Luís Potosí*, second edition. México, D. F.: Instituto Lingüístico de Verano.

Lehmann, Winfred P. 1972. "Contemporary linguistics and Indo-European studies." *Publications of the Modern Language Association of America*. 87(5):976–993.

Lehmann, Winfred P. 1974. *Proto-Indo-European syntax*. Austin: University of Texas Press.

Ochoa Peralta, María. 1984. *El idioma huasteco de Xiloxuchil, Veracruz*. México, D. F.: Instituto Nacional de Antropología e Hístoria.
Pedersen, Holger. 1931[1962]. *The discovery of language. Linguistic science in the nineteenth century*. Bloomington: Indiana University Press.
Pike, Kenneth L. 1954. *Language in relation to a unified theory of the structure of human behavior*, Part 1. Glendale, Calif.: Summer Institute of Linguistics.
Pike, Kenneth L. 1958. "On tagmemes née gramemes." *International Journal of American Linguistics* 24:273–278.
Pike, Kenneth L. 1967. *Language in relation to a unified theory of the structure of human behavior*. The Hague: Mouton.
Pike, Kenneth L., and Evelyn G. Pike. 1977. *Grammatical analysis*. Summer Institute of Linguistics and University of Texas at Arlington Publications in Linguistics 53. Dallas.
Senn, Alfred. 1966. *Handbuch der litauischen Sprache*. Heidelberg: Winter.
Smailus, Ortwin. 1989. *Gramática del maya yucateco colonial*. Hamburg: WAYASBAH.
Warkentin, Viola, and Ruby Scott. 1980. *Gramática ch'ol*. Gramáticas de Lenguas Indígenas de México 3. México, D. F.: Instituto Lingüístico de Verano.
Whitney, William D. 1889. *Sanskrit grammar*, second edition. Cambridge, Mass.: Harvard University Press.
Whittaker, Arabelle, and Viola Warkentin. 1965. *Ch'ol texts on the supernatural*. Summer Institute of Linguistics of the University of Oklahoma Summer Institute of Linguistics Publications in Linguistics and Related Fields 13. Norman.

32

Indo-European and the
Glottalic Theory

In Defense of Ejectives for Proto-Indo-European

Thomas V. Gamkrelidze

It is a great honor and a special privilege to participate in a Festschrift dedicated to Kenneth L. Pike—one of the greater linguists and phoneticians of our time. My generation of linguists has been educated on works by Nikolaus Trubetzkoy, Roman Jakobson, André Martinet, Winfred P. Lehmann, Kenneth Pike, and others, and I am happy to acknowledge that I was privileged on different occasions to render homage to our great teachers. My participation in the *Festschrift* for Kenneth Pike with a contribution involving typological problems of diachronic phonology is a small token of deep respect and admiration for this great man and excellent scholar.

The Indo-European Glottalic Theory notably implies shifting the classical three-series system of Proto-Indo-European (PIE) consonantism specified as: I "voiced" ~ II "voiced aspirates" ~ III "voiceless" to a hypothetical system with the same three phonemic series reinterpreted respectively as: I "glottalized" ~ II "voiced (aspirates)" ~ III "voiceless (aspirates)," with

The present paper was conceived of as a contribution to a volume celebrating the ninetieth birthday of Kenneth L. Pike. Actually, it appears, alas, in his memorial volume. However, I left purposely intact my introductory part, despite the sad news of his passing away, which I received on the completion of the present article.

513

voiced and voiceless stops occurring, in the reinterpreted system, positionally in the form of aspirated and corresponding nonaspirated variants:

Traditional system				Reinterpreted system		
I	II	III	⟶	I	II	III
(b)	b^h	p		(p')	$b^{[h]}$	$p^{[h]}$
d	d^h	t		t'	$d^{[h]}$	$t^{[h]}$
g	gh	k		k'	$g^{[h]}$	$k^{[h]}$
.	.	.		.	.	.
.	.	.		.	.	.
.	.	.		.	.	.

Positing ejectives (glottalized stops) in place of traditional voiced stops accounts naturally for the absence (or near-absence) of the voiced labial b in Proto-Indo-European[1] and of mediae, in general, in Proto-Indo-European inflectional affixes, as well as clarifies some peculiarities in the PIE root-structure (especially, absence of roots combining two traditional mediae).

The proposed comparative reconstruction of the Proto-Indo-European stops, taking into account both synchronic and diachronic typology, differs evidently from the system of Proto-Indo-European consonantism as reconstructed in classical IE comparative linguistics.

In the new interpretation, the Proto-Indo-European system of stops proves to be closer to the systems traditionally defined as those with *Lautverschiebung* (Germanic, Armenian, Hittite), whereas systems which were thought to be close to the Common Indo-European system with respect to consonantism (Old Indian, Greek, Italic, etc.) appear to be the result of complex phonemic transformations of the original language system.

In the latter group of languages, the original glottalized phonemes (Series I) became voiced (a phonemic process that has a parallel in a number of languages with glottalized consonants). A series of voiced stops thus appears, which is necessarily supplemented by the labial member that was regularly missing (or weakly represented) in the original glottalized series.

The traditionally established trajectories of transformations of the Proto-Indo-European stops into the phonemic units of the individual

---

[1] Viewing the highly dubious Proto-Indo-European root *bel- 'force' as an instance of voiced *b cannot, of course, save the situation.

Indo-European languages change accordingly, acquiring—in the new interpretation of the Proto-Indo-European phonological system—a reverse direction. The basic Phonetic Laws of classical comparative IE linguistics, such as Grimm's Law, Grassmann's Law, etc., are also conceptualized anew, acquiring a different meaning in light of the new interpretation of the Proto-Indo-European system of stops.

New methods of comparative reconstruction supplemented by the evidence of modern linguistic typology—both synchronic and diachronic—in effect necessitate a revision of the traditional schemata of classical Indo-European comparative linguistics by advancing new comparative historical reconstructions, essentially a new system of comparative historical grammar of the Indo-European languages (cf. Gamkrelidze and Ivanov 1995).

Indeed, the reconstructed linguistic models of the initial language system—if they claim to reflect in the first approximation a language that really existed in space and time—must correspond, in general, to the typologically determined universal regularities of language established inductively or deductively on the basis of the comparison of a set of various language structures.

Typological verification (both synchronic and diachronic) of the reconstructed linguistic models thus proves to be one of the basic prerequisites in positing initial language structures, indispensable for validating the probability of such structures and their conformity with general linguistic reality. Current methodological premises of language reconstruction thus entail the involvement of typological considerations in the process of comparative and internal reconstruction. Any linguistic reconstruction must naturally be based on comparative evidence, and at the same time take into account the typological plausibility, both synchronic and diachronic, of a linguistic system arrived at by means of comparative and internal reconstruction. To put it another way, comparative reconstruction must go hand-in-hand with typology and language universals, so as not to obtain by comparative reconstruction a system which is linguistically implausible, constituting an exception to typologically verifiable linguistic evidence. The assumption of the thesis of the reality and plausibility of the proposed reconstructions determines, thus, a whole set of methodological principles of comparative-genetic linguistics, primarily its close links with the principles of linguistic typology and language universals.

The criticism levelled at the Glottalic Theory mainly concerns the adopted methodology of linguistic reconstruction, styled by some scholars as "typological reconstruction," as opposed to traditional reconstruction viewed as "comparative reconstruction," which is considered to be the only methodologically legitimate procedure of language reconstruction—typology being "a mere fallacy" (cf. Dunkel 1981).

I consider this to be a misunderstanding of the aims and tasks of linguistic reconstruction, in general, and of Indo-European reconstruction, in particular. There is no such procedure as typological reconstruction as opposed in principle to comparative or internal reconstruction. Consequently, we must speak in Diachronic Linguistics solely of "comparative language reconstruction" aided in some cases by internal reconstruction of the proto-linguistic patterns, typology and language universals appearing merely as verification criteria for the proposed reconstructions.

Typologically verifiable linguistic models arrived at by comparative and internal reconstruction must be given preference over typologically rare and implausible patterns which theoretically may be posited on the basis of language comparison. Among diverse theoretical patterns of linguistic reconstruction arrived at with the aid of genetic comparison of related dialects, typological criteria must give preference to only one of them, considered linguistically most plausible and realistic, explaining a number of historical facts that remain unaccountable from the viewpoint of the alternative reconstructed models.

All these considerations must be involved in the procedure of comparative and internal reconstruction which pays due attention to typological criteria regarding the linguistic plausibility of the theoretically postulated linguistic models that must reflect (in the first approximation) a proto-system existing in space and time.

If we had a linguistic proto-system with highly rare and exceptional characteristics as a historically attested language, we would be called upon to account for its exceptional structural features, setting up pre-stages to justify its peculiar and typologically exceptional traits. This would be a methodologically acceptable procedure, accounting for the typological peculiarities of a historically attested linguistic system which served as a proto-system to a group of related dialects.

This is what is now being done by some scholars, in order to justify by any means the peculiar structural characteristics of the traditionally reconstructed consonantism of the Proto-Indo-European linguistic system (with three series of stops defined as: I "plain voiced," II "voiced aspirates," and III "voiceless"), as if it were not a theoretically posited linguistic construct, but a historically attested and recorded linguistic system whose structural peculiarities should be somehow justified and accounted for.

Our contention is that the Proto-Indo-European stop series from the very beginning should not have been posited in their traditional pattern, this being a mere historical chance due to the influence of the then prestigious Old Indian system and to the absence of a strict reconstructional methodology.

As a matter of fact, in a series of phonemic correspondences $d : d : d : d : t : t :...$, etc., what entity should be posited for the Proto-system, a *d, a *t, or a third unit, different from both the historically attested ones? Logically, all three possibilities may be envisaged, since none of these entities is ruled out a priori. The decision in such cases must rest wholly upon typological considerations, with a view to obtaining a linguistic system which, on the whole, would be linguistically more probable and plausible, and not constitute an exception to general typological evidence. That is why, in these series of correspondences, the preference—for the Proto-Indo-European system—must be given to positing an entity which is phonemically unvoiced and characterized by an additional distinctive feature of "glottalization."

Now, in some attempts to justify and rescue the traditional Proto-Indo-European consonantism, as if it were a historically attested system and not a hypothetical construct like any other linguistic reconstruction, we are advised to view the plain voiced stops with highly marked labial *b and very common and unmarked velar *g as a result of transformation of a system at a pre-Indo-European stage with "voiced implosives" (Haider 1985).

It seems untenable to try to account for this fact by assuming a change of the postulated pre-Indo-European implosive *'b to PIE *m, while *'d and *'g changed to PIE *d, *g, respectively, leaving a gap in the new series of Proto-Indo-European plain voiced stops at the bilabial point which, by the way, is a favored point of articulation in the series of voiced stops, as it is in the series of voiced implosives.

Apart from this, positing voiced implosives, even for the pre-Indo-European stage, leaves unexplained the root-constraint which rules out the cooccurrence of two voiced stops (roots of the *deg-, *ged- type), this being one of the most conspicuous typological inconsistencies of the classical Proto-Indo-European system. This constraint is well accounted for phonetically, on the assumption of a rule of non-cooccurrence of two glottalized consonants (this being widely verified by typological evidence), as distinct from the cooccurrence of voiced implosives.[2]

---

[2]In terms of Natural Phonology, non-cooccurrence of two voiced stops seems rather unnatural, since the feature [+ voice] is assimilatory by nature, as different from the feature [+ glottalization] or [+ pharyngealization], which is phonetically a dissimilatory one. This explains easily, and in a natural way, the cooccurrence of voiced stops in a root or a word-form cross-linguistically and the tendency of ejectives to evade such combinations, which may be illustrated by abundant typological evidence; the examples to the contrary adduced from a number of languages with ejectives, cannot of course refute this evidence since it refers to phonetic *tendency* (not to the

Coming up with new suggestions and alternative theories for Proto-Indo-European has become very popular since the advancement of the Glottalic Theory in the early 1970s by Gamkrelidze and Ivanov (1972, 1973) and Paul Hopper (1973). Concerning the postulation of voiced implosives for pre-Indo-European rather than glottalized stops, as proposed by Haider (1985), we would like to point out that the series of voiced implosives, as shown by Greenberg (1970), is characterized by the same hierarchical relationship of markedness as the plain voiced stops (unmarked labial versus marked—or totally absent—velar member), this being in contradiction to the evidence regarding the traditional plain voiced stops in Proto-Indo-European with highly marked labial *b and unmarked velar *g.[3] The pre-Indo-European voiced implosives simply could not have yielded what is traditionally known in Indo-European as the series of "plain voiced stops."

Another such example, among alternative proposals, is that by Robert Woodhouse (1993) who thinks "that the glottalic hypothesis has nothing solid to recommend it," suggesting, at the same time, to modify traditional reconstructions and posit the PIE tenues as "injectives"(!?) (cf. also Woodhouse 1995).

---

syntagmatic regularity) of the ejectives not to cooccur, as different from the *regularity* of cooccurrence of voiced stops evidenced cross-linguistically by a vast number of languages (as different from traditional Proto-Indo-European!?). The example of the Caucasian Lezgian language adduced to the contrary (cf. Job 1989; Haspelmath 1993) is based on misunderstanding. In Lezgian we attest a tendency of devoicing voiced consonants, and one cannot adduce a great number of lexemes with two voiced consonants, but such words do exist, and not only as loans, cf. Lezgian *gad* 'summer', *guž* 'force', *dad* 'taste', *dugun* 'valley' and others (cf. Talibov 1980:70; Jaraliev 1989).

[3]Opponents of the Glottalic Theory presume to undermine its premises by demonstrating linguistic systems with an absent voiced labial *b* (cf., for example, Hock 1986:625). Even if we admit the existence of certain systems with an absent labial *b*, this being a typological rarity, this would not change anything in the hierarchical relationship of markedness in the series of voiced stops (unmarked b ~ marked g), and this determines methodologically the choice of one concrete reconstructive model from different possible theoretical constructs. However, the fact is that nobody so far has adduced clear and unequivocal evidence of languages with a gap at the bilabial point in the series of voiced stops. Hock's Caucasian evidence is, for example, a misunderstanding since in Dargwa, a Caucasian language, the bilabial voiced *b* is well represented as an unmarked (dominant) phonemic unit (cf. Gaprindashvili 1966:103ff.). On the whole, it must be pointed out that one should refrain from such second-hand examples in support or refutation of any theoretical construct. On the other hand, neither can we agree with the claim that the phoneme *b* was richly represented in Proto-Indo-European, although in noninitial position (cf. Szemerényi 1985). The late Oswald Szemerényi who, by the way, was one of the first scholars to propose "a new look of Indo-European" (Szemerényi 1967), tries to reject the thesis of the absence of a voiced labial *b in Proto-Indo-European by referring to forms with *b* in internal position: Lat. *lūbricus*, *lībō*, Goth. *diubs*, etc. He admits that "initially *b* is rare, perhaps not to be acknowledged at all; but internally it is vigorously represented" (Szemerényi 1985:12). But this vigorous representation of internal *b is restricted mainly to Western ("Ancient European") dialects, thus casting doubts on its Proto-Indo-European provenance.

Setting up such pre-stages for Proto-Indo-European with different sorts of phonemes to account for typological inconsistencies in the traditional system is as old as the first attempts to reinterpret the classical system undertaken by Holger Pedersen (1951), who suggested introducing such changes at the pre-Indo-European stage (*Vorindoeuropäisch*), leaving intact the traditional system of Proto-Indo-European (*Gemeinindoeuropäisch*). Such internal reconstructions of different, typologically consistent, pre-Indo-European stages still leave unexplained the transition from such presumably stable configurations to the highly unstable system known as traditional Proto-Indo-European, which later allegedly transformed once again into typologically stable systems of the historical Indo-European dialects (cf. Cowgill 1984 [1985]: 6).[4]

Let us now evaluate both proto-linguistic models (the Classical and the Glottalic ones) in terms of the economy of diachronic phonemic transformations yielding historical daughter languages from the theoretically postulated original Proto-system. In terms of the number of consonant shifts in historical languages the Classical model is more economic as compared to the Glottalic model, since the former has to assume fundamental consonant transformations (Grimm's Law) only in Germanic, and Armenian (probably also in Hittite), while the Glottalic model implies the shift of ejectives to voiced stops in the rest of Indo-European, Germanic and Armenian (probably also Hittite) being most archaic in this respect (cf. Job 1989; 1995).

---

[4]It must be pointed out at this juncture that it was Holger Pedersen who initiated by his classical investigation of 1951 the premises of the Glottalic Theory, as Férdinand de Saussure laid the foundations by his "Mémoire..." for the Laryngeal Theory. It seems rather peculiar that at the conference organized by the Danish linguist, Yens Elmegård Rasmussen, and dedicated to the memory of Holger Pedersen, there was no mention of this fundamental work of that great Danish scholar (Rasmussen 1995). Nevertheless, there were papers directed against the Glottalic Theory, such as the one by Jost Gippert (Gippert 1995), who reviewed the Indo-European ~ Kartvelian loans and arrived at the conclusion that such lexical borrowings do not confirm the existence of ejectives in Proto-Indo-European. I would like to recall in this connection the methodological principle of comparative linguistics according to which lexical borrowings evince specific phonetic regularities and cannot either corroborate or refute postulated proto-linguistic patterns, and this thesis may be demonstrated on vast cross-linguistic evidence. This is why we did not accept, since they are methodologically impermissible, the examples of Germ. *rīk (a loan of Celtic *rīg) and Arm. *partēz 'garden' (cf. Iranian *pairidaēza-) as an evidence of the *Lautverschiebung* (in the classical sense) respectively in Germanic and Armenian (cf. Gamkrelidze 1995). As for the Indo-European ~ Kartvelian loans referred to in connection with Jost Gippert's article, we (Gamkrelidze and Ivanov) include them in our monograph not in support of the existence of ejectives in Proto-Indo-European, but rather as an illustration of the existence of Indo-European ~ Kartvelian (South Caucasian) language contacts on the proto-linguistic chronological level. And rendering of PIE ejectives in these concrete Kartvelian loans mostly by voiced stops does not, of course, say anything in favor of or against the existence of ejectives in PIE. On the other hand, in Old Egyptian a whole layer of IE loans with ejectives has been singled out by Frank Kammerzell (cf. Kammerzell 1999) that in light of the Near Eastern localization of PIE original habitat becomes especially significant.

On the other hand, as demonstrated by Frank Kammerzell in his above-mentioned highly interesting and insightful review article in *Indogermanische Forschungen* (Kammerzell 1999), in terms of the types of diachronic phonemic transformations, the Glottalic model turns out to be more economic as compared to the classical one. This is why the calculations of Michael Job as to the percentage of voiced → voiceless and ejective → voiced (or vice versa) sound-shifts turn out to be irrelevant to the evaluation of the preference of the proposed models and cannot be adduced as diachronic typological evidence against, or in favor of, any of these assumptions. Thus, the principle of Occam's Razor operates in this case in both directions. At the same time, the calculations of the shifts of ejectives in Caucasian languages, as proposed by Michael Job, are based on shaky historical grounds and cannot be inferred from the linguistic reality attested in Caucasian.[5]

The unfounded criticisms of Michael Job, who is considered to be versed in Caucasian linguistics, are accepted uncritically by some Indo-Europeanists who are scarcely familiar with any linguistic evidence beyond Indo-European, and trusting, therefore, Job's rather dubious statements concerning ejectives in Caucasian. Such statements do not reflect the objective situation in Caucasian and sometimes even distort (I want to hope—unknowingly) our own views on Caucasian [cf., e.g., the adduced list of Georgian examples with two ejectives in a word (Job 1995:241), as if we argued to the contrary for Georgian (however, such forms with two ejectives are scarcely met in Common Kartvelian)].

I am inclined to estimate all such criticisms of the Glottalic Theory as attempts to leave all intact and rescue the traditionally received

---

[5]Thus, in the Northeast Caucasian Nakh languages the positionally motivated sound correspondence Batsbi ejective ~ Chechen, Ingush voiced interpreted by Alf Sommerfelt (Sommerfelt 1938:138ff.) as a result of transition glottalized → voiced is held by Michael Job to be a sound development in the other direction, the voiced being the original phoneme in this correspondence (with a reference to Imnaishvili 1977). The reference to Imnaishvili cannot be in this case a sound indication of the correctness of the established direction of sound transformations, since it is based on the preconceived idea of genetic relationships between North and South Caucasian (Kartvelian) languages forming a common genetic group of Ibero-Caucasian languages, Georgian being held as a language displaying phonologically the most archaic features. The assumption of K. Č'relašvili (1975:276ff.), as well as that of Alf Sommerfelt, reflects more objectively the sound-transformations in the Caucasian languages under review (cf. also Fallon 1993; 1995, who argues that Proto-Nakh lenis ejectives have evolved into modern voiced stops). In general, we may state that the time span recorded in the history of known languages is apparently not sufficient for such changes to occur in an individual language. In the recorded history of languages we find only the final results of such sound changes, their beginning lying beyond their recorded history. What we have is only correspondences between series of different dialects which make it plausible to infer such sound shifts. That is why we have to hypothesize the direction of the prehistorical sound change on the basis of these attested sound correspondences, taking into account of necessity general phonetic considerations and diachronic typological evidence.

Neogrammarian views on Proto-Indo-European at any cost, despite the fact that the contradictory character and the disadvantages of the classical Indo-European paradigm are becoming more and more evident in current Indo-European comparative studies.

On the other hand, much of the argumentation in defense of the Glottalic Theory and the ejectives in PIE is contained in Joseph Salmons' monograph (1993), which has received unjustified criticism on the part of Michael Job (1995). I cannot agree with Job's conclusion that "the author failed to meet the expectations raised by the title of the book and by the author's intention to present a survey from a relatively neutral corner." Salmon's book is one of the best critical surveys and objective evaluations of the Glottalic Theory. If I have any remarks in connection with Salmons' excellent exposition of the Glottalic Theory and its consequences for the Comparative IE, they would be that the author scarcely mentions our work of 1984 (Gamkrelidze and Ivanov) and limits himself to our previous articles of the early 1970s; I have our joint Russian monograph of 1984 in view, where the same comparative IE issues are dealt with at length in light of the glottalic reinterpretation of the system of PIE stops (such as Grassmann's Law, Bartholomae's Law, Lachmann's Law, etc.), with all the structural consequences of such a reinterpretation for the whole of Comparative Indo-European.

One of the main objections on the part of the opponents of the Glottalic Theory to positing glottalized consonants (or ejectives) in Proto-Indo-European in place of the traditional plain voiced stops is, on the one hand, the absence of such stops in historical IE languages (the Armenian evidence being for the proponents of this view due to the Caucasian influence), and, on the other, the phonetic character of the glottalized stops (ejectives) being by their very nature voiceless due to their articulatory characteristics (closed vocal cords during their articulation, the explosion of the outer closure being produced by the air compressed in the space between the oral stricture and the closed glottis). This negative view was advanced notably by Oswald Szemerényi (1985) and repeated later by a number of adversaries of the Glottalic Theory, this being viewed as an insurmountable difficulty for the theory.

The first objection is methodologically inconsistent with the theoretical premises of historical comparative linguistics which do not rule out in principle positing for a proto-language phonemic units that are not found in historical languages descended from the postulated common ancestor. It is rather paradoxical that one can find such objections in works by Indo-Europeanists who posit an unrestricted number of laryngeals in Proto-Indo-European knowing that these postulated hypothetical Proto-Indo-European phonemes never gave segmental reflexes (apart from Hittite) in historical IE languages. I wonder why these scholars are so critical in connection with ejectives and so liberal with respect to laryngeals. In principle, laryngeal sounds are much more exotic for historical IE languages than are glottalized stops, which are met rather frequently in historical IE languages, although in some of them probably in nonphonological status. Furthermore, additional typological evidence might be adduced in favor of the existence of ejectives in PIE: languages with laryngeals tend to contain in their inventory also phonemes with glottalic articulations (cf. Maddieson 1984).[6]

As for other objections concerning the phonetic character of the glottalized consonants incompatible with the feature [+voice], it must be pointed out from the very outset that the glottalized stops being by their very nature voiceless tend, nevertheless, to become voiced or to be perceived as voiced. This phonetic characteristic of the [voiceless] ejectives would justify phonetically the assumption of the shifts of the PIE glottalized consonants to voiced stops in historical Indo-European dialects.

At the International Congress of Phonetic Sciences in Tallinn, J. Ingram and B. Rigsby presented a paper, in which they argue that in Gitskan (spoken in British Columbia) "for non-native listeners, glottalized stops may, in certain instances, be perceptually confused with plain voiced stops" (Ingram and Rigsby 1987).

In this respect highly interesting experimental data are provided also by Mona Lindau. Examining the phonation type of ejectives in different languages, the author arrives at the conclusion that in Hausa and Navaho the ejectives display a great deal of variation between speakers. Some of the speakers realize the ejective /k'/ phoneme as voiced [g] (Lindau 1984). The same is characteristic of nonnative speakers of Georgian, who usually replace Georgian "ejectives" with the respective voiced stops.

---

[6]Usually, in languages with laryngeals, there are glottalics (consonants with glottalized and/or pharyngealized articulations) in the phonological system, as well, and this should be borne in mind by laryngealists dealing with a whole set of laryngeal phonemes in PIE. This is why it is rather amazing that Fredric Otto Lindeman who did an excellent work on IE laryngeals (Lindeman 1997) is so negative towards glottalics in PIE (cf. pp. 145–148), and this not as a result of his own structural analysis of the system, but by reference to some articles by other authors containing unfounded criticisms of glottalics in PIE to which we have already given due responses (cf. Gamkrelidze 1990a, 1990b, 1992, 1995, 1999). This method of refuting the Glottalic Theory is observed also in some other writings adducing critical evaluations of the Glottalic Theory, but never referring to our answers to these rather unfounded and superficial objections. What can I say, for example, about Don Ringe Jr. who, referring merely to the same critical articles concerning the Glottalic Theory, qualifies it as a "monumental error" (1996:3). Although the author seems to be a good specialist in Tocharian, he is apparently (and unfortunately), unaware of the theoretical premises of contemporary Diachronic Linguistics. I wonder whether the author realizes what the term "error" should mean in linguistics and inductive or deductive sciences in general.

The fact that (lax) ejectives may be in free variation with (unaspirated) voiceless and/or voiced stops makes the historical replacement of ejectives by voiced stops phonetically quite plausible (cf. Hayward 1989:47).

Furthermore, in some of the Caucasian languages one may assume in certain cases a regular shift of glottalized consonants into voiced phonemes, as different from nonglottalized consonants. Thus, in Arc'i, a Caucasian language, consonant clusters [c'd] and [č'd] (with glottalized affricates *c'* and *č'*) yield respectively [zd] and [žd] (with voiced spirants *z* and *ž*), while consonant clusters [cd] and [čd] (with nonglottalized affricates *c* and *č*) yield respectively [sd] and [šd] (with voiceless spirants *s* and *š*); cf. Kodzasov (1976).

In Punjabi the voiced phonemes may be viewed as ancient glottalized (cf. Hagège and Haudricourt 1978:165). The same is assumed in the case of preglottalized stops which usually change in the direction of plain voiced stops (p. 164). That is why Haudricourt views the glottalized stops of Armenian as a conservation of the situation characteristic of Proto-Indo-European, while the glottalization of Ossetic and Kurdish is assumed to be a result of language contact and borrowing (pp. 123–125).

In his article on the Northwest Caucasian languages, J. Colarusso (1981) analyzes the phonetic transformations of ejectives as voicing of respective consonants occurring frequently, along with deglottalization and retention of the feature of glottalization.

Good examples implying the consonant shift "ejective" → "voiced" come, as indicated above, from Northeast Caucasian languages:

Batsbi *č'*	~	Chechen *ž*	,	Ingush *ǯ / ž:*	
mač' 'moustache'	~	*maž* 'beard'	,	*moǯ* 'id.'	
Batsbi *k'*	~	Chechen *g*	,	Ingush *g:*	
dok' 'heart'	~	*dwog*	,	*dog* 'id.'	
Batsbi *t'*	~	Chechen *d*	,	Ingush *d:*	
let'ar 'flow'	~	*liedar*	,	*liedar* 'id.'	

Analogous correspondences can be found in other branches of Northeast Caucasian: Avar *c'c'ar* 'name' ~ Rutulian *dur*, Caxur *do*; Archi *moč'or*, Rutulian *mič'ri*, Lak *č'iri* 'beard' ~ Tabassaran *miǯir*, Agul *muǯur* 'beard'. The Proto-Dagestanian fortis glottalized affricates *c'c'*, *č'č'*, *q'q'*, *t¹'t¹'* yield respectively *d*, *ɔ*, *q'*, *g* pretonically and *t*, *č*, *q*, *k* posttonically; i.e., they undergo voicing and deglottalization (cf. Gigineishvili 1974; 1977:106).

In South Caucasian (Kartvelian), Svan has instances of dissimilative voicing of ejectives: *gak'* 'nut' (from *k'ak', cf. Geo. *k'ak'-al-i* 'nut'), *bap'* 'priest' (from *p'ap', cf. Gk. *páppos*). In Ossetic, glottalized consonants in early loans from Georgian are reflected as voiced stops due to dissimilative voicing as in *p'at'ara > bat'ara*, etc. (cf. Gamkrelidze and Ivanov 1995:45–46). Such examples can be multiplied at will from languages of different structures containing ejectives.

The diachronic voicing of the glottalized consonants observed in a number of the languages finds its phonetic explanation in the nature of glottalized sounds, which are pronounced with glottal articulation involving the complete closure of vocal cords. Voiced consonants are also characterized by glottal articulation, with the vocal cords drawn close or closed and vibrating. When the glottal stricture is released in the phonation of glottalized consonants, and in particular before a vowel, there can be a brief vibration (opening after closure) of the vocal cords, as is characteristic of the phonation of voiced sounds. If the period of accompanying vibration is lengthened to extend into the articulation of the glottalized sound, the result can be a voiced preglottalized consonant (or voiced laryngealized consonant, as in Hausa), which otherwise shares the articulatory features of glottalized sounds. In the state of the glottis during phonation, glottalized consonants are more similar to voiced than to voiceless consonants.

An investigation of phonation types of speech sounds indicates that voiced consonants and sounds with glottalic articulation (laryngealized consonants including "ejectives") are related and comprise a single natural class of sounds. They are closer to each other than are consonants with glottal articulation to voiceless consonants (cf. Ladefoged 1971:16ff.; Catford 1977, *passim*). These are articulatorily related sounds in that in both cases the glottalic articulation is actively involved: in the first instance (voiced consonants), this is the vibration of the vocal cords and in the second case (ejectives), their active closure. These sounds are at the extreme poles of the same articulatory process—the articulation of the vocal cords (or active articulatory involvement of the vocal cords as different from their lax position in the process of the articulation of voiceless [aspirated] sounds). This state of active glottalic involvement in case of the articulation of voiced and glottalized consonants conditions their articulatory (and acoustic/auditory) relatedness evidenced in instances of their conditioned interchange and alternation, as well as their diachronic transformations observed in languages of a vast structural spectrum.

The typological approach to linguistic reconstruction led in the early 1970s to the advancement of the Glottalic Theory which has been considered, in view of its fundamentally different interpretation of the Proto-Indo-European linguistic system, a new paradigm in Indo-European comparative linguistics, comparable in its consequences for the views on the derivation and developments of the individual Indo-European dialects to the Laryngeal theory (cf. Baldi 1981; Polomé 1982).[7]

The Indo-European Glottalic Theory has even been considered, alongside the *Palatalgesetz* and the Laryngeal Theory, a stage in the process of digression in Indo-European comparative studies from Old Indian as a model for Indo-European (Mayrhofer 1983). In this famous report to the Göttingen Academy of Sciences, Manfred Mayrhofer views the Comparative Historical Indo-European Studies as a process of digression or deviation from the pattern of Old Indian as a model for Proto-Indo-European. In this process, the author distinguishes between five successive stages reflecting degrees of such a digression. The first stage in this process was presented by Friedrich von Schlegel who identified Indo-European with Old Indian; the second stage is exemplified by August Schleicher who considered Old Indian structurally very close to, but not identical with, Proto-Indo-European. The third stage was presented by *Palatalgesetz* that demonstrated that the Proto-Indo-European vocalism was totally different from Old Indian. The fourth stage was the Laryngeal Theory postulating specific phonemic units that were lost as segmental phonemes in Old Indian, and the fifth and final stage so far in this process of development of Indo-European Comparative Studies is the Glottalic Theory, according to which the consonantism of Proto-Indo-European appears to be totally different from that of Old Indian, presenting thus the whole picture of the IE parent language essentially different from the traditionally assumed Neogrammarian one.

In one of his preprints of 1983, Winfred P. Lehmann made the following statement:

> Major contributions of the past five decades have modified extensively the views on Proto-Indo-European phonology presented in the standard

---

[7]It was a real disappointment to us that one of the earlier supporters of the Glottalic Theory who viewed the theory as a new paradigm in IE comparative historical studies, in his recent fundamental book *The Foundations of Latin* (Baldi 1999), expressed some reservations towards it, noting that "despite initial enthusiasm for the glottalic theory (including that of the present author), evidence against it has mounted" (pp. 57–58). This "mounting evidence" against the theory is, however, limited to the following issues:

1. Assimilation of aspirates in Italic (This is an issue that has been solved satisfactorily by Philip Baldi himself; cf. also my 1999 article, as against Joseph and Wallace (1994). By the way, it must be emphasized that the "Glottalic model" for PIE does not stand or fall dependent on any solution of the issue of "Aspirations in Italic.")

2. Complexity of sound transformations in IE daughter dialects.

3. Change of the (unvoiced) glottalics to voiced stops.

handbooks by Brugmann, Hirt and Meillet. These contributions result on
the one hand from a different approach to the parent language, on the
other, from two far-reaching theories, the Laryngeal Theory and the
Glottalic Theory....What had seemed one of the most solid achievements
of 19th century linguistics is now modified in every section.

How different it is from the mood that reigned at the beginning of our
century, when Antoine Meillet, summing up his views on the situation in
comparative Indo-European linguistics could make the following remark
in his "Introduction": *"En un sens au moins, il semble qu'on soit parvenu à un
terme impossible à dépasser."*
Even the modified version of this statement by Émile Benveniste in the
posthumous edition of Meillet's "Introduction" (1937:479–480) does not
change anything about the established view: *"Même une trouvaille d'espèce
inattendue...n'a pas renouvelé l'idée qu'on se fait de l'indoeuropéen; le
hittite...n'oblige à rien changer d'essentiel aux doctrines exposées ici; il éclaire
nombre de faits, mais il ne transforme pas la théorie générale..."*
The emergence and further development of the Laryngeal Theory,
founded on the method of internal reconstruction, and the advent of the
Glottalic Theory, based on the principle of synchronic and diachronic typological verification in comparative reconstruction, have brought
Indo-European comparative historical studies out of this theoretical
stagnation.
It must be pointed out that the Glottalic Theory has from its very beginning won the support of a number of scholars who proposed interesting explanations—in the light of the new theory—of phonetic developments in
individual Indo-European dialects (cf. especially Bomhard 1975; Normier
1977; Kortlandt 1977, 1978a; 1978b; 1981; cf. also Vennemann 1982, and
others). However, we must admit today—about three decades after our
(Gamkrelidze and Ivanov) first publication on the Glottalic Theory in 1972
and 1973—that, apart from a number of eminent scholars such as André
Martinet, A.-G. Haudricourt, Manfred Mayrhofer, Winfred P. Lehmann, Edgar Polomé, and others, it has gained only a grudging acceptance on the part
of the more established generation of Indo-Europeanists. This fact is fairly
understandable psychologically and testifies once more to the character of
the Glottalic Theory as a "new paradigm" in Indo-European studies. The elder generation is always reluctant to give up old views and ideas and prefers
to continue within the framework of a traditional, time-honored, and hence
more usual paradigm, even if its contradictory character is fairly evident.
One would recall in this connection the famous Max Planck principle:

Eine neue wissenschaftliche Wahrheit pflegt sich nicht in der Weise durchzusetzen, dass ihre Gegner überzeugt werden und sich als belehrt erklären, sondern vielmehr dadurch, dass die Gegner allmählich aussterben und dass die heranwachsende Generation von vornherein mit der Wahrheit vertraut gemacht ist. (Planck 1949:13)

The fate of Saussure's *coéfficients sonantiques* and of the whole of the Laryngeal hypothesis is a brilliant corroboration of the validity of this principle.

We, for our part, firmly believe that the Glottalic Theory as a new paradigm in Indo-European comparative linguistics will gain with time an ever-widening acceptance among Indo-European scholars of all generations, this being a strong impetus to further develop comparative Indo-European studies, making it more theory-oriented and broadening considerably its scope of research.

This is why I cannot agree with Andrew Garrett who upholds the view that "the Glottalic Theory was an exciting proposal but perhaps one…whose time has come and gone" (Garrett 1991). I would oppose to all this the statement by Roman Jakobson who concludes his "Preface" to our (Gamkrelidze and Ivanov) monograph of 1984 (and this, alas, was one of his last writings) by the following remark:

> In the number and magnitude of the questions it asks and [the] answers it proposes this work occupies a unique place. Fully consistent with the highest standards of contemporary theoretical work, the book in turn will certainly provide valuable impetus not only to linguistic analysts of all schools, but also to specialists in related fields, for instance ethnographers, culture historians, and archeologists. A great deal of fruitful discussion will come forth in international science as a result of this momentous work.

Roman Jakobson means here the many firsts in our research on Proto-Indo-European language and culture, as indicated by Johanna Nichols in her "Introduction" to the English version of our monograph (Gamkrelidze and Ivanov 1995:xi). These words by the great Russian-American linguist have been corroborated later by the ensuing research work and appearing publications in the field of Comparative Indo-European.

After our investigations on Proto-Indo-European many similar publications have appeared by authors with an innovative approach to the reconstruction of Proto-Indo-European language and culture, as predicted by Roman Jakobson, although, unfortunately, fairly often without proper reference to, sometimes even without any mention of, their predecessors.

Our present review-article attempts to be, in a sense, a response to some
of those publications.

References

Arbeitman, Yoël L., and Allan R. Bomhard, eds. 1981. *Bono Homini Donum. Es-
     says in historical linguistics, in memory of J. Alexander Kerns.* Amsterdam:
     John Benjamins.
Baldi, Philip. 1981. Review of Brogyanyi, Bela (ed.), *Studies in diachronic,
     synchronic, and typological linguistics: Festschrift for Oswald Szemerényi.* Am-
     sterdam: John Benjamins.
Baldi, Philip. 1999. *The foundations of Latin.* Berlin and New York: Mouton de
     Gruyter.
Bomhard, Allan. 1975. An outline of the historical phonology of Indo-European.
     Orbis 24(2):354–390.
Catford, Ian. 1977. *Fundamental problems in phonetics.* Bloomington: Indiana
     University Press.
Colarusso, J. J., Jr. 1981. Typological parallels between PIE and the Northwest
     Caucasian languages. In Arbeitman and Bomhard (eds.), *Bono Homini
     Donum.*
Cowgill, Warren. 1984[1985] Review of Arbeitman and Bomhard 1981.
     Kratylos 29:1–13.
Č'relašvili, K. 1975. *Naxuri enebis tanxmovanta sist'ema.* Tbilisi: The University
     Press.
Dunkel, George. 1981. Typology versus reconstruction. In Yoël L. Arbeitman
     and Allan R. Bomhard (eds.), 559–569.
Fallon, Paul D. 1993. *Consequences of Nakh obstruent evolution for the Glottalic
     Theory.* Columbus: The Ohio State University.
Fallon, Paul D. 1995. *Synchronic and diachronic typology: The case of ejective voic-
     ing.* Berkeley Linguistic Society 21:105–116.
Gamkrelidze, Thomas V. 1985. The IE Glottalic Theory and the system of Old
     Armenian consonantism. In *Studia Linguistica Diachronica et Synchronica.
     Festschrift für Werner Winter.*
Gamkrelidze, Thomas V. 1990a. Diachronic typology and reconstruction: The
     "archaism" of Germanic and Armenian in light of the Glottalic Theory. In
     Winfred P. Lehmann (ed.), *Language typology 1987. Systematic balance in lan-
     guage,* 57–66. Amsterdam: John Benjamins.
Gamkrelidze, Thomas V. 1990b. The Indo-European Glottalic Theory in the
     light of recent critique. *Folia Linguistica Historica* 9(1):3–12.
Gamkrelidze, Thomas V. 1992. The Indo-European "Glottalic Theory" in the
     light of recent critique: 1972/1991 "KRATYLOS." Kritische Berichts- und
     Rezensionsorgan für Indogermanische und Allgemeine Sprachwissenschaft.

Gamkrelidze, Thomas V. 1995. Recent developments in Indo-European linguistics and a new paradigm in Indo-European Comparative Studies. *On Languages and Language*. Presidential Addresses of the 1991 Meeting of the Societas Linguistica Europaea, ed. by Werner Winter. Berlin and New York: Mouton de Gruyter.

Gamkrelidze, Thomas V. 1999. Italic consonantism in the light of the Glottalic Theory: Language change and typological variation. In Edgar Polomé and Carol F. Justus (eds.), *In Honor of Winfred P. Lehmann on the occasion of his 83rd birthday, Volume I: Language change and phonology*, Journal of Indo-European Studies, Monograph No. 30.

Gamkrelidze, Thomas V. 2000. André Martinet et la "théorie glottalique indo-européenne" *Hommage André Martinet*. La Sorbonne. Université René Descartes, Paris V, 27 Mai, 2000.

Gamkrelidze, Thomas V. and Vyacheslav V. Ivanov. 1972. Lingvistiçeskaja tipologija i rekonstrukcija sistemy indoevropejskix smyçnyx" [Linguistic typology and the reconstruction of Indo-European stop system]. In *Konferencija po sravnitel'no-istoriceskoj grammatike indo-evropejskix jazykov*, 15–18. Moscow: Nauka.

Gamkrelidze, Thomas V. and Vyacheslav V. Ivanov. 1973 Sprachtypologie und die Rekonstruktion der gemein- indo-germanischen Verschlüsse. *Phonetica* 27:150–156.

Gamkrelidze, Thomas V. and Vyacheslav V. Ivanov. 1984. *Indo-evropejskij jazyk i indoevropejcy*. Rekonstrukcija i istoriko-tipologiceskij analiz prajazyka i protokul'tury (tt. I–II). S predisloviem R. O. Jakobsona, Tbilisi: Izdatel'stvo Tbilisskogo Universiteta.

Gamkrelidze, Thomas V. and Vyacheslav V. Ivanov. 1995. *Indo-European and the Indo-Europeans. A reconstruction and historical analysis of a proto-language and proto-culture*, 2 volumes. English version by Johanna Nichols, ed. by Werner Winter, with a Preface by Roman Jakobson. Berlin and New York: Mouton de Gruyter.

Gaprindashvili, Sh. G. 1966. Fonetika darginskogo jazyka. *Mecniereba*. Tbilisi.

Garrett, Andrew. 1991. Indo-European reconstruction and historical methodologies. *Language* 67(4):790–804.

Gigineishvili, B. K. 1974. *Obščedagestanskij konsonantism*. Avtoreferat kandidatskoj dissertacii. Tbilisi.

Gigineishvili, B. K. 1977. *Sravnitel'naja fonetika dagestanskix jazykov*. Tbilisi: Tbilisi State University.

Gippert, Jost. 1995. Die Glottaltheorie und die Frage früher indogermanisch-kaukasischer Sprachkontakte. In Jens Elmegard (ed.), *In Honorem Holger Pedersen*, 107–123. Wiesbaden: Reichert.

Greenberg, Joseph H. 1970. Some generalizations concerning glottalic consonants, especially implosives. *International Journal of American Linguistics* 36:123–145.

Hagège C., and A.-G. Haudricourt. 1978. *La phonologie panchronique: Comment les sons changent dans les langues*. Paris: Presses Universitaires de France.

Haider, Hubert. 1985. The fallacy of typology: Remarks on the Proto-Indo-European stop system. *Lingua* 65:1–27.

Haspelmath, M. 1993. *A grammar of Lezgian*. Berlin and New York: Mouton de Gruyter.

Hayward, K. M. 1989. The Indo-European language and the history of its speakers: The theories of Gamkrelidze and Ivanov. *Lingua* 78:37–86.

Hock, Hans Henrich. 1986. *Principles of historical linguistics*. Berlin and New York: Mouton de Gruyter.

Hopper, Paul J. 1973. Glottalized and murmured occlusives in Indo-European. *Glossa* 7:141–166.

Ingram, U., and B. Rigsby. 1987. Glottalic stops in Gitskan: Acoustic analysis. *Proceedings of the 11th International Congress of Phonetic Sciences*, vol. 6. Tallinn: Academy of Sciences of the Estonian S.S.R.

Imnaishvili, D. 1977. *Istoriko-sravnitel'nyj analiz fonetiki naxskix jazykov*. Tbilisi: Mecniereba.

Jaraliev, M. M. 1989. *Konsonantism lezginskogo jazyka*. Avtoreferat dissertacii na soiskanie ucenoj stepeni kandidata filologiceskix nauk. Tbilisi.

Job, Michael. 1989. Sound change typology and the "Ejective Model." In Theo Vennemann (ed.), 123–136.

Job, Michael. 1995. Did Proto-Indo-European have glottalized stops? *Diachronica* XII(2):237–250.

Joseph, Brian, and Rex E. Wallace. 1994. Proto-Indo-European voiced aspirates in Italic. A test of the "Glottalic Theory." *Historische Sprachforschung* 107:244–261.

Kammerzell, Frank. 1999. Glottaltheorie, Typologie, Sprachkontakte und Verwandtschaftsmodelle: *Indogermanische Forschungen*. Zeitschrift für Indogermanistik und Allgemeine Sprachwissenschaft. B104:234–271.

Kodzasov, S. V. 1976. Model' foneticeskoj sistemy (na materiale arcinskogo jazyka). *Institut Russkogo jazyka AN SSSR*. Problemnaja gruppa po eksperimental'noj i prikladnoj lingvistike, Moscow.

Kortlandt, Frederik. 1977. Historical laws of Slavic accentuation. *Baltistica* 13(2):319–330.

Kortlandt, Frederik. 1978a. Proto-Indo-European obstruents. *Indogermanische Forschungen* 83:107–118.

Kortlandt, Frederik. 1978b. Comments on W. Winter's paper. In: J. Fisiak (ed.), *Recent developments in historical phonology*, 447. (Trends in Linguistics: Studies and Monographs 4, W. Winter (ed.).) The Hague-Paris: Mouton.

Kortlandt, Frederik. 1981. Glottalic consonants in Sindhi and Proto-Indo-European. *Indo-Iranian Journal* 23:15–19.

Ladefoged, Peter. 1971. *Preliminaries to linguistic phonetics*. Chicago: University of Chicago Press.

Lehmann, Winfred P., ed. 1990. *Systemic balance in language*. Amsterdam and Philadelphia.

Lindau, Mona. 1984. Phonetic differences in glottalic consonants. *Journal of Phonetics* 12:147–155.

Lindeman, Fredrik Otto. 1997. Introduction to the "Laryngeal Theory." In Wolfgang Meid (ed.), *Innsbrucker Beiträge zur Sprachwissenschaft*. Innsbruck.

Maddieson, Ian. 1984. *Patterns of sound*. Cambridge: Cambridge University Press.

Mayrhofer, Manfred. 1983. Sanskrit und die Sprachen Alteuropas. Zwei Jahrhunderte des Widerspiels von Entdeckungen und Irrtümern. *Nachrichten der Akademie der Wissenschaften in Göttingen. Philologisch-Historische Klasse*, volume 5.

Meillet, Antoine. 1937. *Introduction à l'étude comparative des langues Indo-européennes*. [Reprinted University of Alabama Press, 1964.]

Normier, R. 1977. Indogermanischer Konsonantismus, germ. "Lautver- schiebung" und vernersches Gesetz. *Zeitschrift für Vergleichende Sprachfor- schung* 91(2):171–218.

Pedersen, Holger. 1951. *Die gemeinindoeuropäischen und die vorindoeuropäischen Verschlusslaute. Det Kongelige Daanske Videnskabernes Selskab*. Hist.-filol. Meddelelser 32(5). Copenhagen: Munksgaard.

Planck, Max. 1949. *Vorträge und Erinnerungen*, fifth edition. Stuttgart.

Polomé, Edgar, ed. 1982. *The Indo-Europeans in the Fourth and Third Millennia*. Ann Arbor: Karoma.

Rasmussen, Jens Elmegård, ed. 1995. *In Honorem Holger Pedersen*. Wiesbaden: Reichert.

Ringe, Don, Jr. 1996. *On the chronology of sound change in Tocharian, vol. I: From Proto-Indo-European to Proto-Tocharian*. New Haven, Conn.: American Ori- ental Society.

Salmons, Joseph C. 1993. *The Glottalic Theory: Survey and synthesis. Journal of Indo-European Studies*. Monograph Series, No. 10.

Sommerfelt, Alf. 1938. Études comparatives sur le caucasique du Nord-Est. *Norsk Tidsskrift for Sprogvidenskap* 9:115–143.

Szemerényi, Oswald. 1967. The new look of Indo-European: Reconstruction and typology. *Phonetica* 17:65–99.

Szemerényi, Oswald. 1985. Recent developments in Indo-European linguistics. *Transactions of the Philological Society* 1–71.

Talibov, B. B. 1980. *Sravnitel'naja fonetika lezginskix jazykov*. Moskva: Nauka.

Vennemann, Theo. 1982. Hochgermanisch und Niedergermanisch. Die Verzweigungstheorie der germanisch-deutschen Lautverschiebung. *Beiträge zur Geschichte der Deutschen Sprache und Literatur* 106:1–45.

Vennemann, Theo, ed. 1989. The new sound of Indo-European: Essays in pho- nological reconstruction. *Trends in linguistics*. Studies and Monographs 41. Berlin and New York: Mouton de Gruyter.

Woodhouse, Robert. 1993. A reformulation of quasi–Gamkrelidzean occlusive typology and its more fruitful application to Indo-European. *Indogermanische Forschungen* 98:1–12.

Woodhouse, Robert. 1995. Some criticisms of the Gamkrelidze/Ivanov glottalic hypothesis for Proto-Indo-European. *Historische Sprachforschung* 108:173–189.

33

The Historical Source of an Irregular Mixtec Tone-Sandhi Pattern

Barbara E. Hollenbach

Introduction

The Mixtec people of Oaxaca, Mexico, trace their history perhaps as far back as the late seventh century A.D. in their pictorial codices, and their language has been written using the roman alphabet since at least 1567, when the Dominican friar Benito Hernández published a Mixtec catechism containing 189 folios. Two other Dominican friars contributed heavily to our knowledge of sixteenth-century Mixtec; in 1593, Francisco de Alvarado published a vocabulary, and in the same year, Antonio de los Reyes published a grammar.

Both Alvarado and De los Reyes were clearly aware that there were tone contrasts in Mixtec. In his prologue Alvarado stated: "In the accent many words vary their meaning, and some not only in having or losing a

I would like to express my appreciation to Bruce Hollenbach, John Daly, Mike Cahill, and Inga McKendry for reading earlier drafts of this chapter and suggesting improvements in it.

533

written accent, but even in pronouncing a word with softness or with the voice full."[1]

De los Reyes (1593) referred to tone in his chapters 17 and 18, which talk about otherwise homophonous pairs or groups of verbs. He said it was necessary to look at the accents, and if there were none, to under- stand that the pronunciation was *llana,* literally, 'flat', but also used in Spanish for a word with penultimate stress (p. 54). One of his example pairs is *sànu* for 'grow, present tense', and *sánu* for 'break, present tense'. These two roots continue to show a tone difference in modern Mixtec; they have the following forms in Mixtec of Magdalena Peñasco, shown in (1). (In this study, high tone is marked with an acute accent, mid tone with a macron, and low tone with an underline, for example, á ā a̲.)[2]

(1)   a. *jā'nū*   'grow'
      b. *jā'nu̲*   'fold, break'[3]

Farther down on page 54, De los Reyes gave a tone triplet: *"Yosacundi,* with the voice low, means 'to laugh', and *yosacundi,* higher, means 'to cry'; *yosacundi,* with mid voice, means 'wear around the neck, like beads' and 'to make noise (wind)', all of which have the future tense form *quacu,* with the difference placed in the pronunciation."[4]

Apart from the above intriguing references to tone, however, no one who wrote in or about Mixtec during the Colonial period made any seri- ous attempt to write tone, or to analyze it. It remained for linguists of the twentieth century to analyze the tonal systems that form an integral part of this language family. The pioneer study of Mixtec tone was carried out by Kenneth Pike in the 1930s and 1940s in San Miguel el Grande, and pre- sented on pages 77–94 of his book *Tone Languages,* published in 1948. Using the techniques for tone analysis developed by Pike, a number of other linguists working with SIL International analyzed tonal systems in

[1]In the original Spanish this is: *"En el acento varian muchas palabras la significacion, y algunas no solamente en tener o perder una tilde pero aun en pronunciar el punto con blandura o con la boz llena."*

[2]Throughout this study Mixtec examples are adapted to the orthography adopted by Ve'e Tu'un Savi *(Academia de la Lengua Mixteca),* the Mixtec language academy. The letter *j* represents a velar fricative, the letter *x* represents an alveopalatal sibilant, the raised vertical stroke (') represents glottal stop, and the letter *n* at the end of a word represents nasalization. Glottal stop is not written at the beginning of a word.

[3]I have chosen to adhere closely to the phonetic facts and write the tone that is pronounced on each syllable. Tone can, of course, be viewed in more abstract ways, but my goal has been simply to present the raw material clearly, and let linguists who have more interest in theory analyze it in the way that they prefer.

[4]In the original Spanish this is: *"Yosacundi, la boz baxa, q. d. reirse y yosacundi, mas alta, q. d. llorar, yosacundi, media voce. q. d. traer al cuello como cuentas y hazer ruido el viento, los quales todos hazen en futuro quacu, con la differencia puesta en la pronunciacion."*

various languages of Mesoamerica, including several other variants of Mixtec.

Tone Sandhi in San Miguel el Grande Mixtec

The San Miguel tonal system has three levels: high, mid, and low. Perhaps the most salient characteristic of this system is the way in which some words raise the tone of the following word. Pike described this by positing an apparently arbitrary classification of words into those which do not cause tone changes (subclass a) and those which do (subclass b) (1948:77–81). More recent approaches to the study of tone posit an unattached (floating) high tone at the end of the words in subclass b, which moves to the following word and affects its tone pattern.

The examples in (2), which Pike gives on pages 77, 80, and 81, show this progressive tone sandhi.

(2) a. *yūkū (b)* 'mountain'   + *vīnā 'now'*   → *yūkū vínā* 'mountain now'
     b. *kēē (b)* 'eat (future)'   + *suchí* 'child'   → *kēē súchí* 'the child will eat'
     c. *kēē (b)* 'eat (future)'   + *kōo̱* 'snake'   → *kēē kóo̱* 'the snake will eat'

In each of the words given so far, the floating high tone replaces the first tone of the following word. In a few cases, however, the change is somewhat less straightforward. The most difficult case is found in words with a mid-low tone pattern and a (C)VCV syllable pattern.[5] The mid-low pattern is changed to mid-high following a word of subclass b, as seen in this example given on page 81.

(3) *kēē (b)* 'eat (future)' + *īso̱* 'rabbit'   → *kēē īsó* 'the rabbit will eat'

Note that mid-low changes to high-low in words with other syllable patterns, as in the example with 'snake' in (2c), which has the syllable pattern (C)VV. What appears to be happening in words like 'rabbit' is that the high tone jumps over the mid tone, leaving it unaffected, and changes the low tone in the second syllable to high.

Even though Pike described this irregular change clearly, he did not offer any explanation for it, and it has remained puzzling to subsequent

---

[5]Pike points out that words with a (C)VV pattern that have dissimilar vowels act like (C)VCV words, rather than like (C)VV words with identical vowels (1948:81). This can be explained historically: San Miguel words like *yáu̱* 'hole' developed from (C)VCV words; the Magdalena form of 'hole' is *yāvi̱*.

generations of linguists working to develop a theory of tonal systems. Goldsmith, for example, in his book on Autosegmental Phonology (1990), presents a theory claiming that tones are on a separate tier from the segments, but that they are associated with one or more segments by rules, and that tone rules can change these associations. The correctness of this formulation is certainly not in doubt. It is essentially a return to Pike's claim that tone is suprasegmental, made in 1945 in his book *The Intonation of American English.* (This return came after a period in which mainstream linguistic theory tried without success to handle tone as a feature of vowel segments.)

One of Goldsmith's major principles is, "Association lines in a given representation may not cross" (1990:47). And yet, when he considered the San Miguel data (1990:20–26), they seemed to violate this principle, and he posited a tonal metathesis rule to associate the high tone to the second syllable of words like *iso* 'rabbit', rather than to the first syllable (1990:24–26).

Chalcatongo de Hidalgo, a Mixtec town located about five kilometers east of San Miguel el Grande, shares this same irregular tone change. In the description of tone in her grammar of Chalcatongo Mixtec, Macaulay (1996:32–39) cited both Pike and Goldsmith, and she essentially adopted Goldsmith's device of a tonal metathesis rule (1996:37).

Tranel (1995), working in Optimality Theory, tried to account for the irregularity by positing that mid tone is transparent to the association of floating high tones. He recognized, however, that not all instances of mid tone are transparent, and he therefore proposed various ranked constraints that interact with this principle.

In this essay I offer a historical explanation for this irregular tone change, based on my study of the Mixtec of Magdalena Peñasco, a town about twenty-three kilometers north of Chalcatongo. I claim that the irregularity is a result of tone movement to the right. Furthermore, based on the tonal behavior of certain loanwords, it seems clear that this movement took place after Spanish contact in the sixteenth century.

Tone Sandhi in Magdalena Peñasco Mixtec

The Mixtec spoken in Magdalena Peñasco (sometimes referred to simply as Magdalena) shows sandhi similar to San Miguel, but the patterns are somewhat more complex. Not only are there floating high tones *(h),* but there are also floating low tones *(l);* and both kinds appear to subdivide depending on how far their influence extends. Some of these features provide clues to the historical development of the current irregular forms.

As in San Miguel, there are words in Magdalena that end with a floating high tone that causes a tone change in the following word. Some of these words have a mid tone followed by the floating high. Just as in San Miguel, the mid-low tone pattern becomes mid-high in following words with a (C)VCV syllable pattern, and high-low in words with other patterns, as shown in (4).

(4) (C)VCV *yū'ū (h)* 'mouth' + *īso* 'rabbit'   → *yū'ū īsó* 'the rabbit's mouth'

    (C)V'V *yū'ū (h)* 'mouth' + *mā'a* 'raccoon' → *yū'ū má'a* 'the raccoon's mouth'

    (C)V'CV *yū'ū (h)* 'mouth' + *ndū'va* 'valley' → *yū'ū ndú'va* 'the edge of the valley'

    (C)VV *yū'ū (h)* 'mouth' + *kōo (h)* 'snake'→ *yū'ū kóo (h)* 'the snake's mouth'

Other words have a low tone followed by a floating high. In these words, the mid-low tone pattern of the following word changes to low-high, rather than mid-high. One way to view this is that the low tone spreads to the first syllable of the next word and takes the place of a default mid.

(5) (C)VCV *kāa (h)* 'will eat' + *īso* 'rabbit' → *kāa isó* 'the rabbit will eat'

There is strong evidence in Magdalena that the two forms of 'rabbit' that result from the sandhi rules end with a floating low tone, and that they should therefore be written *īsó (l)* and *isó (l)*. This floating low tone can be identified historically with the low tone on the final syllable of the basic form of the word. I posit the following scenario.

At some point in the history of Mixtec, words of all syllable patterns with the mid-low tone pattern changed to high-low following a floating high tone. At this stage, the word for 'rabbit' was changed from **īso* to **íso*. Words with the (C)VCV syllable pattern like 'rabbit' then underwent a second change, which involved the movement of the high tone one syllable to the right, i.e., the high tone lagged behind the segments, and it was pronounced with the following syllable. This movement left the first syllable without a tone, and the low tone without a syllable. To supply a tone for the first syllable, either the low tone on the final syllable of the previous word was spread to the right, or a default mid tone was supplied. The "orphaned" low tone that was pushed off the end of the word became a floating low, with the power to effect certain changes in following words.

I turn now to the evidence supporting my claim that there is a floating low tone at the end of these two forms in present-day Magdalena Mixtec. This floating low tone surfaces only in restricted environments, two of which we will consider here.

One environment that shows the effect of this low tone is a possessive phrase with an enclitic pronoun as the possessor. A pronoun like *sá* 'I, me, my' with basic high tone is lowered to low following words with mid-high or low-high that result from this sandhi rule. The original high tone of this pronoun is not, however, lost, but is retained as a floating high tone following the low tone, and it has the power to affect the tone of a following word. Example (6) gives a derivation that shows the results of two rules that move tones to the right (UR = underlying representation; SF = surface form):

(6)   UR   *yū'ū (h)*   'mouth'   +   *īso* 'rabbit' +   *sá* 'my'
       yū'ū   *īsó (l)*   +   *sá*
     SF   *yū'ū*   *īsó*   *sa̱ (h)*
              'the mouth of my rabbit'

First, the floating high tone on *yū'ū (h)* effected a change from *īso* to *īsó (l)*, and then the floating low tone on *īsó (l)* effected a change from *sá* to *sa̱ (h)*.

The derivation shown in example (7) includes a further change effected by the floating high tone at the end of the changed form *sa̱ (h)*, giving three stages of tone movement to the right.

(7)   UR   *ndūkū (h)* 'will look for' + *īso* 'rabbit' + *sá* 'my' + *de̱* 'him'
       ndūkū   *īsó (l)*   + *sá*   + *de̱*
       ndūkū   *īsó*   *sa̱ (h)* + *de̱*
     SF   *ndūkū*   *īsó*   *sa̱*   *dé*
              'my rabbit will look for him'

(The chain of tone changes ends with *dé,* which does not affect the tone of other words that could occur in this sentence, and therefore does not appear to have a floating low tone.)

Pronouns with high tone in their basic form, like *sá,* are not changed to low following an overt low tone on the final syllable, only following a floating low.

(8)   *īso̱* 'rabbit'   + *sá* 'my'   →   *īso̱ sá* 'my rabbit'

The second environment that shows the effect of the floating low tone at the end of words like *īsó (l)* is in a noun phrase that contains an adjective with a high-high tone pattern. These adjectives have the high-high pattern following high[6] or mid tone, and they are changed to low-high following any low tone, including the floating low tone at the end of the mid-high and low-high patterns that result from the sandhi rule. The examples in (9) and (10) show the adjective *kuíjín* 'white' in its basic high-high tone pattern. The examples in (11) and (12) show the adjective *kuíjín* 'white' in its changed low-high tone pattern.

(9) Following high tone:
    ná'nú 'grandmother' + *kuíjín* 'white' → *ná'nú kuíjín* 'white
                                                          grandmother'

    vílú 'cat'   + *kuíjín* 'white' → *vílú kuíjín* 'white cat'

(10) Following mid tone:
    vē'ē 'house'   + *kuíjín* 'white'   → *vē'ē kuíjín* 'white house'

(11) Following a low tone on the final syllable:
    īso 'rabbit'   + *kuíjín* 'white' → *īso kuijín* 'white rabbit'

    mā'a 'raccoon' + *kuíjín* 'white' → *mā'a kuijín* 'white raccoon'

(12) Following a floating low tone:
  a. UR *yū'ū (h)* 'mouth' + *īso* 'rabbit' + *kuíjín* 'white'
          yū'ū   *īsó (l)*   + *kuíjín*
      SF *yū'ū*   *īsó*   *kuijín*
                   'the white rabbit's mouth'

  b. UR *kāa (h)* 'will eat' + *īso* 'rabbit' + *kuíjín* 'white'
          kāa   *īsó (l)*   + *kuíjín*
      SF *kāa*   *īsó*   *kuijín*
                   'the white rabbit will eat'

These examples containing enclitic pronouns and adjectives show that the low tone on the second syllable of the basic form of nouns like *īso* 'rabbit' was not changed to high tone, as it appears to have been from

---

[6]The study of Magdalena Mixtec tone is not yet complete, but it appears that all words that end in a high tone have some sort of floating tone associated with them. The floating tones are not marked in the present study, except for the low tone that follows the mid-high and low-high tone patterns.

synchronic data in San Miguel, but has rather moved to the right to become a floating tone that surfaces under certain conditions.

Tone Patterns in Spanish Loanwords
in Magdalena Peñasco Mixtec

Many Spanish words have entered Mixtec since the sixteenth century, and
in the process they have undergone a variety of phonological adaptations.
One of these adaptations is that each stress pattern found in Spanish
source words correlates with a Mixtec tone pattern. Even though these
correlations are quite consistent, they are not what we might logically expect. Consider the examples of Spanish words with penultimate stress and
their Mixtec form in (13).

(13) *mesa*   'table'   *mēsá*
      lápiz   'pencil'   *lāpí*
      barato   'inexpensive'   *vārātú*
      presidente 'president'   *prēsīdēndé*

In that stressed syllables in Spanish tend to have a higher pitch than unstressed syllables, we might expect the stressed syllable of the Spanish
word to have a high tone in Mixtec, but this is not the case. Instead, we
find a high tone on the syllable following the stressed syllable. Other syllables in the word have mid tone.

A similar pattern is found on words with antepenultimate stress:

(14) *báscula*   'scale'   *vāskúla*
      lámina   'corrugated roofing'   *lāmína*
      máquina   'machine'   *mākína*

As in words with penultimate stress, a high tone occurs on the syllable to
the right of the original stress, and syllables preceding the high have mid
tone. The final syllable has low tone.

When Spanish words that have stress on the final syllable enter Mixtec,
the vowel of the final syllable is doubled, and it takes a high-low tone sequence. Syllables preceding the final syllable take mid tone.

(15)   *mil*   'thousand'   *mı́il*
        fiscal   'a church official' *vēskáal*
        camarón 'shrimp'   *kāmāróon*

Note that there is a low tone at the end of Mixtec words corresponding to two of the three Spanish stress patterns. Only words with penultimate stress lack this final low tone. There is evidence, however, that loanwords with penultimate stress have a floating low tone at the end, because they have the same lowering effect on pronouns and adjectives as the words with the mid-high and low-high patterns that result from tone sandhi. Compare the examples in (16) with those in (6) and (12).

(16)   *mēsá (l)* 'table'   + *sá* 'my'   →   *mēsá sa (h)* 'my table'
       mēsá (l) 'table'   + *kuı̄jín* 'white' →   *mēsá kuı̄jín* 'white table'

The underlying representation of such loanwords should therefore include a floating low tone: *mēsá (l), lāpí (l), vārātú (l), prēsīdēndé (l)*.

Note that the tone pattern found in two-syllable loanwords like *mēsá (l)* and *lāpí (l)* is identical to that found as a result of the tone-sandhi rule described in the previous section. Note also that these words have a (C)VCV syllable pattern. I propose that both groups of words have undergone the same movement of high tone to the right, and I posit the following scenario for loanwords.

Originally, all loanwords entered Magdalena Mixtec with a high tone on the syllable that was stressed in the Spanish source word. All preceding syllables received mid tone (perhaps a default), and the following syllables received low tone. In the case of words with stress on the final syllable, the final vowel was lengthened and received a high tone followed by a low tone. These words had the same form that they now have, but the examples given above with penultimate and antepenultimate stress had the following forms.

(17) With penultimate stress:
      mesa   'table'   *mésa
      lápiz   'pencil'   *lápi
      barato   'inexpensive' *vārátu
      presidente 'president'   *prēsīdénde

(18) With antepenultimate stress:
      báscula   'scale'   **váskula*
      lámina   'corrugated roofing'   **lámina*
      máquina   'machine'   **mákina*

A subsequent sound change moved the high tone in these two groups of words from its original position to the CV syllable to its right. A default mid was placed on the syllable that formerly had the high tone. In the words with antepenultimate stress, the low tone at the end was reduced from two syllables to only one. In the case of words with penultimate stress, the low tone was pushed off the end of the word and became a floating low.

Given that this is exactly the same thing that happened to words with a (C)VCV syllable pattern and a high-low tone pattern that resulted from the tone-sandhi rule described above, it seems highly probable that words from both sources changed together, which means that the change took place since Spanish contact in the first half of the sixteenth century, probably after a corpus of loanwords had become established during the sixteenth and seventeenth centuries.

Another similarity between these loanwords and the forms that result from the tone-sandhi rules is that loanwords undergo a change from mid-high to low-high following a word with a final low tone. This seems to be part of a general process of low-tone spread.

(19) *īñu* 'six'   + *mēsá (l)* 'table'   →   *īñu mẹsá (l)* 'six tables'

Loanwords with the mid-high tone pattern appear to be the only roots in the language that have this pattern in their basic form. Other words with this form are the result of the sandhi described in the third section. (There are also a few forms with mid-high that appear to be compounds, such as *nāsá* 'lest'.)[7]

---

[7]One fact that provides further support for the explanation offered in this study is that loans with the mid-high tone pattern do not undergo a tone change following a floating high tone. Even though they might be expected to become high-high, they do not. In this respect, they behave like words that already have high tone on the first syllable, which are not further changed by the sandhi rule.

Evidence from Other Towns

Published descriptions of Mixtec tone systems include several towns in the western part of the highland Mixtec region. In addition to San Miguel el Grande and Chalcatongo de Hidalgo, which have already been mentioned, there are descriptions for San Esteban Atatlahuca, Santo Tomás Ocotepec, and San Pedro Molinos. A comparison of these five towns with Magdalena reveals a correlation between the existence of the irregular sandhi pattern and the tone pattern found in loanwords. In four of the six towns, the irregular sandhi pattern occurs, and in the other two it does not. In the same four towns that have the irregular sandhi, Spanish loanwords with penultimate stress have a high tone on the syllable following the stress. In the other two towns, Spanish loanwords do not have this pattern.

The four towns that have the irregular sandhi pattern are San Miguel (K. L. Pike 1948), Chalcatongo (Macaulay 1996:34–39), Molinos (Hunter and E. V. Pike 1969), and Magdalena. All four of these towns are located in the Achiutla valley, which is an area of rather broken terrain running north to south, bounded by two ridges, each over 3,000 meters high. Chalcatongo and San Miguel are in the southern part of the valley, Magdalena is in the northern part, and Molinos lies about fifteen kilometers south of Magdalena, and about eight kilometers north of Chalcatongo.

The following examples show the sandhi pattern in which words with a mid-low tone pattern and a (C)VCV syllable pattern become mid-high.

(20) San Miguel (K. L. Pike 1948:78):
  kēē 'will eat' + *īso̱* 'rabbit'   →   *kēē īsó* 'the rabbit will eat'

(21) Chalcatongo (Macaulay 1996:34–35):
  kūu̱n 'four' + *īna̱* 'dog'   →   *kūu̱n īná* 'four dogs'

(22) Molinos (Hunter and E. V. Pike 1969:36):
  síví 'name' + *xīxi̱* 'aunt' + *sán* 'my' → *síví xīxí sán* 'my aunt's name'

(23) Magdalena:
  yū'ū (h) 'mouth' + *īso̱* 'rabbit' → *yū'ū īsó (l)* 'the rabbit's mouth'

(Note that, unlike in Magdalena, the tone of the pronoun *sán* 'my' in Molinos does not lower following the form *xīxí.*)

In all four of these towns, loanwords from Spanish words with penultimate stress regularly have high tone on the final syllable.

(24) San Miguel (Dyk and Stoudt 1973:20, 33; Mak 1953:92):
       arado   'plow'   *lātú*
       paño   'shawl'   *pāñú*
       cuento   'story'   *kuēndú*

(25) Chalcatongo (Macaulay 1996:25):
       primo   'cousin'   *prīmú*
       paño   'shawl'   *pāñú*
       fuerza   'force'   *fuērsá*

(26) Molinos (Hunter and E. V. Pike 1969:26, 29):
       veinte   'twenty'   *vēntí*
       peso   'monetary unit'   *pēsú*
       vara   'staff'   *vārá*

(27) Magdalena:
       mesa   'table'   *mēsá*
       cuento   'story'   *kuēndú*

(A few loans have different patterns. For example, Spanish *cordero* 'lamb'
is borrowed into San Miguel as *lélú* [Dyk and Stoudt 1973:20] and into
Magdalena as *lélū*.)

The two towns that do not have the irregular sandhi rule are Ocotepec
and Atatlahuca. Both are located to the west of the Achiutla valley, but
Ocotepec is considerably farther away than Atatlahuca.

Ocotepec has sandhi rules that change mid-low words to high-low following certain other words. The words that are changed to high-low include those with the (C)VCV syllable pattern, as well as those with the
(C)V'V and (C)VV patterns (Mak 1958:65).

(28) (C)V'V   *yáá* 'tongue'   + *ñū'u* 'fire'   → *yáá ñú'u* 'flame'
       (C)VV   *yū'ú* 'mouth, edge' + *ñūu* 'town'   → *yū'ú ñúu* 'edge of town'
       (C)VCV   *ntīkī* 'horn'   + *īsu* 'deer'   → *ntīkī ísu* 'deer's horns'

Likewise, Ocotepec borrows Spanish words with penultimate stress
with a high-low pattern (Mak 1958:63–64).

(29) *lado*   'side'   *ládo*
       calle   'street'   *káyi*
       marco   'door frame, case' *márku*

In other words, what I have claimed was the original result of the tone-sandhi rule, and the original form of the borrowing, are both found at the present time in Ocotepec. Apparently, the changes that took place in the Achiutla valley to the east did not affect Ocotepec in any way.

Atatlahuca has a four-level tone system, and the tones are written with numbers. The number 1 is used for high tone, and the number 4 is used for low tone. Tone 3 has a limited distribution, and therefore tone 1 generally corresponds to high, tone 2 to mid, and tone 4 to low. The word for 'egg' *(ndi2vi⁴)* is equivalent to mid-low. This word does not become mid-high following a class b morpheme, as it does in the Achiutla valley, but rather high-low, as in Ocotepec (Mak 1953:88–89, 91).

(30)   *ta⁴ka¹ (b)* 'each' + *ndi²vi⁴* 'egg' → *ta⁴ka² ndi1vi4* 'each egg'

Note that the tone of *ta⁴ka¹* 'each' is changed to *ta⁴ka²* preceding the word for 'egg'.

Spanish loanwords with penultimate stress take the tone pattern high-high when they enter Atatlahuca Mixtec (Mak 1953:91–92).

(31)   escuela   'school'   *skue¹la¹*
       cuento   'story'   *kue¹ndu¹*

Mak states that these words cause tone lowering on the first syllable of the following word (1953:93), but, unfortunately, no example is included in the article. This fact provides evidence for a former high-low pattern. The high tone on the first syllable was apparently spread to the second syllable, and the low tone was pushed off the word to the right, where it causes changes in the next word, as it also does in Magdalena.

This pattern may well be an intermediate stage between the original high-low pattern found in Ocotepec, and the mid-high pattern seen in the Achiutla valley to the east, which accords with its intermediate geographical location.

The question naturally arises about tone changes in other parts of the Mixtec region. A preliminary study of available sources shows that the irregular sandhi pattern described in this paper does not extend to towns in other parts of the Mixtec region.

I looked at two studies of tone in towns in the lowland Mixtec region, Huajuapan in western Oaxaca, northwest of the Achiutla valley, and Ayutla in the coastal area of Guerrero at the southwestern extreme of the Mixtec region.

E. V. Pike and Cowan's description of tone for Huajuapan (1967:9) shows a change from mid-low to high-low in (C)VCV words.

(32) k*o̱mi̱* 'four'   + *chīka̱* 'banana'   → k*o̱mi̱ chíka̱* 'four bananas'

In Pankratz and E. V. Pike's description of tone in Ayutla, Guerrero (1967:296), certain words cause the first syllable of a mid-low word to become high.

(33) *yá'á* 'brown'   + *nāma̱'* 'soap'   → *yá'á náma̱'* 'the soap is brown'

In the eastern part of the highland Mixtec region, on the other hand, words that have a mid-low tone pattern in the Achiutla valley have rather different underlying tones. In Daly's unpublished study of Santa María Peñoles, near the eastern boundary of the Mixtec region, words that have the mid-low pattern in the Achiutla valley have either a high-high tone pattern with a floating low, or a mid-high pattern.

(34) *dútú (l)*   'priest'
      ní'í (l)   'find'
      īdú   'deer'
      ñūú   'town'

Inga McKendry is currently carrying out research on the Mixtec of Southeastern Nochixtlán, which is located about halfway between Peñoles and the Achiutla valley. When she compared words with their cognates in San Miguel el Grande, she noted that the tones appear to have shifted one syllable to the right in Southeastern Nochixtlán, leaving many words with toneless initial syllables (personal communication).

Apparently, the shifting of tones one syllable to the right that takes place in limited contexts in the Achiutla valley has taken place in a more general way throughout the eastern part of the highland Mixtec region. The hypothesis that a high tone has moved to the right can perhaps help to account for the rather odd correspondence between Peñoles *dútú (l)* 'priest' and Magdalena *sūtu̱*. If the mid tone on the first syllable of the Magdalena form shifted to high, this high tone could have spread to the right, leaving the original low tone on the second syllable as a floating low at the end of the word.

A further confirmation of movement is found in the fact that Peñoles has a high tone on the syllable following the stress in Spanish loans, just as towns in the Achiutla valley do; an example from Daly's study is *la̱tú* 'plow', from Spanish *arado*.

Closing Remarks

In this section I give a few suggestions for future research, followed by some general musings on the workings of tone languages.

From the tone descriptions that are currently available, I have been able to draw a general picture of certain tone processes that have taken place in Mixtec. This general picture raises many questions that are, unfortunately, not likely to be answered. The nature of tonal systems, with relative levels that shift from speaker to speaker, makes them difficult to analyze, and few linguists choose to take on this arduous task. It is also clear that each town in the Mixtec region differs from its neighbors in tone, as in other respects, and a separate study is needed for each town in order to get a complete picture. To complicate the matter, many variants of Mixtec are now endangered, and they are likely to become extinct before they have been studied.

One question that I have not tried to address in this study is the role of syllable patterns in facilitating and blocking tone movement. There are four different syllable patterns in Mixtec disyllabic couplets: (C)VCV, (C)V'V, (C)V'CV, and (C)VV. Of these, only the (C)VCV pattern shows movement of high tone to the right in the Achiutla valley. The glottal stop in the (C)V'V and (C)V'CV patterns is a laryngeal element closely related to tone, and it could easily have blocked the movement of high tone to the right. What is not clear is why high tone did not move to the right in words with (C)VV, which have no glottal stop. I leave this puzzle to future generations of linguists.

Another topic for research is to what degree the historical process I have described should be reflected in a synchronic description of languages that have it. Should a description of the languages try to recapitulate the historical sequence, or would a completely arbitrary rule result in a simpler description?

Perhaps the most astonishing thing about tonal systems (in addition to their complexity) is the fact that they are managed expertly by native speakers, but in a completely unconscious fashion. My husband and I have studied two languages in the Mixtecan family, Copala Trique and Magdalena Mixtec, and our studies included both an analysis of their tonal systems, and a serious attempt to learn to speak the languages. We have also participated in the process of orthography design for both languages.

The orthography we proposed for Copala Trique included symbols to mark tone, and we have tried to teach native speakers to read and write them. This attempt was largely unsuccessful. It slowly became clear to us that the problem was not that the symbols we had chosen were less than ideal, but rather that Copala Trique speakers did not have any conscious awareness of the tonal system of their language, even though it is used to distinguish among dozens of sets of lexical items, and also grammatical categories like verb tense. Although this should perhaps not have surprised us, it did. But what surprised us even more is that, when we tried to teach them the system, they not only consistently found it hard to learn, but also seemed to resist any attempt on our part to make them bring it to conscious awareness.

This attitude toward tone is not limited to speakers of Copala Trique. Two native speakers of Mixtec who have published grammars of their language have chosen to give tone only minimal attention, and not to write it regularly on their examples. These authors are Gabina Aurora Pérez Jiménez, who has written a grammar of Chalcatongo Mixtec (1988), and Rodrigo Vásquez Peralta, who has written a grammar of the variant spoken in Xayacatlán de Bravo, in the lowland Mixtec region of the state of Puebla (1997). Vásquez Peralta's treatment of tone in his language is limited to the following paragraph on page 1.

> Its peculiar musicality represents another serious obstacle for those who do not have their ears educated to be able to perceive the tone changes that frequently occur; if a different tone is applied to a word that is formed with the same letters, its meaning will change. For such reasons very special attention to its orality is required for the correct understanding.[8]

My husband and I have also watched small children learn to speak Trique, and there is good reason to believe that they learn the tonal system before they learn vowels and consonants. We have heard them track things that are said to them, automatically mimicking the correct tone. And we have heard Trique children say things with little of the segmental structure correctly formed, but with the tone patterns correct, and their mother can usually understand them. Evelyn Pike carried out a study with one of her own children when they were located in San Miguel, away from

---

[8]In the original Spanish this is: *"Su peculiar musicalidad representa otro serio obstáculo para quienes no tienen educado el oído y poder percibir los cambios de tono que frecuentemente se presentan; a una palabra que esté formada con las mismas letras, si le aplicara un tono diferente, cambiará de significado, por tales razones se requiere de atenciones muy especiales en su oralidad para su apropiada comprensión."*

other speakers of English. By controlling the intonation pattern that they used in speaking to the child, she was able to verify that the pattern learned was an imitation of her own pronunciation (1949).

I stand amazed at the complexity of the tone-sandhi changes described in this short study, which form only a very small part of the full—and exceedingly intricate—tonal system of each Mixtec variant. I stand even more amazed at the way the patterns and rules are transmitted to new generations, and the way changes in them take place and slowly spread from town to town, without speakers having any awareness of what is happening. We are truly surrounded by mystery.

References

Alvarado, Fray Francisco de. 1593. *Vocabulario en lengua mixteca*. Facsimile edition, 1962 (Reproducción facsimilar con un estudio de Wigberto Jiménez Moreno y un apéndice con un vocabulario sacado del "Arte en lengua mixteca" de Fray Antonio de los Reyes). México, D.F.: Instituto Nacional Indigenista e Instituto Nacional de Antropología e Historia.

Daly, John. 2000. Tone sandhi in Peñoles Mixtec, manuscript.

Dyk, Anne, and Betty Stoudt. 1973. *Vocabulario mixteco de San Miguel el Grande* (Serie de Vocabularios Indígenas "Mariano Silva y Aceves," 12). México, D.F.: Instituto Lingüístico de Verano.

Goldsmith, John A. 1990. *Autosegmental and metrical phonology*. Oxford: Basil Blackwell.

Hernández, Fray Benito. 1567. *Doctrina christiana en lengua mixteca*. México: Casa de Pedro Ocharte.

Hunter, Georgia G., and Eunice V. Pike. 1969. The phonology and tone sandhi of Molinos Mixtec. *Linguistics* 47:24–40.

Macaulay, Monica. 1996. *A grammar of Chalcatongo Mixtec*. Berkeley: University of California Press.

Mak, Cornelia. 1953. A comparison of two Mixtec tonemic systems. *International Journal of American Linguistics* 19:85–100.

Mak, Cornelia. 1958. The tonal system of a third Mixtec dialect. *International Journal of American Linguistics* 24:61–70.

Pankratz, Leo, and Eunice V. Pike. 1967. Phonology and morphotonemics of Ayutla Mixtec. *International Journal of American Linguistics* 33:287–299.

Pérez Jiménez, Gabina Aurora. 1988. Sain sau: introducción al mixteco de Chalcatongo. In Maarten Jansen, Peter van der Loo, and Roswitha Manning (eds.), *Continuity and identity in native America: Essays in honor of Benedikt Hartmann*, 132–155. Leiden: E. J. Brill.

Pike, Eunice V., and John H. Cowan. 1967. Huajuapan Mixtec phonology and morphophonemics. *Anthropological Linguistics* 9(5):1–15.

Pike, Evelyn G. 1949. Controlled infant intonation. *Language Learning* 2:21–24.

Pike, Kenneth L. 1945. *The intonation of American English*. Ann Arbor: University of Michigan Press.

Pike, Kenneth L. 1948. *Tone languages*. Ann Arbor: University of Michigan Press.

Reyes, Padre Fray Antonio de los. 1593. *Arte en lengua mixteca*. México: Casa de Pedro Balli. Reprinted in 1890 by Comte H. de Charencey. Facsimile edition of the 1890 edition, 1976. (Vanderbilt University Publications in Anthropology, 14). Nashville: Vanderbilt University.

Tranel, Bernard. 1995. Rules vs. constraints: a case study. Paper presented at the conference on Current Trends in Phonology: Models and Methods, Royaumont, France, June 19-21, 1995.

Vásquez Peralta, Rodrigo. 1997. *Gramática popular de la lengua mixteca del sur de Puebla*. Fojas Étnicas, 11/139. Puebla: Secretaría de Cultura.

34

Hierarchy and the Classification of French Verbs

Wolfgang U. Dressler and Marianne Kilani-Schoch

Introduction

Questions of classification have been a constant concern in Kenneth Pike's grammatical studies (e.g., Pike 1967, 1982), be it the establishment of inflectional paradigms and of form classes in general or be it the modeling of grammatical hierarchies. Thus, the hierarchy of verb classes that we put forward finds a predecessor in the division into classes and subclasses within Pike's framework (e.g., Pence 1964). As in Pike's model, such hierarchies express constraints on grammatical complexity, which arises when words are morphologically marked for their syntactic roles. This is one of the two main functions of inflectional morphology within a ternary model of the sign, as in Peirce (1965) or Mel'čuk (1993).

As for any descriptive endeavor, classification must be based on a specific, explicit theory. Our model is the theory of Natural Morphology (cf. Dressler et al. 1987, Kilani-Schoch 1988, Dressler 2000), a functionalist and mentalist model which consists of three subtheories: first, a subtheory based on

We wish to thank Yves-Charles Morin (Université de Montréal) for long and fruitful discussions of our paper and of our approach in general. We would like to thank Narc Xicoira for the tree diagrams.

semiotic and cognitive foundations; second, a subtheory of typological adequacy where French approaches both the ideal inflecting-fusional and the ideal isolating language type in verb morphology, but inflectional noun morphology is much more isolating; and third, a subtheory of language-specific system adequacy. We will focus here on the third.

Dynamic and Static Morphologies

Our morphological model is composed of two, largely overlapping morphologies: DYNAMIC morphology whose core consists of the productive morphological patterns (categories, rules, and classes; cf. Dressler 1997, 1998), and STATIC morphology which consists of the representations of stored morphological forms (cf. Pöchtrager et al. 1998, Enger 2000). The large overlap between rule mechanism and memorized storage results from two factors: on the one hand, most frequently used forms, even when they can be productively processed by a rule mechanism, are stored. On the other hand, the way productive patterns are handled—by a rule mechanism or via abstract patterns—can be extended to unproductive but regular or subregular patterns. This results in something similar to the concept of minor rules in standard generative phonology. Such extension from productive to unproductive patterns is done unconsciously by children in overgeneralizations, e.g., in plural *foot-s,* later *feet-s* with productive -*s* plural instead of, or in addition to, unproductive umlaut *foot - feet.* Similar extensions are consciously done by poets in poetic licence when they form poetic occasionalisms or nonce forms generated by otherwise unproductive patterns. In this contribution we will concentrate on synthetic dynamic morphology.

Its constitutive core property, inflectional productivity, is defined as the capability of using rules, e.g., characterizing inflectional paradigms, with new words. These may be (in order of importance):

1. Loanwords, e.g., English plural *gestalt-s* and not **gestalt-en,* despite German plural *Gestalt-en,* because the -*en* plural is productive in German but unproductive in English.

2. Indigenous neologisms formed via conversion—e.g., noun *grandstand* → verb *grandstand,* preterite *grandstand-ed* and not **grandstood*—or via abbreviation, e.g., plural *fax-es.*

3. Class *change* undergone by old words, prototypically from an unproductive to a productive inflectional class, as in *brethr-en* > *brother-s, roov-es* > *roof-s* (in many dialects of English).

4. *Indigenous* neologisms formed via productive word formation (affixation or composition).

We begin with the productive categories of French inflectional verb morphology. They are:

- Three persons.
- Two numbers, both marked analytically, i.e., cosignalled by proclitics as primary markers, as in /il ɛm/ 'he loves' versus /ilz ɛm/ 'they love'. Second and first person plural are also marked cumulatively by suffixes on the verb, as in: *vous aim-ez, nous aim-ons*, if the first plural is not replaced by the impersonal clitic *on* with third singular.
- Synthetic tenses: present (Pres.), e.g., /ɛm/, /mɛ/ 'put', imperfect, and in written French future and third person simple past (SPast), e.g., /ema/, /mi/.
- Synthetic moods: indicative (Ind.) in all above tenses; imperative (Imp.), as in /ɛm/, /mɛ/); subjunctive present (Subj.), e.g., /ɛm/, /mɛt/; and conditional, e.g., /emrɛ/, /mɛtrɛ/.
- The nonfinite categories: infinitive (Inf.), e.g., /eme/, /mɛtr/; present participle, e.g., /emã/, mɛtã/, which is productive in the analytic gerund construction; and perfect participle, e.g., PP /eme/, /mi/, which is productive in the analytic compound perfect, e.g., /a eme/, /a mi/).

The unproductive categories are: simple past, e.g., /eme/, /emam/, /emat/, /mim/, /mit/ (with the above exception) and imperfect subjunctive, e.g., /emas/, /mis/.

Traditionally, including recent works such as Swiggers and Van den Eynde (1987) and Paradis and El Fenne (1995), French verb paradigms are assumed to be root-based, but nonautonomous roots occur only in unproductive suppletive paradigms, such as: *je dois* [dwa] 'I must', PP [dy], Inf. *dev-oir* [dəvwaʀ], where the traditional root /d/ is the smallest common denominator, whereas [dwa] and [dəv] are considered as suppletive "themes" (cf. Le Goffic 1997). We will consider them as autonomous versus nonautonomous bases: Autonomous bases for *devoir* are: Pres.Sg.Ind. and Imp. [dwa], 3.Pl.Ind. [dwav] and [dy], as in the homophonous Sg. SPast (Pl. /dy + m, dy + t, dy + r/). The only nonautonomous base is [dəv]. This dichotomy cuts across a second dichotomy between short (simple) and long (amplified) bases, the latter being represented by [dwav] = /dwa-v/. As in other modern Indo-European languages, only suffixation is relevant for inflection. Analogously to existing suffixation versus nonexisting prefixation, the outward direction of the base is right-oriented, insofar as its only relevant, class-constitutive parts are the rime or the coda, i.e., its right edge.

As the only or basic lexical entry we assume the infinitive form, either [X + e] or [X + r], as in *parl-er, fini-r* 'to speak, end', and not the respective short bases /parl, fini/. This is justified by the syntactic and semantic basicness of infinitives and by the morphotactic argument of conversion of nouns and adjectives to verbs: *fil* 'thread' *fil-er* 'to spin' can be symbolized as $[X_i]_N [X_j]_V$. In this example, the default is formal identity between X_i and X_j. But in case of consonant insertion, as in *don* 'gift' *don-n-er* 'give', *début* [deby] [deby-t-e] 'make one's debut', this default is overridden. Since this morphonological rule of consonant insertion has the phonological function of eliminating vowel hiatus, it makes sense when it forms the infinitive, but not as the short (simple) base for the lexical entry. In fact, the morpheme boundaries in [X + e] and [X + r] can be automatically derived from the infinitives $[Xe]_{Inf}$ and $[Xr]_{Inf}$, provided that lexical entries are just infinitives of the type $[Xe]_V$ and $[Xr]_V$.

Some further basic concepts and definitions of our classification are:

a. An INFLECTIONAL PARADIGM comprises all inflectional forms of one lemma, e.g., /parl, parl-e, parl-ō, parl-ɛ, parl-jɔ̃, parl-je.../. Paradigms form classes in a hierarchical way from macroclasses down to microclasses.

b. An INFLECTIONAL MICROCLASS is the smallest subset of any inflectional class above the paradigm, definable as the set of paradigms which share exactly the same morphological generalizations (but may differ via the application of phonological processes, in the sense of Natural Phonology). Thus, in English, all weak verbs whose preterite and past participle is formed by mere affixation of *-ed*, form one microclass (the only productive one of English verbs). Since unvoicing of the final dental stop after unvoiced obstruent in *work-ed* is purely phonological, such weak verbs also belong to this microclass. Some microclasses are riming ones, insofar as all paradigms which constitute them rime in all their forms.

b'. A MINIMICROCLASS consists only of two or three paradigms, as in English *light, lit, lit* and *slide, slid, slid*.

b". A MONORADICAL MINIMICROCLASS consists only of verbs formed in a semantically or formally nontransparent way from one single word, as in *come, came, come* and *become, became, become*.

b‴. A BOUND-ROOT MONORADICAL MICROCLASS is root-based, the only base of derivational prefixation being a bound root, e.g., English *-duce* in *re-duce, con-duce.*

c. An ISOLATED PARADIGM (= a paradigm which differs morphologically or morphonologically from all other paradigms) does not form a microclass of its own but is considered a satellite to the most similar microclass, e.g., the isolated English paradigms *go, went, gone; do, did, done.*

d. We define an INFLECTIONAL MACROCLASS differently than Carstairs (1987) or Carstairs-McCarthy (1994:745) do. A macroclass is the highest, most general type of class, which comprises, in hierarchical order, several classes, sub(sub)classes or at least microclasses, i.e., the intermediate ranks of class, subclass, subsubclass, etc. are only posited when needed for a hierarchical description of similarities among microclasses. The nucleus of a macroclass is, prototypically, a productive microclass.

e. The sub(sub)classes of a macroclass share at least one exclusively identical paradigm structure condition, which represents constitutive implicational relations between inflectional forms and bases of the same paradigm (cf. Wurzel 1984). Rules then apply to bases for producing the nonbasic inflectional forms of the paradigm. For example the rule of 2.Pl. formation ($X \rightarrow X + e$) applies to the respective bases of *parl-er, fini-r, val-oi-r* in the present indicative (= imperative) /parl + e, finis + e, val + e/, in the present subjunctive (= imperfect) /parl + j + e, finis + j + e, val + j + e/ and in the future /parl + (ə)r + e, fini + r + e, vo + d + r + e/.

The dynamic morphology of French verbs consists of two macroclasses. Macroclass I comprises the verbs with Inf. *-er* (/e/) and macroclass II those with Inf. /r/. Whereas macroclass I is very homogeneous, contains the only productive microclasses (henceforth: mc), and represents the default (in type frequency), macroclass II is very heterogeneous and complex and includes also minimicroclasses (henceforth: minimc).

The hierarchy in figures 1–4 summarizes the relation of classes, subclasses, microclasses, etc. Each is discussed briefly in sections "Macroclass I" and "Macroclass II."

Macroclass I

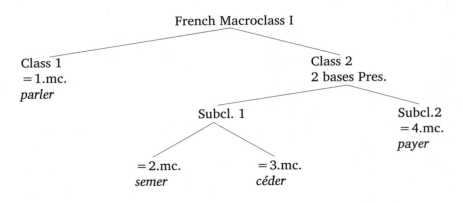

Figure 1.

Macroclass I comprises two phonologically complementary classes, the second of which is again subdivided into two phonologically complementary subclasses. These classes are shown in figure 1. The paradigm structure conditions (PSCs) are:

> PSC A and B: If Inf. /X+e/, then PP /X+e/ and then 1.Sg.SPast /X+e/. (PSC does not have the inverse direction, because the auxiliary *être* 'to be' has also a PP /+e/: été).
> PSC C and D and E: If Inf. /X+e/, then Pres.Sg. /X/ and then 3.Pl.Ind. /X/ and then Pres.Subj. /X/, all defaults (not valid in microclass 4).
> PSC F: If 1.Sg.SPast /X+e/, then 2. = 3.Sg. /X+a/.

As a default, macroclass I verbs have just one invariable base X.

Class 1 = mc 1 (*parl-er* 'talk', lexical entry /parl+e/): the default of the invariable base X holds: 3.Sg.Pres.Ind. *il* [parl] = 3.Pl. *ils* [parl], PP [parl+e] and (formed by rules: Impf. [parl+ε], Fut. [parl+ər+e], etc.). This is the most productive microclass, cf. English loanwords *dribbl-er, flirt-er*, etc.

Class 2: PSC: If base X is stressed, then X → Y.
Subclass 1: PSC: If X → Y, then its last V → /ε/
mc 2 (*sem-er* 'sow'): last V = /ə/: optional phonological rule (PR):ə → Ø, thus Inf. [səme, sme] vs. Sg.Pres. [sεm]. Productive, cf. loanword

cancel-er. But less productive than mc 1, because of class shift from mc 2 to mc 1: *il carrèle* > [kaRl] 'he tiles', *achète* > *ach'te* 'buys' (cf. Le Goffic 1997:38, 46, 53, 82; Morin 1978:127).

mc 3 (*céd-er* 'cede'): last V = /e/, thus Inf. [sede], Sg.Pres. [sɛd]. Productive, cf. loanword *e-mail-er*, pronounced by many speakers as Inf. [imele], Sg.Pres. [imɛl], but by other speakers, with class shift to mc 1: Sg. Pres. [imel].

Subclass 2 = mc 4 (*pay-er* 'pay', *nettoy-er* 'clean', *essuy-er* 'wipe'): PSC: If X → Y, then the morphonological rule (MPR) j → Ø /_# applies. Thus short base [pɛ] in Sg.Pres. and 3.Pl., long antevocalic base [pɛj], but Fut. [pɛRɛ]. There is some variation of this unproductive mc 4 with mc 1, with the invariable longer base [pɛj]. There is also the variant of having the longer base also in the 3.Pl.Pres.Ind. and in the Pres.Subj.: then PSC D and E of macroclass I are blocked and hence the PSC of mc 4 is limited (cf. Morin 1998b, 2000).

The only *isolated paradigm* of macroclass I is a satellite of mc.4: *envoyer* 'send', Fut. *j'enverrai.*

Macroclass II

This heterogeneous and totally unproductive macroclass has no general but only default paradigm structure conditions.

PSC A: If Inf. /X+r/, then default PP /X+i(z,t), X+y(z)/ (exception: mc 14: *offrir*, PP *offert* and isolated paradigm *être* 'be', PP *été*).

PSC B: If Inf. /X+r/, then default more than 1 (2-5) base X (exception: mc 1).

PSC C: If Inf. /X+r/, then (default) 3.Pl.Pres.Ind. = Pres.Subj. (exception: some isolated paradigms).

PSC D: If Inf. /X+r/, then 1. = 2. = 3.Sg.SPast.

Class 1 (with right edge /i/).

The subclasses of class 1 are shown in figure 2. The paradigm structure conditions are:

PSC: If Inf. /Xi+r/, then default /Xi/ = base Sg.Pres.Ind.
PSC: If Inf. /Xi+r/, then PP and SPast default /Xi/.

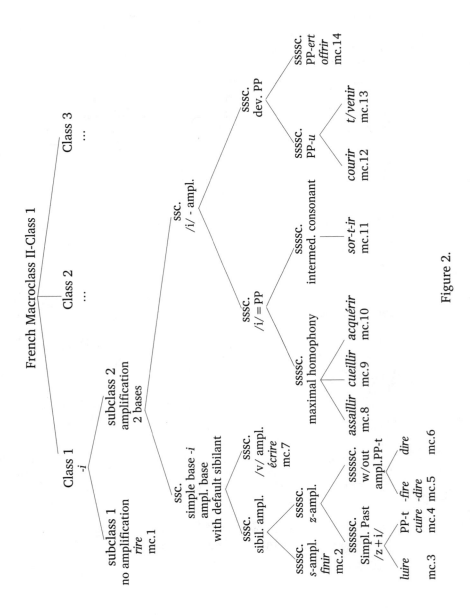

Figure 2.

Subclass 1 = minimc 1 (*(sou)ri-re* 'laugh (smile)', *fui-r* 'flee'): PSC: If Inf. /Xi + r/, then only 1 base X, then class defaults → general. Thus /ri/ is homophonous for 3.Sg.Pres. = SPast *il rit*, 3.Pl.Pres. *ils rient*, PP *ri*. Instead of the unique base /ri/, there exists also the alternation between this short base and a long base /rij/, as in the plurals *nous rions, vous riez, ils rient* (cf. Morin 2000).

Subclass 2: PSCs: If Inf. /Xi + r/, then 2 bases, then default /i/ = right edge of base X', then PSC C triggers an amplification (right-edge insertion) rule.

Subsubclass 1': If default of subclass PSC → general, then the amplification, by default, consists in a sibilant, then class defaults → general.

Subsubsubclass 1": PSC = general.

Subsubsubsubclass 1''' = mc 2 (*fini-r* 'end'): PSC: .., then amplification by /s/. Simple base /fini/: Sg.Pres. = PP = Sg. SPast, long base /finis/ in Subj. = 3.Pl. Ind. *ils finissent*. The last (analogical) neologisms were: analogical *amerrir* 'land on the sea' (1912), *alunir* 'land on the moon' (1921) (after *atterrir* 'land', 18th c.); *vrombir* 'roar' 1908 (onomatopoetic *vroum(b)*). Class shift: defective *brui-re* 'be noisy', 3.Sg.Pres. *il bruit,* Pl. *ils bruissent* > mc.1 *brui-sser* (Le Goffic 1997:49).

Satellite: isolated paradigm: *haïr* [air] 'hate', short base: Sg.Pres. *hais* [ɛ].

Subsubsubsubclass 2''': PSC: ..., then amplification /z/.

Subsubsubsubsubclass 1'''': PSC: ... then same amplification by /z/ in SPast

Riming minimc 3 (*l/nui-re* 'shine, damage'): no further PSC. 3.Sg.Pres.Ind. *il nuit,* Pl. *ils nuisent.* SPast: *je nui-s-is.*

Riming mc 4: (*cui-re* 'cook', *-dui-re* '-duce', *-(s)trui-re* '-struct'): PSC: If class PSC of PP in /i/, then PP amplified by /t/ in fem. (*cui-te*).

Subsubsubsubsubclass 2'''': PSC of sister does not hold; PSC: If class PSC of PP in /i/, then PP amplified by /t/ in fem.

Minimc 5 (*-dire* 'say', *con-fire* 'boil down, make jam'): no further PSC. Thus fem. PP *confite.*

Satellite isolated paradigm: *suf-fire,* PP *suf-fi* 'suffice' (i.e., regularized).

Monoradical minimc 6: (simplex *dire* 'say', *re-dire* 'say again'): ..., then 2.Pl.Ind.Pres. *vous dites.*

Subsubsubclass 2" = monoradical minimc 7 (*écri-re,* Latinate *-scri-re* 'write'): violates PSC of sibilant amplification, instead long base /ekriv/; PSC ..., then PP amplified by /t/ in fem. (/ekri + t/).

Subsubclass 2': If Inf. /Xi + r/, then default more than two bases, then /i/ = base of Inf., then X is base of Pl. Ind.

Subsubsubclass 1": ..., then same /i/ base in PP and SPast (except mc. 10 *acquérir*)

Subsubsubsubclass 1''': ..., then 3.Pl.Ind.Pres. = Sg. = Subj.

Riming minimc 8: (*assaill-i-r* 'attack', *tressaill-i-r* 'wince', *défaill-i-r* 'fail'): ...,
then Pres. without /i/: simple base [asaj]. Class shift to mc 9 possible
in Fut. *j'* [asaj(ə)Rɛ] (Le Goffic 1997:43).

Monoradical minimc 9: (*cueill-i-r* 'pick, collect'): no further PSC. /i/ of Inf.
→ /ə/ in future, like in macroclass I.

Monoradical (bound-root) minimc 10: (*acquér-i-r* 'acquire'): ..., then Fut.
without /i/ and then Sg. base /e/ → /jɛ/ and SPast *acquis* [aki], fem.
PP *acquise*.

Subsubsubsubclass 2''' = mc 11(*sɔr-t-i-r* 'exit'): in addition to sister
subsubsubsubclass 1''': PSC: ...then base before /i/ loses final C in
Sg.Ind. and Imp. (/sɔr/) vs. 3.Pl.Ind. *ils sortent* [sɔrt].

Partial class shift (adoption of /s/-amplification) to mc 1 (*finir*): *répartir*,
as/res-sortir (Le Goffic 1997:107, 109, 111, 115).

Satellites: isolated paradigms: *vêt-i-r* 'wear': bases [vɛ, vɛt], PP [y]: *vêtu*;
partial class shift to mc 1 (*finir*: Le Goffic 1997:125); *mourir* 'die':
1.Sg.Pres. *je meurs*, PP /mɔr(t)/.

Subsubsubclass 2'': ...then PP not in /i/.

Subsubsubsubclass 1''': ...then PP in /y/.

Monoradical mc 12 (*cour-i-r* 'run'): ...then SPast also in /y/

Riming mc 13 (*v/ten-i-r* 'come, hold'): ...then SPast monosyllabic /vɛ̃, tɛ̃/:
1st base [vjɛ̃]: *je viens*; 2nd base: insertive Fut: [vjɛ̃d-r-ɛ]; 3rd base:
3.Pl.Ind. *ils viennent* and Subj.; 4th base [v(ə)n]: 1.Pl.Pres.Ind. *nous
venons*, etc. (incl. PP *venu*); 4th base: SPast *il vint*.

Subsubsubsubclass 2''' = mc 14: ...then PP /ɛr/ (but SPast still in /i/: *offr-i-r*
'offer', *souffrir* 'suffer', *(r)ouvrir* '(re)open', *couvrir* 'cover', PP *offert(e)*,
etc.

Class 2 (*-oi-r* [war]):

The subclasses of class 2 are shown in figure 3.

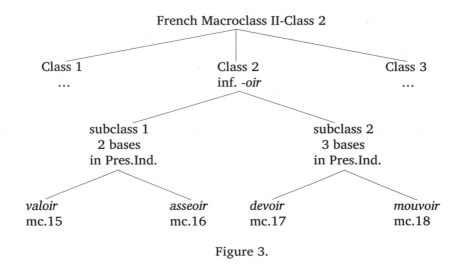

Figure 3.

PSC A and B and C: If Inf. /Xwar/, then default /wa/ belongs to the
Inf. base, i.e., /X + wa + r/, then PP and SPast in /y/.

Subclass 1: PSC: If Inf. /X + wa + r/, then present has two bases:
Riming minimc 15 (monoradical *val-oi-r* 'be valid', plus defective *fall-oi-r*
'need'): PSC:If Inf. /Xl + wa + r/, then class defaults → general and
stressed /al/ → /o/ and Subj. /aj/: 3.Pres.Ind.: Sg. *il vaut* [vo] vs. Pl. *ils
valent* [val] vs. Subj. *il(s) vaille(nt)*, Fut. *vau-d-r-a*.
Satellite isolated paradigms: *pré-valoir* 'prevail', regularized Subj. *pré-vale*;
isolated paradigm with transparent prefixations: five bases: Inf. *voi-r*
'see', 1.Sg.Pres. *je vois*; Pl. *nous voy-ons*; Fut. *ve-rr-ai*; PP *vu*; SPast *il vit*;
morphosemantically opaque prefixed paradigms (regularized, four
bases): *pré-voi-r* 'foresee'; Fut. *pré-voi-r-ai*, and; still more regularized
(three bases): *pour-voi-r* 'provide'; 1.Pl.Pres. *nous pour-voy-ons*; Fut.
pour-voi-r-ai; SPast *il pour-vut*; isolated paradigm with five bases:
voul-oir 'want', 1.Pl.Pres. *nous voul-ons*, PP *voul-u*; 3.Pl.Pres. *ils veul-ent*;
1.Sg. *je veux*; Subj. *veuille* (but 1.Pl. *nous voul-ions*); Fut. *vou-d-r-ai*;
isolated paradigm with five bases: *sav-oir* 'know', 1.PL.Pres. *nous
sav-ons*, 3.Pl. *ils savent*; 1.Sg. *je sais* [sɛ]; Subj. *sache*; Fut. *sau-r-ai*; SPast
/sy/; isolated paradigm with six bases: *pouv-oir* 'can', *nous pouv-ons*; *ils
peuv-ent*; *je peux*; Subj. *puisse*; Fut. *pou-rr-ai*; SPast /py/.
Monoradical minimc *16* (*asseoi-r* 'sit'): PSC: If Inf. /Xswa + r/, (a) then
second and third default does not hold and (b) PP and SPast in /i/

(with /z/ in fem. of PP), c) then /wa/ stressed → /je/, d) unstressed → /ɛj/. Two popular simplifications consist in eliminating PCS c): 3.Sg.Pres. *il s'assied* [asje] > either [aswa] or [asɛj].

Satellite isolated paradigms: *sur-seoi-r* 'postpone': regularized: 1.Sg.Pres. *je sursois*, 1.Pl. *nous sursoy-ons*, Fut. *surseoi-r-ai*; *croi-re* 'believe', *je crois* [krwa], Fut. *croi-r-ai*; 1.Pl.Pres. *nous croy-ons*; SPast /kry/; *pleuv-oir* 'rain': 3.Sg.Pres. *il pleut*, Pl. *ils pleuv-ent*, Fut. *il pleuv-r-a*; SPast /ply/.

Subclass 2: PSC: If Inf. /Xvwar/, then three bases and class defaults hold, loss of /v/ in Sg.Pres.Ind. and Imp., then /Vv/ lost in PP and SPast.

Riming minimc 17 (*dev-oi-r* 'must', *-cev-oi-r* '-ceive'): PSC: If Inf. /Xv + war/, then stressed /ə/ → /wa/: *je dois* = 1st base [dwa]; 2nd base [dwav]: 3.Pl.Pres., Sg. and 3.Pl.Subj.; 3rd base [d(ə)v]: 1. and 2.Pl.Pres., Inf., Fut. [d(ə)vRɛ]; 4th base [dy]: PP, SPast.

Monoradical minimc 18 (*mouv-oi-r* 'move'): PSC: ...., then stressed /u/ → /Ø/: *je meux*.

Satellite isolated paradigm: *boi-re* 'drink', *je bois*, Fut. *boi-r-ai*; 1.Pl.Pres. *nous bu-v-ons*; 3.Pl. *ils boi-vent*; SPast /by/.

Class 3 (Inf. neither *-ir* nor *-oir*).

This class is either a weak default among the three classes, or Class 3 is ordered after the other two classes if one espouses a rule-ordering model. The subclasses of class 3 are summarized in figure 4.

PSC: If Inf. /X + r/, then PP and SPast default /y/.

Subclass 1: PSC: If Inf. /XdentalC + r/, then C lost in Sg.Pres.Ind. and Imp.
Subsubclass 1': PSC: If Inf. /Xd + r/, then /d/ remains default in all other forms.
Subsubsubclass 1": then default → general.

Mc 19 (*ren-d-re* 'render', *per-d-re* 'lose'): ...then defaults → general (except *ba-tt-re* 'hit', *rom-p-re* 'break', *vain-c-re* 'defeat'): Sg.Pres. [pɛr], 3.Pl. and Sg.Subj. [pɛrd], SPast [pɛrdi], PP [pɛrdy].

Monoradical minimc 20: *pren-d-re* 'take', 1.Pl. *pren-ons*, 3. Pl. *prenn-ent*, Impf. *pren-*, SPast = PP *pris*.

Satellite isolated paradigms with transparent prefixation: *vi-v-re* 'live' (PP *vécu* = SPast base); *sui-v-re* 'follow' (PP *suiv-i* = SPast base).

Monoradical bound-root minimc 21 (*ab-sou-d-re* 'absolve'): PSC: If Inf./X-su-d-r/, then SPast and PP /X-su/ (with /t/ in Fem.) and then in other forms /ud/ → /olv/: 3.Pl.Pres.Ind. *ils absolvent*, SPast absol-[y], Fem. PP *absoute*.

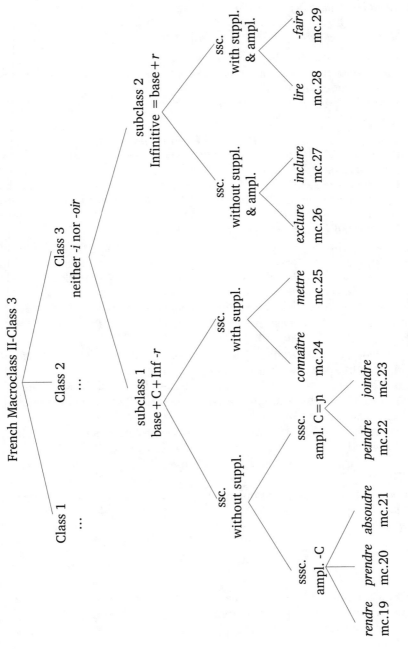

Figure 4.

Satellite isolated paradigms: ré-sou-d-re 'resolve': PP *résol-u; coud-re* 'sow', 3.Pl.Pres. *ils cousent,* PP *cous-u; moud-re* 'grind', *ils moulent,* PP *moul-u* (both with transparent prefixations), SPast *cousis.*

Subsubclass 2': PSC: If. Inf. /Xɛ̃-d-r/, then /d/ remains only in Fut. and Condit. and then PP = Sg.Pres.base (plus /t/ in fem.) and then /d/ → /nj/ elsewhere, also in SPast with /i/.

Riming mc 22 (*pein-d-re* 'paint'): no further PSC: 3.Sg.Pres. *il peint,* Pl. *ils peignent,* SPast *il peignit,* PP *peint.*

Monoradical minimc 23 (*join-d-re* 'join'): …, then /ɛ̃/ → /ã/ before /nj/.

Subsubclass 2': PSC: If Inf. /Xt + r/, then default /t/ → /s/ in derived forms and preceding V lost in PP and SPast

mc 24 (*connaî-t-re* 'be acquainted', *croî-t-re* 'grow'): PSC: If default general, then PP and SPast in /y/: [kɔny]: Sg.Pres.[kɔnɛ, krwa], 3.Pl. [kɔnɛs, krwas].

Satellite isolated paradigm: *naî-t-re* 'be born', SPast *il naquit,* PP *né.*

Monoradical minimc 25 (*me-tt-re* 'put'): PSC: If default violated, then PP and SPast in /i/: [mi].

Subclass 2: PSC: If Inf. /XV + r/ and V = /y, ɛ, i/, then V in PP and SPast substituted by /y/.

Monoradical bound-root minimc 26 (*ex/con-clu-re* 'ex/con-clude'): PSC: If Inf. /Xy + r/, then base invariable: [ekskly] = Sg.Pres. (Ind., Imp., Subj.), 3.Pl.Ind., SPast, PP.

Complementary monoradical bound-root minimc 27 (*in/oc/-clu-re* 'in/oc/-clude'): same, but PP Fem. in [yz].

Minimc 28 (*tai-re* 'be silent', *plai-re* 'please', *li-re* 'read'): PSC: If Inf. /Xɛ,i + r/, then base amplified by /z/ except Sg.Pres.Ind. and Imp.: 3.Pl.Pres. *ils lisent,* PP [ly].

Monoradical bound-root minimc 29 (*-fai-re* '-make'): short base /fɛ/, unstressed [fə] (e.g., Fut. *fe-r-ai*), unstressed longer base /fə)z/ (e.g., 2.Pl.Pres.Ind. *-fais-ez*), 3.Pl.Pres.Ind. *font,* Subj. /fas/, SPast /fi/, PP /fɛ(t)/.

Satellite isolated paradigm: simplex *fai-re* 'make', with 2.Pl.Pres.Ind. *fai-tes* [fɛt].

Conclusion

In conclusion, our model of a language-specific system of the dynamic morphology of French verbs is centered on morphological productivity, i.e., on the productive categories and rules of the fully productive first microclass of macroclass I. The less productive microclasses 2 and 3 of the same macroclass are phonologically complementary to the first microclass. Native speakers of French are bound to induce (or, in our view, better: to abduce) generalizations about the productive-category subsystems of these three microclasses. Our model of productive implicational paradigm structure conditions, which then trigger the application of productive rules, attempts to account for these generalizations.

About unproductive microclasses, native speakers are likely to make generalizations about those forms of productive categories which can be accounted for by productive rules (most likely for the unproductive microclass 4 of macroclass I). But since at least children, during language acquisition, and poets, in poetic license, overgeneralize unproductive patterns, the possibility must be left open that the way productive patterns are handled, can be extended to unproductive ones as well. Our approach to macroclass II models generalizations for the standard inflection in analogy to macroclass I.

However, we cannot exclude the possibility that speakers may make other generalizations or even no generalizations of dynamic morphology at all for smaller or greater parts of macroclass II, i.e., that they entrust those unaccounted forms completely to static, memorized morphology (proposals about its modeling, in terms of phonological similarity, will be given elsewhere). This we must assume especially for those unproductive patterns that are limited to macroclass II: monoradical, bound-root and other minimicroclasses, isolated paradigms, and defective verbs (cf. Morin 1998a, b): those defective verbs that belong to macroclass I have morphologically accidental gaps, due to semantic and pragmatic reasons (e.g., *neig-er* 'to snow') or to phonological obstacles (e.g., *inventori-er* 'to inventory', at least for some speakers).

Our model also allows typological conclusions (cf. Dressler 1999) which go beyond previous work done both in the framework of Natural Morphology (cf. Dressler 1989) and in its predecessor model of Skalička's language typology (cf. Geckeler 1984): richly inflecting languages typically have several productive microclasses (e.g., Polish seven, Croatian five, Russian and Slovene four). Weakly inflecting languages typically have just one productive microclass (e.g., English, Dutch, and German weak verbs), whereas Italian and Spanish have also an additional, but only slightly productive microclass. Thus French (still less approaching the ideal construct of an inflecting type than the other Romance languages), with its three productive microclasses, comes as a surprise. However, as we have seen, these microclasses are phonologically complementary, and can thus be grouped together as a single type. Similarly, agglutinating languages which are less agglutinating than Turkish (where the productive mechanism holds for nearly one hundred percent of all verbs), may show more than one productive microclass, but again they are phonologically complementary (cf. Pöchtrager et al. 1998).

A second typological criterion of the inflecting (or inflecting-fusional) language type is, in contrast to the agglutinating language type, the great depth of the hierarchical ramifications of macroclasses, which, in French, represents the great complexity of macroclass II. In this respect, the French verbal (but not the nominal) system has maintained the complexities of the other Romance languages. This extends also to the considerable number of isolated paradigms.

References

Carstairs, Andrew. 1987. *Allomorphy in inflexion*. London: Croom Helm.

Carstairs-McCarthy, Andrew. 1994. Inflection classes, gender, and the principle of contrast. *Language* 70:737–788.

Dressler, Wolfgang U. 1989. Zur Bedeutung der Sprachtypologie in der Natürlichen Morphologie. In E. Lüdtke (ed.), *Energeia und Ergon III*, 199–208. Tübingen: Narr.

Dressler, Wolfgang U. 1997. On productivity and potentiality in inflectional morphology. *CLASNET* 7. Montréal.

Dressler, Wolfgang U. 1998. What is the core of morphology? In J. Niemi et al. (eds.), *Language contact, variation, and change. Studies in Language* 32:15–32.

Dressler, Wolfgang U. 1999. Ricchezza e complessità morfologica. In *Fonologia e Morfologia dell'Italiano e dei Dialetti d'Italia*. Atti del 21. Congresso, 587–597. SLI. Roma: Bulzoni.

Dressler, Wolfgang U. 2000. Naturalness. In G. Booij et al. (eds.), *Morphology: An international handbook on inflection and word-formation I*, 288–296. Berlin: de Gruyter.

Dressler, Wolfgang U., Willi Mayerthaler, Oswald Panagl, and Wolfgang U. Wurzel. 1987. *Leitmotifs in natural morphology*. Amsterdam: John Benjamins.

Enger, Hans O. 2000. Inflection classes, Norwegian verbs and Cognitive Grammar. *Odense Working Papers in Language and Communication* 19(1):127–137.

Geckeler, Horst. 1984. Le français est-il une langue isolante? - V. Skalička et la typologie du franais. In F. Oroz Arizcuren (ed.), *Navicula Tubingensis, Festschrift for A. Tovar*, 145–159. Tübingen: Narr.

Kilani-Schoch, Marianne. 1988. *Introduction à la morphologie naturelle*. Bern: Lang.

Le Goffic, Pierre. 1997. *Les formes conjuguées du verbe francais oral et écrit*. Paris: Ophrys.

Mel'čuk, Igor. 1993. *Cours de morphologie générale I*. Montréal: Les Presses de l'Université de Montréal.

Morin, Yves-Charles. 1978. The status of mute "e." *Studies in French Linguistics* 1(2):79–140.

Morin, Yves-Charles. 1987. Remarques sur l'organisation de la flexion des verbes français. *ITL Review of Applied Linguistics* 77–78:13–91.

Morin, Yves-Charles. 1998a. De l'acquisition de la morphologie: Le cas des verbes morphologiquement défectifs du français. In H. Bat-Zeef Shyldkrot and L. Kupferman (eds.), *Tendances récentes en linguistique française et générale*, 295–310. Amsterdam: John Benjamins.

Morin, Yves-Charles. 1998b. La flexion du verbe français à l'oral: Morphématique ou analogie? In M. Bilger, Karel Van den Eynde, and F. Gadet. *Analyse linguistique et approches de l'oral: Recueil d'études offert en hommage à Claire Blanche-Benveniste*, 69–78. Leuven: Peeters.

Morin, Yves-Charles. 2000. Les yods fluctuants dans la morphologie française. ms.

Paradis, Carole, and Fatimazohra El Fenne. 1995. French verbal inflection revisited: Constraints, repairs and floating consonants. *Lingua* 95:169–204.

Peirce, Charles S. 1965. *Collected Papers*. Cambridge, Mass.: Harvard University Press.

Pence, Alan ed. 1964. *Verb studies in five New Guinea languages*. Summer Institute of Linguistics Publications in Linguistics and Related Fields 10. Norman: Summer Institute of Linguistics of the University of Oklahoma.

Pike, Kenneth L. 1967. *Language in relation to a unified theory of the structure of human behavior*. The Hague: Mouton & Co.

Pike, Kenneth L. 1982. *Linguistic concepts: An introduction to Tagmemics*. Lincoln: University of Nebraska Press.

Pöchtrager, Markus, Csanád Bodó, Wolfgang U. Dressler, and Teresa Schweiger. 1998. On some inflectional properties of the agglutinating type, illustrated from Finnish, Hungarian and Turkish inflection. *Wiener Linguistische Gazette* 62–63:57–92.

Swiggers, Pierre, and Karel Van den Eynde. 1987. La morphologie du verbe français. *ITL Review of Applied Linguistics* 77–78:151–251.

Wurzel, Wolfgang U. 1984. *Flexionsmorphologie und Natürlichkeit*. Berlin: Akademie-Verlag.

Part VIII

Language in Relation to...

"I am...aware of the danger of leaving one's own discipline and attempting to build a bridge across to another." (Pike 1959)

Ken Pike, using his whistle-flute to help his audience hear how tone works in tone languages, circa 1960. (Archived in the Ken Pike Archives; used with the permission of Vurnell Cobbey.)

35

Redeeming the Time

Pike's Tagmemics and Its Impact on Rhetoric and Composition Theory

Bruce L. Edwards

Reminiscences

Following one of Ken Pike's well-known maxims, I cannot begin this essay without first acknowledging—and, therefore, privileging—the person, and the personal, over the theories and the abstractions endemic to scholarly discourse.

While it is an honor to be included at all in this collection of world-renowned scholars paying tribute to Professor Pike, it is a special privilege to be given the task of deepening the appreciation for his contributions to a discipline outside of linguistics per se.

My career as a publishing scholar and teacher in the field of rhetoric and composition is forever marked by early exposure to Professor Pike's Tagmemics as a graduate student at Kansas State University in the late 1970s; there, under Donald Stewart's direction, I wrote a master's thesis on the impact of Tagmemic theory on composition theory and practice in North American English department classrooms (Edwards 1979).

Often in correspondence (postcards would arrive unexpectedly from around the globe answering my impetuous queries and provocations about language), and, eventually, in several precious, personal visits, Professor Pike and his equally talented and lovely lifelong helpmeet and linguistic collaborator, Evelyn Pike, graciously provided me with insights into the historical development of Tagmemics. More importantly, they helped me better understand and articulate tagmemic applications to teaching writing, and its utility in interacting with and interpreting discourse of all kinds from many different perspectives. (A tagmemicist with text is a bonafide literary theorist, so I have found.)

His work has impacted not only me but a generation of rhetoric students at Bowling Green State University (Ohio); I have been privileged to chair a number of excellent doctoral dissertations at BGSU that explore, employ, and expand tagmemic insights into second-language instruction, propaganda analysis, metaphor, and literary theory and criticism.[1] Ken's ideas and principles have also accompanied me to classrooms and lectures on four continents, most recently in Africa in graduate courses in persuasion and creative writing at Daystar University, Nairobi, Kenya.

Ken Pike's life and legacy bespeak the biblical exhortation to "redeem the time," to make resourceful and productive use of the time, and the times, in which one lives, at the end of the day one being spent for the purposes of the kingdom of God. The scene forever etched in my mind that exemplifies the contribution of "Kenneth L. Pike, Scholar," is his patient and joyful instruction of my then eleven-year-old son, Michael, in how to voice the intricacies of certain sounds in African languages, using a tin whistle to differentiate pitch. The image of the two of them seated on the Pikes' couch in their Duncanville, Texas apartment, Michael totally enthralled, Ken totally engaged, thrills me to this moment; Ken's kindness and his love for dispersing the insights God had given him into human language and culture are therein captured.

My one regret is that Professor Pike did not live long enough to savor this volume celebrating his joyful contributions to many fields of study. My prayer is that Evie, and Ken's children and grandchildren, will see in this essay some small token of the grand indebtedness and gratitude so many of us must express toward his work and toward Ken himself. Selah.

---

[1]See for example, Martin (1989), Yang (1991), Guo (1997), and Cremean (2001). Another dissertation that deserves mention here is one I reviewed and commented on prior to its acceptance. It (Felch 1991) features extensive use of tagmemic theory in proposing a model for analyzing literary texts.

Rhetoric and Tagmemic Premises

It is well known that Kenneth Pike began his career as a virtually self-taught translator among the Mixtec of Mexico and eventually became more formally educated as a linguist under the tutelage of Edward Sapir and others at the University of Michigan (see Eunice Pike 1981). His earliest publications, c.1937–1942, focused on phonetics, as Pike attempted to assist linguists and translators facing the bewildering task of understanding and describing languages in primarily oral cultures that lacked an alphabet or codified grammar. He concluded that this endeavor was not well assisted by existing structuralist and behaviorist models of language, given their limiting conceptual vocabulary, notation system, and field methods. Consequently, Pike and other early tagmemicists, such as Robert E. Longacre, addressed these concerns with an aggressive and innovative inquiry into the social foundations of the phonology, morphology, syntactics, and ethno-epistemology of the peoples among whom the SIL field linguists were living.

How, Pike asked, might language researchers discern and articulate dimensions of human language use that are deeply embedded in culture and not apparent in the surface language behavior of indigenous language users? How do concepts of "sameness" and "difference" operate, not only in the sound and syntactic systems of languages under study but also in larger units of discourse and beyond, into the very fabric of human relationships and behavior between and among various individuals and ethnic groups? Pike's incisive responses to these questions comprised not only his major contribution to twentieth-century linguistics and anthropology, but served also as a significant impetus for the founding of a new theory of discourse within the precincts of the discipline known in Departments of English as "Rhetoric and Composition."

To pursue the implications of his questions further, Pike had to depart from the strictures of the structural linguistics he had been trained in; he could no longer treat language as a *sui generis*, autonomous phenomenon that could be studied in isolation from other, nonlinguistic human behavior—a journey twentieth-century rhetoricians also have had to make. One key result of his inquiry was his conceptualization of the TAGMEME, a neologism for "unit in context," and the foundation for Pike's own linguistic theory, which he labeled Tagmemics to emphasize the centrality of this term. The tagmeme denotes any unit or "chunk" of language or language behavior that can be identified, classified, differentiated, and employed, in itself, in a system, or as a system within a particular universe of discourse or cultural context. That is to say, a tagmeme might be a sound, a word, a sentence, a chapter in a book, a speaker, a writer, a reader, a traditionally recognizable unit or feature of a unit that has distinguishable functions and effects in a particular language situation. The linguist's and, by extension, the rhetorician's task inevitably becomes locating an appropriate "tagmeme" with which to enter a language phenomenon and strategizing how to begin fruitful inquiry into solving a particular language issue or problem.

A rhetoric founded upon such premises is thus preeminently a "social rhetoric," for at the heart of Pike's tagmemic rhetoric is an anthropology that refuses to treat language apart from the human beings as persons who use it, hence the title of Pike's magnum opus, *Language in Relation to a Unified Theory of the Structure of Human Behavior* (1967). Pike believed that traditional linguistics had always been too preoccupied either with micro-level etymological issues (for example, philology), or, after Noam Chomsky, sentence-level operations—thereby excluding necessary context-based analysis. In contrast, Pike's Tagmemics insists upon understanding human language use as a defining feature of human rationality, apart from which neither language nor humanity can be understood.

Important axioms developed alongside his work, none of which was more important for contemporary rhetorical theory than Pike's notion that language users view the world in repeatable units, experiencing the world as particles (discrete bits), waves (merging of units and overlapping borders that change over time), or fields (as points in a set of relationships). From Pike's point of view each of these perspectives may, and in fact must, come into play in understanding the nature of phenomena; they are indigenous to rationality and are not to be understood as mutually exclusive vantage points.

Within tagmemic rhetoric, human communication problems may be thus classified partly according to the perspectives by which language users tend to view the world. An exclusively particle view of the world may yield nothing but discreteness—that is, unconnected, decontextualized, randomized bits of experience. An exclusively wave view may yield nothing but unstable, ever-shifting strings and combinations of experience that elude articulation. An exclusively field perspective may yield nothing but a universe of relations that comprise no substantive, tangible entities that bear discernible features of their own. Inquirers, observers, or writers, assisted by tagmemic theory, are asked to employ such multiperspectival viewpoints to solve misunderstandings, bridge gaps in knowledge, or untangle unnecessary ambiguities in discourse so that an exchange of information can occur and meaningful change may be voluntarily considered or achieved.

Pike often used a game to illustrate such principles and postulates. In attending a baseball game, for instance, a spectator can adopt a particle, wave, or field view of the events and participants. A particle view might focus on the individual acts within the horizon of the stadium: a throw to first base, the pitcher picking up the rosin bag, an outfielder putting on his sunglasses, a vendor tossing a bag of peanuts—oblivious to any continuous action or the larger frame that these individual deeds might play in the game as a whole. A wave view might focus on the flight of a baseball driven over the fence for a home run, the subsequent scramble to retrieve the ball by fans, and the eventual pride of a father and son who return home to show off the ball to neighbor friends—a focus on continuous action and change, again oblivious in some sense to individual components or larger frameworks beyond the changes that occurred as a result of the flight of that particular ball. The field view might focus on the relationships that prevail on a team of nine players, each of whom has his own special prowess, defensive strength, or offensive role; one notes how in the late innings the weak-hitting shortshop uses his turn at bat to sacrifice a runner over to second so the line-drive hitting right-fielder has a better chance to get an RBI so the home team can get an insurance run.

In each case, the perspective employed does not so much exclude or falsify another as subsume it and make the observer temporarily oblivious to other kinds of information that might be received and processed. But the game of baseball is not merely the sum of its parts, and its "meaning" is dependent not only upon what actually occurs on the field but also upon that which the observer has brought to the game. Here Tagmemics enlists the help of Pike's concepts ETIC and EMIC (derived from "phonetic" and "phonemic") to distinguish what he calls the "outsider's view" from the "insider's view." To the novice baseball fan, that is, to the etic observer, much of what occurs on the field goes unnoticed. This observer identifies peak events, such as when runs are scored, and who wins the game, but the subtleties and little dramas and battles of the game escape the novice's vision. If accompanied to the game by an experienced fan (an emic observer), the novice can be directed to watch and absorb other kinds of detail and thereby be assisted in putting a greater number of factors into perspective, thus increasing an understanding of the game.

One could say that the etic observer, the outsider, is confronted potentially with a kind of confusing pluralism when attending the baseball game that must be resolved before "meaning" can take place. In a sense, this observer has too much information, and the most instinctive response to the game is governed by a PARTICLE view, for the novice knows too little about what is supposed to be "seen" to effectively employ an

alternative or interlocking WAVE or FIELD view. Therefore, the etic observer picks up on the minutiae, even though unable to place them in
proper perspective except in the most limited way. For the emic observer,
the potential pluralism of experience is greatly diminished by a greater familiarity and initiation to the game; the insider knows when and how to
move in and out of the various perspectives that yield true insight into the
game.

Pike urges that human beings must, and in fact do, bring multiple perspectives to their communication efforts. But they do so selectively and
often unconsciously, and a tagmemic rhetoric attempts to *systematize* this
multi-perspectival inquiry. In the baseball example, the emic insider's
knowledge of the game is not exhaustive, but it is richer, more realized,
and more sophisticated than that of an etic outsider friend. The emic observer's task is to "translate" for the companion—that is, to use particle,
wave, and field perspectives to move the friend from an etic knowledge
toward an increasingly emic one, in other words, a bridge to new knowledge and unfolding vision.

In summary, a tagmemic rhetoric, derived from Pike's conceptions, ultimately grounds speech, textuality, and communication in a rhetoric of
participation wherein communities of writers and readers are seen as sharing
the responsibility for meaning-making within specific, nonarbitrary historical contexts and in a publicly available discourse, thus rejecting the more dubious, positivistic notion that a static, self-evident, extractable core of
meaning inheres in an utterance or text itself.

Rhetoric: Discovery and Change

It was this aggressively expansive, inquisitive, encompassing quality of
Pike's endeavor and Tagmemics' practical application that made it eventually so attractive, accessible, and malleable for a completely different
audience of academics who would never set foot in one of Professor Pike's
remote seminars for SIL. To many readers of this volume, "Tagmemics" is
a term used by or a theory known primarily to a certain insular group of
linguists, most of them associated with the Summer Institute of Linguistics (now SIL International). Tagmemic theory no doubt seems to the
"insiders" who employ it to be housed almost exclusively within the precincts of one strain of linguistic endeavor: Bible translation. In point of
fact, there has been, since the 1960s, a dedicated and parallel universe of
interested readers, theorists, and practitioners. I speak of rhetoricians op-
erating in Departments of English and Interpersonal Communication who

have attempted to derive from Tagmemics those models and tools that would assist them in bringing literacy skills to as exotic and as needy a group of indigenous people as any faced by the typical SIL translator: *first year writing and speech students at colleges and universities!* How Kenneth Pike's Tagmemics came to be an essential catalyst in a pedagogical revolution is a compelling academic story of desperation colliding with serendipity at just the right time.

Nineteen sixty-three was a momentous year for the study of Rhetoric and Composition—this then fledgling field focused on writing instruction and the impact of literacy on the cognitive and social development of postsecondary writers—in North American universities. An upstart assistant professor, Albert Kitzhaber, published a version of his doctoral dissertation, a critical survey of college composition courses entitled, *Themes, Theories and Therapy: The Teaching of Writing in College*; here, Kitzhaber was brandishing a manifesto for the profession of writing teachers, speaking of "widespread uncertainty about aims, a bewildering variety of content, [and] a frequent lack of progression in the course" (1963:10; see also Kitzhaber 1953, 1960, and 1990). He concluded, "Freshman English in the nation's colleges and universities is now so confused, so clearly in need of radical and sweeping reforms, that college English departments can continue to ignore the situation only at their increasing peril" (1963:26). The early 1960s, a time of foment and upheaval everywhere in higher education, was beginning to witness an intellectual revolution within the means, methods, and meaning of literacy instruction.

The following year, Pike himself published two remarkable essays in the flagship journal of the discipline of Rhetoric and Composition: *College Composition and Communication.* These essays, "A Linguistic Contribution to Composition: A Hypothesis" (Pike 1964a) and "Beyond the Sentence" (Pike 1964b), would take up the gauntlet thrown down by Kitzhaber and proffer insights into language and language instruction drawn from the linguistic fieldwork and biblical translation theory in which he had invested so much of the previous two decades. In the first article Pike provocatively asked, "Would it be possible to explore a number of the axioms of such a language theory [as Tagmemics] in order to develop exercises based on these axioms about language structure, but specifically designed to develop writing competence?" (1964a:82).

Writing teachers had been anticipating, even demanding that some fruitful application for instruction emerge from the growing notoriety of Chomsky's Transformational Theory and his notion of "grammatical competence." Pike was here offering up Tagmemics as a theory that could meet this demand, one that had real world application and classroom value. Pike's work in training linguists to analyze and write descriptions of uncharted oral languages had enabled him to "develop a body of theory general enough to apply to any language whatever...and at the same time to invent exercises which would break down the learning problem into small bits in terms of simulated..." (1964a:82).

Through the 1950s, Pike's collaborations with SIL colleagues had yielded practical tools for investigating the epistemological bases for grammatical competence and rhetorical eloquence in indigenous cultures. Using this toolkit, Pike intuited that just as the resolution of many SIL members' challenges lay both beyond the sentence in discourse and beyond discourse itself in the socio-cultural frameworks in which language is used, the same might be true of the composition classroom. Pike then convinced two colleagues at the University of Michigan—one an English professor teaching writing in the U of M's College of Engineering, and the other, an enterprising graduate student—of the same conclusion, and they would thereafter begin to formulate a theory of discourse based upon the centrality of language use to human rationality and to the building of human community.

The firstfruits of their collaboration was a manifesto issued by Richard E. Young and Alton L. Becker—the professor and graduate student, respectively— in a seminal article in the *Harvard Educational Review*. Their 1965 essay famously debunked the "current-traditional rhetoric" that focused on mere grammatical correctness and ignored the role of invention in the writing process—or refused to see writing as a process in the first place—and concluded by demanding movement "toward a modern theory of rhetoric." Their further collaboration over the next five years resulted in an extremely important textbook, *Rhetoric: Discovery and Change* (1970) that stimulated a large body of research and pedagogical experimentation that made tagmemic theory an essential topic for rhetoric and composition specialists in the 1970s and 1980s.

Rhetoric: Discovery and Change had as its foundation the notion that both rhetorical theory and writing instruction needed liberation from a moribund model that emphasized a product-oriented pedagogy focused primarily on style and arrangement. To accomplish this, the authors sought to restore invention to its proper place at the heart of practical rhetoric and to reconceive writing as a discovery, i.e., "problem-solving," process that could be assisted by systematic heuristic tools—derived from Pike's tested and fruitful tagmemic tools. Young, Becker, and Pike also found the communication strategies derived from the work of psychotherapist Carl Rogers most congenial to their evolving modern rhetoric, specifically his emphasis on reducing an audience's sense of threat so that they are able to understand and then consider alternatives to their own belief system. Rogerian principles meshed well with Pike's concepts of etic and emic perspectives in language inquiry, i.e., the distinction between "alien" and "native" perspectives on discourse generation and reception, and the necessity of finding the right bridge or "tagmeme" that would yield mutual insight.

From *Rhetoric: Discovery and Change*, students would learn every rhetor's task is inevitably analogous to the kinds of challenges "alien" SIL workers in a new cultural environment encounter: locating a point of entry into a particular language ambiguity, problem, or challenge that will provide a true bridge for nonthreatening exchange and that, therefore, might make possible meaningful change. Thus, in tagmemic terms, a rhetorical task involves deliberately leaving behind a default "etic" or outsider's perspective on data under consideration, and employing heuristics that assist a communicator in approximating an "emic" or insider's perspective conducive to reaching the projected audience.

Rhetoric: Discovery and Change, against the grain of the much more staid and static models common to the composition classrooms of the late 1960s and early 1970s, defiantly defined composing in terms of four unique components: (1) preparation; (2) incubation; (3) illumination; and (4) verification. In the preparation stage, a writer seeks to identify and explore the nature of a problem or felt dissonance and is assisted by systematic heuristic inquiry, exemplified in the textbook by the "tagmemic discovery matrix." This nine-celled, multiperspectival grid has become well-known apart from the textbook itself. It is typically included as an essential heuristic device in most composition programs across North America in one form or another, offering users insights into subject matter, document design, and audience analysis through its particle, wave, and field views of data arrayed according to its contrastive/identificational features, its range of variation, and its distribution in context.

The incubation stage names a period of "subconscious" exploration during which a writer is less inclined to perform analytical inquiry and depends more upon the intuitive or "creative" activity of the mind for contribution to the task at hand. During the illumination stage, the writer is poised to hypothesize a solution based upon both analytical and nonanalytical means, producing a "leap," as it were, to imaginative insight that can be neither forced nor placed on a timetable. The fourth stage, verification, consists of some test of the hypothesis, using the criteria of correspondence, consistency, and usefulness, and reflects the tagmemic principle that all hypotheses and theories must ultimately be testable to be productive of insight.

Researchers and theorists such as Janice Lauer (1967) and Lee Odell (1970) investigated the effectiveness of Young, Becker, and Pike's heuristics and related tagmemic principles, attempting to verify experimentally the utility and theoretical soundness of tagmemic postulates for a variety of applications in composition, including, especially, the teaching of invention. Their consistent conclusion was that, indeed, tagmemic principles did advance the cognitive, aesthetic, and rhetorical skill development of writers in composition classrooms.

Rhetoric and Composition

From the vantage point of the twentieth century, there is no question Pike's work has had a continuing and formidable influence on the discipline of Rhetoric and Composition. In their December 1993, *College Composition and Communication* article, "*CCC*: Chronicling a discipline's genesis," Philips, Greenberg, and Gibson document the frequency of citation these three scholars enjoyed over three decades. Their article establishes, for instance that between 1950–1964, the most frequently cited authors in the pages of *CCC* were C. C. Fries (13) and Kenneth L. Pike (11). Between 1965–1979, the most frequently cited authors were Francis Christensen (68), and Kenneth Burke (54), followed directly by Richard Young (54), Alton Becker (34), and Kenneth L Pike (33). Even in the period between 1980–1993, an era dominated by references to the cyber-cognitive rhetorics of Carnegie-Mellon researchers Linda Flower (139) and John Hayes (107), Young (37), Becker (20), and Pike (19) were still cited frequently for the effective theoretical insights Tagmemics might bring to contemporary debates about literacies, technologies, and pedagogical responsibilities in an increasingly diverse collegiate environment.[2]

Nevertheless, in my view, Pike's earliest and most original contributions were and are paradigmatically so far advanced over extant twentieth-century notions of what both linguistics and rhetoric should entail that few within the discipline of Rhetoric and Composition have been equipped to recognize its continuing potential. Instead of its natural destiny—that of shaping and rescuing the field of Rhetoric and Composition from lesser versions of itself—tagmemic rhetoric has been somewhat a victim of its own success. One might say tagmemics was too quickly assimilated, domesticated, and placed on the library shelf as one great idea—a tool for heuristic inquiry. Because of this, the greater contributions that tagmemic rhetoric might have made to the cognitive, constructionist, and empirical debates

---

[2]Another measure of Young, Becker, and Pike's impact in the 1970s and 1980s can be seen in the number of dissertations spawned by their theories. See Rabianski (1979), Ebbert (1980), Tyma (1982), Katz (1984), and Kent (1988).

about the nature of language and written communication, have yet to be advanced.

What Phillips et al.'s survey of *CCC* topics and citations may actually tell us is that while Tagmemics—especially in its incarnation *in Rhetoric: Discovery and Change*—is often thematically part of the obligatory invention sections of contemporary textbooks and continues to be referenced in historical surveys of the development of the discipline of Rhetoric and Composition, the research projects within the discipline too often identify Tagmemics with a "technique" for invention and reveal little cognizance of what unique perspectives Tagmemics might contribute to other aspects of rhetorical theory and pedagogy.

The reason for this status is illustrated in an article by rhetorician and composition historian, Erika Lindemann (1995), in *College English*. Thematically, the essay epitomizes the problems tagmemic theory has had in the last decade in breaking out of its "heuristics" ghetto in rhetoric and composition studies. The essay pays homage to the generational power of the tagmemic perspectives of particle, wave, and field that serve her in her delineation of three kinds of approaches to writing and the use of literature. But Lindemann thereby unwittingly marginalizes Tagmemics, reducing it to its familiar status as merely a template with which to codify existing data. In this, Lindemann so thoroughly associates Tagmemics in the minds of rank and file compositionists with one strand of invention—particularly the fascination with the nine-celled discovery matrix, and with certain conceptions of "writing as process"—that readers could conclude that Tagmemics is therein encapsulated.

I would argue that this marginalization is consistent with the profession's general disposition to reject out of hand wholistic paradigms for inquiry and research that emanate from outside its precincts and to isolate aspects of the theory to be retrofitted into the status quo. It is unfortunate for those who might yet seek in Tagmemics a refreshing alternative to the extremes and non sequiturs to be found in the more closed, monolithic systems currently in operation. But there are profound reasons why Pike's Tagmemics should and can regain, to borrow literary critic Bruce Bauer's term, "a place at the table" of rhetoric and composition theory and practice.

The continuing relevance of Tagmemics has been concealed by the fact that there has been no *succession* of textbooks or textbook writers to follow *Rhetoric: Discovery and Change,* thinkers and dreamers who might have continued to define and refine a pedagogy based primarily upon tagmemic conceptualizations of communication. Further, there is no identifiable, ongoing Tagmemics-related research program associated with any major figures in composition studies emerging thus far in the new century—a situation that can be easily rectified with collaborative effort and skillful grant writing. Finally, there exists no "tagmemic anthology" or general "reader" available that makes readily accessible the key statements and ongoing research of working tagmemicists. Were these deficits to be addressed, one could imagine Tagmemics regaining its status as a theory not with a past, but with a future.

Tagmemic rhetoric, rightly assessed and promoted, emerges as unique among twentieth-century rhetorical theories in its penchant for identifying universals and in its assertion that its axioms hold true for all of human behavior. It therefore is positioned not only to contribute to the study of literacy acquisition skills and related pedagogical issues, but also to greater understanding of how language itself humanizes and orders culture. For tagmemicists, rhetorical models must refrain from abstracting both discourse and language users themselves from the textual, cultural, and social contexts in which they are situated; meaning is always "meaning in use." Tagmemics stood alone for decades against "autonomous linguistics," waiting for scholars and language planners to catch up—supplying both means and ends. In our current, more global educational climate, Tagmemics is well suited to framing and championing inquiry into international, multicultural, transethnic, and gender-based language-use issues so controversial and pronounced in today's academy.

The tagmemic rhetorician, informed by field-tested tagmemic theory, thus can continue to move beyond the narrow applications of Tagmemics to prewriting and invention to apply tagmemic insights to language phenomena that illuminate the taxonomic, epistemic, and heuristic functions of language in human discourse on the way to an ever-more comprehensive theory of human behavior. At the heart of this advance is *not* the nine-celled matrix, which is but a tool or a metaphor for a tool, but Pike's conceptualization of the *tagmeme* and its attendant axioms.

To "redeem the time," I wish to conclude this essay by underscoring some of principles and performance features of Tagmemics that would encourage scholars in Rhetoric and Composition to work toward the development of a full-fledged tagmemic rhetoric for the twenty-first century. These are derived from my own interaction with tagmemic theory, conversations with and the research of many thoughtful students over the last twenty years, and my own intuitions and apprehensions of where Tagmemics' true strengths lie.

Principles and axioms foundational to tagmemic rhetoric

1. We are both *inside* and *outside* of the worlds we inhabit, i.e., we are emic and etic to ourselves and to other selves. We look out at the world as we know it from various locations within those worlds. We are always at once both "different" and "same" to ourselves and others.

2. Truth is ascertainable even by finite creatures, but subject to verification and falsification from references points situated within worldviews to which we can have access via interpretative bridges facilitated by "native" knowers and outside observers.

3. Such truth, though never available exhaustively to us, may tolerably capture the world as it is in ever increasing accuracy, an approximation through language, mediated by personal presence.

4. A concept of objective reality that eludes our complete grasp but rewards those who diligently seek it is essential to good faith inquiry of any kind, including language-based inquiry, and of any communication model which claims insight into humanness.

5. Tagmemics insists on epistemological and ontological bases for the conclusions it draws.

6. Tagmemics demands attention to the situatedness of language and language behavior at every level of inquiry.

7. Tagmemics anticipates observer bias and endeavors to articulate and incorporate it into the investigation as a factor with which to be reckoned.

8. Tagmemics creates a versatile lexicon of useful terms and concepts to identify, describe, differentiate, and contextualize the nature/features of a unit under inquiry—whether it is a linguistic, rhetorical, or behavioral phenomenon. It provides a set of systematic heuristic tools and a consistent notational system to explore, examine, and test the acceptability and accuracy of emerging descriptions of data and relationships within and among it.

9. Tagmemics places no artificial limitation on the subject matter, its form or nature, that can be investigated under its aegis.

10. Tagmemics projects dissonance and/or anomaly as clues and cues to more ultimate levels of reality rather than as negatives to be explained away or subsumed in a contrived, homogenized description.

11. Tagmemics affirms universals of language and behavior that cross cultures, languages, and genders.

12. Tagmemics privileges persons above abstractions, community over autonomy, philosophical wholism over reductionism.

Based on these principles, a *working model of rhetorical inquiry* employing tagmemic rhetoric might look like this:

1. Inquiry begins with well-defined goals, a working hypothesis, or finite set of research questions. The ultimate goal of every tagmemic inquiry is an "emic" understanding or etically-verified hypothesis about the investigated phenomenon.

2. The point of entry may be the somewhat known or recognizable—usually, but not always a "particle"—which serves as the bridge to other contextualized particles, waves, etc.

3. The goal is progressively pursued and modified by incremental progress toward an emic understanding of (or etically-verified hypothesis about) the unit being investigated, with certain universals evoked at appropriate stages to give the inquiry boundaries and landmarks by which to judge progress.

4. The tools of the investigation include, characteristically, the particle, wave, and field *perspectives* whose application yields data that may be classified as contrastive/identificational features, range of variation features, and distribution features.

5. Observations, including initial, projected relations between and among and within particle, wave, and field data are progressively sharpened with references to the four-box (slot, role, class, cohesion) tagmeme notation, which is intended to assist the inquirer

both heuristically *to explore* and in terms of storage as a convenient matrix with which *to record* information.

6.   The tagmemic inquirer continues the inquiry until, in one way or another, the goals of the inquiry are met, modified, or satisfied by other means.

7.   The end of the inquiry is achieved by either (a) corroboration by a reliable or credentialed "native" observer that the description approaches tolerable emicity; or (b) an empirical test, etic-based, that satisfies the criteria of correspondence, consistency, and usefulness.

8.   A tagmemic "report" (a) prefaces the etic/emic description of the investigated phenomena with a discussion of goals and expectations; (b) provides a chronology of the investigation; (c) offers an overview of the data generated and/or explored; (d) states the emic (or, etically-tested) conclusions; and (e) projects further fruitful angles of vision and/or research questions to pursue in follow-up.

9.   The tagmemic inquiry/analysis/report is unique in so far as its final product is intended to be qualified by and sensitive to the maximum context, the discernible intra/inter/outer relationships, and corroborably-identifiable features available to the observer/inquirer. Its claims are never to exhaustive comprehensiveness but to tolerable similitude to "the thing itself," or an emic understanding of it.

Finally, the goals of a general "tagmemic rhetoric syllabus" might look something like this:

1.   Understanding the places of conventions in language within a particular universe/community of discourse: emic/etic exercises; nuclear/marginal exercises; problem-solving exercises.

2.   Conducting inquiries that move from the frame of self (emic) to other (etic), i.e., discourse that moves from personal narrative to other forms; continual movement between private and public, self and other, through language-based bridges.

3.   Text-making that moves from the frame of other (etic, i.e., research) to self (emic, i.e., the incarnation of self in other frames of

reference [worlds], employing, shaping, and reshaping its lexicon, syntax, etc.).

4. Learning new genres of report: the public presentation of self/other in various forms of discourse sensitive to community and projected audience.

Ken Pike was the first among linguists and rhetoricians in the twentieth century to identify comprehensively these working principles and to share their power. His work represents both profundity and humility:

> If language is reflecting deeply the image of God, do not expect it to be simple, now or ever—nor for any theory to exhaust it. God could have made any animal, or any kind of man He chose to make. But man as we know him, and as God wanted him to be, could not have been shaped like an elephant, have burrowed like a worm, been constrained by the mental limits of a bird or the communication restrictions of the moth. (Pike 1967, reprinted in Brend 1972:309)

When all the cataloguing, categorizing, and cannibalizing of Pike's work is done, his lasting legacy will be that of the selfless, servant scholar whose life and love were centered first in the Eternal Word, next in his wife and family, and then, thirdly, in his manly and maverick pursuit of language as an apologetics tool that brings glory to God and supplies the Christian Scriptures to the world.

What C. S. Lewis once said of his friend, J. R. R. Tolkien, might also be said of Ken Pike: "He had been 'inside' language." Yes. And because Ken was, we, too, are privileged to partake of his splendid insights.

Those with "ears to hear" and "eyes to see" ought to pay heed.

References

Brend, Ruth M., ed. 1972. *Kenneth L. Pike: Selected writings.* The Hague: Mouton.

Cremean, David Neal. 2001. *With God obsessed: The novels of Cormac McCarthy.* Ph.D. dissertation. Bowling Green State University.

Ebbert, Genevieve M. 1980. *A comparison of three instructional approaches for teaching written composition: Pentadic, tagmemic, and control treatment.* Ed.D. dissertation. Boston University School of Education.

Edwards, Bruce L. 1979. *The tagmemic contribution to composition teaching.* Occasional Papers in Composition Theory and History 2. Manhattan: Kansas State University. [Posted at < http://personal.bgsu.edu/~edwards/tags.html >.]

Felch, Susan M. 1991. *Paradigms and perspectives: The application of tagmemics and dialogics to religious literary criticism (James Henry, Bakhtin Mikhail).* Ph.D. dissertation. The Catholic University of America.

Guo, Danqing. 1997. *Metaphor in context: Toward a tagmemic linguistic approach.* Ph.D. dissertation. Bowling Green State University.

Katz, Sandra. 1984. *Teaching the tagmemic discovery procedure: A case study of a writing course.* D. A. Carnegie-Mellon University.

Kent, Carolyn Elizabeth. 1988. *A tagmemic analysis of coherence in the writing of descriptive texts by college students.* Ph.D. dissertation. University of North Texas.

Kitzhaber, Albert R. 1953. *Rhetoric in American Colleges, 1850–1900.* Ph.D. dissertation. University of Washington.

Kitzhaber, Albert R. 1960. Death–or transfiguration? *College English* 21:367.

Kitzhaber, Albert R. 1963. *Themes, theories, and therapy: The teaching of writing in college.* New York: McGraw.

Kitzhaber; Albert R. 1990. *Rhetoric in American colleges.* Dallas: Southern Methodist University Press.

Lauer, Janice Marie. 1967. *Invention in contemporary rhetoric: Heuristic procedures.* Ed.D. dissertation. University of Michigan

Linderman, Erika. 1995. Three views of English 101. *College English* 57(March):287–302.

Martin, James. E. 1989. *Towards a theory of textuality for contrastive rhetoric research.* Ph.D. dissertation. Bowling Green State University.

Odell, Camillus Lee. 1970. *Discovery procedures for contemporary rhetoric: A study of the usefulness of the tagmemic heuristic model in teaching composition.* Ph.D. dissertation. University of Michigan.

Phillips, Donna Burns, Ruth Greenberg, and Sharon Gibson. 1993. College Composition and Communication: Chronicling a discipline's genesis. *College Composition and Communication* 44:443–465.

Pike, Eunice V. 1981. *Ken Pike: Scholar and Christian.* Dallas: Summer Institute of Linguistics.

Pike, Kenneth L. 1964a. A linguistic contribution to composition: A hypothesis. *College Composition and Communication* 15:82–88.

Pike, Kenneth L. 1964b. Beyond the sentence. *College Composition and Communication* 15:129–135.

Pike, Kenneth L. 1967. *Language in relation to a unified theory of the structure of human behavior,* second revised edition. The Hague: Mouton.

Rabianski, Nancyanne Elizabeth Munzert. 1979. *An exploratory study of individual differences in the use of free writing and the tagmemic heuristic procedure, two modes of invention in the composing process.* Ph.D. disseration. State University of New York at Buffalo.

Tyma, Deborah Lynne Pierce. 1982. *Tagmemic grammar and reference in the 'pensees' of Pascal: An alternate linguistic framework for literary studies,* volumes I and II. Ph.D. dissertation. University of Michigan.

Yang, Xiao-Ming. 1991. *The rhetoric of propaganda: A tagmemic analysis of selected documents of the cultural revolution in China, 1966–1976.* Ph.D. dissertation. Bowling Green State University.

Young, Richard, and Alton L. Becker. 1965. Toward a modern theory of rhetoric. A tagmemic contribution. *Harvard Educational Review* 35:450–468.

Young, Richard, Alton Becker, and Kenneth L. Pike. 1970. *Rhetoric: Discovery and change.* New York: Harcourt.

36

Language as "Polluted Environment"

Adam Makkai

"Oh, what a tangled web we weave,
When first we practice to deceive..."
Sir Walter Scott, Lochinvar, stanza 17

"But let your communication be Yea, yea; Nay, nay:
for whatsoever is more than these cometh of evil."
Matthew 5:37

Language as Environment

Language has become one of the most important environments: its state of health may play a decisive role in the fate of the entire human race. "Words explode before cannons do," Kenneth L. Pike succinctly remarked. Of equal importance is the fact that *language pollution* does not always reveal itself in actual lingual behavior through words and sentences, but also in images and gestures, which can be brought to consciousness by actors on the stage or screen and through advertisements.

Pike was right when he insisted in his monumental 1967 work, *Language in Relation to a Unified Theory of the Structure of Human Behavior,* that language is not a self-contained structure devoid of human interests. This basic insight may be traced back to Aristotle's rhetoric and may be found to resurface periodically in the works of scholars with an interest in real human societies, such as J. R. Firth and Basil Bernstein. It is understandable that this theme should have been taken up by Systemic-Functionalism headed by M. A. K. Halliday and his colleagues. Pike's Tagmemics and Halliday's Systemic-Functionalism are considered by some scholars to be compatible three-tiered theories that base the description of human languages on semiotics and language use.

Language users exert their will in order to manipulate their environment. So does the infant crying to be nursed or to be changed. Since the infant's cognitive capabilities lie undeveloped, conscious verbalizations aimed at affecting the human environment come later in life.

Nowadays we are well attuned to thinking of the *physical environment* as subject to pollution. The media have made us aware of a long list of dangers, including artificial fertilizers in the soil, mercury poisoning in fish, nuclear waste, and international drug traffic and abuse. Not only are we aware of this aspect of pollution, we are in fact bombarded with information about it. As a result many people have become impervious to "alarmist news casting" and turn off their television sets when the talk turns to protecting the environment.

In this profusion of real and make-believe pollution of various sorts, we seem to have forgotten the fact that people believe what they hear and see, and that what they hear and see comes to them via language and in images. What people believe makes them think and feel in certain predictable and some unpredictable ways. We are influenced by the *information* we receive, whether the source is by word of mouth, the printed letter, radio, television, the Internet or e-mail; they are all recognizable agencies of both correct information and of disinformation. Language which obscures or distorts the meaning and intent so that the "information" imparted is in fact disinformation is "polluted language." In the third millennium, humanity cannot get along without the printed or the broadcast word. Driving on a highway or in a city, one is subliminally spoken to by billboard advertisements or the intermittent advertisements that keep radio stations commercially alive. They are of two kinds: *commercial* and *political persuasion*. Both belong to the *functional tenor of persuasion*—to use Halliday's term (1975). The chief mechanism—at least in English—is the use of *euphemisms*; their task is to make something sinister sound innocuous or even beneficial. The aim of political and commercial persuasion, via the rhetorical devices of euphemism and other figurative language, is to *influence the consciousness of others without their consent*.

In an earlier paper (1993) I tried to characterize idiomaticity cognitively as an attempt to escape de Saussure's principle of the arbitrariness of linguistic signs and an attempt to return to images instead of always having to create a new word from the existing phoneme and morpheme stock. Thus, when we say *seize the bull by the horns* for 'face an issue squarely', *to be all at sea* for 'being lost/confused', *kick the bucket* for 'die', and *pull one's leg* for 'tease', we are using suggestive images whose historical origin may be known or unknown. This is natural idiom creation.

The creation of modern idioms by the computer industry, on the other hand, ranging from *user-friendly* for 'simple/easy', *download* for 'copy', to *surf the net* for 'seek information' seems to have created a highly artificial and special sub-dictionary added to English during the past decades, the terms are akin to the way the computer itself works. Nevertheless, bar codes, compiler language signs, and even the binary code seem relatively innocent as compared to slogans such as *"Proletarians of the world, unite!"* which failed to produce the desired welfare of the working classes throughout the twentieth century.

We now turn our attention to the kinds of language pollution which are caused by *commercial* and *political persuasion*, many of which are brilliantly caricatured in George Orwell's *Nineteen Eighty-Four*.

The Functional Tenor of Persuasion

Personal persuasion can be crooked as when, for instance, a dishonest family member tries to persuade a slow-witted relative to sign a document and thereby relinquish a part of an inheritance. What keeps this from being genuine language pollution is the private nature of the deceit. Language, as the intellectual property of an entire society, becomes truly polluted when lies expressed through language become *culturally institutionalized* to the extent that entire generations of people begin to think in terms of the vocabulary containing the lies and distortions.

Oppressors, while exhibiting the "criminal attitude" in terms of "transactional analysis" (Berne 1966; Harris 1967), are bothered by residual guilt feeling. Euphemisms, therefore, seem just the right hedges to hide behind. The key concept here is that of *disinformation* which is turned into *legitimated societal consciousness* (cf. Berger and Luckmann 1967). Below I will examine some of the most striking cases of such manipulative behavior.

Advertising

One of the commonest types of commercial advertising concerns automobiles. Rarely is one told about the mileage of the car, its mechanical properties, or how many international companies contributed to its parts. One is shown instead a Hercules-like figure outrunning a cannon ball which, in turn, is outrun by a trendy sports car. A van or jeep is precariously balanced on top of a steep rock overlooking a dramatic valley; the car suddenly becomes a submarine and swims under a boat that it would have collided with had it remained on the surface. In ads that use "snob appeal" one sees a luxury car surrounded by classical Greek columns and accompanied by the music of Beethoven. Elegantly dressed men and women emerge from such vehicles in front of European concert halls. The intention of such ads is to make the viewers desire the car by substituting themselves for the actors who are seen on the screen owning such vehicles.

Cigarette commercials have been forbidden on the American screen for several years now (cf. Makkai 1974), but billboards and magazine ads continue to lure adults and children. While such commercials were still permitted, the following mini-drama was aired.

Act I: We are in the compartment of a train somewhere in Europe. Castles and cypresses are seen through the window.

Act II: The protagonist is the male passenger, wearing a turtleneck sweater and streamlined shades. He is faced by the antagonist, the female passenger, sitting opposite him.

Act III: The female passenger reaches for the man's x-brand cigarettes lying on the small table by the train's window. Instead of offering her a light, the man grabs his cigarettes away.

Act IV: He lights one of his cigarettes rescued from the female invader, smirks smugly and looks out the window. The frustrated woman, defeated, sinks into herself.

Message: If you want to be a real man, do not offer a lady a cigarette, but guard your own as fiercely as you should guard your endangered masculinity.

Counter-advertising

Inasmuch as these pro-smoking advertisements work, they may be viewed as a modern kind of "incantation" or "bewitching" of the target audience. The American Cancer Association became aware of the danger inherent in such "spells" and started a counter-propaganda movement, which we may view as acts of EXORCISM. Noticing how effective these four-act mini-dramas were, the health professionals devised their own. Consider the following:

> Act I: A father and his ten-year old son go on a picnic. The father sits down under a tree and opens a sandwich bag. So does the boy. The voice-over says: *"Like father, like son."*
>
> Act II: The father opens a can of coke and takes a sip. So does the boy. The voice-over repeats: *"Like father, like son."*
>
> Act III: The father lies down, stretches and yawns. So does the boy. The voice-over once more repeats *"like father, like son"* in a neutral, declarative intonation.
>
> Act IV: The father reaches for a pack of cigarettes and lights up. The boy also reaches for the cigarettes, at which point the picture freezes and the voice-over asks with an emphatic interrogative intonation: *"Like father, like son?!"*

The implication is that unless you watch what you do in front of immature children, they will imitate you. This ad is intended to arouse the conscience of parents and ask that they stop smoking. It may be compared to an act of *cleaning up a polluted environment.*

Political persuasion

It is common knowledge that in American politics the two major parties continually blame each other for whatever is wrong. The constant theme running through American political rhetoric is that certain things need fixing, but *the other party*—whoever does the talking—goes about it the wrong way. The issues are well known. Both parties use statistics and present documents that to newspaper readers or television viewers appear to be objective.

"Politically Correct" Language

The literature on "Politically Correct Language" (p.c.) is quite extensive; in V. B. Makkai's Presidential Address to the Linguistic Association of Canada and the United States (LACUS) (V. B. Makkai 1996) the number of cited references is 121. I will mention here only some of the best-known cases, which, in my view, constitute obvious cases of language pollution.

Nonsexist language

Along with a host of entirely legitimate issues, such as Equal Pay for Women and Sexual Harassment in the Workplace, the feminist movement has engaged in an attack on the English language branding it "sexist." That the distinction between *Miss* and *Mrs.* was somewhat discriminatory is entirely true, since the male counterpart, *Mr.,* does not identify the person as single versus married; thus the popular abbreviation *Ms.* This is reasonable and fair. Similarly, it makes sense to neutralize German *Frau* versus *Fräulein* to an inclusive abbreviation *Fr.* French *Mme. [Madame]* versus *Mlle. [Mademoiselle]* can be reasonably abbreviated to an inclusive *Me,* Some people, however, go so far as to call themselves *M. X. Y.,* thereby obscuring their sex altogether, which people wanting to know who is male and who is female may consider an act of language pollution.

Language pollution is further committed in English when the word *history* is accused of being sexist and the suggestion is made that the word ought to be **herstory. History* does not contain the morpheme *his;* it comes from the Latin *historia.* The fact that the syllable *his-* sounds like the third person masculine possessive pronoun is pure phonological coincidence.

Future generations of language users as well as technical linguists will have to decide whether generic *they* rather than *he* or *she* is an act of language pollution or a step in the right direction. Being a Hungarian in whose language 'he/she' is always simply *o,* I feel neutral about this issue.

Reverse markedness

In the language of the blind the inability to see is treated as normal, and people who see must be given a marked term, which is *sighted.* Thus you and I who can read this article are *sighted,* as if we had an unusual condition, if not a disease. Similarly, in the language of the deaf, it is their condition that is regarded as normal, and so you and I who can hear, are *hearing people,* as if this were also unusual.

To call a cripple a *cripple* sounds rude and hurtful, thus politically correct jargon created the term *physically challenged.* Why is this an instance of language pollution? Because any healthy person who has to carry a heavy load on his/her back is, under those conditions, "physically challenged." The term disguises the fact that we are talking about someone in a wheelchair or on crutches.

To call a short man a *bantam cock, shorty, wallabee,* or *of stunted growth*—not to mention *midget* or *dwarf*—seems rude; thus politically correct language has coined the semi-serious phrase *vertically challenged.* The pollutant here is the linguistic matrix similar to *X-gate:* any handicap a human being can have may become his/her *being challenged in the X-way,* or being *X-challenged.* A dunce can be called *intellectually challenged;* a mathematics dropout becomes *arithmetically/numerically challenged;* a person who cannot carry a tune *musically challenged,* etc. Could the times be near when a common criminal will graduate to being *morally challenged,* and therefore get a lesser sentence in a court of law? I certainly hope not.

Conclusion

I have tried to show in this paper that language has become the most important environment and that we humans must, therefore, keep a constant vigil over it, since language has the power to alter human consciousness either beneficially—as in teaching and counseling—or in a malefic manner, as in political and commercial exploitation of credulous, gullible people who do not analyze what is being said and react accordingly.

Polluted language manifests itself not only as direct speech or writing, but also as images of false advertising, whether on billboards or on the television screen.

But polluted areas can and have been cleaned up. The Thames in London was once like a sewer, but after the British Government's concentrated efforts to remedy the situation, the Thames is once again fairly clean. The same is true about Lake Erie near Cleveland, Ohio in the U.S.A., which was once declared biologically dead. The city of Cleveland spent hundreds of millions of dollars and literally vacuum cleaned the pollution out of the lake. The fish have returned.

There is still hope that, grave though the situation was throughout the twentieth century, we can take countermeasures to clear up language pollution by telling the truth. The profession of linguistics has a crucial role to play in this regard, since as the late Dwight L. Bolinger has said (1976), "Truth is a linguistic question."

In the spirit of Kenneth L. Pike's entire life's work, I would amplify this admirable statement by adding: "Linguistics is a moral question." Linguistics must not become a subjective field of contentious ideologies, no matter how clever or ingenious at first blush. We must bear in mind that natural languages on earth exist as one of our highest faculties and that their proper or improper use may determine the outcome of war and peace.

References

Berger, P. L., and Luckmann, T. 1967. *The social construction of reality: A treatise in the sociology of knowledge*. London: Allen Lane (The Penguin Press).

Berne, Eric. 1966. *Games people play*. New York: Grove Press.

Bolinger, Dwight, L. 1976. Truth is a linguistic question. *Language* 49:539–550.

Halliday, M. A. K. 1975. *Learning how to mean—Explorations in the development of language*. London: Edward Arnold.

Harris, Thomas A. 1967. *I'm OK, You're OK*. New York: Harper & Row.

Harris, Thomas A. 1993. Idiomaticity as a reaction to *L'Arbitraire du Signe* in the universal process of semeio-genesis. In Cristina Cacciari and Patrizia Tabossi (eds.), *Idioms: Processing, structure, and interpretation*, 297–324. Hillsdale, N.J.: Lawrence Erlbaum Associates.

Makkai, Adam. 1974. Madison Avenue advertising: A scenario. In *The First LACUS Forum*, 197–208. Columbia, S.C.: Hornbeam Press.

Makkai, Valerie Becker. 1996. Correctness in language: Political and otherwise. In Alan K. Melby (ed.), *The Twenty-third LACUS Forum*, 5–25. Chapel Hill, N.C.: The Linguistic Association of Canada and the United States.

Pike, Kenneth L. 1967. *Language in relation to a unified theory of the structure of human behavior*. The Hague: Mouton.

37

Congregations, Coalitions, and Chemicals

A Study in Applied Anthropology

Patricia K. Townsend

The peak years of Kenneth Pike's turn from language to culture coincided with my undergraduate years at the University of Michigan. In the fall semester of 1959, I discovered anthropology simultaneously in an introductory course at the University taught by Marshall Sahlins and in a Sunday morning series at Grace Bible Church on anthropology and Christian missions taught by Professor Pike. A more brilliant teacher can scarcely be imagined, challenging a teenager to sort out the areas of conflict and overlap in her life and learning. (Both Sahlins and Pike in their teaching were explicitly in dialogue with Leslie White, as the personification of anthropological theory at that time and place.) Pike was soon urged by his colleagues to pursue grammar rather than culture. Sahlins, too, shifted away from his theoretical perspective that had captured my interest (with its focus on the interface between environment and technology), but not before I was hooked.

Perhaps more than anything else that Pike conveyed that semester was the notion of scholar-as-servant, the idea that the final test of good work in linguistics and anthropology was that it be *helpful* to one's colleagues and to the minority peoples of the world. In addition to saying it and writing it (Pike 1962), Pike modeled it, spending alternate semesters in the academic setting and in field workshops serving junior colleagues. He also gave me what I took to be an assignment—to find a way to teach beginners, in a single summer's intensive course, the skills to get started on learning and analyzing a culture in the same way that the Summer Institute of Linguistics (now SIL International) got them started on language. I must admit that it was a daunting task to even consider how anthropology might be taught in such a practical and efficient way, and I did not attempt to carry it out. Even so, without that nudge from Pike I would probably not have spent so much of my career in developing textbooks that attempt to bridge the gap between academic anthropology and applied anthropology.

Anthropology has managed to keep its professors and practitioners under a single disciplinary roof to a much greater extent than sociology and social work or other pairs of academic and applied disciplines. Yet all is not well today with the relationship between academic anthropology and applied anthropology. The larger academic departments of anthropology, especially the elite graduate departments, fail to teach applied anthropology, let alone require it, despite knowing that a majority of their students will find their future employment in applied work and the rest will teach such students (Price 2001). Many applied anthropologists cynically view the current call from academic anthropologists for a "public anthropology" as a self-serving attempt from academic anthropologists to get media attention and influence public policy in areas outside their expertise. They fault it with ignoring the policy-relevant work already being done by applied anthropologists (Singer 2000; Young 2001).

In the midst of this era of concern for developing a policy-relevant anthropology, the Society for Applied Anthropology negotiated a five-year collaborative agreement with the Office of Sustainable Ecosystems and Communities (OSEC) of the U.S. Environmental Protection Agency for the period 1996-2001.[1] The agreement was intended to increase anthropological input into environmental planning and problem solving at the agency and in communities. In its early years, the agreement put graduate students and post-doctoral researchers into a wide variety of community and agency settings. Coming along near the end of the five-year agreement, my own project responded to a specific interest expressed by the office of Superfund, the program for cleaning up the most serious of the abandoned hazardous waste sites throughout the United States.[2] The anthropologist's characteristic

---

[1]The Agreement and documents related to the project are posted on the Society's web site (http://www.sfaa.net/eap/) and are discussed in the Summer 2001 issue of the SfAA's publication *Practicing Anthropology*.

[2]Industrial sites that are currently in use are covered by other federal regulations and programs. Also, states have their own Superfund programs for cleaning up additional sites.

ethnographic methods seemed well suited to producing case studies that would explore the role of religious organizations and interfaith coalitions in the communities surrounding Superfund sites.

The Superfund program was established in 1980 by Congress in the Comprehensive Environmental Response, Compensation and Liability Act of 1980 (CERCLA) PL 96-510. Under the program, the government takes action to get the former owners and users of a site to clean it up, using government funds (from a "Superfund" created by taxing the chemical and petroleum industry) only in emergencies or if the responsible parties are bankrupt or cannot be located. The legislation reauthorizing the program in 1986 mandated various reforms, including greater community participation in decisions about Superfund sites.

Grassroots environmental groups seeking the cleanup of existing hazardous waste sites as well as groups resisting proposed new waste disposal sites have attracted much social science research. Most of this research literature comes from the perspective of social movement theory or the role of media in issue formation (Edelstein 1988; Levine 1982; Mazur 1998; Szasz 1994). The role of churches and interfaith coalitions at such sites had not been systematically studied prior to this project, though it was known that church groups and interfaith coalitions had been involved in some locations. Some Superfund locations where religious groups were known to have been a strong influence were the Hanford Reserve in Washington State (Kaplan 1997), Woburn, Massachusetts (Harr 1996), Columbia, Mississippi (where the grassroots group pressing for cleanup was named Jesus People Against Pollution, making it virtually impossible to ignore its religious dimensions), and Carver Terrace, an African-American neighborhood in Texarkana, Texas (Čapek 1993).

The Field Sites

The title of this SfAA project was "The Role of Interfaith Councils and Religious Groups in Superfund Site Identification, Assessment, and Remediation." The project produced an annotated bibliography and three field studies of Superfund sites where religious organizations had been involved to differing degrees (Townsend 2001). The three case studies were the *North Hollywood Dump*, a closed municipal dump in a Black neighborhood on the north side of Memphis, Tennessee, the *Clark Fork* sites, a complex of four Superfund sites in Western Montana that stretches 120 miles from Butte to Missoula along Silver Bow Creek and the Clark Fork River, and *Love Canal* in Niagara Falls, located in western New York state on the Canadian border.

The sites were chosen for a good regional spread—the South, the West, and the Northeast. They also represent different parts of the religious landscape of the United States, including predominantly Baptist Memphis, highly secular Missoula, and the predominantly Catholic, small industrial cities of Butte and Niagara Falls.

All three sites were on the list of some 400 sites that had formed the initial National Priority List when Superfund began, two decades ago. Because the three sites varied in the cost and complexity of remediation they are now at different stages in the Superfund process. Choosing one of several hundred sites more recently added to the Superfund program would have made comparison among the case studies even more difficult.

The North Hollywood site was a city dump containing mostly household rubbish where the Velsicol Corporation had dumped wastes from its manufacture of pesticides. An elementary school and residential neighborhood abutted the site; fortunately, drainage from the site was away from the neighborhood, northward toward the Wolf River. The scope and cost of remediation of the dump were typical for a Superfund site. The site was cleaned up and deleted from the National Priority List in 1997.

Love Canal is well known as a past site of chemical dumping that had become the playing fields for an elementary school adjacent to a residential neighborhood. Its remediation costs came to more than $200 million, which was more than ten times the cost of North Hollywood. The technology used for cleaning up was similar at the two sites; most of the wastes were left right in place and contained by a clay barrier, with monitoring and treatment to continue in perpetuity. Homes at Love Canal were purchased so that residents could relocate if they chose to do so. The Love Canal site had not yet been removed from Superfund at the time of the research, although construction work was completed in 1999, when a second elementary school in the neighborhood was demolished and the sediments that had been cleaned from the creeks and sewers were shipped out of state for disposal.

The four Superfund sites of the Clark Fork in Montana were grouped together by the USEPA for remediation because all are part of the heritage of the Anaconda Company's copper mines, subsequently acquired by the petroleum company ARCO, which is now part of BP Amoco. Cleaning up the mining wastes at the Clark Fork sites may cost ARCO as much as $2 billion, more than ten times what Love Canal cost Occidental Chemical, and more than a hundred times what North Hollywood cost Velsicol. Progress has been made in cleaning the lead and arsenic from residential and industrial areas of Butte and Anaconda and providing alternative water supplies where arsenic had contaminated wells. At the time of this research, the biggest challenges were still ahead—dealing with the contaminated sediments trapped behind a small hydropower dam at Milltown on the Clark Fork River near Missoula and treating the acid lake left from open-pit mining in Butte.

Hysterical Housewives

In each of the three case-study communities, grassroots activists drew attention to the possible health risks that were presented by toxic wastes in their neighborhoods. These activists were women (as is true at many toxic waste sites). The ironically self-deprecating term "hysterical housewife" came to be a widely used expression indicating the political power of such grassroots eco-feminists (Mellor 1997:21; Miller 1997; Newman 1994:58; Pettus 1997:fn.17). What the so-called hysterical housewives have in common is neither hysteria nor being housewives, but that they were *mothers*, passionately concerned about the health of their children. Each of them became an outspoken media figure who drew attention (and government resources) to her community.

The quintessential hysterical housewife was, of course, Lois Gibbs, who dominated media coverage of Love Canal from August 1978 onward. The ironic, self-mocking term is recognizably Gibbs: compare her scathing use of the expression "useless housewife data" to refer to the Department of Health response to her documentation of health problems at Love Canal. Both of her children had illnesses that she connected to the chemical wastes in their neighborhood. More than any other grassroots organizer, Gibbs became the icon of the social movement that Szasz (1994) terms "ecopopulism." The timing of her protests to take advantage of reelection campaigns of New York Governor Carey and then President Jimmy Carter was crucial. She came to be seen as the force behind the creation of the Superfund program in 1980.

Gibbs' contemporary was the hysterical housewife of Memphis, Evonda Pounds. Pounds lived in the white working-class neighborhood of Frayser north of the Wolf River, on the north side of Memphis. She was interviewed on national television in 1980 because her children had rashes and other ailments that she feared were a result of living on an old chemical dump. Tests of the children did show traces of organic phosphates (*Commercial Appeal*, Aug 4, 1979, p.13), indicating possible exposure to pesticides, but despite extensive environmental testing the EPA was never able to discover a source of contamination in Frayser. The citywide Memphis environmental task force set up because of the intense public concern about chemical pollution turned its attention to the North Hollywood site, located not far from Frayser but south of the Wolf River. At the North Hollywood municipal dump, adjacent to a Black neighborhood and elementary school, chemical pollution *was* documented.

A few years later in Montana, the hysterical housewife of the Milltown site was Tina Reinecke-Schmaus. At home near Milltown with her newborn baby, she was disturbed by the noise and dust of trucks moving soils from the Superfund site. Her complaints to the Missoula County department of environmental health revealed that the department had not been aware that there were residences in the area. Coverage of her grassroots environmental crusade headlined her as "the housewife from hell" (*High Country News*, October 30, 1995).

Two of these women became skilled leaders, establishing significant and durable organizations. Reinecke-Schmaus founded MESS, the Milltown EPA Superfund Site committee. MESS evolved into MTAC, the Milltown Technical Assistance Committee. Reinecke-Schmaus chaired MTAC for a decade, while it held a series of USEPA Technical Assistance (TAG) grants that allowed it to employ scientific consultants to help citizens participate effectively throughout the technical review process for remediation of the Superfund site. Constrained by its USEPA funding to represent all viewpoints within the community, and not just those of environmentalists, MTAC worked in close contact with the Clark Fork Coalition, an outspoken and effective environmental organization.

Lois Gibbs left Love Canal in 1981, having achieved relocation on behalf of the Love Canal Homeowners Association. Gibbs then moved to Washington and founded the Citizens Clearinghouse for Hazardous Waste (now called the Center for Health, Environment, and Justice). This organization has been a resource that empowered thousands of similar grassroots environmental groups to resist the siting of new waste facilities or demand the cleanup of existing toxic sites.

Building Coalitions

After identifying the problem of toxic contamination and initially mobilizing resources directed toward solving the problem, effective continuing community involvement in decision-making at a site depends less on hysterical housewives and more on building a broad base of support. Most of the research looking at hazardous waste sites concentrates on the formation of new grassroots organizations such as Gibbs' Love Canal Homeowners Association (Levine 1982). At least equally interesting, though perhaps harder to research, is the formation, and maintenance, of coalitions among such grassroots organizations and *existing* organizations in the community. It is this process of coalition-building that has been of special interest in the current research.

The defining feature of a coalition is that the parties, factions, or organizations that come together retain their individual character. They remain distinct organizations while coalescing around a given issue, an issue to which they bring the influence carried by their larger memberships. An example at the national level is the National Religious Partnership on the Environment, a coalition that is comprised of the United States Catholic Conference Environmental Justice Program, the Coalition on the Environment and Jewish Life, the Evangelical Environmental Network, and the Eco-Justice Working Group of the National Council of Churches of Christ in the USA. While working together on environmental issues, the main religious traditions do not lose any of their organizational distinctiveness. Each of them goes back to their constituencies to interpret the issues in ways that are consistent with their own theology and polity.

Coalition formation at the Clark Fork

At a local level, coalitions may be slippery, shape-shifting things. Some entities bearing the name coalition are no longer coalitions, if they ever were. So, for example, the most influential of the environmental organizations in any of the case study communities is the Clark Fork Pend-Oreille Coalition, which, its legal name notwithstanding, is not a coalition but an individual membership organization. The Clark Fork Coalition, in turn, is one of several environmental organizations that are partners in a fledgling coalition, PLACE, formed during 2000 to advocate for Superfund remediation. The acronym PLACE refers to **P**eople in **L**abor unions, **A**griculture, **C**ommunities of faith, and **E**nvironmental organizations. PLACE's co-founder was Kathy Hadley, Executive Director of the National Center for Appropriate Technology at Butte. She is Lois Gibbs' sister and the person who fought successfully in 1985 to have the 100 miles of the Clark Fork River above the dam included in the Milltown Superfund site. Initial participation from environmental organizations and labor unions was more conspicuous than from the other two sectors, though both the Montana Association of Churches and the Catholic Diocese were represented by John Hart, a theologian at Carroll College. In its first year, PLACE had yet to become a significant voice in the discussion of

Superfund alternatives, but it is poised to do so when the next period for public comment on proposed alternatives for remediation opens.

The challenges to forming coalitions under such circumstances should not be underestimated. Even where there is much shared ideology and a desire to work together, the organizations that come together may have different cultures that affect the way they can work together. Paul Lichterman's study in a West Coast U.S. city of local groups of secular Greens and African-Americans found that the two groups exemplified very different patterns of everyday interaction that made it difficult for them to form an alliance despite sharing a common goal of environmental justice. Briefly, the (largely white and middle class) Greens developed a much more personalized and individualized form of community, while the African-American group was much more unified and communitarian (Lichterman 1995). Another researcher, Fred Rose, is much more encouraged about the ability of labor unions, peace groups, and environmental organizations to form coalitions that cross the class divide. His observations of military sites and the logging industry led him to a guarded optimism, while he acknowledges that labor unions and middle class activists have conflicting patterns of organization and communication (Rose 2000).

Ecumenical cooperation at Love Canal

At Love Canal, the Ecumenical Task Force began as a coalition of parishes, congregations, and judicatories, each sending a representative to meetings. They defined their goals as channeling direct aid to residents, influencing public policy, and educating the religious community on problems related to hazardous wastes. They elected a board, largely of clergy and laypersons officially representing the denominations in the coalition—each with the capacity to go back to the denominations to ask for funds and resolutions. But as the committed board members worked together intensely, meeting every Tuesday morning at 7:30, the ETF was welded into less a coalition and more a tight-knit volunteer organization. The board members came in time to serve more out of personal interest rather than ex officio. The ETF included some residents of the Love Canal neighborhood, but was predominantly comprised of persons of middle-class origins from outside the neighborhood.

The denominations represented in the ETF included the Roman Catholics, Presbyterian, United Church of Christ, United Methodist, Lutherans (ELCA and Missouri Synod), American Baptists, Episcopalian, Disciples of Christ, and Unitarian—as well as councils of churches from both Buffalo and Niagara Falls. The rabbi from one of the local synagogues also served on the board at various times, hence it was more accurately called an interfaith coalition than an ecumenical organization.

Any tension that may have existed between Sister Margeen Hoffman, the nun who was employed as executive director of the ETF, and Lois Gibbs, the president of the homeowners' organization, did not prevent the organizations they headed from working toward the same ends. Eventually, after both had left Western New York, the two organizations virtually spoke with a single voice through former Love Canal residents, Joann Hale and Pat Brown.

Even as the Ecumenical Task Force became an organization with a regional environmental mission broader than the immediate task of disaster relief to Love Canal residents, it became a coalition-building organization. It worked in coalition with grassroots organizations in several Niagara County neighborhoods with toxic sites and with secular environmental organizations. These included Canadian organizations, as pollution from Niagara County sites had implications for Canadian communities along the Niagara River and Lake Ontario. In 1981 the ETF joined with Pollution Probe of Toronto and Operation Clean Niagara to file a joint *amici curae* (friend of the court) brief stating that the Hyde Park Landfill settlement proposal was defective.[3]

The ETF formed another coalition to block the expansion of a hazardous waste landfill. The CECOS facility was an already large hazardous waste landfill (so conspicuous that it was locally referred to as Mount Cecos) that was receiving some of the wastes from Love Canal as well as downstate and out-of-state wastes. The coalition formed for fighting the CECOS permit included the ETF and five other organizations: Campaign to Save Niagara, Great Lakes United, LaSalle and Niagara Demand, Society to Oppose Pollution in Towns, and Evershed Restoration Association (Edelstein 1989:160, fn. 2).

With the sense in the wider community that the Love Canal crisis was over in 1981, after the residents had won relocation, the ETF could no longer count on the level of interest, financial support, or volunteer effort that it had enjoyed initially, though several hundred hazardous waste sites remained throughout Niagara County. The ETF remained very active until the mid 1980s and retained a full-time executive director until 1988. Even after that, the ETF was a strong presence in joining the Homeowners' Association in 1989 and 1990 to delay the resale of the homes in the

---

[3]Hyde Park was another Occident Chemical Superfund site, located on the north side of Niagara Falls.

former Love Canal neighborhood.[4] For more than a decade, the interfaith coalition had worked effectively in coalition with grassroots environmental organizations on issues of environmental justice in Western New York.

The North Hollywood case

The Environmental Task Force that had formed in 1980 to deal with the toxic waste crisis in Memphis, Tennessee, differed substantially from the Ecumenical Task Force at Love Canal. The city and county departments, environmental, religious, and other community groups that came together in the Memphis task force attained no real unity of purpose. The task force was chaired by a Black Baptist minister, the Rev. Hubon Sandridge, Jr., a young minister and employee of the Sheriff's department, who went on to be elected to a successful long-term role on the School Board. MIFA, an inter-faith organization, sent representatives to the Task Force, but their role seems to have been more one of observer/historian rather than an active one. Hostile parties resigned in protest and others drifted away in apathy—the potential for coalition-formation lost. The toxic crisis had gone from being a community-wide concern to the local concern of a poor black neighborhood. The racial politics of the city overwhelmed a short-lived attempt to work together on this issue. Even so, the Task Force accomplished some significant things—notably engaging voluntary, independent scientific input from a Vanderbilt University chemist who worked with the Task Force to identify chemical hot spots in the dump, contamination that had not been located by the official program of testing.

The Value of Faith-Based Responses

Doubtless there are many hazardous waste sites where faith-based organizations have not responded in any way. Yet the case study sites are not unique; it is possible to identify other sites across the country where such involvement appears to be similar to the study communities. The ecumenical task force formed at the dioxin-contaminated community of Times Beach, Missouri, was explicitly modeled after the ETF at Love Canal

---

[4]Opposition to the resale of the homes was finally unsuccessful. The renovated homes in the northern and western portions of the neighborhood were sold with the neighborhood renamed as Black Creek Village. The eastern part of the neighborhood was razed (with the exception of the homes of a few holdout homeowners) and deemed suitable for nonresidential development. Part of this site is currently proposed for the location of an environmental museum that would overlook the central part of the site, containing the waste depository (a fenced grassy knoll) and treatment facility.

(Hoffmann 1987; Reko 1984). PLACE, the new coalition in western Montana, is similar in composition to a highly effective coalition of labor, environmental, educational, and religious organizations that has worked for twenty years on issues of groundwater contamination in the Silicon Valley of Santa Rosa County, California. And the Memphis site was only the first of many Superfund sites scattered across the South from the Carolinas to Texas where African-American ministers took leadership roles. This phenomenon accelerated following the 1993 Black Church Environmental Justice Summit in Washington and the 1994 Executive Order that specified federal government actions to address environmental justice in minority and low-income populations.

This SfAA-sponsored research project was specifically charged with exploring the role of interfaith councils and religious organizations in coalitions surrounding Superfund sites. It is, of course, of some value simply to document that religious groups have been *present* in these coalitions—to compensate for their customary invisibility to media and researchers. Going beyond that initial step, comparison between sites began to suggest the distinctive contribution of religious organizations at Superfund sites.

- Their presence functions to legitimate or broaden concerns about hazardous waste as an issue of the common good rather than the narrow self-interest of a few homeowners or hysterical housewives.
- They have some potential to bridge the class barrier between working-class grassroots groups and middle-class environmental groups, though they are not always successful in doing so, especially where racial-ethnic barriers are high.
- They are not immune from the conflicts that emerge in contaminated communities between those who downplay the risks and those who exaggerate them. When conflicts occur, they often have resources for mediating them and can provide safe spaces for carrying on civil discussion.
- They have traditional concerns with health and particularly with threats to the well-being of children, who are especially vulnerable to toxic chemicals. This background prepares them to engage with the issues of risk from hazardous waste.
- They tend to re-cast the issues in ethical terms rather than purely technical, economic, and political terms.

Existing organizations often move slowly when faced with an emerging social problem, especially one as complex as hazardous waste.[5] "My church was not there for me" was the pained response of many persons undergoing the stresses and uncertainties of living in a contaminated community. In time, many faith-based organizations ranging from local congregations to national denominations crafted varied responses to the emerging problem. They developed resources out of their experience and shared them with other groups (Hoffmann 1987; Ketcham 1999).

As religious groups engaged with the residents of Superfund communities, their pastoral response of comforting the suffering was accompanied by a prophetic one, speaking out against injustice and demanding redress of environmental damage from responsible corporations and government bodies. Engagement of this sort required thinking through the theological rationale for such action. During the 1980s and 1990s, the environment was a significant new emphasis in theology for Catholics, Jews, and mainline and evangelical Protestants.[6] Concepts such as eco-justice emerged as practical theologians and ethicists grappled with how to integrate their concerns for the poor with the responsible stewardship of creation.

Conclusions

As I encountered it in the fall semester of 1959 in Ann Arbor, anthropology was occupied with the villages of Amazonia and Melanesia. This chapter describes a project in applied anthropology that looks instead at North American neighborhoods contaminated by industrial wastes. Though the settings are superficially very different, the communities face formidable challenges that are similar; indeed in some cases it is the same multinational corporation, OXY or AMOCO, that seeks to extract oil or mineral resources from the South while dealing with wastes from past production in the North. Using the same ethnographic toolkit in both

---

[5]With respect to the technical complexity of the issues as well as the stigma associated with the discovery of hazardous waste in a community, perhaps the nearest equivalent social problem emerging in the same era was AIDS. Existing institutions had equal difficulty in responding to AIDS (Perrow and Guillen 1990).

[6]Some figures in discussions of environmental theology include, for example, Sallie McFague, Jay McDaniel, and Larry Rasmussen among liberal Protestants, Calvin DeWitt, and Wesley Granberg-Michaelson among Evangelicals, James H. Cone among the African-American theologians, and Thomas Berry and John Hart among Roman Catholics. This theological development has been reviewed by several authors (Bakken et al. 1995; Fowler 1995; Kearns 1996) and has been examined in conference proceedings (Hessel and Ruether 2000). The Coalition on the Environment and Jewish Life has brought together a wide variety of resources on Jewish thinking about environmental ethics (Coalition on the Environment and Jewish Life, n.d.).

kinds of settings, the anthropologist documents the encounter through fieldwork. The usefulness of anthropology for this task is its built-in interdisciplinarity that encourages the anthropologist to treat as potentially relevant a wide range of factors. From religious beliefs to vegetable gardens, from children's illnesses to commodity prices, from rainfall to neighborhood organizations, each of these phenomena prove as relevant to understanding Love Canal as they are to an ethnographer's grasp of an Amazonian culture. Whether the research problem is a small society resisting the loss of its resource base or a suburban community seeking to participate in decisions for cleaning up wastes, the role of the anthropologist, at its best, may be to identify and affirm the strengths that the community brings to addressing its problems.

References

Bakken, Peter W., Joan Gibb Engel, and J. Ronald Engel. 1995. *Ecology, justice, and Christian faith : A critical guide to the literature.* Westport, Conn.: Greenwood Press.

Brown, Patricia A. 1985. The church was not there. *The Egg: Quarterly Journal of Eco-justice* 5:12.

Čapek, Stella M. 1993. The environmental justice frame: A conceptual discussion and an application. *Social Problems* 40:5–24.

Coalition on the Environment and Jewish Life. n.d. *To till and to tend: A guide to Jewish environmental study and action.* New York: Coalition on the Environment and Jewish Life.

Edelstein, Michael R. 1988. *Contaminated communities: The social and psychological impacts of residential toxic exposure.* Boulder: Westview Press.

Edelstein, Michael R. 1989. Psychosocial impacts on trial: The case of hazardous waste disposal. In Dennis L. Peck (ed.), *Psychosocial effects of hazardous toxic waste disposal on communities,* 153–175. Springfield, Ill.: Thomas.

Fowler, Robert Booth. 1995. *The greening of Protestant thought.* Chapel Hill: University of North Carolina Press.

Harr, Jonathan. 1996. *A civil action.* New York: Vintage Books.

Hessel, Dieter, and Rosemary Radford Ruether. 2000. *Christianity and ecology: Seeking the well-being of earth and humans.* Harvard University Center for the Study of World Religions Publications, Religions of the World and Ecology. Cambridge, Mass.: Harvard University Press.

Hoffmann, Margeen. 1987. *Earthcare: Lessons from Love Canal—a resource and response guide.* Niagara Falls: Ecumenical Task Force of the Niagara Frontier.

Kaplan, Louise. 1997. The Hanford Education Action League: An informed citizenry and radiation health effects. *International Journal of Contemporary Sociology* 34:255–265.

Kearns, Laurel. 1996. Saving the creation: Christian environmentalism in the United States. *Sociology of Religion* 57:55–71.

Ketcham, Jim. 1999. *The silent disaster: People of faith respond to technological disasters.* National Council of Churches of Christ in the USA, Resource Unit on Technological Disasters Church World Service, Emergency Response Program.

Levine, Adeline. 1982. *Love Canal: Science, politics, and people.* Lexington, Mass.: Lexington Books.

Lichterman, Paul. 1995. Piecing together multicultural community: Cultural differences in community building among grass-roots environmentalists. *Social Problems* 42:513–535.

Mazur, Allan. 1998. *A hazardous inquiry: The Rashomon effect at Love Canal.* Cambridge, Mass.: Harvard University Press.

Mellor, Mary. 1997. *Feminism and ecology.* Washington Square: New York University Press.

Miller, Stuart. 1997. Green at the grassroots: Women form the frontlines of environmental activism. *E* 8:34–35.

Newman, Penny. 1994. Killing legally with toxic waste: Women and the environment in the United States. In V. Shiva (ed.), *Close to home: Women reconnect ecology, health and development worldwide,* 43–59. Philadelphia: New Society Publishers.

Perrow, Charles, and Mauro Guillen. 1990. *The AIDS disaster: The failure of organizations in New York and the nation.* New Haven, Conn.: Yale University Press.

Pettus, Katherine. 1997. Ecofeminist citizenship. *Hypatia* 12:132–156.

Pike, Kenneth L. 1962. *With heart and mind: A personal synthesis of scholarship and devotion.* Grand Rapids, Mich.: William B. Eerdmans.

Price, Laurie J. 2001. How good is graduate training in anthropology? *Anthropology News* 42(5):5–6.

Reko, H. Karl. 1984. *Not an act of God: The story of Times Beach.* St. Louis: Lutheran Family and Children's Services.

Rose, Fred. 2000. *Coalitions across the class divide: Lessons from the labor, peace, and environmental movements.* Ithaca, N.Y.: Cornell University Press.

Singer, Merrill. 2000. Why I am not a public anthropologist. *Anthropology News* 41(6):6–7.

Szasz, Andrew. 1994. *Ecopopulism: Toxic waste and the movement for environmental justice.* Minneapolis: University of Minnesota Press.

Townsend, Patricia K. 2001. The Involvement of inter-faith councils and religious groups at Superfund sites. Draft report of an environmental project of the Society for Applied Anthropology.

Young, John A. 2001. Assessing cooperation and change: The SfAA and the EPA. *Practicing Anthropology* 23(3):47–49.

38

Does Language of Instruction Matter in Education?

Stephen L. Walter

Introduction

Efforts to penetrate the relationship between language, thought, and knowledge (or learning) are among the oldest of man's intellectual endeavors. In the Western tradition, the Greeks—Socrates, Plato, and Aristotle—are commonly cited as seminal investigators who articulated the fundamental questions and guided early inquiries.

That more contemporary scholars and intellectuals continue to wrestle with such questions is testament both to the intractability of the questions and to the persistence of scholars devoted to discovering and refining our knowledge of ourselves and our universe. Such investigations comprise not a single perspective but rather, a rich variety of intellectual traditions—behaviorism, rationalism, theism, modernism, postmodernism, naturalism—and numerous academic disciplines—linguistics, philosophy, theology, biology, anthropology, psychology, logic, mathematics, and physics.

As a linguist with an intense interest in the *use* of language as well as its structure, Ken Pike took an interest in the question of the relationship between language and thought. His perspective was clearly influenced by his personal philosophy (theism), the intellectual climate of his early training (behaviorism and structuralism), and his lifelong commitment to the pragmatic applications of linguistic theory (linguistic description, language development, literacy, translation). In his "blue book," for example, Pike states:

> It is concluded...that language is behavior, i.e., a phase of human activity which must not be treated in essence as structurally divorced from the structure of nonverbal human activity. The activity of man constitutes a structural whole, in such a way that it cannot be subdivided into neat 'parts' or 'levels' or 'compartments' with language in a behavioral compartment insulated in character, content, and organization from other behavior. Verbal and nonverbal activity is a unified whole, and theory and methodology should be organized or created to treat it as such. (Pike 1967:26)

While asserting a tight integration between the overt manifestation of language (as a behavior) and its covert essence ("nonverbal activity"), Pike sidestepped the thorny question of the causative relationship between language and this nonverbal activity. As a theist and a realist (cf. Cunningham and Fitzgerald 1997), Pike assumed language to be an "innate feature" of human beings. Of greater interest to Pike was the structure and use of language in the human experience. The actual ontology of language was a given and therefore not readily amenable to investigation.

Theorists from structuralist and poststructuralist perspectives have been more aggressive in their speculations about language, knowledge, and cognition. Whorf, for example, based on his analysis of Hopi verbal inflections, came to the conclusion that "language produces an organization of experience" (Whorf 1956:55). The implication is that language is a lens or filter on the external world which defines what we know or can know of that world. Whorf broadens this assertion when he states:

> Thus, the Hopi language and culture conceals a *metaphysics* [emphasis in the original], such as our so-called naïve view of space and time does, or as the relativity theory does; yet it is a different metaphysics from either. In order to describe the structure of the universe according to the Hopi, it is necessary to attempt—insofar as it is possible—to make explicit this metaphysics, properly describable only in the Hopi language. (1956:58)

In his discussion of Hopi, Whorf appeared to give primacy to Hopi metaphysics in explaining or justifying his analysis of the verbal morphology of Hopi. That is, he assumed or asserted that the Hopi language first reflects and encodes the Hopi metaphysical world and then serves as a vehicle for passing this metaphysical view on to the next generation of Hopi speakers. Maybe Whorf was a realist after all!

A more overtly structuralist perspective was developed by Piaget (1952; 1954) in his well-known work on the cognitive development of children. As a result of his research, Piaget came to the conclusion that the cognitive development of children is tied to a developmental sequence determined by age and physical maturity. Specific cognitive abilities or skills "become available" as the child reaches the appropriate developmental levels.

Lakoff and Johnson (1999) have taken a somewhat Piagetian stance in suggesting that the structure of language reflects fixed cognitive structures which are a part of the genetic makeup of the human being. This accounts, they suggest, for the restricted range of structures to be found in language (relative to what is randomly possible) and the very consistent relationship between sign and signifier found in human language.

Radical poststructuralists such as Foucault (1972) and Derrida (1976) insist that the structuralist notion of "sign" (a word) and "signifier" (meaning, mental representation) implies the existence of a "knowing self" which they prefer to deny. To them, speech events are transitory responses to social circumstances and influences lacking objective content or meaning. (Neither, however, appreciated having their own linguistic expressions characterized as lacking objective content or meaning.)

Cognitive scientists taking a careful empirical look at the process of language development in young children have tended to move away from structuralist and poststructuralist views back towards an innatist position. Gopnik and Meltzoff (1997), for example, marshal substantial evidence in favor of what they term "theory theory." By "theory theory" they propose that language, from the very earliest, is an expression of the child's theorizing about his/her environment. Maturation—linguistically, cognitively, and educationally—reflects growing sophistication in the nature and content of one's theorizing. In this view, children are "mini-scientists" and scientists are merely sophisticated and systematic theorizers. The ability to theorize is inherent or innate. It does not develop in physically wired stages as suggested by Piaget. The ability to theorize grows and develops in degree and sophistication as it is exercised and trained whether in response to environmental influence or the intentional guidance of education and personal focus.

While it may be intellectually interesting to speculate about the ontological relationship between language, cognition, and knowledge, such speculation amounts to little more than word games without the discipline of empirical evidence to sort out the wheat from the chaff. The enduring influence of Piaget's theory depends, in large part, on his extensive empirical research. Similarly, cognitive scientists find support for their theories, as well, in early language development.

Language and Education: How Interdependent?

In this essay, I investigate another line of evidence—that stemming from recent research on the relationship between language of instruction and educational outcomes in the context of bilingual education programs in the U.S. Specifically, the question to be investigated is this: "Can we find, in the education of children, any evidence that language has a determinative role in shaping long-term educational outcomes?" Positive evidence would consist of data showing that language of instruction makes a substantial difference in long-term educational outcomes for those participating in educational programs in which the language of instruction is or is not their first or "best" language. Conversely, negative evidence would consist in demonstrating that long-term educational outcomes are unaffected by language of instruction. The fact that there is a large population of language minority children in the U.S., as well as a wide range of practices in the use of first and second languages in educating this population, provides us with an opportunity to examine the potential dependency between language and educational outcomes in children.

While there is substantial intuitive appeal to the assertion that effective educational outcomes are dependent on the language of instruction, the overwhelming weight of policy and practice both nationally and internationally belies this common intuition. The literature and research on mother tongue (L1) education, while quite substantial, have been uneven and confusing (Crawford 1999; Krashen 1999; Ovando and McLaren 1999; Baker and de Kanter 1983; Rossell and Baker 1996; Porter 1990; Cummins 1998). The majority of published studies (1) examine small samples of data (e.g., comparing the performance of two classrooms when one is the subject of an experimental intervention), (2) look at the results of interventions lasting one to two years (e.g., selective use of the mother tongue for supplemental purposes over a two-year period of time), or (3) examine unusual sociolinguistic situations (e.g., the French immersion programs in Canada).

Much of the experimentation and research done in the U.S. has been based on the assumption that the language minority child can learn the language of education in one to two years and will, from that point on, be on an equal footing with language majority children with respect to potential for succeeding educationally. Few educators have bothered to challenge this assumption.

The research question

One driving force in educational research in the U.S. is the articulation and application of educational policy at state and national levels. Crawford (1999) traces the evolution of federal policy on the education of language minorities.

> The Equal Educational Opportunities Act (EEOA) of 1974 [Section 1703(f)], as interpreted by the Fifth Circuit Court of Appeals in Castañeda v. Pickard...requires school districts to take "appropriate action to overcome language barriers that impede equal participation by its students in its instructional programs."...The court outlined three criteria for a program serving LEP [Limited English Proficient] students:
> - It must be based on "sound educational theory."
> - It must be "implemented effectively," with adequate resources and personnel.
> - After a trial period, it must be evaluated as effective in overcoming language handicaps. (1999:58–59)

Thomas and Collier (1997:7) have interpreted the intent of these statements to mean "English learners reaching eventual *full educational parity* [emphasis added] with native-English speakers in all school subjects (not just in English Proficiency) after a period of at least 5–6 years." Thus, "parity" means not merely equivalence of access and equivalence of educational inputs, but also equivalence of educational outcomes.

How can such parity be achieved? In the U.S., educators have tried numerous approaches. Each has adherents with claims of adequacy. Most of these approaches have been based on the conventional wisdom that 1–2 years of exposure to and instruction in English are sufficient to mainstream language minority children with no educational penalty.

In the 1980s and 1990s, researchers Cummins (1981a, 1981b, 1991) and Collier (1987, 1995) began warning that it appears to take longer than 1–2 years for a child to learn a second language well enough to depend upon that language for educational development. Immediately, two questions arose. First, how long does it take to learn a second language well enough to be effectively educated in that language? Second, which of the various available approaches for educating language-minority children will be most effective in developing the necessary proficiency in English to function effectively in an English-speaking classroom? Obviously, to answer these questions, short-term (1–3 years) research efforts would not serve. Longitudinal research was needed to track students over the course of their primary and secondary school careers.

One of the first major longitudinal studies to appear was that of Wayne Thomas and Virginia Collier of George Mason University (1997). They launched their research to answer the "How long?" question. In the process, they have also made significant and surprising discoveries about the "How effective?" question.

The research question which guided the Thomas and Collier study was the following: *"What approach to education produces educational parity for the language minority student at the end of 12 years of education?"* The resultant research design included the following components:

1.   Only well-implemented programs (six models) were studied. (The purpose of this constraint was to eliminate the confounding effect of poorly implemented instructional programs.)

2.   All studies were longitudinal (tracking children all the way through school).

3.   Sample sizes were very large (700,000 records, 42,000 students, 6 school districts).

4.   No experimental interventions were used. (All assessments are based on standardized tests taken in English. These standardized tests allow objective comparisons between the educational achievement of the native English-speaking population and that of language minority children.)

5.   Detailed information was obtained on each student to test and control for other confounding variables.

Six instructional strategies for language minority students

The Thomas and Collier study compares the differential consequences of six different approaches to providing educational support for language minority children. These are described below.

Program 6 – Language-based (traditional) ESL (approx. 22,000 students). Language minority children receive basic or traditional ESL (English as a Second Language) instruction usually in pullout classes. The objective is sufficient mastery of English to function in the English mainstream. In ESL programs, language minority students receive little or no instruction in or support for their first language.

Program 5 – Content-based ESL (approx. 5,400 students). Language minority children receive ESL training in the context of academic instruction, typically for 2–3 years. Teachers must have special training to deliver ESL via content instruction. The objective is sufficient mastery of English to function in the English mainstream without having gotten too far behind in the content areas.

Program 4 – Transitional bilingual education with language-based ESL (approx. 7,100 students). Language minority children receive 2–3 years of education in their first language from teachers who speak their language and who use their language as a medium of instruction. Initial literacy is provided in L1. In some versions of this program type, English (the L2) is first introduced orally with subsequent instruction in basic English literacy. In other versions, instructional time is split in some structured manner (morning/afternoon, alternating days, different teachers) between L1 and L2. ESL instruction is provided via traditional language-based instruction. The objectives are basic literacy in both languages and sufficient proficiency in English to enter the mainstream by the end of the third grade.

Program 3 – Transitional bilingual education with content-based ESL (approx. 3,700 students). Language minority children receive 2–3 years of education in their first language from teachers who speak their language and who use their language as a medium of instruction. Initial literacy is provided in L1. In some versions, English (the L2) is first introduced orally with subsequent instruction in basic English literacy. In other versions, instructional time is split in some structured manner (morning/afternoon, alternating days, different teachers) between L1 and L2. ESL instruction is provided via academic content. ESL teachers receive special training to teach in this way. The objectives are basic literacy in both languages, sufficient proficiency in English to enter the mainstream by the end of the third grade, and enough academic content to avoid being behind native English students at the time of mainstreaming.

Program 2 – One-way developmental bilingual education (approx. 2,900 students). Language minority children receive 5 or 6 years of education in their first language from teachers who speak their language and who use their language as a medium of instruction. Initial literacy is provided in L1. In some versions, English (the L2) is introduced first orally with subsequent instruction in basic English literacy. In other versions, instructional time is split in some structured manner (morning/afternoon, alternating days, different teachers) between L1 and L2. The objective is full academic proficiency in both languages by the end of the sixth grade. Beyond sixth grade, all students are mainstreamed into regular English-based classes.

Program 1 – Two-way developmental bilingual education (approx. 1,250 students). Language minority children and native English-speaking children are put together in mixed classrooms from the beginning of their education. Both English and Spanish (or other non-English language) are used as languages of instruction for the entire classroom in some structured way (e.g., different teachers, alternating days, by subject, etc.). Language instruction and literacy are provided and supported in both languages. The objective is full academic proficiency in both languages by the end of the sixth grade for both language minority and native English-speaking children. Beyond sixth grade, all students are mainstreamed into regular English-based classes with some effort being made to include the minority language as a subject through secondary school.

Because the sample size for Program 1 is relatively small, the researchers caution that the results reported for this group must be interpreted carefully. Since the original research was published, Thomas and Collier have broadened their database substantially with their findings being only minimally changed as a result (Thomas, personal communicaton).

Interpreting the research findings

Each of the six curves in figure 1 traces the average educational development of children for the indicated program type from first through eleventh grade with respect to national norms (indicated by the dotted line at NCE 50).[1] The numbers on the right-hand side of the figure under the label "Final NCE" represent the average or mean final level of educational development for all of those who participated in a given program type.

---

[1]For the reader unfamiliar (or rusty) with the characteristics of the normal curve, the relationship between an NCE (National Curve Equivalent) and a percentile requires some explanation. The normal curve (more informally referred to as a bell curve) is a statistical construct which has proven to be very useful for understanding and characterizing a broad range of phenomena including performance on standardized tests. In brief, the normal curve reflects the fact that on such a test, we can predict with a high level of confidence that lots of people will achieve scores close to average, but only small numbers of people will score extremely well or extremely poorly with varying percentages of people scoring in between.

Conceptually and mathematically, the area under the normal curve represents the entire population. Fifty percent of the area is below the mean (the peak of the curve) and fifty percent is above the mean. Visually (and mathematically) it is obvious that a fixed unit of movement to the left or the right close to the center of the curve encompasses a larger amount of area than a unit of movement left or right close to the ends of the curve.

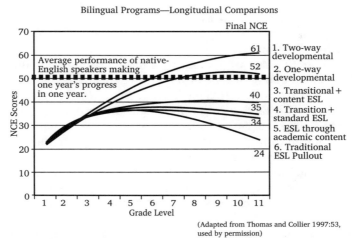

Figure 1. Graph of findings from the Thomas and Collier study.

So, for example, the average final standing of all language minority students who began with traditional ESL pullout programs (Program 6) was NCE 24 (11th percentile), far below national norms. At the other extreme, those in the two-way developmental programs finished 11th grade performing, on average, at NCE 61 (70th percentile) which is well above the

Standardized tests are set up in such a way that performance is measured in equal units whether one performs well, poorly, or about average. The only yardstick of measurement is the test. If one retakes the test and scores ten points better the second time, that person is ten points further towards mastering the content of the test than s/he was the previous time. That person has made ten points of progress regardless of what anyone else did on the test.

Because a normal curve is a mathematical model of the performance of a large population, and a percentile is, by definition, a mathematically defined area under the curve mimicking the performance of a large population, a percentile is a relative measure stating one's position or performance relative to the total population (for the test) rather than one's 'absolute' level of mastery of a defined body of material or knowledge. The NCE construct was developed as a way of capturing fixed progress towards mastering a defined body of knowledge. So, for example, if one scores at an NCE level of 46 on a national standardized test (which is scaled from 0 to 100), then that person has mastered 46 percent of the knowledge the test is designed to measure. If the same person takes the same test the following year and scores an NCE of 55, that person has mastered another 9 percent of the material and is moving in the direction of full mastery. These levels of performance relative to the entire test-taking population are another matter. In terms of percentiles, the test taker may have made no progress, a little progress, or lots of progress depending on how everyone else did who took the test.

For highly reliable national standardized tests, the relationship between NCEs and percentiles is well-defined though the relationship is not linear. In this paper, NCE scores or levels will usually be accompanied by a percentile indicating position or performance relative to the national test-taking population.

national average *for native English-speaking children*. Having looked at the basic facts of the graph in figure 1, we turn now to interpreting and explaining what the graph demonstrates.

First, we note that language minority children begin their education in grade 1 ranked at about NCE 22 or 23 relative to native English-speaking children. This is equivalent to a national percentile of 9. To achieve educational parity with English-speaking children, these language minority children must close the gap by learning more every year than the English-speaking children. The graph shows this happening for the first 3 to 4 years as the gap between the two groups narrows.

Second, we note that there is little difference among the program types during the first four years of school. All show progress in closing the gap with language majority children. Several factors contribute to this finding. (1) The early years of school are not cognitively difficult. (2) Less standardized testing is done at this level so that differences in performance fail to show up. (3) Language minority children are somewhat less likely to be tested with English-based instruments again blurring differences in educational performance. (4) These children do, in fact, learn a significant amount of English and some of the academic content taught in these lower grades. It is this kind of apparent progress which frequently persuades educators and policy makers that the language minority children are "making it" in their first years of school.

Third, by about the fifth or sixth grade when the cognitive content of the curriculum becomes more demanding, a different pattern begins to emerge. Participants in Programs 3, 4, 5, and 6 stop making progress in closing the gap with the language majority children. This does not mean that they are learning nothing, or that they are regressing academically. It simply means that they are no longer closing the gap between themselves and language majority children.

Fourth, students in Programs 1 and 2—one-way and two-way developmental bilingual education—make continuous progress in closing the gap with language majority children which they accomplish around grade 7 or 8. Most significantly, and surprisingly, participants in Program 1—two-way developmental education—actually surpass national norms ending up, on average, at NCE 61, which is equivalent to a national percentile of 70.

The researchers' conclusions

Thomas and Collier identify the following as key factors or predictors of success (defined as "educational parity") for language minority children.

1.   The first predictor of long-term school success is the *inclusion of cognitively complex on-grade-level academic instruction through the student's first language for as long as possible* (at least through grade 5 or 6) and cognitively complex on-grade-level academic instruction through the second language (English) for part of the school day. (p.15)

2.   The second predictor of long-term school success is *the use of current approaches to teaching the academic curriculum* through two languages. (p.16)

3.   The third predictor is *a transformed sociocultural context for language minority students' schooling.* (p.16)

The Prism Model

How does one explain the findings of Thomas and Collier since their findings clearly run counter to much previous thinking about the relationship between language and education? Thomas and Collier propose what they term "the Prism Model" (1997:42–47) to explain their findings. In this model, they propose that desirable educational outcomes depend upon the correlative development of three intellectual dimensions—language, cognition, and academic skill—all in the context of one mediating environmental support system—a nurturing and supportive sociocultural context. The Prism Model suggests that language, cognition, and academic skill are mutually dependent and must develop together and in parallel. When an effort is made to develop one (or two) while ignoring the development of the other(s), there is a net reduction in the overall potential for educational development. When one developmental dimension is stunted, system potential is reduced.

On the basis of this model and their extensive research data, Thomas and Collier suggest that language and education are highly interdependent to a degree not previously suspected in the mainstream educational world. In practical terms, they suggest that primary education will only be successful for language minority children *if* that primary education makes heavy use of the first language of these children for at least 5–6 years. Conversely, the model predicts that educational systems which seek to educate children in a second language only (or primarily) will be characterized by reduced educational outcomes. Not only does submersion not work, it appears to guarantee low levels of educational achievement for 80–90 percent of participants.[2]

Other findings of the Thomas and Collier study

Transitional models

One of the surprising findings of Thomas and Collier was the relatively low performance of transitional programs in which children do, in fact, receive 2–3 years of instruction via their first language. From figure 1 we observe that these program types—Programs 4 and 3—led to average final levels of attainment at NCE 35 and 40 respectively (percentiles 24 and 32). Many have promoted such programs on the assumption that two to three years of instruction in the first language would make a big difference in preparing language minority children to make the transition to language majority classrooms. The counter-intuitive findings of the research data clearly call this assumption into question.

The interactive classroom

Many critics of education decry the so-called "banking models" in which teachers are portrayed as pouring knowledge into students' heads with these (the students) having the responsibility to store and safeguard this knowledge for future reference or recall. A commonly reported (and criticized) variant of the banking model is that of rote learning or rote memorization.

Only slightly evident in figure 1 is the fact that the six program types can be viewed as paired variants—1 and 2, 3 and 4, 5 and 6—in which variants 5, 3, and 1 reflect a stronger emphasis (among other things) on classroom interactivity both vertically between teachers and students and horizontally between students and fellow students. This interactivity includes such classroom phenomena as free use of discussion, the use of group work, peer-to-peer tutoring, a greater emphasis on problem solving, etc.

---

[2]Lockwood and Secada (1999) cite NCES data (1998) indicating that 43 percent of foreign-born hispanic immigrants to the U.S. between the ages of 16-24 failed to finish high school (dropped out). Thomas and Collier report (personal communication) generally comparable levels of attrition among the research populations of Programs 5 and 6, which means they are not included in the final group achieving at the 11th percentile. Since it seems fairly likely that those who drop out are doing more poorly educationally than those who remain in school, the reality is that the population which remains and which finishes, on average, at the 11th percentile represents the cream of the total cohort.

The role of interactivity in the classroom is one of the explanations for the marked difference between the outcomes of Programs 1 and 2. In both programs, learners get 5 or 6 years of first language educational support. In fact, educational support in the first language is probably stronger in Program 2 than in Program 1. Nonetheless, the average outcome for participants in Program 1 is 9 NCEs higher (a 16 percentile difference) than in Program 2. Because two-way developmental programs (Program 1) are based on an approximately equal mix of language minority and language majority students, the high level of interactivity promoted by this linguistic mixture seems to result in a significant educational advantage for the language minority children who finish their secondary educational careers at NCE 61 (70th percentile).

The cognitive advantages of bilingualism

Baker (1996) reviews a number of studies which suggest that bilingualism and bilingual behavior may actually bring subtle but significant cognitive benefits to the bilingual individual whether child or adult. Programs 1 and 2 are the only two of the six program types investigated by Thomas and Collier which sought to promote full and balanced bilingualism for language minority children. Participants in both programs finish their secondary education at levels above national norms (though only minimally so in the case of Program 2).

Not included in figure 1 is an indication of the impact of Program 1 on language majority children (native speakers of English) who participated in two-way developmental programs. According to Thomas (personal communication), language majority children from Program 1 appear to achieve at levels even higher than those reported in the graph (NCE 61). However, the data sample is small and the analysis incomplete. Even if the average scores for language majority children participating in such programs are no higher than that of the language minority children (the 70th Percentile), the educational advantages of this approach are striking.

The Thomas and Collier data clearly reflect marked differences in educational outcomes according to the strategy by which language minority children are educated. At the one extreme—Program 6—where children are educated entirely in a second language (English), the result is a mean group performance at a national percentile of 11. With almost fifty percent of this population finishing in the bottom ten (10) percent nationally, we can hardly characterize this result as "educational parity."

At the other extreme—Program 1 and 2—in which children receive a strong educational foundation in their first language, we find that these two groups score, on average, at or even above national norms. This result looks much more like "educational parity."

Is language of instruction the only variable accounting for this difference? Thomas and Collier carefully explored other potential confounding variables such as socioeconomic status, family support, first language, previous education, length of time in the U.S., etc. In the programs they studied, they conclude that these variables are secondary with respect to explaining the observed differences in program outcomes.

Implications for the Education of Language Minorities in Other Countries

The research reported by Thomas and Collier reflects only data gathered in the U.S. The ethnolinguistic situation of the U.S. is relatively simple compared to that of many developing nations. If language can be demonstrated to play a major role in achieving desirable educational outcomes in the U.S., we would surely expect to find some evidence of the same effect in more linguistically diverse countries. In the sections which follow, I propose to look for evidence of this putative effect from two perspectives. First, do the predictions of the Prism Model accord, in any way, with the conditions of underdevelopment as measured by the generation (or not) of Human Capital (in the form of an educated citizenry).[3] Second, does the existing state of education in linguistically complex developing countries coincide, in any way, with the predictions of the Thomas and Collier model?

Ninety-one (91) countries have populations in which 40 percent or more of the national population consists of ethnic and linguistic minorities most of whom receive their schooling (if any) in a language other than their first language. The total population of these countries is 1.69 billion people. The population of the linguistic or ethnic minorities in these countries is 998.4 million people or 59 percent of the total. The

---

[3]Writers and researchers who investigate issues of education and development in emerging nations often use the terms "human capital" or "social capital" to embrace a cluster of phenomena and behaviors related to the distribution and effects of education, training, and skill development. The intent of these constructs is twofold. First, to portray education as not merely "knowledge and skills" in the cognitive sense, but also as "assets" or "commodities" which individuals and communities of people use or apply to make productive, constructive, and desirable improvements in their lives and the lives of families and communities. Secondly, to provide economists with a construct which they can use to "measure" the relative value and contribution of education to national development.

average literacy rate in these ninety-one countries is approximately 55 percent.

According to SIL research, the average literacy rate among ethnic minorities worldwide is between 20 and 30 percent. Clearly, then, a high proportion of language minority children are not benefiting from the time spent in school using current educational strategies. While these findings are not based on test scores, we can safely note that they do not contradict the Thomas and Collier model. The next step is to hypothesize that the Thomas and Collier model may, in part, explain some of the failings evident in developing countries.

Developing Human Capital (an appropriately educated workforce) in developing countries

By far, the most common approach to educating language minorities remains that of submersion—immediately and completely immersing language minority children in language majority[4] classrooms with no support for or instruction in L1. In the Thomas and Collier research, this is most akin to Program 6 with the difference that such children typically lack even the support of specialized instruction in the majority language in their early years of school.

There is no pragmatic or theoretical reason to assume that language minority children in other countries will perform at a higher level relative to national averages than do language minority children in the U.S. If submersion strategies result in average performance at the 11th percentile in the U.S., we can reasonably expect similar performance under similar educational conditions in other countries. However, we must keep in mind that in countries where language minorities make up most of a country's population, the 11th percentile becomes, in effect, the national norm meaning the consequences may be less obvious (in terms of national standards) than those we see in the Thomas and Collier study.

The graph in figure 2 is a generalization of educational outcomes taken directly from the Thomas and Collier data. The curves in the graph are based on the measured performance of all students coming from three programs in the Thomas and Collier data based on mean performance and the standard deviation (approximately 21 NCEs) incorporated in the standardized test used as a final proxy of educational outcomes for all

---

[4]The term, "language majority" implies the existence of a dominant or majority population which has succeeded in specifying the use of its language as the official language of instruction in formal education. In numerous developing countries, however, no such dominant group exists. Rather, the language of instruction in schools is often a colonial language which is not the first language of any significant population group in the country.

students.[5] The three Program types are (1) ESL pullout (a proxy for sub-mersion education), (2) the English-speaking population (a proxy for nor-mality), and (3) two-way developmentals (a proxy for the optimal use of language for educating language minorities). From this graph, we can make some "projections" of probable educational outcomes (in terms of the development of Human Capital) for a given country (or other sociolinguistic unit).

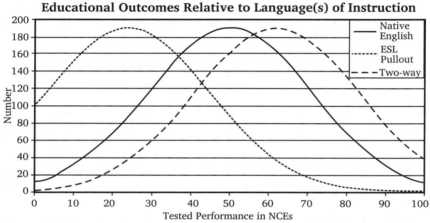

Figure 2. Educational outcomes relative to language(s) of instruction.

The middle curve—indicated by the heavy black line—represents the educational outcome of a majority language population which is edu-cated in the language of that population—English in this case. As in any normal population, a large number will turn out to be "average," able to perform at a level a bit above and below the mean of 50 percent. As we move toward the extremes, we encounter those who do extremely well and those who do very poorly.

The curve to the left of the black line shows the measured performance of those educated entirely in a language other than their first language (the submersion model). We note that the curve for this sub-population does not approach the zero level on the vertical axis until about NCE 90. This means that there will be a few of those educated in this mode who do very well even when their education is entirely in a language other than

---

[5]All three curves assume a normal distribution of the respective populations. The one case where this assumption may need to be taken cautiously is that of the dotted line representing the Two-Way Developmental programs. This is because (a) this sample population is rather small (1,250 students) and (b) in some cases, participation in the program is a matter of choice on the part of students or parents.

their own. Not surprisingly, policy makers in most countries come from this exceptional population. Because they succeeded, despite the limitations of the system, they are prone to assert that everyone else can as well. Similar statements are made by exceptional language minority students who do well in U.S. schools despite an English-only education.

Looking to the far left of the graph, we note that the dotted curve intersects zero on the X-axis—indicative of total educational failure—at a point which corresponds to about 30 percent of the total population educated in this mode (entirely in a second language). This thirty (30) percent is, by any measure, not being educated at all.

The right-most curve—indicated by a broken line—depicts the performance of those educated in two languages with a heavy initial concentration in their first language (actually, a balanced use of L1 and L2 as languages of instruction) and a transition to the language of wider communication after 5 or 6 years of education. At this point, we will note only that the educational outcome of such students is significantly higher than the national average—in this case, native speakers of English in the U.S.

The following table translates the consequences of two of the above curves—Program 6 (ESL by traditional instruction) and the normal English-speaking population—into "real numbers" thus demonstrating the practical educational consequences of the above graph in the development of Human Capital. The table is created by identifying six zones (standard deviations) of achievement which correspond roughly with workforce potential. The numbers in table 1 are based on a block of 10,000 students graduating from secondary in a given year. If a country were graduating 100,000 students from secondary in a given year, the number of students in each category would be increased by a factor of ten.

Table 1. Educational implications of the Thomas and Collier model
in terms of differential outcomes

Standard deviation	NCE equiv.	When educated in a second language only		When educated in one's own language		Differen-tial factor	Social/Professional/ economic potential
		Percent of pop.	No. out of 10,000	Percent of pop.	No. out of 10,000		
Above 2nd	>92	.055	5.5	2.28	228	41.5	Researchers, scientists, top writers, top intellectuals, medical doctors
1st to 2nd	71-92	1.2	120	13.59	1,359	11.3	Professors, business leaders, professionals, journalists
Mean to 1st	50-71	9.5	950	34.13	3,413	3.6	Teachers, mid-level managers, engineers, programmers, bureaucrats
-1st to mean	29-50	29.77	2,977	34.13	3.413	1.1	Skilled factory workers, equipment operators, clerical, service workers
-2nd to -1st	8-29	37.12	3,712	13.59	1,359	-2.8	Blue-collar workers, manual laborers
Below -2nd	<8	22.36	2,236	2.28	228	-9.8	Hard to employ, domestics, menial labor

The data in table 1 is based on the following general assumptions:

1.   The distribution of intellectual ability is essentially the same in all population units (nations, in this case).

2.   The model of educational outcomes with respect to the interdependency of language and long-term educational effectiveness proposed by Thomas and Collier has cross-linguistic and cross-cultural generalizability.

3.   The Thomas and Collier model is highly replicable and will be supported by further research in the U.S.

4.   The proposed "correlation" between professional potential and zones of performance (defined in terms of standard deviation) is

suggestive only, not being based on a formal analysis of longitudinal data tracing this relationship.

5.   Use of the table to make generalizations about educational outcomes in developing countries assumes equivalence in terms of systemic performance, i.e., comparable rates of enrollment, attrition, repetition, and comparable quality in terms of overall educational inputs (instruction, materials, facilities, resources, etc.). Since it is overwhelmingly clear that this assumption is not true, the comparisons set forth in table 1 are optimistic in approximate proportion to qualitative differences in the respective education systems. Simply put, one can expect that "real" educational outcomes in a given, linguistically diverse, developing country will be significantly worse than projected in table 1.

The model developed by Thomas and Collier as rendered in table 1 allows us to make inferences such as the following. When educated in English (or some other majority language in other countries), 228 of 10,000 secondary school graduates who are native English speakers (or speakers of the majority language in some other country) will demonstrate the potential to become top-flight scientists and intellectuals. In contrast, the same population educated in a second language only will produce, at best, 5.5 potential scientists and intellectuals—a differential of 4,150 percent. At the opposite end of the educational spectrum, when majority language speakers are educated in their own language, the model predicts that 228 of 10,000 will be hard to employ or only capable of menial labor. When educated in a second language only, however, this number jumps to 2,236 of 10,000, a difference of 980 percent.

Another way to highlight the "drag" imposed by the language barrier is to compare the two groups with respect to "average" performance. By definition, when educated in the majority language, 50 percent of 10,000 secondary school students (who speak the majority language) will score above average on a standardized national test with an equal percentage scoring below average. However, when educated in a second language, 89.25 percent will score below "average" with only 10.75 percent scoring above average.

The mean performance of English-speakers educated in English is 50 while the mean performance of non-English speakers educated in English only is 23 (with a standard deviation of 21). The obvious implication is that education in a language other than one's own imposes a penalty of 1.29 standard deviations—a massive, massive differential in terms of outcomes for a standardized test administered to a large population (over 22,000 students in the case of Thomas and Collier).

In terms of developing human capital, the Thomas and Collier data suggest a huge advantage for countries providing education in the language of the child. If, for every 10,000 students graduated, Country A can expect to get 1,587 (all those above the first standard deviation) highly capable intellectuals, business leaders, and professionals while Country B gets only 126 such people from a comparably sized pool, Country A is going to have a massive potential (or real) advantage in science, business, industry, and education.

Education in developing countries: do the data support the model?

Based on the data and arguments presented so far, one might conclude from table 1 that language of instruction alone is responsible for large differentials in educational outcomes leading directly to the formation (or nonformation) of Human Capital. Cummins (1999), as well as Thomas and Collier, caution that language of instruction is not a magic bullet that will, by itself, revolutionize the education of language minority children. Such education must take place in a positive environment with strong support from parents, communities, and educational systems.

That said, let us now examine reports from a range of countries looking for support (or counter evidence) for the suggested relationship between language and education.

Table 2. Representative and aggregated data on enrollment and persistence in primary school

Category	N	Mean net enrollment	Mean to 5th grade	Mean cohort to 5th grade	Percent minority population	Mean GNP
Least developed	42	47.04	59.97	26.56	77.62	430
Less developed	68	86.04	80.71	72.14	35.85	3,145
In transition	29	86.81	96.58	85.20	5.93	3,487
More developed	22	95.89	98.55	96.56	.99	20,518

Table 2 is a summary of data from various UNESCO publications on education (1995, 1997, 1998). The only criterion for inclusion in the respective category was the simple fact that complete data for each was available for all relevant variables. In the table, countries are grouped according to their level of development (UNESCO's categorization), and then group means are computed for the following variables: (1) net enrollment in first grade, (2) percent of children enrolling in first grade who reach grade 5, (3) percent of children in fifth grade of those of fifth-grade age, (4) percent of the national population speaking a lesser-known or minority language, and (5) mean GNP.

Looking at the column "Mean net enrollment," we note that the least developed countries show an average enrollment ratio of less than 50 percent. Further, the effect of attrition means that by 5th grade, only 27 percent of chronological 5th graders are actually still in school. In the case of less developed countries, an average of 86 percent of eligible children enroll in first grade with 81 percent of these reaching Level 5. This means that the percent of the total age cohort reaching Level 5 is 72 percent for these countries.

Columns 5 and 6 in table 2 compare (or contrast) the mean cohort to 5th Grade and the size of the language minority population in each group of countries. Curiously, and I believe significantly, the sum of these two columns for each group of countries comes close to being 100 percent.

Statistically, the correlation between "Mean cohort to 5th grade" and "Percent minority population" is $r = -.984$. (The high r is partially due to the fact that there are only four data points). This correlation is extremely high indicating a nearly perfect inverse relationship between the size of a country's language minority population and the percentage of the school-aged population reaching Level 5 in primary. The regression equation of the relationship is percent cohort to 5th grade = -.86 (percent minority) + 95.9. In this equation, the constant—95.9 (percent)—is the predicted percentage of age-level children who will reach level 5 of school when the total population has 0 percent language minority children. The coefficient of -.86 indicates a strong inverse relationship between the two variables.

It is important to note that the data in table 2 are not based on test scores or any other indicator of educational outcome (in the sense of cognitive achievement). Therefore, we cannot demonstrate that the same educational drag or penalty evident in the Thomas and Collier study (resulting from instruction delivered via a second language only) is present in educational outcomes in developing countries. On the other hand, the data in table 2 clearly reflect an association—actually, a tight statistical association—between language and education. While one cannot claim causality on the basis of a statistical correlation, the data in table 2 accord very well—almost too well, in fact—with the predictions of the Thomas and Collier model.

It is also appropriate to note that major differences exist in the GNP of each grouping of countries. This variable is surely salient but is not in focus in this particular analysis.

Discussion and Conclusions

In the development literature of the last twenty years, explanations for the poor performance of education systems in developing countries have ascribed this poor performance to various "developmental" factors such as limited funding, inadequate facilities and materials, poor teaching, familial need for the labor value of the child, etc. The last column in table 2 showing "Mean GNP" for each category certainly lends support to this interpretation. The relationship between "GNP" and "Persistence to fifth grade," however, is not linear ($r = .69$) but rather logarithmic ($r = .947$). What this might mean is beyond the scope of this paper.

The Thomas and Collier study and data make a strong case for the claim that the use of one's first language as a medium of instruction dramatically increases the effectiveness of that education. The data are clear that education in developing countries has been inadequate. The possibility that language—specifically, language of instruction—is a major contributing variable to reduced effectiveness has been almost entirely ignored. The UNESCO data do not contradict the Thomas and Collier model. Indeed, the UNESCO data accord very well with the Thomas and Collier model. It may well be that research on educational effectiveness in developing countries has overlooked the most critical variable of all—that of language.

The data presented certainly lend prima facie evidence to those who would argue for an integral and mediating relationship between language and knowledge/educational achievement (or whatever it is that achievement tests measure). The Prism Model of Thomas and Collier proposes that educational achievement cannot be separated from that of language development and mastery. Further, as Thomas and Collier state (1997:32–33) and others concur (Cummins 1981a), this recent data makes a strong case for the claim that there is a vast difference between basic social proficiency—what Cummins labels Basic Interactive Communication Skills (BICS)—and a level of language proficiency which permits a high level of academic achievement—what Cummins labels Cognitive Academic Language Proficiency (CALP).

Why has educational policy in linguistically diverse developing countries ignored the language factor so completely? The reasons are numerous, often having little to do with educational effectiveness.

Ideological objections to mother tongue education
- Ethnic competition (making education available in language X will give those people opportunities and advantages that people Y do not have.)
- The nation-building construct (We need to leave all of the ethnic languages behind to build a nation based on a common language.)
- Parental (mis)understanding (Our children already know their own language. What they need to learn is the national or official language(s).)
- Professional and institutional biases (Educational officials and functionaries at all levels have a career based on their mastery of the official language. Anything which threatens this security is likely to be opposed.)

Language development challenges
Before a language can be used as a vehicle of instruction in formal education, a lot of work has to be done in language development. This will take skilled manpower and time and is viewed as a major obstacle to programs using the mother tongue.

Curricular limitations
Same issue as stated above under language development.

Teacher development and professional support systems
Same problem.

Size of target communities
If only 10,000 children speak language X, many will assert it is not worth the effort to develop educational support for such a small community.

Demand—side constraints (no jobs available)
In many countries, parents question the value of any education since there are few jobs available for those who do get an education. There is a "chicken-and-egg" problem here that is not going to be solved by denying that it exists.

Significantly, perhaps, few of these factors reflect a concern for educational outcomes. Policy change will come only to the extent that the policy-making "bottom line" is based on educational outcomes rather than ideology or up-front costs. If and when this happens, it is the argument of this paper that the issue of language of instruction will be central to improving educational outcomes and addressing the problem of national development.

References

Baker, Colin. 1996. *Foundations of bilingual education and bilingualism,* second edition. Philadelphia: Multilingual Matters.

Baker, K. A., and A. A. de Kanter. 1983. *Bilingual education.* Lexington, Mass.: Lexington Books.

Collier, V. P. 1987. Age and rate of acquisition of second language for academic purposes. *TESOL Quarterly* 21:617–641.

Collier, V. P. 1995. *Acquiring a second language for school.* Washington, D.C.: National Clearinghouse for Bilingual Education.

Crawford, James. 1999. *Bilingual education: History, politics, theory, and practice,* fourth edition. Washington, D.C.: Privately published.

Cummins, J. 1981a. The role of primary language development in promoting educational success for language minority students. In California State Department of Education (ed.), *Schooling and language minority students: A theoretical framework,* 3–49. Los Angeles: National Dissemination and Assessment Center.

Cummins, J. 1981b. Age on arrival and immigrant second language learning in Canada: A reassessment. *Applied Linguistics* 2:132–149.

Cummins, J. 1991. Interdependence of first- and second-language proficiency in bilingual children. In E. Bialystok (ed.), *Language processing in bilingual children,* 70–89. Cambridge: Cambridge University Press.

Cummins, J. 1998. Beyond adversarial discourse: Searching for common ground in the education of bilingual students. Presentation to the California State Board of Education, Feb. 9, 1998. Also in Ovando and McLaren (eds.), *The politics of multiculturalism and bilingual education: Students and teachers caught in the crossfire.* New York: McGraw-Hill.

Cunningham, James W., and Jill Fitzgerald. 1996. Epistemology and reading. *Reading Research Quarterly* 31(1):36–61.

Derrida, Jacques. 1976. *Of grammatology.* Trans. Alan Bass. Chicago, Ill.: University of Chicago Press.

Foucault, Michel. 1972. *The archaelogy of knowledge and the discourse on language.* Trans. A. M. Sheridan Smith. New York: Pantheon Books.

Gopnik, Alison, and Andrew N. Meltzoff. 1997. *Words, thoughts, and theories.* Cambridge, Mass.: The MIT Press.

Krashen, Stephen D. 1999. *Condemned without a trial: Bogus arguments against bilingual education.* Portsmouth, N.H.: Heinemann.

Lakoff, George, and Mark Johnson. 1999. *Philosophy in the flesh: The embodied mind and its challenge to western thought.* New York: Basic Books.

Lockwood, Anne Turnbaugh, and Walter G. Secada. 1999. *Transforming education for hispanic youth: Exemplary practices, programs, and schools.* National Clearinghouse for Bilingual Education < www.ncbe.gwu.edu/ncbepubs/resource/hispanicyouth/hdp.htm >.

Ovando, Carlos, and Peter McLaren. 1999. *The politics of multiculturalism and bilingual education: Students and teachers caught in the middle.* New York: McGraw Hill.

Piaget, Jean. 1952. *The origins of intelligence in children.* New York: International Universities Press.

Piaget, Jean. 1954. *The construction of reality in the child.* New York: Basic Books.

Pike, Kenneth L. 1967. *Language in relation to a unified theory of the structure of human behavior.* The Hague: Mouton.

Porter, Rosalie. 1990. *Forked tongue: The politics of bilingual education.* New York: Basic Books.

Rossell, C. H. and K. Baker. 1996. The effectiveness of bilingual education. *Research in the Teaching of English* 30:7–74.

Thomas, Wayne C., and Virginia Collier. 1997. *School effectiveness for language minority students.* National Clearinghouse for Bilingual Education < www.ncbe.gwu.edu/ncbepubs/resource/effectiveness/index.htm >.

UNESCO. 1995. *World education report: 1995.* Oxford: UNESCO Publishing.

UNESCO. 1998. *Wasted opportunities: When schools fail.* Paris: UNESCO.

UNICEF. 1997. *The state of the world's children.* New York: Oxford University Press.

Whorf, Benjamin Lee. 1956. *Language, thought, and reality: Selected writings of Benjamin Lee Whorf.* John B. Carroll (ed.). Boston: Massachusetts Institute of Technology and New York: John Wiley and Sons.

About the Contributors

Edwin Arthur (B.Sc. [Hons], Bath University) spent twelve years as a field linguist among the Kouya of Côte d'Ivoire under the auspices of SIL International. He has published several articles, primarily on the Kouya language and culture. His principal linguistic interest is Adult Second Language Acquisition. He is currently serving as SIL's European Training Director.

A. L. Becker (Ph.D., University of Michigan) is Professor Emeritus of Linguistics and Anthropology at the University of Michigan, where he studied with Kenneth Pike and remained, after completing his doctorate in 1965. He studied and taught Southeast Asian Languages and literatures—Burmese, Old Javanese, Indonesian, and Malay—and spent many years in Southeast Asia, studying theater and music jointly with his wife, Judith. He coauthored *Rhetoric: Discovery and Change* with Kenneth Pike and Richard Young, and more recently his collected essays have been published in *Beyond Translation: Essays toward a Modern Philology*. Since his retirement, he has taught descriptive linguistics and translation theory/practice at the Universiti Kebangsaan Malaysia, Princeton University, and Yale University.

Ruth M. Brend (Ph.D., University of Michigan) was Professor of Linguistics at Michigan State University. She was a charter member and past president of LACUS (Linguistic Association of Canada and the United States), organized several annual conferences for LACUS and ILA (International Linguistics Association), and served as editor of *Word* for several years. She was a member of the Summer Institute of Linguistics for more than twenty years. She served as research associate and administrative assistant to Kenneth L. Pike from 1957 to 1968 and continued to collaborate with him on various projects until 1977. Her publications include *A Tagmemic Analysis of Mexican Spanish Clauses* (1968) and several articles. She edited or coedited eight volumes by Pike or about Tagmemic Theory. She died on January 8, 2002.

Robert L. Canfield (Ph.D., University of Michigan) has been Professor of Anthropology at Washington University since 1969 and served as chair of the Department of Anthropology for seven years. He spent nine and a half years in Afghanistan doing educational work and anthropological research. Since the early 1980s he has worked on how the Islamic idioms, dominant in Central Asia, have enabled people to understand their personal experience and provided the justification for collective action. He is currently working on an analytical proposal for how to understand the way symbols inform social action. His publications include *Faction and Conversion in a Plural Society: Religious Alignments in the Hindu Kush* (1973) and about thirty articles, including "Restructuring in Greater Central Asia: Changing Political Configurations." He was editor or coeditor of three volumes.

Eugene H. Casad (Ph.D., University of California at San Diego) is an International Linguistics Consultant with SIL International and a consultant with SIL Mexico. He has carried out extensive fieldwork on the Cora language of Mexico. His publications include *Dialect Intelligibility Testing, Cognitive Linguistics in the Redwoods* (editor, 1986); *Windows on Bilingualism* (editor, 1991), *Sonora Yaqui Language Structures* (coauthored with John Dedrick, 1999); *Uto-Aztecan: Structural, Temporal, and Geographic Perspectives: Papers in Honor of Wick R. Miller* (coedited with Thomas L. Willett, 2000); and *Cognitive Linguistics and Non-Indo-European Languages* (coedited with Gary R. Palmer, 2003). In addition, he has published a number of linguistic papers and book reviews.

Bernard Comrie (Ph.D., Cambridge University) taught previously at Cambridge and the University of Southern California and is currently Director of the Department of Linguistics at the Max Planck Institute for Evolutionary Anthropology, Leipzig, and Distinguished Professor of Linguistics, University of California, Santa Barbara. His main interests are language universals and typology, historical linguistics, and linguistic fieldwork. His publications include *Aspect* (1976); *Language Universals and Linguistic Typology* (1981, 1989); *The Languages of the Soviet Union* (1981); *Tense* (1985); and *The Russian Language in the Twentieth Century* (with Gerald Stone and Maria Polinsky, 1996). He is also editor of *The World's Major Languages* (1987) and managing editor of the journal *Studies in Language*.

John R. Costello (Ph.D., New York University) is Professor of Linguistics at New York University. He is a past president of the International Linguistic Association and currently editor of *Word*, the journal of the association. He is the author of thirty-five articles and two books, *A Generative Grammar of Old Frisian* and *Syntactic Change and Syntactic Reconstruction: A Tagmemic Approach*. He is interested in computer applications in diachronic linguistics, and in this connection, he has written a computer program that detects potential cognates in related languages. His research interests include languages in contact (particularly Pennsylvania German and English), linguistic reconstruction, etymology, and Mayan and Indo-European diachronic syntax.

Wolfgang U. Dressler (Ph.D., University of Vienna) is Professor of Linguistics at the University of Vienna and Research Director at the Austrian Academy of

Sciences; he is an honorary member of the Linguistic Society of America. He has taught in several U.S., Canadian, and Italian universities. His books range from phonology, comparative and text linguistics to his current focus in morphology and psycholinguistics.

Bruce L. Edwards (Ph.D., University of Texas at Austin) is Professor of English and Associate Dean for International and Distance Education at Bowling Green State University (Ohio). He has taught undergraduate and graduate courses in rhetoric, linguistics, and literature at Bowling Green since 1981. In addition, he has traveled and lectured widely on Tagmemic Rhetoric as an S. W. Brooks Memorial Professor at the University of Queensland (1988), a Bradley Fellow at the Heritage Foundation (1989–1990), and as a Fulbright Fellow at Daystar University (1999–2000). He has published and lectured widely on the life and works of C. S. Lewis and is the author or editor of seven books.

Karl J. Franklin (Ph.D., Australian National University) is an Adjunct Professor of Linguistics at the University of Texas at Arlington. He has held various international academic positions with SIL International, including Vice President of Academic Affairs and, at different times, Coordinator for Linguistics, Coordinator for Anthropology, and Coordinator for Training. He has also served as the director of the New Zealand and Australian SIL schools for several years. He and his wife worked in Papua New Guinea for thirty-two years. He is the author or editor of several books and numerous articles on the Kewa language, as well as Tok Pisin.

Peter H. Fries (Ph.D., University of Pennsylvania) is Professor of English and Linguistics and Director of the M.A. TESOL program at Central Michigan University. He has also taught at eleven other universities; in 1990, he was named Lansdowne Professor of the University of Victoria, Canada; and in 1991, he was made permanent Adjunct Professor of Hangzhou University, Peoples' Republic of China. He has served as president of the ESL Assembly of the National Council of Teachers of English and in several other positions in the Council. His research interests include the development of linguistic theory and its application to practical problems, the communication strategies of two bonobo apes, the analysis of discourse and English grammar, and the nature of the reading process. He has written one book and over fifty articles and has edited six books.

Thomas V. Gamkrelidze (Ph.D., Tbilisi State University) teaches at the Oriental Institute of the Georgian Academy and since 1973 has been the Director. He also teaches at the Tbilisi State University. He was president of the Societas Linguistica Europaea (1986–1987) and is an honorary member of several academies. He was awarded the degree of Doctor *honoris causa* by the University of Bonn (1994) and the University of Chicago (1995). He is also a Member of Parliament of Georgia. His main research interests are theoretical and comparative linguistics and semiotics; Caucasian, Indo-European, Semitic, and Ancient Oriental languages and cultures. His publications include *Sibilant Correspondences and Some Questions of the Ancient Structure of Kartvelian Languages* (1960); *A Typology and Provenance of Alphabetic Writing Systems* (1994), and *Indo-European and the*

Indo-Europeans (with V. V. Ivanov, 1984— the monograph was awarded the Lenin prize in 1988; the English translation was published in 1995).

T. Givón (Ph.D., University of California at Los Angeles) teaches linguistics and cognitive science at the University of Oregon and counts as his home a ranch on the Southern Ute Indian Reservation near Ignacio, Colorado. Among his books are *On Understanding Grammar* (1979), *Syntax: A Functional-Typological Introduction* (1984, 1990), *Mind, Code and Context: Essays in Pragmatics* (1989), *English Grammar* (1993), *Functionalism and Grammar* (1995), *Running through the Tall Grass* (a novel, 1997), *Syntax: An Introduction* (2001), and *Bio-Linguistics* (2002).

Joseph E. Grimes (Ph.D., Cornell University) is Professor Emeritus of Linguistics at Cornell University. He is a past president of the Consortium of Social Science Associations and has served as vice president of the Association for Computational Linguistics and as a member of the executive committee of the Linguistic Society of America. He has done fieldwork with the Huichol of Mexico and Hawai'i Pidgin, with research interests in syntax, discourse, the theory of the lexicon, and language diversity. Currently, he is working on a dictionary of Hawai'i Pidgin under the auspices of SIL International. His publications include *Huichol Syntax* (1965), *The Thread of Discourse* (1975), *Language Survey Reference Guide* (1995), and some ninety articles. From 1972 to 2000 he was consulting editor for the *Ethnologue: Languages of the World.*

E. Austin Hale (Ph.D., University of Illinois at Urbana) is an International Linguistics Consultant with SIL International. He has been pursuing his interest in Newar grammar and discourse since 1968. From 1969 to 1973 he collaborated with Pike in linguistics workshops and has benefitted greatly from various periods of learning and collaboration with many Newar friends and scholars. He has served as linguistic consultant for SIL in Nepal 1968–1976, in the Philippines 1976–1989, and currently serves as linguistic consultant for the South Asia Group. His publications include *Research on Tibeto-Burman Languages* (1982) and a number of articles on the Newar language of Nepal. He served as coeditor with K. L. Pike of *Tone Systems of Tibeto-Burman Languages* (1970), as coeditor with David Watters of *Clause, Sentence, and Discourse Patterns in Selected Languages of Nepal* (1973), and as coeditor of *Studies in Philippine Linguistics* (1977–1988).

Jana R. Harvey (M.A., University of Texas at Arlington) is currently a Ph.D. student in English (Applied Linguistics) at Ball State University. Her research interests include discourse analysis, pidgin and creole languages, and second language acquisition.

Thomas N. Headland (Ph.D., University of Hawaii) is an International Anthropology Consultant with SIL International and Adjunct Professor of Linguistics at the University of Texas at Arlington. His primary research interests are in tropical forest human ecology and hunter-gatherer studies. From 1962, he spent eighteen years living in the Philippine rainforest with Agta hunter-gatherer people, with his most recent fieldwork there in the spring of 2002. He has published ten books and over one hundred academic articles. Among his books are *The Tasaday Controversy: Assessing* *the Evidence, Tropical Deforestation: The Human Dimension* (1996), and *What Place for Hunter-Gatherers in Millennium Three?*

Martha Hildebrandt (Doctor en Letras, Universidad Nacional Mayor de San Marcos, Lima). After postdoctoral studies at Northwestern University and at the University of Oklahoma, she began her career in teaching at the Universidad Central de Venezuela. She was awarded the national cultural prize for her book *La lengua de Bolívar*. Later she was awarded the same prize for her book *Peruanismos* She was Professor of Phonetics, and is Professor Emeritus of San Marcos. She was Director General of the Instituto Nacional de Cultura of Peru, 1972–1976, and simultaneously a member of the Consejo Interamericano de Cultura de la Organización de Estados Americanos. From 1976–1978 she was Sub-director General of UNESCO for the Social Sciences. She is a member of the Academia Peruana de la Lengua, served in the Peruvian Congress 1995–2000, and is currently an elected representative of the people of Peru.

Jane H. Hill (Ph.D., University of California at Los Angeles) is Regents' Professor of Anthropology and Linguistics at the University of Arizona. She taught previously at Wayne State University. Her interests include the American Indian languages (especially the Uto-Aztecan family) in grammatical-typological, historical, and sociolinguistic perspective. She has done fieldwork on Cupeño, Nahuatl, and Tohono O'odham. Her publications include *Speaking Mexicano* (with Kenneth C. Hill, 1986). She served as president of the American Anthropological Association 1998–1999.

Barbara E. Hollenbach (Ph.D., University of Arizona) is a field linguist with the Mexico Branch of SIL International. Her research experience includes studies in Copala Trique and, more recently, Magdalena Peñasco Mixtec. She has also served as a consultant and editor, working with other field linguists to produce articles and grammars of indigenous languages of Mexico. Her current research interests include documents written in and about Mixtec during the sixteenth century. She served as coeditor of the four volumes of *Studies in the Syntax of Mixtecan Languages* and contributed a grammatical sketch of Copala Trique to this set.

George L. Huttar (Ph.D., University of Michigan) began fieldwork with SIL International in 1968 in Suriname. He has served as a linguistics consultant with SIL there and in Australia, as SIL International Linguistics Coordinator, and Vice President for Academic Affairs. Currently, he teaches in the M.A. in Translation Studies Program of the Nairobi Evangelical Graduate School of Theology. His primary research interest is in creole languages. He is the author of numerous articles and (with Mary L. Huttar) of *Ndyuka* (1994).

Dell Hymes (Ph.D., Indiana University) is Commonwealth Professor of Anthropology and Commonwealth Professor of English Emeritus at the University of Virginia. He taught previously at Harvard University, University of California at Berkeley, and the University of Pennsylvania, where he was Dean of the Graduate School of Education for twelve years. He is a past president of the American Anthropological Association, the American Association of Applied Linguistics, the

American Folklore Society, and the Linguistic Society of America. He is a Fellow of the American Academy of Arts and Sciences and of the British Academy. His books include *Language in Culture and Society* (1964), *Reinventing Anthropology* (1972, 1999), *Foundations in Sociolinguistics* (1974), *"In Vain I Tried to Tell You"* (1981), and *"Now I Know Only So Far"* (2003).

Barbara Pike Ibach (MLIS, University of Michigan) is the second child of Kenneth and Evelyn Pike. She wrote her contribution in the spring of 2001, shortly after the death of her father. It was posted on the SIL International website in September of that year. She and her husband, David Ibach, live in Livonia, Michigan. They have two adult children and two grandchildren, Jonathan, born in 1998, and Anneke, born in 2000. The Pike family photographs in her chapter are part of her personal photo collection. Her essay and the photographs are reprinted here with her permission.

Linda K. Jones (Ph.D., University of Michigan) is currently serving as linguist for the Yawa language project. Her particular research interest is the grammar of discourse. Her publications include *Theme in English Expository Discourse* (1977); *Discourse Studies in Mesoamerican Languages* (ed., 1979); and numerous articles on topics in discourse and in Yawa linguistics.

Marianne Kilani-Schoch (Ph.D., University of Lausanne), is currently Lecturer in the Foreign Languages Department (EFM) and in the Linguistics Department of the University of Lausanne. Her particular interests are in phonology and morphology. She has done research on French, Arabic, aphasia, and first language acquisition. Among her publications are *Introduction à la Morphologie Naturelle* (1988), and with D. Bittner and W. U. Dressler, *First Verbs: On the way to Mini-Paradigms* (2000).

Mildred L. Larson (Ph.D., University of Texas at Arlington) has served as a linguist-translator, consultant, trainer, and administrator during fifty years with SIL International. For twenty years she did fieldwork which included linguistics, bilingual education, and biblical translation among the Aguaruna of northern Peru. She is the author of several books including *Meaning-Based Translation* (1984, revised 1998), *Meaning-based Translation Workbook* (1998), and *The Function of Reported Speech in Discourse* (1978). She has also authored numerous articles on linguistics, translation, and education topics. She has served on several editorial boards and as editor for several books including *Bilingual Education: An Experience in Peruvian Amazonia* (with Patricia Davis, 1981, also in Spanish, 1979), and *Translation Theory and Practice: Tension and Interdependence* (1991). She is currently retired.

Robert E. Longacre (Ph.D., University of Pennsylvania) taught at the University of Texas at Arlington, the University of Michigan, State University of New York at Buffalo, and several other institutions. He served as an International Linguistics Consultant of SIL International during several decades and carried out extensive field work among the Trique of Mexico. His work on Proto-Mixtecan became the cornerstone for a number of works by others on the Otomanguean language family. His current primary research interests are textlinguistics and Hebrew grammar. He is the founding editor of the *Journal of Translation and Textlinguistics (JOTT)*. He is author of twelve monographs including *Hierarchy and Universality of Discourse Constituents in New Guinea Languages* (2 volumes, 1972), *Joseph: A Story of Divine Providence: A Text Theoretical and Textlinguistic Analysis of Genesis 37 and 39–48* (1989), *Storyline Concerns and Word Order Typology in East and West Africa* (1990), editor of seven volumes, and author of numerous articles.

Ivan Lowe (Ph.D., Cambridge University) has been a member of SIL International since 1958, and has done fieldwork in Brazil with the Nambiquara people. Since 1973, he has been an International Linguistic Consultant of SIL. In the late 1960s and early 1970s, he collaborated with Kenneth L. Pike in developing an algebraic theory of pronominal reference, which described the interactions between the participants in a speech act in terms of algebraic permutation groups. His principal current linguistic interests are discourse analysis, cognitive semantic analysis, and languages of the Kru family of Côte d'Ivoire. He is author of some twenty-five articles.

Adam Makkai (Ph.D., Yale University) was born and raised in Budapest; he came to the United States as a Hungarian refugee in 1957. He was the principal founder of LACUS (Linguistic Association of Canada and the U.S.) in 1974, (of which Ken Pike served as President), and founded the President's Prize for the best paper given that year. Makkai launched Ken Pike's nomination for the Nobel Peace Prize on Pike's seventieth birthday in 1982. Makkai is Professor of English and Linguistics at the University of Illinois at Chicago where he has taught since 1967.

George I. Mavrodes (Ph.D., University of Michigan) was Professor of Philosophy of Religion at the University of Michigan. His publications include *Belief in God* (1970), *Revelation in Religious Belief* (1988), and over one hundred papers, articles, and reviews.

Carol V. McKinney (Ph.D., Southern Methodist University) is an Associate Professor in Ethnology at the Graduate Institute of Applied Linguistics. She has also taught at University of Michigan, Southern Methodist University, the University of Texas at Arlington, and the University of Texas at Dallas. She and her husband Norris began working with the Bajju in Nigeria, under the auspices of SIL International, in 1967 and have continued contact with them since then. Her most recent publication is *Globe-Trotting in Sandals: A Field Guide to Cultural Research* (2000); she is also author of several articles on Bajju language and culture.

Norris P. McKinney (Ph.D., University of Michigan) specializes in Acoustic Phonetics and Communication Sciences. He taught Phonetics for ten years at the Graduate Institute of Applied Linguistics and the Texas SIL School. He has also taught at the University of Oklahoma and the University of Oregon. His publications include articles on acoustic analysis of fortis-lenis consonants and other topics, as well as several titles in Jju, including the translation of the New Testament, which he and his wife Carol, and their Bajju co-workers completed. He is now retired.

Eugene A. Nida (Ph.D., U. of California at Los Angeles) worked with SIL International from 1936 to 1954; he was a consultant with the American Bible Society for many years. He is the author of numerous books and articles, including *Morphology: The Descriptive Analysis of Words* (1943), and *Toward a Science of Translating: Exploring Semantic Structures* (1975). He previously served as editor of *The Bible Translator* and is a past president of the Linguistic Society of America (1968). He currently resides in Belgium.

Herbert Pilch (Ph.D., University of Kiel) teaches at the University of Freiburg. He has also taught at the University of Kiel, University of Cologne, University of Frankfurt/Main, University of Monash, University of Basel, University of Massachusetts, and University of Brest. He received the D.Litt. *honoris causa* from St. Andrews (1984), and Doctor *honoris causa* from Iași. (1993). His areas of special interest are Celtic, English, German, and Slavic linguistics and literature. His publications include *Phonemtheorie I* (1964), *Altenglishche Grammatik* (1970), *Empirical Linguistics* (1976), *Manual of English Phonetics* (1994), several other books, and over one hundred articles.

Vern S. Poythress (Ph.D., Harvard University; Th.D., Stellenbosch University) is Professor of New Testament Interpretation at Westminster Theological Seminary, Philadelphia, and is associate editor of the *Westminster Theological Journal*. He is author of eight books on issues related to biblical interpretation and was a member of the Translation Oversight Committee for the English Standard Version of the Bible. He has a continuing interest in the application of linguistics to translation and interpretation of the Bible.

John R. (Háj) Ross (Ph.D., Massachusetts Institute of Technology) is Professor in the Linguistics Section of the English Department of the University of North Texas. His research interests are poetics and syntax, which for him are one field. He was Professor of Linguistics at MIT from 1973–1985 and has been a visiting professor at universities in Brazil, Germany, Singapore, Egypt, Tunis, Sweden, and Canada, as well as four other U.S. universities. He has also served as research associate of the Max-Planck Institute and as consultant for the Language Awareness Project of the Rhode Island School for the Deaf. He has published several articles in *Papers from the Xth Regional Meeting of the Chicago Linguistic Society* and elsewhere.

Philip Saunders (M.A., in theoretical linguistics from Reading University, 1986) has been a fieldworker with SIL International in Côte d'Ivoire and with his wife, Heather, has been involved in fieldwork among the Kouya people, residing in the villages of Dema and Bahoulifa, near the city of Vavoua, since 1983. His principal linguistic interest is the Kru language family. He is a compiler of a Kouya-French vocabulary.

Kedar P. Shrestha (B.A., Tribhuvan University, Kathmandu) is well known under his pen name, "Situ," as a Newar author and editor. From 1987 to 1990 he served as associate editor of *Àkhe*, a Newar literary journal. For a number of years he contributed a column to the Newar daily newspaper, *Sandhyā Ṭāims* [Evening

Times]. He has published a novel, *Swamhamha Manuu* [The third person], and a collection of short stories, *Dhakā Dhayāwa* [As soon as it was said], in addition to numerous articles and short stories in Newari.

Gary F. Simons (Ph.D., Cornell University) is Associate Vice President for Academic Affairs, an International Linguistics Consultant for SIL International, and Adjunct Assistant Professor of Linguistics at the University of Texas at Arlington. He has done fieldwork in Papua New Guinea and the Solomon Islands. His principal areas of research interest are markup languages and text encoding, computational linguistics, programming languages, historical and comparative linguistics, and Austronesian linguistics. He is cofounder of the Open Language Archives Community and serves on the editorial board of *Markup Languages: Theory and Practice*. His publications include *Language Variation and Limits to Communication* (1979), *Powerful Ideas for Text Processing: An Introduction to Computer Programming with the PTP Language* (1984), and numerous articles.

Joan Spanne (MLIS, University of Michigan) is Director of the Language and Culture Archives and a Library Consultant with SIL International.

V. I. Subramoniam (Ph.D., Indiana University) taught Tamil and Linguistics at Kerala University and was the founder Vice-Chancellor of Tamil University, Tanjavur, Tamil Nadu from 1981 to 1986. He was Pro Chancellor of Dravidian University, Andhra Pradesh from 1999 to 2001. He received the Hon. D.Litt. from Jaffra University, Sri Lanka and Hon. D. Litt. from Tamil University. He received the Rockefeller Fellowship (1955–1957) and a Visiting Fellowship from the Japan Society for the Promotion of Science (1981). He edits the *International Journal of Dravidian Linguistics*. His publications include more than 130 research articles and fourteen books including the *Dravidian Encyclopaedia* in three volumes.

Patricia K. Townsend (Ph.D., University of Michigan) is Research Associate in the Anthropology Department at the State University of New York at Buffalo. Most of her earlier research was in Papua New Guinea. She was formerly Executive Director of a refugee resettlement agency in Buffalo, New York. She is author of two widely-used textbooks, *Environmental Anthropology* (2000), and *Medical Anthropology in Ecological Perspective* (with Ann McElroy, third edition 1996), and numerous articles.

Stephen Walter (Ph.D., University of Texas at Arlington) has worked with SIL International since 1969. After field assignments in Mexico, Guatemala, and Colombia, he took an assignment as International Literacy Coordinator in 1988; he held this position for eleven years. In 1999, he accepted a position as Associate Professor of Applied Linguistics at the Graduate Institute of Applied Linguistics, where he teaches courses in adult literacy methods and social science research methodology. He has traveled and consulted extensively in the developing world on issues related to language, education, and adult literacy.

David J. Weber (Ph.D., University of California at Los Angeles) is an International Linguistics Consultant with SIL International and has done extensive fieldwork on Quechua, particularly Huallaga Quechua. He has taught in SIL programs at the University of North Dakota, the University of Oregon, and the University of Lima. He pioneered CADA (Computer Assisted Dialect Adaptation), now called CARLA (Computer Assisted Related Language Adaptation) and guided its development during its first decade. He is the author (or first coauthor) of *Relativization and nominalized clauses in Huallaga (Huanuco) quechua* (1983), *Estudios quechua: Planificación, historia y gramática* (1987), *AMPLE: A Tool for Exploring Morphology* (1988), *A Grammar of Huallaga (Huanuco) Quechua* (1989), *Ortografía: Lecciones del quechua* (1994), *Rimaycuna: Quechua de Huánuco* (a Quechua-Spanish-English dictionary of Huallaga Quechua, 1998), several other volumes, and some forty articles.

Mary Ruth Wise (Ph.D., University of Michigan) is Senior Editor and a former International Linguistics Consultant with SIL International. She has done fieldwork among the Yanesha' (Amuesha) and Nomatsiguenga of Peruvian Amazonia. She is editor of SIL Peru's Serie Lingüística Peruana, Comunidades y Culturas Peruanas; Documentos de Trabajo; and Coordinator of *Revista Latinoamericana de Estudios Etnolingüísticos*. Her publications include *Identification of Participants in Discourse* (1971); *Los grupos étnicos de la Amazonía Peruana: 1900–1975* (with Darcy Ribeiro, 1978); about eighty articles, and seven publications in the Yanesha' language (with Martha Duff-Tripp). In 1991, the Peruvian Ministry of Education awarded her with *Palmas Magisteriales en el Grado de Maestro*.

Stephen Wurm (Ph.D., University of Vienna) was born in Budapest. He became interested in languages in very early childhood and became a multilingual. In Vienna he mainly studied the Turkic languages. Before he migrated permanently to Australia in 1954, he helped set up the Central Asian Research Institute in London. In Australia he did linguistic research in the southwestern Pacific, Australia, and later also in Siberia and South America. As Research Professor at the Australian National University, he directed large international linguistic research projects and language atlases in the Pacific, China, and South America, as well as in endangered languages worldwide. Many publications resulted from these projects. He was a founding member and the first President of the Linguistic Society of Australia. Professor Wurm died on October 24, 2001.

SIL International and
The University of Texas at Arlington
Publications in Linguistics

Recent Publications

For further information or a full listing of SIL publications contact:

International Academic Bookstore
SIL International
7500 W. Camp Wisdom Road
Dallas, TX 75236-5699

Voice: 972-708-7404
Fax: 972-708-7363
Email: academic_books@sil.org
Internet: http://www.ethnologue.com